BARS | CLUBS | PUBS | HOTEL BARS | RESTAUR

20 02

crushguide

GO OUT IN STYLE

LONDON

BRISTOL | BIRMINGHAM | EDINBURGH | GLASGOW | LEEDS | MANCHESTER

www.crushguide.com

CrushGuide 2002

Contents

London
Birmingham
Bristol
Edinburgh
Glasgow
Leeds
Manchester

Telephone +44 (0)20 7376 9996   Facsimile +44 (0)20 7376 9099
E-mail   info@crushguide.com   Website   www.crushguide.com

CrushGuide ™ is published by Black Book Publishing Limited,
1A Gregory Place, London, W8 4NG
©Black Book Publishing Ltd   ISBN 0-9534714-1-1   ISSN 1476-1262

Publisher/Editor-in-Chief	James Piesse
Editor	Laura Abrahams
Deputy Editor	Joanna Israelsohn
Assistant Editor	Victoria Gill
Art Director	Andrew Debens
Production Director	Victoria Ottewill
Editorial Consultant	Cheryl Westmacott
Contributing Editor	Gemma Elwin Harris
Clubs Editor	Sally Howard
Head of Technology	Alastair Taylor
Managing Editors	Stephanie Pliakas, Sue Tan
Chief Sub-editors	Luke Tracy, Oksana Dashawitz
Proof-reader	Monica Kendall
Principal Contributors	Bethan Ryder, Helen Brown, Richard Clayton, Steve Cleverley, Nick Minter
Other Contributors	James Aufenast, Matthew Baker, Ian Beetlestone, Terry Bergin, Alison Bishop, Bryn Bowden, Jessie Brough, Tim Child, Stephen Cannings, Joannah Connolley, Kate Copstick, Joseph Crilly, Mike Davies, Gerald Foster, Luke Foster, Simon Fry, Daniel Fryer, Alex George, Camilla Goslett, Sarah Garrett, Rob Haigh, Nick Hoare, Ross Holloway, Nadine Kettaneh, Bill Knott, Helen Lamont, George Lees, Kevin Metchear, Andrew Midgley, Nick Minter, Anna Morell, William McCormack, Fergus O'Sullivan, Shiv Paul, Graham Pitts, Oliver Price, Russell Rose, Alexander Ross, Guy Rundle, Alan Sams, Martin Saxon, Vanessa Scott, Anna Smith, Victoria Souter, Amber Tan, Graham Taylor, James Teideman, Sara Teiger, Mat Toor, Hugh Truesdale, Sara Villiers, Ian Wisniewski, Pippa Wight, Tamsin Young
Portraits	Costas Anastasakis (07931 563220) James Pelltekian (07930 301922) and PYMCA (020 7613 3725)
Repro	ITM Graphics
Printing	Polestar Scientific Ltd, Aberdeen

This book may be ordered by cheque or credit card on 020 7376 9996 or via our website at www.crushguide.com

We endeavour to research our recommendations and reviews thoroughly, but they are merely a subjective opinion. Our reviewers are purely expressing their own impressions – no payment of any kind has influenced a review. Readers may come to a different opinion (which we would love to hear). We disclaim liability for any inaccuracies or omissions arising in this publication. All prices quoted were correct in November 2001, but may alter during the currency of this guide. Our printers, sponsors and distributors have accepted this guide in good faith and are blameless for any inaccuracies or mistakes.

FOREWORD

It's six o'clock on a Friday afternoon and you're planning a night out on the town. All you need is your wallet, your keys, your mobile and a copy of CrushGuide.

CrushGuide is no mere bar or drinking guide – it's 272 pages of never-before-published information about London's bars, pubs and clubs, including over 30 pages devoted to the UK's top six cities. If it's not in CrushGuide, it's not worth knowing.

Months of research and hundreds of hangovers have resulted in a unique ratings system whereby every venue is rated for 'ambience', 'eye candy', 'big spenders' and your chances of 'getting lucky'. We tell you what kind of person is likely to be drinking there, what they'll be wearing, what age they are and which celebrities might be in attendance. Follow our chart at the back of the guide to look for the type of person you want to meet (or avoid) and we'll show you where they drink and why they're there, whether it's for a contemplative beer or a serious leer.

Gone are the days when going out for a quick one required no more thought than an episode of Neighbours. We're a fussy lot, and a pint of warm ale and a curled-up sandwich just won't cut it. We know what we want – whether it's a perfectly mixed Martini, a thumping bar with cutting edge DJs or a gastropub meal worthy of three Michelin stars – and CrushGuide tells you where you can get it.

HOW TO USE CRUSHGUIDE

1 Name of bar
2 Type of venue (see glossary)
3 Address
4 Telephone number
5 Opening days and times
6 Nearest underground or rail station
7 Buses that pass the venue or pass nearby
8 How likely you are to pull someone
9 How beautiful the clientele are
10 How rich the clientele are
11 Ratio of men to women
12 Average age range of the clientele
13 Venues are classified as cheap, average, expensive and very expensive.

This classification is broadly based on cost of beer/wine at the venue. Accordingly for beer/ wine, cheap would be £1.75-2.50, average would be £2.30-3.20, expensive would be £3.50-4 and very expensive would be £4 and up

14 One word/phrase to describe venue's ambience (see glossary)
15 Our independent review of the venue
16 Short description of interior/exterior of venue
17 General overview of the venue's clientele
18 Professions/trades of those who use the bar
19 Celebrities who have visited the venue or are regulars
20 General dress of the clientele including labels
21 Type of music played (includes live music, DJs and background music)
22 Door policy: cost of entrance if applicable, including dress code, membership/guest list policy if applicable. Any statement such as 'Smart dress' is the management's words
23 Average price of bottled beer, glass of house wine, glass of house champagne, cocktail
24 Type of food served; average price per main course/snack
25 Credit cards/debit cards accepted. All means the following are accepted: Amex, Diners, MasterCard, Switch, Visa. Otherwise all cards accepted with the exception of stated eg No Amex
26 Max capacity followed by max number of seats
27 Whether you can hire the whole venue and/or a private room is available to book

---

1 **OPIUM**

2 Bar, Members Bar, Restaurant
3 1a Dean Street W1
4 020 7287 9608

5 **OPEN** Mon-Sat 6pm-3am
6 **TUBE/RAIL** Tottenham Court Road, Leicester Square
7 **BUSES** 10, 25, 55, 73, 98, 176

GETTING LUCKY	**3/5**
EYE CANDY	**4/5**
BIG SPENDERS	**5/5**
MIX 40%M 60%F	
AGE 25-35	
PRICE Expensive	

8
9
10
11
12
13

14 **AMBIENCE** Conversation, Exclusive/Chic, Funky, Hip/Fashionable, Jet Set, Late Night Open, Lounge, Opulent, Star Spotting

15 **REVIEW** Oh, so this is where all the beautiful women we never meet in The Ferret and Spanner come to drink – not that moneyed models wearing dresses to make Liz Hurley blush are our cup of tea, you understand. Despite having the air of a members bar, Opium is theoretically open to anyone. Anyone, that is, with the looks of Jude or Sadie and a wallet to rival the Sultan of Brunei's. It's an exceptionally beautiful celebration destination, elegant and funky. But isn't it a bit rich to have a bar menu waffling on about the Vietnamese people's 'decades of struggle' and 'resilience in abundance' whilst flogging bottles of champagne at £625 a pop?

16 **PLACE** An almost stupendously grand(iose) Vietnamese dream palace, with swathes of intricately carved partitions and a muted gold and terracotta colour scheme.

17 **PEOPLE** No one larger than a size 12, no one earning less than £50k and no one beaten by the ugly stick.

18 **PROFS** PRs, artists, music industry professionals, models, fashion designers, advertising, the idle rich
19 **CELEBS** Patsy Kensit, George Clooney, Bryan Adams, Erin O'Connor, John O'Gregor, Mick Jagger, Kate Moss, Liv Tyler
20 **DRESS** Ghost, Prada, Armani, DKNY
21 **MUSIC** Eclectic, House Lounge, Funky Lounge, Funky House, Cabaret Tue-Wed 8pm-10pm, DJ Thu-Sat, from 9pm
22 **DOOR** Smart casual, members and guests, Thu-Sat £15
23 **DRINKS** Beer £4.30, Wine £3.50, Champagne £8, Cocktail £7.50
24 **FOOD** French/Vietnamese, £15
25 **CARDS** All
26 **CAPACITY** 250, seating 80
27 **HIRE** Venue: Yes · Private Room: No

GLOSSARY

GENERAL

All reviews were conducted on either a Thursday, Friday or Saturday night. All reviews are entirely independent and no money was accepted or requested for any of the reviews. Almost all our reviewers arrived unannounced. All venues were subsequently revisited and telephoned to check information and most proprietors or staff were also interviewed.

Chain Bars

London's bar scene is increasingly dominated by bar chains such as All Bar One and Pitcher & Piano. These bars, although in different locations, are physically almost exactly identical. CrushGuide policy is not to review every one of these chain bars but rather to review a selection or even just one.

RATINGS

Bars are rated on several points and are marked out of five – minimum score is one.

Getting Lucky

This rating indicates how likely you are to pull, pick up or meet someone new in a venue. Five out of five for a bar does not necessarily mean you should put your unborn children down for the local school before crossing the doorway. Rather this rating is reserved for venues where we felt that both sexes were actively and clearly out to pull and that – unless you have a ginger beard – there was a high likelihood of achieving success. High rated places have large amounts of singles, who go there to meet other people for friendship, love or sex. Low scores out of five could be places full of smug marrieds or just lack that chemistry and sex appeal which pushes unknowns to pay for each other's drinks.

Eye Candy

Beauty is, of course, in the eye of the beholder. Our reviews rate highest those venues where quantities of beautiful people gather. These are clientele who are blessed with a unique collision of good looks, style and success (well, sometimes). A 1/5 rating means that the place is full of people beaten by the ugly stick.

Big Spenders

People in a venue were graded according to how much they earn. For example, students and the unemployed received a rating of one. Clerical staff, secretaries, labourers, nurses and those earning under £25k would get a rating of two. 3/5 is for places where professionals such as lawyers and accountants earning up to £100K drink. 4/5 is for chief execs, bankers and City boys/girls earning up to £1million. 5/5 is for pop stars who don't use Elton John's former accountant, the aristocracy, fat cats and scions of the oil-rich states.

AMBIENCE DEFINITIONS

Every review contains a series of short one word/phrase descriptions, just before the main review, which provide a snapshot of what's special or of note about a venue.

They are as follows:

Arty/Bohemian: This means the venue attracts the arty or bohemian. These could range from ageing Hampstead intellectuals to artist, musician or writer types whose clothes and appearance either mean they're struggling with the mechanised ethos or they've got a personal hygiene problem. The Vibe Bar on Brick Lane, the Mau Mau on Portobello or the Jazz Café in Camden all offer variations on this theme.

Backpacker: A venue that attracts those who do very little washing and spend their days carrying it around on their backs while knocking us off our feet. Free range traveller types who spend time drinking together when they should be meeting the locals. To assess the soap dodgers, the Fulham Tup is a safe bet.

Basement: Venue is principally underground so no good for sunlight and fresh air lovers – just to let you know in case you suffer from SAD. The crypt that's the Bug Bar in Brixton and the Rumpole-hole of Davy's in the City are polar extremes of subterranean watering holes.

Brightly Coloured/Cheerful: For those whose mood needs lifting without chemicals the venue has been thoughtfully – but not necessarily tastefully – decorated à la Smillie. Sloanetastic Purple fits the DIY bill. 19:20 in Clerkenwell goes for Trainspotting orange – all over.

Bump 'n' Grind: The species of sweat-ridden and music-driven venue that's populated by dirty dancing, shimmying, ass-pinching lads and lasses. Still not sure? Head to Bar Rumba on Shaftesbury Avenue and get down.

GLOSSARY continued

Business: A place that's good for business meetings or even impressing clients. No need to feel embarrassed when loudly discussing the takeover of Megaprofit plc with your new FD. See any bar worth its suits in the Square Mile.

Buzzy: Lots of people, lots of chat and activity. Cantaloupe in Hoxton and The Rhythm Factory in Brick Lane offer lots of diverting opportunities.

Casual: Don't worry about turning up in your tatty old jeans or not putting on any make-up. The Bridge in Fulham or The Bricklayers Arms in hip Hoxton are perfect for Sunday afternoon slouching.

Children: Children are welcomed ie it's not a venue where punters glass each other at closing time. The Mason's Arms in Battersea and The Grove in Hammersmith are pushchair friendly.

Chilled: Special mix of mellow lighting, relaxed music and calm feel to relax your poor stressed city soul. So.uk in Clapham is so chilled you don't even need a wine bucket.

Chin Stroking: A place which caters to musical trainspotters. Y'know, those people who either stand back with folded arms and closed eyes nodding smugly to the 'beats' or continually harass the DJ to discover who did the remix of the track they played 23 minutes ago. Music-orientated places such as Fabric or Plastic People are anorak heaven.

Comfy: Think collapsing into big armchair or prostrating yourself on a bean bag. That lounging at home sensation when out and about. Blakes in Camden and the Front Room Bar in Battersea let you sink into their sofas.

Conversation: Places where you can chat freely without interruption by noise or others. The Castle in Holland Park or The George in the City are great for a chinwag and whinge about the boss.

Cosy: Country style cousin of 'Comfy' above. Could be a candle-lit pub or bar with fireplace and lazy made-for-sprawling sofas. The Drawing Room and Sofa Bar in Battersea is just perfect for cold, rainy nights.

Cute Staff: Refers to good-looking staff who are nice to have around if you're stuck with your quadruple-butted cousin over on a visit from Saskatchewan. The Freedom Brewing Company could certainly provide some distraction.

Destination/Wishlist: Your friends ask if you've been, the papers tell you to get down there and CrushGuide says this is where you need to be. Members bars such as Soho House and The Wellington Club are two favourites that you'd love to go to but probably won't be able to get in.

Dive Bar: Seedy, down at heel, run down, cheap, even grotty but with its own charm. The King's Head and Dive Bar – it's not ashamed – is a classic example.

Elegant/Classic: This refers to decor. Probably smart and often old-fashioned, it's the place you'd take the relatives to celebrate the old man's 50th or the

ambassador would take you for brandy and cigars when the Ferrero Rocher party's over. Refined dens include the Foyer Bar at the Berkeley Hotel or members only Montes in Knightsbridge.

Exclusive/Chic: These are the sort of places where your dress sense, looks, wallet or that urban barbed wire, the red rope, might keep you out. Terence Conran's GE Club at the Great Eastern Hotel knows how to deter the riff raff as does old timer Annabel's.

Friendly: Rare in uptight London. These are venues in cities like Leeds where staff and punters alike are happy to strike up conversations without you feeling that there's been an away-day at the local loony bin. There are exceptions in the capital with pubs such as The Grove and The Chelsea Ram avoiding the hostile attitude curse.

Funky: Not necessarily the music, this refers to laid-back, cool, upbeat venues. The Vibe Bar, the 333 club and Beach Blanket Babylon are good examples.

Futuristic: Hi-tec, or space age decor or gadgets. Alternatively, a venue that is futuristic in theme. Match EC1 and Saint both have a back to the future feel. In Clerkenwell, the manga murals and sushi snacks in Fluid are one step ahead.

Glammed-up: Dressed to kill unwitting prey. Showing off and puckered up to party in flesh-displaying, covetable clothes. The Q Bar and Ministry of Sound are favourites with those for whom a night out is not a night out unless it includes glitter and stilettos.

Groups: Suitable for large get-togethers of mates to celebrate your nose job. Circle Bar in Clapham and the Pitcher and Piano on the King's Road tend not to do the 'one in, one out' thing which leaves you and your 12 best friends on the pavement all night long.

Grunge: Trendier relatives of backpackers but with same allergic reaction to hygiene. Could also apply to decor. The Social on Little Portland Street is a playground for unwashed musos.

High Energy: Characterised by booming, soaring, repetitive beats and sweaty types jumping up and down manically. The End in Covent Garden is somewhere you wouldn't want to forget your trainers.

Hip/Fashionable: The wannabes may not sell their souls to be here and the flash bulbs may have long departed, but the style crowd know it's still going on. Cicada in Clerkenwell and Ling Ling@Hakkasan in Noho are filled with movers and shakers.

Historic: This could be because an historic event took place at the venue or the venue itself could be of historical significance. The Builders Arms in Chelsea and The Anglesea Arms in South Kensington stay true to their past.

Hormone-fuelled Club Kidz: An overt pulling venue driven by the mores of the clientele's pants. Piccadilly Circus stalwart Emporium offers a graphic illustration.

Industrial/Warehouse: Bare-bricked, steel girders, loft-conversion style decor. Clerkenwell club Fabric and newcomer Cargo in Shoreditch are fans of this exposed style.

Jet Set: A place where you'd find people who have homes in three or more different countries. If their parents don't own a Lear, they certainly know someone who does. Paparazzi Lounge, Nicole's and L'Equipe Anglaise are all popular with the multi-passport posse.

Kitsch: Could be cool kitsch/retro kitsch/naff kitsch – bit tacky, maybe a little trashy, not necessarily witty. Pop and Escape in Soho are recent examples of the trend but the all-time London leader of this genre has to be Trader Vics.

Late Night Open: Where the venue stays open after traditional English pub closing hours at 11pm. Ministry of Sound is one of the latest – on Saturday it has an 8am licence.

Legendary: Broad category here. The venue may be a famous person's local, or a first for the city. It may even be infamous as a long-standing pick-up joint. Whatever it is, the event or people are part of the place's mythology. The Palm Court at the Ritz is a leader.

Live Music Venue: A venue with regular bands and/or individual musicians from bongo players to live bands, not solely DJs. From bearded music obsessives in the Jazz Café to um... bearded music obsessives at Fabric.

Lounge/Lounge Atmosphere: Like a designer sitting room. Relaxed, sofas, low lighting, mellow, but comfortable. Bam-bou is a particularly chic example, with lots of dark wood and flickering nightlights.

Luvved-up Clubbers: Good-time girls and boys dancing with arms thrust euphorically into the air, stroking strangers and trying to initiate a lifelong friendship with the bouncer. The tribe can be found at the Limelight on Shaftesbury Avenue and Turnmills in Clerkenwell.

Mashed-up: Where you might encounter people who would struggle to put two and two together and get four. Punters at The Dogstar in Brixton are likely candidates.

Mature/Older Clientele: Where the majority of clientele are over 35 years old and should really be in bed. Most hotel bars (apart from those associated with Mr Ian Schrager) fall into this category, as do many venues in Mayfair – see Annabel's and The Dorchester Bar.

Minimalist: Refers to decor. One of those places where a thief appears to have stolen all the furniture but got disturbed three-quarters of the way through and left some really nice pieces. St John in Clerkenwell is a master of this art; everything is painted white and there are none of those silly extras like art, music or candles.

Network: Business networking joint. Have card, will swap. Brasserie Rocque in the Square Mile is a great place for drumming it up.

Old World: Not necessarily the real thing – that 18th-century inn look is popular in the City. Nevertheless think pre 19th-century interior with beams, flagstones and flagons, gilt mirrors, elm staircases etc. Hack haunt El Vino on Fleet Street is typical.

Opulent/Period: Think plush with class and possibly age. It may be as grand as The Ritz or as decadent as The Cobden Club.

Outdoors: Venue with outdoor area only if the outdoor area (be it terrace/pub garden/deck of boat) is good for al fresco eating/drinking. Not outdoor areas that are just concreted pavement or have a lovely view of a flyover or bus station. The Conran-operated Coq d'Argent in the City gets top marks for this as the only outdoors bar worth queueing for.

Party: Upbeat vibe where spontaneous dancing on tables (not to be confused with table dancing) or shedding of clothes (ditto) could take place. That 'Thank-God-I'm-not-in-TGI-Fridays' feeling. A trip to Cuba in Kensington or The Roadhouse in Covent Garden will get rid of those inhibitions.

Pulling: Gets large number of single people up for meeting others for friendship/love/sex. Lighting must be conducive to pulling. Layout of bar must make it easy to mingle. Music and noise level should be such that chatting up is possible. Crazy Larry's in Chelsea has been a sure thing for over a decade.

Queues: Pack your thermals and flask in winter. This venue gets queues for entry, whether it's just Saturday nights or most of the time. This is an actual physical queue not a waiting list (for members clubs). Red Cube is still leaving people out in the cold.

Retro: Decor relating to the 40s, 50s, 60s or 70s. The Social is a good example. Contradictions are possible; Ether in Bristol is retro and futuristic in a 'Barbarella' kind of way.

Romantic: Atmosphere and lighting, attracts hand-holding couples on first dates or may put a sparkler in the underpants of your relationship if you take your becoming-less-special friend. The Library Bar at the Lanesborough or Julies Bar in Holland Park.

Sports: Good places to watch any type of sport on screen. Nothing to do with the clientele being sporty or wearing jock straps. Sports Academy and Jamies at Pavilion in the City cater to lovers of beautiful games.

Star Spotting: Where the good, the bad and the ugly come to be flashed by paparazzi and enjoy their 15 minutes. Chinawhite, Momo, The Wellington Club, Attica and old favourite the Met Bar pull in the players.

Studenty: Majority of punters are students so beware cheap drinks and medical students performing pranks with bodily fluids. In West London Subterrania and Portobello Gold help loans disappear.

Touristy: Packed with pac-mac types who spend hours scratching their heads wondering why the beer refrigeration unit has broken down. The Roadhouse is a tower of Babel.

Vampire/Gothic: Either the clients are Goths or there's some kind of Vampire/Goth theme going in the decor. Former churches 291 and The Limelight make spooky watering holes.

Views: Not necessarily high up. Could be by the river or with a view of a historic monument or bridge. Scenes of bypasses and traintracks don't count. The riverside scene from the Oxo Tower is a must-see.

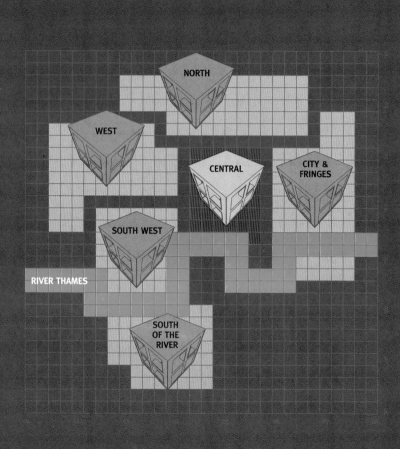

METRO

intro

CENTRAL
bond street/regent street
covent garden
leicester square/piccadilly circus
marylebone
mayfair
noho
soho
st james's
strand/embankment

With over 3,000 licensed premises in Westminster alone, central London has a choice of bars few cities in the world can match. But don't think you can hop off the tube at Leicester Square and find yourself in drinking nirvana – sheer area size and volume of venues mean you've got to know what you want and where to get it. A word of warning – in this part of the world, the distance between cutting-edge style and the edge of a social abyss can be no more than a few paces.

The obvious starting point for a central London drinker is the infamous Soho. Since the war, the area has teemed with artists, musicians, writers, bohemians and misfits. Once deliciously seedy, Westminster Council has slowly but surely sifted out the darker elements, closing down strip clubs and naughty video stores in favour of chic style bars and members clubs. Known as London's gay village, the area has a wide number of gay and gay-friendly bars – look out for **The Edge**, **The Village**, **Manto** and the **Candy Bar**. With the exception of the latter, the majority are male-orientated.

Old stalwart **The Groucho Club** kickstarted the members bar trend and now any exclusive venue worth its weight in Veuve starts life as one. Some operate on a very strict basis, others – including **Momo**, **Chinawhite**, **Noble Rot** and **Opium** – are worth a quick blag. Chances are higher if you're a pretty girl. Same goes for an increasing number of style bars with often baffling door policies, including **The Long Bar**, **10 Tokyo Joe's** and **Attica**. Who said life was fair?

The main Leicester Square and Piccadilly Circus drags are home to many of the rank and file, 'Ikea with beer' chain pubs. Clamber through the burger wrappers and join the unsophisticated punters at **All Bar One** and **Cheers** at your peril. That said, if unsophisticated is your bag and you resent paying a small mortgage on a tiny Martini, there are plenty of venues offering a gloriously tacky night out – we recommend **Tiger Tiger** and **Roadhouse**.

Covent Garden is a perennial favourite with tourists and after-hours professionals, with drinking holes as varied as dull-as-dishwater Bar 38 and chic-as-champagne **Light Bar**. If you want to pump it up a notch, get out your glad rags and go west. Mayfair, St James's and the Strand/Embankment are where it all goes posh-like, with slick style bars **Zeta** and **Che**, and celebrity hang-out **The Met**, as well as Daddy's favourites, **Annabel's**, **Tramp** and **The Dorchester Bar**. Don't forget your wallet.

Young urbanites should head to Noho – North of Soho – an up-and-coming area, home to funky favourites including **Match** and **The Social**, as well as good-looking newcomers **Ling Ling** and **Goodge**. These are Friday feeling places, where advertising/media folk take off their glasses and let their hair down with a foreign beer or three.

Recent and future openings:

Bodecca, Clarges Street
Stork Club, 99 Regent Street
Rivoli, Ritz Hotel, Piccadilly
Shh!, Leicester Square
Revolution, 2 St Anne's Court
Embassy, 2 New Burlington Street

bond street/regent street

CORKS

Bar, Club
28 Binney Street W1
020 7408 0100

OPEN Mon midday-12.30am,	GETTING LUCKY	4/5
Tue midday-1am,	EYE CANDY	3/5
Wed midday-2am,	BIG SPENDERS	2/5
Thu-Fri midday-3.30am,	MIX 50%M 50%F	
Sat 10pm-3.30am	AGE 20-40	
TUBE/RAIL Bond Street	PRICE Average	
BUSES 7, 8, 10, 25, 55, 73		

AMBIENCE Basement, Buzzy, Dancing, Funky, Groups, Late Night Open, Live Music, Party, Pulling
REVIEW Even early on, this place is buzzing, with people crowding round the long tables, chatting and enjoying the mix of Soul, R&B and Garage spun by DJs from Choice (Thursdays) and Starlight Crew (Saturdays). Aye, for real, Ali G could never compete. Around 9pm, the tables are cleared away, the lights go down, and there's a smooth transformation from bar to laid-back club. A lot of bars do this, and end up with distinct crowds either side of the watershed, but Corks just gets fuller, livelier and dressier. Top black music, classy threads and conspicuous champagne consumption comes as a surprise to anyone presupposing the pink neon sign and side street location will lead them to a Delboy-and-Rodney-Go-West style location.
PLACE Large, scruffy basement bar with pick 'n' mix decor, decked out in garish murals. Back room with pool table and big screen.
PEOPLE Loud and friendly, predominantly black and Asian good-time crowd who know their music (and most of each other, apparently) and are here to kick back and be seen.
PROFS Retailers, secretaries, sales execs, PAs, office admin staff, accountants
CELEBS Ian Wright, Lennox Lewis
DRESS Versace, Moschino, Prohibito, Gucci, Prada, Nike, bejewelled, extended nails, hair extensions
MUSIC Hip Hop, Old Skool, R&B, Soul, UK Garage, Reggae, Jazz, DJs
DOOR No tracksuits or trainers. Smart casual. Mon-Sat £4-10
DRINKS Beer £3.20, Wine £2.80, Cocktail £5
FOOD Snacks, £4
CARDS All
CAPACITY 400, seating 130
HIRE Venue: Yes · Private Room: Yes

DOVER STREET WINE BAR

Bar, Jazz Club, Restaurant, Wine Bar
8-10 Dover Street W1
020 7629 9813

OPEN Mon-Thu midday-	GETTING LUCKY	4/5
3.30pm, 5.30pm-3am,	EYE CANDY	3/5
Fri midday-3.30pm,	BIG SPENDERS	3/5
7pm-3am, Sat 7pm-3am	MIX 50%M 50%F	
TUBE/RAIL Green Park	AGE 25-40	
BUSES 9, 14, 19, 22, 38	PRICE Expensive	

AMBIENCE Dancing, Groups, Late Night Open, Live Music, Party, Pulling, Star Spotting, Touristy
REVIEW Years ago, Dover Street was a slightly tawdry joint where middle-aged businessmen tried to pull anything in a skirt to a chorus of squawking secretaries on the razz. It's since had a revamp, but the clientele aren't very different. The live jazz packs them in early on, but after the last trains have left the lights go down and the real action begins. The dancing takes off in front of the main bar and most boogie the night away to up-beat, if old-fashioned, grooves. The atmosphere teeters on the naff, but, like a wedding disco, it's don't-give-a-damn champagne-fuelled fun, so forget your prejudices and join the throng.
PLACE Dimly lit (of course), jazz photos on the walls (of course), but big enough not to feel claustrophobic, with three bars, a diminutive dance area and a raised dais for dining.
PEOPLE Urbane professionals mix with minor celebrities and footballers. A playground for the well off and well oiled, with a lot of good-lookin' gals. This isn't the trendiest place in London, but it doesn't try to be.

PROFS Lawyers, accountants, gallery owners, oil and gas industry execs, insurance brokers, pharmaceutical execs, chartered surveyors, wealthy tourists
CELEBS Vinnie Jones, Lisa Stansfield, Carol Vorderman, Frank Bruno, Timothy Dalton, Dwight Yorke, Andy Cole, Caprice Bourret, Kelly Brook, George Best, Belinda Carlisle, Julian Clary, Elaine Paige, Barbara Windsor, Ross Kemp
DRESS Hugo Boss, Paul Smith, Ghost, Prada, Nicole Farhi, Miu Miu, Jigsaw, Gucci
MUSIC Live Blues and Jazz seven days, DJs playing from 10.30pm Funk, R&B, Soul
DOOR No jeans or trainers; £10 after 10pm
DRINKS Beer £3.75, Wine £3.50, Champagne £6, Cocktail £5.90
FOOD French, Italian, Mediterranean, £13.95
CARDS All
CAPACITY 400, seating 300
HIRE Venue: Yes · Private Room: No

HANOVER SQUARE

Bar, Wine Bar
25 Hanover Square W1
020 7408 0935

OPEN Mon-Fri 11am-11pm	GETTING LUCKY	2/5
TUBE/RAIL Oxford Circus	EYE CANDY	2/5
BUSES 6, 13, 113, 82,	BIG SPENDERS	3/5
159, 11	MIX 55%M 45%F	
	AGE 25-60	
	PRICE Average	

AMBIENCE Basement, Chilled, Conversation, Elegant/Classic, Groups, Old World
REVIEW Attracting a predominantly post-work crowd from the surrounding banks and stores, Hanover Square has an instantly recognisable feel. It's an unremarkable low-key old-style wine bar, the sort you might go to because it's round the corner from your flat and open late. Except no one lives nearby and it shuts at 11pm. It's not somewhere you'd go for a big night out but it does offer a selection of over 200 wines, all vetted by the keen

nose and palate of top buff (and owner) Don Hewitson. Fine wine is obviously a major pull, but one imagines many come simply because it's between office and Tube. **PLACE** Low-ceilinged basement bar, painted a slightly overpowering purple, which serves to accentuate the bar's hard-to-pin-down 70s vibe. Maybe it's the subdued lighting or just that wine-bar sensation of being a random player in a 20th-century sitcom. **PEOPLE** Post-workers, post-shoppers, pre-theatre, all giving a slightly transient feel.

PROFS Property developers, advertising execs, media execs, surveyors, estate agents
CELEBS David Trimble, Richard Ashcroft
DRESS Suits, with women in Sloaney silks. Smart, generally expensive, but rarely particularly stylish. Prevailing colour of decor makes pea-green an unwise choice. Then again, it usually is.
MUSIC Classical (lunchtimes), Pop (evenings)
DOOR None
DRINKS Beer £2.75, Wine £2.75, Champagne £4.40
FOOD International, Mediterranean, £9.50
CARDS All
CAPACITY 160, seating 120
HIRE Venue: Yes · Private Room: No

HAVANA

Bar, Club, Restaurant
17 Hanover Square W1
020 7629 2552

OPEN Mon-Wed 5pm-2am,	GETTING LUCKY	4/5
Thu-Sat 5pm-3am,	EYE CANDY	1/5
Sun 5pm-1am	BIG SPENDERS	3/5
TUBE/RAIL Oxford Circus	MIX 50%M 50%F	
BUSES 6, 11, 13, 113,	AGE 25-30	
82, 159	PRICE Average	

AMBIENCE Basement, Bump 'n' Grind, Dancing, Friendly, Groups, Late Night Open, Live Music, Party, Pulling
REVIEW A heady stream of Latin music from salsa and bossa nova to Ricky Martin-style pop, courtesy of live musicians and DJs from London's best clubs and radio stations. The dance floor is packed with Brazilian bankers, Angolan students, Malaysian accountants and sexy secretaries, all grinding their hips in hot pursuit of the good-natured waiting staff and incidental dancing partners. You'll be hard pushed to find an unsmiling face and the jumpy, infectious feel-good atmosphere is conducive to pairing total strangers off. Be warned though, that the lustier your Latino dance moves, the higher your chances. And competition is tough.

PLACE Large deep, dark basement. An overhead wrought-iron snake winds its way along the ceiling, no doubt the inspiration for a few rum-fuelled congos. Designed by Andrew Shipley, the space maximises the bar area and the dance floor, relegating diners to animal-print banquettes in a back room.
PEOPLE Leave your hang-ups at the door – the refreshing, international mojito-drinking crowd are intent on livin' la vida loca.

PROFS Retailers, students, bankers, accountants
CELEBS Chris Eubank, Graham Gooch, Jo Guest, Scott Michaelson (formerly known as Brad from Neighbours)
DRESS Smart casual: Jigsaw for the chicas, Hugo Boss for the chicos
MUSIC Live Latin American Thu, Sun 9pm-close; DJs Mon, Tue, Wed, Fri, Sat 8pm-close
DOOR Smart dress
DRINKS Beer £3.25, Wine £3.35, Champagne £4.50, Cocktail £4.95
FOOD Mediterranean, £9
CARDS All
CAPACITY 400, seating 180
HIRE Venue: Yes · Private Room: No

HUSH

Restaurant Bar
8 Lancashire Court, Brook Street W1
020 7659 1500

OPEN Mon-Sat 11am-11pm	GETTING LUCKY	4/5
TUBE/RAIL Bond Street	EYE CANDY	2/5
BUSES 8	BIG SPENDERS	4/5
	MIX 55%M 45%F	
	AGE 28-50	
	PRICE Expensive	

AMBIENCE Exclusive, Lounge Atmosphere, Queues
REVIEW Play spot the Moore, ex-007 pops in but really it's the domain of Moore Junior, Geoffrey. A man who doesn't suffer from low self-esteem, what with the gallery of famous mates saying 'hush' like it's some celeb-cult. His cravats, Aspen-Cannes tan and Panavision-shades brings an air of Monte Carlo to lil 'ole Lancashire Court, bless him. Hush packs in the baby blue polo shirt brigade, complete with matching blonde fillies. When the standing room fills, the action ignites. One bravely stupid late 30-something attempts to net three girls, while his two mates watch from a distance. The girls treat him to monosyllabic answers and buckets of disdain – which goes right over his balding head – he is a master of the universe, after all. Bar manager Reece Clarke rules with panache. A Manolo's skip from Bond Street, there's even a cocktail dedicated to Donatella – presumably lurid orange with a peach 'cleavage' garnish.
PLACE Tucked away in cobbled Mayfair courtyard. Ground floor brasserie with first-floor restaurant and lounge cocktail bar. Fusion designed, so comfy sofas, pouffes and rich, warm colours, plus a snug.
PEOPLE James Bond wannabes, Bond girl wannabes, Bond Street devotees, flirty thirty professionals, Fulham and Chelsea guys and gals, a sprinkling of fashionistas, City slickers and Mayfair denizens.

PROFS Bankers, actors, shoppers
CELEBS Roger Moore, David and Victoria Beckham
DRESS Apres-ski Aspen, rockstar denim, office girl nylon – whatever you fancy but to catch Geoffrey's eye think Voyage/Julien Macdonald rather than Next/Zara
MUSIC Chart
DOOR Smart casual
DRINKS Beer £3.80, Wine £3.75, Champagne £6.50, Cocktail £7
FOOD French, £12
CARDS No Diners
CAPACITY 80, seating 40
HIRE Venue: Yes · Private Room: Yes

L'ODEON

Bar, Restaurant
65 Regent Street W1
020 7287 1400

OPEN Mon-Sat 11am-1am	GETTING LUCKY	3/5
TUBE/RAIL Piccadilly Circus	EYE CANDY	4/5
BUSES 3, 15, 159	BIG SPENDERS	4/5
	MIX 50%M 50%F	
	AGE 30-50	
	PRICE Expensive	

AMBIENCE Conversation, Elegant/Classic, Late Night Open, Live Music, Views
REVIEW People-watching on Regent Street doesn't get much better. A catwalk-type approach splits the bar and leads visitors sashaying into the restaurant, a swanky first-floor space with terrific views from the many window tables or the bar by the entrance. The views may be great but customers are just as likely to be looking at each other. Although its cutting-edge trendiness has blunted somewhat since Bruno Loubet's departure, Pierre Condou's huge venue still attracts its fair share of well-known faces. Live jazz comes courtesy of a piano and double bass spanning the cocktail anthems from tempo to smoochy.
PLACE Outside, a listed Grade I building, part of a Nash Terrace. Inside, the long cream-coloured, Art Deco themed room is cleverly broken up with partitions to give the illusion of a much smaller area. There are stools to teeter on in the heart of the bar, but you can get much more comfortable further back.
PEOPLE A diverse selection as one might expect from the location. The bar may look designer but it doesn't attract any particular type, with the stylishly dressed occasionally joined by the woefully attired.

PROFS Professionals, lawyers, management consultants, media execs, musicians, publishers
CELEBS Robbie Williams, George Michael, George Lucas, Annie Lennox, Kevin Spacey, Angelica Huston
DRESS Sleek and smart – lots of power dressing and labels
MUSIC Live Jazz Thu-Sat
DOOR Smart casual
DRINKS Beer £3.50, Wine £3.90, Champagne £6.90, Cocktail £7.50
FOOD Modern European, £14.50
CARDS All
CAPACITY 230, seating 60
HIRE Venue: Yes · Private Room: Yes

MOMO

Bar, Restaurant
25 Heddon Street W1
020 7434 4040

OPEN Mon-Sat 7.30pm-1am	GETTING LUCKY	2/5
TUBE/RAIL Piccadilly Circus	EYE CANDY	5/5
BUSES 12, 23, 53, 94, 139, 159	BIG SPENDERS	4/5
	MIX 50%M 50%F	
	AGE 25-50	
	PRICE Expensive	

AMBIENCE Groups, Late Night Open, Opulent, Party, Souk, Star Spotting, Destination/Wishlist, Exclusive/Chic
REVIEW Once upon a time, the sacred Momo membership keyring was the party scene's equivalent to the keys to heaven's gates. In the Maghreb-themed restaurant/bar's heyday, long supermodel limbs jostled for space in the tiny subterranean Kemia bar-hell, it was even Madonna's nightspot of choice. Now more office girl than It girl, the place is still rammed packed every night and the Momo Special cocktails taste as good as ever.
PLACE Though you can copy the Maghreb-themed Momo look – artfully strewn cushions, low tables, lanterns – from a Freeman's catalogue, it's still one of the prettiest spots around.
PEOPLE Cleavage-baring Middle Eastern slappers, insurance brokers, Eurotrash bankers and glammed-up office girlies have replaced the A-list royalty.

PROFS Lawyers, accountants, bankers, gold-diggers
CELEBS Once upon a time... Naomi Campbell, Sacha Baron Cohen, Meg Ryan, Cameron Diaz, Kevin Spacey, Kate Winslet, Kate Moss, Jonathan Ross, Liv Tyler, Madonna, Tom Jones, Julien Macdonald, Gail Hipgrave (neé Porter)
DRESS Ethnic eclectic
MUSIC World Music – Momo now boasts a handful of own-brand CDs, DJs
DOOR Still tricky after all these years
DRINKS Beer £3.50, Wine £3.50, Champagne £7, Cocktail £6.50
FOOD Couscous, Moroccan, North African, Tagine, £15
CARDS All
CAPACITY 100, seating 50
HIRE Venue: Yes · Private Room: No

NICOLE'S

Bar, Restaurant
158 New Bond Street W1
020 7499 8408

OPEN Mon-Fri 10am-10.45pm, Sat 10am-6pm	GETTING LUCKY	1/5
TUBE/RAIL Green Park	EYE CANDY	4/5
BUSES 8	BIG SPENDERS	4/5
	MIX 50%M 50%F	
	AGE 30-50	
	PRICE Expensive	

AMBIENCE Conversation, Elegant/Classic, Groups, Jet Set
REVIEW The time to visit Nicole's is at lunch, when the bar and restaurant are absolutely packed with either the seriously beautiful or the seriously successful – or that killer combination of both. The attention to detail in the name of elegance is fastidious, with pre-iced

champagne glasses and faultless service. On the down side, the place can seem rather soulless and when Bond Street empties, so does Nicole's. After six, the only customers left are half-a-dozen stalwarts meeting for after-work drinks and a few bag-laden fashion-obsessed Japanese tourists.

PLACE Precisely what you would expect of style guru Nicole Farhi. Muted and luxurious in creams and brown leather with a polished stainless steel top bar. The only stand-out feature is a wall covered in bull's-eye mirrors – useless for people watching, but visually effective.

PEOPLE Coolly cosmopolitan types taking a break from credit card flexing. Though the clientele are unsurprisingly well-coiffed and manicured, Nicole's is surprisingly free of ladies who lunch.

PROFS Bankers, art dealers, management consultants, financiers, publishers, magazine journalists, TV presenters, shop managers
CELEBS Ulrika Jonsson, Belinda Carlisle, Pet Shop Boys, Ralph Fiennes, John Cleese, Lulu, William Boyd
DRESS Nicole Farhi, of course. If not, crisp clean lines and simple but stylish cuts. Nothing too flamboyant or 'unBritish'
MUSIC Classical, Jazz
DOOR Smart casual
DRINKS Beer £3.50, Wine £3.75, Champagne £7.25, Cocktail £5.50
FOOD Modern European, £16
CARDS All
CAPACITY 200, seating 80
HIRE Venue: Yes · Private Room: No

NO. 10

Bar, Club, Wine Bar
10 Old Burlington Street W1
020 7439 2330

OPEN Tue-Fri 6pm-11pm,	GETTING LUCKY	3/5
Thu-Sat 10pm-6am	EYE CANDY	2/5
TUBE/RAIL Piccadilly Circus	BIG SPENDERS	3/5
BUSES 3, 6, 12, 13, 15, 23,	MIX 50%M 50%F	
	AGE 25-45	
	PRICE Expensive	

AMBIENCE Dancing, Groups, Late Night Open, Party, Pulling
REVIEW Tucked away on a quiet street to the west of Regent Street, this relatively hard-to-find bar gets very little in the way of passing trade, which explains its double life. Immediately post-work it operates as a wine bar for the folk from surrounding galleries, marketing consultancies and property and finance houses. It reopens as a club, playing soul, garage, hip hop and R&B to a dressed-up crowd almost 'til sunrise. In both its incarnations, there's a lot of by the bottle Moët consumption, but that's the full extent of crossover between its two faces.
PLACE Roomy upstairs bar, painted in a potentially overpowering mauve with mirrored dance floor at one end and time warp leather furnishing. Smaller, more tranquil downstairs bar.
PEOPLE Two very different looks; after-work drinkers are smart Soho types making the most of happy hour, after-dark drinkers are ghetto fabulous clubbing types making the most of the Champers and the dance floor.

PROFS Music professionals, fashion professionals, magazine publishers, film crews, TV producers, retail staff, travel agents, insurance brokers, footballers, TV presenters
CELEBS John Fashanu, Celestine Babayaro, Alexander O'Neal, Lennox Lewis, Busta Rhymes, Brian Harvey
DRESS Dark suits early on, but then the late shift turns up to add a splash of bling bling glamour
MUSIC Funk, Jazz, Garage, Hip Hop, Reggae, R&B, Soul
DOOR Smart, no trainers or caps; Thu £6-8, Fri £10, Sat £5-10 (after 11pm)
DRINKS Beer £3.50, Wine £3.50, Champagne £7
CARDS No MasterCard, Diners or Amex
CAPACITY 200, no seating
HIRE Venue: Yes · Private Room: No

NOBLE ROT

Members Bar, Restaurant
3-5 Mill Street W1
020 7629 8877

OPEN Tue-Sat 6pm-3am	GETTING LUCKY	5/5
TUBE/RAIL Oxford Circus	EYE CANDY	3/5
BUSES 3, 6, 12, 13, 15, 23,	BIG SPENDERS	5/5
53, 88, 94, 139, 159	MIX 55%M 45%F	
	AGE 25-50	
	PRICE Very expensive	

AMBIENCE Exclusive, Fashionable, Late Night Open
REVIEW Noble by name and by nature, this Hello! society hangout is owned by ex-banker, Danishman Søren Jessen. Parker-Bowles, Dent-Brocklehurst and Nikolaus of Greece are committee members. Perfect gold-digging territory? Our spies sidled past Jerry Springer (looking to expose Eurotrash rather than White Trash?) and grandmaster socialite Nicky Haslam. Men are better served by the patronage of the Kidd sisters. The privilege of sitting costs about £130, but for that you get a bottle of spirits and 2 mixers! Stand and drink cocktails instead. A DJ spins and it all kicks off around midnight. One minute there's a lot of people standing around, not knowing what they're doing and the next you can't see for flailing skinny bodies. Some were beautifully cool and then there was the Hugh Grant type, arms pumping like a frenzied Thunderbird.
PLACE Candlelit-basement members bar below restaurant with pretensions of Marrakech. You know – rugs, louche seating and the odd drape or two.
PEOPLE Double-barrel debs meet German lawyers, the Kidd sisters have a girls' night out, ex-Westminster schoolies run into people they've not seen for absolutely ages.

PROFS Bankers, lawyers, models, It girls, PRs, minor European royalty, fashionistas
CELEBS The Kidd sisters, Jerry Springer, Nicky Haslam, Beverly Bloom, Tom Parker Bowles
DRESS Voyage, Whistles, Pink, Savile Row, Gieves & Hawkes, Burberry, Prada, Hackett, Polo
MUSIC Jazz, R&B, DJs
DOOR Members only, dress to impress
DRINKS Beer £3.50, Wine £5.50, Champagne £8.50, Cocktail £7.50
FOOD Modern European, £20
CARDS All
CAPACITY 120, seating 60
HIRE Venue: Yes · Private Room: No

PAPARAZZI LOUNGE

Bar, Club, Members Club, Restaurant
9 Hanover Street W1
020 7355 3337

OPEN Tue-Wed 6pm-3am, Thu-Sat 6pm-6am	**GETTING LUCKY**	**4/5**
TUBE/RAIL Oxford Circus	**EYE CANDY**	**4/5**
BUSES 3, 6, 12, 13, 15, 23,	**BIG SPENDERS**	**5/5**
	MIX 50%M 50%F	
	AGE 18-35	
	PRICE Expensive	

AMBIENCE Dancing, Late Night Open, Live Music, Jet Set, Party, Basement, Pulling
REVIEW Descend red-carpeted stairs into the subterranean Paparazzi Lounge and leave the swaying beer-guzzlers and battery chicken legs of Oxford Street way, way behind you. Clapping hands, bootylicious hipshaking, the highest of the high-class Russian whores and the sounds of Khaled and Alabina signify this is no ordinary West End bar. Paparazzi Lounge is where the sons, daughters and playmates of the oil-rich states come to party. Hard. Book a table (or risk spending the night in social purgatory by the bar), invite as many of your best-looking friends to crowd on to it, order a Gold Card's worth of bottles and ensure at least five international glamour pusses are dancing on the banquettes around you. Et voilà. Partying, Paparazzi-style.
PLACE Large black-and-white paparazzi snaps of Hollywood legends – Elizabeth Taylor, Sophia Loren, Richard Burton et al line the walls and waiter-served tables surround the tiny dance floor.
PEOPLE An international, mainly Middle Eastern crowd. Seriously beautiful Dior-clad babes wiggle suggestively for rather less attractive men. Guess who picks up the bill.

PROFS Rich kids, ladies of the night, media professionals, fashion designers, account execs, PRs
CELEBS David Coulthard, David Ginola, Belinda Carlisle, Lennox Lewis, Rod Stewart, Jason Donovan, Woody Harrelson
DRESS Versace, Versace, Versace...
MUSIC Arabic, World Music, Latin, R&B, DJs
DOOR No jeans or trainers. £10 for ladies, £15 for gents
DRINKS Beer £3.95, Wine £3.95, Champagne £6.95, Cocktail £7.50
FOOD Full English Breakfast, Italian, Pizza, £8.95
CARDS All
CAPACITY 150, seating 100
HIRE Venue: Yes · Private Room: No

Q BAR

Bar, Club, Restaurant
12 New Burlington Street W1
020 7434 3949

OPEN Mon-Sat 3pm-3am	**GETTING LUCKY**	**4/5**
TUBE/RAIL Oxford Circus	**EYE CANDY**	**4/5**
BUSES 3, 6, 12, 13, 15, 23	**BIG SPENDERS**	**4/5**
	MIX 40%M 60%F	
	AGE 18-50	
	PRICE Average	

AMBIENCE Bump 'n' Grind, Dancing, Glammed-up, Late Night Open, Party
REVIEW Once Sedona, now the Q, it still attracts the same glamorous crowd. The door policy has loosened to make way for evenings dedicated to music, model and PR posses. Weekends rule for the strut-your-stuff in-crowd and flash champagne drinkers. Push your way through the throngs to the packed dance floor or navigate your way downstairs for a chance to rest your stilettos. Guys will find plenty of up-for-it blondes and in-your-face brunettes eager to attract the media mogul of their dreams.
PLACE Q Bar's Moroccan decor blends well with the heady atmosphere. The split-level upstairs bar has a mini 'disco fever' mirrored dance floor and the lower level seats you comfortably on velvet couches; sweet mosaic tables look the part but only just hold a bottle/drink. Downstairs, more ornate gilt furnishings jump out and greet you, while extravagant figures adorn walls and add to the hedonistic feel.
PEOPLE Upmarket glamour junkies with apparent street cred, as well as not-so-subtle page 3 leanings. Eurotrash in full networking mode.

PROFS Bankers, tourists, music industry, PRs, TV and film execs
CELEBS Lennox Lewis, Prince Naseem, Daniella Westbrook
DRESS Smart gigolo-shiny black Versace suits, tacky cleavage enhancers
MUSIC Dance, R&B, Garage, DJs
DOOR Smart casual, Fri before 11pm £3, after 11pm £6, Sat after 10pm £7
DRINKS Beer £3, Wine £2.75, Champagne £5
FOOD Italian, Pizza, £4
CARDS No Diners
CAPACITY 200, seating 40
HIRE Venue: Yes · Private Room: Yes

ROCKET

Bar, Restaurant
4-6 Lancashire Court, Brook Place W1
020 7629 2889

OPEN Mon-Sat midday-11pm	**GETTING LUCKY**	**4/5**
TUBE/RAIL Bond Street,	**EYE CANDY**	**4/5**
Oxford Circus	**BIG SPENDERS**	**4/5**
BUSES 10, 12, 53, 88, 159	**MIX** 50%M 50%F	
	AGE 25-40	
	PRICE Average	

AMBIENCE Elegant/Classic, Groups, Minimalist, Pulling
REVIEW Tucked away in a recently developed area off Bond Street, this chic little bar/restaurant has rapidly

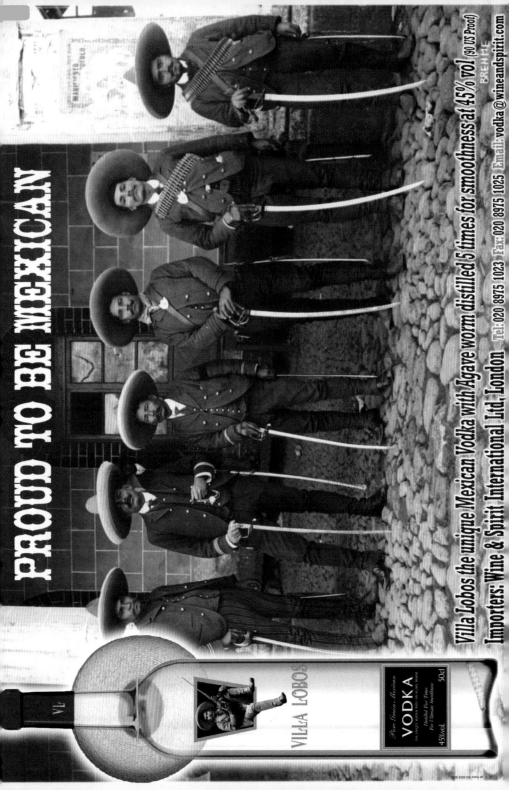

become the in place for nine to five workers craving a quick Cosmopolitan before catching the 20:10 from Victoria. Noisy suits crush into the bar area to eye up the healthy cleavage on show, courtesy of countless pretty PR girls. The friendly staff do their utmost to satiate the masses but the bar's simply too small to cope. A shame, as there's a wonderfully relaxed restaurant and private room upstairs that could, theoretically, ease the mayhem.

PLACE Jaunty little bar with elegant minimalist feel and plenty of orchids. The spiral staircase with rope bannister leads up to a restaurant area where an enormous picture of a mutt looks on. The lavvies are beautiful with elegant glass sinks.

PEOPLE 'Sex and the City' addicts who dream of a local like the ones Carrie and her mates frequent. Pulling does go on around here, but 'Fucking is just so last century dahling.' Overheard: 'Are you giving me inches, honey?' A great phrase, irrespective of meaning.

PROFS Solicitors, accountants, office workers, property developers/surveyors, magazine editors/writers, photographers
CELEBS None
DRESS Power pinstripes, designer everything, Tiffany, Helmut Lang, Chanel, Prada, YSL and the odd 'Oh, it's nothing but you'll never guess what it cost' look
MUSIC Pop, Jazz, Easy Listening
DOOR None
DRINKS Beer £2.70, Wine £2.80, Champagne £6, Cocktail £5
FOOD Italian, Oriental, £7.50
CARDS No Diners
CAPACITY 120, seating 120
HIRE Venue: Yes · Private Room: Yes

STRAWBERRY MOONS

Bar, Club
15-17 Heddon Street W1
020 7437 7300

OPEN Mon-Wed 5pm-11pm,	**GETTING LUCKY**	**5/5**
Thu-Fri 5pm-2am,	**EYE CANDY**	**3/5**
Sat 7pm-3am	**BIG SPENDERS**	**2/5**
TUBE/RAIL Piccadilly Circus	**MIX** 60%M 40%F	
BUSES 3, 6, 12, 13, 15, 23	**AGE** 18-30	
	PRICE Average	

AMBIENCE Dancing, Groups, Late Night Open, Party, Pulling
REVIEW A Croydon nightclub transplanted to the West End. From the Elnette fumes in the gels' toilets to the dodgy looking stains on the stairs – this is scary. Especially for Heddon Street. A vomit's hurl from Momo but a style continent away, this is a full-on, let it all hang out discotheque. It calls itself a 'showbar', and the staff perform groovy impromptu dance routines on a mini-stage behind the bar while a DJ spins partaay classics. Draws a post-pub crowd who are up for unabashed drunken fun in a big way. 'I Will Survive' gets the girls going. Take a tip from Gloria – 'Well, now go, walk out the door' and escape while you can.
PLACE 80s retro. Large ground floor with very long bar and large booths. All showy theatrical with drapes and hints of a French boudoir with red lights. Minute VIP room downstairs. Why?

PEOPLE Unfussy party animals. Young and naive suburbans mix with an older lot who are desperate for more drinking time but should know better.

PROFS Office workers, media employees, actors, salespeople, advertising execs, middle managers, theatrical agents, students, glamour models
CELEBS Lionel Blair, George Michael, Boy George, Tim Vincent, Gail Hipgrave (neé Porter), John Leslie, Linda Robson (Birds of a Feather), Nadia Sawalha, Julia Sawalha, B*witched
DRESS To pull. Scanty attire for the girls and bright shirts for the boys
MUSIC Chart, Pop, R&B
DOOR Smart casual, Thu £3 after 11pm, Fri-Sat £6 after 9pm
DRINKS Beer £3, Wine £2.60, Champagne £6, Cocktail £4.50
FOOD Pizza, snacks, £4.50
CARDS All
CAPACITY 550, seating 50
HIRE Venue: Yes · Private Room: Yes

ZINC BAR AND GRILL

Restaurant Bar, Cocktail Bar
21 Heddon Street W1
020 7255 8899

OPEN Mon-Wed midday-	**GETTING LUCKY**	**1/5**
11pm, Thu-Sat midday-	**EYE CANDY**	**3/5**
11.30pm	**BIG SPENDERS**	**4/5**
TUBE/RAIL Piccadilly Circus,	**MIX** 50%M 50%F	
Oxford Circus	**AGE** 25-45	
BUSES 3, 6, 12, 13, 15, 23	**PRICE** Average	

AMBIENCE Children/Families, Conversation, Elegant/Classic, Groups, Outdoors
REVIEW Zinc sits in the same quiet cul-de-sac as the super fashionable Momo restaurant, just off Regent Street. Neither bar nor restaurant ever seem to get much trade, but they can provide a quiet bolt-hole from the hamburger-munching herds of the West End. What Zinc does attract is money in spades and it certainly helps the service along if it looks like you have a bundle. Not a place to come looking for action – a discreet enquiry to the barman was met with the type of disdain Jeremy Paxman reserves for non-Oxbridge undergraduates. A pleasant enough place to take someone on a date, but clearly not ideal for looking for one.
PLACE Stylish, cool and elegant, the starkly modern bar Conran designed bar/restaurant can appear a little daunting with the predominance of aluminium, glass and hospital-like lighting. The outside tables are great for pavement dining in the summer, though.
PEOPLE Zinc attracts a well-off West End crowd from burnt-out Gold Card shoppers to media lawyers and their clients.

PROFS Film industry, TV producers, advertising execs, PRs, restaurateurs, chefs, shoppers, office workers, bankers, lawyers
CELEBS Denise van Outen, Tim Roth, Chris Tarrant, Samantha Janus, Melanie Sykes, Martin Clunes, Patsy Palmer, Michelle Collins, Sophie Rhys-Jones (Countess of Wessex)

DRESS Ralph Lauren, Donna Karan, Paul Smith, Patrick Cox, Gucci, Prada, Joseph
MUSIC Jazz, Funk
DOOR None
DRINKS Beer £2.75, Wine £2.95, Champagne £6.75, Cocktail £6
FOOD Brasserie, French, £12
CARDS All
CAPACITY 115, seating 75
HIRE Venue: Yes · Private Room: Yes

covent garden

AKA

Bar, Restaurant
18 West Central Street WC1
020 7836 0110

OPEN Mon-Fri 6pm-3am,
Sat 7pm-7am,
Sun 10pm-4am
TUBE/RAIL Tottenham
Court Road, Holborn
BUSES 1, 8, 55, 165, 242

GETTING LUCKY	**2/5**
EYE CANDY	**4/5**
BIG SPENDERS	**3/5**
MIX 60%M 40%F	
AGE 21-40	
PRICE Average	

AMBIENCE Buzzy, Cute Staff, Funky, Late Night Open
REVIEW Those foolhardy enough to venture to the not very special AKA on a Friday or Saturday may well find that if their name's not down then they're not coming in. Once in you may have to feel your way round through the darkness, or alternatively use the thudding basslines to guide you towards the sound system. Movers and shakers do just that in a frenzy of post-work networking, competing to see who has the largest expense account and the occasional fashionista tries a little too hard to look indifferent to the smell of stale ambition in the air.
PLACE Situated right next door to The End, AKA's cavernous interior is an expensive exercise in understated post-industrial chic. A steel mezzanine discretely separates diners from the hoi-polloi trying to appear nonchalant as they struggle to attract the attention of the too funkily uniformed bar staff.
PEOPLE Assorted meeja types too old or too square for Shoreditch, too young for the Hampstead dinner-party circuit.

AKA

Zinc Bar and Grill

PROFS Media, film, TV and music professionals, young creatives
CELEBS Alexander McQueen, Kate Moss, Janet Jackson, Pet Shop Boys, Boy George
DRESS Urban Outfitters, the odd suit, Boxfresh, Hope and Glory, Diesel
MUSIC Latin House, Funky House, Detroit House, New York House, Deep House, Tech House, top name DJs Wed-Sun from 10pm
DOOR Admission Wed-Sun from £2-9
DRINKS Beer £3.25, Wine £2.95, Champagne £6, Cocktail £5
FOOD Tapas Platters, £7
CARDS No Diners
CAPACITY 300, seating 100
HIRE Venue: Yes · Private Room: No

BAR 38

Bar, Chain
1-3 Long Acre WC2
020 7836 7794

OPEN Mon-Sat 10am-11pm,	**GETTING LUCKY**	**4/5**
Sun midday-10.30pm	**EYE CANDY**	**2/5**
TUBE/RAIL Leicester Square	**BIG SPENDERS**	**3/5**
BUSES 14, 19, 24, 29,	**MIX** 60%M 40%F	
38, 176	**AGE** 22-35	
	PRICE Average	

AMBIENCE Groups, Pulling
REVIEW This bar attracts punters the way Posh and Becks attract the tabloids. Populated by the mainstream masses, it may be soulless but it serves its purpose well. Bar 38 houses its customers in bland surroundings named after nothing more exciting than its street number (originally from Manchester, now in Leeds as well as London). Teams of blokes hunt out the girls wearing the shortest skirts and the girls are equally happy because there are plenty of men. A nouveau pub for the not yet nouveau riche.
PLACE Two huge beechwood floors heave on busy nights, the curved chrome staircase alone is a social mountain to climb with all those who stop and chat. Little alcoves can get interesting late at night.
PEOPLE FHM readers and Cosmopolitan sex maniacs who fill out all the multiple orgasm, multiple choice pages. By day they're low budget meeja/PR types.

PROFS Office girls and boys, admin staff, confused tourists
CELEBS None
DRESS Shiny satin slips, leopard prints, lace trims and strappy shoes with bleached highlights for the girls. Bright Johnny Vaughan shirts and TV-set glasses with shirts with Gap jeans/khakis for the lads
MUSIC Chart, Pop, Dance, Easy listening
DOOR No large groups of men
DRINKS Beer £2.85, Wine £2.95
FOOD Asian, Traditional British, £6
CARDS All
CAPACITY 460, seating 100
HIRE Venue: Yes · Private Room: No

THE BOX

Bar, Gay
32-33 Monmouth Street WC2
020 7240 5828

OPEN Mon-Sat 11am-11pm,	**GETTING LUCKY**	**3/5**
Sun midday-10.30pm	**EYE CANDY**	**4/5**
TUBE/RAIL Covent Garden,	**BIG SPENDERS**	**3/5**
Leicester Square	**MIX** 95%M 5%F	
BUSES 24, 29, 38, 176	**AGE** 20-35	
	PRICE Average	

AMBIENCE Casual, Conversation
REVIEW How brown is your tan, how white are your teeth and have you been down the gym lately? No? Oh dear. Anyone ugly or overweight visiting this café-bar will be in for a night of inferiority complex hell. It's not that The Box is unfriendly. It isn't. The freely-given smiles alone would make the rank and file of American dentistry proud. It's just that male grooming is considered a matter of life and death at this intimate venue. A bigger Box it may be after a recent revamp, but things are still a little tight. There's hardly room to change your mind here, let alone shake your little tush, although that doesn't stop the boyz from trying.
PLACE Done up in neutral shades of cream and brown, with regularly changing artwork on the walls. By day, The Box is more Mediterranean café than bar; when night falls, it's party time – get blinded by disco lights or deafened by thumping house, then shout yourself hoarse chatting someone up.
PEOPLE With more happy campers than a weekend at Butlins, The Box caters to a theatrical crowd of muscle Marys and disco bunnies who are no strangers to the beauticians. These lot have been UVd, primped, preened, plucked and primed to perfection.

PROFS Marketing execs, sales reps, media execs, actors
CELEBS Julian Clary, Rupert Everett, Alexander McQueen, Graham Norton, Kylie Minogue, Dannii Minogue, Emma Bunton, John Cleese, Glenda Jackson
DRESS Gucci, D&G, Moschino, Nicole Farhi, Helmut Lang and Calvin Klein with a smattering of Gap, Next and Levi's
MUSIC Funk, Chart, House, Disco, Dance
DOOR None
DRINKS Beer £2.80, Wine £3, Champagne £5, Cocktail £5
FOOD Mediterranean, Modern Eclectic, £8.50
CARDS No Diners
CAPACITY 200, seating 90
HIRE Venue: No · Private Room: No

BRASSERIE MAX

Hotel Bar
Covent Garden Hotel, 10 Monmouth Street WC2
020 7806 1000

OPEN Mon-Sat 7am-11pm,	**GETTING LUCKY**	**1/5**
Sun 7am-10.30pm	**EYE CANDY**	**3/5**
TUBE/RAIL Covent Garden,	**BIG SPENDERS**	**4/5**
Leicester Square	**MIX** 60%M 40%F	
BUSES 14, 19, 24, 23,	**AGE** 28-50	
59, 68	**PRICE** Expensive	

AMBIENCE Conversation, Elegant/Classic, Groups, Hip/Fashionable, Romantic
REVIEW An averagely chic little hotel bar hermetically sealed against the bustle of Covent Garden. Small groups of young, mixed Sloanes lisp at the tables: 'It's the only place we could think of where we could sit down and, you know, actually have a conversation.' Meanwhile at the bar, steam rushes up from the dishwasher and older, solitary types gaze reflectively into their drinks. You could picture Bogart slipping in from the rain, loosening his mac and leaning one elbow on the romantically underpopulated bar. He'd have all the time and space to drink long and slow, and to tell the bartender all about it.
PLACE They describe the decor as 'Anglo-French', but I imagine that's how they describe the Channel Tunnel. Both are dark, expensive and make the English look rather slow. The large peacock's tail mirror behind the bar gives you the chance to speculate on your neighbours with the advantage of dimming them ever so slightly.
PEOPLE Lone males nurse spirits and ponder romantic regrets while small groups of 30-somethings swap investment opportunities.

PROFS Bankers... investment bankers, merchant bankers, banking lawyers, traders, stockbrokers, fashion designers, girls living in Mummy's town flat
CELEBS Drew Barrymore, Jon Bon Jovi, Sheryl Crow, Kevin Kline, former All Saints, Christina Ricci, Sadie Frost, Jude Law
DRESS Classic cuts, no conspicuous labels. 'I mean, God, if you're in design the last thing you want to do is look at the same name on the lapel of the guy opposite you'
MUSIC Acid Jazz, Funk
DOOR Smart casual
DRINKS Beer £2.75, Wine £3.75, Champagne £7.50, Cocktail £8
FOOD Modern British with European influences, £15
CARDS All
CAPACITY 70, seating 50
HIRE Venue: Yes · Private Room: Yes

CAFÉ DES AMIS DU VIN

Wine Bar
22-24 Hanover Street WC2
020 7379 3444

OPEN Mon-Sat 11.30am-11pm	**GETTING LUCKY**	**3/5**
TUBE/RAIL Covent Garden	**EYE CANDY**	**3/5**
BUSES 6, 9, 13, 23, 59, 68	**BIG SPENDERS**	**3/5**
	MIX 50%M 50%F	
	AGE 25-50	
	PRICE Average	

AMBIENCE Basement, Conversation, Groups
REVIEW A no spirits or beers policy has effectively segregated wine buffs from lager louts and cocktail babes, ensuring that nearly all tipplers are regulars popping in for an after-work bottle. This means that the genial French barman Jean Luc knows most of the middle-aged single men propping up the bar, and has a pretty sure sense of whom to matchmake with whom. Not that he has any real need to with so many Sauvignon-fortified PFAs (personal financial advisers) pouncing on the first fresh piece of totty they see.

Behaviour is generally restrained though – this is, après tout, a bar that only plays classical music.
PLACE A smoky basement, decorated in London's most ubiquitous style: light-wood floors, cube stools and tables and, yawn, it's those black-and-white photographs again, this time with a Covent Garden ballet and opera theme.
PEOPLE A Joe-average crowd of local office workers and the odd corps de ballet dancer or chorus member. Mercifully free of the hordes that descend upon this part of town on weekends.

PROFS Marketing staff, insurance brokers, publishers, opera staff, theatre technicians, shop staff
CELEBS Amanda Barry, Placido Domingo
DRESS Men: City suits (Hugo Boss, Pierre Cardin) with the odd flashy Hèrmes/Ede & Ravenscroft tie. Women: dark, tailored suits, little black velvet numbers and court shoes, lush perfume, Louis Vuitton bags in abundance
MUSIC Classical
DOOR None
DRINKS Beer £2.75, Wine £3, Champagne £5.50
FOOD French, International, Modern European, £8
CARDS All
CAPACITY 100, seating 40
HIRE Venue: No · Private Room: No

COVENT GARDEN BRASSERIE

Restaurant Bar
1-2 The Piazza WC2
020 7240 6654

OPEN 7 days 9am-midnight	**GETTING LUCKY**	**1/5**
TUBE/RAIL Covent Garden	**EYE CANDY**	**1/5**
BUSES 6, 9, 13, 23, 59, 68	**BIG SPENDERS**	**2/5**
	MIX 20%M 80%F	
	AGE 20-60	
	PRICE Average	

AMBIENCE Casual, Conversation, Touristy, Late Night Open
REVIEW Some bars offer outdoor seating because it's continental, spontaneous and sexy. And others do it because there isn't enough room inside. Even if the interior of the Covent Garden Brasserie was big enough to swing a cat, any self-respecting moggy would recoil in horror at the thought of claws caught in plastic ivy. So most people do tend to drink alfresco, 'even in the rain' say the waitresses. But don't worry about distinguishing this bar from the plethora of pavement cafés in Covent Garden: you'll recognise it by the (mainly female) clientele who are noticeably more provincial than their neighbours. If they're not tourists delving into girth-enhancing moneybelts, then they're saying 'Spaghetti Bolognese, Justine? Feeling frisky are you?' Frankly, no.
PLACE Anonymous alcove inspired less by the Piazza than Pizza Hut. Plastic-coated, duvet-patterned tablecloths adhere to the elbows, fluorescent lighting filters through faux foliage, and 'bohemian' blackboards boast banality.
PEOPLE Middle-aged Boots blondes with handbag straps bisecting their be-jumpered breasts. Tourists, shop assistants, people who got tired of walking and picked the wrong moment to say 'Oh, let's just sit down'.

PROFS Local theatre staff, students
CELEBS Deepak Verma (Sanjay from EastEnders)
DRESS Littlewoods and their German/Italian/Austrian etc. equivalents
MUSIC Easy Listening, Chart, Pop

DOOR None
DRINKS Beer £2.80, Wine £2.50
FOOD American Breakfast, Brasserie, Continental Breakfast, £6.95
CARDS All
CAPACITY 110, seating 55
HIRE Venue: Yes · Private Room: No

DETROIT

Bar, Cocktail Bar, Restaurant
35 Earlham Street WC2
020 7240 2662

OPEN Mon-Sat 5pm-midnight	GETTING LUCKY	5/5
TUBE/RAIL Covent Garden	EYE CANDY	4/5
BUSES 6, 9, 13, 23, 59, 68	BIG SPENDERS	3/5
	MIX 40%M 60%F	
	AGE 20-35	
	PRICE Average	

AMBIENCE Basement, Buzzy, Casual, Cute Staff, Dancing, Groups, Hip/Fashionable, Late Night Open, Pulling
REVIEW A trendy, subterranean cave of a cocktail bar/restaurant, this is the sort of place casting directors and modelling agencies die for. Beautiful men everywhere. At the door, behind the bar, in private alcoves, and even in the kitchen, it's packed wall-to-wall. Although some customers seem to suffer from a terminal case of vanity, this isn't enough to dampen the bar's buzz; girls in pairs may well spend an entire evening swaying by the DJ unnoticed.
PLACE Underground Mad Max designer apocalyptic cave meets Star Wars bar, with spiral staircase, sand-covered walls and lots of alcoves thrown in for good measure.
PEOPLE Professional dancers rub shoulders with TV producers, no doubt plotting the Beeb's next thrilling docu-drama 'The Royal Ballet, Uncovered'.
PROFS Media, PRs, film employees, advertising execs, dancers, fashion employees, musicians, money brokers, artists, bar and restaurant staff
CELEBS Alexander McQueen
DRESS Wear a suit and stand out like a sore thumb. Gaultier wannabes, Boxfresh, Outrage, Diesel, Prada
MUSIC House, Jazz, Ambient, DJs Thu-Sat
DOOR None
DRINKS Beer £3, Wine £3.50, Champagne £5.90, Cocktail £5
FOOD Mediterranean, £9.50
CARDS All
CAPACITY 200, seating 150
HIRE Venue: Yes · Private Room: Yes

THE END

Club
16a West Central Street WC1
020 7419 9199

OPEN Mon 10pm-3am, Thu 10pm-4am, Fri 11pm-6am, Sat 10pm-7pm, Sun varies	GETTING LUCKY	3/5
TUBE/RAIL Tottenham Court Road, Holborn	EYE CANDY	3/5
BUSES 1, 8, 55, 165, 242	BIG SPENDERS	3/5
	MIX 50%M 50%F	
	AGE 18-35	
	PRICE Expensive	

AMBIENCE Basement, Buzzy, Dancing, High Energy, In-yer-face, Late Night Open, Mashed-up, Party
REVIEW Mr C's purpose-built club for clubbers, heavy on the techno, breakbeat, drum 'n' bass and UK garage. The End is a club for people who know exactly what they want from a night out. And a lot of them do. The queues outside may be huge but the door policy is relaxed and so too is the security. The crowds are nearly always chilled and friendly but then, not many of them are on the beers. The End was built for dancing and therein lies its one and only real fault. Namely that, when it gets packed, and it does get packed, there's no real escape.
PLACE Blue and brick vaulted. The two dance floors (one long, narrow and sprung, the other surrounded by seating) are big but occasionally not big enough to service such a popular venue.
PEOPLE The well dressed mix with the usual dressed-down drum 'n' bass crowd. Dancing is the key, with romancing usually a long way from anyone's mind.
PROFS Music industry executives, flight attendants, architects' assistants, printers, accountants, musicians, producers, students, DJs
CELEBS Prince, Puff Daddy, Robbie Williams, Björk, former Spice Girls, Lennox Lewis, Carl Cox, Mr C, Cat Deeley, Janet Jackson, Norman Cook (Fatboy Slim)
DRESS Karen Millen, Venom, Adidas, Cyberdog, Jigsaw, Duffer, Diesel, Oasis, FCUK, Boxfresh, Gucci and a lot of combats
MUSIC Dedicated nights, cutting-edge DJs include Jazzy Jeff, Laurent Garnier and Carl Cox
DOOR From 10pm, £3-20
DRINKS Beer £3.25, Wine £2.90, Champagne £8
FOOD None
CARDS No Switch
CAPACITY 1000, seating 100
HIRE Venue: Yes · Private Room: No

FREEDOM BREWING COMPANY

Pub
41 Earlham Street WC2
020 7240 0606

OPEN Mon-Sat midday-11pm, Sun midday-10.30pm	GETTING LUCKY	3/5
TUBE/RAIL Covent Garden	EYE CANDY	3/5
BUSES 6, 9, 13, 23, 59, 68	BIG SPENDERS	3/5
	MIX 60%M 40%F	
	AGE 25-40	
	PRICE Average	

AMBIENCE Basement, Cute Staff, Groups
REVIEW The mother bar of Freedom in Ganton Street and a mother of a bar in its own right. A big, blond wood basement with an impressively shiny wall of copper vats and an impressively shiny clientele with copper tans. Freedom was one of London's first 'brew bars' and the beer is the reason to come – top-quality stuff, whether you're necking Organic, Wheat or Soho Red. And for the indecisive, there is a sampler selection. Freedom has a better-than-OK restaurant section and (perhaps unwisely from the management's point of view, if they want to fill the dining area up) the most moreish bar snacks in this postcode.
PLACE Airy and very pale. A mix of high stools around the 'look at me' middle tables and the 'actually I've

already got a boyfriend' banquettes. It's nicely relaxed during the day, pleasantly cool in summer and more packed at night.
PEOPLE Designer Suits enjoying a post-work pint, Saturday shoppers and Sunday chillers.

PROFS Solicitors, marketing executives, musicians, TV professionals, actors, media professionals, fashion designers
CELEBS Julianna Marguiles, Brendan Fraser
DRESS Whistles, Hugo Boss suits, Boxfresh, FCUK
MUSIC Pop, Jazz, Funk, Dance
DOOR None
DRINKS Beer £2.95, Wine £3.35, Champagne £5.50, Cocktail £5.85
FOOD Mediterranean, £8.50
CARDS All
CAPACITY 350, seating 100
HIRE Venue: Yes · Private Room: No

FREUD

Bar
198 Shaftesbury Avenue WC2
020 7240 9933

OPEN Mon-Sat 11am-11pm,	**GETTING LUCKY**	**3/5**
Sun midday-10.30pm	**EYE CANDY**	**3/5**
TUBE/RAIL Covent Garden,	**BIG SPENDERS**	**3/5**
Tottenham Court Road,	**MIX** 55%M 45%F	
BUSES 8, 19, 24, 55,	**AGE** 25-35	
134, 176	**PRICE** Cheap	

AMBIENCE Basement, Casual, Chilled, Conversation, Funky, Live Music, Student
REVIEW This high-ceilinged but intimate basement bar does not advertise as a matter of policy. Pretentious? Well, perhaps just a tad, but it really doesn't need to be. Opened in 1986, Freud was one of the quintessential 80s hang-outs and still seems to be going strong, even if now they may rely more on passing tourist and shopping trade. The interior-designed, distressed-chic decor looks a bit dated now but can still impress, if you like that sort of thing. Despite the evident trendiness of many punters the atmosphere is chilled and informal. People keep more or less to themselves, although the closeness of the tables would make it easy to strike up conversations if you could get a word in. The ice-cube-down-yer-trousers cool staff serve up large and delicious cocktails and Freud's famous Bloody Marys are better than ever before.
PLACE Small basement bar in minimalist Gothic style, subdued lighting and de rigueur uncomfortable chairs.
PEOPLE Creative types, Neal Street refugees, funky sophisticates who aren't bothered that this place has been going longer than is strictly acceptable.

PROFS Advertising employees, interior designers, art students
CELEBS Alex James, Tim Roth, Saskia Reeves, Lenny Henry, Damien Hirst, Steven Berkoff
DRESS A few suits, voguish grungy kit, Duffer, Maharishi, casual combats, Stüssy, Vans, FCUK
MUSIC Jazz, Dance, 70s
DOOR None
DRINKS Beer £2.35, Wine £1.75, Cocktail £3.55
FOOD Snacks, £4.50

CARDS All
CAPACITY 90, seating 45
HIRE Venue: Yes · Private Room: No

FUEL

Bar, Cocktail Bar
21 The Market WC2
020 7836 2137

OPEN Mon-Sat 10am-1am,	**GETTING LUCKY**	**5/5**
Sun 10am-midnight	**EYE CANDY**	**3/5**
TUBE/RAIL Covent Garden	**BIG SPENDERS**	**3/5**
BUSES 6, 9, 13, 23, 59, 68	**MIX** 60%M 40%F	
	AGE 21-48	
	PRICE Average	

AMBIENCE Basement, Conversation, Dancing, Late Night Open, Pulling
REVIEW Patrons of the Market Café crêperie, one of the alfresco focal points of the Piazza, probably have no idea about the groovy, original basement bar throbbing downstairs beneath the cobbles. Covent Garden's jeunesse argentée are to be found glugging down cocktails to an eclectic soundtrack from 70s grooves to garage and drum 'n' bass. The men are all a bit Aftershavey Davy, mind, but as far as the women are concerned, well, we all know wannabe-supermodels look just as good as the real thing. Standing in front of the 'fishtank feature' (the fishtank) is unwise: proprietor Adam Davies will start telling you about it and then at some point finish telling you about it.
PLACE Subterranean, wilfully trendy cocktail-cum-everything bar converted from a labyrinthine cellar with plenty of nooks and crannies to suit discretion-seekers.
PEOPLE Fresh-faced model types wearing extra long scarves, earnest young guns with Che emblazoned across their chests.

PROFS Advertising account execs, PR agents, music industry, models
CELEBS Chris Eubank, Nigel Benn, Melanie Sykes, Stephen Dorff, Robert De Niro, Harvey Keitel
DRESS No-blue-jeans policy, though what doorman could refuse 'Bobby' De Niro in his favourite set of snow-washeds?
MUSIC Dance, Funk, 70s, DJs Fri-Sat
DOOR Smart casual, no jeans
DRINKS Beer £3.25, Wine £3.75, Cocktail £5.50
FOOD Modern European, £7.50
CARDS All
CAPACITY 200, seating 80
HIRE Venue: Yes · Private Rooms: No

THE LIGHT BAR

Hotel Bar, Members Bar
St Martin's Lane Hotel, 45 St Martin's Lane WC2
020 7300 5500

OPEN Mon-Sat 5.30pm-	**GETTING LUCKY**	**2/5**
3am, Sun 5.30pm-midnight	**EYE CANDY**	**5/5**
TUBE/RAIL Covent Garden,	**BIG SPENDERS**	**5/5**
Leicester Square	**MIX** 55%M 45%F	
BUSES 6, 9, 13, 23, 59, 68	**AGE** 25-55	
	PRICE Expensive	

REVIEW A case of 'don't believe the hype' with one
of those baffling 'guest list only, phone and beg' door
policies. The bar can be found in the surreal surrounds
of St Martin's Lane Hotel, a theatrical production brought
to London by New Yorker Ian Schrager (Mr Studio 54)
and eccentric magician/designer Philippe Starck. There
is no actual bar – too passé – instead a clear glass
cabinet displays various crystal glasses. High stools and
banquettes make for perching cocktail rendezvous rather
than all-night lounging; if you sit between two different
light zones the contrasting colours render your face the
reincarnation of Picasso's Crying Woman. Fruit cocktails
are meaty muddles and some come with sexy, slithery
flakes of ice.
PLACE Clinical, minimal rectilinear space bathed
in red, yellow and green with one long communal
table and darker alcoves along each wall; tealights
flicker everywhere.
PEOPLE Fash mag slags, skinny fashionistas, musos,
bankers, Eurotrash.

PROFS Fashion, music, TV, film and advertising execs,
magazine publishers, photographers, Wall Street and
City moneymakers
CELEBS Boyzone, Goldie, Helena Bonham-Carter,
Jade Jagger, Kate Moss, Julien Macdonald
DRESS Pencil thin, razor sharp and don't give a damn.
Cutting-edge fashion girls meet hip, sneaker-toed
Londoners and frumpy besuited Americans
MUSIC Easy Listening
DOOR Hotel Clientele and Guest List Only
DRINKS Wine £4.50, Champagne £7.50, Cocktail £12
FOOD Asian/Cuban Fusion, Modern Italian, £8.50
CARDS All
CAPACITY 180, seating 140
HIRE Venue: No · Private Room: No

LONG ISLAND ICE TEA BAR

Restaurant Bar
1 Upper St Martin's Lane WC2
020 7240 3734

OPEN Mon-Sat midday-3am,	GETTING LUCKY	5/5
Sun midday-10.30pm	EYE CANDY	3/5
TUBE/RAIL Leicester Square	BIG SPENDERS	3/5
BUSES 14, 19, 24, 29,	MIX 60%M 40%F	
38, 176	AGE 20-35	
	PRICE Average	

REVIEW All cocktails and no kudos, all this venue is
missing is a cocky 1980s Tom Cruise lookalike shakin'
it up behind the bar. I'd bet straight cash that half the
female clientele once blue-tacked Athena black and
white man-with-baby posters to their bedroom walls.
A distinctly Euro feel; young blonde Danish, French,
Italian tourists and City bankers mingle happily while
bar staff lament the business lost from regulars who
now sink their drink at the topless bar opposite.
PLACE Two-storey bar with a pungent 80s theme.
Downstairs is more formal with heavy steel chairs,
upstairs is about as cosy as the power-dressing 80s
with black sofas on steel frames. Steel rails running
around the bar provide support after one cocktail
too many.
PEOPLE The girls here sang Madonna songs into their
hairbrushes when they were getting ready and know
all the movements to 'Vogue'. The lads all came
together in a K-reg Sierra with a souped-up stereo.
The boyz are back in town.

PROFS Administrative staff, secretaries, nurses,
police officers, insurance brokers, building surveyors
CELEBS EastEnders cast, Ian Wright
DRESS High Street labels – from Benetton to TopShop,
Reiss, FCUK, Dorothy Perkins, Nine West and Gap
MUSIC Commercial Dance, 70s, 80s, 90s, House,
DJs Thu-Sun 9.30pm-3am
DOOR No football colours/baseball caps
Mon-Wed £3 after 9pm, Thu £6, Fri/Sat £8-10
DRINKS Beer £2.85, Wine £2.60, Champagne £4.20,
Cocktail £4.95
FOOD Snacks, £5
CARDS All
CAPACITY 490, seating 90
HIRE Venue: Yes · Private Room: Yes

NAVAJO JOE

Bar, Restaurant
34 King Street WC2
020 7240 4008

OPEN Mon-Sat midday-	GETTING LUCKY	3/5
midnight, Sun midday-9pm	EYE CANDY	3/5
TUBE/RAIL Covent Garden	BIG SPENDERS	3/5
BUSES 6, 9, 13, 23, 59, 68	MIX 50%M 50%F	
	AGE 25-45	
	PRICE Average	

AMBIENCE Casual, Groups, Late Night Open, Party
REVIEW In spite of the bar's speciality – a choice of over 200 tequilas and mezcals – it has successfully transcended the 'theme bar' tag. Lunchtime can be quiet but evenings hot up when Euro-barmen get pumped up and launch into cocktail mode. The early evening crowd is a mix of City boys ready to sink some and Covent Garden media types ready to think some. The more casually attired club crowd looking to put a dent in the tequila menu turn up towards the weekend. Meanwhile, the bar's nostalgic music compilations generate a party spirit, without intruding on conversation. Single-sex groups abound so there's plenty of scope, whether it's girls having a good gossip or guys talking shop.
PLACE Industrial chic setting majors on exposed brickwork, hung with vibrant native American-Indian art. An impressive marble-topped counter, some decorative Mexican tiles and plenty of pierced metalwork complete the picture.
PEOPLE Combination of after-work and pre-club crowds.

PROFS Bankers, brokers, PR agents, editors, TV employees, advertising agents, property developers, graphic designers, solicitors
CELEBS Arsenal Football Club, Alan Parker, EastEnders cast, Ryan Giggs, Sid Owen, Kelly Brook
DRESS Suits rub shoulders with casual club gear: Cecil Gee, Burton, TopShop, Oasis, FCUK, Ted Baker, Moss Bros, Blazer
MUSIC Funk, Alternative, Jazz, Dance
DOOR None
DRINKS Beer £2.95, Wine £3, Champagne £5.25, Cocktail £4.85
FOOD Southwest American, £12
CARDS All
CAPACITY 250, seating 150
HIRE Venue: Yes · Private Room: No

LE PALAIS DU JARDIN

Restaurant Bar
136 Long Acre WC2
020 7379 5353

OPEN Mon-Sat 10am-midnight, Sun midday-11pm	**GETTING LUCKY**	**2/5**
	EYE CANDY	**4/5**
TUBE/RAIL Covent Garden, Leicester Square	**BIG SPENDERS**	**4/5**
	MIX 50%M 50%F	
BUSES 6, 9, 13, 23, 59, 68	**AGE** 25-60	
	PRICE Expensive	

AMBIENCE Conversation, Groups, Late Night Open
REVIEW It's all part of the Palais du Jardin's authentic French experience to ensure that Brit customers feel thoroughly patronised by their cultural superiors, and it can be rather fun to watch. The waitairze mince disdainfully between tables replacing ashtrays with a bang. The majority of female guests are dressed up as Left Bank caricatures in classic black polo necks, sipping Chablis and gesticulating with YSL Rouge smudged extra-long cigarettes. The senior Suits are clearly moneyed, and we all know how the rich and powerful love a bit of public humiliation at the hands of London's night-shift. Moi, non plussed.
PLACE The narrow bar directly opposite the door serves as a chilly foyer for the two-storey restaurant. It's decked out like a minimalist, upmarket Dôme: all right angles and hard white edges, cheap chipped chairs and wobbly tables.
PEOPLE City sloggers who just want to release the Sartre inside, older women in gaudy Chanel, Nicole and Papa adulterers with an age-gap problem.

PROFS Bankers, media execs, models, advertising execs, film producers
CELEBS Dustin Hoffman
DRESS Pinstriped suits, Issey Miyake, Tiffany
MUSIC Easy Listening, Jazz
DOOR None
DRINKS Beer £3.50, Wine £3.50, Champagne £4, Cocktail £7
FOOD Brasserie, French, Seafood, £13.50
CARDS All
CAPACITY 450, seating 350
HIRE Venue: No · Private Room: No

PORTER'S BAR

Bar
16 Henrietta Street WC2
020 7836 6466

OPEN Mon-Sat midday-11pm, Sun midday-10.30pm	**GETTING LUCKY**	**3/5**
	EYE CANDY	**3/5**
TUBE/RAIL Covent Garden, Leicester Square, Charing Cross	**BIG SPENDERS**	**3/5**
	MIX 40%M 60%F	
BUSES 6, 9, 13, 23, 59, 68	**AGE** 25-40	
	PRICE Average	

AMBIENCE Basement, Chilled, Comfy, Conversation
REVIEW This proactively woman-friendly ale-serving Covent Garden bar (obvious fanny-grabbers are likely to have their lecherous shell-likes bent by the management) is, ironically, packed with media women dying to be pulled by media men who are simply too

free-spirited or Zen to hang around Covent Garden bars. Civilised and chilled ambience, although if you want one of the sought-after seats in the comfy basement room, blessed with armchairs and waiter service, turn up early (think sun-loungers, think Bundesrepublik Deutschland). If not, wooden recliner seats in the distinctly un-macho lilac and white ground-floor bar will have to do.

PLACE Air-conditioned street-level bar that looks expensive enough to keep out the riff-raff, while serving 18 wines by the glass at riff-raff prices, all brought to you by a company called Exciting Biting Ltd.

PEOPLE A healthy mix of ABC1s – media professionals all close to or over the 30.

PROFS PRs, recruitment consultants, solicitors, barristers, financial advisers, bankers
CELEBS Philippa Forrester, Melanie Sykes, Julia Sawalha, Hugh Grant, Diana Rigg
DRESS Non-strobing TV suits; nice middle-class mediawear, pashminas, Whistles, Hobbs, Jigsaw, Nicole Farhi
MUSIC Easy Listening
DOOR Smart casual, no soiled clothes
DRINKS Beer £2.60, Wine £2.75, Champagne £5.75, Cocktail £5.50
FOOD International, Modern British, £6.50
CARDS All
CAPACITY 140, seating 40
HIRE Venue: Yes · Private Room: No

THE ROADHOUSE

Bar, Live Music Venue, Restaurant
The Piazza, Covent Garden WC2
020 7240 6001

OPEN Mon-Sat 5.30pm-3am, Sun 5.30pm-10.30pm	GETTING LUCKY	**3/5**
	EYE CANDY	**3/5**
TUBE/RAIL Covent Garden	BIG SPENDERS	**4/5**
BUSES 6, 9, 13, 23, 59, 68	MIX 55%M 45%F	
	AGE 20-40	
	PRICE Average	

AMBIENCE Basement, Dancing, Kitsch, Party, Live Music, Touristy, Late Night Open, Pulling

REVIEW Call us old-fashioned, but this rollicking bar reminds us of everything that was good about the 80s – neon Americana, Del Boy cocktails, crash-bang-wallop live music, tarty women, pissed men, Tex-Mex muck, furious snogging and non neo-Nazi doormen. Let's face it, everyone loves a bit of tack. That's why The Roadhouse appeals to such an incredibly broad range of punters. A bit touristy maybe, but non-pretentious late-night venues are few and far between around here. Besides, where else in the West End can you dance the night away to appalling never-weres such as Limahl and Sonia, watch posey barmen chuck bottles around, get a snog off a drunken hen-night victim and wash down your fajitas with a cut-price radioactive cocktail?

PLACE Large basement filled with US road memorabilia. The dance floor is located to the left of the pinball machines and the dining carriage serving up Tex-Mex food doubles up as a rather convenient snog-booth.

PEOPLE Well up for it waifs and strays, blokes who haven't a hope in hell of getting a late drink anywhere else, girls who arrive from Essex in stretch limos.

PROFS Media professionals, tourists, secretaries
CELEBS Bob Geldof, Frank Skinner, Bill Wyman, members of Damage, Penny, Brian and Bubble from Big Brother, Pat Sharp, Meg Matthews, Vinnie Jones's other half Tanya, Vanessa Feltz
DRESS Polyester, non-designer denim, topaz jewellery and heavy metal hair
MUSIC 70s, 80s, 90s, Rock, Pop, DJs, Live Music
DOOR Smart casual, no ripped jeans or combats
DRINKS Beer £3.30, Wine £3, Champagne £5, Cocktail £3.80
FOOD American, £9
CARDS All
CAPACITY 575, seating 40
HIRE Venue: Yes · Private Room: Yes

STRINGFELLOWS

Bar, Club, Club/Strip
16-19 Upper St Martin's Lane WC2
020 7240 5534

OPEN Mon-Sat 8pm-3.30am	GETTING LUCKY	5/5
TUBE/RAIL Leicester Square	EYE CANDY	2/5
BUSES 6, 9, 13, 23, 59, 68	BIG SPENDERS	4/5
	MIX 45%M 55%F	
	AGE 25-50	
	PRICE Expensive	

AMBIENCE Groups, Cute Staff, Kitsch Decor, Late Night Open, Legendary, Pulling, Views
REVIEW Chris Quinten meets Dirty Den at the gloriously 1980s Stringfellows. Entertainment involved two bored-looking Barbie dolls sliding up and down poles in rather alarming positions. Topsy-turvy spreadeagled, in the air spreadeagled and legs behind the head on the floor spreadeagled. All in fetching plastic pants, matching bras and gloves. Why bother with accessories? When the guy came on in his white, sock-bulging Ralph Lauren he just looked gay and the audience lost interest. The 'laydeez' loo attendant wearing the attractive gilt and velvet Alice band was a living breathing, fake-tanned waxwork. Pop in for a make-over, the lipstick range is astounding. Watch out for bar staff: we didn't tip ours and she poured champagne – accidentally – down us.
PLACE Gilt and red velvet seating, mirrors and a downstairs dance floor that lights up. Dark but not enough to pretend you're elsewhere.
PEOPLE Women in white with big hair and an overheard request by a 'Moaay' drinker, 'Ah nah, can you get us a straw, it'll get me pissed quicker.' Need we say more?

PROFS Bankers, lawyers, C-list celebs, sweatshop owners, hairdressers, aerobics instructors, Essex City boys
CELEBS Peter Stringfellow, Chris Quinten (Brian Tilsley from Coronation Street)
DRESS Men in suits and women in not much (but short skirts, handbags and little white numbers will do)
MUSIC Chart, Varied, DJs Mon-Sat 8pm-3.30am
DOOR Smart casual. Free before 10pm, £15 after 10pm
DRINKS Beer £4, Wine £3.80, Champagne £8, Cocktail £6.50
FOOD French, English, £12
CARDS All
CAPACITY 800, seating 100
HIRE Venue: Yes · Private Room: No

SWAY

Bar, Club, Members Bar
61-65 Great Queen Street WC2
0207 404 6114

OPEN Mon-Fri 5pm-3am,	GETTING LUCKY	5/5
Sat 6pm-3am	EYE CANDY	2/5
TUBE/RAIL Covent Garden	BIG SPENDERS	3/5
BUSES 1, 59, 68, 91, 168	MIX 60%M 40%F	
	AGE 25-40	
	PRICE Expensive	

AMBIENCE Basement, Conversation, Groups, Friendly, Late Night Open, Party, Pulling
REVIEW This new bar on the site of the short-lived

10 Covent Garden has gone for cheerful corporate rather than super-slick. Tiger operator Chorion pounced on the place when City Bars went under and are still working out what they should do with the barn-like rooms. One-off fashion and music events help fill the labyrinthine basement. A VIP room replaces the female-only bar gimmick which generated press for the former tenant. The one-way mirrors or 'love shutters' are still in place, but feel more like an ID room on The Bill than an exclusive retreat.
PLACE The main bar has deep purple walls and free-form pods to perch on, but loses marks for the grotty carpet. The adjoining club room is still finding its feet in much the same way as the ties-off Friday night boys. Chaises longues and chandeliers in the VIP bar make you yearn for a cigarette holder.
PEOPLE Early evening is the preserve of middle-management office types who think they've found something swish. Later on the backroom boys get down and dirty much to the disgust of Linda from personnel.

PROFS Bankers, lawyers, PRs, secretaries, IT consultants, advertising, accountants
CELEBS Puff Daddy, Boy George
DRESS The odd Gucci or Prada bag spotted but this is mainly top-end of the High Street territory, Karen Millen, Coast, Reiss
MUSIC Chart, R&B, Party, DJs
DOOR No trainers. Mon-Thu £3 after 10pm, Fri-Sat £10. Membership on application
DRINKS Beer £3.50, Wine £2.95, Champagne £6.25, Cocktail £5.75
FOOD Tapas, £4
CARDS No Diners
CAPACITY 700, seating 250
HIRE Venue: Yes · Private Room: Yes

WILD

Members Club
Wesley House, 4 Wild Court WC2
020 7419 9928

OPEN Wed-Sat 8pm-2am	GETTING LUCKY	3/5
TUBE/RAIL Covent Garden,	EYE CANDY	5/5
Holborn	BIG SPENDERS	5/5
BUSES 1, 59, 68, 91,	MIX 50%M 50%F	
168, 171,	AGE 20-40	
	PRICE Average-Expensive	

AMBIENCE Exclusive, Hip/fashionable, Late Night Open
REVIEW Sean Cronin – the ex Hollywood stunt stud-muffin and Hoxton-scene progenitor behind Wild – cites this stylish new central London sweatpit as a 'New York Style Clubbing experience'. Alas, the hip hop hoorays and greased-up boy band wannabes slouching around to R&B and reworked easy listening greats in this school hall/brothel of a venue wouldn't know Studio 54 high living if it bashed them around the head with a gold lamé dildo. Nevertheless, the Wild bunch are as gorgeously outré as you'll find amid the sweaty-creviced tourists of Covent Garden. The venue – all parquet, banquette areas, champers bars and wood panelling – makes for a comfortable night's supping and shimmying, just mind you don't slip on the fake-tan residue.
PLACE More Debbie does Dallas than Brooklyn block party, Wild is an exploration into high-ceilinged, high

www.crushguide.com

campness with ketchup-hued walls, Abigail's Party shagpile and Art Deco plaster work, tarted up with bleary shots of a post-coital-looking Debbie Harry and leather sofas straight from a Columbo film set.
PEOPLE Media desk desperados, luvvies who launch and 10-minutes away ad boys throwing worryingly thrusting moves or ligging about in the stairwell performing impromptu a capellas.

PROFS Actors. musicians, artists, models, advertising
CELEBS Boy George, Mick Hucknall, Robbie Williams, former All Saints
DRESS High-end style meets youthfully funky, titfers, smoking jackets, the accessory du jour and an overt label
MUSIC Breakbeat, Funky House, Glam House, monthly Miss Moneypennys hosted nights, R&B, DJs
DOOR Look cool. Members only £8-20, apply 48 hours in advance
DRINKS Beer £3, Wine £3, Champagne £8, Cocktail £6
FOOD Modern European, £10
CARDS All
CAPACITY 2000, seating 500
HIRE Venue: Yes · Private Room: Yes

green park

10 TOKYO JOE'S

Bar, Cocktail Bar
85 Piccadilly W1
020 7495 2595

OPEN Wed-Thu 8pm-3am,	**GETTING LUCKY**	**5/5**
Sat 8pm-4am,	**EYE CANDY**	**4/5**
Sun 8pm-1am	**BIG SPENDERS**	**5/5**
TUBE/RAIL Green Park	**MIX** 55%M 45%F	
BUSES 9, 14, 19, 22, 38	**AGE** 22-45	
	PRICE Expensive	

AMBIENCE Basement, Cute Staff, Dancing, Funky, Futuristic, Groups, Hip/Fashionable, Late Night Open, Party, Pulling, Star Spotting
REVIEW If you can get past possibly the most impenetrable door girl in London, who would deny your name was on the guest list even if it was written in blood, you'll find yourself in a luminous den of sexy posturing. The Gucci'd and Prada'd young guns go for it, proud to be 'getting jiggy' in surroundings that have appeared in countless Hype Williams' style music videos. Oh, and the cocktails are top notch too.

PLACE This spacious basement bar features low ceilings, seating units upholstered in Evisu denim (yes, really), net drapes plus a very millennial multi-coloured lighting system. Customers willing to flash the cash take over one of the four arched booths where they can control their own light hues and music levels.
PEOPLE Puff Daddy meets Prince Naseem and anyone big in UK Garage. Well, almost. Mainly a well-groomed London crowd living it up in a laid-back stylee.

PROFS Footballers, models, dancers, hairdressers, retailers, rag traders, beauticians
CELEBS Stevie Wonder, Steffen Iversen, Rio Ferdinand, Frank Sinclair, Robbie Williams, Eddie Irvine, Jay Kay, Emma Bunton, Meg Matthews, Goldie, Trevor Nelson, EastEnders cast
DRESS Touches of Gucci/Prada/Versace shine against a backdrop of Oasis, Karen Millen and TopShop
MUSIC R&B, Soul, Garage, Funk, House, Rare Groove, DJs Wed-Sun
DOOR Funky and Fashionable, Guest List
DRINKS Beer £3.50, Wine £3.50, Champagne £7, Cocktail £6.50
FOOD Snacks, £7
CARDS All
CAPACITY 280, seating 100
HIRE Venue: Yes · Private Room: No

CECCONI'S

Restaurant Bar
5a Burlington Gardens W1
020 7434 1500

OPEN 7 days 10am-11pm	**GETTING LUCKY**	**2/5**
TUBE/RAIL Oxford Circus	**EYE CANDY**	**3/5**
BUSES 3, 6, 12, 13, 15, 23	**BIG SPENDERS**	**5/5**
	MIX 60%M 40%F	
	AGE 30-70	
	PRICE Very expensive	

AMBIENCE Cigar Lounge, Cocktail bar, Italian
REVIEW The return of this 70s favourite, Cecconi's is a Victor 'I liked it so much I bought the company' Kiam story. Its 21st-century transformation is all down to the impeccably groomed Hani Farsi and a few million. The handsome Farsi likes the finer things in life and conducts himself like a mafia don (without the 'fugedaboutit' gratuitous violence). He may be a man of few words but he's firmly in control. The family business (property and art, natch) and his father led him to Cecconi's as a boy – he loved it so much that now he's bought it. Like its sibling Che, it has a mindboggling range of spirits and hefty cocktail list, their forte is the Bellini. Just don't expect a booty-shaking, foot-stomping party hoe down, it's a civilised affair, attracting aperitif drinking diners, and customers who've been coming for years. Entertainment is guaranteed by the cheeky bartender Chin whose jokes occasionally skim the butt of decency.
PLACE Tiny elegant bar at the recently revamped über-pricey Italian restaurant, spruced up by David Collins (yawn). Dosh is in the details; marble bar top, lush onyx corner lamps, leather seating, etc.
PEOPLE Two attractive 50-something couples meet up for dinner, she in a colourful Warhol Monroe Versace skirt, he Mr Grecian 2000, while a less discreet foursome splashing out bigtime chat loudly in the corner.

PROFS Art dealers, property dealers, auctioneers
CELEBS You wouldn't recognise them
DRESS The 80s are back, tanned bodies (real & roll-on) in designer jeans, or little dresses, business suits, Boateng shirts. Mayfair meets Knightsbridge
MUSIC Instrumental, Pianist Thu-Sat
DOOR Smart casual
DRINKS Beer £4, Wine £5, Champagne £9, Cocktail £10
FOOD Italian, £12
CARDS All
CAPACITY 30, seating 20
HIRE Venue: No · Private Room: No

PALM COURT AT THE RITZ

Hotel Bar
The Ritz Hotel, 150 Piccadilly W1
020 7493 8181

OPEN 7 days 8am-10.30pm	**GETTING LUCKY**	**1/5**
TUBE/RAIL Green Park	**EYE CANDY**	**3/5**
BUSES 9, 14, 19, 22, 38	**BIG SPENDERS**	**4/5**
	MIX 55%M 45%F	
	AGE 35-90	
	PRICE Very expensive	

AMBIENCE Children/Families, Conversation, Groups, Legendary, Live Music, Mature/Older, Romantic

REVIEW The British version of the ambassador's reception, 'Oh Monsieur with these Rocher, you are really spoiling us'. Regal and romantic it may be, but this doesn't mean you'll meet your prince – and even if you did, he'd probably be 70 years old. It's My Fair Lady post-flower girl and gutter, which is perhaps why ol' Rex Harrison loved it so. Busy early evenings with post-work and pre-dinner/theatre drinks, don't expect riotous fun and games, do expect establishment cameos; the Foreign Secretary and the Swiss PM marched through in a penguin parade en route to dinner while we were there.
PLACE Glide through the hotel lobby to the mirror and gilt drawing-room where the bar is concealed behind mirrored French-style doors. If Dame Barbara Cartland was a bar, she'd be the Palm Court.
PEOPLE Bastions of the establishment. Old school business meetings, upper-middle-class families on special occasions, estranged rich fathers indulging sulky offspring, wealthy foreigners.

PROFS Politicans, diplomats, landed gentry, aristocrats, MPs, property, CEOs, lawyers, bankers, PRs, publishers
CELEBS Harry Hill, John Hurt, Lord Lamont, Tony Curtis, Michael Foot, David Mellor, Vinnie Jones, Joan Collins, Sir Terry Waite, Joan Rivers, Nanette Newman, Gloria Hunniford, Ronnie Corbett, Sir Trevor MacDonald, Tim Bell, David McAlpine, Rockefeller family
DRESS Either business wear with Hermes tie/Vuitton bag or evening wear with dickie bows/diamonds/family heirlooms
MUSIC Live Classical, Jazz Pianist Mon-Fri, Harpist Sat-Sun
DOOR Jackets and ties, no jeans
DRINKS Beer £5, Wine £6, Champagne £11, Cocktail £11
FOOD Light Snack Menu, £12
CARDS All
CAPACITY 120, seating 120
HIRE Venue: No · Private Room: No

10 ROOM

Cocktail Bar, Members Club
10 Air Street W1
020 7734 9990

OPEN Mon-Fri 5pm-3am, Sat 6pm-3am	**GETTING LUCKY**	**5/5**
	EYE CANDY	**3/5**
TUBE/RAIL Piccadilly Circus	**BIG SPENDERS**	**4/5**
BUSES 3, 15, 19, 22, 38, 159	**MIX** 50%M 50%F	
	AGE 25-36	
	PRICE Expensive	

AMBIENCE Comfy, Dancing, Funky, Groups, Late Night Open, Live Music, Party, Pulling, Star Spotting
REVIEW London's first New York-style lounge bar, 10 Room in its heyday was a veritable smorgasbord of football stars, fashionistas, models, singers and actors served up alongside London's finest selection of professional party people. For about eight months they sipped Cosmopolitans in a venue nearly as glamorous as themselves. Then the inevitable happened, and Earl Jeans made way for Warehouse, third division footballers took over from the premiership and matching Karen Millen skirt-and-bustier combos moved in en

masse. Still, the predatory air remains and the open layout is perfect for the lower grade peacocks to strut their stuff. Bizarrely, it seems no-one has informed the door whores of the bar's change in status, and they're as prickly as ever.

PLACE The artist formerly known as Prince would love the vast, purple painted room – one, not ten – with Grecian pillars and an abundance of red and purple sofas and easy chairs.

PEOPLE Smart, slick, flash. Dudes in white Prada loafers and blue linen suits, girls in beaded, customised jeans, sequin boob tubes and too much make-up.

PROFS Rag trades, office types, TV producers, music biz

CELEBS Emma Bunton, Michael Jordan, Spike Lee, Louise Redknapp, Chris Evans, Robbie Williams, Pierce Brosnan, Alicia Silverstone, Jay Kay, Trevor Nelson, Goldie, Andy Cole, Westlife, Audley Harrison, Backstreet Boys, Damage, Thierry Henry

DRESS Richard James, Versace, Prada, Whistles, Chloe, Jigsaw, Zara, Warehouse, Oasis, Karen Millen

MUSIC Old Skool, Live Jazz, Funk, Soul, R&B, DJs Gigs Mon-Thu

DOOR Smart

DRINKS Beer £2.80, Wine £3.50, Champagne £6, Cocktail £5

FOOD Snacks and canapés, £15

CARDS All

CAPACITY 300, seating 150

HIRE Venue: Yes · Private Room: No

ALL BAR ONE

Bar, Chain
48 Leicester Square WC2
020 7747 9921

OPEN Mon-Sat midday-11pm, Sun midday-10.30pm	GETTING LUCKY	**4/5**
TUBE/RAIL Leicester Square	EYE CANDY	**2/5**
BUSES 14, 19, 24, 29, 38	BIG SPENDERS	**2/5**
	MIX 60%M 40%F	
	AGE 18-35	
	PRICE Average	

AMBIENCE Backpacker, Casual, Groups, Party, Pulling

REVIEW The further west you go, the more laddish All Bar One's punters become, without ever quite reaching pub-ugly. On Saturday nights the Leicester Square branch is brimming with exactly the sort of blokes you'd expect to tube it all the way into town and spend the evening necking lager in the Square. They come in hordes with their surprisingly attractive, pint-drinking totty and mix in with the usual disoriented backpackers. The warning 'CCTV CAMERAS IN OPERATION' as you go in suggests that like many in this part of the West End, it's not a venue for the faint-hearted. Even less so on certain nights of the year – eg when England have just lost 7-0 at home to Borneo, Beckham o.g. 7.

PLACE Big, high-ceilinged, split-level chain boozer with all the advantages of a pub, while just managing not to be one. Friday and Saturday nights are Club 18-30 for people who'd never dream of going.

PEOPLE Morrissey & Clunes fan club members who know every episode of 'Men Behaving Badly' by heart. Fräulein Bettina Railpass wit her Svedish friends Sven und Sven und their enormous rucksacks.

PROFS Office workers, recruitment consultants, shop assistants, cinema staff, cameramen, TV journalists, bank cashiers, bank clerks, accountants

CELEBS Les Ferdinand, Ian Wright, Nadia Sawalha

DRESS The sort of low-flying labels that pile high and sell cheap in suburban shopping centres

MUSIC Easy Listening, Dance

DOOR Smart Dress, Over 21s

DRINKS Beer £2.90, Wine £3.70, Champagne £5.50

FOOD Mediterranean, Modern British, £7.50

CARDS All

CAPACITY 350, seating 120

HIRE Venue: No · Private Room: No

ATLANTIC BAR AND GRILL

Cocktail Bar, Restaurant, Restaurant Bar
20 Glasshouse Street W1
0207 734 4888

OPEN Mon-Fri midday-3am, Sat 5pm-11.30pm, Sun 5pm-10.30pm	GETTING LUCKY	**3/5**
	EYE CANDY	**3/5**
	BIG SPENDERS	**4/5**
TUBE/RAIL Piccadilly Circus	MIX 50%M 50%F	
BUSES 3, 15, 19, 22, 38, 159	AGE 30-50	
	PRICE Expensive	

AMBIENCE Basement, Cute Staff, Elegant/Classic, Groups, Late Night Open, Mature/Older, Opulent, Retro

REVIEW Even in its heyday Atlantic was outcooled by its own arbitrary door policy. One day you'd breeze past the bouncers' clipboards like Liz Hurley at a mothercare, the next you'd be treated like something that just stepped in. Popularity has waned to such a degree that bouncers no longer need to cordon off the hordes and the mighty gates of Atlantic are open to all and sundry. London's original style bar now attracts out-of-towners on the razzle but remains one of the most glamorous spots in London to wet your whistle.

PLACE The decor still impresses and the original Art Deco interior has been augmented with clever lighting and variously successful examples of pop art. Dick's Bar (named after cocktail legend Dick Bradsell) with its wood panelling, deep velvet sofas and low leather armchairs remains a low-key place for a drink.

PEOPLE Suburban 'bridge and tunnel' dressed-up wannabes at weekends, a slightly younger, funkier crowd late nights towards the end of the week, snappily dressed wide boys and otherwise hip Londoners for whom this will always be a favourite.

PROFS Bankers, film, TV and fashion professionals
CELEBS Jerry Springer, Spice Girls, Jeremy Irons, Madonna, Dave Courtney, Lawrence Llewelyn-Bowen
DRESS Ozwald Boateng, Emporio Armani, Hugo Boss, Richard James, Jimmy Choo, Karen Millen, Whistles, Press & Bastyan, Gucci, Kookaï, Earl, Evisu, Warehouse, Nine West
MUSIC Jazz, Funk, Soul, House, Garage, Latin
DOOR Smart casual
DRINKS Beer £3, Wine £4.60, Champagne £7.50, Cocktail £6.75
FOOD Mediterranean, Modern British, South East Asian, £15
CARDS All
CAPACITY 500, seating 200
HIRE Venue: Yes · Private Room: No

BAR RUMBA

Bar, Club
36 Shaftesbury Avenue W1
020 7287 6933

OPEN Mon-Thu 5pm-3pm, Fri 5pm-4am, Sat 9pm-6am, Sun 8pm-2am	**GETTING LUCKY**	**4/5**
	EYE CANDY	**3/5**
	BIG SPENDERS	**2/5**
TUBE/RAIL Piccadilly Circus	**MIX** 60%M 40%F	
BUSES 3, 15, 19, 22, 38, 159	**AGE** 22-35	
	PRICE Average	

AMBIENCE Basement, Bump 'n' Grind, Dancing, Groups, Late Night Open, Party, Pulling
REVIEW This small basement club/bar on Shaftesbury Avenue offers dirt cheap two-pint cocktails (until 9pm, Mon-Fri) and world-famous house, garage and drum 'n' bass promotions. The dearth of late-licensed bars in the heart of London dictates Rumba's curious mix of Trocadero tourists, office suits and budgeting clubbers. It's become a favourite for after-work 'dos' and the loose-tie lechery and boozy bonhomie mixes surprisingly well with the weekend Garage City massive, bumping and grinding at the capital's oldest and most highly lubricated garage night. The shortage of space and seats makes it very easy to meet people but when you wake up bleary-eyed the next day you'll probably find you've done something with someone you'll regret.
PLACE Small, long, low-ceilinged room with a sound system at one end and bar along the side. The only notable decoration is the graffiti scratched into the tables ('Kate likes monkeys' is a typical example).
PEOPLE Tourists, clubbers and office workers mingle in the dark, sipping frothy fluid from unfeasibly large cocktail jugs. Most people are blind drunk by the time happy hour ends at 9pm.

PROFS Retail workers, advertisers, sales, publishing, secretaries, recruitment consultants, students, music industry
CELEBS Björk, Bono, Andy Cole, Wesley Snipes, Goldie, DJ Spoony, Paul Ince, Ian Wright, Lauryn Hill, Wyclef Jean, Roni Size, Armand van Helden, Mel C, Darryl Hannah, Kele Le Roc, Missy Elliot, Slum Village, Kenny Dope
DRESS Karen Millen, Next, TopMan, Firetrap, Mango, Gap, FCUK

MUSIC Drum 'n' Bass, US Garage, Deep House, Salsa, African, Breakbeat, Funk, Soul, R&B, Rap, Hip Hop
DOOR No jeans or trainers on Sat; Thu £3-6
DRINKS Beer £2.90, Wine £2.60, Champagne £4.60, Cocktail £4.50
FOOD Snacks, £3
CARDS All
CAPACITY 455, seating 70
HIRE Venue: No · Private Room: No

CAFÉ DE PARIS

Club, Restaurant
3 Coventry Street W1
020 7734 7700

OPEN Wed-Sat 10pm-4am	**GETTING LUCKY**	**4/5**
TUBE/RAIL Piccadilly Circus	**EYE CANDY**	**3/5**
BUSES 3, 15, 19, 22, 38, 159	**BIG SPENDERS**	**4/5**
	MIX 45%M 55%F	
	AGE 22-35	
	PRICE Expensive	

AMBIENCE Basement, Conversation/Dancing, Elegant/Classic, Party, Pulling, Jet Set, Star Spotting, Late Night Open, Live Music
REVIEW Everyone wants to be seen to be in the C de P, but no one knows exactly why, as it's little better than the Ilford Palais. They're willing to queue for it, too. And queue and queue and... well, you get the picture. So what do you get for your 15 quid entrance fee? Well, insulting door whores aside, you get very impressive decor – think crimson velvet and Interview with a Vampire – served alongside bad attitude, sad music and expensive drinks. Whatever this place has to offer can be found at a dozen clubs across London: similar music, similar decor, same drinks, and only a quarter of the price.

PLACE From street level everything is down. Down to reception, down a sweeping staircase to the oval dance floor and bar area, then if you're really lucky, even further down into the claustrophobic VIP room.
PEOPLE Media dahlings, fashion things, suburbanites, Eurotrash, hairdressers and self-made movers and shakers.

PROFS Account execs, PRs, fashion execs, software designers, sales execs, shoe designers, accountants, restaurant managers, entrepreneurs, media execs
CELEBS Mark Wahlberg, Kate Moss, Emma Bunton, Al Pacino, Caprice Bourret, Thierry Henry, Kanu, Marcel Desailly, Steffen Iversen, Trevor Sinclair, Dwight York
DRESS Patrick Cox, Donna Karan, Joseph, Armani, Hugo Boss, Valentino, Versace, Paul Smith
MUSIC Hip Hop, R&B, Dance DJs Wed-Sat
DOOR Wed £10, Thu-Sat £15
DRINKS Beer £3.75, Wine £4, Champagne £8, Cocktail £8
FOOD International, Modern British, £34.50 (2 courses)
CARDS All
CAPACITY 715, seating 120
HIRE Venue: Yes · Private Room: No

CHEERS

Bar, Restaurant, Theme
72 Regent Street W1
020 7494 3322

OPEN 7 Days 11am-3am	**GETTING LUCKY**	**4/5**
TUBE/RAIL Piccadilly Circus	**EYE CANDY**	**1/5**
BUSES 3, 9, 15, 22, 38, 159	**BIG SPENDERS**	**1/5**
	MIX 60%M 40%F	
	AGE 25-35	
	PRICE Average	

AMBIENCE Casual, Children/Families, Dancing, Groups, Late Night Open, Party, Touristy, Pulling
REVIEW Tacked on to the side of the Café Royal in Regent Street, Cheers is a mock-up of the TV bar of the same name. Unfortunately in this case reality does not imitate TV and Cheers is full of people who don't know your name and staff who couldn't give a shit whether you came or not. However, weekend queues of tourists, office and shop types suggest the uncomplicated, stereotypically American bar, like Robin Cook to his wife, has some unfathomable appeal. Perhaps punters have fond memories of happy times spent in provincial US airports where the American bar chain rules supreme. Fortunately we've only got one in the UK, and we'd like it to stay that way. Cheers.
PLACE Faithful representation of TV's Cheers bar, minus Sam, Woody, Norm and the gang, in unlikely proximity to the Café Royal.
PEOPLE A workaday cocktail of businesspeople, office workers and confused tourists who don't know the difference between Boston, New England and London, England.

PROFS Office workers, builders, retail staff
CELEBS Chris Evans, David Schwimmer
DRESS TopShop, Next, Nike, Billabong, general waterproof tourist tat
MUSIC Chart, 80s, 90s, DJ after 10.30pm
DOOR Smart casual, no trainers, no caps.
Sun-Wed £3, Thu-Sat £6-8

DRINKS Beer £2.90, Wine £2.90, Champagne £5, Cocktail £4.50
FOOD American, £10
CARDS All
CAPACITY 600, seating 150
HIRE Venue: Yes · Private Room: No

CHINAWHITE

Members Club
6 Air Street W1
020 7343 0040

OPEN Mon-Sat 8pm-3am	**GETTING LUCKY**	**3/5**
TUBE/RAIL Piccadilly Circus	**EYE CANDY**	**5/5**
BUSES 3, 9, 15, 22, 38, 159	**BIG SPENDERS**	**5/5**
	MIX 40%M 60%F	
	AGE 25-45	
	PRICE Very expensive	

AMBIENCE Destination/Wishlist, Party, Exclusive/Chic, Funky, Groups, Hip/Fashionable, Late Night Open, Opulent, Star Spotting
REVIEW After three years Chinawhite is still enjoying peak position at the top of the club desirability stakes. It has a host of celebrity members and a list of those clamouring to join. As a result the club is about as easy to get into as free-form jazz. To men who arrive after 11pm the doors may as well be barricades of re-inforced concrete, such is the emphasis on maintaining a respectable banking baron to model ratio. They may fondly nickname it Chinashite, but members are viciously protective of their territory, so the trick is to arrive early and bring a small and slickly-dressed posse. An interesting cocktail menu (try the lychee house special) and skilled barmen will keep you amused for as long as it takes for your credit card to melt.
PLACE Decadent and louche, this Oriental-Indonesian den is a Po Na Na for the really rich. The main room includes curtained dens, a separate snug draped in silks, dance floor and expensive tables manifesting as pedestals for wannabe podium dancers.
PEOPLE Models and little rich girls come here to bathe in the drool of chiselled jawed execs, plump millionaires and demi-monde semi-celebs.

PROFS Music execs, internet execs, TV execs, models, bankers, film producers
CELEBS Kate Moss, Alexandra Aitken, Jemma Kidd, Lady Victoria Hervey, Gordon Ramsay, Carmen Electra, Leonardo DiCaprio, William Orbit, Madonna, Patrick Cox, Mick Hucknall, Robert Hanson, Mel B, Mel C, David Schwimmer, Backstreet Boys, Jude Law, former All Saints
DRESS Prada, Gucci, Armani for the boys and obscure designer label jeans/stilettos/diaphanous top combo for the girlies
MUSIC Funk, Dance, House, Soul, Salsa, DJs Mon-Sat
DOOR Open to non-members Mon, Tues £15; Thurs £20
DRINKS Beer £3.50, Wine £3.50, Champagne £6, Cocktails £7
FOOD Indonesian, Thai, £11.50
CARDS All
CAPACITY 400, seating 300
HIRE Venue: Yes · Private Room: Yes

CLINIC

Bar
13 Gerrard Street W1
020 7734 9836

OPEN Mon-Fri 5pm-3am,	**GETTING LUCKY**	**3/5**
Sat 5pm-4am	**EYE CANDY**	**3/5**
TUBE/RAIL Leicester Square	**BIG SPENDERS**	**2/5**
BUSES 24, 29, 176	**MIX** 50%M 50%F	
	AGE 21-40	
	PRICE Average	

AMBIENCE Arty, Conversation, Romantic, Dive Bar, Cosy, Funky, Late Night Open
REVIEW There's nothing clinical whatsoever about this gloriously quirky and dilapidated little bar tucked above the Chinese restaurants (buffet £5!!! Come eat ducks here!!) of Gerrard Street. Reminiscent of the dimly lit student bars of yore, the place is packed out with alternative comedians, musicians and philosophy graduates, gobbling peanuts and debating the merits of the latest David Byrne album. You can never be entirely sure of what to expect at Clinic – you could show up for an evening of South American films, a Druids convention or a drum 'n' bass night, but before you know it you'll be passionately identifying with the plight of the grandmothers of Venezuelan emerald smugglers, building scale models of Stonehenge with matchboxes or dancing like a tasmanian devil on amphetamines to Viennese drum 'n' bass. This is one crazy clinic you'll never want to check out of.
PLACE Up the Singapore Fried Rice-scented stairs to a tiny little room, papered in anaglypta and painted a dull red. A few tiny round tables over by the large 19th-century window are draped in red cloth. A bit like a miniature version of the Magic Club in 'Desperately Seeking Susan'.
PEOPLE They watch old videos of Saturday Night Live, Blackadder and Not the Nine O'clock News and can probably recite dozens of sketches by heart... 'What are four bean and four beans, Baldrick?'

PROFS Media, IT, shop workers, advertising, students, DJs
CELEBS Chrissie Hynde, Mark Thomas, Tony Parsons, Gomez, Nick Hancock, Sean Hughes
DRESS Firetrap, Diesel, Carhartt, Evisu
DOOR None
MUSIC Funk, Soul, House, Drum 'n' Bass, Breakbeat, DJs
FOOD They have an arrangement with the Chinese downstairs
CARDS No Amex
CAPACITY 120, seating 40
HIRE Venue: Yes · Private Room: No

CONRAD GALLAGHER

Bar, Restaurant
179 Shaftesbury Avenue WC2
020 7836 3111

OPEN Mon-Sat 10am-12pm	**GETTING LUCKY**	**1/5**
TUBE/RAIL Covent Garden,	**EYE CANDY**	**3/5**
Tottenham Court Road,	**BIG SPENDERS**	**3/5**
Leicester Square	**MIX** 50%M 50%F	
BUSES 38, 19, 14	**AGE** 24-40	
	PRICE Expensive	

AMBIENCE Business, Conversation, Exclusive/Chic
REVIEW Acres of glass filter urban light from Shaftesbury Avenue into the ground-floor bar above Irish chef Conrad Gallagher's new haute cuisine dining room. Retro brown leather armchairs and 50s-style glass-topped tables dotted around the lounge area lend an upmarket airport feel. As for the crowd... well, that's optimistic. On the night we visited the smattering of people were vague and varied – a few couples, a handful of leggy girls doing the pissed bambi on ice teeter, a trio of 'When I was in Hong Kong' men and some fashionista Twiglets comparing arms. The cocktails aren't bad though.
PLACE Overwhelmingly brown. A rather grubby cream floor which could do with a wipe-down, groovy glass tables and bulky chairs not conducive to intimate conversation.
PEOPLE Passers-by, shoppers and cocktail swigging professionals who live to lounge, from check-shirted City boys to Covent Garden retailers and presumably a few Irish.

PROFS Bankers, retailers, legal secretaries, solicitors
CELEBS Graham Norton, Mick Hucknall, Lady Victoria Hervey, Dean and Brian from Big Brother, Bono, Moloko, Andrew Lloyd Webber
DRESS The return of the smart casual, anything from jeans and Converse to black lace tops and mini skirts. Jigsaw, FCUK, Whistles
MUSIC Background
DOOR Smart casual
DRINKS Beer £3.50 Wine £5, Champagne £8, Cocktail £7.50
FOOD Light snacks, £5
CARDS All
CAPACITY 160, seating 80
HIRE Venue: Yes · Private Room: No

DENIM

Bar, Restaurant Bar
4a Upper St Martin's Lane WC2
020 7497 0376

OPEN 7 days 5pm-2am	**GETTING LUCKY**	**4/5**
TUBE/RAIL Leicester Square	**EYE CANDY**	**5/5**
BUSES 14, 19, 24, 29, 38	**BIG SPENDERS**	**5/5**
	MIX 50%M 50%F	
	AGE 25-35	
	PRICE Expensive	

AMBIENCE Dancing, Groups, Late Night Open, Party, Pulling
REVIEW This place could be summed up with one simple four-letter word. Pose. Denim is a typical Soho identikit style bar – all smooth shiny interior, crammed bar, dodgy cocktails and moody staff. The upstairs bar is for standing and posing, while downstairs is reserved for dancing and posing. Both floors are filled with cheap Madonna wannabes in gold lamé, snakeskin boots and cowboy hats. They make a career of sipping cocktails, sidling up to the owners of private clubs and generally clawing their way up the guestlist ladder with perfectly manicured false nails. The men aren't much better, sporting bulging sleeveless vests, too-tight trousers and Craig David-stylee facial hair.
PLACE Outside is like the monkey enclosure at Regent's Park Zoo, the plate-glass front providing brilliant views of the clonettes within. Padded walls surrounding the

dance floor lend a slight loony bin feel, while pink neon lighting reflects off more shiny surfaces than Patrick Bateman could find a use for.
PEOPLE Mobile-toting smoothies letch after scantily-clad women. Scantily-clad women letch after Platinum Card waving men.

PROFS Brokers, traders, models, D-list celebs, PR types, media whores
CELEBS Billie Piper (pre-Chris), EastEnders cast, Holby City cast
DRESS Joseph, Ozwald Boateng, anything expensive and/or 'sexy'
MUSIC Dance, R&B, DJs
DOOR Smart casual
DRINKS Beer £3.50, Wine £3, Champagne £3.50, Cocktail £6
FOOD International, Snacks, £10
CARDS All
CAPACITY 300, seating 20
HIRE Venue: Yes · Private Room: No

EMPORIUM

Club, Restaurant
62 Kingly Street W1
020 7734 3190

OPEN Mon-Sat 9pm-4.30am	**GETTING LUCKY**	**4/5**
TUBE/RAIL Piccadilly Circus,	**EYE CANDY**	**2/5**
Oxford Circus	**BIG SPENDERS**	**3/5**
BUSES 12, 13, 94, 139, 159	**MIX** 45%M 55%F	
	AGE 18-30	
	PRICE Expensive	

AMBIENCE Bump 'n' Grind, Dancing, Groups, Hormone-fuelled Club Kidz, Late Night Open, Party, Pulling, Star Spotting
REVIEW There's something oddly nostalgic about Emporium. Maybe it's the gangs of dolled-up teenage girls scanning the room as they slink sexily to Mis-teeq. Perhaps it's the predatory packs of lads roaming around in shiny shirts and weekend-best trousers, looking well-hard to the sounds of So Solid Crew. Maybe it's the fact most of these adolescent lovelies have spent two years' lunch money on their new Moschino trousers, in the hopes of pulling that fit bloke/bird from college. Whatever it is, Emporium has shrugged off the challenge of dedicated house and garage clubs, and is thriving on young punters buying into its old-style 'bright-night-out' ethos. Things are very much what they used to be.
PLACE Past the industrial Gothic door, up the stairs to the dance floor, surrounded by a vaguely Eastern lattice. The restaurant is often curtained off for private parties, leading to the nagging suspicion that they're having a better time on the other side.
PEOPLE Young burbites, footballers and weekenders looking for a slice of up-West glamour, with a few older wannabe playboys – the line between 'suave' and 'sleazy' is oh so thin.

PROFS Footballers, boxers, shop staff, students, PAs, soap stars, office administrators, models, TV, music and media professionals
CELEBS Leonardo DiCaprio, Sean Combs (aka Puff Daddy, P Diddy, Bobby), Cat Deeley, Tamzin Outhwaite, Lennox Lewis, Prince Naseem, Rio Ferdinand, B*witched,

Jamie and Louise Redknapp, Michael Owen, David and Victoria Beckham, Denise van Outen, N-Sync, Patsy Palmer
DRESS Designer labels with the tags still on. Proves they're kosher, innit?
MUSIC Garage, R&B, Hip Hop, Dance, DJs
DOOR Smart/glam; no jeans or trainers. Mon-Fri before midnight £10, after £15
DRINKS Beer £3.50, Wine £3.50, Champagne £7, Cocktail £3.50
FOOD International, Modern Eclectic, £27.50 (3 courses)
CARDS All
CAPACITY 500, seating 350
HIRE Venue Yes · Private Room: No

KING'S HEAD AND DIVE BAR

Pub
48 Gerrard Street W1
020 7437 5858

OPEN Mon-Sat 10am-11pm,	**GETTING LUCKY**	**2/5**
Sun midday-10.30pm	**EYE CANDY**	**3/5**
TUBE Leicester Square,	**BIG SPENDERS**	**3/5**
Oxford Circus	**MIX** 65%M 35%M	
BUSES 14, 19, 24, 29, 38	**AGE** 30-65	
	PRICE Average	

AMBIENCE Casual, Conversation, Arty/Bohemian, Dive Bar, Grunge
REVIEW More colourful than an argument between Gordon Ramsay and Alf Garnett, The King's Head is one of Soho's most genuinely diverse drinking dens. Where else can you find elderly road sweepers chatting about nothing to Triad gangsters? Lycra-squeezed gay men sipping Guinness with brandy-soaked pensioners? Womb-like in its power to make you stay, it resembles a 'Lock, Stock' back-drop where the resolutely no-bullshit punters gather to extraordinary effect. It's not uncommon for tourists to walk in and straight back out, as this is really a pub for people who have dedicated their services to the capital, dubious or otherwise. The next time you hear a politician spouting off about social inclusion and multi-cultural integration in London, just remember it can happen. The King's Head proves so.
PLACE Paying absolutely no heed to modernity whatsoever, and all the better for it. Dimly lit, deep, walnut-lacquered wood panels, dark blinds – imagine the shabbiest Las Vegas rat pack bar.
PEOPLE Scammers, blaggers, war veterans, slumming urbanites, young, old, male, female, gay, straight, and every shade in between. People who have been through it all, and still don't feel a day over 21. People with nicknames, and a story about how they earned them.

PROFS Everything, anything and nothing
CELEBS None
DRESS Work overalls, grey suits, cheap leather, battered raincoats and lots of gold. If a style mag decides to invent post-prole-glamour-villain chic, this is where the photo shoot will take place
MUSIC 80s, 90s, Classic Rock
DOOR None
DRINKS Beer £2.30, Wine £2.30
FOOD None
CARDS None
CAPACITY 160, seating 90
HIRE Venue: No · Private Room: No

PROFS TV employees, retailers, shop assistants, publishing employees, caterers, students
CELEBS Michelle Collins, Leo Sayer, Michael Barrymore, Steps, Boy George, Jean Paul Gaultier
DRESS Smart casual is the official line, though lagered-up, suit-clad office workers and the jeans and t-shirts brigade break up a smattering of Calvin Klein, FCUK and TopShop
MUSIC Commercial House, Garage, Dance, Soul, R&B, Brazilian, Bhangra, 70s and 80s trash
DOOR Smart; no trainers, no sportswear, admission from £3-12
DRINKS Beer £3, Wine £2.70
FOOD Snacks, £3
CARDS All
CAPACITY 860, seating 50
HIRE Venue: Yes · Private Room: Yes

LIMELIGHT

Club
136 Shaftesbury Avenue W1
020 7434 0572

OPEN Mon-Thu 10pm-3am,	**GETTING LUCKY**	**4/5**
Fri-Sat 9pm-3.30am,	**EYE CANDY**	**3/5**
Sun 3pm-midnight	**BIG SPENDERS**	**2/5**
TUBE/RAIL Leicester Square,	**MIX** 60%M 40%F	
Tottenham Court Road	**AGE** 20-50	
BUSES 19, 24, 25, 38, 19	**PRICE** Average	

AMBIENCE Bump 'n' Grind, Dancing, Groups, Haunted, Late Night Open, Luvved-up Clubbers, Party, Pulling, Student, Touristy
REVIEW State-of-the-art lighting rigs and a varied musical policy have pulled this former Welsh Presbyterian chapel back from clubland's brink and Limelight now packs 'em in seven nights a week. The club's various themes – anything from 70s and 80s pop to Bhangra and Brazilian – attract an eclectic mix of students and pissed-up tourists on the pull. Given its religious affinity, decor is decidedly Transylvanian parish church and the place is reportedly haunted by two priests and a nun. The dome and gallery areas work best, as the rest can feel quite claustrophobic. Plenty of shadowy recesses provide privacy for those more intimate moments.
PLACE Domed ceilings, an abundance of arches, narrow passages and castle-like balconies. What else do you expect from a 300-year-old church?
PEOPLE Clubbers raving to the latest in Italian Eurohouse, Italian, Spanish and French clubbers hunting for the latest in English totty, terrifyingly sexy Brazilians putting everyone to shame and a motley crew of obliterated tourists who should be ashamed.

ON ANON

Bar, Café, Club, Restaurant
The London Pavillion, 1 Shaftesbury Ave W1
020 7287 8008

OPEN Mon-Sat 5pm-3am	**GETTING LUCKY**	**4/5**
TUBE/RAIL Piccadilly Circus	**EYE CANDY**	**2/5**
BUSES 14, 19, 38	**BIG SPENDERS**	**3/5**
	MIX 50%M 50%F	
	AGE 20-40	
	PRICE Expensive	

AMBIENCE Dancing, Groups, Late Night Open, Party, Pulling
REVIEW This is Bar Disneyland, just about as sincere but not as much fun. Seven different styles of bar, from gents' club through to jazz lounge, are squashed on to three floors. The punters look like they've been shipped in as part of the set, too – paunchy suits in the 'study', angular mods in the 'lounge', and a couple of middle-aged women rummaging through their Dorothy Perkins bags in 'Raffles'. It'd be a good place to bring a bunch of disparate office workers with nothing in common. Great for schizophrenics, just a tad confusing for the rest of us.
PLACE Deep breath: think of every bar cliché and here is its imperfect incarnation. The rather ordinary café's on the ground floor, Raffles upstairs is all wood panelling and wicker seating, the lounge is bright colours and modern art. The lodge has fake stuffed animals, the loft is a bit more groovy while the club section is more over-the-top and hi-tec. The study... yawn... yawn... has 'battered' leather chairs and fake gilt-framed oils
PEOPLE Tourists and others who should know better.

PROFS Bankers, accountants, stockbrokers, traders, management consultants
CELEBS None
DRESS Like Kraft slices: tasteless
MUSIC Dance, DJs Mon-Sat
DOOR Over 25s only. Smart casual, no trainers Mon-Wed after 11pm £3, Thu after 10pm £5
DRINKS Beer £3.25, Wine £3.50, Champagne £5.25, Cocktail £4.85
FOOD Modern European, £5
CARDS No Amex or Diners
CAPACITY 1300, seating 300
HIRE Venue: No · Private Room: Yes

OXYGEN

Club, Cocktail Bar, Theme
18 Irving Street WC2
020 7930 0907

OPEN Mon-Wed 4pm-1am, Thu 4pm-2am, Fri-Sat 4pm-3am, Sun 4pm-10.30pm	**GETTING LUCKY**	**4/5**
	EYE CANDY	**3/5**
	BIG SPENDERS	**2/5**
TUBE/RAIL Leicester Square	**MIX** 60%M 40%F	
BUSES 14, 19, 24, 29, 38, 176	**AGE** 20-30	
	PRICE Average	

AMBIENCE Dancing, Late Night Open, Party, Pulling, Student
REVIEW This three-floor theme bar takes its inspiration from Star Wars and Bladerunner with a bit of The Addams Family thrown in. Nevertheless it's more zitfest than zeitgeist. Busy Friday and Saturday nights see cocktail fans taking full advantage of happy hour jugs. The much-hyped oxygen canisters are a waste of space. When will bar owners understand that gimmicks neither work nor last? Upstairs is 'haunted house' – it certainly made us scream with horror at its sheer naffness: cast-iron tables and chairs 'complement' glowing candle-cum-wall lights and heavy chandeliers. It clearly has a Transylvanian effect on the punters judging by the amount of bloody necking going on.
PLACE The ground floor is all metal 'rock' walls and chrome bar. By the time you get upstairs it's almost impossible to see anything except for the glowing jugs of sticky alcohol and fruit juice mixes masquerading as cocktails.
PEOPLE If they're young, post-college, pre-mortgage and not bothered about 'anything long term' you'll probably find them in here.

PROFS Students, comedians, bar staff, secretaries, accountants, City types
CELEBS Rob Newman
DRESS Lycra, corset-style dresses (always short), Morgan, Miss Selfridge, lairy shirts and jeans, Burton suits, Ben Sherman, Levi's, Gap, River Island, H&M, TopShop
MUSIC Chart, Dance, Garage, R&B, DJs Fri-Sat
DOOR Smart casual; no caps or hats; Fri £5, Sat after 10pm £5, after 11pm £7
DRINKS Beer £2.95, Wine £2.75, Cocktail £4.25
FOOD None
CARDS No Diners
CAPACITY 286, seating 100
HIRE Venue: Yes · Private Room: Yes

RED CUBE

Club, Bar, Restaurant
1 Leicester Place WC2
020 7287 0101

OPEN Tue-Fri 5pm-3am, Sat 6pm-3am	**GETTING LUCKY**	**4/5**
	EYE CANDY	**2/5**
TUBE/RAIL Leicester Square	**BIG SPENDERS**	**3/5**
BUSES 24, 29, 176	**MIX** 50%M 50%F	
	AGE 20-35	
	PRICE Expensive	

AMBIENCE Groups, Party, Pulling, Queues, Late Night Open
REVIEW In Red Square, Moscow, the proletariat queue up to see a pickled person plastered with lurid make-up, and it costs them £1 million per annum for the pleasure. At Red Cube, London, the proletariat queue up to see pickled people plastered with lamentable make-up, and it costs a lot more than it should for their pleasure. Like Lenin's visitors, they're all wowed-up for a glimpse of something incredible – they think they're getting cutting-edge London nightlife, when all that's on offer is low-grade suburban shite life. As any discerning Londoner will know, it was mission impossible for the team behind Sugar Reef to create a cool bar bang smack in the middle of Leicester Square. But if it makes provincial middle-management types and their secretaries happy, then who are we to complain.
PLACE Impressively renovated at a cost of £1.5 million and designed to intimidate the impoverished, Red Cube is decked out in chic scarlet, black and marble. Ironically funky touches include a disco ball over the staircase and an enormous print of a bikini'd Bond girl.

PEOPLE Brenda and Mandy have pulled on their new cleavage-baring Morgan tops after a hard days' work on the Midland's division budgets. They're keeping an eye out for soap stars, and if they see anybody from EastEnders they'll ask them to autograph a photocopied spreadsheet for the girls back in Birmingham HQ.

PROFS Secretaries, admin girls, traders, soap stars
CELEBS EastEnders cast, Hollyoaks cast, S Club 7
DRESS Next and equivalent High Street office gear, Morgan, Kookaï, Giant, Jane Norman
MUSIC Dance, Pop, Disco
DOOR Smart casual. Over 21s. Entrance £10 after 9pm
DRINKS Beer £3.75, Wine £3.75, Champagne £7.50, Cocktail £7.50
FOOD International, £15
CARDS All
CAPACITY 700, seating 360
HIRE Venue: No · Private Room: Yes

SAINT

Bar
8 Great Newport Street WC2
020 7240 1551

OPEN Mon-Tue 5pm-1am,	GETTING LUCKY	4/5
Wed-Thu 5pm-2am,	EYE CANDY	4/5
Fri-Sat 5pm-3am	BIG SPENDERS	3/5
TUBE/RAIL Leicester Square	MIX 40%M 60%F	
BUSES 14, 19, 24, 29, 38	AGE 25-36	
	PRICE Expensive	

AMBIENCE Basement, Casual, Conversation, Dancing, Elegant/Classic, Funky, Futuristic, Groups, Hip/Fashionable, Late Night Open, Party, Pulling
REVIEW One of London's first 'style' bars, popular back in the day when clubbers slowed down, stopped rushing and fancied a drink instead. But the professional party crowd have been usurped by Essex try hards who have begun to shift in, although the beauty set still cameo. The haughty door policy deters tourists, the pissed and poorly dressed; those damned by all three should just walk on by. Early evening booths are sprinkled with groups chilling after work. Later these provide refuge from the heady mingling among interactive, proactive hypesters. Be prepared to queue (stylishly) if you arrive late on Thursday-Saturday (though Wednesday is also hot).

PLACE Paul Daly's ode to timber, purple and space-age organic shapes. Basement bar with raised right-side restaurant area and a circular bar surrounded by plenty of posing room. Booth diner-style seating lines the walls.
PEOPLE Soigné, sophisticated London club crowd mixed with Essex wannabes and generic cocky cockney creatives.

PROFS Fashion executives, music industry, models, fashion students, media executives, TV promoters, artists, hospitality staff, designers, restaurant staff, bankers, actors
CELEBS Rick Parfitt from Status Quo, Jenson Button
DRESS Understated designer or kooky fashion: LK Bennett, Dolce & Gabbana, FCUK, Paul Smith, Karen Millen
MUSIC Funk, Soul, Disco, R&B DJs Tue-Sat 9pm-3am
DOOR Smart, trendy dress
DRINKS Beer £3, Wine £3, Champagne £6, Cocktail £6.50
FOOD Soul Food, £22 (2 courses)
CARDS All
CAPACITY 290, seating 100
HIRE Venue: Yes · Private Room: No

SALSA

Bar, Club, Restaurant, Theme
96 Charing Cross Road WC2
020 7379 3277

OPEN Mon-Sat 5.30pm-2am	GETTING LUCKY	4/5
TUBE/RAIL Leicester Square,	EYE CANDY	2/5
Tottenham Court Road	BIG SPENDERS	3/5
BUSES 14, 19, 38, 24,	MIX 60%M 40%F	
29, 134	AGE 20-35	
	PRICE Average	

AMBIENCE Dancing, Groups, Late Night Open, Live Music, Party, Pulling, Student
REVIEW Although Latino-themed clubs are usually hellishly full of drunken accountants in sweaty groups shouting 'arriba' while swinging their arses in what they believe to be a sinuous Hispanic way, Salsa succeeds by getting the basics spot on. Good music provided by live bands, bar staff who appear to be having a great time and a good balance between dance floor, table

areas and bar space create an atmosphere where slinky experts, stunning South Americans and total novices can comfortably dance side-by-side. Minglers can mingle to their hearts' content, and people who are just out for an evening drink can sit and chat without feeling as if they are missing out. Tuition is provided early in the evening – Tuesday's Brazilian night comes highly recommended. **PLACE** Huge high-ceilinged underground club with raised bar areas, dance floor and stage, all done out in the West End version of a Cuban cantina. **PEOPLE** Large office parties mix with dedicated salseros of all shapes and sizes. High quota of Latin American expats, tourists and students.

PROFS Students, office workers, PAs, shop assistants, solicitors, diplomats, dancers, musicians
CELEBS Mambo Boys, Made in Brazil, Jo Guest, Chris Evans, Nick Hancock
DRESS Idiosyncratic mix of casual stuff, short dresses, baggy pants, suits and lycra
MUSIC Latin, Salsa Dance Classes Mon-Sat
DOOR No Sportswear, Mon-Thu £4 after 9pm, Fri-Sat £2 7-9pm, £8 after 9pm
DRINKS Beer £2.50, Wine £3.45, Champagne £4.65, Cocktail £4.95
FOOD Latin American, £17.95 (3 courses)
CARDS All
CAPACITY 375, seating 90
HIRE Venue: Yes · Private Room: No

SUGAR REEF

Bar, Club, Restaurant
Great Windmill Street W1
020 7851 0800

OPEN Mon-Sat 5pm-1am	GETTING LUCKY	4/5
TUBE/RAIL Piccadilly Circus	EYE CANDY	3/5
BUSES 9, 14, 19, 22, 38	BIG SPENDERS	3/5
	MIX 45%M 55%F	
	AGE 18-30	
	PRICE Expensive	

AMBIENCE Party, Pulling, Late Night Open, Groups
REVIEW Jordan's favourite nitespot, this is where Hugh Hefner celebrated his 75th with his one-for-every-day-of-the-week girlfriends. Welcome to the Valley of the (Silicone) Dolls, where the Loooey Vweeton-bag toting horrors make Janine off EastEnders look like Grace Kelly. After-work crowds throw shapes on the dance floor, throw up in the loos and then get thrown out of the club, making way for suburbia's finest Birds-of-a-Feather-types who are thrilled to be drinking in the same place what once had The Spice Girls' afterparty. Sugar Reef's clientele operate on a strictly less is more basis – less clothes, less taste, less charm, less brain and less chance of getting in anywhere remotely cooler. **PEOPLE** With bodies like Baywatch and faces like Crimewatch, remove your beer goggles before doing anything you might regret. **PLACE** The nautical, tropical-island theme is evident from the turquoise walls, wicker chairs, blond wood floor, downstairs waterfeature... and pictures of Mickey Mouse and Al Pacino on the walls.

PROFS Glamour models, admin staff, estate agents, solicitors, shop assistants
CELEBS S Club 7, Jordan, EastEnders cast, David Coulthard
DRESS Loafers for the boys, customised denim and leather outfits for the girls (if you do it yourself you can make it as short and flesh-baring as you want)
MUSIC Commercial Dance
DOOR Over 21, Smart casual
DRINKS Beer £3.70, Wine £3.35, Champagne £6.50, Cocktail £6.95
FOOD Modern European, £17
CARDS All
CAPACITY 1000, seating 1000
HIRE Venue: Yes · Private Room: Yes

TIGER TIGER

Bar, Club, Restaurant
29 Haymarket SW1
020 7930 1885

OPEN Mon-Sat midday-3am,	GETTING LUCKY	4/5
Sun midday-midnight	EYE CANDY	2/5
TUBE/RAIL Piccadilly Circus	BIG SPENDERS	2/5
BUSES 19	MIX 60%M 40%F	
	AGE 25-40	
	PRICE Average	

AMBIENCE Basement, Dancing, Groups, Late Night Open, Party, Pulling
REVIEW Coming on like an explosion in a theme pub factory, Tiger Tiger, whether it realises it or not, is a celebration of all that is joyously naff with the London bar scene. Almost strictly a boozer for the after-work posse that don't have homes to go to or, if they do, prefer to stagger back late and vomit all over their MFI. The occasional Moschino-clad oily foreigner can be found weaving in and out of the dons and doyennes of the secretariat, ready with the cash, but redundant in taste. Here it's white wine spritzers for the ladies, beer bottles for the boys and tequila shooters for anyone who cares to push the boat out. Surreal, silly, daft, boisterous and, above all, fun. **PLACE** A cavernous temple to tackiness. A subtle smoky glass exterior gives way to wild abandon – nouveau Baroque downstairs, Thai upstairs, stripped-pine and wacky zebra-patterned seating in the middle. There's also a restaurant and a basement club. **PEOPLE** Suited and booted, shirted and skirted, either on the pull, on the piss, or both. Watch Wayne from Accounts cop off with Michelle from Sales, with both sorry in the morning.

PROFS Bankers, solicitors, insurance, accountants, travel consultants, nurses, admin staff
CELEBS English rugby team, EastEnders cast, James Nesbitt, Toby Anstis, Steps
DRESS Suits, open-necked shirts and smart dress with the odd bit of Diesel and FCUK thrown in for good measure. Mainly a Gap and Next wearing, Daily Mail reading mass
MUSIC Chart, 70s, 80s, 90s, Commercial Dance, House, DJs 7 days
DOOR Smart casual, No Trainers or Scruffy Jeans. Over 25s. Fri-Sat after 10pm £10
DRINKS Beer £3.25, Wine £2.95, Champagne £4.95, Cocktail £4.75
FOOD Modern British, £11.95
CARDS All
CAPACITY 1770, seating 120
HIRE Venue: Yes · Private Room: Yes

TITANIC

Bar, Restaurant
81 Brewer Street W1
020 7437 1912

OPEN Tue-Sat 5.30pm-3am	GETTING LUCKY	**5/5**
TUBE/RAIL Piccadilly Circus	EYE CANDY	**3/5**
BUSES 6, 16, 22, 38,	BIG SPENDERS	**3/5**
94, 139	MIX 50%M 50%F	
	AGE 26-55	
	PRICE Expensive	

AMBIENCE Dancing, Groups, Late Night Open, Minimalist, Party, Pulling
REVIEW This place opened in December 1998 and it's been up sh*t creek somewhere outside the M25 pretty much ever since. For a brief period the enormous monster of a room with acres of terrazzo floor had 'em all crushing through the doors. Now, like the liner, it's sinking fast, taking the majority of its cattle class crew down with it. Poor Marco Pierre White. The furore over the name, that legal wrangle with Peyton over the proximity to the Atlantic, and all he's left with is the West End's equivalent of Hollywoods, Romford.
PLACE Vast cavernous restaurant-cum-nightclub loosely based on the Queen Mary ocean liner. Original rosewood panelling and Art Deco light details have been (ahem) brought to life by eight giant revolving glitterballs, two TV screens and disco lighting. Kind of like the Atlantic meets Sugar Reef or Jane Austen meets Jackie Collins.

PEOPLE If you were wondering where all those swaggering pony-tailed shiny-suited men and tottering peroxide, nylon-wrapped women had gone, look no further. You've pulled.

PROFS Fashion designers, musicians, council workers, radio DJs, secretaries, Essex boys, brokers, hairdressers, beauticians, fitness instructors, actors, models
CELEBS Louise Redknapp, Michael Stipe, Noel Gallagher, Lawrence Llewelyn-Bowen, Cornelius Carr
DRESS Conspicuous fakes eg baby blue shiny Vuitton bags and conspicuous High Street eg Ben Sherman, River Island, Kookaï, Warehouse, Burtons, Next, Karen Millen, Morgan
MUSIC 70s, Pop, House, Garage, Hip Hop, Thu-Sat 11pm-3am
DOOR Smart casual
DRINKS Beer £3.50, Wine £3.50, Champagne £6.95, Cocktail £6.95
FOOD Modern British, £13.50
CARDS All
CAPACITY 350, seating 334
HIRE Venue: Yes · Private Room: No

L'EQUIPE ANGLAISE

Club, Members Club
23 Duke Street W1
020 7486 8281

OPEN Thu-Sat 9.30pm-5am	GETTING LUCKY	**4/5**
TUBE/RAIL Bond Street	EYE CANDY	**5/5**
BUSES 6, 7, 10, 23, 73	BIG SPENDERS	**4/5**
	MIX 50%M 50%F	
	AGE 20-55	
	PRICE Expensive	

AMBIENCE Dancing, Jetset, Late Night Open
REVIEW Much like the Jordanesque breasts sported by many of its regulars, L'Equipe can be a pumped-up annoyance that gets right up the average punter's nose. But if you're after the kind of gaudy, lordy treacle sweet clubbing experience that would give Jean Paul Gaultier a stiffy then it's worth its weight in wipe-clean zebra print. Top of the pops for holidaying oil barons, L'Equipe is full to the velvet brim of old money with a predilection for tasteless attire and honey blondes of both genders. The club's owner protects his luvvlies from baying salivators by imposing strict big breast/big budget entry requirements, so stag do's need not apply.
PLACE L'Equipe boasts the biggest disco ball outside the Grimsby WI's disco revival night. Well-manicured feet rest up in the tarty black and ivory leather VIP room, framed by wallprints of lingerie-clad women smoking fags.
PEOPLE Fresh-faced Freddie Windsor types, page three show and tell sapph-if-u-likes and fat wallets labouring against the cruel misfortunes of genetics.

PROFS Bankers, ladies who lunch, oil fat cats, estate agents
CELEBS Mick Hucknall, Prince Andrew, Naomi Campbell, Eddie Irvine, David Coulthard, Patrick Cox
DRESS Mini skirts, maxi boots, expensive suits
MUSIC Disco, House, Dance

DOOR Entrance £10
DRINKS Beer £5, Wine £5, Champagne £10
FOOD Eclectic, £25 (2 courses)
CARDS All
CAPACITY 400, seating 150
HIRE Venue: Yes · Private Room: Yes

mayfair

photo: James Balston

ALLORO

Restaurant Bar
19-20 Dover Street W1
020 7495 4768

OPEN Mon-Fri midday-	GETTING LUCKY	1/5
11.30pm, Sat 7pm-11.30pm	EYE CANDY	3/5
TUBE Green Park	BIG SPENDERS	4/5
BUSES 8, 9, 14, 19, 22, 38	MIX 50%M 50%F	
	AGE 30-80	
	PRICE Expensive	

AMBIENCE Exclusive/Chic, Conversation, Couples, Network, Romantic
REVIEW The elegantly elderly rub not-quite arthritic shoulders with Dolce & Gabbana debutantes. The place discreetly whispers money. Understatedly upscale, it's full of groups and couples. There is practically no chance of pulling – they come for conversation and fine Italian food. The decor is unpretentious – no old-school chandeliers and Ritz-style gaudiness in this corner of Mayfair. A slight bubble of conversation and barely discernible wallpaper jazz ensure the atmosphere is upbeat, in a quiet fashion. Seductive sophisticated and selective – the restaurant only accommodates a cosy 70; the bar, a mere seated 20. But what an oasis of deep blue heaven – all navy, dark woods, burgundy and chocolate – perfect for pre-dinner drinks – there's a range of Campari-based cocktails, but don't think Lorraine Chase – Alloro is all luxury, and no Luton Airport.
PLACE Chequerboard wooden floor, illuminated concrete wall panels with leaf imprints and lime light, chocolate banquettes, burgundy leather dining chairs, warm, dim lighting. Private back areas with brushed suede chocolate banquettes. Wave-effect frosted and mirror glass-backed bar, lilies galore and understated chic in cream, brown and navy.

PEOPLE Think the ambassador's party from the Ferrero Rocher ads, but without the parody, irony and shoulder pads. Class, in all its guises, from horn-rimmed hommes to Left Bank ladies of all ages. Designer labels, but don't forget, Bond Street is the local High Street.

PROFS Bankers, lawyers, CEOs, full-time lunchers, PR
CELEBS Manager of Tottenham FC
DRESS Chanel, YSL, tweed, or if it's cheap, it has to be black, well cut and well pressed
MUSIC Background Jazz
DOOR Smart casual
DRINKS Beer £3, Wine £5, Champagne £6, Cocktail £6
FOOD Italian, £8
CARDS All
CAPACITY 40, seating 20
HIRE Venue: No · Private Room: Yes

ANNABEL'S

Club, Members Club
44 Hays Mews, Berkeley Square W1
020 7629 2350

OPEN Mon-Sat 7.30pm-3am	GETTING LUCKY	4/5
TUBE/RAIL Green Park,	EYE CANDY	3/5
Bond Street	BIG SPENDERS	5/5
BUSES 8	MIX 50%M 50%F	
	AGE 28-65	
	PRICE Very expensive	

AMBIENCE Dancing, Elegant/Classic, Exclusive/Chic, Groups, Jet Set, Late Night Open, Pulling, Star Spotting
REVIEW Annabel's is beyond comprehension unless you're a penthouse hooker, cholesterolly rich Arab or royalty. It's some kind of underground parallel universe where money is no object but women are. Blondes could be lost for 40 camels. Service comes plural with several kowtowing men in white coats shadowing your every move. The drinks list is actually a wealth certificate and if you spill the entire table gets removed and replaced, spotless. Top 40 pop dross is played by a DJ wearing a DJ for mostly dubious couples of the Lolita variety and a few clueless youngsters.
'Oh yah, this is more like it' said one floundering deb about a Celine Dion song, just before she accidentally headbutted the glass divide, startling onlooking diners. Men salivate, fuelled by the possibilities of Viagra, and girls gravitate towards those with the fattest cigars, usually the overweight from Kuwait.
PLACE Descend a deckchair-canopied stairway to be greeted by old boys. Enter the small bar and drawing-room with a fireplace, gilt-framed paintings covering the walls and regal chairs and sofas. Beyond the saloon doors is the restaurant separated by a glass division from the glittery dance floor with starry ceiling. The dog portrait gallery will blow your mind.
PEOPLE Sheikh rather than chic, sugar daddies and their scantily clad 'offspring'. Countesses, viscounts, double-barrel couples, European royalty and American nouveau riche equivalents, Arabs, powder puff oldies with cigar-puffing husbands.

PROFS Oil tycoons, rulers of countries, royalty
CELEBS The Duchess of York, Prince Andrew, Ivana Trump, Rupert Murdoch, Lord Andrew Lloyd Webber, Michael Heseltine

DRESS Men in ties and jackets; women in horrendous suits or not much else, leopard mini skirts, strappy stilettos and backless white satin gowns.
MUSIC Chart, DJs
DOOR Members Only
DRINKS Beer £5, Wine £5, Champagne £9, Cocktail £8
FOOD International, £25
CARDS All
CAPACITY 100, seating 60
HIRE Venue: No · Private Room: No

THE DORCHESTER BAR

Hotel Bar, Restaurant
The Dorchester Hotel, 53 Park Lane W1
020 7629 8888

OPEN Mon-Sat 11am-11pm,	**GETTING LUCKY**	**2/5**
Sun midday-10.30pm	**EYE CANDY**	**4/5**
TUBE/RAIL Hyde Park Corner	**BIG SPENDERS**	**5/5**
BUSES 2, 10, 16, 36,	**MIX** 60%M 40%F	
73, 137	**AGE** 25-65	
	PRICE Very expensive	

AMBIENCE Business, Conversation, Destination/Wishlist, Elegant/Classic, Live Music, Romantic, Mature/Older
REVIEW The typical customer profile is a stylish, self-assured, international achiever – people who know they've made it and don't need to underline the fact. The setting is too elegant and restrained for any obvious manoeuvring – you've got to be a really smooth operator, particularly as it's mainly table seating and table hopping is not the norm. The bar itself is segmented with plants and furniture arrangements, so you don't get the full picture in one easy reconnaissance and businessmen seem to be conducting meetings which have sprouted into social occasions. The mezzanine area, being less formal with stools at the counter, provides greater scope. Live music flows from a flamboyant grand piano (previous owner: Liberace), while an excellent Italian menu means that at lunchtime the bar is virtually a restaurant.
PLACE All the inherent grace of high Art Deco-mirrored walls and decorative tiles depicting caged birds, combined with a mirrored ceiling, and softly lit atmosphere in which everyone looks their best.
PEOPLE International jet set, hotel residents, local international residents.

PROFS Celebrities, bankers, ambassadors, sports stars, international elite
CELEBS Tom Cruise, Robbie Williams
DRESS Joseph, Jaeger, Chanel, Donna Karan, Aquascutum, Prada, Gucci
MUSIC Classical, Jazz band Wed-Sat, Classical Pianist Sun-Tue
DOOR Smart Dress
DRINKS Beer £4.50, Wine £6, Champagne £12, Cocktail £10
FOOD Italian, £22
CARDS All
CAPACITY 80, seating 70
HIRE Venue: No · Private Room: No

THE LIBRARY

Cocktail Bar, Hotel Bar
The Lanesborough Hotel, Hyde Park Corner W1
020 7259 5599

OPEN Mon-Sat 11am-11pm,	**GETTING LUCKY**	**3/5**
Sun midday-10.30pm	**EYE CANDY**	**3/5**
TUBE/RAIL Hyde Park	**BIG SPENDERS**	**5/5**
Corner	**MIX** 60%M 40%F	
BUSES 9, 10, 14, 19, 22, 52	**AGE** 27-70	
	PRICE Very expensive	

AMBIENCE Comfy, Conversation, Elegant/Classic, Live Music, Mature/Older, Romantic
REVIEW At the epicentre of rush-hour mayhem, it's hardly surprising that this bar is best enjoyed as a posh post-work pitstop. Mayfair PAs fight off vultures, sip cocktails peacefully alongside smart, sensible suits, bald pates and cigars. Award-winning bar manager extraordinaire, Salvatore Calabrese, will deftly keep any unwanted attention at bay. In fact, Salvatore's personal attention is renowned, let alone his incredible cigar and cognac collections; some have paid up to £500 a cigar and £1,000 for a gulp of his 1789 cognac. The place picks up the pace (as far as it is possible in a place like this) after 9pm, when the lights dim and City boys and a Middle Eastern mix looking to bag a blonde take over.
PLACE Faux Regency library/drawing-room. Cocktail of Ralph Lauren and Versace. Nouveau riche gentleman's club feel. Mahogany panelling, plush sofas and chairs, oh, and books.
PEOPLE Multi-generational smart professionals. Very rich City boys and a corporate cross-section of Brits, Americans and YSL Euros. Later more sheikh chic, alongside a smattering of George Michael/ Versace'esque gay crowd.

PROFS Lawyers, tourists, bankers, musicians, movie stars, international businessmen, PR agents, headhunters, estate agents
CELEBS George Melly, Sly Stallone, Lord Spencer Churchill, Madonna
DRESS After-work smart office kit, pinstripes and brogues, Harvey Hudson, Gieves & Hawkes; girls in Euro chic, Prada, Gucci and Joseph; grandes dames in Chanel, Jaeger, pearls and brooches
MUSIC Dance Fri-Sat, Jazz Pianist Mon-Sat 6.30pm-11pm, Sun 6.30pm-10.30pm
DOOR None but you'll need your Gold card
DRINKS Beer £4.90, Wine £6, Champagne £12, Cocktail £9.50
FOOD Snacks, £10
CARDS All
CAPACITY 150, seating 100
HIRE Venue: No · Private Room: No

THE MET BAR

Hotel Bar
The Metropolitan Hotel, 19 Old Park Lane W1
020 7447 5757

OPEN Mon-Sat 10am-3am, Sun 10am-10.30pm		
TUBE/RAIL Green Park, Hyde Park Corner	**GETTING LUCKY**	**5/5**
BUSES 2, 8, 9, 10, 14, 19	**EYE CANDY**	**5/5**
	BIG SPENDERS	**5/5**
	MIX 50%M 50%F	
	AGE 25-45	
	PRICE Expensive	

AMBIENCE Star Spotting, Destination/Wishlist, Late-Night Open, Party, Pulling, Hip/Fashionable
REVIEW This bar adjoining the still hip Metropolitan Hotel has been open now for over three years. When slick host Ben Pundole left for NYC (since returned to oversee Schrager's hotel bar operations) and pretty head-mixologist Ben Reed went west to Woody's there were low points. If there was a Priory cure for bars the Met would have checked in. However, with new guy James Stewart and membership recently streamlined the place occasionally gets some old faces returning for late night fun and games. It remains a steady pop, film and fashion favourite and is difficult to frequent unless you're a hotel resident, friend of the staff, or miraculously blessed and invited to join. It's the designer baby of ex-empress of Bond Street, Mrs Ong, and attracts the Prada-clad, Voyage fashionistas and Boateng dandies. Wear whatever's in Vogue but not DKNY or you'll be mistaken for a mixologist (barman to the layman) and asked to shake one of their Martini cocktails. Thursday thru' Saturday a DJ spins lazy drum 'n' bass down one end and the odd popstar may join in. Large red leather banquettes and deep tub chairs provide deep comfort, but late in the evening you may be left standing. When stumbling out at 3am, don't forget your card behind the bar as you pass the Big Issue seller who may have a camera tucked inside his coat for those paparazzi shots.
PLACE The Emperor has lost his clothes. The bar's once sharp edges, reflective tables, shiny chocolate walls and New York skyline need new expression. In-house entertainment provided by newcomers striding headfirst into the mirror at the far end.
PEOPLE Boasts celebrity members and 'movers and shakers' drawn from movies, modelling, meeja and music, all of whom get messy. Fewer celebs than in its heyday, still gets major US stars who stay in hotel. Don't go on a bad hair day.

PROFS Media professionals, models, musicians, film execs, fashion victims
CELEBS Former Spice Girls, Louise Redknapp, Robbie Williams, Steve Coogan, Fun Lovin' Criminals, Kevin Spacey, Ingrid Casares, Tamara Beckwith, Tara Palmer-Tomkinson, Patsy Kensit, Meg Matthews, Fran Cutler, Kylie Minogue, Gwyneth Paltrow, Goldie, Jamiroquai, Liam Gallagher, Noel Gallagher, Madonna, Guy Ritchie, Finley Quaye, Helena Christensen, Christy Turlington, Tom Jones, Prince Andrew, Janet Jackson, Andrea Corr, Denise van Outen, Bruce Willis, Martine McCutcheon
DRESS Expensive catwalk labels, chi chi shabby, the odd Trilby or whatever Vogue decrees and some suits from Boateng to Boss, Boyd, Prada, Gucci, Voyage, Whistles, Nicole Farhi, Maharishi, Armani
MUSIC Drum 'n' Bass, Funk, Jazz, Pop, R&B
DOOR After 6pm hotel residents and members only
DRINKS Beer £4, Wine £3.50, Champagne £6.50, Cocktail £7.75
FOOD International, Sushi, £25
CARDS No Diners
CAPACITY 157, seating 80
HIRE Venue: No · Private Room: No

SCOTTS

Bar, Restaurant
20 Mount Street W1
020 7629 5248

OPEN Mon-Sat midday-11pm, Sun midday-10pm		
TUBE/RAIL Bond Street, Green Park	**GETTING LUCKY**	**2/5**
BUSES 2, 8, 10, 16, 36, 73	**EYE CANDY**	**3/5**
	BIG SPENDERS	**4/5**
	MIX 50%M 50%F	
	AGE 28-50	
	PRICE Expensive	

AMBIENCE Basement, Business, Conversation, Elegant/Classic, Exclusive/Chic, Groups, Historic, Old World, Romantic
REVIEW Scotts the restaurant has always been a bit of a Mayfair legend. Since 1851, it's served oysters and champagne to almost every 20th-century star and monarch from Dietrich to Burton. A few years ago, it underwent a £2.5 million refit, in an attempt to recreate its past glories, courtesy the owners of Chez Gerard better known for their 'steak frites' and Livebaits. The bar itself is under the restaurant and is a stylish little haven if you want a sophisticated pre-dinner or post-work drop in. You walk past a Beverly Hills column of bubbling water which descends like a massive lava lamp to the cocktail/champagne bar below. Relax to Sinatra in corduroy chairs and spot Mayfair businessmen, antique dealers and rich tourists knocking back the champagne.
PLACE At the Park Lane end of incredibly swanky Mount Street, a 24-carat stone's throw from Purdeys and Thomas Goode's. Bar is in the basement. Quiet, subterranean with a 20 feet or so marble-lined bar. Special little booths with curtains that you can draw – great for quiet business or assignations.
PEOPLE Money talks, walks, drinks and eats here. Rich property developers and antique dealers rub shoulder-pads with City gents, tourists and local residents.

PROFS Bankers, socialites, traders, lawyers, property developers, antique dealers, tourists
CELEBS Patsy Kensit, Claudia Schiffer, the Zagats
DRESS City suits, sheikh chic, blazers for men and Aquascutum, MaxMara, Jaeger for women
MUSIC Jazz & Classical, Pianist Mon-Sat 7pm-11pm
DOOR Smart casual
DRINKS Beer £3, Wine £3.25, Champagne £6.75, Cocktail £6.50
FOOD Fish, Seafood, Traditional British, £10 (2 courses)
CARDS All
CAPACITY 167, seating 135
HIRE Venue: Yes · Private Room: Yes

TRADER VIC'S

Cocktail Bar, Hotel Bar, Theme
The London Hilton, 22 Park Lane W1
020 7493 8000

OPEN Mon-Thu 11.30am-1.30am, Fri, Sat 5pm-3am, Sun 5pm-10.30pm	GETTING LUCKY	3/5
	EYE CANDY	2/5
	BIG SPENDERS	4/5
TUBE/RAIL Green Park, Hyde Park Corner	MIX 60%M 40%F	
	AGE 26-60	
BUSES 2, 10, 16, 73, 137	PRICE Expensive	

AMBIENCE Conversation, Groups, Legendary, Kitsch, Live Music, Pulling, Late Night Open
REVIEW It's still 1972 in Trader Vic's, the subterranean temple of Riki-Tiki Polynesian kitsch in the basement of the Hyde Park Hilton. The kind of place your dad took your mum for their first anniversary, it's a sort of rum-fuelled flower-laden Happy Days. On any given evening a table of PAs tap their feet to Alan Partridge renditions of The Girl From Ipanema, West End tarts and their 'international businessman' escorts sip Planter's Punch through shared 49cm straws and loaded international teenagers make serious dents in the 150-strong cocktail list. Order a Mai Tai, created by bar founder Victor 'The Trader' Bergeron, tuck into a plate of crispy duck pancakes and drift back to a time when cheese and pineapple cubes on sticks were the cat's pyjamas.

PLACE A Hawaii 5-0 heaven of straw and bamboo walls, South East Asian artwork and pretty foreign waitresses in flowered cheongsams. All that's missing is Elvis in a bright shirt surrounded by a bevy of hula-skirted beauties.
PEOPLE Hotel guests, tourists, ironic drinkers and anyone who wants a brown plastic cocktail stick as a souvenir.
PROFS Fashion designers, Metropolitan hotel staff, bankers, arms dealers
CELEBS Michael Douglas, Tony Curtis, Madonna, Guy Ritchie, Rod Stewart, Diana Ross, Sting, Bono, Nicky Haslam, Anita Dobson, David Ginola
DRESS A mind-boggling mixture of Savile Row suits, combat trousers and Prada dresses
MUSIC Latin, Jazz, Cuban, Brazilian; Live Music Mon-Sat 10.30pm-1am
DOOR Smart casual
DRINKS Beer £4, Wine £6.50, Champagne £8, Cocktail, £7
FOOD International, Pacific Rim, South East Asian, £8
CARDS All
CAPACITY 330, seating 180
HIRE Venue: Yes · Private Room: Yes

WINDOWS BAR

Hotel Bar
Hilton Park Lane, 22 Park Lane W1
020 7493 8000

OPEN 7 days 5pm-2am	GETTING LUCKY	2/5
TUBE/RAIL Green Park, Hyde Park Corner	EYE CANDY	3/5
	BIG SPENDERS	4/5
BUSES 2, 10, 16, 36, 73, 137	MIX 55%M 45%F	
	AGE 27-55	
	PRICE Expensive	

AMBIENCE Business, Conversation, Exclusive/Chic, Groups, Late Night Open, Live Music, Mature/Older, Views
REVIEW Total antithesis to the neighbouring Met Bar, this is what hotel bars used to be. Once you get past the Vegas voltage and 28 floors of nine-carat-gold elevator, you are rewarded with quite staggering views of London, including the Queen's backyard. This piano cocktail bar offers, quite unwittingly, a hypertrendy, horrendously passé 70s interior – as recognised and endorsed by Pulp, who shot the photos for 'This is Hardcore' here. Derek the pianist plays all those easy listening greats by Elton John and Billy Joel. Fortunately,

few here appreciate the irony that keeps this sky-high sanctuary safe from pretension. Snogging middle-aged couples make entertaining appearances. Staff are blighted with Star Trek uniforms. Boldly go and beam up for the view.

PLACE 70s VIP airport lounge meets Towering Inferno, built in 1961. Bring on Burt Bacharach and Steve McQueen. If you need more style head downstairs to Zeta bar in the basement.

PEOPLE An equal mix of hotel residents and non-residents. Half English, half Euro, Americano Arabs. After-work crowd en route home and classic Hiltonesque hotel guests.

PROFS Prime Ministers, world leaders, bankers, financiers, travel agents and salesmen
CELEBS Emmanuel Pettit, John Major
DRESS Tight-suited men who wouldn't leave home without aftershave and women whose logos come attached to handbags
MUSIC Easy Listening Bands Fri-Sat
DOOR £6 for non-residents after 11pm
DRINKS Beer £3, Wine £3.50, Champagne £8.35, Cocktail £9
FOOD French, £25
CARDS All
CAPACITY 300, seating 150
HIRE Venue: Yes · Private Room: No

ZANDER

Bar, Restaurant
45 Buckingham Gate SW1
020 7379 9797

OPEN Mon-Wed 11.30am-11pm, Thu-Fri 11.30am-1pm, Sat 5pm-1pm, Sun 5pm-10pm
TUBE/RAIL St James's Park, Victoria
BUSES 11

GETTING LUCKY	**2/5**
EYE CANDY	**3/5**
BIG SPENDERS	**4/5**
MIX 60%M 40%F	
AGE 27-60	
PRICE Expensive	

AMBIENCE Business, Conversation, Exclusive/Chic, Groups, Network
REVIEW The Bank Restaurant Group, which opened this bar and restaurant in March 2000, claims its purpose is to service the bar-and-restaurant starved 'heart of Westminster'. Perhaps politicians – not renowned for their collective sobriety – should not be exposed to

the temptations of this, the longest bar in Europe (48 metres long). That said, you can just see a Rt Hon Member checking his pager at the door and treating a puce-Chanel-wearing Miss Party Whiplash to one of the mixologist's powerful Thai Sapphires. Delicious, but your MP wouldn't be able to stand up and be counted after more than two. sober politios beware: Friday and Saturday evenings see a funkier clubby crowd.

PLACE Spacious 'Victorian masterpiece' is unrecognisable after its modernising £18 million conversion. Colours and lines are just this side of industrial. The conservatory area out the back affords a delightful view of a cherubic fountain. This view is far more appealing than the pervasive Barratt Home paintings. Strangely-lit globes add a surreal touch to the disorientating design.

PEOPLE Chic and cheerful. Small talk and flirtation are the order of the day. Do discuss Margaret's Ascot headgear, darling, or Giles's revealing after-dinner speech. Do not discuss the Inland Revenue. A haven for the early middle-aged. Groups of mid-30s career women, businessmen in their 40s and the odd hotel resident from next door Crowne Plaza.

PROFS Advertising agents, solicitors, civil servants, MPs, bankers, accountants, consultants
CELEBS Boy George, Vinnie Jones, Kate Moss, Steve Cram, Lord Coe, Andrew Neil, Claudia Schiffer, Anna Kournikova
DRESS Ladies wear Chanel, Gucci, Pied à Terre, Armani, jewellery picked up from a darling little man in Bali who makes it himself. Gents in traditional bespoke suits. Everyone has a man on Bond Street. Some of them aren't sleeping with him. For men, smart dark suits and Ralph Lauren shirts are the order of the day
MUSIC Funk, Breakbeat, Jazz, Easy Listening, Mellow, Soul DJs Wed-Sat
DOOR None
DRINKS Beer £3, Wine £3.20, Champagne £7, Cocktail £7
FOOD Modern British, Modern Eclectic, £12
CARDS All
CAPACITY 250, seating 150
HIRE Venue: Yes · Private Room: Yes

ZETA

Bar, Hotel Bar
The Hilton Hotel, 35 Hertford Street W1
020 7208 4067

OPEN Mon-Tue 4pm-1am, Wed-Fri 4pm-3am, Sat 5pm-3am
TUBE/RAIL Marble Arch, Green Park
BUSES 2, 9, 10, 14, 16, 19, 22, 36

GETTING LUCKY	**5/5**
EYE CANDY	**4/5**
BIG SPENDERS	**5/5**
MIX 50%M 50%F	
AGE 28-60	
PRICE Expensive	

AMBIENCE Cute Staff, Dancing, Destination/Wishlist, Groups, Jet Set, Late Night Open, Live Music, Minimalist, Party, Pulling
REVIEW Zeta Jones and sugar daddy Douglas spring to mind as you witness old men slavering over nubile young girls who seem only too pleased to frolic, pout and perform pseudo-lesbian acts for their leery admirers. Nevertheless the £5 door after 11pm is cheap for Mayfair and Met club rejects. Prepare to be chatted up at the

bar as you wait forever for an arduous concoction from bartenders who are far too pretty to work quickly. The DJ tries desperately to make it hip, spinning discs from behind a beaded curtain; thanks to the suited men wandering past giving pathetic 'groovy 70s' shuffles, you know there's no hope.

PLACE Designed by NYC architects, Tony Chi & Associates. Asia 'n' bamboo meets minimal marble and Egyptian teak screens that resemble beaded car seats; the window detail appears to be a mobile fabricated from steel coke straws.

PEOPLE Rich old men and young women dressed in nothing but St. Tropez. Businessmen, Versace-clad American women with puffed-up hair, a few London hip kids and people who can't get into The Met.

PROFS Footballers, models, tycoons, It boys and girls, bar staff, personal trainers, TV presenters, beauty therapists, make-up artists

CELEBS Björk, Julian Clary, EastEnders cast

DRESS Smart 'n' tart. Women dress to kill in tiny little numbers and Prada shoes, men dress for business in suits or shirts

MUSIC Jazzy House, DJ Mon-Sat 9pm-3am, Percussion Fri 11pm-3am

DOOR Stylish and funky; Mon-Sat after 11pm £5

DRINKS Beer £3.50, Wine £3.50, Champagne £7.50, Cocktail £6.50

FOOD Asian based, £8.50

CARDS All

CAPACITY 200, seating 70

HIRE Venue: Yes · Private Room: No

noho

BAM-BOU

Bar, Restaurant
Percy Street W1
0207 323 9130

OPEN Mon-Sat 6pm-1am	GETTING LUCKY	2/5
TUBE/RAIL Goodge Street	EYE CANDY	3/5
BUSES 10, 24, 29, 73, 134	BIG SPENDERS	4/5
	MIX 50%M 50%F	
	AGE 28-50	
	PRICE Expensive	

AMBIENCE Exclusive, Opulent, Network, Business, Lounge, Conversation, Elegant

REVIEW According to some Feng Shui experts, the best way to achieve Zen is to stick bamboo flutes to your ceiling, but that's frankly daft. We suggest a visit to French Vietnamese restaurant bar Bam-bou instead. Some of its initial kudos may have faded, but it's still one of the chicest drinking holes in the locale with a refined but mellow ambience perfect for impressing a date or wowing employees. Head up the narrow staircase and you'll find yourself in a series of little bars which fit together like the compartments in a chinese calligrapher's box. The designers had to blow dry the paint in the member's bar with hairdryers to get the cracked porcelain effect, though some of its ditzy PR girl clientele were clearly cracked long before they got to theirs.

PEOPLE Eva and Gerard have been married for five years and live in a three-bedroom Islington terrace with original artwork on the walls and organic herbs growing in terracotta window-boxes. Gerard works in film production while Eva is a designer for an advertising agency. They're spending August in Tuscany at the farmhouse which Gerard's university friend is turning into a ceramics studio.

PLACE Four floors of classily classic chinoiserie, seductively low lit by nightlights flickering through red and green glass candle holders. The area over the upstairs bar looks like a complex knick-knackery, or the window dispay in Neal Street East.

PROFS Media, film industry, PR, post production

CELEBS Tim Burton, Jerry Hall, Jilly Goulden, Danny Boyle

DRESS Whistles, Jigsaw, Selfridges first floor, Oeuf, Levi's

MUSIC Lounge, Jazz

DOOR None

DRINKS Beer £3.50, Wine £3.50, Champagne £7.50, Cocktail £7

FOOD French Cantonese, £10

CARDS All

CAPACITY 300, seating 69

HIRE Venue: Yes · Private Room: Yes

BAR MADRID

Bar, Club, Restaurant
4 Winsley Street W1
020 7436 4649

OPEN Mon-Sat 4.30pm-3am	GETTING LUCKY	5/5
TUBE/RAIL Oxford Circus	EYE CANDY	4/5
BUSES 10, 24, 29, 73, 134	BIG SPENDERS	3/5
	MIX 65%M 35%F	
	AGE 21-40	
	PRICE Average	

AMBIENCE Basement, Bump 'n' Grind, Dancing, Late Night Open, Live Music, Party, Pulling

REVIEW English is most people's second or even third language at Bar Madrid but that doesn't matter because everyone is fluent in the language of dance. It's a salsa bar but don't think about shouting 'arriba' or 'andale' – this is the real thing and should be enjoyed as such. If you can't dance, sit back and spectate – the sexual politics of the dance floor are fascinating. Will the Fabio lookalike start pouting after the wiry, dark Pacino character cuts in on his bird? Not a chance – he just dives into the crowd and picks out another beautiful woman and they segue together in a dizzyingly intricate salsa that has the audience cheering. It's like that scene in Swingers brought to life. The air is thick with egos, sweat and sexuality – and whoever said that dancing was the vertical expression of horizontal intention was bang on. Me? I'm off to get some lambada lessons and hair extensions pronto...

PLACE Low-ceilinged basement bar with kindergarten Dali decor. There's a raised central dance floor but people salsa, samba and shake their booties on every available square foot of floor.

PEOPLE Mainly Spanish, Italian and Portuguese. The English are the ones swigging bottles of beer, standing still and looking sheepish.

PROFS Foreign students, dance instructors, tourists, latin footballers, restaurant staff, media employees

CELEBS None

DRESS Men: vests, tight trousers, hair extensions and cowboy boots. Women: halter tops and hot pants

MUSIC Brazilian, Latin American, Pop, Salsa, Spanish, DJs 7 days

DOOR Smart casual, £3-5 after 9pm

DRINKS Beer £2.90, Wine £2.85, Cocktail £4.50

FOOD Spanish, Tapas, Tex Mex, £3

CARDS All

CAPACITY 575, seating 80

HIRE Venue: Yes · Private Room: Yes

THE CHURCHILL BAR & CIGAR DIVAN

Bar, Hotel Bar, Members Bar
Churchill Inter-Continental Hotel, 30 Portman Square W1
020 7486 5800

OPEN Mon-Sat 11am-11pm (Non-Residents), (Until 2am Residents and Members), Sun 5pm-10.30pm (Non-Residents), (Until 1am Residents and Members)	**GETTING LUCKY**	**2/5**
	EYE CANDY	**1/5**
	BIG SPENDERS	**3/5**
	MIX 70%M 30%F	
TUBE/RAIL Marble Arch	**AGE** 35-65	
BUSES 2, 10, 16, 23, 36, 98	**PRICE** Very expensive	

AMBIENCE Business, Conversation, Elegant/Classic, Late Night Open, Live Music, Mature/Older, Network, Touristy

REVIEW So cigar bars have had their 15 minutes of fame but remain popular all the same, especially with US tourists and anyone oblivious to the wanky connotations and desperate to appear an entrepreneur. Locating a friendly, low-key venue to commence one's apprenticeship of the Cuban missile arsenal has become a priority for cigar novices. Cue The Churchill Bar & Cigar Divan at the

Inter-Continental Hotel. Anyone who can overcome the double handicap of the bar's name and location is on to a winner. An extensive and reasonably-priced cigar list is backed by equally impressive whisky and bar menus, so that aficionados and their Montecristos, once ensconced in deep armchairs, need only resurface at closing time. Mercifully, the suckers here don't show off, so keep that cigar-lickin', mouth-smackin'-style for a more nouveau venue.

PLACE Comfortable in that classic hotel interpretation style of 'this is what a gentleman's smoking room should look like'. That is: wall-to-wall mahogany panelling and leather sofas with the added benefit of air conditioning so that, amazingly, the bar never smells of stale cigar smoke.

PEOPLE Hotel residents and members of the bar's cigar club. The hotel is a favourite of the US State Department and Embassy so score ten points if you see a US official puffing on a Cuban cigar. Score double if said official is accompanied by an intern.

PROFS Government employees, MPs, lawyers, auditors, ambassadors, embassy staff

CELEBS Geoff Boycott, Viscount Portland, Tom Jones, Dolly Parton

DRESS Barneys and Saks 5th Avenue for the Americans; Harvey Nicks and Harrods for the Brits

MUSIC Jazz, Pianist, Singer, Mon-Fri 8pm-midnight

DOOR None

DRINKS Beer £4, Wine £4.50, Champagne £10.50, Cocktail £9

FOOD Continental, Snacks, £7

CARDS All

CAPACITY 80, seating 50

HIRE Venue: No · Private Room: No

DK BAR

Bar, Restaurant, Chain
40 Charlotte Street W1
020 7636 1576

OPEN Mon-Sat 11am-11pm	**GETTING LUCKY**	**4/5**
TUBE/RAIL Tottenham Court Road, Goodge Street	**EYE CANDY**	**3/5**
	BIG SPENDERS	**3/5**
BUSES 10, 24, 29, 73, 134	**MIX** 45%M 55%F	
	AGE 25-35	
	PRICE Average	

AMBIENCE Basement, Brightly Coloured/Cheerful, Buzzy, Casual, Conversation, Friendly, Pulling

REVIEW There's something decidedly refreshing about DK, like it's been freshly doused in zesty lemon Fairy Liquid. Even at closing time, it feels like midday thanks to acres of pine, yellow tables and clever lighting. In fact, upstairs feels more like a café than a bar and the Guardian-reading clientele play up to this. No sweaty hordes of lager swillers here, just relaxed, civilised groups sipping long, tall glasses of Stella and discussing the pitfalls of privatisation. Downstairs regularly holds private parties and provides a sweltering, windowless hole of a bar. This is undoubtedly the place to pull as long as you can convince your target that you really are best mates with whoever the hell's party it is.

PLACE Light 'n' bright upstairs, hot 'n' horny downstairs; reminiscent of an adolescent party, parents keeping a polite distance from the drunken debauchery taking place below.

PEOPLE Young, relaxed Charlotte Street types. Mercifully free of mobile-wielding media negotiators.

PROFS Media, advertising and TV execs

CELEBS A variety of BBC jocks from nearby Broadcasting House, Blue Peter presenters, EastEnders cast

DRESS Nothing fancy or precious; few labels on display, but co-ordinated, colourful high street semi-chic, Adidas trainers, Eastpak, Reef, Kookaï

MUSIC Everything from Disco to Rock, DJs Sat

DOOR None

DRINKS Beer £2.85, Wine £2.55, Cocktail £4.75

FOOD Mediterranean, £8.75

CARDS All

CAPACITY 150, seating 40

HIRE Venue: Yes · Private Room: Yes

THE EVE CLUB

Club
189 Regent Street W1
020 7734 4252

OPEN Thu-Sat 9pm-3am	**GETTING LUCKY**	**4/5**
TUBE/RAIL Oxford Circus	**EYE CANDY**	**3/5**
BUSES 6, 13, 23, 88, 159	**BIG SPENDERS**	**3/5**
	MIX 40%M 60%F	
	AGE 25-35	
	PRICE Expensive	

AMBIENCE Basement, Kitsch, Dancing, Late Night Open

REVIEW Man walks into a bar. Bangs his head. Instead of feeling pain and frustration, he laughs, and starts nodding appreciatively whilst stroking his chin. You see... it's an ironic bar. If the Eve Club was in Benidorm, you would give it the widest of berths, having been repelled by its trashy 'It Ain't Half Hot Mum' decor. But because it's closeted away in an unprepossessing office block on Regent Street, and because it's only announcement is a discreet brass plaque, and because the staff are reasonably surly, the fact that there's a palm tree in the middle of the dance floor suddenly goes from being insufferably naff to knowingly naff. And as any style guru will tell you, that's cool.

PLACE The combination of zebra and leopard skin furniture makes it look like a John Woo-directed episode of Wildlife on One. There's a Saturday Night Fever chequered dance floor, and you enter the bar via a long red love tunnel. Saucy.

PEOPLE Despite some top-notch funk and soul mixing, most people content themselves with idly shifting their weight from one foot to another, suggesting that they might not quite be the VIP party elite the organisers hope for.

PROFS Music, TV, media, advertising, fashion

CELEBS Denise van Outen, Boy George

DRESS Jennifer Lopez – the TopShop years

MUSIC House, Disco, Funk

DOOR Guest list

DRINKS Beer £3.50, Wine £3.50, Champagne £6, Cocktail £7

FOOD None

CARDS All

CAPACITY 300, seating 100

HIRE Venue: Yes · Private Room: Yes

GOODGE

Bar
62 Goodge Street W1
020 7436 9448

OPEN Mon-Fri midday-11pm,	**GETTING LUCKY**	**4/5**
Sat 5pm-11pm	**EYE CANDY**	**3/5**
TUBE/RAIL Goodge Street,	**BIG SPENDERS**	**3/5**
Oxford Circus	**MIX** 50%M 50%F	
BUSES 10, 24, 29, 73, 134	**AGE** 25-40	
	PRICE Average	

AMBIENCE Groups, Conversation, Casual, Chilled, Funky

REVIEW A local bar for local after-work drinks for locals to drink after work. Max Shepherd and Matt Nesbitt are the two young guns behind Goodge, and you get the feeling it's a place for their mates as much as the above-mentioned locals. The bartender in the groovy Hawaiian shirt serves up a mean watermelon Martini, as fine as you'd find down the road at the Sanderson but considerably less expensive. Here it's less high gloss transatlantic glam, more turned-up denim and wacky slackeresque t-shirts from the Charlotte Street set. Location means it attracts a media savvy crowd that hate all that posh Botox crap but still eye up your trainers knowingly.

PLACE Funky, narrow little bar, with DJ on the decks and raised seating area at the back.

PEOPLE 150 of Max and Matt's mates and various Noho professionals.

PROFS Media professionals, graphic designers, retail staff

CELEBS None

DRESS Suits to t-shirts and low slung jeans. Hugo Boss, Emporio Armani, M&S, Hysteric Glamour, Evisu, Levi's, Carhartt, Ben Sherman, Nike, Adidas

MUSIC Electronic Funk, Hip Hop, House

DOOR Over 21s

DRINKS Beer £2.80, Wine £2.80, Champagne £6, Cocktail £5

FOOD Modern British, Bar Food, £5

CARDS No Amex

CAPACITY 150, seating 60

HIRE Venue: Yes · Private Room: Yes

HOME HOUSE

Members Club, Bar, Restaurant
20 Portman Square W1
020 7670 2000

OPEN 7 days 7am-midnight	**GETTING LUCKY**	**3/5**
TUBE/RAIL Marble Arch	**EYE CANDY**	**4/5**
BUSES 2, 13, 30, 74,	**BIG SPENDERS**	**4/5**
82, 113	**MIX** 40%M 60%F	
	AGE 25-45	
	PRICE Expensive	

AMBIENCE, Dancing, Conversation, Elegant/Classic, Historic, Exclusive/Chic, Groups, Jet Set, Late Night Open, Outdoors

REVIEW Home House was for one all too brief moment the temple at which paper rich dotcommers came to worship. It had everything to impress: history, 18th-century swagger and extreme elegance wrapped in one of London's most famous Adam buildings. It was the ultimate classical town mansion for those who worked with technology or in the media but longed for a bit of class when their mouse was weary. New money, old style. But just about the time new economy paper proved to be, well, just paper, Home's stock started to fall. The food's overpriced and not much cop and the people seem all too impressed to create a genuine clubby feel. Nevertheless the surroundings are fantastic and we can think of few better places to sit and sneer at the poor unfortunates excluded by this country's drinking laws. **PLACE** Classic elegance. Marble floors and sweeping staircases with original frescos and statuary. Huge Scottish mansion of a bar with stags' heads and three giant widescreen screens. An outside garden with mini-marquee which should be great but feels like the champagne tent at Sandown on a Tuesday afternoon. **PEOPLE** Dot-bombers, media, show-biz, professionals, North London flash cash boys who don't care about the food, just want to feel the equality.

PROFS Media, what's left of new media, law, finance, banking, film, TV
CELEBS Boy George
DRESS From hippy chic to City suit
MUSIC Background Music
DOOR Full membership by invitation only – £1,500 joining fee and £1,500 annual subscription.
DRINKS Beer £3.25, Wine £4.40, Champagne £9.50
FOOD British, Seasonal, Far Eastern Influence, £17.50
CARDS No Switch
CAPACITY 120, seating 60
HIRE Venue: No · Private Room: Yes (for Members)

JERUSALEM

Bar, Restaurant Bar
33-34 Rathbone Place W1
020 7255 1120

OPEN Mon-Fri midday-11pm,	**GETTING LUCKY**	**5/5**
Sat 7pm-11pm	**EYE CANDY**	**3/5**
TUBE/RAIL Tottenham	**BIG SPENDERS**	**3/5**
Court Road	**MIX** 55%M 45%F	
BUSES 8, 10, 25, 55,	**AGE** 22-45	
73, 176	**PRICE** Average	

AMBIENCE Casual, Conversation, Dancing, Groups, Hip/Fashionable, Party, Pulling

REVIEW Buying a drink here on a Friday night is hot and sweaty work – get triples instead. Pulling malarkey involves the old shoulder tap and then look the other way technique. Works every time. Jerusalem is not a promised land of models and moviestars. However, the Lord would be proud because this place seems to open its arms to anyone and everyone in spite of the bouncers, who are simply stopping an overcrowding crush. There's a genuine weekend-starts-here party atmosphere generated mainly by the Suits; the few inconspicuous trendies keep to themselves. The music's loud and pumping with much lip synching in practice. **PLACE** Stylish womb-like basement, prerequisite gilt-framed-food-and-drinks blackboards above the bar. Exposed brickwork lends it a rough edge, softened by velvet drapes in the dining area, candles & chandeliers. Awkward, uncomfortable, refectory-size tables and benches intended for seating – most stand. **PEOPLE** Some suburbanites 'up West' for the weekend and a smattering of Soho creatives.

PROFS PRs, TV and record producers, publishing, advertising executives, printers, pharmacists
CELEBS Liam Gallagher, Noel Gallagher, Ulrika Jonsson, Dennis Wise
DRESS Jane Norman, Next, TopShop, Moss Bros
MUSIC Funk, Soul, Jazz, DJs Wed-Sat
DOOR Over 21s
DRINKS Beer £2.60, Wine £2.70, Champagne £6, Cocktail £5.50
FOOD Asian, Modern European, Oriental, £8
CARDS All
CAPACITY 200, seating 90
HIRE Venue: Yes · Private Room: No

LING LING @ HAKKASAN

Bar, Restaurant
8 Hanway Place W1
020 7927 7000

OPEN Mon-Wed 6pm-1am,	**GETTING LUCKY**	**2/5**
Thu-Sat 6pm-3am,	**EYE CANDY**	**4/5**
Sun 6pm-11.30pm	**BIG SPENDERS**	**4/5**
TUBE/RAIL Tottenham	**MIX** 40%M 60%F	
Court Road	**AGE** 26-45	
BUSES 10, 24, 29, 73, 134	**PRICE** Very expensive	

AMBIENCE Destination/Wishlist, Exclusive/Chic, Hip/Fashionable, Late Night Open, Wish List

REVIEW Not to be confused with a sexual practice, Ling Ling is the cocktail bar adjoining top eaterie Hakkasan. It was just the bar on the side, but evidently felt left out and demanded a name of its own. It's all very beautiful, with baby blue leather furniture bearing embroidered dragon motifs, though quite uncomfortable for 'me-love-you-long-time' lounging, so bag a banquette. A DJ spins tunes at the end of the bar; occasionally everyone dances, but generally it's just one drunken rich girl desperate for the attention. Full of Eastern promise and attempting that Buddha Bar vibe, it never quite surpasses the fantastic first impression upon arrival.

PLACE Cavernous basement with speakeasy promise tucked down a seedy back alley. Opulent Asian temple meets moody Manhattan loft, designed by Parisian Christian Liagre, with glowing blue wall panels and a towering carved timber screen/cage surrounding diners.
PEOPLE Persian princesses and British princes have made cameos, otherwise expect plenty of posh boys and girls and industry types, bartenders and drinks company bods gossiping and late-night London's usual jaded shakers and movers.

PROFS Royalty, actors, businessmen, models, doctors
CELEBS Tom Parker-Bowles, Giles Baker, Joanna Lumley, Mick Jagger, Naomi Campbell, Lennox Lewis, Caprice, Jude and Sadie, Lady Victoria Hervey
DRESS Avoid Maharishi's: you'll be mistaken for a chair. Abercrombie, Levi's, Gucci, Selfridges, Harvey Nichols
MUSIC DJs Mon-Sat
DOOR Guest List, Smart Dress
DRINKS Beer £4, Wine £4.20, Champagne £7.50, Cocktail £8
FOOD Modern, Chinese, £12
CARDS No Diners
CAPACITY 100, seating 70
HIRE Venue: Yes · Private Room: No

THE LONG BAR &
THE PURPLE BAR

Cocktail Bar, Hotel Bar
The Sanderson Hotel, 50 Berners Street W1
020 7300 9500

OPEN Long Bar: Mon-Sat 10am-1am, Sun 10am-10.30pm.
Purple Bar: Mon-Sat 5pm-3am, Sun 5pm-1am
TUBE/RAIL Oxford Circus, Tottenham Court Road
BUSES 8, 10, 25, 55, 73, 176

GETTING LUCKY 3/5
EYE CANDY 5/5
BIG SPENDERS 5/5
MIX 50%M 50%F
AGE 26-50
PRICE Very expensive

AMBIENCE Buzzy, Conversation, Cute Staff, Destination/Wishlist, Elegant/Classic, Exclusive/Chic, Groups, Hip/Fashionable, Jet Set, Minimalist, Late Night Open, Outdoors, Star Spotting
REVIEW Starck and Schrager's sequel to the clinically disappointing Light Bar is brasher and flasher, attracting a wealth of money makers, money chasers and Eurotrash. It's located to the right of the lobby in the new Sanderson hotel, just past the illuminated screen that appears to display a frenzy of wriggling maggots. Net curtains, sorry, I mean diaphanous sheer drapes – line the walls and during summer the pretty courtyard is accessible. The slimline space surrounding the bar makes everyone a barfly and fellow voyeur. Drinks are extortionate with 15% service included on the bill (in the Purple Bar, for guests and VIPs only, a glass of bubbly leaves you nada, nil, zilch from £25), nothing is optional here, it's all for the taking. So grab, grab, grab if you've got the wallet and wardrobe for it.
PLACE Bright and shiny flash showcase adjoining the crazeee, kitsch-Baroque lobby. The 40-seater, more exclusive Purple Bar is a plush velvet darker den, all purple and candlelight with Venetian mirror detailing and a hideous rocky bar front.
PEOPLE A rash of Eurotrash, City boys trying to buy a sip of taste, skeletal style vampires desperate to suck some cool from the Schrager/Starck dream. Overly-groomed single Eastern European women and Botox-happy, gym-cruising Conde Nasties.

PROFS Music industry staff, brokers, traders, arms dealers, PRs, models, accountants, wealthy tourists, fashion professionals, property developers, film and TV professionals, photographers, stylists, pretenders
CELEBS Jerry Springer, Hugh Grant, Christy Turlington, Jade Jagger, Dan MacMillan, Paul Smith, Philippe Starck
DRESS Show all, flash and brash; suits from Boateng to Gieves & Hawkes, Gucci, Prada, Voyage, Jimmy Choo, Manolo Blahnik, Fendi, Burberry, Nicole Farhi, a touch of Jigsaw and Whistles
MUSIC Jazz, Funk
DOOR Long Bar: none, Purple Bar: residents only and at door host's discretion
DRINKS Long Bar: Beer £4.68, Wine £6.05, Champagne £9.90, Cocktail £9
Purple Bar: Beer £8, Wine £10.50, Champagne £25, Cocktail £15

FOOD French, £12
CARDS All
CAPACITY 800, seating 120
HIRE Venue: Yes · Private Room: Yes

MASH

Bar, Restaurant,
19-21 Great Portland Street W1
020 7637 5555

OPEN Mon-Tue midday-		
midnight, Wed-Sat	GETTING LUCKY	**2/5**
midday-2am	EYE CANDY	**3/5**
TUBE/RAIL Oxford Circus	BIG SPENDERS	**2/5**
BUSES 8, 10, 24, 29,	MIX 50%M 50%F	
73, 134	AGE 19-35	
	PRICE Expensive	

AMBIENCE Brightly Coloured/Cheerful, Futuristic, Groups, Late Night Open, Party, Pulling, Retro
REVIEW Buck Rogers gets it on with Burt Reynolds. Mash is futuristic, weird and camp. A curvy-bendy entrance propels you via the 1950s into a 70s bar area, both trying to survive the start of the 21st-century. It's all a bit confusing, but restaurant mover and shaker Oliver Peyton (Atlantic, Isola, Admiralty) knows what he's doing with his ironic time and space games. It may seem like the final frontier for good taste but, despite the closure of the original Mash in Manchester, that hasn't stopped him from 'rolling out the concept' in London. Peyton's place is designed for modern, shiny, happy people, but the crowd now hails from well beyond the M25, and they're all very much up for it. The girlies think it's a giggle because the ladies' has video screens showing views of the gents'.
PLACE Huge backlit photos depict a 70s-style Burt Reynolds lookalike, with moustache and Pringle shirt, yachting with his wife and kids. It's the ideal happy family, except everyone around the central man is pulling hilariously revolted faces. Whatever he's done to deserve the disgust, it can't be worse than what goes on in the bar itself, such is the state of the clientele.
PEOPLE Groups of office workers from the 'burbs hunting in packs.

PROFS Accountants, salesmen, recruitment consultants, receptionists, media planners, students
CELEBS Davina McCall, Paul Whitehouse, Armand van Helden, Graham Norton, Terry Wogan, Sarah Cracknell
DRESS Short-sleeved Tommy shirts, shiny tight Armani tops, thin-strapped, low-cut FCUK vest tops
MUSIC Funk, Blues, Ambient, DJs Thu and Sat
DOOR None
DRINKS Beer £2.80, Wine £4.50, Champagne £7.50, Cocktail £5.50
FOOD International, Mediterranean, Modern European, Pizza, £9
CARDS All
CAPACITY 430, seating 160
HIRE Venue: Yes · Private Room: Yes

MATCH

Bar
37-38 Margaret Street W1
0207 499 3443

OPEN Mon-Sat 11am-		
midnight	GETTING LUCKY	**3/5**
TUBE/RAIL Oxford Circus	EYE CANDY	**3/5**
BUSES 113, 137, 189	BIG SPENDERS	**3/5**
	MIX 50%M 50%F	
	AGE 25-40	
	PRICE Expensive	

AMBIENCE Lounge, Conversation, Groups
REVIEW Welcome to Marlboro country. Not only are the walls designed to resemble the cool, tumbleweed Marlboro roads, but the air is thick with 'em too. When Match W1 joined the original Clerkenwell branch, the West End's working girls found their spiritual home. Finally, a stylish bar within staggering distance of the office for showing off lunchtime purchases, smoking cartons of you-know-what's, wasting entire salaries on alcohol and living out Sex and the City fantasies. Problem is, it's been a long time since that Pret sandwich, the MAC mascara is beginning to run and Mr Big's nowhere in sight. What the hell. Another round of Cosmopolitans, please, barman.
PLACE You have to hand it to the Match design team: the Marlboro walls are a perfect blend of scenery and irony, the soft low lighting from candles and hessian-effect lampshades casts a warm glow on office-pale faces, and the leather banquettes were made for lounging.
PEOPLE Movers, shakers and wigglers, although the highest quality shaking takes place behind the bar where the boys and girls in black mix up superb cocktails.

PROFS Media employees, retail staff, magazine staff
CELEBS None
DRESS Karen Millen, Warehouse, Uth, Reiss, Levi's
MUSIC Lounge, Jazz, Ambient, Funk, DJ Thu-Sat
DOOR None
DRINKS Beers £2.75, Wine £3.25, Champagne £5.75, Cocktail £5
FOOD Modern European, Oriental, Platters, £7
CARDS All
CAPACITY 300, seating 120
HIRE Venue: Yes · Private Room: Yes

NORDIC

Bar
25 Newman Street W1
020 7631 3174

OPEN Mon-Sat 6pm-11pm		
TUBE/RAIL Tottenham	GETTING LUCKY	**5/5**
Court Road	EYE CANDY	**1/5**
BUSES 8, 73	BIG SPENDERS	**2/5**
	MIX 70%M 30%F	
	AGE 20-40	
	PRICE Average	

AMBIENCE Kitsch, Pulling
REVIEW It's astounding that a bar so bad can open in 2001. Nordic is tragically themed around Viking territory check the alluring photo-mural behind the bar, Danish bacon clock and ABBA references. It's about as Nordic as a dire shifty pub full of saddo's in the depths of Salford, or a dreggy student bar north of Watford. The laminated menu belongs in motorway Harvester wilderness or better – butt-f**k Iowa. Cocktails include the Lapp Dance, beneath which it says 'Girls get one free if they strip' (you would be insane to even take your coat off in this

dump), followed by Elkie Brooks 'Where moose go to drink' – you couldn't make it up. The warm white wine didn't help. A chalk blackboard gives it that King's Head touch, which probably explains the male overload, all hiding behind their pints like true Norsemen. We didn't hang around to see what happens when they find their Dutch courage.

PLACE Basement bar that keeps on unfolding, café style room leads into narrow bar area with another room at the back. Shoddy Viking/Danish theme.

PEOPLE Too many men for comfort. People without an ounce of self-respect or notion of style. The pitiful ones.

PROFS Media, TV and advertising professionals, Scandinavians

CELEBS Various actors from The Bill

DRESS It really doesn't matter, make as little effort as humanly possible

MUSIC Background, ABBA

DOOR None

DRINKS Beer £3, Wine £3, Champagne £4.50, Cocktail £6

FOOD Scandinavian, £7.75

CARDS No Diners

CAPACITY 180, seating 75

HIRE Venue: Yes · Private Room: Yes

OFFICE

Bar
3-5 Rathbone Place W1
020 7636 1598

OPEN Mon-Sat midday-3am,	**GETTING LUCKY**	**5/5**
Sun 6am-2pm	**EYE CANDY**	**2/5**
TUBE/RAIL Tottenham	**BIG SPENDERS**	**1/5**
Court Road	**MIX** 40%M 60%F	
BUSES 7, 8, 10, 25, 55, 73	**AGE** 21-35	
	PRICE Cheap	

AMBIENCE Dancing, Party, Basement, Dive bar, Groups, Grunge, Kitsch decor, Pulling, Queues

REVIEW Somewhere between a Student Union bar and a public toilet, Office Bar is always incredibly popular with the post-work admin and wannabe media whores. The punters are, to paraphrase REM, slimy happy people, groping hands. The secret to its success must be the jugs of saccharine cocktails and the feelgood music – a memory-fest of cheesy 8os, indie, disco and rock. But why anyone would choose to queue to get beyond the dog-gnawed red rope to hang out in a festering concrete basement with no nod to even passable decor, or even chairs, is beyond us. Maybe the clue is at the bottom of the council towerblock-alike stairs – as you go to yank open the heavy utility-issue door, there's a reminder sign just above the handle – 'pull'.

PLACE Nothing to see even if you could. Dingy, dank, concrete basement painted in back-of-a-lorry paint – possibly blue or purple. Grey-tiled toilets that smell bizarrely of old people and cats. Dance floor in the corner, but who needs that – no tables, no chairs, no worries. Standing room only.

PEOPLE Office people, as in the BBC comedy, The Office – with life parodying art parodying life: it's obviously cool to have a complexion that suggests too many Pot Noodles, a baguette bag full of Rimmel and tottery heels for the girls, and Steve Coogan's character lists cast-offs for the boys.

PROFS They wish! Assistant this, that or the other – one toe on the career ladder if they're lucky. Media, film, PR if they're bragging

CELEBS None

DRESS High Street all the way, baby. Glitter and flab-fighting corsets for girls. Forgettable shirts and trousers for boys. Didn't John Collier close a decade ago?

MUSIC New Romantic, Pre-Guy Madge, Britney – cheese, rock, pop and disco. Hard House on Sundays

DOOR None

DRINKS Beer £3, Cocktail £4

FOOD None

CARDS No Diners

CAPACITY 300, seating 20

HIRE Venue: Yes · Private: Yes

THE SOCIAL

Bar
5 Little Portland Street W1
020 7636 4992

OPEN Mon-Fri midday-2am	**GETTING LUCKY**	**2/5**
TUBE/RAIL Oxford Circus	**EYE CANDY**	**3/5**
BUSES 7, 8, 10, 22	**BIG SPENDERS**	**2/5**
	MIX 65%M 35%F	
	AGE 19-50	
	PRICE Cheap	

AMBIENCE Buzzy, Minimalist, Industrial, Grunge, Legendary, Basement

REVIEW The Social's house cocktail is composed of frangelico, teichenne, butterscotch schnapps and cream, topped off with a sprinkling of chocolate flakes. It's a frilly, camp confection and, in character, entirely at odds with the stark concrete bunker in which it is infrequently served. The Social is a bar with a function, a place for the music industry to hear up-and-coming bands and catch the curl of new waves before things go all mainstream on them. Underground in every sense, on any given night it'll be packed out with muso hacks in battered leather jackets knocking back pints and mentally masticating phrases like 'swooping, gull-like guitars' or – and we actually overheard this one – 'condescending synth samples'. Before the bands come in they mainly hang out in the booths of the upstairs bar, puffing on Lucky Strikes and ploughing through rival journals and obscure sleevenotes to Finnish alt country bands. Occasionally they dive outside to call their girlfriends and explain laconically why hearing a revolutionary new kind of drum 'n' bass from the Scilly Isles has to take precedence over that romantic evening in with a curry.

PLACE Stylish minimalism in basic materials: glass, concrete and a smattering of wood. The upstairs bar looks a bit like a sauna while the concrete cavern down the starkly lit fluorescent stairs looks a little like the basement of an NCP carpark.

PEOPLE The kind of people who alphabetise the vast CD collections which dominate their tiny North London flats. They can tell you who played bass on the most obscure of early 80s Detroit punk, but they never remember their mother's birthday and are congenitally unable to operate a washing machine.

PROFS Music industry: A&R, producers, engineers, journalists, graphic designers
CELEBS The Manic Street Preachers, Chemical Brothers, Lambchop, Primal Scream
DRESS Music industry types either dress according to music taste (checked shirts for Neil Young fans, bizarre rubber trousers for acolytes of German techno thrash) or they don't give a toss and opt for the Bryan Adams greyish t-shirt, leather jacket and old jeans combo
MUSIC The full monty from Scandanavian lounge kitsch to seriously heavy metal
DOOR None
DRINKS Beer £2.80, Wine £2.50, Cocktail £4.80
FOOD Traditional British, £3.50
CARDS No Diners
CAPACITY 300, seating 100
HIRE Venue: Yes · Private Room: Yes

TSAR BAR

Bar
Langham Hilton, 1c Langham Place W1
020 7636 1000

OPEN Mon-Fri 5pm-11.30pm	**GETTING LUCKY**	**2/5**
TUBE Oxford Circus	**EYE CANDY**	**4/5**
BUSES C2, 88	**BIG SPENDERS**	**5/5**
	MIX 50%M 50%F	
	AGE 30-70	
	PRICE Expensive	

AMBIENCE Business, Conversation, Elegant/Classic, Exclusive, Groups, Historic, Mature/Older, Opulent/Period
REVIEW Sweep back the red velvet curtain and step into timeless decadence – mahogany panelling hung with still lifes in oils and rustic impressionist art. Balalaika folk music gives it the requisite Russian feel. Kalinka (geddit?) glasses with aficionados of the finest

vodka – there are over 100 on offer. On the menu – hot and cold zakuski, okroschka, Siberian ravioli and caviar. It's not exactly revolutionary (well it wouldn't be, would it?) in concept, decor or atmosphere, but you do feel you're getting the best. There's also a rather large humidor in the corner with a modest selection of Cuban cigars (now we're getting closer to revolution). And how many venues can claim the rare honour of having played host to both Gloria Hunniford and the Beastie Boys? Now that is radical.

PLACE Expensive, exclusive, exemplary. Banquette fabrics and patterned carpet in rich, regal colours: reds, blues, bottle greens – all in the best possible taste. Mahogany, brass and leather gent's club chairs. Black, polished stone tables.

PEOPLE Older, discerning clientele. Business people in suits. You wouldn't undo the top button in here. Keep it refined – even regal. Think Dynasty, but easy on the glitz and shoulder pads.

PROFS BBC execs, film execs, City types, finance, law, a handful of dotcommers
CELEBS Michael Schumacher, Gloria Hunniford, Adam Horowitz and Beastie cohorts, Robert Duvall, Princess Di
DRESS Black cocktail dresses, some sequinned labelled glamour, suits, ties
MUSIC Da! Peasant folk!
DOOR Smart – this is the Hilton
DRINKS Beer £4.25, Wine £6, Champagne £11.50, Cocktail £10
FOOD Russian, £15
CARDS All
CAPACITY 60, seating 30
HIRE Venue: Yes · Private Room: Yes

6 DEGREES

Bar
56 Frith Street W1
020 7734 8300

OPEN Mon-Fri midday-11pm,	**GETTING LUCKY**	**3/5**
Sat 6pm-11pm	**EYE CANDY**	**3/5**
TUBE/RAIL Tottenham Court	**BIG SPENDERS**	**2/5**
Road	**MIX** 60%M 40%F	
BUSES 14, 19, 24, 29,	**AGE** 25-35	
38, 176	**PRICE** Average	

AMBIENCE Dance, Conversation, Friendly, Funky, Comfy, Buzzy, Chilled
REVIEW Flava-ful, feelgood nu-soul bar with a contemporary black street vibe but a mixed bunch of punters. The music is unashamedly urban USA, but you're spared the full-on Gap/Hilfiger ad feel from the down-to-earth crowd who come here to see each other, rather than to be seen. The vermillion lighting lets you know you're in the heart of Soho – but the scarlet signals lifeblood rather than light district. Cocktails border on the predictable, and there are a couple of duds – who'd still want, yeah really, really want a Ginger Spice (rum and ginger beer) or a Chocolate Martini? Don't even ask. Stick to the standards and you're in, as Kelis would say, for the good stuff.

PLACE Low-slung chocolate brown leather sofas. Red backlighting anywhere it can be hidden – in metal half-barrel coffee tables under frosted glass tops and in the bar frontage. Upstairs is a mahogany-panelled, pared down, warmed up room with cosy sofas and wax-dripping candles.
PEOPLE Take your pick from EastEnder's Slater sisters – that denim casual look in all its variations works, especially with a midtown Manhattan twist. Boys – go a little 'Lock Stock'. Sorted.

PROFS Film production workers, new media, PR, actors, session musicians, trendy admin
CELEBS EastEnders, Sly Stallone
DRESS Black open-necked shirts, black trousers, twisted Levi's, chino's for men. Anything between trendy office suits and Kelis/Macy Gray style for women
MUSIC Soul
DOOR None
DRINKS Beer £3, Wine £4, Champagne £6, Cocktail £7
FOOD Bar Snacks, £4
CARDS All
CAPACITY 350, seating 100
HIRE Venue: Yes · Private Room: Yes

ABIGAIL'S PARTY

Members Bar
25-27 Brewer Street W1
020 7434 2911

OPEN Mon-Fri 5pm-3am,	GETTING LUCKY	**3/5**
Sat 9pm-3am	EYE CANDY	**4/5**
TUBE/RAIL Piccadilly Circus	BIG SPENDERS	**3/5**
BUSES 3, 6, 12, 13, 15, 23,	MIX 45%M 55%F	
53, 88, 94, 139, 159	AGE 27-40	
	PRICE Expensive	

AMBIENCE Buzzy, Casual, Comfy, Funky, Hip, Late Night Open, Network
REVIEW If bars were twinned with towns, then Abigail's Party would be Brighton; a curious mixture of pure tack for the tourists and cliquey cutting-edge chic. There's a lot of boyish banter of the Jamie Oliver order but with a heavy networking twist: 'You've met Greg haven't you? He did that amazing website for irony.com. Yeah, well he's doing a few things for us now... actually he could be lots of use on your TV project – why don't I get in another round while you two exchange numbers? Hey! Paul-mate! Great jacket, man. You still with Andrea at Random House?'
PLACE Rothko pastiches on the wall by Mark Wood and a Tiffany window featuring a pyramid and one of the china camels you used to get in crackers.
PEOPLE Alex and Jeremy share a flat on Wardour Street from which they jointly run a design consultancy. Jeremy's currently dating Lola, who he met at Abigail's; she works as an inhouse PR for a publishing company. She thought 'Amelie' was the best film she'd ever seen. He is appalled.

PROFS Local media (particularly advertising), funky IT companies, artists and designers, publishing execs, PRs
CELEBS Neil Morrissey, Leonardo DiCaprio, Cilla Black, Kate Moss, Ronnie Wood, Atomic Kitten, S Club 7
DRESS Lots of funky post-work gear: lots of clientele come in after work and stay on through the night.

Miss Sixty, Hobbs, DKNY, random chic and lots of black suits. Higher percentage of purple ties here than in any other bar. Also some yahoo lads in chinos and loafers
MUSIC House, Funk, Rare Groove, Ambient, Disco
DOOR Members only. Entry will be refused to the excessively scruffy and 'smelly people'
DRINKS Beer £4.50, Wine £3.50, Champagne £7, Cocktail £6.50
FOOD Modern Mediterranean, £5
CARDS No Diners
CAPACITY 125, seating 45
HIRE Venue: Yes · Private Room: No

AKBAR

Bar, Restaurant
77 Dean Street W1
020 7437 2115

OPEN Mon-Fri midday-1am,	GETTING LUCKY	**3/5**
Sat 6pm-1am	EYE CANDY	**4/5**
TUBE Tottenham	BIG SPENDERS	**4/5**
Court Road	MIX 50%M 50%F	
BUSES 7, 8, 10, 25, 55, 73	AGE Average	
	PRICE Expensive	

AMBIENCE Basement, Conversation, Exclusive/Chic, Chilled, Comfy, Cosy, Cute Staff, Wishlist, Funky, Lounge atmosphere, Romantic
REVIEW A spice-tinged chill-out zone somewhere between Kashmir and the Kasbah, located underneath the newly-refurb'ed The Red Fort, renowned for its Mughal court cuisine. Akbar, named after the Mughal emperor, only drank water from the Ganges If he'd popped over to his tribute bar, he'd have given up purity for the exquisite range of cocktails – delicate, decadent, and fruit-rich – some of the best in the capital. Boasting a ridiculously long and exotic list of liqueurs, vodkas, martinis, shorts and champagnes, Akbar is neither short on liquor nor atmosphere. From the low-key in-house DJs, the proliferation of candles, the subtle smell of sandalwood, the cushioned alcoves and the minimal blend of dark wood, red accents and cool white walls, Akbar is subtle, but vibrant. Forget the 'gracious me', this Indian-inspired jewel is pure 'goodness'.
PLACE Richly minimalist – the key is in the detail. Tealights light the way downstairs to the floating candle and gerbera pond. Low, chocolate leather armchairs and cubes, York stone floor, American walnut, Italian tile and Indian rugs in the main area. Bolsters and cushions in the alcoves.

PROFS Media, music, film, TV, IT, finance
CELEBS None
DRESS Black cocktail dresses, subtle but glam. Think Cat Deeley at a funeral. Sophisticated but understated
MUSIC Ethnic Electronica, mellow to moveable
DOOR No dress code, but stay smart
DRINKS Beer £3, Wine £4, Champagne £6, Cocktail £6
FOOD Bar food, £6
CARDS All
CAPACITY 80, seating 40
HIRE Venue: Yes · Private Room: Yes

ALPHABET

Bar, Cocktail Bar
61-63 Beak Street W1
020 7439 2190

OPEN Mon-Fri 11am-11pm,	GETTING LUCKY	3/5
Sat 4pm-11pm	EYE CANDY	4/5
TUBE/RAIL Oxford Circus,	BIG SPENDERS	3/5
Piccadilly Circus	MIX 50%M 50%F	
BUSES 3, 6, 23, 53,	AGE 21-35	
139, 159	PRICE Average	

AMBIENCE Casual, Conversation, Cute Staff, Funky, Groups, Hip/Fashionable, Pulling, Retro, Warehouse/Industrial

REVIEW More Urban Outfitters than haute couture. Just as London got into the overtly designed 'style bar' phenomenon, Alphabet made its debut. Adorning one of the first and most successful DIY, rough 'n' ready bars, the ABC crew are stylish and over-effortlessly hip: they've got Attitude, Beauty and Cool in equal measures and don't need telling. The ground floor is more vertical; people sit or stand, whereas downstairs they practically lie flat out in the louche basement. Here's where the DJ resides and beanies and car seats provide laid-back seating as the patrons rest their fashionably scuffed trainers upon the (now famous) A-Z of Soho floor map. The bar walls display art that changes regularly and a mute and moody barman serves at an industrial-looking counter.

PLACE Lively and unpretentious atmosphere, Alphabet can proudly boast of being most people's cup of tea, though not in a bad way. Upstairs' bench seating is good for groups, whilst downstairs' eclectic chair range is good for, um, sitting.

PEOPLE Laid-back mockneyed meeja stars. One too many and all the Evisu logos will have you thinking you're actually on Brighton beach.

PROFS Media employees, musicians, fashion employees, account execs, caterers, film and TV employees, PRs, film runners, researchers, photographers

CELEBS Mr and Mrs David Bowie, Johnny Depp, Cat Deeley, Sophie Dahl

---

DRESS Streetwise, skateboard boys, Maharishi, Mandarina Duck, Nike, Adidas, unisex urbanites and boho babes

MUSIC Breakbeat, Dance, Drum 'n' Bass, Funk, Jazz, Latin, Opera, World Music, DJ Thu-Sat, from 7.30pm

DOOR None

DRINKS Beer £3.10, Wine £2.95, Champagne £6.00, Cocktail £4.50

FOOD International, Modern Eclectic, Pacific Rim, £10

CARDS No Amex or Diners

CAPACITY 150, seating 50

HIRE Venue: Yes · Private Room : Yes

AMBER

Bar, Restaurant
6 Poland Street W1
020 7734 3094

OPEN Mon-Sat midday-1am	GETTING LUCKY	4/5
TUBE/RAIL Tottenham	EYE CANDY	3/5
Court Road	BIG SPENDERS	3/5
BUSES 3, 6, 23, 53,	MIX 50%M 50%F	
139, 159	AGE 24-34	
	PRICE Average	

AMBIENCE Basement, Buzzy, Casual, Funky

REVIEW It was a while in coming, but the boys behind Alphabet finally pulled off their second bar. Although Amber doesn't, and probably never will, have the cred of its older cousin, that's not important as the feel is completely different. A Latin-themed bar – no really, it's much better than that sounds – there are no mullet-topped Butlins girls trying to feed groups of civil servants tequila slammers. Nor are there novelty maracas, bandit hats or framed El Paso adverts featuring genial-looking moustachioed Mexican men. Instead there's rotating artwork that ranges from installation pieces to 60s photography and a media-savvy crowd of post-production workers sipping inspired cocktails while discussing the latest Chris Cunningham video.

PLACE Small tapas eaterie upstairs with DIY designed booths and a bar in the basement with mosaic floor, booth seating, trendy arc lamps and a vague Amber theme.

PEOPLE 20 to 30-something Londoners that know their music and Mojitos, don't want to drink with the chain gang and can't afford members' clubs.

PROFS Media lovelies, PRs, runners, art directors, production assistants
CELEBS Saffron Alldridge, England Rugby Team, Brand New Heavies, Mark Strong, Nick Moran
DRESS Soho work gear (leisure wear to most people), dirty denim, Nike, Levi's, Carhartt, Jigsaw, TopShop, Evisu
MUSIC Samba, Latin House, DJ Thu-Sat from 8pm
DOOR £5 after 11pm
DRINKS Beer £3.50, Wine £3, Cocktail £5
FOOD Latin, £5.50
CARDS All
CAPACITY 120, seating 60
HIRE Venue: Yes · Private Room: No

ATTICA

Club, Restaurant
24 Kingly Street W1
020 7287 5882

OPEN Wed-Sat 9pm-3.30am	GETTING LUCKY	5/5
TUBE/RAIL Oxford Circus	EYE CANDY	5/5
BUSES 3, 6, 23, 53,	BIG SPENDERS	5/5
139, 159	MIX 55%M 45%F	
	AGE 25-45	
	PRICE Very expensive	

AMBIENCE Destination/Wishlist, Exclusive/Chic, Futuristic, Hip/Fashionable, Late Night Open, Party, Pulling, Retro
REVIEW This late-night den of outlandish egos has usurped the Met Bar as the Friday night place to preen, pose and party with the absurdly arrogant and stupidly rich. Beware, mere mortals may be refused entry, but if you're one of the beautiful ones then in-house entertainment is guaranteed. Scoff at Aspen-tanned toffs braying like bloated chipmunks in gold-buttoned blazers. Witness the Gatecrasher-style gropings of an older-enough-to-know better It-boy with a drunk-enough-to-know-nothing blonde sprawled across his lap. Parking your butt will cost ya' Manhattan-style – learn to love buying booze by the (litre) bottle, though if you're an attractive female fun comes for free. The loaded live it up in glowing glory while the oiks mill around in the standing-room only cattle class, playing their 'onlookers' part in the VIP circus.
PLACE Think 80s, think Gucci, think posh marble hotel loo meets downtown New York late night lounge bar. Four large VIP cube booths, separated by glam, illuminated glass screens overlook a glowing L-shaped bar.

PEOPLE Princes, popstars, posh gits and twits, producers, pretty boys, pretty girls and poseurs all round, this place is not for the shy: get out there and strut it baby, preferably with Panavision shades, Botox-face and a Collagen pout.

PROFS Popstars, entrepreneurs, record producers, bankers, traders, models, stylists, fashion designers
CELEBS Piers Adam, Donatella Versace, Lady Victoria Hervey, Jay Kay, Tom Jones, Kylie, Matthew Williamson, Kelis, Robert De Niro, Nell McAndrew, Robbie Williams, Mick Jagger
DRESS Couture ad campaign. Glitzy, flashy and frivolous mixed in with the casual jean clad billionaire; Voyage, Gucci, Levi's, Jimmy Choo, Manolo Blahnik, Nike, Matthew Williamson, Whistles
MUSIC R&B, Dance, Hip Hop, Old Skool, DJ seven days
DOOR Members and Guest List Only, £20
DRINKS Beer £4.50, Wine £4, Champagne £8, Cocktail £8
FOOD Modern European, £13
CARDS All
CAPACITY 450, seating 100
HIRE Venue: Yes · Private Room No

BAR CHOCOLATE

Bar
26-27 D'Arblay Street W1
020 7287 2823

OPEN 7 days 10am-11pm	GETTING LUCKY	3/5
TUBE/RAIL Oxford Circus	EYE CANDY	4/5
BUSES 3, 12, 53, 88,	BIG SPENDERS	3/5
139, 159	MIX 50%M 50%F	
	AGE 20-35	
	PRICE Average	

AMBIENCE Buzzy, Casual, Conversation, Minimalist
REVIEW If this really was a bar of chocolate, it would be a Galaxy that had been left in the fridge: simple, unpretentious, satisfying and chilled. Bar Chocolate manages a rare Soho feat in being stylish without being judgmental. No single tribe dominates, allowing a mixture of centred 20 and 30-somethings with plenty of energy but precious little attitude to relax in a cosy and unobtrusive environment. The music – mellow trip-hop, jazz and urban R&B – offers an aural Shiatsu massage, and it's easy to settle in for the whole evening. The conceptual artwork says a lot about who drinks here – creative, inspired individuals with lots to say but no need to shout about it.
PLACE Small (seating for about 40), simple set-up with claret, vanilla and chocolate walls. Good attention to detail thanks to the wood/metal tables, bookcases and church chairs.
PEOPLE While most Chocaholics work in media, they're at the more creative end. Talk is of screenplays and experimentation, not bonus-related airtime sales targets.

PROFS Publishers, sound engineers, broadcasters, music industry execs, students, PRs, film production staff, graphic designers
CELEBS Lisa l'Anson, Eddie Izzard
DRESS Diesel, combats, trainers, Nike, Hackett, Evisu, Hope and Glory, Firetrap

MUSIC Hip Hop, Trip-hop, Jazz, R&B
DOOR None
DRINKS Beer £2.60, Wine £2.75, Cocktail £4.99
FOOD Mediterranean, English, Snacks, £6.50
CARDS No Amex or Diners
CAPACITY 100, seating 40
HIRE Venue: Yes · Private Room: No

BAR ITALIA

Bar, Restaurant
21 Frith Street W1
020 7734 4737

OPEN Mon-Sat midday-4am,	GETTING LUCKY	**5/5**
Sun midday-11.30pm	EYE CANDY	**3/5**
TUBE/RAIL Tottenham Court	BIG SPENDERS	**3/5**
Road, Piccadilly Circus,	MIX 50%M 50%F	
Leicester Square	AGE 25-50	
BUSES 14, 19, 24, 29,	PRICE Average	
38, 176		

AMBIENCE Casual, Friendly, Late Night Open, Legendary, Party, Pulling
REVIEW Immortalised by Pulp in their tribute of the same name, Bar Italia's authentic Nu-Yawk Italian atmosphere is generated by the simple interior of this unpretentious café-style bar. Air of nostalgia with a 50s slant, Sophia Loren would fit here. Sinatra croons as waiters serve, often too attentively, on top-ups. Frequented by various Londoners and Italians, and appreciated by Bohemians and Soho-dwellers for its 4am food licence. Post-pub hours, tables are removed, music is turned up and it becomes jammed solid. Easy to mix, due to sardine-like proximity and good-time mood. Girls should aim to exit clinging to a gigolo on the back of a Lambretta.
PLACE Compact, pleasantly claustrophobic two-tier space. Drinkers crowd at the tile-floored bar; diners perch on their seats trying to avoid them at ground level. Black and white photos of stars like Sinatra and Travolta.
PEOPLE Groups of noisy girls and boys throwing wine on the floor and down their throats, plus older Suits trying to get in on the act. Look out for the cameos of young Donnie Brascos, Italian stallions in fine, black suits.

PROFS Media employees, actors, singers, headhunters, sales managers, journalists, PR agents, fashion directors, producers, advertising executives, film editors, accountants
CELEBS Dani Behr, Emma Bunton, Mickey Rourke, Ruud Gullit, Gail Hipgrave (neé Porter), Paul Nicholls, Victoria Beckham, Mel B, Jamie Theakston, Robbie Williams, Jerry Hall
DRESS Jigsaw zip tops, Gap cardigans, Hugo Boss suits or Da Fonz style waist-banded leather jackets, obligatory white t-shirts and lots and lots of gel
MUSIC Jazz, Soul, Pop, Italian, Dance, South American
DOOR Smart casual, Fri-Sat £3 after 11pm
DRINKS Beer £3, Wine £4.50, Champagne £8, Cocktail £5
FOOD Italian, £8.50
CARDS No Diners
CAPACITY 95, seating 80
HIRE Venue: Yes · Private Room: No

BAR RED

Bar, Restaurant
5 Kingly Street W1
020 7434 3417

OPEN Mon-Sat midday-	GETTING LUCKY	**3/5**
midnight	EYE CANDY	**3/5**
TUBE/RAIL Oxford Circus,	BIG SPENDERS	**4/5**
Piccadilly Circus	MIX 30%M 70%F	
BUSES 3, 6, 23, 53,	AGE 18-40	
139, 159	PRICE Expensive	

AMBIENCE Buzzy, Dancing, Elegant/Classic, Groups, Hip/Fashionable
REVIEW Since the spate of post-millennial openings (Bar Red, Attica) joined old-timer Emporium, Kingly Street's now got more clipboarded door sentries than a cold war checkpoint. Quite why this chilled-out bar/ restaurant needs a peremptory, cross-questioning Goldie/Donna Air wannabe on the door is beyond us. Still, once you're past the blood-red frontage, the rest of the young, aesthetically pleasing staff are far from frosty. And it's clear from the happy mix of skewed ties, Jarvis Cocker specs, lamé halternecks, lamé balding pates and ho-chic nylon wigs that there's no hefty door policy in action. Leather-coated sugar daddys and cleavage exposing disco dollys have a good time whilst sipping decent cocktails.
PLACE Red Perspex filter over full glass frontage casts a crimson light. Rectilinear space on two floors, both with red walls and stainless steel bar.
PEOPLE Media youth – more West End sassy than East End garage geek. Networking creatives, animated shop assistants, pencil pushers and glitzy girls just out of gym-slips with older suitors in their cups (literally).

PROFS Account execs, PRs, graphic designers, post-production workers
CELEBS Mick Hucknall and a bevy of pre-Attica soap lovelies
DRESS LK Bennett boots, Paul Smith, Adidas trainers, Lycra tops, low-slung diamante belts, camel macs, black polo necks, halter necks, silver-studded jeans
MUSIC Breakbeat, R&B, Hip Hop, Electronica, DJ Thu-Sat from 7.30pm
DOOR Smart casual
DRINKS Beer £2.95, Wine £3.75, Champagne £7, Cocktail £6
FOOD Modern European, £13
CARDS No Diners
CAPACITY 250, seating 40
HIRE Venue: Yes · Private Room: No

BLACKS

Members Club
67 Dean Street W1
020 7287 3381

OPEN Mon-Sat 9am-1am,	GETTING LUCKY	**2/5**
6pm-1am	EYE CANDY	**3/5**
TUBE/RAIL Piccadilly Circus	BIG SPENDERS	**5/5**
BUSES 9, 14, 22, 53,	MIX 50%M 50%F	
94, 139	AGE 25-60	
	PRICE Expensive	

AMBIENCE Basement, Conversation, Cosy, Exclusive/Chic, Late Night Open, Old World, Romantic
REVIEW A private club, discreet and hidden away. Originator Tom is a curator of Georgian style and has created something magical here. Enter at basement level where the arrangement of heavy wooden bench tables prompts expectations of a hearty wench slapping a silver tankard of ye olde ale before you. On the first-floor delicious three-course menus are served at Dickensian prices of £18 per head, £9.50 per bottle of wine. The second-floor is where quiet conversation occurs; take over the bedroom if you feel riotous, otherwise behave as children should and be seen and not heard. On the landing dried flowers conjure up memories of Miss Haversham and cobwebbed chandeliers. Blacks offers genuine escapism, and we defy anyone to not be seduced by its romanticism, if you can find a way in.
PLACE Mysterious and secretive Georgian townhouse set on three floors. Dark and mysterious with candle sconces and Hogarth prints hanging on murky green walls. Antique furniture. So authentic it could be haunted.
PEOPLE Romantics and nostalgics. Cultured, sensitive, creative types who value good conversation, food and wine.

PROFS Artists, account execs, antique dealers, journalists, actors, art dealers, aristocrats, film professionals, music industry execs, financial types
CELEBS John Rocha, Miranda Sawyer, Mark Strong
DRESS Too dark to see but really not important
MUSIC No Background Music
DOOR Members Only
DRINKS Beer £2.50, Wine £2.50, Champagne £4
FOOD Modern European, £8.50
CARDS None
CAPACITY 100, seating 20
HIRE Venue: Yes · Private Room: No

BLUES BAR & BISTRO

Bar, Restaurant
42-43 Dean Street W1
020 7494 1966

OPEN Mon-Thu midday-midnight, Fri midday-1am, Sat 5.30pm-1am, Sun 5.30pm-midnight **TUBE/RAIL** Piccadilly Circus **BUSES** 9, 14, 22, 53, 94, 139	**GETTING LUCKY**	**3/5**
	EYE CANDY	**3/5**
	BIG SPENDERS	**3/5**
	MIX 50%M 50%F	
	AGE 20-55	
	PRICE Average	

AMBIENCE Groups, Late Night Open, Pulling
REVIEW In the same way that Durham University is for failed Oxbridge candidates, the Blues Bar offers consolation to those unable to Noel Coward it at the neighbouring Groucho Club. Surrounded by varied media haunts, this bar/restaurant is agreeably unselfconscious. Tucked into the narrow, neon streets of Soho, this Tardis-sized bar is normally packed by 7pm, but if you're visiting at peak boozing time, it's usually worth battling your way through to a table. Fancy-Dan distractions are kept to a minimum, both in terms of the menu and understated interior. Add the obliging service, decent grub and wine list and you've found an affordable, reliable place to eat and drink.

PLACE Woody ground-floor bar and restaurant offset with pastel shades; downstairs is good for parties. MTV and the occasional bit of footy at the bar.
PEOPLE Usual Soho hybrid, although it should be said that this isn't the hippest hang-out on the block; good for out-of-towners who fancy risking a non All-Bar-Pitcher-Parrot visit. Big on girls' nights out.

PROFS Middling ad execs, sales teams, PR agents, occasional film bods, advertising agents, TV post-producers, tourists
CELEBS None
DRESS Smart casual: more Gap and FCUK than Prada or Joseph. Oasis, Jigsaw, Hugo Boss suits, Moss Bros
MUSIC Funk
DOOR None
DRINKS Beer £3, Wine £3.25, Champagne £6.95, Cocktail £5.95
FOOD International, Modern British, Modern Eclectic, Modern European, £12
CARDS No Diners
CAPACITY 160, seating 100
HIRE Venue: No · Private Room: Yes

BOARDWALK

Bar, Restaurant
18 Greek Street W1
020 7287 2051

OPEN Mon-Sat 5pm-3am **TUBE/RAIL** Tottenham Court Road **BUSES** 14, 19, 24, 29, 38, 176	**GETTING LUCKY**	**4/5**
	EYE CANDY	**2/5**
	BIG SPENDERS	**2/5**
	MIX 55%M 45%F	
	AGE 20-35	
	PRICE Average	

AMBIENCE Casual, Dancing, Groups, Late Night Open, Party, Pulling
REVIEW This busy Soho destination never seems to disappoint. People come here to drink and get drunk and, sure enough, that seems to be the most pronounced effect. The large drinking space is inevitably full of a mix of office-types, bar hoppers and grown-ups who should know better. Any bar like this provides ample opportunity to meet and greet, and the boisterous crowd adds to the general air of revelry. If you aren't saving yourself for a supermodel or filmstar, this friendly bar may just be for you. Two long staircases provide easy promenading and scanning of fellow boozers. Unpretentious and honest, but best seen through the bottom of a glass.
PLACE From the outside it's an attractive period building, inside it's fallen prey to the one-style-suits-all mauve walls and chrome furniture job.

PEOPLE Sensibly funky meeja types who have to catch the last Tube back to Streatham to feed the cat. Ben Shermanites luvvin' it luvvin' it at the weekend.

PROFS Media executives, artists, office and service workers, business executives, tourists, actors, TV producers

CELEBS Brian Moore, Kathy Lloyd, Tony Hadley, Johnny Vegas

DRESS Suits and ties, M&S, Ralph Lauren, Jane Norman, Miss Selfridge, Carhartt

MUSIC Commercial Dance, Chart, Pop, DJ Mon, Thu-Sat, from 11pm

DOOR Smart casual. No trainers at weekends. £3-5 after 11pm Mon, Thu-Sat

DRINKS Beer £3, Wine £2.85, Champagne £5.25, Cocktail £4.50

FOOD Modern European, £10

CARDS No Diners

CAPACITY 209, seating 60

HIRE Venue: Yes · Private Room: Yes

CAFÉ BOHEME

Bar, Café, Music Venue, Restaurant
13-17 Old Compton Street W1
020 7734 0623

OPEN Mon-Sat 8am-3am, Sun 8am-11pm TUBE/RAIL Tottenham Court Road, Leicester Square BUSES 14, 19, 24, 29, 38, 176	GETTING LUCKY	3/5
	EYE CANDY	3/5
	BIG SPENDERS	3/5
	MIX 50%M 50%F	
	AGE 25-40	
	PRICE Average	

AMBIENCE Buzzy, Groups, Late Night Open, Live Music, Outdoors, Party, Romantic, Student

REVIEW This café/restaurant/bar has permanently steamy windows as it's packed tighter than Tom Jones's trousers, and chairs seem to be for diners only. The corner-site prominence guarantees tourists vying for space next to maturer media Soho types, regulars from Soho House above and a few middle-class, middle-aged theatregoers. Known for its fast-paced, lively atmosphere in the week and prime viewing of the Soho strutters' main drag in summer at pavement tables. Okay for couples but hectic otherwise; you may stay all afternoon in August, but no one stays all night during winter.

PLACE Small bar with tiny table section and larger restaurant area adjoining. Slightly baroque and dark with the bohemian flicker of candlelight, an antique wooden dresser and ornate mirror.

PEOPLE High-heeled media babes, slick City suits, bohemian Soho wanderers, office workers on a girls' night out, couples catching a quick bite.

PROFS Restaurateurs, club owners, music industry employees, actors, dancers, media employees, journalists, publishing employees, artists, students, marketing employees, film company employees, account execs, tourists

CELEBS Stephen Fry, Anna Friel, Tiger Woods, Woody Harrelson, Tom Cruise, Nicole Kidman

DRESS Suits, jeans, shirts and ties, Jigsaw, Boss, Armani, Dior

MUSIC House, Live Jazz Tue-Fri, Sun, 3pm-6pm

DOOR Smart casual. £4 after 10pm Fri-Sat
DRINKS Beer £2.80, Wine £3, Champagne £5.50, Cocktail £5.50
FOOD Brasserie, French, £10
CARDS All
CAPACITY 60, seating 60
HIRE Venue: No · Private Room: No

CANDY BAR

Bar, Lesbian
23-24 Bateman Street W1
020 7437 1977

OPEN Mon-Thu 2pm-1am, Fri-Sat 2pm-3am TUBE/RAIL Tottenham Court Road BUSES 3, 6, 12, 53, 139, 159	GETTING LUCKY	5/5
	EYE CANDY	3/5
	BIG SPENDERS	3/5
	MIX 5%M 95%F	
	AGE 18-35	
	PRICE Average	

AMBIENCE Basement, Buzzy, Late Night Open, Outdoors, Pulling

REVIEW A London lesbian scene stalwart, Candy Bar's latest incarnation – all honey low lighting and mop clean minimalism – has been servicing capital city lickers and their Stripe swigging consorts for two years. And candy is an apt moniker if you're in the girl-girl trade: wised-up moneyed media pariahs skulk around the recently outed teen and twenty-something sweet treats on the dance floor downstairs, as those fond of a different breed of candy sniff menacingly at the entry and exit routes of the bar area upstairs. Homo-hop ain't reached this neck of the woods, so bumping and winding tunes are invariably of the über-camp disco diva school. Beware: dungarees and rowdy holidaying heteros are about as welcome as Pat Butcher in a g-string and nipple tassels.

PLACE Candy Bar downsized on its last move, allowing ample frotting opportunities as you squeeze through the girl pile-ups to the loo. A narrow corridor of outsized seating and a lengthy stooled bar area upstairs gives way to a dank, dark stew of bodily odours and pumping rhythms below.

PEOPLE Worldly-wise lesbians buzzing around new scene queens ripe from the provinces. Also the first port of call for city-hopping, Gucci-clad sophisticats.

PROFS Media professionals, accountancy executives, PRs, directors, movie stars, journalists

CELEBS Sarah Waters, Martina Navratilova, Samantha Fox, Belinda Carlisle, Sophie Ward

DRESS Paradiso, Calvin Klein, Diesel

MUSIC Old Skool, R&B, Soul, Hip Hop, House, Indie, Rock

DOOR Females with gay male guests only. Fri-Sat £5 after 9pm

DRINKS Beer £2.80, Wine £2.80, Cocktail £2.70

FOOD Snacks, £4

CARDS All

CAPACITY 140, seating 110

HIRE Venue: No · Private Room: No

CIRCUS

Bar, Restaurant
1 Upper James Street W1
020 7534 4000

OPEN Mon-Wed midday-1am, Thu-Sat midday-3am
TUBE/RAIL Oxford Circus
BUSES 9, 14, 19, 22, 38, 159

GETTING LUCKY	**4/5**
EYE CANDY	**4/5**
BIG SPENDERS	**4/5**
MIX 60%M 40%F	
AGE 30-60	
PRICE Average	

AMBIENCE Business, Conversation, Dancing, Elegant/Classic, Hip/Fashionable, Jet Set, Late Night Open, Minimalist, Star Spotting
REVIEW People keep to themselves in this temple of icy metropolitan eating and drinking. White walls, a bit of black and the odd splash of beige are reflected in the gear of the cool brigade of shaven-headed architects and gay designers in tight t-shirts, black suits and linen trousers. There is a performance of sorts going on, nonetheless. Circus is like a Sunday supplement photo shoot, with frosted glass free-standing screens and people turned to show their best side. What a perfect example of late 90s minimalism, and what a pity it's just gone out of date.
PLACE High ceilings and big windows, big on 90s metropolitan chic. Like a party in Smeg fridge.
PEOPLE Snappily-dressed media moguls with their scriptwriters.

PROFS Bankers, media, film and TV execs, architects, graphic designers
CELEBS Guy Ritchie, Madonna, Jude Law, Ridley Scott
DRESS Calvin Klein, Giorgio Armani, Ermenegildo Zegna
MUSIC DJs Thu-Sat after 10pm
DOOR After 11pm there is a charge of £3 from Mon-Wed and £5 on Thu-Fri
DRINKS Beer £3.75, Wine £3.75, Champagne £6.95, Cocktail £6
FOOD Bar Food, £5
CARDS All
CAPACITY 286, seating 136
HIRE Venue: Yes · Private Room: No

DIGRESS

Bar, Cocktail Bar
10 Beak Street W1
020 7437 0239

OPEN Mon midday-midnight, Tue midday-1am, Wed-Thu midday-2am, Fri-Sat midday-3am
TUBE/RAIL Oxford Circus, Piccadilly Circus
BUSES 3, 6, 23, 53, 139, 159

GETTING LUCKY	**3/5**
EYE CANDY	**2/5**
BIG SPENDERS	**2/5**
MIX 50%M 50%F	
AGE 20-40	
PRICE Average	

AMBIENCE Brightly Coloured, Groups, Late Night Open, Lounge Atmosphere, Pulling
REVIEW Imagine someone who goes on safari in an armoured truck dressed in chain mail, views big cats through a peep hole from a three-mile distance and comes back raving about how it was 'like scary but brilliant'. That person's fabbest bar in London is Digress. Get the picture? A safe option – perfectly harmless and inoffensive but that's the problem. It likes to think it's trendy but still isn't convinced. Incapable of committing an opinion, it uses several decorative styles in an effort to please all tastes. Secretaries whinge over wine and bar snacks while middle-agers on a day trip to The Big City come in to eat, seduced by its generic style. A comforting haven for couples, it's an alcoholic Noah's Ark. God help us if these are the people left to repopulate the planet after WW3.
PLACE Bright, multi-coloured front room, trying to be a designer lounge with velour sofas for two and abstract art deco. Downstairs, Moroccan cushioned booths are set in alcoves with soft lighting so you can just, you know, chill.
PEOPLE Office workers from the surrounding area stopping by to slag off their jobs to their mates before picking up a copy of Heat on their way home.

PROFS Tourists, civil servants, support staff workers
CELEBS None
DRESS Casual credibility, suited and booted types
MUSIC REM, The Verve, Travis, anything bland and vaguely melancholic
DOOR Smart casual
DRINKS Beer £3.25, Wine £2.60, Champagne £5.50, Cocktails £4.75
FOOD International, £5
CARDS All
CAPACITY 390, seating 90
HIRE Venue: Yes · Private Room: No

THE DOG HOUSE

Bar
187 Wardour Street W1
020 7434 2116/2118

OPEN Mon-Fri 5pm-11pm, Sat 6pm-11pm
TUBE/RAIL Leicester Square
BUSES 24, 29, 176

GETTING LUCKY	**3/5**
EYE CANDY	**3/5**
BIG SPENDERS	**3/5**
MIX 50%M 50%F	
AGE 25-35	
PRICE Average	

AMBIENCE Basement, Conversation, Cosy, Hip/Fashionable
REVIEW Due to its central Soho location you are more than likely to find a whole TV crew in here on a busy Friday night; certainly young trendy media types use it frequently to meet other Beta-literate creatives. The atmosphere can get quite lively and if you prefer close-quarters socialising, this place is for you. Given its small confines, trendy urbanites and men in suits (with ties removed, please) tend to gather rapidly towards the end of the week; after a sharp early evening influx it generally stays jammed. Come back Saturday evening and a more relaxed tourist crowd come down the stairs for a look.

PLACE This tucked-away underground media den has a seedy air about it. Discreet but surprisingly spacious alcoves make for lively private sessions with 10-15 people around a table. Watch out for low archways. **PEOPLE** Media moguls, post-production workers, Hoxton anoraks, bemused tourists and opinionated music industry insiders.

PROFS Sales assistants, solicitors, publishers, music and media employees, accounting and TV execs **CELEBS** Cat Deeley, Gail Hipgrave (neé Porter), The Christians **DRESS** Stüssy, FCUK, DKNY, Base, Nike, Diesel, Firetrap, Mambo **MUSIC** Funk, Garage, Jazz, Rare Groove **DOOR** No ties **DRINKS** Beer £2.70, Wine £2.60, Champagne £6, Cocktail £4.50 **FOOD** Snacks £4 **CARDS** No Amex or Diners **CAPACITY** 120, seating 50 **HIRE** Venue: Yes · Private Room: No

THE EDGE

Bar, Café, Gay
11 Soho Square W1
020 7439 1313

OPEN Mon-Sat midday-1am,	GETTING LUCKY	**3/5**
Sun midday-10.30pm	EYE CANDY	**4/5**
TUBE/RAIL Tottenham	BIG SPENDERS	**3/5**
Court Road	MIX 70%M 30%F	
BUSES 10, 25, 55, 73,	AGE 21-35	
98, 176	PRICE Average	

AMBIENCE Casual, Gay, Dancing, Groups, Student **REVIEW** Why anyone would wish to be assaulted by advertising all night is beyond us. We thought that was one of the strong arguments for going out. Sadly The Edge, an otherwise OK but unremarkable gay bar attracting an affluent and aesthetically pleasing gay clientele, has succumbed to the money machine and installed large video screens looping commercials all night. And guess what they advertise? Drinks, sausage snacks and other bar-related products. So if you happen to find yourself in The Edge thinking 'Cor I really fancy a Pepperoni and a Smirnoff Ice, I wonder how the tabby's doing?', you'll know why. **PLACE** An endless succession of stairs takes you to an endless succession of identical floors which all have the same semi-circular bars, the same wooden tables and chairs and even the same people sitting at them. Rumour has it that if you keep going on up the stairs, you eventually end up inside the head of Dale Winton. **PEOPLE** The Edge is nominally a gay bar, but if it wasn't for the bar staff's tendency to suddenly camp it up from time to time, you probably wouldn't realise it. Attracts a very mixed crowd and its fair share of tourists.

PROFS Tourists, media employees, dance and theatre workers, young professionals **CELEBS** None **DRESS** FCUK, Diesel, Hugo Boss. During summer posing topless males prance about under the pretext that they've just come in from Soho Square to get out of the heat

MUSIC Latin, House, Disco, Soul, Garage, Dance, DJ Thu-Sat, 8pm-1am **DOOR** None **DRINKS** Beer £2.90, Wine £3, Cocktail £3 **FOOD** Snacks, Mexican, Healthy, Modern European, £5 **CARDS** All **CAPACITY** 350, seating 50 **HIRE** Venue: Yes · Private Room: No

ESCAPE DANCE BAR

Bar, Gay
10a Brewer Street W1
020 7734 2626

OPEN Mon 3pm-2am,	GETTING LUCKY	**4/5**
Tue-Sat 3pm-3am,	EYE CANDY	**4/5**
Sun 3pm-10.30pm	BIG SPENDERS	**4/5**
TUBE/RAIL Piccadilly	MIX 80%M 20%F	
BUSES 3, 6, 23, 53,	AGE 18-35	
139, 159	PRICE Average	

AMBIENCE Brightly Coloured/Cheerful, Cute Staff, Kitsch, Late Night Open, Party, Pulling **REVIEW** Cruise the preening Latino boys and crème de la scene a-strutting and a-posing against a backdrop of Kylie and Mariah. Those who don't know the difference between Suzanne and Faye may not wish to glue their eyes to one of the ten TV screens all night, as the regulars tend to do in this rather small venue. Spot the occasional drag queen, rent boy, sugar daddy, and Mr Gay UK winner. When you're sick of candy-coloured pop videos monitor the bronzed and buff clientele instead. Every night is themed and the bar area is dressed appropriately: Hawaiian, Schooldays or Western. Always popular, its close proximity to the recently opened Shadow Lounge may mean that it is forced to now take a humble second best or at least accommodate its competitor's rejects. **PLACE** Don't even think about talking; the idea here being that there's so much to look at you won't need to. At 11 sharp the tables and chairs are abruptly whisked away to clear the floor for the dancing queens. **PEOPLE** Dexter Wong'ed bronzed Adonises, shady looking guys in baseball caps and drag queens confuse the odd tourist couple who've wandered in for a quiet drink after sex shopping.

PROFS Shop assistants, businessmen, students, unemployed, tourists, judges, legal, medical and media professionals **CELEBS** Brian and Josh from Big Brother, Martine McCutcheon **DRESS** Less is more seems to dominate the unofficial dress code. Dolce and Gabbana tank-tops, Helmut Lang, Gucci, H&M, Gap, Diesel, Chaps **MUSIC** MTV, Chart, Dance, Gay Anthems, DJs Wed, Fri-Sat 11pm-3am **DOOR** £2 after 7pm **DRINKS** Beer £2.95, Wine £2.95, Cocktail £5 **FOOD** Snacks, £3 **CARDS** No Diners **CAPACITY** 120, seating 40 **HIRE** Venue: Yes · Private Room: No

FORM

Bar, Members Bar
4-5 Greek Street W1
020 7434 3323

OPEN Mon 5pm-midnight, Tue 5pm-1am, Wed 5pm-2am, Thu 5pm-1am, Fri-Sat 5pm-3am **TUBE/RAIL** Tottenham Court Road **BUSES** 10, 23, 73, 98	GETTING LUCKY	2/5
	EYE CANDY	4/5
	BIG SPENDERS	3/5
	MIX 60%M 40%F	
	AGE 22-35	
	PRICE Expensive	

AMBIENCE Basement, Casual, Conversation, Cosy, Groups, Late Night Open
REVIEW Clerkenwell meets Soho with this venture from the Clerkenwell House crew. The no-nonsense absence of cocktails and gaggle of cynical ad-kids wearing cool logo t-shirts and supping beer from bear size, fuck-off-you-lightweight Hoegaarden glasses says it all. Form follows function with simple furniture and basic drinks (wine in a Duralex school canteen glass anyone?) and mocks function with scratchy Del-boy inspired wallpaper and seating jutting into a postage stamp sized, Seabreeze-sticky dance floor. Downstairs for run-of-the-mill Soho types, from creative after-workers to rowdy birthday celebrators and a few hip, young things, recreating their aerobo-salsa moves to nu-funk and Italian house. Basement for cosy seated table service, mwah mwah work posses and cross-eyed canoodlers.
PLACE Grey ground-floor bar and low-lit basement with alcoves and group tables for all. The members bar above is a cross between a pub and curryhouse with gilt-framed oil paintings and Warhol's wet dream wallpaper.
PEOPLE 'When I make my first £1 million award-winning advert' said the cocky upstart from the MDMA FHM ad agency round the corner. Yup, it's meeja 20-somethings attracted by the retro wallpaper and dotcomish graphics.

PROFS Advertising executives, designers, musicians
CELEBS None
DRESS Sloppy urban outfits from cords and combats to jeans and more dressed-up girlies. FCUK, Carhartt, Levi's, Warehouse, Oasis, Adidas, Nike, Stüssy, Zara
MUSIC Breakbeat, Funk, Hip Hop, Soul, Jazz
DOOR £5 after 9pm Fri-Sat
DRINKS Beer £3.50, Wine £3.50, Champagne £7.20
FOOD Bar snacks, £4
CARDS All
CAPACITY 270, seating 50
HIRE Venue: Yes · Private Room: Yes

FREEDOM BREWING CO.

Bar, Restaurant
Ganton House, 14-16 Ganton Street W1
020 7287 5267

OPEN Mon-Sat 11am-11pm **TUBE/RAIL** Oxford Circus **BUSES** 3, 6, 23, 53, 139, 159	GETTING LUCKY	1/5
	EYE CANDY	4/5
	BIG SPENDERS	3/5
	MIX 50%M 50%F	
	AGE 25-35	
	PRICE Average	

AMBIENCE Basement, Casual, Cute Staff, Groups, Party
REVIEW The baby of the Freedom Brewing Company in Covent Garden, where half the space on the ground floor is taken up by huge brewing vats. The beers are the thing here – organic, wheat, – all lovingly nurtured by Freedom's in-house German brewmaster. and several notches up the taste scale from the average Soho offering. An impressive bar menu offers several ways to help absorb the 5% ABV afforded by the beer. It feels like a happening place for people who do real joined-up thinking. The gorgeous Italian barman says that people tend to come to Freedom rather than any of the other five or six similar bars in the area specifically for the quality of the product.
PLACE 'Red Nevada desert style cocktail bar circa 1960'. Floor to ceiling windows open on to the street. The effect is very clean and light, like a cosmetic dentist's waiting room, and much less claustrophobic than you might expect a basement bar to be.
PEOPLE A hugely attractive lot: multinational, young and very cute. But enough about the staff. The customers vary from tourists on the Carnaby trail at lunchtime through to Soho boys in suits having a quick one after work, to a younger, clubbier crowd later in the evening.

PROFS Office workers, businessmen and their secretaries, tourists, the occasional media mogul
CELEBS None
DRESS Principles, TopShop, Miss Selfridge, suits, sandals
MUSIC Funk, Progressive House, Ambient
DOOR None
DRINKS Beer £3.10, Wine £3.35, Champagne £6.50, Cocktail £5.85
FOOD Modern European, Oriental, Snacks, £8.50
CARDS No Diners
CAPACITY 250, seating 100
HIRE Venue: Yes · Private Room: No

THE FRENCH HOUSE

Bar
49 Dean Street W1
020 7437 2799

OPEN Mon-Sat midday-11pm, Sun midday-10.30pm **TUBE/RAIL** Leicester Square **BUSES** 24, 29, 176	GETTING LUCKY	2/5
	EYE CANDY	2/5
	BIG SPENDERS	3/5
	MIX 70%M 30%F	
	AGE 25-75	
	PRICE Cheap	

AMBIENCE Arty/Bohemian, Casual, Conversation, Historic, Intellectual/Literary, Legendary, Mature/Older, Old World
REVIEW Not many London pubs are as distinctive as the French House. A meeting point since the 20s for London's French community, the bar was General de Gaulle's wartime local. Though the clientele are now mostly Anglo-Saxon, much of the original bawdy atmosphere still remains. Ageing bohemians and would-bes rub shoulders with advertising people (whose mobiles are banned) and period drama actors who spend the evening shouting in each other's ears over the noise. With a high quotient of intellectual punters, it is possible for the innocent bystander to become engrossed in a spot of verbal sparring with

one of the tweedy soaks who've been here for years. Though some might be put off by the dense smoke and the regulars' sniffy attitude, you can't beat the French House for character.
PLACE Small, smoky, wood-panelled bar that's brightly lit and lined with photos documenting the progress of London's French community. Small restaurant upstairs.
PEOPLE Arty old Soho residents, moneyed professionals, verbose actors and advertising types. Packed to the hilt most evenings. Tip for avoiding sneers from barstaff: don't ask for a pint, they only serve beer in halves.

PROFS Actors, artists, advertising, music and film execs, lawyers
CELEBS Lucien Freud, Timothy Spall, Tim Woodward, Robert Plant, George Melly, Robbie Coltrane, Michael Elphick
DRESS Decaying tweeds and old cords meet their trouser-suited grandchildren. M&S, DKNY, House of Fraser, Linea
MUSIC No background music
DOOR None
DRINKS Beer £2.60, Wine £2.20, Champagne £5.50, Cocktail £4
FOOD Snacks, £5
CARDS No Diners
CAPACITY 150, seating 30
HIRE Venue: No · Private Room: No

GARLIC AND SHOTS

Bar, Restaurant, Theme
14 Frith Street W1
020 7734 9505

OPEN Mon-Wed 5pm-midnight, Thu-Sat 6pm-1am, Sun 5pm-11.30pm	**GETTING LUCKY**	**2/5**
	EYE CANDY	**1/5**
	BIG SPENDERS	**1/5**
TUBE/RAIL Leicester Square	**MIX** 55%M 45%F	
BUSES 24, 29, 176	**AGE** 20-80	
	PRICE Cheap	

AMBIENCE Casual, Late Night Open, Student, Vampire/Gothic
REVIEW Virginal maidens desperate to be ravished by Dracula give this a miss, he'd wither at the door just from the fumes. But then you could drown your sorrows fang-tastically in 101 different flavours of vodka. This dark and dingy den attracts a real mixture of people, of which many are Metallica-loving regulars. Perching at the restaurant bar you'll hear tall Soho stories and time will fly like a bat out of hell. But creep downstairs and it all goes horribly wrong. Angst-ridden teenager Jim Morrison fans have assaulted the vaulted snug, complete with a coffin, and defaced the wall with graffiti willies and expletives. The deafening heavy/thrash metal could drive you to add your own poetry.
PLACE Only nine years old but could be 90 as junky artefacts, from garlic to snipped-off old ties, hang everywhere. Garlic grub upstairs, drinking vault downstairs with dungeonesque feel. The beer garden opens in summer.
PEOPLE Garlic and vodka lovers, craggy Soho characters, stoodents, fellow bar traders, occultists, teenage blood-letters, visiting Scandinavians, elderly Swedes, tourists and anyone else from bikers to bankers.

PROFS Civil servants, musicians, PRs, journalists, actors, advertising execs, bankers, bikers
CELEBS Lemmy (Motorhead), Nine Inch Nails, Primal Scream
DRESS Just don't dress up and forget your suit as you may be castrated by your tie. Leather or black with a skull tattoo is your best shot
MUSIC Thrash, Rock, Heavy, White, Soft and Death Metal
DOOR None
DRINKS Beer £2.50, Wine £2.30, Champagne £4.95
FOOD Garlic, Modern Eclectic, Tapas, £11.50
CARDS No Amex or Diners
CAPACITY 100, seating 45
HIRE Venue: No · Private Room: No

GLENFIDDICH BAR

Bar, Cocktail Bar
93-107 Shaftesbury Avenue W1
020 7494 3040

OPEN Mon-Fri midday-3pm, 5.30pm-midnight, Sat 5.30pm-midnight	**GETTING LUCKY**	**5/5**
	EYE CANDY	**3/5**
	BIG SPENDERS	**4/5**
TUBE/RAIL Leicester Square	**MIX** 50%M 50%F	
BUSES 14, 19, 24, 29, 38, 176	**AGE** 25-40	
	PRICE Expensive	

AMBIENCE Business, Conversation, Late Night Open, Network, Pulling
REVIEW Question: what do you do when your members bar's seen better days, your restaurant's going down the pan and there's a big, ugly recession looming? Answer: turn part of the restaurant into a drinking establishment that those sniffling insignificants, the general public, can frequent. Brilliant! So now all and the high-maintenance sundry get to savour the kind of environs that are bound to score with 40-something American and Japanese businessmen. The creators have kindly installed a round window between the two bars, so that those not fortunate enough to possess one of the much-coveted swipe cards can see how the other half drink. And frankly it's much better. 'Ooh Christine – I think I just saw that girl from Men Behaving Badly walk in.'
PLACE Naff, faux Shanghai businessman's retreat, non-ironic 80s. Red and wood theme, with nasty 30s-style etched glass windows. Big, comfy curved leather seating.
PEOPLE Predatory female singletons on a minesweeper mission. Media men not batting an eyelid.

PROFS PRs, film producers, copywriters, recruitment consultants
CELEBS Too soon to say, but guaranteed Lee's football chums and other C-listers will be here for the first 60 minutes
DRESS Prada (bought on a binge buy), Saks, Benetton, Karen Millen
MUSIC Background
DOOR None
DRINKS Beer £3, Wine £3.50, Champagne £7.50, Cocktail £7
FOOD Modern European, Snacks, £6.50
CARDS All
CAPACITY 80 seating 30
HIRE Venue: Yes · Private Room: No

GOLD BAR CAFÉ

Bar, Café
23a Ganton Street W1
020 7434 0109

OPEN Mon-Sat 11am-11pm	GETTING LUCKY	**2/5**
TUBE/RAIL Oxford Circus	EYE CANDY	**4/5**
BUSES 3, 6, 23, 53,	BIG SPENDERS	**3/5**
139, 159	MIX 40%M 60%F	
	AGE 21-35	
	PRICE Average	

AMBIENCE Brightly Coloured/Cheerful, Casual, Chilled, Friendly, Funky, Groups
REVIEW This is how the bar at Ibiza airport should feel. There are hints of sun-soaked hedonism everywhere, from the beach bum bar staff and thoroughly chilled drinkers through to the varied, funked-up music choice and rainbow-coloured retro decor. Different early-evening clubs run most nights of the week and although the layout doesn't lend itself to largin' it, it's a good warm-up to get you in the mood for a club. Also recommended for a bite to eat thanks to generous portions, and the fact that the staff look happy to be dealing with the general public. Because it's preposterously small you may not end up staying very long, but it's clearly the best bar in the Carnaby Street area.
PLACE Great, brash, gaudy decor. Retro-pop airport icons point your way around, although the huge technicolor lightbox photos may be familiar to regular Mash-goers.
PEOPLE Sure, Carnaby Street has become a bit of a tourist-trap hellhole resting on its former glory, but it still attracts friendlier visitors than most of the surrounding streets, and the Gold Bar Café gets the cream of them.

PROFS Media execs, advertising execs, retail staff, tourists, musicians
CELEBS None
DRESS Light colours and soft fabrics faded by the sun
MUSIC Chart, Funk, DJs Mon-Sat, from 7.30pm
DOOR None
DRINKS Beer £2.75, Wine £2.50, Champagne £4.25, Cocktail £5.25
FOOD Veggy, American, Pacific Rim, £5
CARDS No Amex or Diners
CAPACITY 100, seating 75
HIRE Venue: Yes · Private Room: No

THE GROUCHO CLUB

Members Club
45 Dean Street W1
020 7439 4685

OPEN Mon-Sat 8am-2am	GETTING LUCKY	**1/5**
TUBE/RAIL Leicester Square,	EYE CANDY	**4/5**
Tottenham Court Road	BIG SPENDERS	**5/5**
BUSES 10, 25, 55, 73,	MIX 50%M 50%F	
98, 176	AGE 28-65	
	PRICE Average	

AMBIENCE Arty/Bohemian, Business, Casual, Conversation, Lounge Atmosphere Destination/Wishlist, Exclusive/Chic, Groups, Hip/Fashionable, Late Night Open, Legendary
REVIEW Exclusive, original luvvie darlins' den and as classic as a 60s orange Penguin paperback. Warm, familiar and escapist. Celebrities and serious industry execs retreat from the Soho sprawl to strike deals without interruptions. Sit back and watch the wheels of British media turn. For all this, the atmosphere is relaxed and laid-back. Staff are discreet, professional and unfazed by it all. Pick any of the best in film, art, comedy and literature and they will have sipped and supped here. Pulling could be a major career move, but it's not quite the done thing, my dear.
PLACE Imagine Melvin Bragg's ideal retirement home. A colourful boho house. Slink into easy armchairs and sofas in the main lounge downstairs or opt for the mellower 'new bar' upstairs. There are two dining rooms, a snooker room on the 2nd floor, various function rooms and at the top, guestrooms for members.
PEOPLE Overtly middle-class. Grown-up, intelligent and successful artsy media types. From establishment dinosaurs to petulant popstars and mischievous piss artists, whose business is pleasure and who come here to get blotto away from the pestering public.

PROFS Meeja moguls, stars of stage, screen (big and small), producers, directors, writers (good and bad), singers, songwriters, musicians, managers, PRs, chefs, comedians, actors, journalists, TV presenters, bankers, lawyers, painters, artists and, as Damon Runyon said, 'just people with money'
CELEBS Keith Allen, Robbie Williams, Barry Norman, Kate Moss, Stephen Fry, Kathleen Turner, Kevin Costner, George Michael, Sarah Lucas, Tom Cruise, Madonna, Jay Jopling, Vic Reeves, Bob Mortimer, Jonathan Ross, Sir Cameron Mackintosh, Jack Nicholson, Lady Caroline Conran, Chris Evans, Helen Fielding, Tracey McCloud, Robbie Coltrane, Miranda Sawyer, Damien Hirst, Blur, Richard Wilson, Anna Friel, Liam Gallagher, Noel Gallagher, Mike Leigh, Mariella Frostrup, Fast Show cast, George Dawes, Melvyn Bragg, Harvey Keitel, Brad Pitt, Jarvis Cocker, Lee Chapman, Leslie Ash, Dawn French, Lenny Henry, Caroline Aherne, Paul Young, Joanna Lumley
DRESS Hey, it's not what you wear, it's what you do and who you know. Miu Miu, Armani, Ghost, Diesel, Combats, Donna Karan, Katherine Hamnett, Nicole Farhi
MUSIC Jazz, Pop, Chart, Funk, Classical, Jazz Pianist Tue-Sat, from 6.30pm
DOOR Members Only
DRINKS Beer £2.80, Wine £3, Champagne £6.60, Cocktail £5.40
FOOD Brasserie, Modern European, £12
CARDS All
CAPACITY 400, seating 110
HIRE Venue: Yes · Private Room: Yes

K BAR

Bar
84-86 Wardour Street W1
020 7734 5447

OPEN Wed, Thu, Sun 10pm-	GETTING LUCKY	**4/5**
3am, Fri-Sat 10pm-4am	EYE CANDY	**4/5**
TUBE/RAIL Piccadilly Circus,	BIG SPENDERS	**3/5**
Oxford Circus	MIX 50%M 50%F	
BUSES 14, 19, 38	AGE 20-35	
	PRICE Expensive	

AMBIENCE Basement, Dancing, Groups, Late Night Open, Party, Pulling
REVIEW Once Piers Adam's place and Tara P-T's home-from-home, the K Bar's once heaving VIP area now features about as many recognisable faces as Crimewatch UK. If you can get past the pathologically rude door crew then be prepared for a sensory adjustment: very loud, very dark and the suggestive signature K Bar fragrance (Czech & Speake 88) blasting through the air conditioning. The venue itself may not have changed, but one look at the more-average-than-Special K crowd demonstrates how the mighty have fallen.
PLACE K Bar chain flagship. Large, dark blue-walled basement bar with dance floor. Easy to lose someone when busy. A few dark intimate tables for the erotically involved or dates that improve with the lights off.
PEOPLE Eurotrash bankers who haven't yet heard of the K Bar's demise, West End girls and East End boys.

PROFS Bankers, PRs, office gels
CELEBS Michelle Collins, Chris Evans, Lisa I'Anson, Tottenham Hotspur Football Club, Chris Quentin, Julian Clary, Graham Norton, Rupert Everett
DRESS Smart casual bankers in button-down shirts and chinos, girls in high street not-particularly-chic
MUSIC Commercial Dance, Garage, R&B
DOOR £5-10
DRINKS Beer £3.50, Wine £3.50, Champagne £5, Cocktail £5
FOOD None
CARDS All
CAPACITY 450, seating 100
HIRE Venue: Yes · Private Room: No

KABARET

Members Club
16-18 Beak Street W1
020 7287 8140

OPEN Tues, Thu-Sat 10.30pm-3am	**GETTING LUCKY**	**4/5**
	EYE CANDY	**5/5**
TUBE/RAIL Piccadilly Circus	**BIG SPENDERS**	**4/5**
BUSES 14, 19, 38	**MIX** 45%M 55%F	
	AGE 25-50	
	PRICE Expensive	

AMBIENCE Basement, Dancing, Exclusive/Chic, Groups, Jet Set, Late Night Open, Party, Hip/Fashionable
REVIEW What is it with the London glitterati and the Ks? Now The K Bar has headed down the alphabet, Kabaret has stepped in to fill its well-heeled place. Not surprising really, given the club is run by 'It' boy about town Ben Elliott. Most nights are something akin to a Priory reunion, with Tom Parker Bowles and Freddie Windsor thrusting suede-covered booties to their own personal rythms. Still, the question remains – what is it about Kabaret that keeps Bono, Mick Jagger, Rod Stewart and a whole host of A-list rock wrinklies rooted in place for entire Thursday nights? Perhaps it's the permanent throngs of Gucci-thonged St. Tropez'd lovelies dressed for the 90s. Degrees, that is.
PLACE Subterranean bunker with tiny bar, where drinks-buying is a men-only occupation. If you can't get a table you're screwed – apart from hovering in social Siberia you won't get service, and once full, there's no escape from the wrestling-ring dance floor.

PEOPLE Think ET – that's Euro-trash and Euro-totty, with lashings of society boys and girls getting flirty. Young aristos mix with journos and restauranteurs such as Mogens Tholstrup showing off his latest platinum duvet warmer or looking for replacements.

PROFS Spending family cash, media employees, fashionistas, bankers, journos
CELEBS Bono, Mogens Tholstrup, Freddie Windsor, Kate Moss, Nicky Haslam, Rolling Stones, Hugh Grant, Sheryl Crow, Stephen Dorff, Meg Mathews
DRESS The men start in jackets and sharp suits but end up slit to the waste. The girls start slit to the waste and end up leaving in their men's jackets
MUSIC Hip Hop, Dance, 80s, 90s
DOOR Guest list and members only
DRINKS Beer £4, Wine £4.50, Champagne £8, Cocktail £8
FOOD None
CARDS No Amex
CAPACITY 100, seating 60
HIRE Venue: Yes · Private Room: No

KETTNER'S

Bar, Restaurant
29 Romilly Street W1
020 7734 6112

OPEN 7 days 11.30am-midnight	**GETTING LUCKY**	**2/5**
	EYE CANDY	**3/5**
TUBE/RAIL Tottenham Court Road, Leicester Square, Piccadilly Circus	**BIG SPENDERS**	**3/5**
	MIX 45%M 55%F	
BUSES 22, 24, 29, 94, 139, 176	**AGE** 28-58	
	PRICE Average	

AMBIENCE Business, Casual, Conversation, Groups, Historic, Live Music
REVIEW Kettner's is the faded old grande dame of Soho, the head chef of Napoleon III having set up shop circa 1867. Today, sadly, it is a champagne bar gone slightly to seed, serving Pizza Express-style pizzas (owner is ex-PE boss Peter Boizot) in a grandiose setting to the accompaniment of a tinkling piano. The champagne bar could certainly do with a few touch-ups of gilt paint and a new carpet, but the ice buckets still get dragged out for the local demi-monde and, more commonly, local businessmen out on the piss. Its best days seem to be behind it, but it's still an experience unlike any other. The smarter restaurant and private dining rooms are upstairs.

PLACE Legend has it that once upon a time an underground passage ran from the cellar here to the Palace Theatre in Shaftesbury Lane. Nowadays no such mystique prevails but a dusty old school grandeur sits in its place.

PEOPLE Casual mix of tourists, local businessmen in scuffed suits on champagne, and Soho-goers who want a quick pizza without the chain experience.

PROFS Firefighters, sales people, travel agents, PRs, shop managers

CELEBS EastEnders, David Blunkett, Charles Kennedy, Les Ferdinand, Cliff Richard, Edward VII, Oscar Wilde

DRESS Moss Bros, Burton, Next suits, DKNY, tourists in jeans and trainers

MUSIC Light Jazz, Live Pianist Mon-Sat, from 8pm

DOOR None

DRINKS Beer £3.10, Wine £3.40, Champagne £6.25

FOOD Pizza, Steakhouse, £10

CARDS All

CAPACITY 200, seating 200

HIRE Venue: Yes · Private Room: Yes

LAB

Bar, Cocktail Bar
12 Old Compton Street W1
020 7437 7820

OPEN Mon-Fri midday-midnight, Sat 4pm-midnight, Sun 4pm-10.30pm	GETTING LUCKY	3/5
	EYE CANDY	4/5
	BIG SPENDERS	3/5
TUBE/RAIL Tottenham Court Road, Leicester Square	MIX 55%M 45%F	
BUSES 14, 19, 24, 29, 38, 176	AGE 24-35	
	PRICE Expensive	

AMBIENCE Buzzy, Groups, Hip/Fashionable, Party, Retro

REVIEW 'From strip joint to hip joint' runs the blurb for Lab, one of the few straight bars on Old Compton Street. Indeed this narrow, one-up one-down, cocktail bar is so proud of its heterosexual status that visiting the loo requires an identification with 'bitch' or 'bastard'. Like Paul Daly's retro design, these gender pole positions hark back to the 70s – luckily the drinks don't. You'll find no flair juggling of bottles, flouncy brollies, candy-striped straws or sweet insipid concoctions here. This place makes serious, on the money, noughties style and substance cocktails. And so it should, as Lab stands for the London Academy of Bartending which, like the bar was set up by mix-meisters Douglas Ankrah and Richard Hargroves. Only three years old, it attracts a liberal measure of regulars, mainly spirited Soho creatives muddled together with a garnish of Suits propping up the bar.

PLACE There are no surprises here, it's signature Paul Daly, the king of purple and brown. Rough-textured brown walls, curvaceous bar stools and a handy bar front that houses shelves for bags. Upstairs is for barflies, downstairs for minglers and swingers with sofas and lots of standing room.

PEOPLE Cocktail lovers, West End drinkers, party-minded professionals (way-hey!), Elle-reading, latte drinking, Jigsaw-wearing, Prada-aspiring Londoners.

PROFS Media employees, TV producers, PRs, bar staff, graphic designers, advertising execs

CELEBS Dave Courtney, Tara Palmer-Tomkinson, Courtney Cox-Arquette

DRESS Anything from pinstripes to snakeskin

MUSIC Chart, Dance, Drum 'n' Bass, House, Trance, Mon-Sat, from 9pm

DOOR None

DRINKS Beer £3.10, Wine £3.50, Champagne £5.50, Cocktail £5

FOOD Snacks, £5

CARDS No Diners

CAPACITY 200, seating 70

HIRE Venue: Yes · Private Room: No

LUPO

Bar, Restaurant
50 Dean Street W1
020 7434 3399

OPEN Mon-Tue midday-1am, Wed-Thu midday-2am, Fri-Sat midday-3am	GETTING LUCKY	3/5
	EYE CANDY	4/5
	BIG SPENDERS	3/5
TUBE/RAIL Leicester Square	MIX 60%M 40%F	
BUSES 22, 24, 29, 53, 94, 176	AGE 20-35	
	PRICE Average	

AMBIENCE Conversation, Cosy, Dancing, Funky, Groups, Late Night Open, Party

REVIEW Two distinct crowds provide contrasting atmospheres at this popular bar. Early evening sees a healthy mix of 30-something creatives with uniform TV-frame specs mingling with more pedestrian, non-meeja literate drinkers. Pre-clubbers and teeth-grinding nocturnals pile into this surprisingly capacious bar, where intimate corners offer refuge from the general crush. For the uninitiated it's perhaps a little too cliquey to offer opportunities for making new friends, but if you are lucky enough to be one of Soho's finest, you will not need enlightening on the fun to be had here. Regulars prefer Mondays and Tuesdays.

PLACE Two main bar areas, a dining section and two party rooms. As cliquey and cosy as some members' clubs, with subdued lighting, dark timber panelling and terracotta flooring. Fraying a bit at the edges these days.

PEOPLE All and sundry of Soho, from creative ad boyz to TV producers, exotic beauties from neighbouring strip joints and suburbanites who bar-crawl Dean Street every Saturday.

PROFS Media, advertising, PR and film employees

CELEBS Mick Hucknall, Beth Orton, Richard Branson, M People, Kylie

DRESS Diesel, Maharishi, Burro, Jigsaw, FCUK, Nike, Muji, well-cut leather jackets

MUSIC Funk, Jazz, House, Garage, DJ Thu-Sat, from 9pm

DOOR Mon-Sat £3-5 after 11pm

DRINKS Beer £3, Wine £2.50, Champagne £5.50, Cocktail £6.50

FOOD Modern European, £12

CARDS All

CAPACITY 280, seating 100

HIRE Venue: Yes · Private Room: Yes

MADAME JOJO'S

Club, Live Music Venue
8-10 Brewer Street W1
020 7734 3040

OPEN Mon-Sat 10pm-3am	GETTING LUCKY	**4/5**
TUBE/RAIL Piccadilly Circus	EYE CANDY	**4/5**
BUSES 6, 12, 23, 53,	BIG SPENDERS	**2/5**
88, 139	MIX 60%M 40%F	
	AGE 20-45	
	PRICE Average	

AMBIENCE Casual, Cosy, Dancing, Groups, Kitsch Decor, Late Night Open, Legendary, Live Music, Opulent, Party, Student, Pulling
REVIEW With nights as varied as the visitors to a West End swinger's pants, Madame JoJo's – an old puckered hag of a capital institution – has survived the Soho stripped pine and stripper groundswell with admirable ease. The famed drag act cabarets are now augmented by Mixamatosis (for hip hopping, boot-shuffling midweek dis-ease) and Deep Funk on Fridays, where painfully hip sideburned DJs showcase the fruits of a youth misspent rifling through old vinyl at car boot sales. Unpretentious sophisticats meld with studenty first jobbers and i-D models, all intent on shimmying on the paving slab of a dance floor before necking vodka and Red bull and tripping over the human breakdancing exhibits en route to the bar.
PLACE Seventeen years on and JoJo's red decor teeters on the knackered/distressed hip divide. Part bar, part theatre, part club and part 1970s low-budget porn set. Small, intimate tables cluster around the small dance floor and even smaller stage.
PEOPLE A none-too-subtle blend of gay and straight go-getting Sohoers, pissed-up tourists who think they've made it to the Met and funk fiends in their best baggies.

PROFS Actors, typing pool types, fashion people, pop stars, students, journalists, advertising employees
CELEBS Jamiroquai, Jasper Conran, Belinda Carlisle, Robbie Williams, Brand New Heavies, Oasis, Tina Hobley
DRESS The suited and booted meet the glammed-up but downbeat Dieselites
MUSIC Jazz, Funk, Disco, Alternative, Roots, Underground Hip Hop, DJs Live Music, 7 nights
DOOR £5-8
DRINKS Beer £3, Wine £2.50, Champagne £6.50, Cocktail £4
FOOD None
CARDS All
CAPACITY 220, seating 80
HIRE Venue: Yes · Private Room: No

MANTO

Bar, Gay, Restaurant
30 Old Compton Street W1
020 7494 2756

OPEN Mon-Sat midday-	GETTING LUCKY	**3/5**
midnight, Sun midday-	EYE CANDY	**4/5**
10.30pm	BIG SPENDERS	**4/5**
TUBE/RAIL Tottenham	MIX 70%M 30%F	
Court Road	AGE 21-40	
BUSES 14, 19, 24, 29,	PRICE Expensive	
38, 176		

AMBIENCE Basement, Casual, Comfy, Dancing, Groups, Party, Student
REVIEW Manto would make a better name for a deodorant than a bar. But Manto it is, and with one bar already established on Manchester's Canal Street, the name's obviously not too much of a deterrent. The cast of Queer as Folk made regular visits to the Manchester version, but if they visited its Soho equivalent, Vince would undoubtedly emit a trademark yelp of 'Oh my God' at the sheer size of the place. There are three huge floors and you could easily spend an entire evening just trying to locate the lounge bar. It even has its own restaurant, which, according to their adverts, has a 'global style menu', ie you pay for Eggs Florentine and get egg on toast.
PLACE In the ground-floor bar house music blasts out at an uncomfortable volume and the Manto logo is flashed on to every available space. Those fortunate enough to find the lounge bar get to recline on luxurious sofas or sit at candle-lit tables.
PEOPLE Gay guys in designer clothes drink designer bottled beer in the ground-floor bar and then head upstairs to eat designer food. Eventually they retire to the comforts of the lounge bar to discuss their designer-led lives.

PROFS Law students, journalists, accountants, shop workers, bankers, media employees, club promoters
CELEBS Rupert Everett, Melinda Messenger, Ian McShane, Jonathan Ross
DRESS Diesel, Gap, Hype
MUSIC House, Garage, Funk, Disco, Funk, House, Garage DJs 7 days from 9pm, 6pm weekends
DOOR None
DRINKS Beer £2.70, Wine £3.50, Champagne £6, Cocktail £4.95
FOOD International, Modern British, £7.95
CARDS No Diners
CAPACITY 800, seating 200
HIRE Venue: Yes · Private Room: Yes

MEAN FIDDLER

Live Music Venue, Club
165 Charing Cross Road WC2
020 7434 9592

OPEN Mon-Thu 10.30pm-	GETTING LUCKY	**3/5**
4am, Tue-Thu 7pm-11pm,	EYE CANDY	**3/5**
Fri 11pm-4am,	BIG SPENDERS	**2/5**
Sat 10.30pm-6am	MIX 60%M 40%F	
TUBE/RAIL Tottenham	AGE 18-40	
Court Road	PRICE Average	
BUSES 14, 19, 24, 29,		
38, 176		

AMBIENCE Bump 'n' Grind, Buzzy, Dancing, Hormone-fuelled Club Kidz, Late Night Open, Legendary, Live Music, Party, Pulling

REVIEW The Mean Fiddler's mirrored walls and neon signs make you think you've been transported to an Essex nightclub or one of those old-school discotheques you find on cruise ships. But the Astoria's younger sibling is a popular central London venue for clubs and bands alike. It is home to both the weekly G.A.Y. Pink Pounder and the Saturday night 70s, 80s and big beat thrash, Atomic. It's seen some notorious gigs in its often chequered past. GWAR raised eyebrows on tubes and night buses across London by covering the place and its inhabitants in fake blood, while Kenickie caused tears in literally tens of bedrooms across the country with a legendary last ever performance.

PLACE Linking Mean Fiddler's two floors are the world's most confusing stairs – whether you go up or down you always seem to end up by the main entrance. There is also a food stall for those of you who suddenly feel the need for a cheese omelette in the middle of a gig or club.

PEOPLE G.A.Y. Pink Pounder is invaded by camp, lithe young things, invariably with an even more camp girlfriend – known in the trade as a fag hag – dangling off one arm. Scruffy indie/pop types take over for the other club nights, but the Mean Fiddler also sees its fair share of hoary old rockers and scary looking punks.

PROFS Bikers, musicians, students, music industry types scouting for talent. They come to see the bands here too sometimes

CELEBS None

DRESS Levi's, Adidas, Ben Sherman, combats, Prowler, biker jackets

MUSIC Commercial Dance, Club Anthems, Hi-NRG, Pop, Disco, Indie, House

DOOR Varies

DRINKS Beer £2.50, Wine £3.50, Cocktail £4.50

FOOD Snacks, £3

CARDS No Amex or Diners

CAPACITY 1000, seating 70

HIRE Venue: Yes · Private Room: No

MEZZO

Bar, Restaurant
100 Wardour Street W1
020 7314 4000

OPEN Mon-Thu midday-12.30am, Fri-Sat midday-2.30am, Sun midday-10.30pm	**GETTING LUCKY** **4/5**
	EYE CANDY **4/5**
	BIG SPENDERS **4/5**
TUBE/RAIL Piccadilly Circus, Leicester Square	**MIX** 60%M 40%F
	AGE 25-35
BUSES 9, 24, 29, 176, 53, 139	**PRICE** Average

AMBIENCE Chilled, Dancing, Elegant/Classic, Groups, Jet Set, Late Night Open, Pulling, Star Spotting

REVIEW A palace of a bar – vast, plush and crammed to the hilt with languid champagne-swigging lovelies. It's got Conran's 90s scrawl all over it, from the lazy curving bar to the perfumed bogs (complete with towel-brandishing attendant). PR chicks fondle fingerfood while their well-coiffed chaps talk showreels and toy

with a variety of potent cocktails. From a chrome and silver alcove, Mr Funky DJ spins his tunes at high volume, moving from 70s disco to mellow R&B as the evening unwinds. Close proximity in the crush makes it easier to sidle up to your target, and the loud music gives you an excuse for the morning after. You were so sure your score had a brain – who wouldn't have mistaken 'I've got an itch' for 'I'm reading Nietzsche'.

PLACE Think New York retro with a 90s fascination with chrome. Conran generation yups sprawl on leather banquettes against a vast backdrop of groovy black-and-white prints of Soho life. Two floors, including vodka bar and dance floor.

PEOPLE In the media, darling. The bar attracts Simply Everyone, or at least their upwardly mobile assistants. The fizzy stuff is eagerly glugged by designer suits and their sleekly hip girlfriends, while sharks hunting in pairs cruise the fringes of the room.

PROFS Film producers, account execs, media professionals, music professionals, film editors, sound technicians

CELEBS Sean Bean, Martin Clunes, Mel Smith, Talvin Singh, Kelly Brook, Jack Dee, Peter O'Brien, Marc Almond, Gail Hipgrave (neé Porter), Denise van Outen, Skin, Jamiroquai, Chemical Brothers, Björk, Rowan Atkinson, Graham Norton

DRESS Designer jeans, stylish leather skirts, dark tailored suits, elegant handbags. Jigsaw, Paul Smith, MaxMara, Miu Miu

MUSIC DJs from Black Market Records upstairs Tue-Sun, from 9pm, live music downstairs 7 days, times vary

DOOR Smart casual

DRINKS Beer £3, Wine £3.50, Champagne £7.50, Cocktail £7

FOOD Oriental, Tapas, £7

CARDS All

CAPACITY 200, seating 50

HIRE Venue: Yes · Private Room: Yes

MONDO

Bar, Club
12-13 Greek Street W1
020 7734 7151

OPEN Mon-Sat 10pm-4am	GETTING LUCKY	3/5
TUBE/RAIL Tottenham Court	EYE CANDY	3/5
Road, Leicester Square	BIG SPENDERS	2/5
BUSES 9, 14, 22, 53,	MIX 60%M 40%F	
94, 139	AGE 20-40	
	PRICE Average	

AMBIENCE Basement, Chilled, Cute staff, Funky, Late Night Open, Minimalist, Party, Queues
REVIEW Drawing London nightlife's depraved, decadent and devilish, Mondo is, fittingly, a labyrinthine basement of infernal rooms. A claustrophobic's nightmare – this could very well be a vision of hell in the 21st century. It gets so hot in this lair that the walls sweat and even the devil would be forced to put ice in his red shorts. Yet the night-eyed and bushy-chinned occupants don't bat an eyelid, so intent are they on recreating that Barcelonian house experience while eyeing up the 'fit birds'. Nice girls are strangers to Mondos and chivalry is non-existent as Italiano wideboys and smooth, besuited gangsters elbow their way around. Not for the faint-hearted, the nooks and crannies are ideal for intimate behaviour and f**k-off stares should any outsider dare to intrude the private party.
PLACE Catatombical enclosure that only just avoids erring on the side of sleaze by resembling the back room of a continental gay club. It exudes less-is-more style throughout.
PEOPLE Nightleeches. The genuinely debauched as opposed to the wannabe debauched.

PROFS Media and music industry types, promoters, singers, night owls
CELEBS Boy George
DRESS Diesel, FCUK, Zara, Daniel Poole
MUSIC Chilled Ibiza, Funk, House, Dance, DJs Wed-Sat
DOOR Smart casual
DRINKS Beer £3.30, Wine £3.30, Champagne £6.50, Cocktail £7
FOOD Bar snacks, £6
CARDS No Amex
CAPACITY 240, seating 80
HIRE Venue: Yes · Private Room: Yes

O BAR

Bar
83-85 Wardour Street W1
020 7437 3490

OPEN Mon-Fri 5pm-3am,	GETTING LUCKY	4/5
Sat 4pm-3am,	EYE CANDY	2/5
Sun 4pm-10.30pm	BIG SPENDERS	3/5
TUBE/RAIL Piccadilly Circus	MIX 60%M 40%F	
BUSES 3, 6, 23, 53,	AGE 20-35	
139, 159	PRICE Expensive	

AMBIENCE Dancing, Groups, Late Night Open, Party, Pulling, Touristy
REVIEW O Bar scores no points for subtlety. Loud chart sounds pound in this big, thumping pick-up

joint. Drunk girls and boys from the 'burbs, the heavy City wide boys and tourists pack this place every weekend to down bottled American beer and chat each other up. Though O Bar amusingly pretends to be a high-class cocktail bar, it's neither particularly tasteful nor very stylish. At the same time, it's not pretentious either, and with the right attitude you may well have fun. However, if you're even slightly sober, the heavy security and dense crowds make you feel like a well-behaved sheep obediently following the next one's arse into the pen to be fleeced.
PLACE A big downstairs bar best described as Beverly Hills meets Cleopatra, with purple velvet sofas and leopard print chairs. The upstairs bar is (slightly) more subdued.
PEOPLE Gangs on the pull, professional swingers, bewildered tourists.

PROFS Media employees, PRs, students, retailers, TV employees, tourists, journalists, film employees, bankers, footballers
CELEBS Gary Kemp, Sid Owen, Matt Goss, Frankie Fraser, cast of Big Brother, Rio Ferdinand, Atomic Kitten
DRESS Girls dress up, guys don't bother, unless they're still in their suits. Plenty of Oasis, Karen Millen, Hugo Boss, TopShop, Mango, Miss Selfridge, Calvin Klein, YSL
MUSIC Chart, 70s, 80s, House, Trance, DJs Mon-Sun, from 9pm
DOOR Smart casual
DRINKS Beer £3, Wine £3, Champagne £5.50, Cocktail £5
FOOD Snacks, £5
CARDS All
CAPACITY 350, seating 120
HIRE Venue: Yes · Private Room: Yes

OPIUM

Bar, Members Bar, Restaurant
1a Dean Street W1
020 7287 9608

OPEN Mon-Sat 6pm-3am	GETTING LUCKY	3/5
TUBE/RAIL Tottenham Court	EYE CANDY	4/5
Road, Leicester Square	BIG SPENDERS	5/5
BUSES 10, 25, 55, 73,	MIX 40%M 60%F	
98, 176	AGE 25-35	
	PRICE Expensive	

AMBIENCE Conversation, Exclusive/Chic, Funky, Hip/Fashionable, Jet Set, Late Night Open, Lounge, Opulent, Star Spotting
REVIEW Oh, so this is where all the beautiful women we never meet in The Ferret and Spanner come to drink – not that moneyed models wearing dresses to make Liz Hurley blush are our cup of tea, you understand. Despite having the air of a members' bar, Opium is theoretically open to anyone. Anyone, that is, with the looks of Jude or Sadie and a wallet to rival the Sultan of Brunei's. It's an exceptionally beautiful celebration destination, elegant and funky. But isn't it a bit rich to have a bar menu waffling on about the Vietnamese people's 'decades of struggle' and 'resilience in abundance' whilst flogging bottles of champagne at £625 a pop?

PLACE An almost stupendously grand(iose) Vietnamese dream palace, with swathes of intricately carved partitions and a muted gold and terracotta colour scheme.
PEOPLE No one larger than a size 12, no one earning less than £50k and no one beaten by the ugly stick.

PROFS PRs, artists, music industry professionals, models, fashion designers, advertising, the idle rich
CELEBS Patsy Kensit, George Clooney, Bryan Adams, Erin O'Connor, John O'Gregor, Mick Jagger, Kate Moss, Liv Tyler
DRESS Ghost, Prada, Armani, DKNY
MUSIC Eclectic, House Lounge, Funky Lounge, Funky House, Cabaret Tue-Wed 8pm-10pm, DJ Thu-Sat, from 9pm
DOOR Smart casual, members and guests, Thu-Sat £15
DRINKS Beer £4.30, Wine £3.50, Champagne £8, Cocktail £7.50
FOOD French/Vietnamese, £15
CARDS All
CAPACITY 250, seating 80
HIRE Venue: Yes · Private Room: No

PAPA GAIO

Club, Members Club
61 Poland Street W1
020 7565 1620

OPEN Mon-Sat 9pm-3am, Sun 9pm-2am TUBE/RAIL Oxford Circus, Piccadilly Circus BUSES 3, 12, 23, 53, 88, 139		
GETTING LUCKY		**4/5**
EYE CANDY		**4/5**
BIG SPENDERS		**4/5**
MIX 50%M 50%F		
AGE 20-26		
PRICE Expensive		

AMBIENCE Hip/Fashionable, Basement, Business, Cute Staff, Exclusive/Chic, Late Night Open, Pulling
REVIEW Former favourite of Billy Evans (neé Piper), pre collapsing, marrying and going to seed, Papa Gaio has something of a hit and miss history. Hailed as the next big thing on opening it's never quite lived up to its promise. Like the Hamiltons – big news for three weeks then not a peep for six months until the next scandal erupts. Currently going through hard times, a rather grim selection of lap dancers were recently employed to entertain the rapidly diminishing clientele. Set across three cramped floors (plus an infamous apartment), upstairs would be a VIP section if it ever had any to house. Still, the later you stay, the better it gets. Arabian princes shove bottles of Möet down blondes' throats; on the middle floor banquettes and dark lighting help to give the place a lounge atmosphere, while the frequently empty subterranean dance floor is the social basement in every sense.
PLACE Three-floored, red and purple velveteen club with a sense of Studio 54 style. Named Madame Louise in the 70s, it was the venue where punk evolved. How ironic that nowadays it attracts the most pretentious brats in London.
PEOPLE Young, gifted and loaded professional party set. Lots of Tony Montana wannabes, into white suits and Eastern European models.

PROFS Models, music/media types, teenage movers 'n' shakers, fashionistas

CELEBS Atomic Kitten, EastEnders cast, footballers
DRESS Uth, Karen Millen, Sid Rhule, FCUK
MUSIC R&B, Funk, House, Dance
DOOR Members, £10
DRINKS Beer £4, Wine £4, Champagne £7, Cocktail £6.50
FOOD None
CARDS No Amex
CAPACITY 180, seating 50
HIRE Venue: Yes · Rooms: Yes

PITCHER & PIANO

Bar, Chain
69-70 Dean Street W1
020 7434 3585

OPEN Mon-Sat midday-11pm TUBE/RAIL Tottenham Court Road BUSES 14, 19, 24, 29, 38, 176		
GETTING LUCKY		**4/5**
EYE CANDY		**3/5**
BIG SPENDERS		**3/5**
MIX 60%M 40%F		
AGE 23-34		
PRICE Average		

AMBIENCE Groups, Network, Pulling
REVIEW Caught in the glare of Soho, trainee City types all make a dive for familiar P&P territory. Out of their native EC1 environment, they're self-conscious but exhilarated, gulping down the booze like sixth formers. Everyone's lashed by about 7pm, with beer on their lapels and sex on their brains. This branch is bland enough to suit the tastes of all the office after work, loud enough to cover the gaps and gaffes and expensive enough to reassure you that buying a round makes a statement. The City's young hopefuls stagger, bewildered, into Leicester Square station at 11.30pm mumbling incoherently, unable to read the Tube map.
PLACE Oddly corporate in design for Soho. The decor and upstairs/downstairs layout give the impression that you're at a houseparty where you can't find the host.
PEOPLE Amateur City types booming with bravado. Girls trying to look sexy in clothes bought with the intention of putting the kibosh on any harassment-in-the-workplace action.

PROFS Bankers, PRs, tourists, secretaries, advertising employees
CELEBS None
DRESS Burton, TopMan, Miss Selfridge, Cotton Traders
MUSIC Funk, Blues, Dance, Pop, Chart, Jazz
DOOR Smart casual
DRINKS Beer £2.95, Wine £2.75, Champagne £4.50, Cocktail £4.95
FOOD Mediterranean, French, English, American, Snacks, £7
CARDS No Diners
CAPACITY 400, seating 125
HIRE Venue: Yes · Private Room: Yes

POP

Bar
14 Soho Street W1
020 7734 4004

OPEN Mon-Thu 5pm-3am, Fri 5pm-4am, Sat 8pm-5am, Sun 7pm-11.30pm
TUBE/RAIL Tottenham Court Road
BUSES 8, 10, 25, 73, 98, 176

GETTING LUCKY	5/5
EYE CANDY	4/5
BIG SPENDERS	5/5
MIX 40%M 60%F	
AGE 22-30	
PRICE Expensive	

AMBIENCE Basement, Dancing, Groups, Late Night Open, Live Music, Party, Pulling, Student
REVIEW Ignore the politely stubborn but dapper doorman's attitude and descend into a sticky, hormonal pit of Poptastic proportions. On Fridays the technicolor bar jumps with pissed-up 20-somethings with hazy glints in their eyes and saliva bubble on their lips. Trouble is, with 'Can I Kick It', followed by 'Blame It on the Boogie', and 'Last Night a DJ Saved my Life', it's hard not to join the festering throng and bump thongs with the best of 'em. Guaranteed you'll end up stuck next to the flailing, lanky sod who thinks other people exist as bounce-guards to keep him vertical. Sudden bouts of well-directed slam dancing often keep idiots at bay. Whilst the random Slumped Suit decides throwing glasses at the wall is hilarious, the rest of the grinning and steaming Pop kids pant and leg-hump the night away.
PLACE Funky basement clubby-bar designed by Shaun Clarkson, featuring a woodland photo mural along the back wall, U-shaped banquettes, furniture units, glowing plastic-clad support columns and a very red VIP lounge. The women's urinal, protected only by a shower curtain, provokes much hilarity in the ladies.
PEOPLE Drunk and drooling, sloshed and swaying Pop tarts out to have fun until 3am. Cooler characters and a few young models hang about the edges and in the VIP lounge, safe from the fray.

PROFS Advertising gurus and fashionistas, models, graphic designers, salespeople, PRs, students
CELEBS Westlife, EastEnders, Atomic Kitten
DRESS High Street interpretations of what's cool now. Miss Sixty, DKNY
MUSIC House, R&B, Hip Hop, Dance, DJs nightly
DOOR Smart casual, Guest list only Sat; £3-10 Mon-Sun
DRINKS Beer £3.20, Wine £3.50, Champagne £6, Cocktail £5.50
FOOD Pacific Rim, Tapas, Platters, £9
CARDS All
CAPACITY 260, seating 100
HIRE Venue: Yes · Private Room: Yes

SAK

Bar, Cocktail Bar
49 Greek Street W1
020 7439 4159

OPEN Mon-Tue 5pm-2am, Wed-Sat 4pm-3am
TUBE/RAIL Tottenham Court Road
BUSES 14, 19, 24, 29, 38, 176

GETTING LUCKY	3/5
EYE CANDY	4/5
BIG SPENDERS	3/5
MIX 40%M 60%F	
AGE 24-35	
PRICE Expensive	

AMBIENCE Funky, Late Night Open, Lounge, Retro
REVIEW Brainbabe of young, hip sharpster, James Roccelli, Sak is small, a little bare and has seen livelier days, but still appeals with its late licence. Reminiscent of a Wallpaper fashion shoot with its Burro-clad staff and beautifully groomed clientele. The W11 fashion crowd and Soho 'meeja' lounge, laugh and chat across low brown and cream leather sofas and coffee tables. The glass-encased waterfall, which serves as a pièce de resistance in otherwise bland surroundings, prompts regular visits to the novelty loos. Look for the foot pedal to operate the watertrough taps. Despite claims that it's really mixed, Sak feels cliquey and style-conscious but it's narrow enough to throw people together.
PLACE The Perrier-Jouet etched glass entrance is a delicate foil for the functional look beyond. Sexy furniture with curved finishes generates a futuro-retro feel. Cool style on a shoestring.
PEOPLE An arty and creative Soho bunch, joined by a sprinkling of fashionistas and trustafarian visitors from W11 and their neighbouring Portobello lounge lizards. Boy band boys with spiky hair and skimpy girls.

PROFS Fashion students, graphic and interior designers, film and music professionals
CELEBS Mick Hucknall, Finley Quaye, Alexander McQueen
DRESS Gucci, DKNY, Armani
MUSIC Funk, Jazz, House DJ Wed-Sat, 10.30pm
DOOR None
DRINKS Beer £3.50, Wine 3.50, Champagne £5.50, Cocktail £6
FOOD Snack, Mediterranean, Asian, £4.50
CARDS No Diners
CAPACITY 150, seating 100
HIRE Venue: Yes · Private Room: Yes

THE SHADOW LOUNGE

Club, Gay, Members Club
Brewer Street W1
020 7287 7988

OPEN Mon-Sat 7pm-3am
TUBE/RAIL Leicester Square
BUSES 6, 12, 15, 23, 53, 88

GETTING LUCKY	5/5
EYE CANDY	4/5
BIG SPENDERS	4/5
MIX 95%M 5%F	
AGE 20-50	
PRICE Expensive	

AMBIENCE Destination/Wishlist, Hip/Fashionable, Pulling
REVIEW Sally Bowles would be in her element here; so would Madonna, Kylie, Ricky Martin and any other self-respecting disco diva or dance floor dandy. It's a Tuesday night, 'Absolutely Flawless' plays to a packed dance floor

full of shiny luvvlies shimmying their gym-slim bodies. Two guys, one dressed à la Gatsby (trilby and all) pose about the pole. A new, trimmed-down Alexander McQueen slips past two slick-haired dykes as they perform finger-licking, body-rubbing moves. It's one gorgeous pop-video parade. It has the electric atmosphere of a private party with attitude, not arrogance. And it would be absolutely flawless if only the boy band-cutie bartenders were a bit quicker on the draw – when it comes to service, that is.
PLACE Former lap-dancing club The Astral, now a gay members club, still complete with pole and stage. Seating alcoves line the perimeter of this basement space with a sunken dance floor in the middle.
PEOPLE Scan the room, it's a lawn of tufty-haired pretty young things, stylish twenty and thirty-year-olds plus a few older guys that can't believe their luck (but are willing to try it later).

PROFS Psycho-therapists, fashion designers, stylists, journalists, hotel and restaurant staff, hairdressers, lawyers, interior designers, concierges
CELEBS Lady Victoria Hervey, Big Brother's Brian, Alexander McQueen, Graham Norton, Pet Shop Boys, Paul O'Grady, Julien Macdonald, Cilla Black
DRESS From Hoxton urbanite to Milan catwalk, from Lock Stock to Moulin Rouge, aesthetics matter. Dolce & Gabbana, Helmut Lang, Gucci, Boateng, Uth, FCUK, Levi's, Evisu, Maharishi
MUSIC House, Chart, Disco, DJs
DOOR Non-members Fri-Sat £5 before 10.30pm, £10 after
DRINKS Beer £3, Wine £3.80, Champagne £6.50, Cocktail £6.50
FOOD None
CARDS No Diners
CAPACITY 280, seating 100
HIRE Venue: Yes · Private Room: Yes

SOHO HOUSE

Members Club
40 Greek Street W1
020 7734 5188

OPEN Mon-Sat 8am-3am,	GETTING LUCKY	3/5
Sun 10am-6pm	EYE CANDY	5/5
TUBE/RAIL Leicester Square	BIG SPENDERS	4/5
BUSES 14, 19, 24, 29,	MIX 50%M 50%F	
38, 176	AGE 20-70	
	PRICE Expensive	

AMBIENCE Conversation, Elegant/Classic, Exclusive/Chic, Hip/Fashionable, Late Night Open, Destination/Wish List
REVIEW If propping up the bar with Rufus Sewell, working on your film script over dinner and queuing for the loo with Mrs Merton sounds like your idea of a life less ordinary, then join the club, or try to. With 2,000 members and over 800 waiting, Soho House is proving to have a very successful formula. With a young, relaxed anti-establishment feel, good food, personal service and hip reputation, it's not hard to see why. A networking haven and stylish office extension, a day can begin with business breakfasts, followed by lunchtime meetings, private screenings and after-hours fun until 3am. With its country cousin, Babington House in Somerset, a yacht at Cannes and Hollywood stars wanting membership before they arrive to film in town, there is no doubting its continuing credibility.

PLACE Old school with contemporary touches. Each of the six floors differs in feel and decor, from old world through to fresh and contemporary. Includes a cinema and three floors of restaurants.
PEOPLE Media and film, darling. See contracts exchanged, news breaking, affairs exposed and luvvies air kissing.

PROFS Film industry, actors, directors, media moguls, photographers
CELEBS How long have you got?
DRESS Miu Miu, Adidas, Ghost, Nicole Farhi
MUSIC Dance, Lounge
DOOR Members Only
DRINKS Beer £3.50, Wine £3, Champagne £6
FOOD International, Snacks, £8
CARDS All
CAPACITY 300, seating 100
HIRE Venue: Yes · Private Room: Yes

SOHO SPICE

Bar
124-126 Wardour Street W1
020 7434 0808

OPEN Mon-Thu 5pm-	GETTING LUCKY	3/5
12.30am, Fri-Sat 5pm-3am	EYE CANDY	2/5
TUBE/RAIL Leicester Square,	BIG SPENDERS	3/5
Tottenham Court Road	MIX 65%M 35%F	
BUSES 10, 24, 29, 176	AGE 18-40	
	PRICE Average	

AMBIENCE Basement, Casual, Groups, Late Night Open
REVIEW Occupying the basement beneath the restaurant of the same name, this Indian bar has taken a low-key approach to the thorny issue of themeing – its theme not really extending beyond the fantastic bar snacks and informative marketing paraphernalia that adorn the walls. Chart music, R&B and hip hop please a generally smartish, after-office crowd, who, if the truth be told, are verging on the 'lacklustre' side of polite and the 'not very' side of exciting. Maybe everyone is waiting for their table upstairs or for last orders to be called so they have no option but to face the streets of Soho, because it can feel a little like a holding bay, albeit a smartly turned-out one. Bland enough to make the name slightly ironic.

PLACE Shared entrance with the restaurant leads to a basement bar. Rich colours, pleasantly subdued lighting, inoffensive decor with good attention to detail.
PEOPLE Weary Soho desk-jockeys and smart pre-eaters mix with more casual night-outers but fail to create that distinct buzz that the best bars have.

PROFS Accountants, ITs, bankers, PAs, doctors, property developers, account execs, students, tourists
CELEBS None
DRESS Oasis, Karen Millen, Suits
MUSIC Chart, Pop, R&B, Hip Hop DJ Fri-Sat, from 11pm
DOOR Smart casual, £5 after 11pm Fri-Sat
DRINKS Beer £2.95, Wine £2.95, Champagne £7, Cocktail £6.50
FOOD Indian, Snacks, £2.50
CARDS All
CAPACITY 100, seating 60
HIRE Venue: Yes · Private Room: Yes

TEATRO

Members Club, Restaurant
93-107 Shaftesbury Avenue W1
020 7494 3040

OPEN Mon-Fri 9am-3am,	**GETTING LUCKY**	**2/5**
Sat 5.30pm-3am	**EYE CANDY**	**4/5**
TUBE/RAIL Leicester Square,	**BIG SPENDERS**	**4/5**
Tottenham Court Road	**MIX** 50%M 50%F	
BUSES 14, 19, 24, 29,	**AGE** 30-50	
38, 176	**PRICE** Expensive	

AMBIENCE Business, Casual, Chilled, Comfy, Conversation, Elegant/Classic, Exclusive/Chic, Groups, Hip/Fashionable, Late Night Open, Romantic, Star Spotting
REVIEW This Soho media club (attached to the restaurant) comes courtesy of Lee Chapman and Leslie Ash. It's all a bit out of character as you won't find any shiny-suited footballers or men behaving badly. Although the press vultures circled for a while awaiting its failure, they've had to flap off elsewhere. After three years this remains strictly stylish, quietly cool and definitely grown-up, with a loyal membership. It's a calmer

alternative to the Groucho and Soho House, and although once you could always find a seat, nowadays you may have to snuggle up close to a well-connected stranger. Used mostly as an after-work haven or home-away-from-home for TV, media, comedians and theatricals, who relax on the leather sofas or amongst scatter cushions. Candlelight flatters all.
PLACE Noughties take on a gents' club by United Designers. Like a hip hotel lounge, low ceilings (in a former multistorey carpark). A cubist-type mural runs behind the bar, with complementary earth tones all round. Dark wood, leather sofas and chairs. Banquettes and low tables. Peaceful and dimly lit.
PEOPLE Grown-up media, TV soap stars, friends of Lee and Leslie.

PROFS TV execs, film producers/directors, theatrical agents, account execs, journalists, editors, fashionistas, musicians
CELEBS Lee Chapman, Leslie Ash, Anna Walker, Trevor Beattie, Rowland Rivron, Mick Hucknall, Wayne Hemingway, Lulu, Minnie Driver, George Michael, Ben Elton, Keith Allen, Lord Andrew Lloyd Webber, Shane Ritchie, Tim Roth, Les Dennis, Catherine Zeta-Jones, Ant & Dec, Gail Hipgrave (neé Porter), Tom Jones, Craig Charles, Talvin Singh, former All Saints
DRESS Media smart casual, some suits, though more Ozwald Boateng than Moss Bros, Chris Evans specs. Paul Smith, Joseph
MUSIC Progressive House, Ambient
DOOR Members only (bar)
DRINKS Beer £3.50, Wine £3.75, Champagne £7.50, Cocktail £6.50
FOOD Modern European, £7.50
CARDS None
CAPACITY 150, seating 80
HIRE Venue: Yes · Private Room: No

TWO FLOORS

Bar
3 Kingly Street W1
020 7439 1007

OPEN Mon-Sat 11am-11pm	**GETTING LUCKY**	**3/5**
TUBE/RAIL Oxford Circus	**EYE CANDY**	**4/5**
BUSES 3, 6, 23, 53,	**BIG SPENDERS**	**2/5**
139, 159	**MIX** 50%M 50%F	
	AGE 20-35	
	PRICE Average	

AMBIENCE Basement, Casual, Conversation, Groups, Hip/Fashionable
REVIEW At seven years old, Two Floors, so named because there are, erm, two floors, is well established and has kept itself thriving on a steady diet of 20-something hip media kids and their slightly older cousins who seem to be successfully holding middle age at bay with a mix of lager and expensive urban skatewear. Its constant midweek 'bustling' status switches to 'v. busy' at the weekends, with punters spilling out into the back street in all but the most inclement weather, the fresh air and reduction of volume making it a great spot for cooling off and mingling. The lively vibe serves well as either a pre-club nursery or an evening out in itself, all in a refreshingly suit-free environment.

PLACE Large glass-fronted ground-floor room, simple modern look. The smaller basement has huge leather benches. Good place to arrange a rendezvous with someone you don't like because they'll never find it.
PEOPLE Young, fun and full of booze, from the creative side of Soho, with perhaps the odd fashion-conscious, foreign student – the sort of people likely to make older revellers feel their age.

PROFS Direct marketing reps, recruitment consultants, sales execs, post-production people, music and fashion industry profs, models, PRs
CELEBS Tim Roth, Björk, Tony Kaye, Sean Pertwee, Ewan McGregor, Jason Priestley, David Schwimmer, The Charlatans, Super Furry Animals
DRESS Maharishi, anoraks, wraparound bags, trainers, Levi's, Hysteric Glamour, Kookaï, DKNY, Carhartt, Evisu
MUSIC Indie, Rock, Hip Hop, Rap
DOOR None
DRINKS Beer £2.80, Wine £2.80, Champagne £5, Cocktail £5
FOOD Sandwiches, £4
CARDS No Amex or Diners
CAPACITY 220, seating 50
HIRE Venue: Yes · Private Room: Yes

THE VELVET ROOM

Club
143 Charing Cross Road WC2
020 7734 4687

OPEN Mon-Thu 10pm-3am,	GETTING LUCKY	3/5
Fri-Sat 10pm-4am,	EYE CANDY	3/5
Sun 7pm-midnight	BIG SPENDERS	3/5
TUBE/RAIL Tottenham	MIX 50%M 50%F	
Court Road	AGE 18-40	
BUSES 14, 19, 24, 29,	PRICE Average	
38, 176		

AMBIENCE Dancing, Friendly, Late Night Open, Party
REVIEW Laid-back managers Jonathan and Billy maintain a relaxed policy, with a dress code of wear what you want, but wear it well. A diverse range of nights provides a variety box of sweet sounds and occasionally not so sweet days. The deep down, dark and dirty b-lines of Fabio's Wednesday weekly Swerve run through to the pumped-up, thrust-out disco and garage grooves of the weekend. Despite it's lush interior and 'place to be' kudos, this club is refreshingly attitude free. Sit back and let The Velvet fluff you up, for few central London clubs do it so goddamned well.
PLACE A small, intimate space with a small, intimate dance floor that's broken up by Art Deco pillars, so you can always hug them if you fail to pull. And, on the subject of l'amour, intimate booths – low-lit by glowing, bubbling, water-filled cylinders – provide privacy should cupid strike.
PEOPLE Thursday is media types and students, Fridays and Saturdays more fashion and music industry people, coupled with dressed-to-kill club kittens. When managers Jonathan and Billy are on the door, you get a mainly female crowd.

PROFS Students, DJs, PRs, advertising agents, musicians
CELEBS None

DRESS Whistles, Karen Millen, Ted Baker, Boxfresh, Nike, Adidas, denim, TopShop, New Look, Gap
MUSIC R&B, Drum 'n' Bass, Tribal House, US & UK Garage, Soul, Techno
DOOR Smart dress Sat
DRINKS Beer £2.90, Wine £2.50, Cocktail £6
FOOD None
CARDS No Amex or Diners
CAPACITY 200, seating 50
HIRE Venue: No · Private Room: No

VILLAGE

Bar, Gay
81 Wardour Street W1
020 7434 2124

OPEN Mon-Sat 4pm-1am,	GETTING LUCKY	4/5
Sun 1pm-10.30pm	EYE CANDY	4/5
TUBE/RAIL Piccadilly Circus	BIG SPENDERS	3/5
BUSES 9, 14, 22, 24,	MIX 80%M 20%F	
29, 176	AGE 18-70	
	PRICE Average	

AMBIENCE Basement, Casual, Dancing, Late Night Open, Party, Pulling
REVIEW The nicest door staff ever let you in, but inside it's disappointing to discover that it isn't literally a village. There's no quaint postcard shop, they don't do cream teas and Barclays hasn't tried to close any of it down. Instead there are video screens that no one seems to be watching, DJs playing tunes no one appears to be listening to (there's no dance floor, so why have decks?), and an attendant in the toilets trying to fleece you of your pink pound purely for the pleasure of handing you a paper towel. Once a dark, cruisey alternative to Freedom, Village has tried to go upmarket by installing the said video screens, DJs and attendant and also by actually turning the lights on. The atmosphere has become rather muted as a result.
PLACE There are three downstairs bars: one is decked out café style, with candlelit wooden tables and chairs and a wooden bar. The other bar has a more modern feel, with video screens and a silver metallic look. A new, alcoved basement bar is perfect for louche fraternising.
PEOPLE Single guys half-heartedly stare at the video screens while eyeing up their night's conquest; friends enjoy a quiet drink and casually flick through Boyz or the Pink Paper. Upstairs, the capital's camp young things congregate preparing for a night at G.A.Y. or Heaven.

PROFS Retail staff, students, businessmen
CELEBS Brian from Big Brother,]Paul O'Grady (Lily Savage), Graham Norton, Julian Clary
DRESS FCUK, Prowler, Adidas, Hackett, Prada
MUSIC Chart, Dance, DJ Mon-Sat, from 8pm
DOOR None
DRINKS Beer £2.90, Wine £3, Champagne £5.50, Cocktail £4
FOOD Snacks, £5
CARDS No Amex
CAPACITY 300, seating 70
HIRE Venue: No · Private Room: Yes

YO! BELOW

Bar, Restaurant
52 Poland Street W1
020 7439 3660

OPEN Mon-Wed 5pm-midnight, Thu-Sat 5pm-1am, Sun 5pm-10.30pm	GETTING LUCKY	1/5
TUBE/RAIL Oxford Circus, Tottenham Court Road	EYE CANDY	3/5
BUSES 3, 6, 23, 53, 139	BIG SPENDERS	2/5
	MIX 50%M 50%F	
	AGE 25-40	
	PRICE Average	

AMBIENCE Basement, Business, Buzzy, Futuristic, Late Night Open

REVIEW From the moment you descend the metal steps, you get a funny feeling as if you've suddenly been transported into Alien 3 and the loud humming noise is actually a rotary blade towards which you're being thrust for the obligatory supporting-character-death-scene. In fact, you're in for something far more technically advanced as you enter what aims to be an oasis in the city. It should have views of mountains and fresh water lakes and delicate, minimalist statements. Instead it's a set of excellent ideas that haven't been quite as solidly executed. The clientele seem happy enough to believe that this Digimon screening, low stool seating, seventies-esque bar is 'awfentik Japnise kulcha' – but is it? Uncomfortable, Liliputian seating, an exposed cleaning area at the back, plus the faint smell of stale urinals doesn't quite cut it. Nevertheless the massages are fun and staff-led karaoke impresses.

PLACE Drink as much as you like and keep a note of your own tab, courtesy of beer buttons on the tables. Fantastic. Seventies, anglicised version of Japan à la Bond, with music to match. TV screens showing the next generation of animated action.

PEOPLE Media types catching up with mates. Reborn hippies. Sushi virgins and beginners.

PROFS Media and music employees
CELEBS Björk, Catherine Deneuve, Robbie Williams, Dido
DRESS Armani, Zara, Carhartt, Miss Sixty
MUSIC Chart, Karaoke
DOOR None
DRINKS Beer £3, Wine £3, Champagne £5, Cocktails £5
FOOD Japanese, £9
CARDS All
CAPACITY 150, seating 60
HIRE Venue: Yes · Private Room: Yes

ZILLIBAR

Bar
40 Dean Street W1
020 7734 1853

OPEN Mon-Sat midday-midnight	GETTING LUCKY	2/5
TUBE/RAIL Piccadilly Circus	EYE CANDY	3/5
BUSES 9, 14, 22, 53, 94, 139	BIG SPENDERS	3/5
	MIX 50%M 50%F	
	AGE 25-45	
	PRICE Average	

AMBIENCE Groups, Star Spotting

REVIEW Tucked in next to All Bar One and Pitcher and Piano, Zillibar is an authentic-feeling Italian bar, acting as a bit of a jewel among a couple of rather dreary chain pubs. Reaching back off the street, this elegant walnut-clad joint has a long curving bar, which, thanks to table service, you can actually stand and drink at, without people continually breathing down your neck, waving £20 notes in your face and then spilling Chianti all over you. The shape of the place limits mingling, particularly when it's busy (most of the time), so come with friends and let the excellent staff do their stuff. In the summer the whole front opens out on to the street.

PLACE Refurbished by Sam Ogilvy (Café de Paris), it has the clean lines of a classic Italian bar. The end furthest from the street can seem a long way away when full, but this in itself grants it a degree of increased calm. Makes more sense with smaller groups.

PEOPLE Definitely a stop on the Italian Soho crawl, where occasional stylish expats are pressed up against the smarter media suits and slightly younger (but still well-heeled) post-work gaggles.

PROFS Actors, advertising directors, media employees, marketing agents, PR agents, music producers, salespeople, journalists, models, film directors, DJs, art directors
CELEBS Chris Evans, George Michael, Mick Hucknall, Teddy Sheringham, Cat Deeley, Michael Greco, Michelle Collins, Sir Paul McCartney, Paul Young, Sid Owen
DRESS Predominantly black (either suit-based or Italian chic) and generally smarter than cutting-edge cool
MUSIC Pop, Ambient
DOOR None
DRINKS Beer £3, Wine £3, Champagne £5.50, Cocktail £7
FOOD Italian, £12
CARDS No Diners
CAPACITY 100, seating 40
HIRE Venue: Yes · Private Room: No

st james's

57 JERMYN STREET

Members Club
The Basement, 57 Jermyn Street SW1
020 7495 5570

OPEN Monday-Friday 7pm-3am, Saturday 8pm-3am	GETTING LUCKY	**3/5**
	EYE CANDY	**3/5**
TUBE/RAIL Green Park	BIG SPENDERS	**4/5**
BUSES 9, 14, 19, 22, 38	MIX 50%M 50%F	
	AGE 25-50	
	PRICE Expensive	

AMBIENCE Basement, Conversation, Dancing, Exclusive/Chic, Groups, Jet Set, Late Night Open
REVIEW 'Louche' is the word the owners of this SW1 members' bar use to describe their underground enterprise. Skulking down the stone steps after dark you get an illicit thrill that you're in for something a bit murky; like bumping into Jeffrey Archer at midnight in Shepherd's Market with a grin on his face. But pass into the inner sanctum and you'll be surprised at how 70s Scorsese it is. All booth seating, cheesy, sleazy sounds and lighting, with Sharon Stone/Robert De Niro wannabes oozing over the tables, laconically lighting each other's cigarettes. It's rich kitsch on a small, after-work-drinkies scale. But for all that, we couldn't help being reminded of an underground carpark. Beyond the Muzak and the walls you can feel the tonnage of foundation concrete pressing down on you, altogether far more stifling than the pretensions of the clientele.
PLACE Subterranean lounge decked out in an expensively 'seedy' late 70s style. Booth banquette seats are like shiny cocoons, with red lacquered tables. Step down to a dance floor with a more intimate snug and snogging zone off to the left.
PEOPLE They pay three hundred pounds a year to come down here. Monied, second generation media with their entourages and neuroses in tow. But definately decadent. I bet the half of them who aren't on the Ryvita diet ate smoked salmon on rye for breakfast, catching crumbs on their copies of Cosmopolitan.

PROFS Lawyers, bankers, musicians, media execs
CELEBS Meg Matthews, Leonardo DiCaprio, Christy Turlington, Jennifer Lopez, Jude Law, Sadie Frost, Noel Gallagher, Gordon Ramsay, Thierry Henry, Les Ferdinand, Rio Ferdinand, Kelis
DRESS A label stable: Joseph, Gucci, Ralph Lauren, Prada, Armani
MUSIC Funk, Jazz, R&B, Soul, DJs Tue-Sat
DOOR Smart casual, no trainers
DRINKS Beer £3.50, Wine £3.50, Champagne £7, Cocktail £8
FOOD European, £12
CARDS All
CAPACITY 120, seating 60
HIRE Venue: Yes · Private Room: No

THE AVENUE

Bar, Restaurant
7-9 St James's Street SW1
020 7321 2111

OPEN Mon-Fri midday-11pm, Sat midday-11pm, Sun midday-9pm	GETTING LUCKY	**2/5**
	EYE CANDY	**4/5**
	BIG SPENDERS	**4/5**
TUBE/RAIL Green Park	MIX 60%M 40%F	
BUSES 9, 14, 19, 22, 38	AGE 25-65	
	PRICE Expensive	

AMBIENCE Business, Buzzy, Conversation, Groups, Live Music, Minimalist
REVIEW When people talk about minimalist modern, sparse, white restaurants, this is the one they're probably thinking of. It was one of the first genuinely modern restaurants, built back in the mid-90s, and one of the biggest. For the denizens of St James's, it was all a bit of a shock. Even the flickering TV screens at the front of the all-glass entrance seemed deliberately placed as an affront to local sensibilities. But it's changed a bit now. The locals seem to have got used to it. The bar fizzes with effervescent blondes and their silver-haired menfolk. As far as the bar goes probably only worth a stop if you're eating here so head for Che next door.
PLACE Big, bright and gleaming white. Not a wine, egg or blood stain in sight. Spooky.
PEOPLE Wealthy St James's businesspersons and City bankers who need to get out a bit (or at least out of the Square Mile).

PROFS Bankers, advertising execs, businessmen from large multinationals, bankers, fine art dealers, auctioneers, media sales reps, MPs, property developers, secretaries, PAs, MDs
CELEBS Jodie Kidd, Tania Bryer, Michael Portillo
DRESS Like a funeral for an Italian suit designer. Lots of labels in attendance, all black
MUSIC Live music every evening
DOOR None
DRINKS Beer £3.50, Wine £3.65, Champagne £6.95, Cocktail £5.50
FOOD Bar Food, £3.50
CARDS All
CAPACITY 300, seating 180
HIRE Venue: Yes · Private Room: No

CHE

Bar
2 St James's Street SW1
020 7747 9380

OPEN Mon-Fri 11am-11pm, Sat 5pm-11pm	GETTING LUCKY	**2/5**
	EYE CANDY	**2/5**
TUBE/RAIL Green Park	BIG SPENDERS	**4/5**
BUSES 9, 40	MIX 60%M 40%F	
	AGE 28-70	
	PRICE Very expensive	

AMBIENCE Business, Conversation, Groups
REVIEW Unsuitably named after Che Guevara, Hani Farsi's swanky St James's Street restaurant and bar once housed that organ of capitalism, The Economist. The wine selection is far from egalitarian. There are two lists; one is limitlessly priced. The only thing señor Guevara would approve of would be the cigar lounge which has won many plaudits for its massive range of smokes. In the main bar, you can order a magical mojito from the comfort of your chocolate leather armchair.

PLACE A large, high-ceilinged room with overtones of Moscow airport in its 60s look, though not its facilities. As you might suspect from the superbly-stocked cigar lounge downstairs, cheroots frequently battle with the air con after lunch. Don't fall down the escalator after you've had a bottle or three.
PEOPLE Amidst the business groups and local poshos there are some unexpectedly normal, late-20s eaters and drinkers. But don't blink or you'll miss them.

PROFS Bankers, auctioneers, staff to royalty, hotel staff
CELEBS George Michael, Terry Wogan, Kylie
DRESS Bond Street suits, Savile Row shirts
MUSIC Pop, Chart
DOOR None
DRINKS Beer £3.20, Wine £3.90, Champagne £9.50, Cocktail £6.50
FOOD International, £5.95
CARDS All
CAPACITY 120, seating 50
HIRE Venue: Yes · Private Room: Yes

DUKE'S BAR

Hotel Bar
Dukes Hotel, 35 St James's Place SW1
020 7491 4840

OPEN 7 days 11am-11pm	**GETTING LUCKY**	**0/5**
TUBE/RAIL St James's Park	**EYE CANDY**	**2/5**
BUSES 9, 14, 19, 22, 38	**BIG SPENDERS**	**4/5**
	MIX 55%M 45%F	
	AGE 28-78	
	PRICE Expensive	

AMBIENCE Conversation, Mature/Older Clientele, Old World
REVIEW Suave Gilberto Preti is proud master of ceremonies at Duke's Bar. He's been the resident silver-haired, smooth-talking bar-steward here (ladies beware) for over 15 years and is living proof that Italians do it better. Making dry Martinis that is. Apparently 'the best in London' and such a fuss they make anyone would think it was rocket science. The bow-tied Preti brings a tray to your table, bearing his props; a lemon, a frosty glass, chilled gin/vodka and a bottle of vermouth. Like Paul Daniels it's all sleight of hand and twist of wrist. But don't ask him to shake it, that's sacrilege – it's stirred Martinis only here. And spare the praise, Preti knows his worth, you'll only be regaled with endless stories of the international visitors who flock to Duke's 'because they give the people the good thing'. Indeed. The 'good thing' is lethal, do not attempt more than one.
PLACE Old school hotel bar hidden away in a quiet St James's courtyard, more posh, hushed drawing room that serves booze than bar. Ox-blood red leather arm chairs and fuddy duddy interior.
PEOPLE Americans, middle-aged couples from the home counties, bar industry anoraks, youngsters eager for the gin-addled Martini experience.

PROFS Bartenders, drinks journalists
CELEBS None
DRESS Smartly. Blue blazers, Pink shirts, Laura Ashley, Prada, Jaeger
MUSIC None

DOOR None
DRINKS Beer £3.50, Wine £5, Champagne £10.50, Cocktail £12.50
FOOD Sandwiches, £5
CARDS No Switch
CAPACITY 40, seating 40
HIRE Venue: No · Private Room: No

ICA

Bar, Café, Restaurant
12 Carlton House Terrace, The Mall SW1
020 7930 2402

OPEN Mon midday-11pm,	**GETTING LUCKY**	**2/5**
Tue-Sat midday-1am,	**EYE CANDY**	**2/5**
Sun midday-10pm	**BIG SPENDERS**	**3/5**
TUBE/RAIL Charing Cross,	**MIX** 50%M 50%F	
Piccadilly Circus	**AGE** 18-50	
BUSES 3, 11, 12, 24, 53, 77a	**PRICE** Average	

AMBIENCE Arts/Entertainment, Arty/Bohemian, Casual, Conversation, Dancing, Hip/Fashionable, Late Night Open, Star Spotting, Student
REVIEW With British contemporary artists the frontline infantry in Labour's cultural march, you would be right in assuming the ICA to be full of people full of themselves. They seem to fall into two groups based on success. Those without it, the backbone of the ICA, slouch around the pubby-bar planning their next conceptual comment on modern life. The rest have achieved success in their field but still ache for the 'instant cool' of the struggling artist. The vibe alters depending on the happenings, ranging from alternative film events, live Internet broadcasts or someone 'unplugged'. Pulling is possible if you are prepared to flirt your way through the defensive art-scene stance, probably easiest if you're interestingly bisexual. Well recommended for culture clubbers, but it may confirm suspicions that although art is sexy, real artists aren't.
PLACE At the end of the entry corridor there are about seven white tables. Up the stairs to the parqueted main bar there's a large mirror which makes the place look twice as big as it is. Round and square tables, spongy, shiny ceiling.
PEOPLE Eccentric artists and intellectuals, mixed with hangers-on and a sprinkling of cerebral celebrities.

PROFS Artists, musicians, media, fashion and advertising employees, film students, civil servants, art students
CELEBS Björk, Eric Clapton, Stevie Wonder, Madonna, David Bowie, Mick Jagger, Anita Pallenberg, Peter Gabriel, Bryan Ferry, Jarvis Cocker, Damien Hirst, Tracey Emin, Beth Orton, Sneaker Pimps, Dave Stewart, Natalie Imbruglia
DRESS Contemporary bohemian, from ultra techno trainers and anoraks to 'I'm in my black period, man,' ripped jeans, painting clothes, anti-High Street trendy
MUSIC Chart, Pop, R&B, Rock, Dance, Ambient, DJs Thu-Sat
DOOR None
DRINKS Beer £2.70, Wine £2.50, Champagne £6, Cocktail £5.25
FOOD Italian, Middle Eastern, £6.50
CARDS All
CAPACITY 250, seating 125
HIRE Venue: Yes · Private Room: Yes

PAGE'S

Bar
75 Page Street SW1
020 7592 9901

OPEN Mon-Fri 11.30am-11pm, Sat 5pm-11.30pm
TUBE/RAIL Pimlico, Victoria
BUSES C11, 88

GETTING LUCKY 3/5
EYE CANDY 1/5
BIG SPENDERS 2/5
MIX 60%M 40%F
AGE 18-30
PRICE Cheap

AMBIENCE Conversation, Futuristic, Groups
REVIEW It's a bar, Jim, but not as we know it. Decorated exclusively with Star Trek memorabilia, and showing episodes of the same on its big-screen TV, the bar plays host to regular meetings of London's resident Klingons, Romulans and Borgs every Saturday night. For most grown adults this would mean engaging warp factor ten faster than the thought of waking up next to Robin Cook. However, in between Trekkie fests people with lives do come here, from the numerous workers in government-related offices in the area to enjoy the karaoke nights, as well as punters wfrom the local Grosvenor Housing Estate. This intergalactic mix, results in a thoroughly enjoyable experience. Generally, Page's is a worthwhile place to meet the opposite sex, especially after work, and more especially on karaoke nights. But remember – whenever Kirk pulled a gorgeous bird she always turned into a seven-headed mucous-mouthed alien by the end of the show. Now there's a metaphor for the beer goggle wearers among us.
PLACE Modern bar dedicated to the celebration of all things Star Trek.
PEOPLE Curious mix of local government office workers, less well-off local residents and members of the Star Trek cast. Jokes about pulling Klingons may result in Vulcan deathgrips.

PROFS Civil servants, politicians, lawyers, security officers, accountants
CELEBS None
DRESS Suits, Gap, Ben Sherman, Warehouse, TopShop/Man, Star Trek fancy dress, Next, Principles
MUSIC Funk, Chart, Rock, Pop, Karaoke with twice-monthly Sci-Fi nights
DOOR None

DRINKS Beer £2.50, Wine £3
FOOD Bar food, £4.50
CARDS All
CAPACITY 150, seating 70
HIRE Venue: Yes · Private Room: No

QUAGLINO'S

Bar, Restaurant
16 Bury Street SW1
020 7930 6767

OPEN Mon-Thu midday-1am, Fri-Sat midday-2am, Sun midday-10.30pm
TUBE/RAIL Piccadilly Circus, Green Park
BUSES 9, 14, 19, 22, 38

GETTING LUCKY 3/5
EYE CANDY 3/5
BIG SPENDERS 4/5
MIX 50%M 50%F
AGE 25-55
PRICE Expensive

AMBIENCE Basement, Business, Groups, Late Night Open, Live Music
REVIEW Quaglino's has all the elegance of a once-great cruise liner that has been invaded by English day-trippers. You stand at the balcony by the bar, looking down into a vast, sleekly-decorated room. Row after row of tables are packed with eaters; large, angled mirrors reflect back glances and towering flower arrangements. From a distance all seems well. Close up, it's not. The first contact you get with your fellow drinkers and diners is at reception where eager eaters, more used to TGI Fridays, queue to be shown to their tables. The bar offers customers the chance to sample this once most-talked-about destination, safe from the financial and culinary commitments. Successful geezers and their gals from East London mix with banking and legal fixtures. Big single-sex groups are often out to celebrate and provide the best pulling opportunities.
PLACE An elegant, bright and glitzy mezzanine bar overlooking a vast sunken dining room with mirrors, plants and spotlights. The height of fashion in the 90s it's heading bargain basement.
PEOPLE Westward-bound, upward-looking and confident individuals in pursuit of Conran 'sophistication'.

PROFS Travel execs on a freebie, bankers, tourists, accountants, management consultants
CELEBS Jerry Springer, Minnie Driver, Richard Wilson, Rio Ferdinand, Peter Egan, Mo Mowlam, Joan Collins
DRESS From sartorially-challenged Austrians in collarless shirts and cheap-jacket-wearing Brits to bespoke suits
MUSIC Jazz, Classical, Jazz Pianist Mon-Thu, Sun, Live Jazz Band Fri-Sat
DOOR Smart casual
DRINKS Beer £3.25, Wine £3.75, Champagne £6.95, Cocktail £5
FOOD Bar snacks, £10
CARDS No Solo
CAPACITY 340, seating 70
HIRE Venue: Yes · Private Room: Yes

TRAMP

Club, Members Club
40 Jermyn Street SW1
020 7734 0565

OPEN Tue-Sat 8pm-3am	**GETTING LUCKY**	**4/5**
TUBE/RAIL Green Park	**EYE CANDY**	**5/5**
BUSES 9, 14, 19, 22, 38	**BIG SPENDERS**	**5/5**
	MIX 50%M 50%F	
	AGE 21-51	
	PRICE Expensive	

AMBIENCE Basement, Dancing, Exclusive/Chic, Late Night Open, Legendary, Opulent, Pulling
REVIEW 'Heeeeeeeere's Johnny!' And if anyone else could qualify for this legendary chatshow introduction it would be Johnny Gold, owner of Tramp. For at his table over its 30-year history has sat an impressive line-up of the rich and famous, from Dodi Fayed to Bruce Willis. Why? Well, while generally regarded today as an Annabel's for the young where those of a hipper persuasion would not dare set a trainer, it's a bit of a London institution, whose long association with the mega rich means it can still command the odd cameo from recognisable models and veteran Hollywood stars. A mix of those that are here because they think it's cool, or because they're too old to be bothered. It's mainly a haven for 30-something Euro and Arab professionals who feel comfortable enough to dance and misbehave in their Gucci loafers.
PLACE Large basement nightclub in the heart of Mayfair. Brighter bar/restaurant off darker reception and big dance floor. The latter is generally heaving; banquettes, low tables and stools surround the dance floor. Very dark, red lights, wood panelling, oil paintings – decaying old mansion feel. Grown-up yet decadent.
PEOPLE Brits, Eurotrash, Americans, Arabs, City slickers. It girls to Essex girls, Harley Street doctors to Hollywood film stars. Chelsea, Holland Park, Hampstead to Dubai.
PROFS Bankers, property developers, international businessmen, doctors, models, film stars
CELEBS Andrew Neil, Terry O'Neil, Tara Palmer-Tomkinson, Petrina Khashoggi, Sophie Dahl, Yasmin Le Bon, Brigitte Nielsen, Laurence Fishburne, Michael Douglas, Jeremy Beadle, Jim Davidson, Jilly Johnson, Bruce Willis
DRESS Girls in Jane Norman to Joseph; boys in navy jackets, blue Ralph Lauren shirts, jeans and chinos
MUSIC Chart, Dance, Pop, DJs Tue-Sat

DOOR Members only
DRINKS Beer £4, Wine £5, Champagne £9, Cocktail £9
FOOD International, £10
CARDS All
CAPACITY 300, seating 100
HIRE Venue: Yes · Private Room: No

THE AMERICAN BAR

Hotel Bar
The Savoy, Strand WC2
020 7836 4343

OPEN Mon-Sat 11am-11pm	**GETTING LUCKY**	**1/5**
TUBE/RAIL Embankment	**EYE CANDY**	**2/5**
BUSES 6, 9, 11, 13, 15, 23	**BIG SPENDERS**	**4/5**
	MIX 60%M 40%F	
	AGE 30-90	
	PRICE Very expensive	

AMBIENCE Legendary, Conversation
REVIEW One of the best-known and longest established bars in London, to those who know how to waltz at least, this place exudes a faded glamour redolent of another era. The immaculate waiters, the live jazz piano tinkling standards, the feeling that you're never quite sure who might walk down the steps – all these contribute to a unique drinking experience, made all the more piquant because you know nothing has changed for years. Fabulous nibbles and classy cocktails – well worth the exorbitant prices.
PLACE When we say nothing has changed, this includes the decor. Art deco prints assist the time-war illusion; the migraine-inducing orange and blue swirls on the carpet do not.
PEOPLE Three types of punters soak up the gin here: suits wooing clients, loud tourists and a set of very old, very rich people who have been coming here for ever, the epitome of (occasionally battered) elegance.
PROFS Politicians, lawyers and accountants schmoozing clients, bankers trying to spend their bonuses in the efficient way, the odd table of media types, probably being ironic
CELEBS All the way from Chris Patten to Brian Ferry via... er... Richard Littlejohn
DRESS Generally J&T (jacket and tie) territory, although given the disparity of customers these vary between Next and Savile Row
MUSIC Pianist in the evenings from 7pm-11pm
DOOR Relaxed dress
DRINKS Beer £4.75, Wine £5, Champagne £10.75, Cocktail £10
FOOD Light lunch, sandwiches, £7
CARDS All
CAPACITY 100, seating 90
HIRE Venue: No · Private Room: No

AXIS

Cocktail Bar, Hotel Bar
One Aldwych Hotel, 1 Aldwych WC2
020 7300 0300

OPEN Mon-Fri midday-11pm,	GETTING LUCKY	**1/5**
Sat 6pm-11pm	EYE CANDY	**4/5**
TUBE/RAIL Covent Garden,	BIG SPENDERS	**4/5**
Temple	MIX 60%M 40%F	
BUSES 6, 9, 13, 23, 77	AGE 25-50	
	PRICE Expensive	

AMBIENCE Conversation, Elegant/Classic, Exclusive/Chic, Star Spotting

REVIEW For those of you yearning to take part in a Wallpaper* shoot forget calling Tyler Brulé. Come to Axis. Spy the cool reception girls in black hipsters, white shirts and loafers. Wander nonchalantly over the Bill Amberg leather flooring. Ruminate upon a clinical host of design touches conceived by someone who probably sources loo paper from remote Guatemalan pine forests. Welcome to design on the edge of the City. Okay, you may feel let down by the lack of paparazzi outside and find fault in the stale cashews and finally feel that this place has had its day in the fun. Nevertheless when the alternative is the Pig & Poke in Chancery Lane rammed to the gills with spotty legal clerks you'll savour this oasis of cool.

PLACE Mezzanine bar over the restaurant, designed in renewal 1930s style with black leather armchairs, marble tables and Art Deco style columns. Panoramic view of a gigantic ochre, yellow and brown wall painting – do not look at it after a couple of Martinis.

PEOPLE Fashion victims, MDI with big expense accounts and famous people with attitude. On the fringe of the City, some try-hards.

PROFS Lawyers, bankers, stockbrokers, traders, musicians, interior designers, stockbrokers, management consultants, journalists, media professionals

CELEBS Tom Cruise, Jerry Hall, Paco Rabanne, Mick Hucknall, Alan Rickman, Ricky Martin, Billy Connolly

DRESS If it's in it's in here. Boateng, Jimmy Choo, Paul Smith, Prada. Labels for les belles

MUSIC Acid Jazz, Jazz

DOOR Smart casual

DRINKS Beer £3.25, Wine £4.50, Champagne £7, Cocktail £7.50

FOOD None

CARDS No Solo

CAPACITY 75, seating 25

HIRE Venue: Yes · Private Room: No

BANK

Cocktail Bar, Restaurant Bar
1 Kingsway, Aldwych WC2
020 7379 9797

OPEN Mon-Sat midday-	GETTING LUCKY	**3/5**
11pm, Sun midday-10.30pm	EYE CANDY	**3/5**
TUBE/RAIL Holborn,	BIG SPENDERS	**4/5**
Temple, Covent Garden	MIX 50%M 50%F	
BUSES 6, 9, 13, 23, 77	AGE 24-40	
	PRICE Expensive	

AMBIENCE Business, Buzzy

REVIEW From its beginnings as an overwhelmingly masculine, City and Inns of Court crush bar, Bank has become a draw for a wider variety of slick townies. The number of celebrities may have dived over the last year, but the staple, day-to-day bar proppers are less corporate than they used to be. Girls can now feel comfortable going to the bar for a vodka Martini and a gossip – and will give any significant-looking male a come on that could stir a Trappist monk. Some of the flusher overseas students from the nearby LSE have adopted the horseshoe bar as a post-lecture recovery point and it is also not uncommon to overhear the droning of BBC World Service newsreaders getting tanked up before the next edition of Outlook.

PLACE Entrance through a mighty revolving door. Vast space nearly completely taken up by the bar itself and dominated by an enormous mural of Coney Island. (Coney Island? Well might you ask.) Hundreds of rectangular panes of glass hang menacingly from the ceiling, forming a 20-ton chandelier. A very late 90s feel by Julyan Wickham.

PEOPLE London City and legal trendies, Euro-sophisticates and tourists. Bankers, solicitors and barristers are still a regular feature of the restaurant area.

PROFS Insurance agents, brokers, advertisers, media professionals, bankers, lawyers

CELEBS Lord Andrew Lloyd Webber, Diana Rigg, Mick Hucknall

DRESS Thomas Pink, Chester Barrie, Boss. Occasional label princess in Prada or Gucci

MUSIC Ambient sounds

DOOR Smart dress

DRINKS Beer £3, Wine £3.40, Champagne £7.65, Cocktail £5.50

FOOD Modern British, Modern European, Seafood, £6.50

CARDS All

CAPACITY 150, seating 50

HIRE Venue: Yes · Private Room: No

GORDON'S

Bar, Wine Bar
47 Villiers Street WC2
020 7930 1408

OPEN Mon-Sat 11am-11pm	GETTING LUCKY	**2/5**
TUBE/RAIL Embankment	EYE CANDY	**2/5**
BUSES 6, 11, 15, 23, 77	BIG SPENDERS	**3/5**
	MIX 60%M 40%F	
	AGE 25-60	
	PRICE Average	

AMBIENCE Basement, Conversation, Cosy, Historic, Legendary, Romantic, Outdoors
REVIEW The oldest bar in town, this genuinely Dickensian haunt attracts an equal mix of City and literary types. Funky in authenticity, the ultracool sit table to table with crusty bankers (possibly under the impression that they're 'atmospheric'). Serious wine lovers come here for the pure unadulterated alcoholism of the place: the wine list is as long as the musty staircase which seduces you down to the cellar. You should buy by the bottle, not the glass and settle in for the evening. It's no coincidence that Rudyard Kipling wrote 'The Light that Failed' here as it's not the brightest of venues. Ideally lit for that date who might appeal more after a few glasses... look out for letchers leering through the gloom.
PLACE You expect to see tide marks on its crumbling interior brickwork. Nookish and cosy with dilapidated candlelit recesses. Can get smoky. Sit out on the Watergate Walk by Embankment Gardens in the summer.
PEOPLE Older crowd of City types and female shoppers who get thirsty earlier and are giggly/confessional by 8pm. A young media/retail crowd in sharp blacks ooze in later. Patronised by Vivien Leigh and Sir Laurence Olivier.

PROFS Financial brokers, accountants, lawyers, journalists, actors, media, literary agents, tourists, authors
CELEBS None
DRESS From high heels and short Versace skirts to dark jeans and polo necks. Well-cut suits from Paris and Milan. Odd broadsheet journalist in tweedy jacket, Aran jumper and gold-rimmed specs
MUSIC No background music
DOOR None
DRINKS Wine £2.70, Champagne £4
FOOD Modern British, Continental, £5.50
CARDS No Amex or Diners
CAPACITY 125, seating 60
HIRE Venue: Yes · Private Room: No

HEAVEN

Club, Gay
The Arches, Villiers Street WC2
020 7930 2020

OPEN Mon, Wed 10.30pm-3am, Fri 10.30am-5am, Sat 10pm-5am	**GETTING LUCKY**	**3/5**
	EYE CANDY	**4/5**
	BIG SPENDERS	**3/5**
TUBE/RAIL Charing Cross, Embankment	**MIX** 70%M 30%F	
BUSES 6, 9, 11, 13, 15, 23	**AGE** 18-35	
	PRICE Average	

AMBIENCE Casual, Cute Staff, Dancing, Groups, Hormone-fuelled Club Kidz, Late Night Open, Luvved up Clubbers, Party
REVIEW There are, quite literally, three steps to heaven, or three bits to it anyway. On the ground-floor, groups of skimpily dressed lads and girls ignore the cold blasts of air sweeping the dance floor to shimmy to house and garage or, in some cases, make ill-advised attempts at the Macarena. A floor up, in the Star Bar, Heaven's resident gender benders take to the stage or gyrate on podiums. The top-floor Dakota Bar is invariably rammed with people, mainly because the bar takes up most of the room, leaving everyone to cram in around the

edges. Heaven is more like a village than a club. As well as a myriad of dance floors and bars, it has a café and even its own shop flogging Heaven merchandise.
PLACE In the downstairs bar there are alcoves convenient for plonking yourself down next to someone you fancy and plenty of pews dotted around the place (church pews for Heaven – geddit?).
PEOPLE Japanese tourists, mostly with spiky hair and shades, dominate the downstairs bar, while the younger clubbers on the dance floor strike an array of poses with glow sticks. Those without light sticks wave cigarettes around in much the same manner.

PROFS Japanese tourists, office staff, PAs, retailers, DJs, musicians, fashion designers, publishing staff
CELEBS Boy George, Barbara Windsor, Tracey Shaw, Jesse Wallace, Julian Clary, Graham Norton, Marc Almond, Pet Shop Boys, Dolce & Gabbana
DRESS FCUK, Levi's, Gucci, Hype, Diesel, Boy, Prowler
MUSIC House, Garage, Chart, R&B, Trance, 70s, 80s, DJs
DOOR Behavioural policy, Mon-Sat £1-12
DRINKS Beer £3, Wine £3.20, Cocktail £5
FOOD Snacks, £3
CARDS No Diners
CAPACITY 1,300, seating 300
HIRE Venue: Yes · Private Room: Yes

ROCK

Club
Hungerford House, Hungerford Lane,
Victoria Embankment WC2
020 7976 2006

OPEN Mon-Sat 6pm-3am, three Sundays monthly 5pm-midday	**GETTING LUCKY**	**4/5**
	EYE CANDY	**3/5**
	BIG SPENDERS	**3/5**
TUBE/RAIL Embankment	**MIX** 60%M 40%F	
BUSES 4, 26, 76	**AGE** 21-32	
	PRICE Expensive	

AMBIENCE Bump 'n' Grind, Buzzy, Dancing, Hormone-fuelled Club Kidz, Late Night Open, Pulling, Student
REVIEW Once the chosen locale of the London's eye candy party parasites, Rock somehow lost its wings during the metamorphosis into fully-fledged music club. A pasty, aurally-challenged crowd – somewhat optimistically referred to as a 'young Chelsea lot' – skirt around each other sullenly to the sort of 'commercial house' that a) doesn't deserve to be placed in a genre and b) makes you wonder why this lot didn't stay at home with the Playstation. Sunday's Factor 25 continues to get a good-looking gay crowd hot under the scanties – so, I'm assured, they definitely got the name right.
PLACE 90s urban chic industriana, with 21st-century squishy bits for those weary of traipsing around provocatively on the strappies. The Chillout Zone on the second level witnesses the real action and – blessings – is fitted with the sort of lighting that would throw a favourable glow on Marilyn Manson.
PEOPLE Temping Antipodeans seeking respite from eight hours of photocopying. Sloaney Accenture secs trying to disguise the fake-tan stains on their pencil skirts in the hope that Matt and Chris from Accounts will stop mirthfully spilling beer on each other's trousers and attempt to chat them up. Groomed gay boys in their best skin tights on Sundays.

PROFS Students, insurance, office workers, professionals and trustafarians
CELEBS Piers Adam, Lady Victoria Hervey, Stephen Dorff
DRESS Best office attire, strappy top and nylon trouser combos, transparent skin tights. Occasional loitering twin set and the odd Country Casuals shirt
MUSIC House music for rich kids and a touch of R&B
DOOR Smart dress, no trainers. Admission from £8-12
DRINKS Beer £3.50, Wine £3.50, Champagne £7, Cocktail £7.50
FOOD Tapas, £3.50
CARDS No Diners
CAPACITY 650, seating 350
HIRE Venue: Yes · Private Room: Yes

ROCKWELL

Bar, Hotel Bar
Trafalgar Hotel, 2 Spring Gardens SW1
020 7870 2959

OPEN Mon-Sat 9am-1am,	**GETTING LUCKY**	**1/5**
Sun 11am-10.30pm	**EYE CANDY**	**2/5**
TUBE/RAIL Charing Cross	**BIG SPENDERS**	**4/5**
BUSES 3, 11, 12, 24, 53, 88	**MIX** 60%M 40%F	
	AGE 25-45	
	PRICE Very expensive	

AMBIENCE Business, Elegant/Classic, Late Night Open, Opulent
REVIEW The hotel market is revived, with independently owned designer-boutique numbers housing groovy hotspot bars and, before you know it, the corporate big boys are chasing the action. Yup, the Hilton group has opened shop in a location more commonly associated with flocking pigeons and swarming tourists than style hotels and cocktail consumption. Rockwell lacks a certain je ne sais quoi: mainly people. Which is a shame, because it's a cool name and it's gotta lotta bottle, as in Bourbon. Rows of the stuff line the acres of back bar, but it's not quite the crowd magnet it was hoped it might be. Maybe this town ain't big enough for yet another impersonal though impressive 5-star lobby, or just maybe the hotel bar's day has come.
PLACE Cavernous lobby-bar-cum-reception at the Hilton's new 'lifestyle' hotel (as opposed to a 'deadnaff' hotel we assume) on the south side of Trafalgar Square. Day beds, sofas and lounge chairs with upholstery akin to tube seating.
PEOPLE Smart guests of the hotel, Bourbon lovers, business bods. Ratio of staff to guests, 2:1.

PROFS City boys, ladies-who-lunch, PRs
CELEBS Tamara Beckwith, Jarvis Cocker, Luciana Morad
DRESS Ghost, Saks 5th Avenue, Richard James, Voyage, Nicole Farhi
MUSIC Classical, Ambient, House
DOOR None
DRINKS Beer £4.50, Wine £4.50, Champagne £9, Cocktail £8
FOOD Continental, Bar Snacks, £8
CARDS All
CAPACITY 400, seating 100
HIRE Venue Yes · Private Room Yes

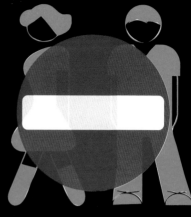

THE EVE club

Club nights

Tuesday
Thursday
Friday
Saturday

Available for
private hire

Tel: 020 7734 4252
www.theeveclub.com

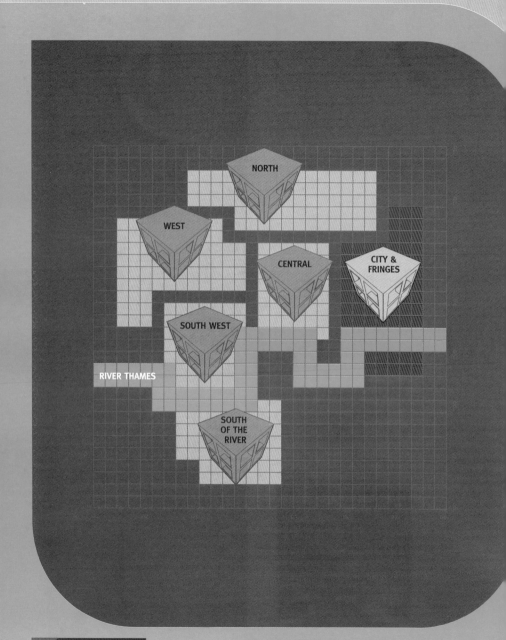

METRO

intro

The City of London is unique: a medieval street map home to some of the richest businesses on the planet, the most loaded guys in town and the dullest drinking spots known to mankind.

This is odd given that underneath almost every building in the Square Mile lurk after-work and lunchtime boozers which should, in theory, provide as much choice as a Cosmo questionnaire.

However, with so much disposable income on tap, the chain bars have flexed their financial muscle and moved in faster than a trader chasing his coke dealer on a Friday. Beware. The City bars are male-dominated, old boys clubs full of suited and booted money machines who work together, drink together and share a collective lack of imagination. How else can you explain their fraternising in these ghastly places?

That said, there are a few stand-out gems in amongst the tat. If you're after an expense account bashing in classic chic surroundings, then the **Coq d'Argent** (fab views), **La Grande Marque**, **Pacific Oriental** and **Prism** are sure to please. Likewise, the big boys on the South Bank are particularly good if you're with someone who likes views and paying bills – see **Baltic** and **Oxo Tower**.

If it's Sex and the City you're yearning for, there are a handful of stylish venues floundering in the sea of sawdust and chrome: **Fuego**, **Nylon Bar** and the **GE Club** at the Great Eastern Hotel are recommended, particularly for their late licences.

Like tramps sitting on Bill Gates' doorstep, the City's neighbours include some of the country's poorest and most ethnically mixed communities, in Hackney, Southwark and Tower Hamlets. Despite, or perhaps because of this, there are some pockets of urban cool on the City fringes.

To the north, Clerkenwell and Farringdon are filled with a strange combination of funky media types and City slickers. Guardian and Observer hacks in battered denim drink side by side with Duffer-sporting graphic designers and pinstriped portfolio managers, but the groups mix surprisingly well. Clerkenwell and Farringdon are a game player's paradise. Quit talkin', start chalkin' because **19:20** and **Clerkenwell House** are where you rack 'em up. If you can't cut it as a hustler, head for **Café Kick**, where table football rules. Bars here show a tendency towards invention and a pleasing desire to present a USP. They know it takes a bit more than a brace of foreign beers and some leather cubes to please this lot. The area has a number of high-quality style bars, led by the original 'God is a cocktail' **Match EC1**. Other favourites include **Cicada** and **Mint 182**. A handful of good gastropubs, including the legendary **Eagle** and **The Peasant**, make good filling stations, alongside more up-market eateries **St John** and **Smiths of Smithfield**. It's not just mussels and Martinis though. **Dust** and **Fluid** do the 'am I a bar or a club?' thing, and music lovers come from all over the country to dance their socks off at leading dance club **Fabric**.

Further east is Brick Lane, just a few blocks away in distance but light years away in style. The area's venues are the jack-of-all-trades of the bar scene, often wacky hybrids of bar-cum-art-gallery-cum-restaurant-cum-concert-hall-cum-club. Mixed-bag music policies – at **93 Feet East** and the **Rhythm Factory** – attract a mixed-bag crowd of out-there day-glo fashionistas, Stan Smith slackers and East End geezers.

Recent and future openings:

Living Room, 2–3 West Smithfield
Bonds, Tabernacle Street
Ruby Lounge, 34 Lower Marsh Street
Mint on Montague, 6–10 Borough High Street
Aurora Bar, 40 Liverpool Street

brick lane

93 FEET EAST

Bar, Club, Music Venue
150 Brick Lane E1
020 7247 6095

OPEN Mon-Wed 6pm-11pm,	GETTING LUCKY	**3/5**
Thu-Sat 6pm-2am,	EYE CANDY	**4/5**
Sun midday-10.30pm	BIG SPENDERS	**3/5**
TUBE/RAIL Shoreditch,	MIX 55%M 45%F	
Liverpool Street	AGE 20-35	
BUSES 8, 25, 67, 253	PRICE Average	

AMBIENCE Arts/Entertainment, Asian Underground, Buzzy, Dancing, Funky, Hip/Fashionable, Late Night Open, Live Music, Student, Warehouse/Industrial

REVIEW 93 Feet East kung-fu kicked its way into Brick Lane folklore in September 2000, when Ninja Tunes took over the whitewashed minimalist East End space for their 10th birthday party and caused a road block. Although 93's promotional logistics remain somewhat sketchy (letting in a usurper posing as the director of Eurostar to a Vogue party is amongst the faux pas top ten), in-house director/designer Natalie Tate has adeptly revamped the former warehouse shell, creating a multi-layered venue with excellent acoustics and a suitably Shoreditch attitude. Lord of the Asian underground Talvin Singh and breaks meister Andrew Weatherall number amongst the East End swanksters planning regular club nights at the venue.

PLACE Directly opposite the Vibe Bar and in strict contrast far as decor goes. Where the Vibe has apathetically settled for distressed, 93 has gone all-out for the standard East End-dun-good ductwork and plumped soft furnishings. An exposed ventilation system and spartan paint job in the main hall surrenders to all manner of squidgy seating in all shades of genitalia in the bar area.

Plans for expansion include a members bar upstairs, extended mezzanine level and a new basement room.

PEOPLE Its location in the up 'n' coming reaches of the East End means the Cool Britannia tourists haven't quite got to grips with this one yet, so it's still a proppa Shoreditch crowd. You know the drill: camp haircuts, lots of denim, a few anoraks and heavily-stylised skinny birds in the ludicrous accessory of the week. Where are all the post-punk reactionary outfits though? I wanna see lumo-pastel tight leather and multi-coloured kipper ties. And that's just on the bouncers.

PROFS Artists
CELEBS Andrew Weatherall, Finley Quaye, Bez, Groove Armada, Talvin Singh, Jarvis Cocker, Sneaker Pimps, Aphex Twin, David Holmes
DRESS Straight out of i-D and The Face, fashion slaves here are truly daring – headgear is de rigueur. Current combos include trainers and suits, ankle socks and winklepickers, trilby hats and Magnum moustaches
MUSIC Great hip hopping shakester Mr Scruff keeps it unreal bi-monthly on Friday. Other nights on rotation include award winning London Xpress, Way Out East and the Sonic Mook Experiment
DOOR Thu-Sat £5-10
DRINKS Beer £2.80, Wine £2.80, Champagne £5.50, Cocktail £4.50
FOOD Bar Food, £5
CARDS No Amex or Diners
CAPACITY 700, seating 120
HIRE Venue: Yes · Private Room: Yes

THE RHYTHM FACTORY

Bar, Club, Music Venue
16-18 Whitechapel Road E1
020 7375 3774

OPEN Mon-Thu 11am-2am,	GETTING LUCKY	**3/5**
Fri 11am-3am, Sat 8pm-3am	EYE CANDY	**3/5**
TUBE/RAIL Aldgate East	BIG SPENDERS	**3/5**
BUSES 25, 253	MIX 50%M 50%F	
	AGE 20-35	
	PRICE Average	

AMBIENCE Bump 'n' Grind, Buzzy, Dancing, Late Night Open, Luvved-up Clubbers, Pulling

REVIEW Although the name Rhythm Factory conjures up a surreal image of hundreds of Trevor Nelsons dancing in an industrial estate, this is actually a fine, friendly club where ego free DJs weave a relaxed funky/housey/jazzy aural backdrop. The laid back atmosphere is more typical of South than East London, with the DJs decks propped up by the dance floor rather than sealed off in a self important booth.

PLACE Although you'd never guess from the outside, there are three sizeable rooms within. The first has a bit of a student bar feel, but in the best possible way with comfy leather seats, white brick walls, arty photos and projected visuals. The second has a huge glitterball, dense dry ice and funky divas shaking their moneymakers. The third has red walls, chiffon drapes and the languid atmosphere of someone's sitting room at the end of a house party.

PEOPLE Subtly trendy twenties and a few gnarled East End geezers awkwardly grasping their beers by the scruff of the bottleneck.

PROFS Students, meeja, designers
CELEBS Brand New Heavies, Noel Gallagher,
Irvine Welsh, Gary Crowley
DRESS Girls: flared denim, hoop earrings, little vests,
Adidas Stan Smiths. Boys: faded denim, retro shirts,
Adidas Stan Smiths
MUSIC Indian, House, Punk, Ska, Jazz, Soul, Uplifting
House, Akaash the Bollywood Experience – Indian Vibe
Sitar Funk, Live Music DJs Club Night Thu – DJ Open
Night Sat fortnightly – Footloose House Mod Scene
Night Thu – Live Bands, DJs, Scansoul Hullabuloo 1st
Sat monthly – Whistlebump 3rd Sat monthly – Soulful
Dance, Jazz, Punk, Ska, House with Simon Haggis and
Andy Crowther plus guests
DOOR £6 before 11pm, £8 after 11pm
DRINKS Beer £2.50, Wine £2.50
FOOD Mediterranean, £5
CARDS No Diners
CAPACITY 420, seating 45
HIRE Venue: No · Private Room: No

VIBE BAR

Bar
Brick Lane E1
020 7377 2899

OPEN Mon-Thu 11am-	**GETTING LUCKY**	**3/5**
11.30pm, Fri-Sat 11am-1am,	**EYE CANDY**	**3/5**
Sun 11am-10.30pm	**BIG SPENDERS**	**4/5**
TUBE/RAIL Shoreditch,	**MIX** 50%M 50%F	
Liverpool Street	**AGE** 22-35	
BUSES 8, 25, 67, 253	**PRICE** Average	

AMBIENCE Arty/Bohemian, Chin Stroking, Funky,
Hip/Fashionable, Late Night Open, Retro, Student
REVIEW Firmly on the verdant side of fashion's electric
fence, the Vibe terms itself 'a space where the borders of
reality and virtual reality meet'. Although any challenges
to drinkers' doors of perception are largely sought at the
bottom of a glass or via the internet portals. This is
a funky bar moulded for relaxed layabout creatives,
stampeded by the designer voddy herds at weekends.
PLACE The large mural/graffiti wall and informal
arrangement of arcade games, trestle tables, leather sofas
and internet terminals in the spacious main room creates
an atmosphere somewhere between art school common
room and a loft party. When the sun shines, all the action
moves to the outside courtyard, kitted with a barbie,
steel band and tequila girls.
PEOPLE Art school students and ill defined media jobs
mingle with a few suited Liverpool Street refugees.
Daddy's gold card goes East.

PROFS Media company employees, film and
entertainment industry players, musicians, performers
CELEBS Andrew Weatherall, Talvin Singh
DRESS 101 ways with dirty denim, batwing jumpers,
studded belts and fringes, t-shirts bearing meaningless
slogans such as 'oeuf'
DOOR Fri £2 after 9pm
MUSIC From Deep House to more relaxing Jazz and Afrobeat
DRINKS Beer £2.80, Wine £3, Cocktail £5
FOOD Modern British, £6
CARDS All
CAPACITY 300, seating 150
HIRE Venue: Yes · Private Room: Yes

ALL BAR ONE

Chain, Bar
34 Threadneedle Street EC2
020 7614 9931

OPEN Mon-Fri 11am-11pm	**GETTING LUCKY**	**1/5**
TUBE/RAIL Bank	**EYE CANDY**	**1/5**
BUSES 8, 11, 23, 25, 26, 35	**BIG SPENDERS**	**2/5**
	MIX 60%M 40%F	
	AGE 26-35	
	PRICE Average	

AMBIENCE Conversation, Groups
REVIEW This member of the 'wood, wine and windows'
chain gang is kept ticking over almost exclusively by
employees of the Bank of Scotland, whose gargantuan
HQ is more or less opposite. Now you know what they
do with all those bank charges. Food is not too bad
for the money – how far we've come in 20 years from
70s 'pub grub' – and the service is, as in all ABOs,
as hyperactive and obsequious as you could wish for
PLACE Huge converted bank in typical All Bar One
mode. Quite possibly the most characterless of them
all – something of an achievement.
PEOPLE Suits, suits and more suits but 'dress-down
Friday' sees them in mufti (you can still tell though).

PROFS Bankers, support staff
CELEBS None
DRESS Tailored suits reflecting workplace hierarchy.
From Pink to Principles
MUSIC Fades into background
DOOR No workmen's or soiled clothes. Over 21s
DRINKS Beer £2.90, Wine £3.80, Champagne £6.50
FOOD Modern British, £7
CARDS All
CAPACITY 250, seating 100
HIRE Venue: Yes · Private Room: No

BALLS BROTHERS

Wine Bar, Chain
3 King's Arms Yard EC2
020 7796 3049

OPEN Mon-Fri 11am-11pm	**GETTING LUCKY**	**1/5**
TUBE/RAIL Bank	**EYE CANDY**	**2/5**
BUSES 8, 11, 76, 133	**BIG SPENDERS**	**3/5**
	MIX 60%M 40%F	
	AGE 20-45	
	PRICE Average	

AMBIENCE Basement, Business, Conversation, Groups
REVIEW This typical member of the Balls Bros chain
cultivates the sort of ambience normally described
as 'womb like' – that is, if you can handle imagining
yourself inside a 600ft wooden woman with some
very odd ideas about storing wine. This particular
branch attracts a slightly younger set than sighted in
similar set-ups. It's popular with local white-collareds
for birthday booze-ups, as well as long lunches.
Romantic cubbyholes abound, occupied by couples
so deep in conversation we doubt they live together.

PLACE Smallish basement wine bar in traditional English style circa 1820.
PEOPLE Porn stars and philosophers. Sorry, only joking. This is the heart of the City after all.

PROFS Lawyers, bankers, stockbrokers, fund managers, insurance agents, brokers
CELEBS None
DRESS Gieves & Hawkes suits, Thomas Pink and Jermyn Street shirts
MUSIC No Background Music
DOOR None
DRINKS Beer £3, Wine £4.30
FOOD Snacks, £4.20
CARDS All
CAPACITY 100, seating 40
HIRE Venue: No · Private Room: No

BRASSERIE ROCQUE

Bar, Brasserie
37 Broadgate Circle EC2
020 7638 7919

OPEN Mon-Fri 11.30am-11pm	**GETTING LUCKY**	**2/5**
TUBE/RAIL Liverpool Street	**EYE CANDY**	**3/5**
BUSES 11, 42, 133, 214	**BIG SPENDERS**	**4/5**
	MIX 60%M 40%F	
	AGE 23-50	
	PRICE Average	

AMBIENCE Business, Conversation, Network
REVIEW If you hired a visually impaired Ukrainian architect to design a young offenders institution in the 1970s he'd have come up with the award-winning Broadgate Circle. So it's nice to find a civilised spot from which to admire the breeze-blocks. Although you can only eat at Brasserie Rocque at lunchtime, drinkers have the run of the place in the evenings, where weather willing they sit under the five plane trees and imagine themselves in Barcelona. Staff, flatteringly, are as attentive as sentries, only a lot more mobile. No dress code as such, but thin-skinned casual wearers may feel a bit exposed up against all the £300+ Whistles outfits.
PLACE Chic, purpose-built (Design House) drinkery in Liverpool Street's neo-yuppie heartland. Outdoor terrace is a summer hotspot.
PEOPLE Curious mixture of senior City-zen and young, spivvy types that put the 'oi' in hoi polloi.

PROFS Stockbrokers, lawyers, bankers, management consultants, marketing execs, financial advisers
CELEBS Famous on Bloomberg
DRESS Ted Baker, DKNY, Polo
MUSIC Classical at lunchtimes, Pop in the evening
DOOR None
DRINKS Beer £2.80, Wine £2.65, Champagne £5.25
FOOD Bar Food, £6
CARDS No Diners
CAPACITY 110, seating 100
HIRE Venue: Yes · Private Room: No

COQ D'ARGENT

Restaurant Bar
1 Poultry EC2
020 7395 5000

OPEN Mon-Fri 7.30am-11pm,	**GETTING LUCKY**	**1/5**	
Sat 6.30pm-10pm,	**EYE CANDY**	**2/5**	
Sun Midday-4pm	**BIG SPENDERS**	**4/5**	
TUBE/RAIL Bank	**MIX** 65%M 35%F		
BUSES 25, 8, 11, 26, 242	**AGE** 25-75		
	PRICE Expensive		

AMBIENCE Business, Elegant/Classic, Groups, Jet Set, Live Music, Minimalist, Outdoors, Views
REVIEW This slick Conran outfit offers the best outdoor drinking experience in the City. Having seen the summer queues stretching from the lifts into the tube station it's fair to assume that Sir T must be laughing all the way to Bank. An expense accounter's paradise. This is where the ebbs of that zillion-dollar syndicated loan deal with 'Old Edgers in HK' flow with the bubbly. Weeknights are the preserve of groomed 30-something Square Milers who've left town by Friday 5pm. Martini glasses and champagne flutes vie for space alongside Gucci bags and 3G mobiles and appalling acoustics make Derek in Derivatives all the more audible.
PLACE Boardroom teak all over makes the City punters feel at home, with a little concession to the fact it's a restaurant, in the form of a few white, plastered curves. The bar reflects neighbouring Conran establishments: clean, contemporary, minimalist with Oasis bar stools, Habitat'y tables and uncomfortable chairs. In the summer the fabulous rooftop terrace, an eyrie above the heart of the city, makes it the only place for a City drink.
PEOPLE 'Look, there's Marcus,' said Barnaby in braces to Charlie in cufflinks. Here the City Slicker isn't just a cocktail. The rich City types behave themselves in the restaurant. If you go in quite tanked up and all set for a laugh you're unlikely to have a good time.

PROFS City boys, bankers, stockbrokers, traders, CEOs, lawyers
CELEBS Lord Andrew Lloyd Webber
DRESS Men: surprisingly a few open necked shirts, but generally expensive suits from US and London tailors. Turnbull & Asser, Savile Row, off the peg Giorgio Armani. Women: department stores rule.
MUSIC No Background Music
DOOR None
DRINKS Beer £3, Wine £3.50, Champagne £8, Cocktail £7
FOOD French, Modern British, £13
CARDS All
CAPACITY 410, seating 200
HIRE Venue: Yes · Private Room: No

Coq d'Argent

CORNEY & BARROW

Bar, Wine Bar, Chain
5 Exchange Square EC2
020 7628 4367

OPEN Mon-Fri 8am-11pm	GETTING LUCKY	**2/5**
TUBE/RAIL Liverpool Street	EYE CANDY	**2/5**
BUSES 8, 11, 23, 214	BIG SPENDERS	**4/5**
	MIX 70%M 30%F	
	AGE 25-50	
	PRICE Average	

AMBIENCE Conversation, Groups
REVIEW Panamas off to Corney & Barrow for finding a cracking location on the edge of the City in the Broadgate development. If you have to work in these Blitz and architect ravaged parts of London, there are not that many better places to be. What other wine bar offers you a ringside seat for the annual Veuve Clicquot Croquet League which takes place under the gaze of a nine foot giant fat female sculpture, while a panoramic view of your last train home leaving Liverpool Street without you is but a neck's swivel away to the rear?
PLACE Praise for this bar's outside seating area cannot be overstated: it basically is a seating area. The bar itself is about the size of one of those security data boxes you trip over outside Argos or somewhere, so unsurprisingly it's 'very quiet' in the winter. But for a few months in the summer it's Henley-on-breezeblocks: highly recommended.
PEOPLE A heaving (sometimes literally) tableau of young City types, viz brokers, bankers and middle-ranking lawyers.

PROFS Lawyers, bankers, financiers, traders, insurance brokers, recruitment consultants, City professionals
CELEBS None
DRESS Natty City suits with bright shirts straight out of Hackett's front window, women in Austin Reed
MUSIC Chart
DOOR Smart casual
DRINKS Beer £2.90, Wine £2.95, Champagne £5.95
FOOD Brasserie, Full English Breakfast, Snacks, £8
CARDS All
CAPACITY 220, seating 100
HIRE Venue: No · Private Room: Yes

DAVY'S

Bar, Wine Bar, Chain
10 Creed Lane EC4
020 7236 5317

OPEN Mon-Wed 11am-9pm, Thu-Fri 11am-11pm	GETTING LUCKY	**2/5**
	EYE CANDY	**2/5**
TUBE/RAIL St Paul's, Blackfriars	BIG SPENDERS	**3/5**
	MIX 60%M 40%F	
BUSES 11, 15, 26	AGE 25-65	
	PRICE Average	

AMBIENCE Basement, Conversation, Groups
REVIEW Davy's does 'ye olde' decor – horse brasses, sherry casks and what not. As a result it is hugely popular with ye oldies. Paunchy bankers and lawyers with projection Windsor Davies would envy exchange work-related unpleasantries, swill claret and Old Wallop by the pewter tankard – and that's only the women. During the week, lunchtimes attract older customers, entertaining clients: evenings are a younger bunch on the afterwork razz, as far as that's possible in here. Friday nights are quiet as, according to the management, 'Most of our customers have gone down to the country by 3pm.'
PLACE Sawdust-in-the-turn-ups time again, in a largish basement, one of the faux-Victorian/rustic members of Davy's chain.
PEOPLE The pompous one from Kavanagh QC and his just-acquitted attractive lady fraudster client.

PROFS Solicitors, barristers, court staff, office workers, financial advisers, tourists
CELEBS None
DRESS Men: chalkstripes, pinstripes, basically the whole Austin Reed catalogue. Women: ditto.
MUSIC Classical, Acid Jazz, Easy Listening
DOOR Smart dress
DRINKS Beer £2.30, Wine £2.75, Champagne £4.80
FOOD Modern British, Traditional British, £8.95
CARDS All
CAPACITY 300, seating 50
HIRE Venue: Yes · Private Room: No

EL VINO

Bar, Wine Bar
47 Fleet Street EC4
020 7353 6786

OPEN Mon-Wed 8.30am-9pm, Thu-Fri 8.30am-10pm	GETTING LUCKY	**1/5**
	EYE CANDY	**1/5**
TUBE/RAIL Chancery Lane, Blackfriars, Temple	BIG SPENDERS	**3/5**
	MIX 85%M 15%F	
BUSES 11, 15, 26, 76, 172, 341	AGE 25-80	
	PRICE Average	

AMBIENCE Business, Conversation, Cosy, Intellectual/Literary, Mature/Older, Old World
REVIEW If you want to bag a brace of barristers, toddle down to the venerable El Vino where legal types foregather to souse themselves amidst a few die-hard journos, who trained here. Expect rambling war stories aplenty as the booze bites. This is the lawyer and journalist as cliché, as sideshow freak, as antediluvian throwback. The lunchtime crowd is far more mixed than

in the evenings. Do not believe the myth: women are very welcome and will be served (even those in trousers). Sadly this was not always the case and the evening crowd reflects the effects of former daftness. Question: do the chaps miss having the ladies around or is this a happy oestrogen-free haven? It's a tricky one to answer. **PLACE** The aesthetic is crusty gentleman's club manqué with huge and decorative wine racks. Millennia of hot air and cigar smoke lend a louche patina. The main seating area at the back is table service only. The sandwiches come well recommended. **PEOPLE** If they've been in the High Court they've probably been in El Vino. Lawyer land for both sexes.

PROFS Barristers, solicitors, bankers, accountants, journalists
CELEBS David Mellor, Richard Branson
DRESS Dress code of Mistress Whiplash style strictness; expensive ill-fitting suits, even three-piece (men), expensive drab suits and demure couture (women)
MUSIC No Background Music
DOOR None
DRINKS Beer £2.75, Wine £3, Champagne £5
FOOD Bar Food, £5
CARDS No Diners
CAPACITY 200, seating 90
HIRE Venue: Yes · Private Room: No

EXTRA TIME

Bar
1 Long Lane, Smithfields EC1
020 7726 8292

OPEN Mon midday-2am,	GETTING LUCKY	**3/5**
Tue midday-11pm,	EYE CANDY	**3/5**
Wed-Fri midday-2am	BIG SPENDERS	**3/5**
TUBE/RAIL Barbican	MIX 60%M 40%F	
BUSES 4, 56	AGE 25-40	
	PRICE Cheap	

AMBIENCE Basement, Casual, Dancing, Groups, Late Night Open
REVIEW Three bars in one, all adding much needed colour and zest to an area not exactly known for either. Upstairs offers a fair shot at Manhattan minimalism, the basement goes for spilt lager, sports bar bonhomie and the ground floor is, appropriately, somewhere between the two. Still too young to be fully established, there's a slight jarring between the clued-up clientele grateful for a good local joint and the beered-up boys here to watch the footy. It's clearly following in the footsteps of certain nearby factory-conversion bars rather than leading, and there's something of an 80s MTV vibe to it, thanks to the omnipresent TV screens. That said, Extra Time isn't cooler-than-thou, it's right by Barbican tube, large enough to lose your friends in and always feels friendly. As such, recommended. **PLACE** The three floors offer options, but all are clean and well designed. The ground and first floors let in plenty of light and feel relatively sophisticated, but the basement is best for intimacy and fun. There are TV screens everywhere, which makes it look a little like the Croydon branch of Dixons. **PEOPLE** Some pre-club party apostles gearing up for their big night, but many more mainstream drinkers who live or work in the Barbican's concrete labyrinth.

Probably more suits during the week than the owners would ideally like.

PROFS Bankers, lawyers, arts administrators, marketing managers, students
CELEBS None
DRESS Smartish playwear, smooth and perfectly 'du jour', but not alienatingly trendy. Adidas, Levi's, Ben Sherman, Nike
MUSIC Chart
DOOR No dirty work clothes
DRINKS Beer £2.50, Wine £2.50, Cocktail £3.35
FOOD Pizza, £4.50
CARDS No Diners
CAPACITY 350, seating 100
HIRE Venue: Yes · Private Room: Yes

FIRST AND LAST

Bar, Café
175 Bishopsgate EC2
020 7786 9251

OPEN Mon-Thu 11am-11pm,	GETTING LUCKY	**3/5**
Fri 11am-1am	EYE CANDY	**2/5**
TUBE/RAIL Liverpool Street	BIG SPENDERS	**3/5**
BUSES 8, 26, 35, 47, 48	MIX 70%M 30%F	
	AGE 25-35	
	PRICE Average	

AMBIENCE Dancing, Groups, Late Night Open
REVIEW Some people get a bit light-headed if they walk under electricity pylons: fighting your way through the mobile phone users squawking around the entrance is enough to turn your stomach. A blast of indistinct thumping music greets your entrance to the smoke-choked interior which is stocked with all manner of high disposable income yoof. Think PA-to-the-MD meets Mr-Administration-Manager-whose-acne-has-very-nearly-cleared, both live at home and need something to do with their money of an evening. Serious boozing and serious flirting before the last train home. Not for punters of a delicate disposition, but great if your chat-up lines work best when bellowed in smog. Would-be sinners wanna kiss would-be angels. **PLACE** Party party party in this super-charged open plan dancing den. **PEOPLE** The evening crew are largely backroom boys and girls, and, being fairly new to the joys of human interaction, are as much concerned with getting sauced as getting laid. Drop a bomb and decimate the mobile phone population of EC2. Brash, loud, louche, smoky and unremittingly young on the northern extreme of Broadgate.

PROFS Bankers, stockbrokers, PAs, admin managers
CELEBS None
DRESS Lots of baggy, shiny suits with button-down collars, girls that have made the most out of living close to suburban high streets
MUSIC Dance, Chart, Live DJ Fri 70s, 80s, 90s, Pop
DOOR None
DRINKS Beer £3, Wine £3.75
FOOD Bar Food, £6
CARDS All
CAPACITY 500, seating 70
HIRE Venue: Yes · Private Room: No

FUEGO

Bar, Restaurant, Chain
1a Pudding Lane EC3
020 7929 3366

OPEN Mon-Fri 11.30am-2am	**GETTING LUCKY**	**5/5**
TUBE/RAIL Monument	**EYE CANDY**	**2/5**
BUSES 15, 25	**BIG SPENDERS**	**3/5**
	MIX 60%M 40%F	
	AGE 25-40	
	PRICE Average	

AMBIENCE Basement, Dancing, Groups, Late Night Open, Party, Pulling, Warehouse/Industrial

REVIEW A mild-mannered tapas bar by day, Fuego is an inferno of sexual activity by night. Its aim is to fuel the City's 'work hard, play hard' ethic, reliably releasing the built-up tensions (and hormones) of the day in a blaze of lust, noise and alcohol. After 8pm, when the cappuccino crowd have moved on, the volume goes up, the clubby lighting comes on and the City's ambitious youth come on to each other. The Great Fire of London started here in 1666, and these boys seem to want to get it going again. Girls show up later because they've gone home to change into something more slinky, but by 9pm ties are loosened, shirts are ripped and mascara runs. Beer drinkers flail about on the terracotta tiles, as random couples crush frantically against the walls. A 2am licence leaves them staggering, sweat soaked into the street long after most cabs have vacated the City, clutching empty bottles or broken shoes.

PLACE Compact, custard-coloured cellar, divided into three small sections accessed by short, individual staircases. Glass-topped bar is central. Fuego's industrial girders reveal that the venue was once part of Monument station. When the volume's down 'Mind the gap' echoes through the floor.

PEOPLE Unsubtle, ambitious City sorts of both genders. Influences: money and sex (in that order). Fairly flashy. When they grow up, they want to make partner, drive an Aston, own a racehorse, spend weekends in the country and sleep with their best friends' wives/husbands.

PROFS Bankers, brokers, insurance agents, estate agents, lawyers, rugby players, traders, accountants
CELEBS None
DRESS For the men: Next, Principles, Cecil Gee, odd designer shirts/ties. Lime green and purple shirts are popular. Women in Selfridges. Matching lipstick and nail varnish are de rigueur
MUSIC DJs from 8pm every night except Mon, spinning party tunes
DOOR Smart casual, £5 after 10pm Thu-Fri
DRINKS Beer £2.60, Wine £2.50, Champagne £4.50, Cocktail £5
FOOD Tapas, £4.50
CARDS All
CAPACITY 150, seating 60
HIRE Venue: Yes · Private Room: No

GE CLUB

Club, Members Club
The Great Eastern Hotel, 40 Liverpool Street EC2
020 7618 7070

OPEN Mon-Fri 11am-2am, Sat 8pm-2am	**GETTING LUCKY**	**2/5**
	EYE CANDY	**3/5**
TUBE/RAIL Liverpool Street	**BIG SPENDERS**	**4/5**
BUSES 11, 23, 42, 133, 141, 271	**MIX** 50%M 50%F	
	AGE 25-45	
	PRICE Expensive	

AMBIENCE Dancing, Elegant/Classic, Exclusive/Chic, Late Night Open

REVIEW Known as the Great E Club but it's far from a 'right on one matey' raver's den. Nevertheless, the music policy harks back to the good old days when clubs were 'clubs' and not posh, private drinking lounges. This long, chi-chi room of serious duty, dark-grained wood, butterscotch suede banquettes and low black leather chairs is a soothing cushion against the stripped bare brick and exposed silver ducting of S'ditch warehouse bars nearby. God-guru of design Conran went East End with his mighty hotel and multiple satellite ventures including this bar, so cool that residents aren't guaranteed entry. The Chosen Ones receive a choo-choo train charm-cum-Monopoly talisman, to be dangled on arrival at reception. Some nights things pass slowly like a push 'n' pull, but other times things get steamy and boys and gals end up shimmying and flailing around the dance floor towards the red altar that dispenses drinks, like some spontaneous choreographed Gap ad.

PLACE Tucked above Terminus restaurant, this rectilinear charcoal, carpeted lounge is split down the middle by a blonde oak catwalk. Plush grey-blue drapes keep the world at bay, and the subdued lighting grows ever dimmer – to the point of repression – over the course of an evening. Look out for the Patrick Caulfields en route to the loo.

PEOPLE Sneakered, down-at-heel arty guys from Shoho mixing with players: from captains of industry to those who stroke the egos of the would-be-famous. Sort of Monopoly meets Playstation.

PROFS Graphic/interior designers, account execs, PRs and someone's 'people'
CELEBS Jarvis Cocker and somebody else's entourage
DRESS Whatever denim is in season, suits or ankle socks and pointy shoes
MUSIC Old Skool, Disco, Easy Listening as well as occasional multi-media shindigs
DOOR Members Only
DRINKS Beer £3.30, Wine £4.50, Champagne £7.50, Cocktail £6
FOOD Modern British, Modern European, £12.50
CARDS All
CAPACITY 150, seating 100
HIRE Venue: No · Private Room: No

GEORGE

Pub, Restaurant
The Great Eastern Hotel, 40 Liverpool Street EC2
020 7618 7300

OPEN Mon-Sat 11am-11pm, Sun midday-10.30pm	**GETTING LUCKY**	**2/5**
	EYE CANDY	**2/5**
TUBE/RAIL Liverpool Street	**BIG SPENDERS**	**4/5**
BUSES 35	**MIX** 60%M 40%F	
	AGE 25-55	
	PRICE Average	

AMBIENCE Conversation, Old World

REVIEW Like the saint, George offers the 'best of British', serving premium beers and (I mean, really) ciders soaked up by good, old-fashioned comfort food. The punters are young, dynamic Liverpool Street types, often out to treat foreign clients to a 'British heritage' meal in what could almost be a Merchant Ivory set. During the course of the day, the punters get portlier and arguably less dynamic. 'City gents', as they'd like to think of themselves, although some ladies like to pop in here after work because it's quieter than the more rowdy local bars.

PLACE In all the slightly camp magnificence of the Great Eastern Hotel, George epitomises the late Victorian predilection for historical pastiche. Oak panelled walls and ceiling, it was described by its original architect, Colonel R W Edis, as 'Tudorbethan'.

PEOPLE City, although mercifully not all slickers. They might get the Alan Clark Diaries from their wives for Christmas or perhaps vouchers for a day hot air ballooning, complete with a champagne hamper. They read The Daily Telegraph and listen to Radio 4.

PROFS Bankers, financiers, lawyers, IT professionals, accountants
CELEBS None
DRESS City workwear, except on dress-down Friday, obviously, when confusingly, everyone wears the same clothes
MUSIC None
DOOR Smart casual
DRINKS Beer £2.75, Wine £3.20, Champagne £7.95
FOOD Comfort Food, Traditional British, £7.50
CARDS All
CAPACITY 120, seating 68
HIRE Venue: No · Private Room: No

HEELTAP AND BUMPER

Bar, Café
2-6 Cannon Street EC4
020 7248 3371

OPEN Mon-Fri 8am-11pm	GETTING LUCKY	3/5
TUBE/RAIL St Paul's	EYE CANDY	3/5
BUSES 4, 11, 15	BIG SPENDERS	3/5
	MIX 70%M 30%F	
	AGE 20-45	
	PRICE Average	

AMBIENCE Conversation, Groups

REVIEW In total contrast to its SE1 sister, this branch of Heeltap and Bumper successfully achieves the atmosphere of Habitat with a bar. This café-bar along with others of its ilk seems to have achieved the feat of moving the City boys away from the traditional City pubs and into these pretentious 'I think the 80s are coming back' style. They should be applauded for the not-insignificant achievement of replicating a departure lounge in a Swedish airport. The saddest part of this venue is the projector screen showing not MTV or sporting events but stock indices – presumably to give the local traders the familiar feeling of being drunk at work.

PLACE In the shadow of St Paul's, this bar in a post-WWII office block goes for a cold and detached

atmosphere with bland nowewheresville decor. Purposeless display cabinet filled with Ikea-blue glasses and bottles, and food cooked in a Wimpy-style open kitchen area adjacent to the bar don't help.

PEOPLE Traders strain their necks to view the share prices, watched in awe and pity alternately by the upwardly mobile City women who are straining to hear the barely audible music.

PROFS Bankers, traders, media, PAs, secretaries, financiers, lawyers
CELEBS None
DRESS High street heaven for the most part
MUSIC Easy Listening, Jazz, Chart, Dance
DOOR None
DRINKS Beer £2.85, Wine £2.90, Champagne £5.30, Cocktail £4.50
FOOD Pub Food, £8.50
CARDS All
CAPACITY 450, seating 200
HIRE Venue: Yes · Private Room: Yes

JAMIE'S AT PAVILION

Bar
Finsbury Circus Gardens EC2
020 7628 8224

OPEN Mon-Fri 11.30am-11pm	GETTING LUCKY	2/5
TUBE/RAIL Moorgate,	EYE CANDY	2/5
Liverpool Street	BIG SPENDERS	4/5
BUSES 133	MIX 65%M 35%F	
	AGE 30-60	
	PRICE Average	

AMBIENCE Conversation, Groups, Sports, Views

REVIEW As a piece of post-colonial bourgeois whimsy, Jamie's at Pavilion just about takes the biscuit (Carr's Water or Bath Oliver, naturally). Overlooking the sacred turf of the City of London Bowling Club, this bar has retained the atmosphere of the sports pavilion it once was. City of London bowlers are now relegated to a sort of garden shed thing at the side if they want to change into their funny galoshes, but at least they can take their drinks outside. Inside financiers are noisily at play decanting Chablis into their chortling PAs – but you don't have to look at them if you don't want to. Large observation windows mean you can watch the bowls or the creosote dry.

PLACE Converted bowls pavilion in unlikely situ slap in middle of Finsbury Circus, mostly hidden by trees.

PEOPLE Hugo and Henry accompanied by Isobel and Victoria, without whom the whole office would simply collapse.

PROFS Lawyers, merchant bankers, chartered surveyors, stockbrokers
CELEBS Jimmy White... apparently
DRESS Afterwork City threads of noticeably senior quality
MUSIC None
DOOR Smart casual
DRINKS Beer £2.95, Wine £4.85, Champagne £5.95
FOOD Snacks, Spanish, Tapas, £8
CARDS All
CAPACITY 125, seating 63
HIRE Venue: Yes · Private Room: Yes

LA GRANDE MARQUE

Bar
47 Ludgate Hill EC4
020 7329 6709

OPEN Mon-Fri 11.30am-9.30pm	GETTING LUCKY	2/5
TUBE/RAIL St Paul's	EYE CANDY	2/5
BUSES 11, 15, 23, 73	BIG SPENDERS	3/5
	MIX 50%M 50%F	
	AGE 30-50	
	PRICE Average	

AMBIENCE Business, Conversation, Network
REVIEW Thank goodness for the customer services culture. Big old banks all over London have turned into boozers, and La Grande Marque is no exception. Inconvenient, of course, for the bank's customers (you've seen the Nat West ad), but so convenient for those in search of a half decent bar in the City – of which La Grande Marque is one. With 23 different champagnes it is clear just what clientele the bar's aimed at – they are suited and it suits 'em.
PLACE Old Lloyds bank. High-ceilinged wine bar adjoining restaurant of repute. The wood-panelling is distinguished, but amplifies normal conversations to a deafening pitch when full so you may as well be standing next to a tone deaf town-crier.
PEOPLE The professionals: basically, anyone who doesn't think La Grande Marque means 'the big tent'.

PROFS Bankers, lawyers, accountants, financiers, brokers, barristers
CELEBS None
DRESS Suits. That's about it
MUSIC Jazz, Easy Listening
DOOR None
DRINKS Beer £3, Wine £3.50, Champagne £6.50
FOOD Snacks, £4
CARDS All
CAPACITY 200, seating 80
HIRE Venue: Yes · Private Room: No

MOORGATE ORIENTAL

Bar
45 London Wall EC2
020 7638 2288

OPEN Mon-Fri 11.30am-11pm	GETTING LUCKY	2/5
TUBE/RAIL Moorgate	EYE CANDY	3/5
BUSES 100, 141, 214, 271	BIG SPENDERS	4/5
	MIX 60%M 40%F	
	AGE 25-45	
	PRICE Average	

AMBIENCE Conversation, Groups
REVIEW Opened in mid-98 this oriental café/bar still gets a fair proportion of its custom from people who've arranged to meet in the now-defunct yuppie hang-out Coates, but didn't realise it closed three years ago. Original it certainly is: if someone had suggested they were going to open up what can only be described as a noodle-cum-sports-cum-doubles bar in the heart of the City, you'd probably have said they were mad, or a genius. Clientele are upmarket and corporate, and by the look of them, pining for the two years they spent in Hong Kong. When the conversation runs dry, City boys turn to the giant TV screens playing football, cricket and rugby.
PLACE Modern 25 foot marble-topped bar painted in Far Eastern reds and yellows dispensing a broad range of Oriental snacks (approved by consultant chef Ken Hom) and occidental booze.
PEOPLE Hard core City slickers who don't buy the FT just because it matches the loo roll.

PROFS Bankers, financiers, brokers, lawyers
CELEBS None
DRESS Expensive City suits (sometimes colourfully lined) plus a few Hong Kong copies
MUSIC Pop, Easy Listening
DOOR None
DRINKS Beer £2.80, Wine £2.95, Champagne £5.75, Cocktail £4.95
FOOD Asian, Malaysian, Oriental, South East Asian, Thai, £8
CARDS All
CAPACITY 100, seating 20
HIRE Venue: Yes · Private Room: No

NYLON BAR

Bar, Restaurant, Club
1 Addle Street EC2
020 7600 7771

OPEN Mon-Wed 12.30pm-11pm, Thu-Fri 12.30pm-2am	GETTING LUCKY	3/5
TUBE/RAIL Moorgate	EYE CANDY	3/5
BUSES 76, 100, 141, 153, 214, 271	BIG SPENDERS	4/5
	MIX 60%M 40%F	
	AGE 25-35	
	PRICE Average	

AMBIENCE Futuristic, Hip/Fashionable, Kitsch, Late Night Open, Retro
REVIEW Hip stockbrokers may be as thin on the ground as cream buns in Calista Flockhart's fridge, but the ones that do exist can be found here. It's an unquestionable improvement on the Corney & Barrow/Balls Brothers joints that would normally mop up this kind of clientele, but Nylon still falls between two stalls somewhat – it's too funky for the City, yet far too City to be funky. The cosy circular banquettes which surround seductively lit tables suggest loose living, but listen carefully and you realise that the only mergers being proposed are financial ones.
PLACE Some seriously swanky touches – red plastic space chairs, tropical fish projections on the net curtains – help to transform an outstandingly ugly concrete building. Good use of space, with more than enough room to mingle.
PEOPLE Stylistically and intellectually sharp City slickers who appreciate the bar staff's encyclopaedic cocktail knowledge and the world-funk soundtrack.

PROFS Bankers, lawyers, stockbrokers, secretaries, executives, financiers
CELEBS None
DRESS City casuals, Hackett shirts, chinos
MUSIC Jazz, Soul, 70s, Funk, DJs Tue-Sat
DOOR None
DRINKS Beer £3, Wine £2.80, Champagne £6.50, Cocktail £5.50
FOOD Bar Snacks, £12
CARDS All
CAPACITY 800, seating 200
HIRE Venue: Yes · Private Room: Yes

PACIFIC ORIENTAL

Restaurant Bar
1 Bishopsgate EC2
020 7621 9988

OPEN Mon-Fri 11.45am-	GETTING LUCKY	1/5
9.30pm	EYE CANDY	2/5
TUBE/RAIL Liverpool Street	BIG SPENDERS	3/5
BUSES 8, 26, 35, 43,	MIX 80%M 20%F	
47, 48	AGE 25-50	
	PRICE Average	

AMBIENCE Business, Buzzy, Groups
REVIEW The blue sign outside makes it look like a travel agency but inside awaits a 100% busy City eaterie with a brasserie and microbrewery downstairs. Movers and shakers slip from their top-notch tables into the hustle and bustle of the bar. The home-brewed bitters, wheat beer and Pils slide down nicely although most diners here head for the wine list. In a bit of a desert Pacific Oriental is a real find.
PLACE Pacific has a sea of big backers with other famous eateries in the Square Mile. Kitchen takes centre stage, surrounded by high-stooled circular bar. Modern mashed coral reef art is there on the walls to remind you of somewhere exotic in contrast to the sounds of Bing Crosby, Andy Williams and Petula Clark that are not. Evenings go candlelit, attracting City couples and sit-downs of 15-20 corporate execs.

PEOPLE Can't you guess? It's suits, suits, suits.

PROFS Brokers, bankers, event planners
CELEBS Ken Hom, Tony Blair, Jacques Chirac
DRESS Ladies: MaxMara, Windsmoor, Jaeger.
Gents: Savoy Tailor's Guild, Austin Reed, Aquascutum, Jaeger
MUSIC Jazz, Motown, Big Band, Soul
DOOR None
DRINKS Beer £2.50, Wine £2.95, Champagne £5.95, Cocktail £5.50
FOOD Pacific Rim, £15
CARDS All
CAPACITY 500, seating 300
HIRE Venue: Yes · Private Room: Yes

THE POET

Bar
20 Creechurch Lane EC3
020 7623 3999

OPEN Mon-Fri 11am-11pm	GETTING LUCKY	3/5
TUBE/RAIL Liverpool Street	EYE CANDY	1/5
BUSES 8, 26, 35, 43,	BIG SPENDERS	3/5
47, 48	MIX 60%M 40%F	
	AGE 26-60	
	PRICE Average	

AMBIENCE Buzzy, Casual, Conversation, Groups, Lounge Atmosphere, Party
REVIEW Psychics are no earthly use to the military and should be obliged by statute to work in bars to save the hapless punter the trouble and delay of actually having to order. Until that happy day The Poet will hold the record for speed of service. An order placed here is regarded as a team undertaking by the young and lovely staff. Having worked his magic at The Water Poet, Dubliner Peter Dunne sold up and moved all of 200 yards down the road to set up the next phase of his empire which will, in due course, consist of ten bars. The Poet is a chameleon: by day a bar-cum-restaurant for all ages, but by night a bustling two-level bar with pounding music and shoulder to shoulder conditions that would upset even French lamb farmers.
PLACE The Poet is located in the relative quiet of Creechurch Lane. In the evenings the dimly lit space is opened up to allow the hordes to mingle, while the sore-footed can sink into the comfy chairs and sofas.
PEOPLE A broad cross-section from the insurance and legal worlds, from the fairly high to the lowly low. Upstairs sees the jacket and tie crowd while downstairs is the preserve of the dress-down Friday mob.

PROFS Insurance underwriters, lawyers, stockbrokers, traders, bankers
CELEBS None
DRESS Conventionally well dressed for the most part. Even the occasional bit of designer flair
MUSIC Easy Listening, Pop
DOOR None
DRINKS Beer £2.75, Wine £3.75, Champagne £5.50
FOOD Brasserie, £7
CARDS All
CAPACITY 300, seating 70
HIRE Venue: Yes · Private Room: No

PRISM

Bar, Restaurant
147 Leadenhall Street EC3
020 7256 3888

OPEN Mon-Fri 11am-11pm	**GETTING LUCKY**	**2/5**
TUBE/RAIL Bank, Monument	**EYE CANDY**	**2/5**
BUSES 25	**BIG SPENDERS**	**5/5**
	MIX 60%M 40%F	
	AGE 22-65	
	PRICE Expensive	

AMBIENCE Business, Elegant/Classic, Groups
REVIEW Harvey Nichols's City offshoot has proved a lot more consistent in its early days than Oxo over the river. The former Bank of America has been impressively converted to provide a hugely swanky setting for dealmaking, backstabbing and redundancy-planning. Be it in the library, main room, mezzanine or bar section there's an intense sense of affluence from pillared portico to white leather seating.
PLACE The room is spectacular: neo-classical columns, huge ceilings and a marble floor livened up by red leather Mies van der Rohe chairs. Fine when the place is packed – usually at lunch – but a little intimidating, not to say a touch deathly, when the place is quiet.
PEOPLE Neighing City types sporting cufflinks and phones inversely proportional to their bonuses. Less dressy in the basement bars. Fashionistas occasionally pay homage.

PROFS Bankers, traders, stockbrokers, lawyers, accountants, insurance agents, entrepreneurs, financial consultants. Some fashion parties
CELEBS David Jensen, Michael Portillo, Jono Coleman, Mario Testino
DRESS Savile Row, Gieves & Hawkes, Principles, Thomas Pink, Harvey Hudson
MUSIC Relaxing background surround sounds
DOOR None
DRINKS Beer £3.25, Wine £3.50, Champagne £7.50, Cocktail £8
FOOD Modern British, £17
CARDS All
CAPACITY 200, seating 150
HIRE Venue: Yes · Private Room: Yes

SPORTS ACADEMY

Pub
24 King William Street
020 7397 9861

OPEN Mon-Fri midday-11pm	**GETTING LUCKY**	**1/5**
TUBE/RAIL Monument	**EYE CANDY**	**1/5**
BUSES 21, 43, 133, 501	**BIG SPENDERS**	**2/5**
	MIX 80%M 20%F	
	AGE 20-30	
	PRICE Average	

AMBIENCE Casual, Groups, Sports
REVIEW Lad-tastic to the max. When lads die and go to heaven it must look something like this. A variety of expensive beers, huge TVs, smaller TVs, video games and pool tables. In case you hadn't guessed, it's all about sport; any sport but especially footy. So it's little surprise to find the punters are almost exclusively young males doing what they do best and then wondering why they never pull. To try and even things out, the Academy offers a Ladies Privilege Card with associated special offers and is justly proud of achieving an 80/20 gender ratio – admittedly the fairer sex is mainly spotted at lunchtime.
PLACE In the commuter wasteland of London Bridge. Mega-big screen upstairs; pool tables, video games and Naugahyde benches in booths downstairs.
PEOPLE Lads

PROFS Bankers, stockbrokers, traders, insurance salesmen, accountants, students, retail assistants
CELEBS None
DRESS Mostly Cecil Gee, what the cast of EastEnders would wear if they had to work in the City, M&S, Ben Sherman
MUSIC Chart
DOOR Smart casual
DRINKS Beer £2.80, Wine £3.50, Cocktail £4
FOOD Snacks, £5
CARDS All
CAPACITY 330, seating 80
HIRE Venue: Yes · Private Room: Yes

VERTIGO 42 SEAFOOD & CHAMPAGNE BAR

Bar, Restaurant
42nd Floor, Tower 42, 25 Old Broad Street EC2
020 7877 7842

OPEN Mon-Fri midday-3pm, 5pm-11pm	**GETTING LUCKY**	**2/5**
	EYE CANDY	**2/5**
TUBE/RAIL Bank, Liverpool Street	**BIG SPENDERS**	**3/5**
BUSES 11, 23	**MIX** 60%M 40%F	
	AGE 25-50	
	PRICE Expensive	

AMBIENCE Conversation, Views
REVIEW Tower 42 is easy to find because it looks like a huge packet of Lambert & Butler – exit Liverpool Street station and head for the largest thing in sight (egos and bank balances excluded). Once you've figured out where to check in, you'll be ushered into a lift and up to Vertigo where breathtaking views await (that is if you can get past the three boring blokes involved in some

sort of power meeting). As the sun sets, the staff might slip in the latest Café del Mar CD – perfect for watching London go all dark and twinkly.
PLACE Wrapped around the shoulders of the 42nd floor, Vertigo has seating lined up facing views of Tower Bridge and Tate Modern. Bank foyer decor – navy-blue furniture with perspex ledges and mirrors. Some interesting touches include compass bearings on the walls and, at each table, little blue plastic binoculars to play with.
PEOPLE Mostly arsey City traders, bankers and other finance types. Overheard: 'I heard they closed Sweden,' spoken in a deep and genuinely serious tone. For fun, try to convince nearby strangers of your own business prowess by toasting a non-existent venture again and again in a loud voice.

PROFS Bankers, stockbrokers, traders, lawyers, accountants, financial journalists
CELEBS None
DRESS Serious suit wearers (Principles to Savile Row), but feel free to go jeans-and-trainers casual – no one seems to mind
MUSIC Ambient
DOOR Smart casual
DRINKS Wine £4.75, Champagne £8
FOOD Seafood, Snacks, £15
CARDS No Diners
CAPACITY 100, seating 66
HIRE Venue: Yes · Private Room: No

clerkenwell and farringdon

19:20

Bar, Pool Bar
19-20 Great Sutton Street EC1
020 7253 1920

OPEN Mon-Fri midday-11pm,	GETTING LUCKY	**2/5**
Sat 6pm-1am	EYE CANDY	**2/5**
TUBE/RAIL Farringdon	BIG SPENDERS	**3/5**
BUSES 4, 55, 56, 505	MIX 60%M 40%F	
	AGE 20-40	
	PRICE Average	

AMBIENCE Basement, Brightly Coloured/Cheerful, Business, Buzzy, Casual, Live Music, Late Night Open
REVIEW Question: what do you do with an Asian/French menu and a reputation for showcasing feng shui design? Dump it, like every other London bar did three years ago. 19:20 have gone back to basics with a short modern British menu and allowed people to take it for what it is – a bright, vibrant venue bar, restaurant and pool venue. Think classic Irn Bru. Just like the fizzy drink – it's all about bright orange and steel girders (fortunately the food does not taste like steel girders). Padded walls are ideal for frustrated business folk to bang their heads against when deals fall through, plus orange tables and a peach wavy wall with mirrored portholes give them that away from it all feeling.
PLACE The large, bright orange pool room, which glows like a neon oasis in a desert of cool industrialism, is visible from the street, and has begun to lure Hoxton hustlers.
PEOPLE Clerkenwell tribes, laid-back chattering office types, chilled-out design creatives.

PROFS Printers, lawyers, account execs, media execs, film industry employees, accountants, shipping brokers, journalists
CELEBS Lisa Faulkner, Sir Bob Geldof, Alan McGee, Jools Holland, Brett Anderson, Björk, Mick Hucknall
DRESS Mostly neat and sometimes street. Thomas Pink, Cecil Gee, Carhartt and Firetrap with some Episode classics and Principles for the smarter women
MUSIC Modern Jazz, Latin, Live Jazz every Wednesday, DJs Thu-Fri
DOOR None
DRINKS Beer £2.70, Wine £2.70, Champagne £5.60, Cocktail £5.50
FOOD Modern British, Bar Snacks £8
CARDS No Diners
CAPACITY 150, seating 80
HIRE Venue: No · Private Room: No

THE BEAR

Gastropub
2 St John's Square EC1
020 7608 2117

OPEN Mon-Fri 11am-11pm	GETTING LUCKY	**2/5**
TUBE/RAIL Farringdon	EYE CANDY	**4/5**
BUSES 55, 243, 505	BIG SPENDERS	**4/5**
	MIX 50%M 50%F	
	AGE 27-50	
	PRICE Average	

AMBIENCE Comfy
REVIEW Hello, it's the 21st century calling. Blakes, a solid, if unremarkable pub, is hauled down and The Bear built in its place. The pub draws on Anytown, Euroville with fruit prints and Mediterranean theme. After a couple of pints you'll be hard pressed to tell which European city you're actually in. Although this makes the homeward journey after a long night more intellectually absorbing ('I know we're in Stuttgart, but I could've sworn I saw a London taxi'), it is likely to make you feel like you've spent the evening in a chain store.
PLACE The style is unrelentingly 90s – lots of glass, mirrors and subdued tones – except for an incongruous pile of old books. A stab at the ironic?
PEOPLE Almost exclusively peopled by office types on their lunch hour/way home or skiving off. Bosses flirt haplessly with secretaries whilst liquid lunches decide the fate of the nation (or at least Clerkenwell). A few lost freelancers from The Guardian.

PROFS Lawyers, stockbrokers, journalists, estate agents, designers, secretaries
CELEBS Anna Friel
DRESS Smart office clothes rule: trouser suits, skirt suits, white blouses, ties – no labels on show here, which would suggest that everyone's afraid of getting their D&G caught in the photocopier. Quite right, too
MUSIC Pop, Dance
DOOR None
DRINKS Beer £2.40, Wine £3.10
FOOD Bar Snacks, Mediterranean, £5
CARDS No Diners
CAPACITY 100, seating 40
HIRE Venue: Yes · Private Room: Yes

CAFÉ KICK

Bar
43 Exmouth Market EC1
020 7837 8077

OPEN Mon-Sat 11am-11pm,	**GETTING LUCKY**	**3/5**
Sun 11am-10.30pm	**EYE CANDY**	**2/5**
TUBE/RAIL Angel,	**BIG SPENDERS**	**3/5**
Farringdon	**MIX** 40%M 60%F	
BUSES 19, 38, 341	**AGE** 30-55	
	PRICE Average	

AMBIENCE Arty/Bohemian, Casual, Conversation, Groups, Outdoors, Sports, Student
REVIEW Crazy ideas, crazy guys. Babyfoot is the name of the game and if you can't kick it, there's no place for you in this Iberian table football café. Formica tables, second-hand junk shop chairs and scrubbed floors lend it the air of being the life and soul of a remote Spanish village. Although most floor space is given over to the beautiful game, Kick will also appeal to those whose hand/eye co-ordination has been developed with bottles of Bud rather than soccer balls. Customers are spoilt for choice with the bar's extensive range of Spanish, Portuguese, French and Belgian beers and spirits, as well as an eye-widening range of yucky continental soft drinks.
PLACE Romantic air of faded decay, wooden floors washed with the colours of national flags, two TVs (no cable or satellite as yet) showing international football coverage. Mixed groups swarming around the football tables do not disturb the more intimate Gallic feel around the cosy booths next to the main bar area.
PEOPLE They may look like overgrown student grants, but the secret is that they're all creatives and freelancers stopping off after a quick meeting with the record label people. Also a hit with slackers from the journalistic fraternity.

PROFS Journalists, graphic designers, artists, market stallholders, lawyers, bankers, students
CELEBS None
DRESS Urban sportswear, grungy Fair Isle jumpers, Euro dress minus the backpacks, student clobber
MUSIC Brazilian, Latino, Portuguese
DOOR None
DRINKS Beer £2.70, Wine £2.75, Cocktail £5
FOOD Mediterranean, £5
CARDS No Amex or Diners
CAPACITY 100, seating 30
HIRE Venue: Yes · Private Room: No

CAFÉ LAZEEZ

Bar, Restaurant
88 St John Street EC1
020 7253 2224

OPEN Mon-Fri 11am-	**GETTING LUCKY**	**2/5**
10.30pm, Sat 6pm-10.30pm	**EYE CANDY**	**2/5**
TUBE/RAIL Farringdon	**BIG SPENDERS**	**3/5**
BUSES 55	**MIX** 60%M 40%F	
	AGE 30-60	
	PRICE Average	

AMBIENCE Business, Children/Families, Conversation, Groups, Minimalist
REVIEW The first offshoot of the famous Knightsbridge Indian restaurant and bar is self-consciously minimalist throughout. Part of this can't be helped as the former paint factory is listed so the bricks and metalwork had to stay. The private room tucked off the bar is ideal for parties and the stunning, large back room/conservatory making for an interesting, yet often empty, socialising space.
PLACE Large, spartan, industrial chic interior which will make those living in Clerkenwell loft apartments feel at home. The rear conservatory space is architecturally gorgeous and lightens up what would otherwise be a dark interior.
PEOPLE Anything that works locally in a suit, particularly lawyers; also local photographers and genuine and immaculately dressed Indians (which always boosts cred). Younger crowd in the evening dress down a fraction and down Cobras at lightning pace.

PROFS City workers, lawyers, photographers, watchmakers, textiles magnates, solicitors, PAs
CELEBS None
DRESS Well-cut suits, saris, leather jackets
MUSIC No Background Music
DOOR Smart casual
DRINKS Beer £2.50, Champagne £6.90, Cocktail £5
FOOD Indian, £8
CARDS All
CAPACITY 200, seating 110
HIRE Venue: Yes · Private Room: Yes

CICADA

Bar, Restaurant
132-136 St John Street EC1
020 7608 1550

OPEN Mon-Fri midday-11pm,	**GETTING LUCKY**	**2/5**
Sat 6pm-11pm	**EYE CANDY**	**3/5**
TUBE/RAIL Farringdon	**BIG SPENDERS**	**3/5**
BUSES 55	**MIX** 60%M 40%F	
	AGE 25-40	
	PRICE Average	

AMBIENCE Casual, Conversation, Groups, Hip/Fashionable, Minimalist
REVIEW Cicada exudes a warm glow. It's earthy, natural and worn-in like a pair of soft leather Campers. It caters for all, champagne City boys and Chardonnay

businesswomen are overruled by a relaxed, loafing cool Clerkenwell contingent. Unisex trainer – combatters and anorak dudes hang out with delicate, fashion groupie girls. Flattering lighting, muted wall sconces, candlelight and an intimate, raised dining area with banquette seating is illuminated from below. Designed with tongue in cheek, check out the 'face wall' fireplace. It's Suzie Wong on opium with low antique furniture, oversized orange Chinese lanterns, wooden screens and leather low stools. Summer sees most idling outside on the pavement.
PLACE Rough 'n' ready designer half-diner with horseshoe bar to the centre. Parquet floor, slabs of soft brown leather on concrete for banquettes, low block timber and matching funky bar stools.
PEOPLE Laid-back lofties, People who make things with computers and read Dazed and Confused.

PROFS Clerkenwell creatives, publishers, editorial staff, graphic designers, advertising execs, solicitors, brokers, artists, fashion designers, photographers and a sprinkling of accountants
CELEBS Justin O, James Lavelle
DRESS Anything goes from chic to geek and back again. Keep it hip though and you'll be in with a chance with the boy who looks like he's stepped out of a Diesel ad
MUSIC Asian Lounge
DOOR None
DRINKS Beer £2.70, Wine £2.60, Champagne £5.80, Cocktail £5.50
FOOD South East Asian, £10
CARDS All
CAPACITY 220, seating 50
HIRE Venue: No · Private Room: Yes

CLERKENWELL HOUSE

Bar, Restaurant, Pool Bar
23-27 Hatton Wall EC1
020 7404 1113

OPEN Mon-Sat midday-11pm, Sun 1pm-10pm	GETTING LUCKY	1/5
	EYE CANDY	3/5
TUBE/RAIL Farringdon, Chancery Lane	BIG SPENDERS	2/5
	MIX 55%M 45%F	
BUSES 17, 55, 243	AGE 25-45	
	PRICE Average	

AMBIENCE Buzzy, Casual, Conversation, Retro
REVIEW At night the bar's blue neon façade floods an unassuming City side street with Close Encounters of the Third Kind light. However, the futuristic razzmatazz of the exterior has nothing to do with the interior's carelessly thrown together retro-chic. A jumbled arrangement of leather couches, modern art and 70s wallpaper creates perfect lounging conditions, with young professionals, new media types and tortured poets slumping over random pieces of furniture. A winding cast-iron staircase leads to what feels like the hippest youth club on the planet, with murals depicting scenes from classic American TV shows, purple-baized pool tables and scruffy boys and girls loitering with intent.
PLACE The loose, relaxed feel of a carelessly arranged house party without any of the mayhem. If anything, it is a little too relaxed for some, but great if you like your bars horizontal.

PEOPLE Not the proliferation of pool-crazy men you might expect. Instead, a pleasing amalgam of new cool, old-skool and straight-laced City drink and chat happily side by side.

PROFS New media, lawyers, business, locals, students
CELEBS Alexander McQueen, Mel from Big Brother
DRESS Anything you want
MUSIC Funk, Soul, Ambient, Jazz
DOOR No
DRINKS Beer £2.70, Wine £2.50
FOOD Mediterranean, £8
CARDS All
CAPACITY 500, seating 80
HIRE Venue: Yes · Private Room: No

DUST

Bar
27 Clerkenwell Road EC1
020 7490 5120

OPEN Mon-Wed midday-midnight, Thu midday-2am, Fri midday-2am, Sat 7.30pm-2am	GETTING LUCKY	2/5
	EYE CANDY	3/5
	BIG SPENDERS	3/5
	MIX 50%M 50%F	
TUBE/RAIL Farringdon	AGE 25-35	
BUSES 55, 243, 505	PRICE Average	

AMBIENCE Arty/Bohemian, Dancing, Late Night Open, Live Music
REVIEW The name's a reference to the tumbleweed that fills Clerkenwell after 6pm. But it's not so much 'dust' as 'ashes to ashes', as nearly everyone here smokes: 100 per cent of Dust smokers prefer Marlboro Lights above any other tobacco. Bring a super-reliable lighter as a pulling prop. This is a young, urban mooch verging on the arrogant but grounded enough to save each other. Very much a laid-back local for the Clerkie crew, workers and residents who are more bottled beer than Martini, and carry their bike saddles for security's sake. A few loungey sofas at the back for DJ groupies but most sit on plywood bar stools or at tables.
PLACE Bare and basic with exposed brickwork and floorboards. One long wooden banquette to the left and art-studio-style tables. The triple-height space at the end features a full-height copper back wall with windows exposing the 2nd-floor kitchen activities.
PEOPLE Meeja boys, the odd Rasta, East End blokes, elfinly hip alternative girls and the occasional smooth ad exec.

PROFS Photographers, shop assistants, designers, publishers, graphic designers, architects
CELEBS Pet Shop Boys, Damon Albarn, Janet Street-Porter, Kate Moss
DRESS Casual streetwear, vintage shirts, corduroy, Firetrap, Boxfresh
MUSIC Drum 'n' Bass, Hip Hop, House, Latin, Occasional live Jazz, DJs Fri-Sat
DOOR £3 after 10pm Fri-Sat
DRINKS Beer £2.60, Wine £3, Champagne £6, Cocktail £4.50
FOOD Mediterranean, Tapas, £6
CARDS All
CAPACITY 220, seating 60
HIRE Venue: Yes · Private Room: No

clerkenwell and farringdon

THE EAGLE

Gastropub, Pub
159 Farringdon Road EC1
020 7837 1353

OPEN Mon-Sat midday-11pm, Sun midday-5pm	**GETTING LUCKY** 1/5
	EYE CANDY 3/5
TUBE/RAIL Farringdon	**BIG SPENDERS** 3/5
BUSES 38, 63	**MIX** 60%M 40%F
	AGE 25-35
	PRICE Average

AMBIENCE Arty/Bohemian, Business, Buzzy, Casual, Conversation, Cosy, Network
REVIEW The Eagle is one of London's notorious media haunts, thanks to its proximity to the Guardian newspaper offices on Farringdon Road. Inevitably, it's slightly pretentious – there's a record player rather than those newfangled CDs – with a studied shabbiness that suits its chattering class clientele down to their Camper shoes. It can't seem to make up its mind whether it's a pub, wine bar or restaurant (people jostle each other to get to the front of the food queue, though) but that matters not a jot to the punters – they come here to trade media gossip and network. It's not a place to party or make new friends, but if you want to drink overpriced imported beer and talk bollocks about the Third World (sorry, darling, 'the developing world'), you'll be more than welcome.
PLACE An open plan pub conversion with simple, French-style decor; dark wood, blinds, overhead fans, huge colourful paintings and food cooked on a bloody great stove and grill range behind the bar.
PEOPLE Saffron has just finished a piece about the Native Americans' battle with alcohol in South Dakota. She abhors Nestle and is a fervent StopEsso campaigner.

PROFS Publishers, chemical engineers, journalists, artists, ITs, bankers, accountants, secretaries, photographers, designers – the usual self-appointed delegates of the chattering class
CELEBS Suggs, James Brown, Sean Hughes, Graham Coxon
DRESS Down to earth – these people would never spend a fortune on a designer item except for when they just have to have the latest Philippe Starck/micro-scooter/palm pilot
MUSIC World Music, Jazz, Funk, Spanish
DOOR None
DRINKS Beer £2.60, Wine £2.40, Champagne £4.50, Cocktail £4
FOOD Mediterranean, Modern European, £10
CARDS No Amex or Diners
CAPACITY 100, seating 60
HIRE Venue: No · Private Room: No

FABRIC

Club, Live Music Venue
121-123 Charterhouse Street EC1
020 7336 8898

OPEN Fri 10pm-5am, Sat 10pm-7am, Sun 10pm-5am	**GETTING LUCKY** 4/5
	EYE CANDY 3/5
TUBE/RAIL Farringdon	**BIG SPENDERS** 3/5
BUSES 17, 45, 46, 63	**MIX** 50%M 50%F
	AGE 20-30
	PRICE Average

AMBIENCE Cavernous, Dancing, Destination/Wishlist, Hip/Fashionable, Chin Stroking, Late Night Open, Mashed up, Warehouse/Industrial
REVIEW Unveiled to break in the noughties with a resounding beat, Fabric is perhaps the most excellently conceived amongst the new breed of 'serious' London dance clubs. From the ordered queuing systems to in-house taxi services for those worn by the groove, all club-kid comforts are in evidence. One of the world's best sound systems seduces the world's greatest turntablists: residents James Lavelle and Terry Francis are joined by big-name monthly guests including Paul Daly of Leftfield and progressive house man of the moment Lee Burridge. Friday's Fabric Live pursues a policy of booking up-and-coming acts. DTPM attracts the predominantly gay and glammed-up posse. Well-deserved of its numerous industry plaudits.
PLACE Victorian cold (wear your thermals, it really is) former slaughterhouse refashioned as a multi-level chrome and brickwork complex revolving round a central staircase. The unisex loos become predictably chaotic as the night's shenanigans progress.
PEOPLE Parka-clad, work-shy creatives, clubbed-to-death excitable Northerners and a smattering of ironic mullets. People for whom music is not a laughing matter. Overheard: 'I keep meanin' to get a job but I keep, like, getting way too wrecked...'

PROFS Students, musicians, DJs, PRs, journalists, retail staff, postmen, models, electricians. With a 1500 capacity, quite a good mix
CELEBS Julien Macdonald, Noel Gallagher, Howard Marks
DRESS Trainers du jour and Vexed Generation for Friday's Fabric Live; Slick house cats and the odd shiny shirt in evidence on Saturdays
MUSIC Breakbeat, Progressive House, Drum'n'Bass
DOOR Fri £10-12, Sat £12-15, Sun £9-13
DRINKS Beer £2.50, Wine £3.50, Champagne £7
FOOD None
CARDS No Amex or Diners
CAPACITY 1500
HIRE Venue: Yes · Private Room: Yes

FLUID

Bar, Club
40 Charterhouse Street EC1
020 7253 3444

OPEN Mon-Wed midday-midnight, Thu-Fri midday-2am, Sat 7pm-2am, Sun midday-6pm	**GETTING LUCKY**	**4/5**
	EYE CANDY	**3/5**
	BIG SPENDERS	**2/5**
TUBE/RAIL Farringdon, Barbican	**MIX** 60%M 40%F	
	AGE 22-35	
BUSES 17, 45, 46, 63	**PRICE** Average	

AMBIENCE Basement, Casual, Cute Staff, Dancing, Futuristic, Groups, Late Night Open, Live Music, Minimalist, Party, Student, Warehouse/Industrial
REVIEW Tucked away but doing okay with a club-cult following, especially since Fabric opened round the corner. After a morning of no-holds-barred hedonism at Trade, this place becomes a major pulling paradise for the boys on a Sunday afternoon. Hardcore. Otherwise it's a young, straight, studenty and creative crew hanging out and playing at DJing. Go for cheap sushi, to play pinball or Space Invaders, or to pull the staff who are usually pretty fine. The music generally dissuades suits from staying late, and it's ideal for clubby kids reminiscing about their Chopper/Grifter/BMX while supping on bottled beers. Busiest Thu-Sun, and if you can recall that 80s classic, 'Hey Mickey you're so fine, you're so fine you blow my mind' and understand the old skool humour in playing it – come and dig your scene.
PLACE All futuristic Japanese-inspired graphics, set on two floors. The ground floor has typical EC1 exposed ducting and a silver minimal, industrial-metallic look with a few plants to soften the edges. Basic basement for clubbing.
PEOPLE Art students, people that make stuff, fashion-gadget Japanese, Clerkenwell locals, musos, The Scene, i-D and SleazeNation readers.

PROFS Fashion and music execs, art students, students, DJs, web designers, photographers, graphic designers, journalists
CELEBS Ewan McGregor, Zoë Ball
DRESS Urban ruffians, Ted Baker, Diesel, Sharp-Eye, Adidas Old Skool, Boxfresh, Nike, Duffer, DKNY, Calvin Klein, Levi's, O'Neill, Stüssy and Converse. Tarts not looked upon kindly
MUSIC Breakbeat, Funk, Hip Hop, House, Jazz, Reggae, Soul, Deep House, Tech House, Techno, Live Hip Hop, DJs Thu-Sun
DOOR Fri-Sat £3 after 10pm
DRINKS Beer £2.40, Wine £2.70, Cocktail £5
FOOD Japanese, Sushi, £8
CARDS All
CAPACITY 220, seating 90
HIRE Venue: Yes · Private Room: Yes

JACOMOS

Bar, Gay
88-89 Cowcross Street EC1
020 7553 7641

OPEN Mon-Fri Midday-11pm	**GETTING LUCKY**	**1/5**
TUBE/RAIL Farringdon	**EYE CANDY**	**1/5**
BUSES 63, 243	**BIG SPENDERS**	**2/5**
	MIX 50%M 50%F	
	AGE 18-40	
	PRICE Average	

AMBIENCE Dancing, Groups
REVIEW Take the elements of the bar separately, and you have a sure-fire success. It's a bar. It's in one of the trendiest areas of London. It's gay. What could possibly go wrong? From the outside it looks like it should be called the Ritzy or Rio's and located in Middlesborough, a facade it bravely maintains inside. It's almost certainly the straightest gay bar in London, with ugly blokes and miniskirted harridans snogging like sixth-formers. Add to that the presence of four lads who can't take their drink and their buck-toothed birds, all of whom are compelled to jump on every item of furniture, bare their flesh, and 'dance' to Louise songs, and you have the answer. Jacomos closes at 11pm. Thank God.
PLACE It's not that it's too tacky, nor that it's too bare, nor indeed that it looks revolting, it's just so under-imagined that it's become a nothing-place and if it were to disappear totally then nobody would really notice. Like Middlesborough.
PEOPLE Don't start.

PROFS Investment bankers
CELEBS Toyah Wilcox came here once
DRESS Boyz in tight tops. Birdz in tight tops
MUSIC Easy Listening, Pop, Dance
DOOR None
DRINKS Beer £3, Wine £2.75
FOOD Bar Snacks, £3.50
CARDS No Amex or Diners
CAPACITY 120, seating 70
HIRE Venue: Yes · Private Room: No

MATCH EC1

Bar, Cocktail Bar, Restaurant
45-47 Clerkenwell Road EC1
020 7250 4002

OPEN Mon-Fri 11am-midnight, Sat 5pm-midnight	**GETTING LUCKY**	**3/5**
	EYE CANDY	**3/5**
TUBE/RAIL Farringdon	**BIG SPENDERS**	**3/5**
BUSES 55, 243, 505	**MIX** 50%M 50%F	
	AGE 24-40	
	PRICE Average	

AMBIENCE Buzzy, Casual, Funky, Futuristic, Groups, Hip/Fashionable, Late Night Open, Lounge
REVIEW Match has come a long way since opening in 1998, thrust ever forward into the award-winning limelight by unstoppable owner, ex-solicitor Jonathan Downey and his business partner, the cocktail maestro Dick Bradsell. They have bought professional bar service, cocktails and well-made drinks to the masses. This is the original Match and it's pleasant enough. Hearty fuel food joins the array of cocktails that range from classics to the Matchnificent Seven, a list named after cool guys like Steve McQueen and James Coburn. There's even a cocktail devised by a Match bartender and named after Downey's daughter, 'the lady baby jesus'. Roadside tables are available for summer

pollution. Sparsely populated, busier on Thursdays and Fridays, attracting a steady stream of regulars at lunch and early evening. Music has improved somewhat from the early days, watch out for the Match CDs.
PLACE Loungey, warm and lazy. The entry level forms an L-shaped mezzanine overlooking the lower barpit; there are three horseshoe banquettes and some beaten-up leather sofas for lounging on the upper level. During summer the entire frontage opens up for roadside drinking.
PEOPLE 'Who do you know in your neighbourhood, in your neighbourhood, in your neigh-bour-hood?' A broad EC1 mix; think straight office crew, a few hyper-cybercoolies and far-out artistes. Lofty couples, some rowdy male solicitors, foursomes dining, a gaggle of girlies and a trio of ponytailed lairy lads.

PROFS Media employees, account execs, solicitors, art gallery staff, shop assistants, secretaries, photographers, printers, accountants, estate agents
CELEBS Massive Attack, Richard Bacon, Mitch Johnson
DRESS River Island, Hawaiian shirts, Combats, Levi's, Camper, Warehouse, Calvin Klein, Nike, TopMan, FCUK, Hysteric Glamour
MUSIC Funk, Garage, Jazz, Soul, Live Funk, Garage, Jazz, Soul
DOOR None
DRINKS Beer £2.85, Wine £3.50, Champagne £6, Cocktail £6
FOOD Modern European, British, £8
CARDS No Diners
CAPACITY 200, seating 60
HIRE Venue: Yes · Private Room: No

MINT 182

Bar, Cocktail Bar, Restaurant
182-186 St John Street EC1
020 7253 8368

OPEN Mon-Tue midday-11pm, Wed-Fri midday-midnight, Sat 6pm-midnight	**GETTING LUCKY**	**1/5**
	EYE CANDY	**5/5**
	BIG SPENDERS	**3/5**
TUBE/RAIL Farringdon	**MIX** 50%M 50%F	
BUSES 153	**AGE** 25-35	
	PRICE Average	

AMBIENCE Casual, Children/Families, Groups, Hip/Fashionable, Late Night Open, Live Music
REVIEW Dust, Match, Mint. Clerkenwell has a whole list of venues whose terse names complement the miniature size of their interiors. Size does matter, but in this case it's all about being small. Graphic designers work out of tiny modern Clerkenwell one-room offices whose most distinguishing feature is that you reach them by twirling metal staircases. And graphic designers, youngish, well-dressed and reasonably sexy are Mint's patrons. Every building oozes loft-conversion potential, so Mint offers an equally light room for its clientele. Plus there are the tensile metal balconies that divide the eating area from the less salubrious bar. It's aimed at rich, trendy locals and, judging by the way it looks, it won't have to try very hard to please.
PLACE A small, compact venue that concentrates its efforts into a large bar area, squeezing banquettes for eating on a raised area. Downstairs there's a bar with a glass waterfall and bamboo feng-shui (yawn) area.
PEOPLE Youngish designers with sticky-up hair, the odd metal piercing and combat trousers.

PROFS Graphic designers, designers, bankers, businesspeople
CELEBS Kate Moss, Chris Evans, Chris Cleverley, S Club 7
DRESS Duffer, Firetrap T-Shirts, Camper shoes
MUSIC Jazz, Garage, Dance, Pop
DOOR None
DRINKS Beer £2.60, Wine £3, Champagne £6, Cocktail £5
FOOD Asian, Modern European, £10
CARDS All
CAPACITY 120, seating 32
HIRE Venue: Yes · Private Room: Yes

THE PEASANT

Gastropub
240 St John Street EC1
020 7336 7726

OPEN Mon-Fri midday-11pm, Sat 6pm-11pm	**GETTING LUCKY**	**3/5**
	EYE CANDY	**4/5**
TUBE/RAIL Farringdon, Angel	**BIG SPENDERS**	**3/5**
	MIX 50%M 50%F	
BUSES 153	**AGE** 28-38	
	PRICE Average	

AMBIENCE Casual, Chilled, Conversation, Groups, Student
REVIEW The Peasant's notoriety stems primarily from its acclaimed Mediterranean menu, popular since this place was first lovingly turned into a relaxed gastropub. Good though the food is, it's still a venue for unadulterated drinking. A former gin den, The Peasant retains a palatial air and the atmosphere strikes a good balance between cool and convivial: chilled enough to lose the pretentiousness other Clerkie institutions seem to pride themselves upon and sophisticated enough for that all

important first date. Due to proximity with City University and Sadler's Wells, there's a steady stream of almost stereotypically suave young Islingtonians.
PLACE Restored mosaic floor, turquoise exterior and ceiling, large wood-framed mirrors and Aero-style silver lampshades.
PEOPLE Arty, crop-haired bright young things and strappy-sandal-wearing girls who're tired of fad bars but enjoy dressing up a little.

PROFS Bankers, brokers, solicitors, IT consultants, theatre staff, students
CELEBS None
DRESS Diesel, Hope and Glory, Paul Smith
MUSIC Jazz, Pop, Latin, Soul, Reggae
DOOR None
DRINKS Beer £2.70, Wine £2.60, Champagne £6,
Cocktail £5
FOOD Mediterranean, £11.50
CARDS All
CAPACITY 140, seating 120
HIRE Venue: Yes · Private Room: Yes

POTEMKIN

Restaurant, Bar
144 Clerkenwell Road EC1
020 7278 6661

OPEN Mon-Fri midday-	GETTING LUCKY	3/5
midnight, Sat 6pm-midnight	EYE CANDY	3/5
TUBE/RAIL Farringdon,	BIG SPENDERS	3/5
Chancery Lane	MIX 45%M 55%F	
BUSES 55, 243	AGE 25-40	
	PRICE Average	

AMBIENCE Conversation, Late Night Open, Minimalist
REVIEW Vodka: it's Russian for 'water' and English for 'Aargh! Aargh! My bloody mouth's on fire!' Leaving aside the professional purists who blather on for hours about premium distillation techniques, it's fair to say that we're a nation of tonic-adders. If you've ever wondered why some people get so fired up about the difference between blue, black and red brands – or if you just want to get laughably drunk in under 20 minutes – then head for Potemkin. There are over 130 brands to sample, from the smooth-smooth house Cristall Superlux to oddities such as cannabis, rose petal and St John's Wort flavours. Drinks are served as 25ml singles or – gulp – 100ml measures. Best of all, the friendly, unpretentious staff won't laugh when your legs stop carrying you to the places you want to go.
PLACE Cool, clear design, softened by tactile wooden tables and warm brown leather banquettes and a vase of dried twigs.
PEOPLE Russians may drink vodka before, during and after every meal, but frankly they're used to it. Sit at the bar and watch the cool, collected professional types who've come for dinner get riotously drunk over a pre-meal tipple.

PROFS Media, IT, advertising, accountancy
CELEBS Pet Shop Boys, Ralph Fiennes
DRESS Smart but simple, plenty of black and white
MUSIC Chill-out, Ambient
DOOR None

DRINKS Beer £2.75, Wine £2.50, Champagne £6.50,
Cocktail £5
FOOD Russian, £12
CARDS All
CAPACITY 50, seating 34
HIRE Venue: Yes · Private Room: Yes

SMITHS OF SMITHFIELD

Bar, Cocktail Bar, Restaurant
67-77 Charterhouse Street EC1
020 7236 6666

OPEN Mon-Fri 7am-11pm,	GETTING LUCKY	2/5
Sat 10.30am-11pm,	EYE CANDY	3/5
Sun 10.30am-10.30pm	BIG SPENDERS	4/5
TUBE/RAIL Farringdon,	MIX 60%M 40%F	
Barbican	AGE 25-65	
BUSES 17, 45, 46, 63	PRICE Average	

AMBIENCE Business, Buzzy, Gourmet/Foodie, Groups, Hip/Fashionable, Views, Warehouse/Industrial
REVIEW You'd think it was pretty obvious why a restaurant specialising in all things carnivorous would want to open next to Smithfield meat market. Suits and their girls feel safe in this establishment as it's obviously geared towards them, which is good because when it's not sell, sell, sell, it's me, me, me. The ground floor is a kind of All Bar-Pitcher-Lettuce venture, ie chalk blackboards and empty space just waiting to be filled with Pinks and Richard James. However, upstairs is a much more flash champagne lounge in which to woo the laydeez. Rumour has it that if you peek between the red velvet curtains that surround the room you'll find Bob and a dancing dwarf.
PLACE A four-level brownstone block conversion: loud ground-floor bar with refectory tables and benches; sexy red leather cocktail bar; more keenly priced brasserie and top-floor restaurant with huge windows and terrace.
PEOPLE Scantily-clad women with floppy-haired City boys in the cocktail bar and 3rd-floor brasserie while real high rollers dine on the top floor.

PROFS Bankers, solicitors, designers
CELEBS Ewan McGregor, Ronnie Wood, Guy Ritchie, Jamie Oliver
DRESS Feather boas and high heels, black body warmers and FCUK t-shirts, Savile Row suits
MUSIC Hip Hop, Funk, Rare Groove, Breakbeat, Jazz, Dance, House, DJs Mon-Sun
DOOR None

DRINKS Beer £2.75, Wine £2.75, Champagne £5.75, Cocktail £5.50
FOOD Traditional British, £4
CARDS All
CAPACITY 300, seating 100
HIRE Venue: Yes · Private Room: Yes

ST JOHN

Bar, Restaurant
26 St John Street EC1
020 7251 0848

OPEN Mon-Fri 11am-11pm, Sat 6pm-11pm	**GETTING LUCKY**	**1/5**
TUBE/RAIL Farringdon	**EYE CANDY**	**3/5**
BUSES 153	**BIG SPENDERS**	**3/5**
	MIX 50%M 50%F	
	AGE 30-40	
	PRICE Average	

AMBIENCE Arty/Bohemian, Buzzy, Casual, Conversation, Minimalist, Star Spotting
REVIEW A former smokehouse which has been converted by painting everything white into a bar-cum-restaurant-cum-bakery. Deliberately little has been done to mask the original use of the premises or to prettify the interior: no music, no art, no candles. The distinctly mixed clientele hankering over the tables around the busy bar provides a snapshot of Clerkenwell in transition: office workers on the way home, young lovers down from their loft apartments and full-on meeja types with designer glasses towing artists in the wake of their expense accounts. There is little interaction between the small groups despite the fairly cramped space available. Wear sturdy shoes – some pretty heavy names are dropped here.
PLACE So minimal and unaffected that it just had to grab the Brit art crew. Because I've had enough of this up-yer-arse bollocks. Junowataimeeen.
PEOPLE A combination of Joe and Joette Normal in transit from job to train and multi-media glitterati preparing to chow down in the separate dining-room.

PROFS Graphic designers, writers, journalists, artists, architects, writers, luvvies
CELEBS Sam Neil, Ralph Fiennes, Sir Elton John, Janet Street-Porter, Terry Gilliam, David Bowie, David Hockney, Damien Hirst, Luella Bartley,

Anthony Bourdain, Jarvis Cocker, Tracey Emin, Sam Tatler-Wood, Michael Clarke, Sarah Lucas
DRESS FCUK, Gap, Adidas Trainers and mostly designer wear during the evening. More artists than you can shake a suckling pig at. Come as you are, as you were, or as you want. From River Island work suits to dungarees
MUSIC None
DOOR None
DRINKS Beer £2.60, Wine £2.50, Champagne £6, Cocktail £5.50
FOOD Modern British, £7
CARDS All
CAPACITY 100, seating 40
HIRE Venue: Yes · Private Room: Yes

TURNMILLS

Club
63b Clerkenwell Rd EC1
020 7250 3409

OPEN Tue 6.30pm-midnight, Fri 10.30pm-7.30pm, Sat 10pm-5am, Sun 4am-1pm	**GETTING LUCKY**	**3/5**
	EYE CANDY	**2/5**
	BIG SPENDERS	**3/5**
TUBE/RAIL Farringdon	**MIX** 60%M 40%F	
BUSES 55, 243, 505	**AGE** 20-35	
	PRICE Average	

AMBIENCE Dancing, Hormone-Fuelled Club Kidz, Industrial/Warehouse, Late Night Open, Luvved Up, Mashed Up
REVIEW Once the epitome of 'avin-it-large clubbing suave for London's disaffected, beat-infected youth, Turnmills met its nemesis in leaner, meaner (and substantially cleaner) cousin Fabric. But like that greying pair of y-Fronts you'd never cast aside for slicker, arse-itching synthetics, Turnmills retains a place in every clubkid's heart. Those who rant about such things (usually after a little too much of the enlivening stuff) reckon that Turnmills has the most 'northern' vibe amongst the capital's night-spots. But the connotations of white-skirted lovelies dancing with side-parted beaus to an 'Everything But the Girl' remix 6785 is too misleading. Turnmills is merely proof that London's clubbing cognoscenti shouldn't be indiscriminately lumbered with the pouting misery tag.
PLACE A decade ago Turnmill's decor was the best thing since MDMA, but now it feels almost quaint. Plenty of seating in discreet alcoves for tired legs and canoodlers drinking their student loans dry.
PEOPLE A friendly bunch of up-for-its restore your faith in the inherent blinking niceness of humanity at Turnmills on a weekly basis.

PROFS Students, promoters, retail staff, the disaffected
CELEBS EastEnders cast, David Furnish, Chemical Brothers
DRESS Trainers, t-shirts, just don't dress up
MUSIC House, Garage, Techno – you name a dance music sub-genre – they'll play it
DOOR Varies, £6-15
DRINKS Beer £3, Wine £2.50, Cocktail £5
FOOD None
CARDS Cash Only
CAPACITY 1000, seating 250
HIRE Venue: Yes · Private Room: Yes

VIC NAYLOR'S BAR & GRILL

Bar, Restaurant
38-40 St John Street EC1
020 7608 2181

OPEN Mon-Wed midday-midnight, Thu-Sat midday-1am	**GETTING LUCKY**	2/5
	EYE CANDY	3/5
	BIG SPENDERS	3/5
TUBE/RAIL Farringdon	**MIX** 55%M 45%F	
BUSES 55, 152, 243	**AGE** 28-45	
	PRICE Average	

AMBIENCE Casual, Conversation, Groups, Late Night Open
REVIEW One of Farringdon's original bars as seen in 'Lock Stock and Two Smoking Barrels'. This does its best trade in the winter. Probably because it feels like New Orleans with its timber shutters, long bar, neon signs in the window, distressed brickwork and heavily lacquered wood. Frequented by surrounding office workers and more of the 30-something financial and legal smart suits than the young, hip creatives who probably prefer Cicada or Dust. Bartop accoutrements included the 8210 resting on the Psion and a fiver floating around casually unclaimed. Residents pop by and ask staff whether friends have been in. This is a bar where they'd know your face and your drink after a few visits. You'll probably end up eating too, as fat juicy sausages and mash are whisked past from the dumb waiter behind the bar to waiting tables. Ideal winter comfort zone.
PLACE Vic's has taken over the next-door property with its eight leather booths. It's the kind of amiable place that has tried to keep up with the Farringdon scene but still remains more akin to Cheers (the sitcom, not the rank Leicester Square rip-off joint).
PEOPLE Clerkies and Farringdon sensible professionals.

PROFS Lawyers, marketing execs, designers, solicitors, journalists
CELEBS Elton John, Janet Street-Porter, Pet Shop Boys, Tracey Emin, Sam Taylor Wood
DRESS Straight from the office, shirts and ties and some trainer trendies with wallet-chains
MUSIC Disco, House, Hip Hop, DJs Fri-Sat
DOOR None
DRINKS Beer £3, Wine £3, Champagne £7, Cocktail £6
FOOD Traditional English, Bar Snacks £8
CARDS No Diners
CAPACITY 200, seating 50
HIRE Venue: Yes · Private Room: No

THE WELL

Bar, Restaurant
180 St John Street EC1
020 7251 9363

OPEN 7 days 11am-11pm	**GETTING LUCKY**	1/5
TUBE/RAIL Farringdon	**EYE CANDY**	2/5
BUSES 55, 153, 243	**BIG SPENDERS**	3/5
	MIX 65%M 45%F	
	AGE 25-45	
	PRICE Average	

AMBIENCE Buzzy, Comfy, Cosy, Friendly
REVIEW The Well is aptly named. Why? Well, judging by

the amount of 'reserved' signs sitting on the distressed-wood tables it must do extremely, er, well. And why shouldn't it? It's owned by a pair of one-time City boys, so failure's just not an option. It's definitely more restaurant than bar – a fact made abundantly clear by the hyperactive, klaxon-voiced staff who, come late afternoon (and with scant regard for lunchtime hangers-on), busy themselves playing with various evening table configurations. Downstairs, leather banquettes house guffawing ladies who sit sniggering as Flavio lookalikes fail to locate the bog and then pretend to be fixated by the somewhat superfluous tropical fishtanks. Poor things; stuck in there all day with bugger all else to do – the women, not the fish.
PLACE Pleasant corner bar with huge, floor to ceiling windows. Chrome beer pumps and coffee machines combined with exposed brick walls and distressed old furniture to create a kind of modern/rustic feel.
The basement is a bit of a claustrophobic affair lightened by the aforementioned aquariums. Not really an evening kinda place unless, like everyone else, you're eating.
PEOPLE Clerkenwell creatives who pretend they can tell the difference between Heineken and Staropramen, account managers who love a bit of pretentious pub grub, ex-City boys done good, hungry locals and poncey EC1 foodies.

PROFS Advertising, sales
CELEBS None, unless you call journalists celebrities
DRESS Straight out of work, which round these parts can mean anything
MUSIC Dance, Latin, DJs Fri-Sat
DOOR None
DRINKS Beer £2.70, Wine £2.50, Champagne £6, Cocktail £5
FOOD Modern European, £10
CARDS All
CAPACITY 150, seating 100
HIRE Venue: Yes · Private Room: No

south bank

BALTIC

Bar, Restaurant
74 Blackfriars Road SE1
020 7928 1111

OPEN Mon-Sat 11am-11pm, Sun 11am-10.30pm
TUBE/RAIL Southwark
BUSES 344, 381

GETTING LUCKY	**1/5**
EYE CANDY	**3/5**
BIG SPENDERS	**3/5**
MIX 45%M 55%F	
AGE 25-60	
PRICE Average	

AMBIENCE Conversation, Historic, Old World, Romantic
REVIEW John 'Wodka' Woroniecki's Eastern European restaurant and bar was a long time coming. Flickering candlelight and jazz music give the somewhat stark and narrow bar a warm and sophisticated feel. This is the place to down Baltic's naturally infused vodkas, stored in large vats behind the counter; flavours range from Karmelowka (caramel) to Gingrowka (ginger) and even Koperkowa (dill). Attracting the attention of the Polish bar staff's about as easy as finding a parasol on the Steppe; they may see you but 'hey, what's the rush?' Situated just a stone's throw away from Tate Modern, Baltic attracts a thespian, cultured-looking lot; apparently SE1 is a pink pound mecca. One guy in a shawl effortlessly carried off that terribly chic Claire Rayner meets Oscar Wilde look.
PLACE Slender, candlelit vodka bar, with illuminated amber panel detailing at each end, leads through to lofty restaurant offering Eastern European fare in a former 18th-century coach-builder's barn.
PEOPLE Middle-aged middle-class couples, flirty thirties, Guardian reading, jazz loving, theatre-going Southwark locals, plus a few Suits early evening.

PROFS Actors, academics, choreographers, Tate employees
CELEBS Joanna Lumley
DRESS Spotted: two unconnected guys in numbered t-shirts, coincidentally '27' and '72'; weird. Monsoon, Levi's, Hugo Boss, Jigsaw, Uth
MUSIC Jazz
DOOR None
DRINKS Beer £2.75, Wine £2.60, Champagne £5.75, Cocktail £4.50
FOOD Polish, £5
CARDS All
CAPACITY 150, seating 90
HIRE Venue: Yes · Private Room: Yes

LE PONT DE LA TOUR

Bar, Restaurant
36d Shad Thames, Butler's Wharf SE1
020 7234 3651

OPEN 7 days 11.30am-11pm
TUBE/RAIL London Bridge, Tower Hill
BUSES 47, 381

GETTING LUCKY	**2/5**
EYE CANDY	**3/5**
BIG SPENDERS	**5/5**
MIX 60%M 40%F	
AGE 25-50	
PRICE Expensive	

AMBIENCE Business, Conversation, Elegant/Classic, Jet Set, Outdoors, Romantic, Star Spotting, Views
REVIEW Tony and Cherie chose Le Pont de la Tour to entertain Bill and Hillary in an 'unofficial' foursome. That should give you a pretty good idea of what this restaurant and bar is all about. Providing reliable, and by now trademark, Conran food, design and service, it's the kind of place which fits middle-aged 'We're still hip' hopefuls best. A pianist crooning 'My Way' will often get the whole bar joining in, and cashmere-clad couples go home stuffed with oysters and champagne, feeling chuffed that they still have it in them to sing along.
PLACE This is the understated and elegant side of Conran that you never see in his gastro-empire's other venues. It even has a romantic bent to it, with wide-angle views of the Thames and Tower Bridge.
PEOPLE New Labour, residents starved of decent watering holes and City folk crossing the bridge during the week.

PROFS Media professionals, design buffs, popstars, politicians, City movers and shakers
CELEBS Sir Terence Conran, Lady Caroline Conran, Tony Blair, Cherie Blair, Bill Clinton, Hillary Clinton, Michelle Collins, Pierce Brosnan, Vic Reeves, Sir Michael Caine, Jack Dee, Rio Ferdinand, Sol Campbell, Andie Macdowell, Renee Zellweger, Geri Halliwell, Michael Barrymore
DRESS The powerful meet the power dressers and power suits — only trainers are of the personal variety
MUSIC Jazz Pianist Mon-Sat, Sun Lunch
DOOR Smart casual
DRINKS Beer £3.25, Wine £3.95, Champagne £6.95, Cocktail £6.50
FOOD French, Mediterranean, Modern European, Seafood, £17
CARDS All
CAPACITY 100, seating 40
HIRE Venue: No · Private Room: Yes

OXO TOWER

Bar, Brasserie, Restaurant
8th Floor, Oxo Tower Wharf, Bargehouse Street SE1
020 7803 3888

OPEN Mon-Sat 11am-11pm,	**GETTING LUCKY**	**2/5**
Sun midday-10.30pm	**EYE CANDY**	**3/5**
TUBE/RAIL Waterloo,	**BIG SPENDERS**	**4/5**
Blackfriars, Southwark	**MIX** 50%M 50%F	
BUSES 45, 63, 100, 381	**AGE** 30-60	
	PRICE Expensive	

AMBIENCE Business, Conversation, Jet Set, Live Music, Romantic, Views
REVIEW 'Oh, I've just decided what we should have – a Cosmo,' said one shoulder-padded, coiffeured middle-aged woman to her identikit friend. 'Two Seabreezes, Absolut yah,' ordered the floppy hair gent. 'If it's any consolation I lost £200 at Charles Chesters last week,' boomed the trader as he entered. Bonfire of the Vanities eat your Tiffany heart out. Look out for the diamanté initial on the heel of those Gucci loafers and that's just the boys. Here cufflink City is matched by shiny cleavages and drag superstrength lipliner. High-profile visibility is unavoidable due to the wonderful abundance of natural light. The old ivories tinkle later as the sun sets, sky darkens and the boys get bolder, especially on the alfresco viewing gallery which is standing room only.
PLACE An English oak-floored goldfish tank with vast glass front and back. The wide blue leather bar shelf is great to lean on and matches the blue designer Eames chairs. Best London cityscape.
PEOPLE A smooth 'n' easy ebb and flow of diners (mainly couples), meeting for pre-dinner drinks, plus the odd tourist – either style-literate Italians or wealthy Asian/American moneymen. More relaxed crowd at weekends.

PROFS Bankers, television producers, arts administrators, publishing execs, lawyers, media execs, accountants, marketing execs, PR execs, managers, chairpeople
CELEBS Naomi Campbell, Anna Friel, Natalie Imbruglia, Tony Blair, Bruce Willis, David and Victoria Beckham, Catherine Zeta-Jones, Liz Hurley, Richard Madeley,

Judy Finnegan, Denise van Outen, Sophie Dahl, Sir Bob Geldof, Laurent Garnier, David Blunkett
DRESS Conventional suits – not pinstriped, but smart modern executive style, mostly black and brown, DKNY, Louis Vuitton, Gucci, Valentino, Chanel
MUSIC Jazz, Blues, Latin, Soul, Ambient, Live Jazz, Blues Mon-Fri 7pm-11.30pm, Sun 7.30pm-10pm
DOOR Smart casual
DRINKS Beer £3.35, Wine £3.60, Champagne £7.50, Cocktail £7.50
FOOD Japanese, Italian, Bar Snacks, £7
CARDS All
CAPACITY 80, seating 28
HIRE Venue: No · Private Room: No

STUDIO SIX

Bar, Restaurant
Gabriel's Wharf, 56 Upper Ground SE1
020 7928 6243

OPEN Mon-Sat midday-11pm	**GETTING LUCKY**	**3/5**
Sun midday-10.30pm	**EYE CANDY**	**4/5**
TUBE/RAIL Waterloo	**BIG SPENDERS**	**3/5**
BUSES 1, 68, 168, 171,	**MIX** 60%M 40%F	
172, 176	**AGE** 20-40	
	PRICE Average	

AMBIENCE Conversation, Groups, Outdoors
REVIEW A stockbroker's suicide leap away from the expense account atmosphere of the Oxo Tower's corporate view. Gabriel's Wharf is where the more laid-back beautiful people come to relax on a summer evening over a pint or two of Hoegaarden and some homemade chips. The bracing air swishing off the Thames, the heady fumes of money drifting over from the City, and all those arty vibes emanating from the Tate Modern and Globe Theatre – it's all the headiness of the capital at once... or maybe that's just the Belgian beer talking. It's not overpriced and, anyway, what you're paying for here is location, location, and intoxication.
PLACE Rather like a country summerhouse or boathouse, with the sort of wooden-framed all-round windows that women in Chekhov plays like to gaze existentially out from.
PEOPLE After Zac and Greg's internet company crashed they realised London had become stale, so spent the summer in South East Asia. They now run a lifestyle management consultancy in Hammersmith.

PROFS Theatre staff, newscasters, ITs, journalists, American and Canadian tourists, TV producers, actors, newscasters, journalists, computer analysts, engineers, publishers, stockbrokers
CELEBS Jonathan Ross, Richard Madeley, Judy Finnegan, Emma Bunton, Chris Evans, Billie Piper, Ant & Dec, Cat Deeley, Jack Nicholson
DRESS Next suits, Hobbs straight-laced dresses, FCUK, Moss Bros, Whistles
MUSIC Latin, House, Jazz
DOOR Smart casual
DRINKS Beer £2.60, Wine £2.50
FOOD Continental, £8
CARDS All
CAPACITY 150, seating 60
HIRE Venue: Yes · Private Room: No

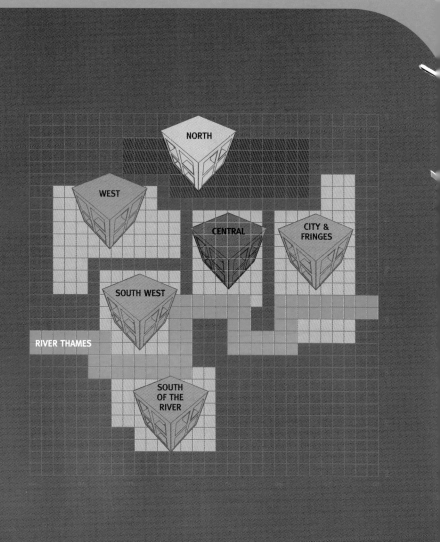

METRO

intro

camden
chalk farm
hampstead
hoxton/shoreditch
islington
primrose hill

Once the butt of London and the butt of too many jibes, North London has in recent years emerged shining – like Kylie standing up in a mudbath. It's home to three glossy urban villages, possibly the most famous market in the world and the birthplace of Brit-Art. North London, don't you just love it?

First came the artists, then the art galleries, then the obscure boutiques and bars and the Hoxton and Shoreditch scene was born. **333** and the **Bricklayers Arms** led the way, but it was soon cranked up a notch with the **Great Eastern Dining Rooms** and the **Electricity Showrooms**. As more and more money pumped into the area, impoverished artists have packed up their rubbish to make way for swish new arrivals **Pool Bar**, **Sosho** (from the Match stable), **The Light** and **Cargo**. No longer the centre of cutting-edge cool, this is where dirty denim'd girls and boys talk art installations, wonky haircuts and expensive foreign beer. Bring your wad, there isn't a cashpoint for miles. Heard it all before? Look out for Hoxton, the movie, starring Jake and Dinos Chapman, Alexander McQueen and Julia Roberts.

Just next door is Islington, home to the chattering classes and enough luvvies to cast an entire Christmas panto. The explosion of Tony Blair, New Labour and the meeja darlings upon the national conscience brought a lick of paint and a whole new rash of bars to Upper Street and its leafy environs. Now the area is something of a chain-bar-u-like, but **Embassy**, **The Elbow Rooms**, **Medicine Bar** and **The Social** stand out.

Camden, like Glastonbury but without the mud, is the home of second-hand jeans and leather emporia, tramps, tourists and the baggiest and skinniest trousers known to man. In recent years the area round the station has become one of the most depressing spots in London, crawling with crackheads, pissheads, Goths

and herbal vendors. Avoid the pubs near the tube and High Street and head further afield. Inverness Street is home to quirky favourites **Bar Gansa** and **Bar Vinyl** and new kid **Singapore Sling** while funky pubs like the **Camden Brewing Co.**, **Mac Bar** and **The Lord Stanley** are luring drinkers away from the main drag. Up the road is classier Chalk Farm, where classical music joint **Bartok** and the laid-back **Lounge-jing** attract a more sophisticated market crowd.

Primrose Hill is gastropub heaven, where you're likely to be sipping your Guinness and chewing ciabatta alongside Natural Nylon members and nice North London boy Sacha Baron Cohen. If you like your pub food posh, **The Engineer** and **The Landsdowne** are unbeatable.

If it's not just good food you're after but glossy venues packed with glossy people, then look no further than Hampstead. No longer the boho village of 20 years ago, Hampstead is now a fully paid-up member of the flash-pack with more celebrity faces than The Priory. Famous NW3ers including Frank Skinner and Cat Deeley and a stadium load of footballers. You can catch these lot living the life at **House on the Hill**, the **Bar Room Bar** and **Toast**.

Recent and future openings:

Living Room, 18–26 Essex Road

camden town

ARIZONA BAR & GRILL

Restaurant Bar
2 Jamestown Road NW1
020 7284 4730

OPEN Mon-Thu midday-	**GETTING LUCKY**	**3/5**
1am, Fri-Sat midday-2am,	**EYE CANDY**	**2/5**
Sun midday-midnight	**BIG SPENDERS**	**2/5**
TUBE/RAIL Camden Town	**MIX** 50%M 50%F	
BUSES 24, 27, 31, 168	**AGE** 20-45	
	PRICE Average	

AMBIENCE Buzzy, Casual, Comfy, Groups, Late Night Open, Live Music
REVIEW What? A bar in Camden almost completely free of the hordes of Liam-a-likes, Britpop survivors and music industry reptiles so often found in these parts? Hard to believe, but true. By day, Arizona is filled with drinkers fleeing the armies of Peruvian hair-wrappers and Jamaican incense vendors camped out on the bridge. Early in the evening, the pleasantly dark Mexican bar attracts a mix of after-workers and night-outers desperate to escape the Goth and tourist-infested streets. Late on Fridays and Saturdays DJs up the tempo, packing in a raring-to-go after-hours crew. Don't go expecting fireworks – it's not sophisticated or particularly stylish, but it gets its well-mixed crowd mingling and they all seem to come back for more.
PLACE Large L-shaped bar, with cyan benches, nicotine orange walls and wooden floors. Sitting at the bar is an option, although you may well be confronted by a soundless TV showing sumo or European ten-pin bowling.
PEOPLE Early on gets office groups of varying sizes (seemingly the lifeblood of Latin-themed bars), while later in the evening a smarter crowd come for the music and the more-relaxed-than-Camden's-hipper-bars feel.

PROFS Tourists, market traders, office workers, musicians, producers, actors
CELEBS Stella McCartney, Nicole Appleton, Aqua
DRESS The odd suit but mostly Camden street style, from market hand-me-downs to urban surf labels
MUSIC 70s, 80s, Easy Listening, Funk, Soul, DJs Fri-Sat
DOOR Smart casual
DRINKS Beer £2.60, Wine £2.60, Cocktails £3.95
FOOD Caribbean, Tex Mex, £8
CARDS All
CAPACITY 150, seating 90
HIRE Venue: Yes · Private Room: No

BAR GANSA

Restaurant Bar
2 Inverness Street NW1
020 7267 8909

OPEN Mon-Wed 10am-	**GETTING LUCKY**	**2/5**
midnight, Thu-Sat 10am-	**EYE CANDY**	**2/5**
1am, Sun 10am-11pm	**BIG SPENDERS**	**2/5**
TUBE/RAIL Camden Town	**MIX** 50%M 50%F	
BUSES 24, 27, 31, 168	**AGE** 18-30	
	PRICE Average	

AMBIENCE Buzzy, Casual, Dancing, Groups, Late Night Open, Party
REVIEW You've heard of Spanish Harlem, but here you have it: Spanish Camden. In the blackest corner of Inverness Street lies the inauspicious-looking Bar Gansa. It's painted black, it's small and narrow, the lighting's poor, but it's better than the name suggests. As ever-pounding Ricky Martin-free Latin rhythms raise the roof, body heat in this claustrophobic speakeasy also rises a few notches more. Revellers here – and they do revel – are manifold and multicultural. A high percentage of exchange students down cheap margaritas, a few hopeful London girls search for London boys who don't like the beer at these foreign places and up-for-it couples relive their summer-in-Spain shagfests with pitchers of lethal sangría.
PLACE The blackness of this corner site is all-enveloping, and subsequently welcoming, once you know your way around. Tables are small and mostly meant for two, but larger parties can be accommodated toward the back where there is just about room to salsa with a very small cat.
PEOPLE Young, buoyant, studenty, cosmopolitan crowd into music to bolt tapas by.

PROFS Theatre staff, music managers, actors, film directors, photographers, artists, students, retail workers
CELEBS Boy George, Robbie Williams, Eurythmics, Suede, Sneaker Pimps
DRESS Casual jeans, roll neck jumpers, leather jackets, long flouncy skirts, patterned waistcoats
MUSIC Spanish, Latin
DOOR None
DRINKS Beer £2.75, Wine £2.50, Champagne £3.50, Cocktail £5.50
FOOD Spanish, Tapas, £6
CARDS No Amex or Diners
CAPACITY 100, seating 80
HIRE Venue: Yes · Private Room: No

BAR VINYL

Bar, Café
6 Inverness Street NW1
020 7681 7898

OPEN Mon-Sat midday-	**GETTING LUCKY**	**4/5**
11pm, Sun midday-10.30pm	**EYE CANDY**	**3/5**
TUBE/RAIL Camden Town	**BIG SPENDERS**	**2/5**
BUSES 24, 27, 31, 168	**MIX** 70%M 30%F	
	AGE 18-35	
	PRICE Average	

AMBIENCE Casual, Funky, Party, Student, Pulling
REVIEW A mere slip of a bar that tends to get busy on weekends when lack of competition drives the natives towards Inverness Street. Past the corridor-like bar area, a slightly wider space doubles as a restaurant where the politically preoccupied, left-leaning staff will look hurt if you ask for ketchup. That said, the bar person was genial enough to warn off bag snatchers, for among the moaning Trustafarians and urban surfers winds a darker underbelly of Camden society. There's a record store downstairs, but don't bother looking unless you're sporting the prerequisite Technics headphones

round your neck and possess a fine set of dreadlocks. Or a skinhead. Especially if you're female.
PLACE Narrow ground-floor bar with café at rear and record store downstairs. Austere, post-industrial decor with grubby emulsioned walls, stripped fag-end laden floors, metallic staircases.
PEOPLE Girls called Sahara, dodgy-looking toothless guys in baseball caps, khaki'd Japanese electro fans, aspiring DJs loaded down with 20 tonne record bags.

bar.vinyl.cafe

PROFS DJs, musicians, clubbers, record producers, market retailers, film production
CELEBS Fun Lovin' Criminals, Boy George, Howie B, Björk, Kahuna Brothers, Freestylers
DRESS Well-scrubbed Camden retro and grunge dress prevalent but not de rigueur. Plenty of second-hand cardigans, combats, trainers, clam diggers, skimpy t-shirts, singlets and a smattering of hot pink – body piercing optional
MUSIC Breakbeat, Hip Hop, Deep House, House, Techno, Trip Hop
DOOR None
DRINKS Beer £2.60, Wine £2.50, Champagne £4, Cocktail £4
FOOD International, Modern European, £4.95
CARDS All
CAPACITY 80, seating 80
HIRE Venue: Yes · Private Room: No

BLAKES

Restaurant Bar
31 Jamestown Road NW1
020 7482 2959

OPEN 7 days 11am-11pm, 11am-10.30pm	GETTING LUCKY	2/5
TUBE/RAIL Camden Town	EYE CANDY	3/5
BUSES 24, 27, 31, 168	BIG SPENDERS	3/5
	MIX 50%M 50%F	
	AGE 25-35	
	PRICE Average	

AMBIENCE Casual, Conversation, Groups, Comfy
REVIEW Blakes is one of the few bars in Camden you can feel at home in without half a packet of Lambert & Butler and a black frightwig. As grunge (and Camden) got cool and its supporters turned professional, it left a gap in the market for what owner Robert Blake describes as 'something a bit more chilled for the more affluent'. And Blakes is. He bought a sofa, some (still fairly studenty) artwork, chucked out all the Levellers records in favour of de-stressing jazz and soul and put

a rather good restaurant upstairs. But it still feels like a pub. The bar staff slouch over the counter to pull pints which you sip at pubby tables. The door gapes on to the street, where takeaway refuse reigns and local tramps sip Special Brew.
PLACE Basic pub set-up gradually evolving into a bar. Washed plaster walls, heritage-style-spiral-legged chairs, and that battered leather sofa. Muted lighting from arty hempen table lamps soften the rough edges.
PEOPLE Creative Camdenites with cash. They take McClaren Vale wine to dinner parties, where they listen to Dido and Macy Gray and discuss Ali G's autobiography over guacamole and Kettle Chips.
PROFS Musicians, media execs, TV production, publishers, restaurateurs, advertising execs
CELEBS Zoë Ball, Kylie
DRESS Levis, Duffer, Nike, Adidas. Urban sportswear fresh from the office, trendy tags on the trainers and bags
MUSIC Classical, Jazz
DOOR None
DRINKS Beer £2.80, Wine £2.70, Champagne £5, Cocktails £4
FOOD International, Mediterranean, Modern Eclectic, £10
CARDS All
CAPACITY 250, seating 50
HIRE Venue: Yes · Private Room: No

CAMDEN BREWING CO.

Pub, Bar
1 Randolph Street NW1
020 7267 9829

OPEN Mon-Fri midday-11pm, Sat midday-1am, Sun midday-10.30pm	GETTING LUCKY	3/5
	EYE CANDY	3/5
	BIG SPENDERS	3/5
TUBE/RAIL Camden Town	MIX 50%M 50%F	
BUSES 29, 46, 253	AGE 25-40	
	PRICE Average	

AMBIENCE Brightly Coloured/Cheerful, Comfy, Conversation, Cosy, Late Night Open
REVIEW The angular snapping dog on the Camden Brewing Co.'s sign looks spookily like the evil robotic canine in Wallace & Gromit's 'A Close Shave'. While on the one hand this is a seemingly modern, lounge pub, on the other it's also as Nick Park-English as knitted sweaters and Wensleydale. Amid the groovy baby sofas and the style savvy clientele, there are a few old geezers watching the footy on a remarkably uncool TV, and beside the fairy-lit spiral staircase two expensively blue-rinsed ladies play a genteel game of gin rummy on Sunday afternoons. Later in the evening young guns take full advantage of the unusual beers on offer – watch City bankers snogging dreadlocked marketstall holders after one too many jars of Golden Duck.
PLACE A bright cream-tiled pub in the Camden Road hinterland. Inside it's très nouveau with a small, modern Japanese-style bar surrounded by comfy chairs and sofas. The cigarette machine reads 'Ciggies' in case you were unsure.
PEOPLE Nonchalantly wealthy locals who read the Sunday supplements over M&S half-baked croissants plus a smattering of locals whose artificial hips won't take them much further.

PROFS Music, media, TV employees
CELEBS Graham Coxon, Jude Law, Sadie Frost, Ewan McGregor, Suggs
DRESS High street to designer casuals, Diesel, Duffer, Boxfresh, Fake London
MUSIC House, Dance
DOOR None
DRINKS Beer £2.60, Wine £3, Champagne £3.60, Cocktails £5
FOOD Snacks, £5
CARDS All
CAPACITY 350, seating 50
HIRE Venue: No · Private Room: No

EDWARD'S

Bar, Chain
1 Camden High Street NW1
020 7387 2749

OPEN Mon-Sat 10am-11pm,	GETTING LUCKY	2/5
Sun midday-10.30pm	EYE CANDY	2/5
TUBE/RAIL Mornington	BIG SPENDERS	2/5
Crescent	MIX 50%M 50%F	
BUSES 24, 27, 29, 88, 134,	AGE 18-28	
168, 253	PRICE Average	

AMBIENCE Casual, Conversation, Dancing, Groups, Outdoors, Party, Student
REVIEW Pick the time of day you visit Edward's with care. Evenings are party time with thumping choons played by the resident DJ and an up-fer-it crowd of raucous students downing two for one offers. Visit at lunchtime and you'll find yourself hemmed in by suits on an office politics rant. During the afternoon Edward's empties out. The only punters are weighed down with superstrength Argos and Woolworths carriers, light from the high windows reflects on empty formica tables and laminated menus, and Edward's becomes a Royle-Family-goes-to-Littlewoods-Café hell.
PLACE There's a corner here for everyone, whether you're after a quiet chat in the corner, a space to eye up the talent at the bar or a brickwork alcove for a covert boogie to 80s party classics.
PEOPLE Good-natured, evening party crowd getting down to M People's 'Moving On Up' after four measures of Aftershock. Afternoon gets the not-so-happy-shoppers, lunchtimes it's suit city.

PROFS Estate agents, solicitors, retailers, office workers, students, opticians, doctors, financial advisers, business managers, supermarket checkout workers
CELEBS Sean Bean, Joe Cole
DRESS Oasis, River Island, Principles, Next, Ben Sherman
MUSIC Commercial Dance, Garage DJs Thu-Sun
DOOR No sportswear after 7pm
DRINKS Beer £2.80, Wine £2.80, Cocktail £4
FOOD Snacks, £5
CARDS All
CAPACITY 240, seating 125
HIRE Venue: No · Private Room: No

JAZZ CAFÉ

Bar, Club, Jazz Club, Live Music Venue
5 Parkway NW1
020 7916 6060

OPEN Mon-Thu 7pm-1am,	GETTING LUCKY	2/5
Fri-Sat 7pm-2am,	EYE CANDY	3/5
Sun 7pm-midnight	BIG SPENDERS	3/5
TUBE/RAIL Camden Town	MIX 65%M 35%F	
BUSES C2, 274	AGE 25-45	
	PRICE Average	

AMBIENCE Arty/Bohemian, Chin Stroking, Dancing, Funky, Groups, Hip/Fashionable, Late Night Open, Live Music, Warehouse/Industrial
REVIEW Are these people really young or have Laboratoires Garnier set up a covert test centre in Camden? The Jazz Café – not just great for jazz but also blues, soul and latin – attracts a funky-looking crowd. Young musos with more money than most, lithe things in trim leather jackets and bespectacled former start-up upstarts. Appearances are misleading, though; the look may be Uth, but the behaviour is definitely pipe and slippers. You would expect this lot to get down a little, but when the band strikes up everyone's foot-tapping and nodding like a bunch of Thunderbird marionettes. Even the guy in the corner who strikes out on his own with some cool and contrapuntal moves is actually, on closer inspection, just making his way to the loo. They could all do with some serious lubrication from the blue neon bar, but prefer to sip their Asahi slowly, with eyes fixed firmly on the stage. Of course, drinking's not the priority here, and anyway, it's tricky applauding improv with a bottle in your hand.
PLACE Two-level, neon and chrome live music venue. The main area gratifyingly close to the small stage is standing room, with a few stools to perch on by the wall. Book a table in the industrial-style dining area overlooking the stage to ensure a seat.
PEOPLE Gifted music bods and trendsters with sharp hairdos. They're serious about music and don't appreciate raucous antics: it only takes one loud, bug-eyed bint to get the most amenable of jazz fans muttering death threats through clenched teeth.

PROFS Musicians, students, lawyers, creatives
CELEBS Julia Sawalha, Tracy Shaw, David Bowie, Samuel L Jackson, Robbie Williams, Mark Knopfler, Noel Gallagher, Britt Ekland, Beverley Knight, LTJ Bukem, Roachford
DRESS Leather jackets, polonecks, utility wear, fleecy sleeveless jerkins, needle cords. Ill-fitting jeans and t-shirts for the few uncool
MUSIC Jazz, Gigs Mon-Sat
DOOR £8-20
DRINKS Beer £3, Wine £3, Champagne £3.50, Cocktail £7
FOOD Modern European, £15
CARDS No Amex
CAPACITY 300, seating 80
HIRE Venue: Yes · Private Room: No

THE LORD STANLEY

Pub
51 Camden Park Road NW1
020 7428 9488

OPEN Mon 6pm-11pm,	**GETTING LUCKY**	**3/5**
Tue-Sun midnight-11pm,	**EYE CANDY**	**3/5**
Sun midday-10.30pm	**BIG SPENDERS**	**3/5**
TUBE/RAIL Caledonian	**MIX** 55%M 45%F	
Road, Camden Road	**AGE** 25-45	
BUSES 10, 29, 253	**PRICE** Cheap	

AMBIENCE Casual, Groups, Live Music
REVIEW A pop star's local. When Blur aren't Groucho-ing it up you might catch them here, sprawling on the beyond-battered leather armchairs by the fire, being visibly regular guys. Certainly, Graham Coxon lives locally, as do a host of pop's new aristocrats. It's a gourmet, Chablis sort of pub with a rough nonchalance, a hint of self-consciousness and a Marlboro Light bouquet. Music biz and media types in their early thirties debate the appeal of Audrey Tautou, Le Creuset pans and Hackney over steady pints, a middle-aged man in an Aran sweater wades diligently through The Guardian, and everything seems right with the world.
PLACE Lots of light and space for a Camden pub with seven feet of magnolia-topped wood panelling round the walls and a glistening green ceiling. Minimal expense was the apparent motive for the standard but comfy decor.
PEOPLE Posh broadsheet readers who like nothing better than settling down in front of Channel 4 with an organic ready-meal and their long-term partner. Friends, Will & Grace and South Park. Oh, goody.

PROFS Media execs, musicians, photographers, IT profs
CELEBS Donna Air, Blur
DRESS Three-quarter-length leather jackets, bootcut cords, Diesel, Gap, Urban Outfitters and variations on the Hoxton fin
MUSIC Soul, African, Caribbean
DOOR None
DRINKS Beer £2.70, Wine £2.50, Cocktail £2.70
FOOD New World, £7
CARDS All
CAPACITY 200, seating 50
HIRE Venue: No · Private Room: No

MAC BAR

Bar
102-104 Camden Road NW1
020 7485 4530

OPEN Mon-Sat midday-	**GETTING LUCKY**	**3/5**
11pm, Sun midday-10.30pm	**EYE CANDY**	**3/5**
TUBE/RAIL Camden Town,	**BIG SPENDERS**	**3/5**
Camden Road	**MIX** 50%M 50%F	
BUSES 29, 253	**AGE** 18-30	
	PRICE Average	

AMBIENCE Casual, Conversation, Groups, Live Music
REVIEW More kebab 'n' gig land than bar nirvana, Camden has never been known for the quality of its drinking holes – unless you like your beer from the can served in a puddle of piss. Which is why this revamped pub is probably the best NW1 has to offer. Put together by guys who've done their time at slick style bars like Atlantic and Momo, it shows in the quality of service and drinks. A Sunday visit revealed a t-shirt and denim-clad spread of under thirties, more belly flesh flashing than a pre-natal clinic and a general display of insouciant youthful posturing.
PLACE Scarcely recognisable as its former boozy old self, Rosie O'Grady's, Mac Bar has been positively reformed and revamped with stripped floorboards, cushy leather lounge seating and changing artwork on display.
PEOPLE Despite its location in the heartland of the great unwashed, the crowd are as squeaky clean as their funky retro Juliette-Lewis-in-that-Gap-jeans ad look will allow.

PROFS Students, bartenders, meeja types, i-Mac users
CELEBS Graham Coxon, Sophie Ellis-Bextor
DRESS A dippy chick is practically tripping over her petticoats trying to pull off a Little House on the Prairie/radical slash punk goth rock look. Don't try to compete with the 'creativity', go for the jeans/combats t-shirt combo
MUSIC Jazz, Funk, Soul, Blues, Wed live music
DOOR None
DRINKS Beer £2.50, Wine £3.60, Champagne £6, Cocktail £5
FOOD World Cuisine, £7.95
CARDS All
CAPACITY 250, seating 140
HIRE Venue: No · Private Room: No

SINGAPORE SLING

Restaurant bar, Cocktail Bar
16 Inverness Street NW1
020 7424 9527

OPEN 7 days midday-	**GETTING LUCKY**	**3/5**
midnight	**EYE CANDY**	**3/5**
TUBE/RAIL Camden Town	**BIG SPENDERS**	**3/5**
BUSES 24, 27, 29, 88	**MIX** 30%M 70%F	
	AGE 25-35	
	PRICE Average	

AMBIENCE Conversation, Late Night Open, Opulent
REVIEW Camden may well be the centre of all things student, but some people seem strangely reluctant to fight their way through unwashed hoards of dope-addled, goatee-bearded, skateboarding Slipknot fans just to have a beer. Singapore Sling – clearly based on Singapore's legendary Raffles bar – is so un-Camden, the owners are either entrepreneurial mavericks or barking mad. But judging by the buzzy atmosphere ten days after opening, the gamble seems to have paid off. With a sumptuous, sensual drinks menu – ginger Martini, Malaysian tea, young coconut juice – and acres of dark wood, it's hard not to feel relaxed once inside. Sit by the water feature on the back balcony, sip a delicately fragrant cocktail, and forget all about the one-armed man shouting obscenities at his can of Red Stripe you had to step over to get here.
PLACE Perched directly above the restaurant, there's an immediately intimate feel to this cocktail bar. The low-lit natural decor feels homely, but there are enough flashes of golden exotica to make you feel you're somewhere special.

PEOPLE Possibly the only drinking den in NW1 where it's not compulsory to discuss bass guitars. A million professional and conversational miles away from the stereotypical Camden bedsit boys and girls.

PROFS Media, advertising
CELEBS None yet – recent opening
DRESS Smart
MUSIC Background Jazz and Funk
DOOR None
DRINKS Beer £2.60, Wine £2.65, Cocktail £4.85
FOOD Malaysian, £7
CARDS All
CAPACITY 30, seating 20
HIRE Venue: Yes · Private Room: Yes

WKD

Bar, Café, Club
18 Kentish Town Road NW1
020 7267 1869

OPEN Mon-Thu 4pm-2am,	**GETTING LUCKY**	**4/5**
Fri-Sat 2pm-3am,	**EYE CANDY**	**3/5**
Sun 1pm-midnight	**BIG SPENDERS**	**3/5**
TUBE/RAIL Camden Town	**MIX** 50%M 50%F	
BUSES 134, 29, 24, 253	**AGE** 18-35	
	PRICE Average	

AMBIENCE Groups, Industrial/Warehouse, Party, Pulling
REVIEW The acronym 'Wisdom, Knowledge, Destiny' is overstating it somewhat, but WKD has become a popular haunt amongst North Londoners looking for decent tunes and intimacy. Cramped into an uninspiring corner of Camden Town, it is, in turns, a bar, a club, a café, a live music venue and a gallery. Despite its chameleon-like nature it's been attracting the same old characters for almost a decade. If you can tolerate the dick-in-hand machismo and growling bouncers then the imaginatively disparate range of 'nights' will get the adrenaline flowing. The most notable of these are 'Juicy', a sweaty excursion through the classic funk of the 70s and 80s, and the jazz and Brazilian swing of Sunday evenings. There's a lazier feel during the day and the Thai and Cajun cuisine is surprisingly good.
PLACE A functional arrangement of bars over two floors. WKD is all twisted metal and dark rooms enlivened by spinning neon. They could have filmed Red Dwarf here.
PEOPLE Dancing the windmill in the darkest corner of the room with your shades on could earn you big-time respect; cats dressed to kill cut silly shapes to the latest sounds.

PROFS Music industry, advertising, PR, media and fashion execs, gangsters
CELEBS Dandy Warhols, Beverley Knight
DRESS Moschino, TopShop, Karen Millen, Versace, Bernini
MUSIC Soulsonic, R&B, Drum 'n' Bass, Brazilian, Latin, Retro, House, Jazz, DJs
DOOR Smart casual, free-£8
DRINKS Beer £2.95, Wine £2.50, Champagne £5.50, Cocktail £5
FOOD Thai, £8
CARDS No Amex or Diners
CAPACITY 300, seating 40
HIRE Venue: Yes · Private Room: Yes

chalk farm

BARTOK

Bar
78 Chalk Farm Road NW1
020 7916 0595

OPEN Mon-Thu 5pm-	**GETTING LUCKY**	**1/5**
midnight, Fri midday-1am,	**EYE CANDY**	**3/5**
Sat midday-1am,	**BIG SPENDERS**	**2/5**
Sun midday-midnight	**MIX** 50%M 50%F	
TUBE/RAIL Chalk Farm	**AGE** 20-40	
BUSES 24, 27, 31, 168	**PRICE** Average	

AMBIENCE Comfy, Conversation, Late Night Open, Live Music, Lounge
REVIEW Anyone who thought Camden was the haunt of Gothed-up suicidal stoodentz, ex-roadie nutters, pink-haired snot-nosed teenagers, stoned wasters, scoundrels, hawkers, vinyl-anoraks and backpackers called Sven on their way to Glastonbury would be bang on. However, trot just a few hundred yards north to Chalk Farm, away from the market scrum and the raggle taggle hordes of the main drag, and life drastically improves. Named after the Hungarian composer Bela and owned by the Mean Fiddler, Bartok is music by name and music by nature. If you're after banging choons and happy hardcore you're in the wrong place, for Bartok plays strictly classical, from modern contemporary to old skool dead people's stuff. Bring on the noise.
PLACE Very red, Shaun Clarkson-designed classical meets modern lounge bar. Dramatic window drapes, a chandelier and William Morris-style upholstered sofas and highbacked chairs, mixed with noughties cube pouffes and hip graphics.
PEOPLE Generally a 20-something local crowd, a few students and first-jobbers, plus a few middle-aged locals and some downright ancient geezers making a cameo appearance on quieter nights.

PROFS Actors, nurses, graphic designers, trainee doctors, musicians
CELEBS Vanessa Feltz, Patrick Stewart, Cat Deeley, Les Dennis, Dale Winton
DRESS Duffer, Levi's, Adidas, FCUK
MUSIC Classical, Live Wed-Sun
DOOR Smart casual
DRINKS Beer £2.90, Wine £3, Champagne £5.50, Cocktail £3.50
FOOD Bar snacks, £4.95
CARDS No Diners
CAPACITY 100, seating 30
HIRE Venue: No · Private Room: No

LOUNGE-JING

Bar
89-91 Chalk Farm Road NW1
020 7485 8222

OPEN Mon-Sat 6pm-11pm,	**GETTING LUCKY**	**2/5**
Sun 6pm-10.30pm	**EYE CANDY**	**4/5**
TUBE/RAIL Chalk Farm	**BIG SPENDERS**	**3/5**
BUSES 24, 27, 31, 168	**MIX** 50%M 50%F	
	AGE 30-50	
	PRICE Average	

AMBIENCE Casual, Groups, Late Night Open
REVIEW With its white goat hair banquettes, Indian Kitsch paintings, giant leather bean bags, hanging baskets, incense, throws and modern European and space age touches, Lounge-jing looks more like a branch of Urban Outfitters than a bar. The atmosphere upstairs is designed to encourage a degree of mixing, although the middle-class reserve of the drinkers often belies this. Downstairs is filled with ethnic banquettes, divided by screens punched with star-shape holes – perfect for spying on your fellow drinkers.
PLACE A scantily lit two-tier collage of kitsch and boho. Textures and ethnic touches aplenty, although with a slightly contrived feel. There's an office which turns into a computer games viewing room, but best of all is the cubbyhole for two under the stairs, cut off by a beaded curtain and designed for seduction.
PEOPLE Primrose Hill locals, funky shoppers who only came to Camden for the vintage jeans.

PROFS Music and media employees, office workers
CELEBS None
DRESS Smart, casual, subtly fashionable. The girls are more adventurous than the men, but this is still Camden. Know what I mean?
MUSIC Dance, Drum 'n' Bass, Garage, House, DJs Fri-Sat
DOOR None
DRINKS Beer £2.60, Wine £2.30, Champagne £5.50, Cocktail £4.50
FOOD None
CARDS No Amex
CAPACITY 170, seating 60
HIRE Venue: Yes · Private Room: Yes

BAR ROOM BAR

Bar
48 Rosslyn Hill NW3
020 7435 0808

OPEN Mon-Sat 11am-11pm, Sun midday-10.30pm	**GETTING LUCKY** **4/5**
	EYE CANDY **4/5**
TUBE/RAIL Hampstead	**BIG SPENDERS** **3/5**
BUSES 46, 268	**MIX** 50%M 50%F
	AGE 22-40
	PRICE Average

AMBIENCE Casual, Conversation, Friendly, Funky, Groups, Pulling

REVIEW During the day it's a typical Hampstead writers' haunt, popular for its wood-burned pizzas. Early evening, the literary ghosts are chased away by a glamorously uninhibited clique whose expansive gestures are something akin to hippy vogue. A local hairdresser in cheesecloth dances by herself to the acid-jazzy garage, lads discuss their favourite gory bits from 1950s B-movies, a group of models talk olive oils by the door while a bunch of out-of-NW3ers who heard the birds in Hampstead were really fit clutch bottled beers and gawp.
PLACE Mid-sized glass-fronted showcase bar, with a sort of nouveau vague chandelier made from granny's old silver. Look out for the claw-hand coat hook on your right as you enter – it's by the same guy who made the metal tree in the small back garden.
PEOPLE An eclectic crowd of after-work drinkers, Hampstead honeys and pony-tailed, leather-waistcoated eccentrics.

PROFS Lawyers, media profs, students, artists, estate agents
CELEBS Mandy Smith, Annie Lennox, Michael Greco
DRESS Funky threads – the clientele are out to be seen
MUSIC Funk, Jazz, Garage, House, DJs Fri-Sat
DOOR None
DRINKS Beer £2.60, Wine £2.50, Champagne £3.50, Cocktail £4
FOOD Pizza, Snacks, £6.50
CARDS No Amex or Diners
CAPACITY 100, seating 60
HIRE Venue: Yes · Private Room: No

THE HOUSE ON THE HILL

Restaurant Bar
34 Rosslyn Hill NW3
020 7435 8037

OPEN Mon-Sun 10.30am-midnight	**GETTING LUCKY** **4/5**
	EYE CANDY **4/5**
TUBE/RAIL Hampstead	**BIG SPENDERS** **4/5**
BUSES 46, 268	**MIX** 50%M 50%F
	AGE 26-40
	PRICE Average

AMBIENCE Conversation, Groups, Live Music, Hip/Fashionable, Star Spotting
REVIEW Übercool and überrated, the House on the Hill is still one of *the* places to be seen in Hampstead, and the absurd superficiality makes for addictive viewing. In the summer, regulars display themselves on outside tables, with large heaters warming Marbella sun-kissed shoulders. Later in the year the in-crowd move indoors where the seating is more formal. Balloons are tied around all the chairs at one table. We assumed a birthday, but then around here who knows? Could be an album deal, or a major share buyout, or even the second anniversary of somebody's breast enlargements.
PLACE Modern (by Hampstead standards) little bar with a gaggle of aluminium chairs and tables behind picket chains on the pavement. Inside it's large, cream-walled and mellow with fabric looped from the ceiling for that authentic marquee effect.
PEOPLE Pretty, privileged and pretentious but likeable all the same. It's not their fault they have bags of cash, style and the sort of CV the rest of us couldn't get away with faking. It's tough having it this easy, you know.

PROFS Trustafarians, estate agents, ladies-who-lunch, divas, bankers, stockbrokers, footballers
CELEBS Kevin Spacey, Thierry Henry, Nicole Appleton, Noel Gallagher, Emma Bunton, Gianluca Vialli
DRESS Ghost, Voyage, Joseph, Prada, Gucci, Armani
MUSIC Funk, Soul, Latin American, Jazz, Live Musician Tue, Thu, Sat
DOOR None
DRINKS Beer £2.75, Wine £2.95, Champagne £5.25, Cocktail £3.50
FOOD Anglo-Mediterranean, £12.50
CARDS No Diners
CAPACITY 90, seating 90
HIRE Venue: Yes · Private Room: No

TOAST

Bar, Cocktail Bar, Members Club, Restaurant
50 Hampstead High Street NW3
020 7431 2244

OPEN Mon-Fri 6pm-midnight, Sat-Sun 11am-midnight	**GETTING LUCKY**	**3/5**
	EYE CANDY	**4/5**
	BIG SPENDERS	**4/5**
TUBE/RAIL Hampstead	**MIX** 45%M 55%F	
BUSES 46, 268	**AGE** 17-35	
	PRICE Expensive	

AMBIENCE Conversation, Elegant/Classic, Hip/Fashionable, Groups, Late Night Open, Star Spotting
REVIEW The West End comes to Hampstead with this chi-chi little number, a home-from-home for the groomed and moneyed NW3 Mafiosi. More restaurant than members bar, although for some reason they've still got a hulking doorman purporting exclusivity. Witness the professional daddy's girls with French manicures and sleek Daniel Hersheson hair chat at volume and giggle over champagne while their significantly less attractive consorts talk (lots of) money and look generally pleased with themselves. Monday night is ghetto fabulous, when the Hampstead hotties come to shake their expensive booties to R&B and hip hop in the safe confines of the High Street. A place for locals who want to show off their blow-drys but can't possibly face the frightful cab ride into town.
PLACE A small oak-lined, triangular-shaped restaurant above Hampstead tube station with small cocktail bar, trendy mirrored disc inset ceiling detail, padded leather walls and swanky marble loos.
PEOPLE Glossy, Gucci shade-wearing NW3 princesses and their escorts, plus well-to-do locals, House on the Hill regulars and a smattering of footballers.

PROFS Lawyers, bankers, property developers, models
CELEBS Janet Street-Porter, Michelle Collins, Thierry Henry, Sol Campbell, Emma Bunton, Damage
DRESS Flashy trashy labels revealing St. Tropez'd skin for the girls and Gucci loafers for the boys
MUSIC Classical (day), R&B, Soul (evening), DJ Mon 10pm
DOOR Smart casual
DRINKS Beer £3, Wine £4, Champagne £8, Cocktail £7
FOOD Modern British, Modern European, £12.50
CARDS No Diners
CAPACITY 125, seating 80
HIRE Venue: Yes · Private Room: No

hoxton/shoreditch

291

Restaurant Bar
291 Hackney Road E2
020 7613 5676

OPEN Tue-Wed 6.30pm-midnight, Thu-Sat 6.30pm-2am	**GETTING LUCKY**	**3/5**
	EYE CANDY	**4/5**
	BIG SPENDERS	**2/5**
TUBE/RAIL Old Street, Liverpool Street	**MIX** 50%M 50%F	
BUSES 26, 48, 55	**AGE** 18-60	
	PRICE Average	

AMBIENCE Arty/Bohemian, Conversation, Dancing, Groups, Late Night Open, Live Music, Vampire/Gothic
REVIEW The gaping Gothic architecture of this converted church arches up into the night. The striking clientele, self-created artists living in a permanent state of performance art, play backgammon and drink bottled beer beside a stage on which two naked girls struggle inside an enormous, flesh-tone PVC cube. It's hard to tell, in this postmodern environment, where the art ends and the 'just popping out for a drink' begins. But the voyeuristic thrill of the place is infectious, and in no time you'll catch yourself sipping syncopatedly or only answering every third question you're asked.
PLACE A vast, converted Gothic church, eerie at night. The bar is on the opposite side of the foyer to the door – it's long, narrow and bustling during the live event nights that are staged in the galleries.
PEOPLE Beautiful, unusual, fleeting types with a curiously contrived fashion sense. Overheard: 'My God, she has the most heartbreakingly jointed fingers. Is she the one who did that piece with the toilet flushing montage?'

PROFS Media professionals, artists, design consultants, wholesalers, interior designers, solicitors
CELEBS Soon to be Brit Artists – watch their space
DRESS Textures and colours in all standard and geometrically-challenging combinations. Thrift-store chic, Junk, Diesel
MUSIC Electro, House, Live Music
DOOR None
DRINKS Beer £2.60, Wine £2.50, Cocktail £4.25
FOOD International, Modern Eclectic, Snacks, £6
CARDS No Amex or Diners
CAPACITY 150, seating 30
HIRE Venue: Yes · Private Room: Yes

333

Club, Live Music Venue
333 Old Street EC1
020 7739 5949

OPEN Fri-Sat 10pm-5am, Sun 10pm-4am	**GETTING LUCKY**	**3/5**
	EYE CANDY	**3/5**
TUBE/RAIL Old Street	**BIG SPENDERS**	**2/5**
BUSES 43, 55, 76, 141, 214, 243	**MIX** 50%M 50%F	
	AGE 21-35	
	PRICE Average	

AMBIENCE Arty/Bohemian, Casual, Chilled, Dancing, Funky, Late Night Open, Live Music

REVIEW A kaleidoscopic cornucopia of delights, though somewhat reminiscent of a tatty party in a dilapidated house. The varied music continually surprises the unwary and the crowd is remarkably unpretentious for one of Hoxton's hippest hang-outs. Three floors, each with its own theme, decor and vibe, give you a money's worth feel, and both management and security are so laid-back as to be practically non-existent. Unveiled in 1998 as an ironic experiment in eclecticism and clubbing anti-commercialism, promoters Perverted Science and Off Centre consistently meet their remit, sating an audience's hunger for a hip hop, jazz and house stir fry that would send other promoters scuttling for the Rennies. Ultra trendy, yes, but no need to suffer for your suave, 333 has a funky, laid-back groove.
PLACE Projection city as you walk in at ground level, with more than enough visual entertainment to keep you interested should the music hit a lull which, generally, it doesn't. The basement is your typical drum 'n' bass UV warehouse affair. Upstairs Mother joins 333 for small hours partying.
PEOPLE Chilled-out boho beatniks, students, musos and arty types who come here because, as one clubber so eloquently put it, 'it's down to earth, with no pretentious bullshit'. Hasn't yet suffered from the rise of the über-slick Hoxtonite.

PROFS Artists, actors, actresses, exotic dancers, financial analysts, graphic designers, musicians, students, media types, sales people
CELEBS Jarvis Cocker, Beastie Boys, Zoë Ball
DRESS Hysteric Glamour, Mambo, Firetrap, TopShop
MUSIC From Big Beat to Break Beat to Freestyle, legendary nights include All Night Schlong, Off Centre and Perverted Science
DOOR Fri-Sat £5 before 11pm, £10 after 11pm, Sun £5 before midnight, £7 after midnight
DRINKS Beer £2.60, Wine £3, Champagne £3.50
FOOD None
CARDS Mastercard and Visa only
CAPACITY 650, seating 60
HIRE Venue: Yes · Private Room: No

BLUU

Bar
Hoxton Square N16
020 7613 2793

OPEN Mon-Thu 11am-	GETTING LUCKY	**3/5**
11.30pm, Fri-Sat 11am-	EYE CANDY	**3/5**
midnight, Sun	BIG SPENDERS	**3/5**
midday-10.30pm	MIX 55%M 45%F	
TUBE/RAIL Old Street	AGE 24-36	
BUSES 55, 242	PRICE Average	

AMBIENCE Basement, Dancing, Groups, Hip/Fashionable, Live Music, Warehouse/Industrial
REVIEW The proximity to Jay Jopling's Brit Art temple White Cube² could mean a few transatlantic visitors to this Fat Cat owned bar. The chances are they may gravitate to the premeditated, ubiquitous warehouse look, although true locals can spot the difference and stick to the original, bonafide indie-bars sprinkled in the area. This is part of the slippery alco-circuit that runs from Home on Leonard Street to Herbal on Kingsland Road. The basement has a clubby vibe with cosy

alcoves while the ground floor is more of a café/bar. When you're done reflecting on New Neurotic Realism you can always regress by initiating a pinball session.
PLACE Once the legendary Blue Note, it was revamped by the Fat Cat group in a rough 'n' ready Hoxton style. Zinc bar, second-hand furniture, exposed brick and ducting, concrete and some comfy leather banquettes.
PEOPLE The usual Hoxton suspects, architects and designers wearing streetwise clothes with 'difficult' haircuts. Lofties plus some West London visitors searching for cutting edge away from familiar territory.

PROFS People who create and design, graphically, magically, whatever. Media execs, musicians, editors, lawyers, accountants
CELEBS Jarvis Cocker, Dinos Chapman, Jake Chapman, Natalie Imbruglia
DRESS The funnel-necked Maharishi, Niked-up posse with fishnets for the girlie girls. Always a few sartorially-challenged sticking out a mile like court shoes and pencil skirts in a dotcom workspace
MUSIC Funk, Dance, Ambient, DJs Thu-Sat
DOOR None
DRINKS Beer £2.70, Wine £2.65, Champagne £5, Cocktail £5
FOOD American, Snacks, £6
CARDS No Diners
CAPACITY 300, seating 100
HIRE Venue: Yes · Private Room: No

THE BRICKLAYERS ARMS

Pub, Restaurant
63 Charlotte Road EC2
020 7739 5245

OPEN Mon-Sat 11am-	GETTING LUCKY	**4/5**
midnight, Sun midday-11pm	EYE CANDY	**2/5**
TUBE/RAIL Old Street	BIG SPENDERS	**2/5**
BUSES 35, 48, 55, 171, 242	MIX 50%M 50%F	
	AGE 22-30	
	PRICE Cheap	

AMBIENCE Arty/Bohemian, Casual, Friendly, Funky, Groups, Pulling, Retro, Student
REVIEW Down a dark, dark alleyway, in the dark, dark not quite East End... is a funky little pub. The Bricklayers is a down at heel, up-tempo haunt for the local art students and studio-apartment types who live, work and study in the area. They mix with some genuine old, East End geezahs, the very friendly staff and a few young Suits (who appropriately dress down). Various DJs with a decent record selection (at its worst bordering on wacky) are far more interesting than the wall-to-wall garage you hear in most places these days. No, the DJs here are all unique, and have the flair to try something different. The result is largely successful. It's a noisy pub after about 7pm, so not the place to bring a date.
PLACE Small, fairly grub-standard pub downstairs, with decks at the back, strung over with fairy lights. Upstairs the restaurant is more hip in its design with 70s brown leather seats and brick walls adorned with some avant-garde artwork.
PEOPLE Serena and Ian are performance artists, working on a project to do with Victorian pornography and have just bought a fox-fur stole at Brick Lane Market for a

fiver. They are taking turns to wear it tonight. Neil and Rob have just come to 'chill and listen to the music, you know?'

PROFS Designers, artists, media employees, musicians, architects, fashion employees, students, TV production staff, art students

CELEBS Jarvis Cocker, Manic Street Preachers, Orbital, Sid Owen, Robbie Williams, Happy Mondays, Coldplay, Vinnie Jones

DRESS Dressing down for this place is a time-consuming fine art. Band and logo t-shirts, Carhartt, TopShop, Nike, Adidas

MUSIC House, Jazz, Funk, Techno, DJs Thu-Sun

DOOR None

DRINKS Beer £2.10, Wine £2.40, Cocktail £4

FOOD Thai, Traditional British, £6

CARDS No Amex or Diners

CAPACITY 150, seating 50

HIRE Venue: Yes, Private Room: No

CANTALOUPE

Bar
35 Charlotte Street EC2
020 7729 5566

OPEN Mon-Fri 11am-midnight,	**GETTING LUCKY**	**5/5**
	EYE CANDY	**3/5**
Sat-Sun midday-midnight	**BIG SPENDERS**	**2/5**
TUBE/RAIL Old Street	**MIX** 65%M 35%F	
BUSES 26, 35, 47, 48, 55, 67	**AGE** 20-40	
	PRICE Average	

AMBIENCE Buzzy, Casual, Dancing, Groups, Party, Pulling, Warehouse/Industrial

REVIEW Approach with caution; females should not travel in pairs. The men are as subtle as window-cleaners and as charming as builders, dressed in either Reiss suits or 'casj' gear. That said, it's an unpretentious place to escape the regional label slaves and neighbouring Shoreditch Twats. One of the first warehouse bars to open in the area; the original designer and arty crafty crowd prefer the neighbouring Bricklayers Arms. The only escape from Friday night leching is the restaurant, which is well recommended for hassle-free and inexpensive noshing. Some alternative characters make fleeting appearances, mainly for the food, before schlepping onwards for an EC1 crawl. One-night-stand addicts and girls looking for the proverbial dumb sexist bastard may think they've found nirvana. Less carnivorous midweek.

PLACE Enter the pubby bar, step through to a red lounge with Chesterfields and rough 'n' ready seating, step under a garage door to another bar and adjoining mezzanine diner. The grafitti-filled loos are 1,000 breezeblocks away and are straight out of Grange Hill.

PEOPLE East End swaggering lads, brash City boys and strutting girlies outnumber the sassy i-Ders and aloof, Agnès B Lolitas.

PROFS Bankers, accountants, account execs, graphic designers, craftspeople, PAs, photographers, musicians, students, models

CELEBS Tim Roth, Alexander McQueen, Natalie Imbruglia, Matt Johnson, Mel Smith, Kylie, Mark Strong, Radiohead

DRESS Think Ricky from EastEnders invites Paul Calf for a party. Diesel, Carhartt, Camper

MUSIC Funk, Soul, Jazz, Reggae, Rare Groove, DJs Fri-Sat

DOOR None

DRINKS Beer £2.50, Wine £2.80, Champagne £5, Cocktail £4.50

FOOD Modern Mediterranean, Tapas, £4

CARDS No Diners

CAPACITY 350, seating 70

HIRE Venue: No · Private Room: Yes

CARGO

Bar, Club
83 Rivington Street EC2
020 7739 3440

OPEN Mon-Thu 5pm-1am,	**GETTING LUCKY**	**4/5**
Fri-Sat 5pm-3am,	**EYE CANDY**	**4/5**
Sun 5pm-12am	**BIG SPENDERS**	**2/5**
TUBE/RAIL Old Street, Liverpool Street	**MIX** 60%M 40%F	
BUSES 26, 35, 47, 48, 55, 67	**AGE** 20-35	
	PRICE Cheap	

AMBIENCE Cavernous, Hip/Fashionable, Late Night Open, Live Music, Underground, Warehouse/Industrial

REVIEW Evidence, if necessary, that Hoxton's young creatives mainly enjoy creating ironic puce pavement pieces. The Monday night launch of club-cum-street-caf-cum-enjoyment-space Cargo, on a tide of free voddy and the promise of short film screenings of phallic explosions, effortlessly garnered the standard Shoreditch bitches: those painfully asymmetrical DJs and all manner of spun-out fringes. If downtempo beats and an upbeat humour temper the propensity to mawkishly lounge – and they've made a definite start with the kitten heel traps posed by unsanded MDF – Cargo, with its new 3am licence may soon become one of the underground clubs of the decade.

PLACE A Flintstones porn set tacked on to a 70s Habitat showroom with all of the cumbersome tools of the industrial revolution. Truly innovative touches include a video relay screen between the two arches and the combat pant-moistening, honey-warm, low-level lighting.

PEOPLE The odd horny EastEnd gangsta and dirty-denimmed, 'early Madge', fingerless gloved pseudo rock chick. The half-cut and the expensively cut.

PROFS Hoxton creatives, students, designers, promoters, musicians
CELEBS Jarvis Cocker, Normski, Noel and Liam Gallagher, Craig David, Kate Moss, Anastacia
DRESS Denim A-lines with torn waistbands, designer puffa/parkas with fur trim and hobble-garter inspired ankle gatherers, haircuts reminiscent of Anne Widdecombe after a heavy night with the deep fat fryer
MUSIC From Hip Hop to Latin Afro Beats, DJs 7 nights
DOOR Guest List, £4-8
DRINKS Beer £2.90, Wine £2.40, Cocktail £5.50
FOOD International, Snacks, £3.25
CARDS No Amex or Diners
CAPACITY 500, seating 60
HIRE Venue: Yes · Private Room: No

COCOMO

Bar, Café, Cocktail Bar
323 Old Street EC1
020 7613 0315

OPEN Mon-Sun 11am-11pm	**GETTING LUCKY**	**3/5**
TUBE/RAIL Old Street	**EYE CANDY**	**3/5**
BUSES 26, 35, 47, 48,	**BIG SPENDERS**	**2/5**
55, 67	**MIX** 50%M 50%F	
	AGE 26-35	
	PRICE Average	

AMBIENCE Basement, Casual, Conversation, Cosy, Hip/Fashionable
REVIEW Unique not only in its haphazard, let it happen kitsch design but also in the fact that it's owned by two girls. Attracts a kooky clique of creative types from DJs to graphic designers and all those after an unusual, unpretentious place to call their own. It's a zillion stuffed sharks away from commercial and so informal and laid-back it feels weird exchanging money for drinks. Not for the precious barfly who desperately wants to strike out and pose, more for those that know the meaning of postmodern but don't feel the need to discuss it.
PLACE Ex-launderette, very small but richly textured with yellow flock wallpaper and Moroccan metal, coloured glass lamps upstairs. Café seating and a makeshift Marrakech downstairs with leather pouffes, cushions and fairylights.
PEOPLE Sharp-toed hipsters chasing alcoholic oblivion, with great chat on the ground floor and up-close boogying in the basement.

PROFS Music industry employees, artists, fashion execs, graphic designers, website designers, students
CELEBS None
DRESS Ironic chic with a Pringle jumper and Farahs, the latest skinny-toed stilettos and jeans for girls, t-shirts with hip, retro or obscure logos, very urban slash subversive cool.
MUSIC Funk, Hip Hop, Dub, House, DJs Wed-Fri
DOOR None
DRINKS Beer £2.20, Wine £2.60, Cocktail £4.50
FOOD Snacks, Tapas, £5
CARDS None
CAPACITY 100, seating 70
HIRE Venue: Yes · Private Room: Yes

DRAGON

Bar
5 Leonard Street EC2
020 7490 7110

OPEN Mon-Sat midday-	**GETTING LUCKY**	**2/5**
11pm, Sun midday-10.30pm	**EYE CANDY**	**3/5**
TUBE/RAIL Old Street	**BIG SPENDERS**	**3/5**
BUSES 35, 55	**MIX** 50%M 50%F	
	AGE 26-35	
	PRICE Average	

AMBIENCE Basement, Casual, Conversation, Dive Bar, Funky, Groups, Grunge, Lounge
REVIEW In Lower East Side Nu Yawk style, this once derelict shell has been dusted down, resuscitated and picked up by owner Justin Piggott. The decorative wooden doorway has a slightly Oriental look, but Eastern influences stop there. A kind of living artwork with bleak, beautiful views over a deserted carpark, the staff are more than happy behind the decks or the counter, so don't be surprised when the bartender becomes the DJ. This place is so subversively cool that the interior and regulars could well be the next Turner Prize winners. Even the toilet graffiti is encouraged by the proprietor – as long as your tag's good you can join in the odd scrawling session. Prim and proper goodie two shoes types should steer well clear.
PLACE Low-key, brickwork-exposed narrow bar with bare floorboards and a basement lounge area. Invitingly tattered and torn leather sofas surround it and a Jake and Dinos Chapman piece has pride of place in the basement.
PEOPLE Strictly no suits, an esoteric clan of creative people sporting difficult haircuts who are more than prepared to stand out from the crowd either for their art or just as an intellectual statement.

PROFS Artists, designers, photographers, media professionals, editors, musicians, graphic designers, Hoxtonites, students
CELEBS Jarvis Cocker, Alexander McQueen, Kate Moss, Danny from Hear'Say
DRESS Low down and dirty, free and easy, quirky fashion queens, jeans and retro ironic t-shirts
MUSIC Hip Hop, Funk, Drum 'n' Bass, Rock 'n' Roll, DJs and Live Bands Fri-Sat
DOOR No suits
DRINKS Beer £2.50, Wine £2.50, Cocktail £6
FOOD None
CARDS No Amex or Diners
CAPACITY 150, seating 50
HIRE Venue: No · Private Room: No

THE FOUNDRY

Bar
84-85 Great Eastern Street EC2
020 7739 6900

OPEN Tue-Fri 4.30pm-11pm,	**GETTING LUCKY**	**3/5**
Sat 2.30pm-11pm, Sun	**EYE CANDY**	**2/5**
2.30pm-10.30pm	**BIG SPENDERS**	**2/5**
TUBE/RAIL Old Street	**MIX** 70%M 30%F	
BUSES 55	**AGE** 18-45	
	PRICE Cheap	

AMBIENCE Casual, Outdoors
REVIEW This ex bank turned bar-and-art-venue has become a magnet for anyone sick of having other people's money rammed in their faces by the Shoreditch Twat crowd (and that must include the many local strippers who have to cope with City-boy overflow). Recent installations/experiments include controlled explosions and mushroom growing in the basement; this place is no stranger to maggot racing. The regulars have frequent Fight Club style punch-ups, and poetry night on Sundays ('Come down and read your poems if you think you're hard enough') attracts punters more up for the craic than chin-stroking.
PLACE The decor is very, very basic – not a galvanised steel-recessed light or rubber floor tile in sight, and the bar looks like it was transplanted from a youth club disco. There's a huge space downstairs and a vault complete with airlock door (good for fetishists).
PEOPLE The average weekday night yields a mixture of drunken, shouting, Noo-Meeja types, grant-funded video artists and assorted large, rollie-toting mutes. Weekends bring a younger, trendier digerati.

PROFS Artists, programmers, designers, musicians, maniacs
CELEBS Bill Drummond, Mark Manning
DRESS Varied; though distinctly lacking in suits. For those who feel insecure when too far away from a designer label, Fridays and Saturdays provide a fuller quota of Japanese girls in huge shoes and young geezers with last week's mini-mohican
MUSIC Easy Listening, Chart, Dance, Rock, Pop, Eclectica, DJs Tue-Sat. Pints, Piss Artists and Poets, Sun
DOOR None
DRINKS Beer £2, Wine £2.50
FOOD None
CARDS None
CAPACITY 150, seating 50
HIRE Venue: No · Private Room: No

GRAND CENTRAL

Bar, Cocktail Bar, Cafe
93 Great Eastern Street EC2
020 7613 4228

OPEN Mon-Fri 7.30am-midnight,	**GETTING LUCKY**	**2/5**
	EYE CANDY	**3/5**
Sat 6pm-midnight,	**BIG SPENDERS**	**3/5**
Sun 10.30am-10.30pm	**MIX** 55%M 45%F	
TUBE/RAIL Old Street	**AGE** 22-34	
BUSES 55, 243	**PRICE** Average	

AMBIENCE Buzzy, Late Night Open, Network
REVIEW Set in a former corner site previously inhabited by The Shoreditch Eating House, Grand Central was snapped up by Eric 'Breakfast Group' Yu and smartened up by cool design agency Block. All brightness and natural light, it works better as a daytime café than a happening hotspot for late-night adventures – you want to go to Yu's Pop bar for that sort of 20-something free-love cavorting. No, this is a fairly muted affair with groups of Post Office drinkers sinking a few before heading home to their M&S ready meals. For some reason the cocktail list is preoccupied with Bourbon, so if that rocks your world make a beeline.
PEOPLE Spacious corner restaurant, café bar and deli with café style seating and a few raised areas. 'Go faster' multi-coloured stripes on illuminated panels lend that Paul Smith circa 2000 feel.
PEOPLE A scattering of types also found grazing in Sosho, Home, Electricity Showroom and Bluu.

PROFS Web designers, media employees, journos, photographers
CELEBS Jarvis Cocker
DRESS It's Shoreditch, so dress like a DJ or a City suit
MUSIC Latin, House, Disco, Funk DJ's Wed-Sun
DOOR None
DRINKS Beer £2.40, Wine £2.50, Champagne £6.50, Cocktail £4.50
FOOD All Day Breakfast, Deli, Grill, £6
CARDS All
CAPACITY 300, seating 100
HIRE Venue: Yes · Private Room: Yes

GREAT EASTERN DINING ROOM/ BELOW 54

Bar, Cocktail Bar
54 Great Eastern Street EC2
020 7613 4545

OPEN Thu-Sat 7.30pm-1am	**GETTING LUCKY**	**3/5**
TUBE/RAIL Old Street	**EYE CANDY**	**3/5**
BUSES 43, 55, 243	**BIG SPENDERS**	**3/5**
	MIX 55%M 45%F	
	AGE 22-38	
	PRICE Average	

AMBIENCE Arty/Bohemian, Basement, Comfy, Conversation, Funky, Groups, Hip/Fashionable, Late Night Open, Lounge, Student
REVIEW A cocktail lounge bar with art cred. The location inspired name could refer to its cool quota in degrees Centigrade, but it does more than that with its nod to stellar-hip NYC club Studio 54. Queues form outside the Great Eastern Dining Room towards the end of the week, when the area's arty-party posse fancy living it up underground. Those who look intense, offbeat, perhaps a tad creatively insane but pretty tasty too, should feel at home here, though blandsters and Suits won't stand a chance. Full of folk with 'difficult' haircuts, matched by the edgy-looking staff who look like art students or quirky Nordic pop stars. DJs spin music, and strange visuals, ranging from disturbing performance art to comic imagery, make for great mobile wallpaper.
PLACE Slate-grey basement sporting two hot pink floor stripes with lots of soft leather cubes and modular low

sofas for louche behaviour. Two walls play host to arty videos supplied by curators from the Lux cinema.
PEOPLE Hoxton's creative elite and Soho refugees searching for decent drinks, music and a credible scene. Arty desperados trying to escape the increasing invasion of drink tourists and carnivorous, slavering Suits above ground.

PROFS Music industry executives, graphic designers, fashion execs, publishers, magazine execs, writers, photographers, art students
CELEBS Kylie, Jarvis Cocker, Alexander McQueen, Vernon Kaye
DRESS Strictly no suits. Down and out in a Hoxton style. Utility wear, Nike, Firetrap
MUSIC Funk, Jazz, House, Hip Hop, Trip Hop, DJs Thu-Sat
DOOR No suits
DRINKS Beer £2.60, Wine £3.50, Champagne £5.80, Cocktail £5
FOOD Pasta, Salads, £5
CARDS All
CAPACITY 200, seating 80
HIRE Venue: Yes · Private Room: No

HERBAL

Bar, Club
12-14 Kingsland Road E1
020 7613 4462

OPEN Tue-Thu 7.30pm-11.30pm, Fri-Sat 7.30pm-2am	**GETTING LUCKY**	**2/5**
	EYE CANDY	**4/5**
	BIG SPENDERS	**3/5**
TUBE/RAIL Old Street	**MIX** 50%M 50%F	
BUSES 38, 55, 67, 149, 242, 243	**AGE** 20-35	
	PRICE Average	

AMBIENCE Chin Stroking, Funky, Hip/Fashionable, Late Night Open
REVIEW 'Spark up your chalis in Buckingham Palace', so croaked Howard Marks in the '97 chart 'stormer' of the same name. On the revolutionary antagonism front, Marks makes these Hoxton herbalists – herbs that you smoke, that is – look like geriatrics. The place is crammed with the sort of ironic Shoreditch bitches who

wouldn't understand irony if it rained on Alanis Morissette's wedding day. They congregate in Herbal to talk philosophical shop and look fashionably confused. Their soundtrack is jazzy/funky/breakbeaty, anything glad of the fusion tag and nothing to dent their mock-angst. Don't forget your Rizla.
PLACE The venue is all fairy light salesroom transplanted into a late 80s discotheque. Pocket-sized dance floor area, squishy red cube seats reminiscent of a kids section in a provincial library and a function room downstairs for the weekend overspill.
PEOPLE It's too early to say whether Herbal will be party to an Old Street cult breakaway, but early signs are promising. Whereas nondescript music policies draw the standard sneerophiles, on nights such as Groove Armada's Nearest and Dearest the revellers gather more for the tunes than to showcase the latest word in utility wear. A smattering of unlikely looking tourists skulk at the peripheries.

PROFS Artists, musicians, photographers, designers
CELEBS Groove Armada, Samantha Janus, Dave Courtney, Kate Moss, Helen Adams
DRESS Firetrap, Carhartt, Paul Smith, Portobello market curiosities
MUSIC Funk, House, Breakbeat, Old Skool, Ska, Drum 'n' Bass, Hip Hop, Funky House
DOOR Entry £5-7
DRINKS Beer £2.80, Wine £2.50
FOOD None
CARDS All
CAPACITY 250, seating 50
HIRE Venue: Yes · Private Room: Yes

HOME

Bar, Restaurant
100-106 Leonard Street EC2
020 7684 8618

OPEN Mon-Sat 5.30pm-midnight	**GETTING LUCKY**	**4/5**
	EYE CANDY	**4/5**
TUBE/RAIL Old Street, Liverpool Street	**BIG SPENDERS**	**3/5**
	MIX 50%M 50%F	
BUSES 43, 76, 141, 214, 271	**AGE** 25-30	
	PRICE Average	

AMBIENCE Arty/Bohemian, Basement, Buzzy, Chilled, Comfy, Cosy, Dancing, Groups, Late Night Open, Pulling
REVIEW Forerunner of a new 'concept': catering for the bohemian crowd who trip hop between Portobello, Soho and EC2. Blurring the distinction between restaurant, bar and lounge, Home is still a buzzing success. It captures City suits for lunch and early evenings, but by 9pm the laid-back posse moves in. Relaxed, though rehearsed, posing as mixed groups sprawl across the eclectic collection of sofas and coffee tables. It's a hip magazine photo shoot. The conversational hum is suggestive of intellectual types- probably meeja zeitgeist topics and favourite ads. There's some attitude and self-conscious style snobbery, but it's generally friendly. Reclined, idle posing is possible due to physical proximity. Feels like home but without a parent in sight.
PLACE Distinctive house logo announces 'Home' on the otherwise anonymous entrance (it's difficult to find). Suburban wooden banisters and carpeted stairs lead

to a subterranean space comprising stripped wooden floors, deep sofas and club chairs.
PEOPLE Creative and streetwise. Lofties (Clerkenwell loft dwellers), grown-up clubbers, aspiring Manhattanites and Soho lovers sick of the invasion of chain pubs who have moved to EC2.

P Tyagi & Craig Moffat, Architects

PROFS Publishers, advertising execs, restaurant and bar staff, designers (graphic, fashion, interior), prop makers, style writers, TV researchers and editors
CELEBS Ralph Fiennes, Talvin Singh, Ted Baker, Erin O'Connor, Boyzone, Kylie, Jemma Kidd, Paul Rothschild, Sacha Baron Cohen, Tamsin Outhwaite
DRESS Urbanite NYC leisure wear. Snowboard cool. The latest Nike/Adidas trainers (not yet available in the UK), Addict, Diesel, Carhartt and Firetrap mixed with DKNY and fleamarket staples like Lee cords and Hawaiian shirts
MUSIC Hard House, US Garage, Funk, DJs Fri-Sat
DOOR None
DRINKS Beer £2.80, Wine £3.50, Champagne £4.50, Cocktail £5.75
FOOD Modern European, £13
CARDS All
CAPACITY 250, seating 50
HIRE Venue: Yes · Private Room: Yes

HOXTON SQUARE BAR & GRILL

Bar
2 Hoxton Square N1
020 7613 0709

OPEN Mon-Sat 11am-midnight, Sun 11am-10.30am	**GETTING LUCKY**	**2/5**
	EYE CANDY	**3/5**
	BIG SPENDERS	**2/5**
TUBE/RAIL Old Street	**MIX** 60%M 40%F	
BUSES 242	**AGE** 25-35	
	PRICE Average	

AMBIENCE Casual, Conversation, Groups, Star Spotting, Student
REVIEW Andreas and Patrick's follow-up to Two Floors in Soho, this was an instant hit among the hip Hox crew. On the Home and Electricity Showrooms alco-circuit, it's rammed on a Friday and brimming with energy, a rough cut mix of locals, students, Soho refugees and craftspeople from surrounding studios and collective art spaces. Look out for transatlantic visitors thirsty after a trip to the White Cube² (that's squared – geddit). Pulling? Perhaps if you wear your gear right and 'you know your shit'. Ex-BMX riders and the Star Wars generation gather and natter under ambient street light flickering in through the mezzanine-height windows at the back.
PLACE The rear view is 'Starsky & Hutch' in downtown New York; when it rains you expect James Dean to skulk by in his overcoat. When it's sunny the louche spill out on to the front.
PEOPLE People who take their irony seriously. Icy kohled-up Scandinavian chicks with their photographer boyfriends.

PROFS Designers, students, musicians, writers, models
CELEBS Tracey Emin, Alexander McQueen, Kylie
DRESS Retro woman: ironic sweatshirts, goth boots and Miss Sixty jeans. Balenciaga, Diesel, Levi's
MUSIC From Rock to R&B
DOOR None
DRINKS Beer £2.50, Wine £2.80, Champagne £5, Cocktail £5.50
FOOD Continental, English, £7.50
CARDS No Diners
CAPACITY 300, seating 100
HIRE Venue: Yes · Private Room: No

KATABATIC

Bar, Club
89 Great Eastern Street EC2
020 7739 5173

OPEN Mon-Wed 4pm-11pm, Thu 4pm-midnight, Fri 4pm-2am, Sat 8pm-2am	**GETTING LUCKY**	**4/5**
	EYE CANDY	**3/5**
	BIG SPENDERS	**3/5**
TUBE/RAIL Old Street	**MIX** 50%M 50%F	
BUSES 43, 55, 243	**AGE** 20-40	
	PRICE Average	

AMBIENCE Party, Late Night Open, Pulling
REVIEW This new £1.5 million supervenue has laid claim to the swarm of easy-to-please barflys who frequent the drinking holes of Old Street. Despite its distinctively modern blend of music and design Katabatic proves that money can't buy you love. Set over three floors, including a main bar, basement club and mezzanine, there is a peculiar soullessness to the proceedings. Despite the aesthetic beauty of tropical fish-tanks and rainbow strobes, Katabatic is full of no-hopers intent on getting humourlessly and hopelessly drunk. It's early days for Old Street's latest hotspot, but the fact that it's a more vibrant experience by day than night speaks volumes. Do yourself a favour and save the five pound entrance fee for somewhere round the corner.
PLACE Like a show home – faultlessly presented, full of gleaming edges and modern furniture but not somewhere you'd ever choose to live.
PEOPLE A young pre-club crowd, City boys and girls in expensive threads and older men in the throes of a mid-life crisis.

PROFS City types, media employees, secretaries
CELEBS None

DRESS Woodhouse, Reiss, Ben Sherman, Kookaï,
Whistles, Karen Millen
MUSIC Club Nights, House, Latin, Funk
DOOR £5 after 10pm at weekends
DRINKS Beer £2.70, Wine £3.20, Champagne £7,
Cocktails £5.70
FOOD Pizza, £6.50
CARDS All
CAPACITY 350, seating 100
HIRE Venue: Yes · Private Room: Yes

THE LIGHT

Bar, Restaurant, Members Bar
233 Shoreditch High Street EC2
020 7247 8989

OPEN Mon-Wed midday-midnight, Thu-Sat midday-2am, Sun 12.30pm-10.30pm	**GETTING LUCKY**	**2/5**
	EYE CANDY	**2/5**
	BIG SPENDERS	**4/5**
TUBE/RAIL Old Street	**MIX** 60%M 40%F	
BUSES 26, 35, 43, 47, 48, 55, 149, 242	**AGE** 25-50	
	PRICE Average	

AMBIENCE Buzzy, Comfy, Cute Staff,
Industrial/Warehouse, Hip/Fashionable, Lounge
REVIEW An impressive-looking new venue lingering on
the City borders, with high ceilings, exposed brickwork
and timber rafters left over from the power station that
once existed in its place. Unfortunately, the ambience of
this bar, restaurant and members club fails to match the
grandeur of the building. There is a trivial arrogance to
the staff that makes ordering a beer feel like grand
larceny, the clientele are never quite as good looking
as they ought to be and the minimalist furniture is
arranged with a strange lack of perspective so you feel
either Lilliputian or Gulliver-like depending on where you
sit. On the plus side, The Light acts as an effective
barrier, the last line between City bars for City boys and
Hoxton bohemia. Why do you think they made it so big?
PLACE Suffers through its size. There's an unruly and
painstaking stampede to the huge bar on Friday nights.
It's worth checking out for the brilliant restoration work
on one of Shoreditch's most dilapidated industrial
buildings but you may not want to stay too long.
PEOPLE A definite corporate feel. It's generally City hell,
although Shoreditch and Hoxton locals do pop in for
Sunday lunch.

PROFS Traders, brokers, analysts
CELEBS None
DRESS Anything goes, although the members bar has
a refreshing 'no suits' policy
MUSIC Dance, Club Classics, DJs Thu-Sat
DOOR None
DRINKS Beer £2.70, Wine £2.50, Cocktails £5
FOOD French Mediterranean, £12.50
CARDS All
CAPACITY 585, seating 350
HIRE Venue: Yes · Private Room: Yes

MOTHER

Bar, Club, Cocktail Bar, Live Music Venue
1st Floor, 333 Old Street EC1
020 7739 1800

OPEN Sun-Wed 6pm-1am, Thu-Sat 6pm-2am	**GETTING LUCKY**	**3/5**
	EYE CANDY	**2/5**
TUBE/RAIL Old Street	**BIG SPENDERS**	**2/5**
BUSES 26, 48, 55, 253	**MIX** 51%M 49%F	
	AGE 20-36	
	PRICE Average	

AMBIENCE Buzzy, Casual, Dancing, Groups,
Hip/Fashionable, Late Night Open, Lounge, Retro
REVIEW If Shoreditch is the home of lounging,
then 'Mother' is the mother of the lounge lizard.
From the pierced eyebrow jetset to the lush lowbrow
lo-fi, there are no restrictions and its late licence
ensures a refreshing mix of clientele. Sunday to
Thursday sees the local breed of 'lost' Hoxtonians
blending down with Italian disco funk DJs, deutsche
sound design engineers, multimedia meddlers, ('we
invented IT, darlin'), and rock chic barflies. Mullets strut
their stuff at the weekend along with transient clubbers
downloading from the overcrowded West End, so come
early to avoid queues. Having the same owner as the
Bricklayers Arms guarantees Hoxton hardcore credentials
with a big, wild welcome mat. From a Guinness to a
Manhattan, drinks are inexpensive and add to the
louche atmosphere.
PLACE On the T-junction of Old Street and Curtain Road.
Distinctly lacking ostentation. Flock wallpaper, 70s decor,
but the view over the road and moody lighting adds to
the Brooklyn international flavour. Sofas and chaises
longues are hard to come by after 9pm.
PEOPLE International estuary 20-36ers. Musicians and
designers mix with St Martin's flunkies and Notting Hill
downsizers. MTV will probably relocate from the Café
Grove shortly.

PROFS DJs, sound engineers, IT consultants, musicians
CELEBS None
DRESS Diesel, Maharishi, Carhartt, Levi's, Camper shoes,
thrift-store chic
MUSIC House, Rare Groove, Hip Hop, Drum 'n' Bass,
Soul, Funk, Garage, Global Beats, Psychedelic Rock,
Reggae, DJs Wed-Sat
DOOR No ties or suits; Mother is part of 333 club,
for entrance after 10pm see 333
DRINKS Beer £2.80, Wine £2.40, Cocktail £4.50
FOOD Snacks, £3
CARDS No Amex or Diners
CAPACITY 600, seating 50
HIRE Venue: Yes · Private Room: No

PLASTIC PEOPLE

Club, Live Music Venue
147-149 Curtain Road EC2
020 7739 6471

OPEN Thu-Sat 10pm-3am	**GETTING LUCKY**	**3/5**
TUBE/RAIL Old Street	**EYE CANDY**	**2/5**
BUSES 8, 26, 55, 242	**BIG SPENDERS**	**2/5**
	MIX 50%M 50%F	
	AGE 20-35	
	PRICE Average	

AMBIENCE Basement, Buzzy, Chin Stroking, Friendly,
Funky, Hip/Fashionable, Late Night Open, Live Music,
Mashed-up, Queues

REVIEW No frills basement clubbing in the heart of Hoxton, servicing electro fiends with asymmetrical haircuts, monied students, Essex tourists and anyone brave enough to risk a boogie on the power-cut dark dance floor. On poor nights little more than an overspill for big daddies 333 and Cargo, pokey old Plastic occasionally comes up trumps with the sort of DJ sets that leave you battling the tinnitus to eulogise on their greatness for, ooh, weeks afterwards. The seating deficit in the bar area makes for interesting musical chair games and the area is lit so well you can watch the panic set in when newly formed dance floor tongue-tusslers witness the pockmarked realities of their new beaus.

PLACE Small, low-ceilinged and sparse with about one table and three chairs. A dance floor negotiable only by cigarette light, somewhat baffling for the see and be seen Hoxton contingent, who resort to flailing windmill motions to elicit attention from the brooding cyber-geek in the corner.

PEOPLE Despite its proximity to Shoreditch Twat territory the clientele are not as fiercely trendy as many of their 80s revivalist compadres, but if you trip over mini scooters on entry, think again.

PROFS Musicians, artists, graphic designers, computer programmers, copywriters
CELEBS Normski, Steven Leather
DRESS Nike climbing boots and combat trousers for the boys – perfect for the great indoors. On girls, the latest in denim and asymmetrical tops
MUSIC Electro, Jazz, Funk, Breakbeat, Latin, Afro, Brazilian
DOOR Entry £6-10
DRINKS Beer £2.50, Wine £2.75, Cocktail £3.50
FOOD None
CARDS No Amex
CAPACITY 150, seating 40
HIRE Venue: Yes · Private Room: No

THE POOL

Pool Bar
104-108 Curtain Road EC2
020 7739 9608

OPEN Mon-Tue midday-11pm, Wed-Thu midday-1am, Fri midday-2am, Sat 5.30pm-2am, Sun midday-10.30pm	GETTING LUCKY	**4/5**
	EYE CANDY	**4/5**
	BIG SPENDERS	**3/5**
	MIX 60%M 40%F	
	AGE 20-30	
TUBE/RAIL Liverpool Street, Old Street	PRICE Average	
BUSES 26, 35, 47, 48, 55, 67		

AMBIENCE Basement, Hip/Fashionable, Party, Pulling
REVIEW They were on my left as I walked in. Two total stunners, sat on their own. Men were milling around them, making awkward approaches, but they only had eyes for me. As the strains of music and conversation filtered across from the other end of the bar, I heard one of them murmur play with me... play with me... bend over, take that big stick in your hand and play with me all night long. Sorry, but if falling in love with pool tables is a crime, then lock me up and throw away the key. Yes, it's clearly a great place to meet people, dance, get chatted up, enjoy the company of friends and all that. But please, there's pool to be played.

PLACE A spacious shell with enough elbowroom for an octopus to play. The huge roadside windows allow passers-by to appraise your every move, which entirely explains why I lost five games on the trot. There's a dance bar downstairs with – thank you God – another sumptuous slab of baize.
PEOPLE Standard issue gorgeous, trendy, 20-year-old Shoreditchers whose idea of a hard day's work involves DJing at two of their friends' nightclubs in one evening.

PROFS IT professionals, DJs, journalists
CELEBS Kylie, Sol Campbell, Big Brother girls, Jimmy White, Ronnie Wood
DRESS Evisu, Stüssy, retro Adidas
MUSIC Hip Hop, House, Reggae, DJs Wed-Sun
DOOR None
DRINKS Beer £2.50, Wine £2.50, Cocktail £4.50
FOOD International, £6.50
CARDS No Amex
CAPACITY 350, seating 100
HIRE Venue: Yes · Private Room: No

SHOREDITCH ELECTRICITY SHOWROOMS

Bar, Restaurant
39a Hoxton Square N1
020 7739 6934

OPEN Tue-Wed midday-11pm, Thu midday-midnight, Fri-Sat midday-1am, Sun midday-10.30pm	GETTING LUCKY	**4/5**
	EYE CANDY	**4/5**
	BIG SPENDERS	**3/5**
	MIX 55%M 45%F	
	AGE 25-35	
TUBE/RAIL Old Street	PRICE Average	
BUSES 38, 55, 67, 149, 242		

AMBIENCE Casual, Dancing, Groups, Late Night Open, Pulling, Star Spotting
REVIEW Basic interior decorated by murals. Currently a Land Rover advert featuring two bathing hippos sits behind the bar, and Swiss mountains, like a Lindt chocolate box cover, one wall. Rammed with smoky arrogance on a Friday night, cliques congregate on the sofa and around the café tables. Freaks with 'tude barge by, so cuttin' edge that excusing themselves is not an option. Be gratified to rub shoulders with them. A very pretty crowd who know it, and anything else worth knowing too for that matter. If you're finger snappin' hip, a 'life-space creator', a 'structural fabric manipulator', or 'just, like, play around with stuff' come down and explore your own backside or bounce some concepts off

fellow vainguards of style. Otherwise FCUK off and get a life, or at least the latest Nikes.
PLACE Rectilinear with huge windows. Electricity showroom parody, from illuminated dome exterior to standard bulb box lampshades inside and electronic display menu inside.
PEOPLE If you asked 'Is there a designer in the house', you'd be artfully trampled. Life is a magazine. Talented, young and razor-sharp, probably the ones-to-watch in Wallpaper, i-D, Dazed and Confused and The Scene.

PROFS A designer's wet dream: fashion, web, interiors, furniture, graphics. Artists, TV professionals, account execs, architects, musicians
CELEBS Kylie, Damien Hirst, Paul Daly, Gavin Turk, Tracey Emin, Malcolm McLaren, Neil Tennant, Richard Ashcroft, Sade, Jarvis Cocker
DRESS Original and alternative, just like the clientele; Prada, trainers, Brick Lane meets Hoxton Boutique
MUSIC Garage, Soul, Jazz, R&B, Hip Hop, Dub, Dance, DJs Fri-Sat
DOOR None
DRINKS Beer £2.70, Wine £3.10, Cocktail £5.50
FOOD Modern European, £8.50
CARDS All
CAPACITY 400, seating 80
HIRE Venue: Yes · Private Room: Yes

SOSHO

Bar, Cocktail Bar
2 Tabernacle Street EC2
020 7920 0701

OPEN Mon-Wed midday-midnight, Thu-Fri midday-2am, Sat 7pm-2am	**GETTING LUCKY**	**4/5**
	EYE CANDY	**3/5**
	BIG SPENDERS	**4/5**
TUBE/RAIL Old Street	**MIX** 55%M 45%F	
BUSES 55, 243	**AGE** 24-45	
	PRICE Average	

AMBIENCE Arty/Bohemian, Funky, Groups, Hip/Fashionable, Late Night Open, Pulling, Warehouse/Industrial
REVIEW Caught between the creative hipsters of Hoxton and the straight-laced Square Milers, Sosho somehow manages to cater to both parties. It can be suit City hell, but luckily the bar's art gallery slant encourages

some more interesting characters. That, and cocktail guru Mr Dick Bradsell, who worked as spirit consultant when the bar opened a year ago. He won't be serving you behind the bar, but the rest of the Bradsell-trained team are pretty damn hot. With a helping hand from US drinks maestro Dale Degroff, Sosho guarantees top-notch tipples. They've named it Sosho, by the way, after the urban slang for South Shoreditch. Try saying that after a Match Spring Punch too many.
PLACE Match no. 3 is the largest of the lot. Warehouse loft interior with plenty of brown leather banquettes and sofas, some café style seating and huge photo-murals of crocodile swamps and roads.
PEOPLE Loud and lairy office workers who make a 10pm exodus to Liverpool Street, leaving the more louche and laid-back creative lot who only have to start nudging their mouse back to life around 10am the next day.

PROFS Media professionals, bankers, lawyers, solicitors, management consultants, artists, graphic designers, photographers, marketing managers, journalists
CELEBS None
DRESS Suits to sneakers; Next, Reiss, Boss, M&S, Stüssy, Adidas, FCUK, Levi's, Maharishi, Uth
MUSIC Jazz Fusion, Funk, DJs Thu-Sat
DOOR Fri £5 after 10pm, Sat £5 after 8pm
DRINKS Beer £2.85, Wine £3.25, Champagne £5.75, Cocktail £6.20
FOOD International, £6.50
CARDS All
CAPACITY 260, seating 68
HIRE Venue: Yes · Private Room: Yes

islington

25 CANONBURY LANE

Bar
25 Canonbury Lane N1
020 7226 0955

OPEN Mon-Fri 5pm-11.30pm,	**GETTING LUCKY**	**2/5**
	EYE CANDY	**3/5**
Sat midday-11.30pm,	**BIG SPENDERS**	**3/5**
Sun midday-10.30pm	**MIX** 50%M 50%F	
TUBE/RAIL Highbury &	**AGE** 23-35	
Islington, Angel	**PRICE** Average	
BUSES 4, 19, 30, 43		

AMBIENCE Casual, Chilled, Comfy, Conversation, Cosy
REVIEW Once an old man's boozer with a knocking shop upstairs, the millennium heralded a new era for 25 Canonbury Lane. Transformed from a pints 'n' prossies hellhole into a relaxed, laid-back hangout, it's a particular fave of eminent playwrights, Big Breakfast presenters and hunky actors (all of whom wish to remain nameless). These days, house specialities are the cocktails at a fiver a go, though most people seem happy quaffing lager on tap or working their way through the extensive wine list. It's a smallish room with an ad hoc feel which has thankfully avoided the BBC's ever popular 'Changing Islington Bars' mosaic and mirrors treatment.
PLACE Blend of cold turquoise and warm red. A certain Art Deco influence in the beautiful mirrored cabinet behind the bar, but no dominating style or philosophy.

PEOPLE Cool but not desperately hip and happening. They've heard of two-step but would never dream of buying any.

PROFS Fashion professionals, lawyers, estate agents, bar and restaurant staff, retailers, media executives, insurance agents, actors, playwrights
CELEBS Jay Kay, Denise van Outen, Fine Young Cannibals, Kate Winslet, Cassandra (Only Fools and Horses), Cate Blanchett, Jarvis Cocker
DRESS FCUK, Ted Baker, Firetrap, Diesel, Jigsaw
MUSIC Soul, Jazz, Funk, Chill-out
DOOR None
DRINKS Beer £2.60, Wine £3, Champagne £4, Cocktail £5
FOOD Tapas, Modern British, £7
CARDS No Amex
CAPACITY 70, seating 30
HIRE Venue: No · Private Room: No

ALL BAR ONE

Bar, Restaurant, Chain
1 Liverpool Road N1
020 7843 0021

OPEN Mon-Sat 11am-11pm, Sun midday-10.30pm **TUBE/RAIL** Angel **BUSES** 19, 30, 38, 73, 153, 341	GETTING LUCKY	**2/5**
	EYE CANDY	**3/5**
	BIG SPENDERS	**3/5**
	MIX 65%M 35%F	
	AGE 25-35	
	PRICE Average	

AMBIENCE Casual, Conversation, Groups
REVIEW This laid-back hangar-sized branch of the ever-expanding All Bar One chain comes as a pleasant surprise. Populated by a slightly older and more polite crowd than the Pitcher & Piano down the road, it's not so packed, the atmosphere is relaxed and clever positioning of tables means that people don't camp around the bar. It features all the usual Ikea with beer suspects – refectory-large wooden tables, long bar, comfy sofas, brass fittings, bla bla bla. Music is subdued, although the enthusiastic crowd, pumped up by pitchers of vodka and Red Bull, makes enough noise on its own. There are a few hopeful stragglers by the bar, but generally people drink in packs, so pulling potential is limited.
PLACE The bar itself is impressive if you like that sort of thing – long and lined with wine bottles in the house style. There's the de rigueur skylight, and overhead fans keep the drinkers cool. More wood than a Scandinavian sauna.

PEOPLE Lots of after-work drinkers in suits and professional women secure in the knowledge that they're trendier than their Fulham counterparts. Even the bouncers (whose presence seems a little unnecessary) are polite.

PROFS Architects, shop staff, bankers, doctors, music executives
CELEBS Johnny Vaughan, Denise van Outen
DRESS Lewin shirt and tie combos, Hugo Boss suits, whizzy cufflinks a must. Gap polo shirts for those in mufti. Karen Millen and Whistles for the girls
MUSIC Easy Listening, Funk, Jazz, Chart
DOOR Over 21s, Smart casual
DRINKS Beer £2.90, Wine £2.70, Champagne £7
FOOD Traditional British, £7.50
CARDS No Diners
CAPACITY 200, seating 100
HIRE Venue: No · Private Room: No

BABUSHKA

Bar, Restaurant, Chain
125 Caledonian Road N1
020 7837 1924

OPEN Mon-Thu midday-11pm, Fri midday-midnight, Sat 6pm-midnight, Sun midday-10.30pm **TUBE/RAIL** King's Cross **BUSES** 17, 91, 259, 274	GETTING LUCKY	**2/5**
	EYE CANDY	**3/5**
	BIG SPENDERS	**3/5**
	MIX 60%M 40%F	
	AGE 18-35	
	PRICE Average	

AMBIENCE Cosy, Dancing, Live Music, Opulent, Party
REVIEW All mock baroque and bijou, this cosy bar pulls in a similar though slightly more savvy crowd to the nearby Ruby Lounge. It's got a get-pissed-quick policy and during the evenings it's packed with budding party girls perfecting their excited arm-waving and lip-glossy air kisses, while young lads cruise through the crowd with pints in hand. Older, local logo-designers and netheads come to boogie and wash away their corporate selves in a fast-flowing stream of cheap beers and weird vodka shooters. 'Crazy' flavours like rhubarb 'n' custard and garlic are a Babushka speciality.
PLACE Large windows overlook the canal. The Midas touch has been applied to everything: windows, doors, pictures, etc. Burning candles sit atop large wooden tables, flanked by pewlike benches.
PEOPLE Creatives and local, bar-circuit trendsters mix with a slightly younger, nervous crowd who may just be discovering boozers for the first time. Tease with impunity.

PROFS Media execs, advertising account execs, marketing staff, graphic designers, publishers, bankers
CELEBS None
DRESS DKNY, Ted Baker, Nicole Farhi, Karen Millen. Scruffy Portobello Market second-hand chic meets up-to-the-minute label trendy
MUSIC Easy Listening, DJs Wed-Sat, Jazz Sun
DOOR None
DRINKS Beer £2.60, Wine £2.60, Champagne £5.95, Cocktails £5
FOOD Mediterranean, Modern British, £6
CARDS All
CAPACITY 400, seating 220
HIRE Venue: Yes · Private Room: Yes

BABUSHKA

Bar, Restaurant, Chain
188-190 New North Road N1
020 7354 5400

OPEN Mon-Fri midday-11pm,	**GETTING LUCKY**	**3/5**
Sat 4pm-11pm,	**EYE CANDY**	**4/5**
Sun midday-10.30pm	**BIG SPENDERS**	**3/5**
TUBE/RAIL Highbury &	**MIX** 40%M 60%F	
Islington, Essex Road	**AGE** 25-40	
BUSES 30, 73, 271	**PRICE** Average	

AMBIENCE Casual, Chilled, Funky, Groups
REVIEW The newest member of the Babushka family circle is awkwardly situated in the darker fringes of Islington, stuck in a no-mans land between the alluring lights of Upper Street and the popular hedonism of Hoxton. Babushka's USP is the widest range of vodkas known to man, although many barflys seemed more excited by what they simply described as 'wall-to-wall cleavage'. Although there is enough to recommend the latest version of Babushka – not least a debauched Saturday night House and Funk-fest – it remains to be seen if it can lure drinkers away from neighbouring hotspots on a regular basis.
PLACE A Lawrence Llewellyn-Bowen clone has been given free reign over the interior design. The cumulative effect of open fires, chestnut floorboards, halogen lighting, pristine bar, eclectic furniture and dubious Moroccan drapes can be cloying.
PEOPLE Drunken fools in Ben Sherman shirts stumble off the beaten track and end up here, hoping to find vodka and women in ample supply. The suited and booted arrive from nearby new media offices and Katherine Hammnett's London base in search of an alcohol fix.

PROFS New media, fashion executives
CELEBS Katherine Hammnett
DRESS Smart casual
MUSIC Dance, Funk, House DJs Thu-Sun
DOOR None
DRINKS Beer £2.70, Wine £2.60, Cocktails £5.50
FOOD Modern European with Asian twist, £6
CARDS All
CAPACITY 350, seating 150
HIRE Venue: Yes · Private Room: Yes

DUKE OF CAMBRIDGE

Gastropub
30 St Peter's Street N1
020 7359 3066

OPEN Mon-Sat midday-	**GETTING LUCKY**	**2/5**
11pm, Sun midday-10.30pm	**EYE CANDY**	**2/5**
TUBE/RAIL Angel	**BIG SPENDERS**	**4/5**
BUSES 38, 56, 73, 341	**MIX** 60%M 40%F	
	AGE 38-65	
	PRICE Average	

AMBIENCE Casual, Conversation, Groups, Mature/Older
REVIEW One of the noisiest pubs in London, and there isn't a loud speaker or television screen in sight. The sonic racket comes from something called conversation, that last resort of human beings when

there's nothing to gawp at or hum along to. The clientele are generally older and wiser than in your average Islington boozer – in some cases, so much older you get the feeling they're frantically articulating everything they've ever thought before Alzheimer's sets in. Thousand-page memoirs of wartime Blighty are dictated over a couple of pints, while a genuine pearly king munches on a bowl of nuts. Maybe it's something they put in the beer. Or leave out, because what really puts this bar on the map is its exclusively organic food and drink. With most main courses priced in two figures, you do pay through the nose, but the quality is such that at least you won't be paying through any other orifice the following morning.
PLACE Big, glass window and classy pillars. Lots of big wooden tables nicked from French farmhouses.
PEOPLE Retired factory farmers who always eat free range because they can afford it and 30-somethings panicking about all the rubbish they ate in their 20s, calming their nerves with vast quantities of organic alcohol.

PROFS Media employees, publishers, photographers, painters, PR agents, architects
CELEBS Kylie, Ralph Fiennes, Cate Blanchett, Jennifer Ehle
DRESS Ted Baker sweatshirts, Nike trainers, Stüssy, Ben Sherman, retro Adidas trainers, NB trainers, Liberty, Austin Reed, M&S
MUSIC No Background Music
DOOR None
DRINKS Beer £2.75, Wine £2.75, Champagne £7.25
FOOD Modern British, Modern European, Organic, £12.50
CARDS No Diners
CAPACITY 250, seating 150
HIRE Venue: No · Private Room: No

THE ELBOW ROOM

Bar, Pool Bar Chain
89-91 Chapel Market N1
020 7278 3244

OPEN Mon-Wed midday-	**GETTING LUCKY**	**4/5**
2am, Thu-Sat midday-3am,	**EYE CANDY**	**3/5**
Sun midday-10.30pm	**BIG SPENDERS**	**2/5**
TUBE/RAIL Angel	**MIX** 60%M 40%F	
BUSES 4, 19, 30, 43, 73	**AGE** 19-35	
	PRICE Average	

AMBIENCE Casual, Groups, Late Night Open, Pulling
REVIEW This young, brutish addition to the snooker-themed Elbow Room bar stable emits a shade of vomitous neon welcoming light redolent of the worst excesses of cheap 20th-century pop culture (see Fanny Craddock's dyed duchesse potato, American motels et al). No respite upon entry: the brasher-than-Bet-Lynch's-bazookas theme continues with the music policy – wedding greats and house tunes reminiscent of two blokes killing each other with dustbin lids. Not the place to come for a date then, but great for pulling: cue the cue length jokes and crisp snacks down cleavage game. Oh, and ladies can size up their potential sparring partners through the one-way mirrors in the loos — what was that about knowing how to hold your stick?

PLACE Cross between Ed's Easy Diner, Stringfellows and a teen disco circa '89. Ten pool tables fronting on to a parquet dance floor area punctured by stand/perch circular tables.
PEOPLE The inevitability of entropy gets 'em young here. Smooth elbow action swiftly deteriorates into flayed limbs and buttock groping as gelled, lowered-Golf boys compete with Islington media geeks in pulling birds with full head highlights.

PROFS Record industry workers, PRs, boy band wannabes
CELEBS Neneh Cherry, Robbie Williams
DRESS Jennifer Aniston haircuts, overpriced sportswear and middle-league high street clobber married with Chapel Market and boutique fare
MUSIC Hip Hop, US Garage, House, DJs 7 nights
DOOR Smart casual; Thu £3 after 10pm, Fri-Sat £4 after 10pm
DRINKS Beer £2.40, Wine £3, Cocktail £4.75
FOOD Grill, £6
CARDS No Amex or Diners
CAPACITY 600, seating 300
HIRE Venue: Yes · Private Room: Yes

EMBASSY BAR

Bar
119 Essex Road N1
020 7359 7882

OPEN Mon-Thu 5pm-11pm,	GETTING LUCKY	3/5
Fri-Sat 5pm-1am,	EYE CANDY	3/5
Sun 5pm-10.30pm	BIG SPENDERS	2/5
TUBE/RAIL Angel	MIX 50%M 50%F	
BUSES 38, 56, 73, 341	AGE 20-35	
	PRICE Average	

AMBIENCE Buzzy, Conversation, Late Night Open
REVIEW Once the nucleus of North London's fly posting mafiosas (and accompanying Babs Windsorlikes), this welcoming Islington bar retains a certain beer, spittle and nosebleed ambience, despite the gentrification imposed by its proximity to the Pizza Express and Piña Colada marauders of nearby Upper Street. The Embassy's breed of fallen angel is no boozy barfly-by-night; punters come here for the music. DJs from the greatest of the capital's club nights play a mixed bag of funk,

northern soul, breakbeat and music to stroke beards by from Thursday to Sunday. This place is offbeat cool, pulling may therefore be dependent on face furniture, or appreciation thereof. A more chilled atmosphere during the week gives way to a clubby be-seen feel at weekends.
PLACE Snug, low-ceilinged, battered and reminiscent of a 60s Krays hangout with subdued lighting concealing beery residue. Long, V-shaped bar gives necessary room for punters to lounge artfully. Black and white photos of a young Michael Caine betray retro-chic hankerings.
PEOPLE Proto-nerds to funky clubbers and more laid-back drinkers. Lots of goatees, shaved heads and Richard Ashcroft hairdos.

PROFS Students, musicians, media professionals
CELEBS Sara Cox, Sharleen Spiteri, The Verve, Jarvis Cocker, Paul Weller, Kate Winslet
DRESS Duffer, Carhartt, scruffy oiks, unisex casual
MUSIC Downbeat, Ambient, Funk, Breakbeat, DJs Thu-Sun
DOOR None
DRINKS Beer £2.60, Wine £3.40, Cocktail £4.50
FOOD None
CARDS No Diners
CAPACITY 240, seating 140
HIRE Venue: Yes · Private Room: No

MATT & MATT BAR

Bar, Cocktail Bar
112 Upper Street N1
020 7226 6035

OPEN Tue-Thu 5pm-	GETTING LUCKY	4/5
midnight, Fri 6pm-2am,	EYE CANDY	3/5
Sat 8pm-2am	BIG SPENDERS	3/5
TUBE/RAIL Angel,	MIX 50%M 50%F	
Highbury & Islington	AGE 24-35	
BUSES 4, 19, 30, 43	PRICE Average	

AMBIENCE Casual, Dancing, Groups, Pulling, Student, Late Night Open
REVIEW Described as Islington's answer to Ibiza, Matt & Matt's is a must for the kitsch-konscious. It's the girls on tour in 'Napa and the lads on the rage in Rhodes, and loving every minute of it. Luminous colours and fake sunflowers kaleidoscope deliriously around after a few flavoured vodkas, deeply tanned girls laugh lopsidedly in strappy white tops and heels while guys in black make their dead cert moves. One of the owners leans over the bar, a little worse for wear, and starts telling us of his plans to develop a 'Matt & Matt's tequila'. After all, their own flavoured vodkas, including Jelly Baby, Toblerone, Refresher and Galaxy, have taken off like a rocket. Boom boom.
PLACE There's a weird little alcove with a blue-topped pool table on your right as you go in leading through to a lurid and whimsically coloured bar, filled with little touches like a dressmaker's dummy and a sign on the wall reading 'Plan A'. Sit at the bar for best pulling opportunities.
PEOPLE Caroline works in a local estate agents and loves the 'totally mad' atmosphere which, she says, kicks off from about 7pm. She'd like us to say (since she just split up with her boyfriend) that she's 5'5", almost naturally blonde, a C-cup and likes clubbing,

drinking and ER. Tall, Latin-looking lover with GSOH required ASAP.

PROFS Office workers, students, shop workers, music and TV professionals, lawyers, City bankers, PR, advertising
CELEBS Lennox Lewis, Kevin Spacey, Jason Orange, Paul Whitehouse, Sara Cox
DRESS Miss Selfridge, Kookaï, Morgan, Nicole Farhi, Dolce & Gabbana, Diesel, Stüssy
MUSIC Dance, House, Trance, Funk, DJs Thu-Sat
DOOR None
DRINKS Beer £2.60, Wine £2.60
FOOD Members free; non-members £4 after 10pm Fri-Sat
CARDS No Amex or Diners
CAPACITY 100, seating 40
HIRE Venue: No · Private Room: No

MEDICINE BAR

Bar
181 Upper Street N1
020 7704 9536

OPEN Mon-Thu 5pm-midnight, Fri 5pm-2am, Sat midday-2am, Sun midday-12.30pm	**GETTING LUCKY**	**3/5**
	EYE CANDY	**4/5**
	BIG SPENDERS	**3/5**
TUBE/RAIL Angel	**MIX** 60%M 40%F	
BUSES 4, 19, 30, 43	**AGE** 25-30	
	PRICE Average	

AMBIENCE Arty/Bohemian, Buzzy, Casual, Comfy, Conversation, Cosy, Cute Staff, Dancing, Friendly, Funky, Groups, Hip/Fashionable, Late Night Open
REVIEW Could this be the best bar in Islington? Answers on a postcard, please. Small but vibrant, it's got that Lower East Side Manhattan effortless hip/relaxed chic feel. Brilliant staff are quick, charming and funny, DJs play a heady mix of urban funk and 70s soul at not impossible volume and the management care about their clientele. A no suit policy is applied

politely but firmly and a (free) membership scheme operates on Fridays and Saturdays to deter the less palatable elements of the Upper Street melée.
PLACE Renovated on the site of one of the oldest pubs in London. Funky colours and subdued lighting. Deceptive amount of space. Excellent chilling area at the back where people sprawl on low sofas.
PEOPLE Arty, self-possessed crowd. Creative types abound.

PROFS Models, fashion designers, artists, DJs, stylists, graphic designers
CELEBS Denise van Outen, Jay Kay, former All Saints, Norman Cook, James Dean Bradfield, Paul Whitehouse, Kate Winslet, Jamie Theakston, Death in Vegas, Martine McCutcheon
DRESS Urban scruffians, sneakers, turn-ups
MUSIC Soul, Funk, Jazz, House, Drum 'n' Bass, DJs 7 nights
DOOR None
DRINKS Beer £2.80, Wine £2.80, Champagne £4.50, Cocktail £4.50
FOOD Breakfast, £4.50
CARDS All
CAPACITY 250, seating 90
HIRE Venue: No · Private Room: Yes

RUBY IN THE DUST

Bar, Restaurant, Chain
70 Upper Street N1
020 7359 1710

OPEN Mon-Wed 10.30am-11pm, Thu-Sat 10.30am-2am, Sun midday-10.30pm	**GETTING LUCKY**	**4/5**
	EYE CANDY	**4/5**
	BIG SPENDERS	**2/5**
TUBE/RAIL Angel	**MIX** 50%M 50%F	
BUSES 43, 75, 274, 279	**AGE** 20-40	
	PRICE Average	

AMBIENCE Casual, Cosy, Cute Staff, Dancing, Pulling Groups, Friendly, Late Night Open
REVIEW Aptly named, Ruby is a shining jewel of a joint nestling in the grimy hustle, bustle and corporate monotony of Upper Street. Part of a small chain of five, attention to bohemian detail is still apparent. More chic than shabby, it's still got a bit of beguiling roughness around the edges. The waiters and waitresses positively glow with beauty, youth and friendliness, and they all speak Italian, even if they're not, for reasons beknownst only to themselves.
PLACE Upstairs, it has a Latin/Cuban feel, painted with bright reds, purples and yellows. Despite the Mediterranean flavour, it's Disco, rather than Dante's Inferno – the music has a high-to-mellow energy semi-retro flavour. Downstairs, the boho feel continues, with a distressed brass bar and wackily shaped mirrors.
PEOPLE Laid-back family types getting away from the kids. Single boys and girls who don't want to be scene, but don't want to be invisible. Sexy party animals who look like they'll be dancing on the ceiling with roses between their teeth before midnight.

PROFS Lawyers, estate agents, TV producers, PRs, journalists, students, office workers, designers, graphic artists, scriptwriters
CELEBS Kylie, Fun Lovin' Criminals, Howard Marks, Alexander McQueen, Jennifer Saunders, Ade Edmondson, Jo Whiley, Denise van Outen

DRESS Gap, Ralph Lauren, Nicole Farhi, Karen Millen, 70s retro dresses and cardis, moleskin trousers, tactile fabrics.
MUSIC Funk, Disco, Chart, Rock, Pop, 80s, DJs Thu-Sat,
DOOR Smart casual; £3 after 11pm
DRINKS Beer £2.55, Wine £2.95, Cocktail £3.55
FOOD International, Modern Eclectic, £8
CARDS All
CAPACITY 115, seating 115
HIRE Venue: Yes · Private Room: Yes

RUBY LOUNGE

Bar
33 Caledonian Road N1
020 7837 9558

OPEN Mon-Thu midday-midnight,	**GETTING LUCKY**	**3/5**
	EYE CANDY	**4/5**
Fri-Sat midday-2am	**BIG SPENDERS**	**2/5**
TUBE/RAIL King's Cross,	**MIX** 60%M 40%F	
St Pancras	**AGE** 20-35	
BUSES 17, 19, 259, 274	**PRICE** Average	

AMBIENCE Casual, Funky, Groups, Party, Retro
REVIEW A local with ideas above its grotty location, the Ruby Lounge is a bizarre hybrid of languid posturing and 'don't give a toss' attitood. Still, it pulls a few very beautiful punters and fills the need for some middle ground between Scala cool and Upper Street commercialism. The pub interior looks like it's been hastily vamped-up with a job lot of red leatherette and a staple gun. The music is banging: loungey, dancey or deep house, with regular DJs from The White House and The Cobden Club. Cocktails are courtesy of Alphabet Bar, so you don't need to schlep over there for some style in a glass.
PLACE Grubby 19th-century corner pub, glammed up with a liberal coat of deep pinky-red paint and a plastic wall-fixture made up of eight shiny moulded red half-balls. Uplights look like sheet-at-a-time toilet paper holders.
PEOPLE Media-savvy pre-clubbers, skateboard kids, drama students.

PROFS Designers, ad agents, PR agents, skateboarders
CELEBS Richard Blackwood, Gabrielle, Irvine Welsh, Mike Figgis, Saffron Burrows, Gabrielle
DRESS Skate style baggy pants and slogan t-shirts, glam and clubby little bright dresses, jeans and basic tops
MUSIC Hip Hop, House, Rare Groove, Soul, DJs Thu-Sat
DOOR None
DRINKS Beer £2.60, Wine £2.80, Cocktail £5
FOOD Modern Tapas, £3
CARDS No Amex
CAPACITY 125, seating 85
HIRE Venue: Yes · Private Room: No

SALMON AND COMPASSES

Pub, Club
58 Penton Street N1
020 7837 3891

OPEN Mon-Wed 5pm-midnight, Thu-Sat 5pm-2am, Sun 1.30pm-10.30pm	**GETTING LUCKY**	**3/5**
	EYE CANDY	**3/5**
	BIG SPENDERS	**2/5**
TUBE/RAIL Angel	**MIX** 60%M 40%F	
BUSES 38, 43, 73, 214	**AGE** 21-35	
	PRICE Cheap	

AMBIENCE Buzzy, Casual, Conversation, Dancing, Friendly, Funky, Hip/Fashionable, Late Night Open, Mashed-up, Queues
REVIEW Little more than a beery belch of a North London pie, pint and fight pub dun good, the Salmon and Compasses has managed to put itself on the clubby bar map with a hearty roster of underground house and hip hop nights and a Caffreys ad meets Manchester Uni reunion vibe. As sexy as twitchy Red Bull jumping and winding ever gets, the dance floor is the main attraction and is usually stocked with an odd assemblage of parka-clad beat freaks, bemused Upper Street refugees and shiny skirted/pastel shirted totty. Perhaps George Michael should have the last word on this place. As he memorably sang in that timeless classic Wham Rap 'Young guns having some fun, crazy ladies keep 'em on the run'. That's the Salmon and Compasses in a nutshell.
PLACE Oil paintings of horses, a cartoony mural of an elephant being drowned in a lake of fire, an imposing bar, low-slung, battered seating and lots of sticky dance/walk/talk space.
PEOPLE Casual professionals, graduate drunks, flirty thirties, graphic designers with portfolios in their bags and city boys who've still got a life.

PROFS Musicians, tattoo artists, advertising employees, office workers, students, market research, IT consultants, runners, copywriters
CELEBS None
DRESS Kick flares, tiny tees bearing ambiguous slogans, Oxford Street sportswear, battered leather. Bench, Diesel and Miss Sixty jostle with bargain basement finds
MUSIC Commercial Dance, Hip Hop, Live Music/Events: House, Hip Hop, R&B, Soul, Garage
DOOR £3 entry Fri-Sat
DRINKS Beer £2.50, Wine £2.50
FOOD No
CARDS All
CAPACITY 150, seating 40
HIRE Venue: No · Private Room: No

SLUG AND LETTUCE

Bar, Chain
1 Islington Green N1
020 7226 3864

OPEN Mon-Sat 11am-11pm,	**GETTING LUCKY**	**2/5**
Sun 11am-10.30pm	**EYE CANDY**	**3/5**
TUBE/RAIL Angel	**BIG SPENDERS**	**2/5**
BUSES 4, 19, 30, 43	**MIX** 50%M 50%F	
	AGE 25-35	
	PRICE Average	

AMBIENCE Casual, Conversation, Groups
REVIEW 'A chain bar as a chain bar does', my grandmother was fond of saying and the Slug and Lettuce is no exception. It's a cheese sandwich, fuel food kinda bar, filling a hole when you're on the move.

Use The Slug and Lettuce as a compromise, a place to meet before moving on somewhere groovy. Let's face it, everybody knows where it is and it's an unthreatening location for a swifty while you're waiting for your mates. Considering you're slap bang in the middle of Islington's main drag, there are a lot of better places for a bev but hell, there are a lot of worse ones, too.

PLACE Swizzed up pub-cum-bar. Weirdly there's never anywhere to sit even though it's quite big. Worth knowing about the cheeky second bar hidden away on the first-floor room, furnished with loungey sofas and some group tables.

PEOPLE Martin from Sales and Linda from Accounts get beltered at a mutual friend's leaving do and snog in a taxi all the way home.

PROFS Designers, estate agents, architects, secretaries, admin staff
CELEBS Robbie Williams
DRESS Heaving with fresh-from-the-office casual and suits, Ben Sherman, Next, River Island, Ted Baker
MUSIC Rare Groove, Indie, DJ Sun
DOOR Over 21s
DRINKS Beer £2.85, Wine £3.70
FOOD Modern European, £6
CARDS No Diners
CAPACITY 200, seating 75
HIRE Venue: No · Private Room: Yes

THE SOCIAL

Bar, Restaurant
33 Linton Street N1
020 7354 5809

OPEN Mon-Fri 5pm-11pm, Sat 11am-11pm, Sun 11am-10.30pm	**GETTING LUCKY** 3/5
	EYE CANDY 4/5
	BIG SPENDERS 3/5
TUBE/RAIL Angel	**MIX** 50%M 50%F
BUSES 38, 56, 73, 271	**AGE** 25-40
	PRICE Average

AMBIENCE Buzzy, Cosy, Conversation, Friendly, Lounge Atmosphere, Party, Retro
REVIEW While you were blissfully gurning in a field in Milton Keynes, the person on the bar stool next to you was preparing for the eleven plus. Meet The Social mark II, where grown-ups drink when they've given up free parties. Formerly an old man's pub (some of the original punters still drink here, making for an interesting contrast to the meeja and muso regulars), it's retained most of the original wood panelling and tables but with some Socially retro touches thrown in. Photography features dishevelled landscapes and hope-inspiring messages on Evangelical churches... Martin Creed, ya better watch out...
PLACE Two floors – upstairs has battered old sofas. Beautifully kitsch ten grand jukebox provides music during the week until St Etienne, Bugged Out and Jockey Slut turn up to turn it up at the weekend.
PEOPLE People travel far and wide for this out-of-the-way venue, resulting in an up for it crowd hell bent on growing old disgracefully. Don't let them down.

PROFS Musos, graphic designers, photographers, meeja crowd
CELEBS Sara Cox and Jon Carter, Miranda Sawyer, Lowri Turner, Sarah Cracknell, Chemical Brothers, Beth Orton, Martine McCutcheon
DRESS Firetrap, Urban Outfitters, Relic, Evisu, Jigsaw, Johnny Loves Rosie, Erin O'Connor style, Asymmetrical haircuts
MUSIC Jukebox, 80s Rock through to Happy House with some Burt Bacharach in between, DJs Fri-Sun
DOOR None
DRINKS Beer £2.60, Wine £2.55, Champagne £5, Cocktail £4.50
FOOD Modern Scottish/British, £9
CARDS All
CAPACITY 300, seating 60
HIRE Venue: No · Private Room: Yes

primrose hill

THE ADELAIDE

Pub
143 Adelaide Road NW3
020 7722 3777

OPEN Mon-Sat midday-11pm, Sun midday-10.30pm	**GETTING LUCKY**	**4/5**
	EYE CANDY	**2/5**
TUBE/RAIL Chalk Farm, Swiss Cottage	**BIG SPENDERS**	**2/5**
	MIX 50%M 50%F	
BUSES C11, 31	**AGE** 18-35	
	PRICE Average	

AMBIENCE Brightly Coloured/Cheerful, Outdoors, Pulling
REVIEW It wouldn't be surprising if The Adelaide has caused a few crashes in its time. Positioned at the Swiss Cottage end of Adelaide Road, this pub sticks out like a... well, like a blindingly bright yellow pub incongruously planted on a grey, fumy, concrete road. The reverently placed tequila bottles, whirring overhead fans and distressed (distressing) terracotta and turquoise walls look like they've been put together by a colour-blind designer with a penchant for Mexicana. It gets better towards the back, though, with a pretty red conservatory leading on to a large beer garden, the pub's most popular feature in summer when young Kappa Slappers from the tower blocks across the road come in droves to pull.
PLACE The main room is large and airy with a big central bar. Round tables with mosaic tiling are littered randomly around the large floor space, and palm trees stand in corners, looking desperate for a hot drink and a woolly jumper.
PEOPLE Young locals popping in for a quick mid-week pint and cheapie Pad Thai, illicit NW3 couples avoiding the Hampstead crowds.

PROFS Bank clerks, secretaries, travel agents, actors, media types
CELEBS None
DRESS Girls wear frilly Hennes tops, Miss Selfridge spray-on trousers and obligatory sparkly accessories. Boys opt for smart 'holiday' casual, short-sleeved shirts, clashing trousers and the odd baseball cap
MUSIC Soul, Ambient, Latin Jazz
DOOR None
DRINKS Beer £2.60, Wine £2.75, Cocktail £4.50
FOOD Thai, £4.95
CARDS No Amex
CAPACITY 200, seating 100
HIRE Venue: Yes · Private Room: Yes

THE ENGINEER

Gastropub
65 Gloucester Avenue NW1
020 7722 0950

OPEN Mon-Sat 9am-11pm, Sun 9am-10.30pm	**GETTING LUCKY**	**1/5**
	EYE CANDY	**3/5**
TUBE/RAIL Chalk Farm	**BIG SPENDERS**	**4/5**
BUSES C11, 24, 27, 31, 168	**MIX** 40%M 60%F	
	AGE 35-60	
	PRICE Average	

AMBIENCE Conversation, Friendly, Gourmet/Foody, Hip/Fashionable, Outdoor
REVIEW The Engineer is definitely up there with The Eagle when it comes to London's best gastropubs. One of the first and still a favourite, not only with local luvvies but paperweight politicos too. Bordering on restaurant territory, forget about a swift half here – the rule is book, book and book again. Although not ideal for a hot date, it's the perfect place to show your parents how far you've come. An extensive wine list raises the stakes, but the food really is the business. Anyway, drinks are on Daddy.
PLACE Stylishly gloomy canalside setting. An element of 'olde-English tea room' is offset by overpriced art on the wall.
PEOPLE Polished intellectuals, glamorous grannies and refugees from St John's Wood.

PROFS Media, luvvies, computer geeks and gadget freaks
CELEBS Sacha Baron Cohen, Sadie Frost, Neneh Cherry, Jude Law, Derek Draper, Alastair Campbell, Jonathan Glazer
DRESS Keep the olds happy – have a laugh, wear a scarf
MUSIC Background Easy Listening
DOOR None
DRINKS Beer £2.60, Wine £2.35, Champagne £6.50, Cocktail £5
FOOD Modern European, £12
CARDS No Amex or Diners
CAPACITY 120, seating 70
HIRE Venue: No · Private Room: Yes

THE LANDSDOWNE

Gastropub
90 Gloucester Avenue NW1
020 7483 0409

OPEN Mon-Sat midday-11pm, Sun midday-4pm, 7pm-10.30pm	**GETTING LUCKY**	**2/5**
	EYE CANDY	**3/5**
TUBE/RAIL Chalk Farm	**BIG SPENDERS**	**3/5**
BUSES 274	**MIX** 50%M 50%F	
	AGE 27-60	
	PRICE Average	

AMBIENCE Casual, Children/Families, Conversation, Groups, Mature/Older
REVIEW Like you probably didn't know about the Dian Fossey (Gorillas in the Mist) Centre in Camden, you probably aren't aware of this glorious gastropub a few doors down. That's because The Landsdowne, like the indigenous gorillas, is one of Primrose Hill's best-kept secrets. And the locals want it to stay that way. The food at this pub stands out like a Big Issue seller in Prada. It's unexpectedly gorgeous, wholesome and served by straight-up Londoners who have never felt the need to fake a French accent to convince you of how great their fare really is.
PLACE Outside, standard picnic tables line the cream-tiled frontage. Inside it's a bit like an upmarket school dining room, all plain walls and solid chairs scraping rough wooden floors.
PEOPLE Rich local trendies and Natural Nylon wannabees sip their Guinness alongside genuine old-timers who lived in the Hill when you could still buy a one-bedroom flat for less than £500,000.

PROFS Writers, architects, designers, artists, media and radio personalities
CELEBS Johnny Depp, Tom Cruise, Nicole Kidman, Jude Law, Kate Winslet, Boy George, Sacha Baron Cohen, Robert Plant, Neil Morrissey, Blur, Jon Bon Jovi, Vanessa Feltz, Noel Gallagher
DRESS Prada, Duffer, Maharishi, Zara, Whistles, Christy Turlington's yoga pyjamas
MUSIC No Background Music
DOOR None
DRINKS Beer £2.70, Wine £2.80
FOOD Organic Rustic, £11.50
CARDS No Amex
CAPACITY 200, seating 90
HIRE Venue: Yes · Private Room: Yes

ODETTE'S WINE BAR

Bar, Wine Bar
130 Regent's Park Road NW1
020 7722 5388

OPEN Mon-Sat 5.30pm-	GETTING LUCKY	**1/5**
midnight	EYE CANDY	**2/5**
TUBE/RAIL Chalk Farm	BIG SPENDERS	**4/5**
BUSES 31, 274	MIX 50%M 50%F	
	AGE 30-60	
	PRICE Average	

AMBIENCE Basement, Chilled, Conversation, Romantic
REVIEW This is a bar for types who'd spend £800 on Bose noise-cancelling ear phones. It's quiet tranquil, not quiet dead. It's ironically named 'Mad Max Bar' – cellar nook tables, candles, in no way whatsoever mad – attracts sedate local professionals who fill it up early. Food, a good wine list and erratic service make the bar feel like a cut-price version of the famed ground-floor restaurant. Good for an intimate evening à deux, or just a great way to prepare for the yawning waste of middle age.
PLACE Low basement bar, covered in classic black-and-white photos and posters of root vegetables.
PEOPLE Wealthy young couples playing at being grown-ups, smart locals and their families, the unhip rich of Primrose Hill.

PROFS Writers, music and film industry employees, doctors, lawyers, accountants, academics, artists
CELEBS Noel Gallagher, Liam Gallagher, Ewan McGregor, Michael Palin, Joan Collins, Bob Hoskins, George Michael, Zoë Ball
DRESS If a Volvo could dress itself – safe, sensible and definitely not cheap
MUSIC No Background Music
DOOR None
DRINKS Beer £2.95, Wine £3.25, Champagne £6.95, Cocktail £6.50
FOOD Brasserie, £8
CARDS All
CAPACITY 40, seating 40
HIRE Venue: No · Private Room: No

THE QUEENS

Gastropub
49 Regent's Park Road NW1
020 7586 0408

OPEN Mon-Sat midday-	GETTING LUCKY	**1/5**
11pm, Sun midday-10.30pm	EYE CANDY	**4/5**
TUBE/RAIL Chalk Farm	BIG SPENDERS	**3/5**
BUSES 31, 274	MIX 50%M 50%F	
	AGE 30-60	
	PRICE Average	

AMBIENCE Conversation, Outdoors, Views
REVIEW With it's A-list location on the corner of Primrose Hill, The Queens is very much an affluent local's local, especially now the departure of Liam and Patsy has thinned out all but the most out-of-touch Oasis-spotters. It's a better-than-average gastropub, perfect for a post-yoga rocket and parmesan salad or burger if you're feeling naughty. Less self-consciously pretty than The Engineer up the road, it's the kind of place you could take the lads for a post-footie sausage and mash and still get change from a tenner. The pub really comes into its own on Bonfire Night, when frazzled parents sedate shell-shocked children with vats of mulled wine and locals rue the day Guy Fawkes played around with a box of matches.
PLACE Well-preserved Victorian corner pub with high ceilings and ornate fixtures. Head to the terrace with a set of binoculars in the summer for a spot of topless star-spotting on the Hill.
PEOPLE Wealthy boho types with the emphasis on music and media people and their lawyers.

PROFS Music and media professionals, estate agents, lawyers, bankers
CELEBS None
DRESS Significantly less flashy than other Primmy Hill locals
MUSIC Easy Listening
DOOR None
DRINKS Beer £2.60, Wine £2.50, Champagne £7, Cocktail £5
FOOD Traditional Pub Fare with Modern British twist, £8
CARDS No Amex or Diners
CAPACITY 100, seating 35
HIRE Venue: No · Private Room: Yes

© James Pelltekian

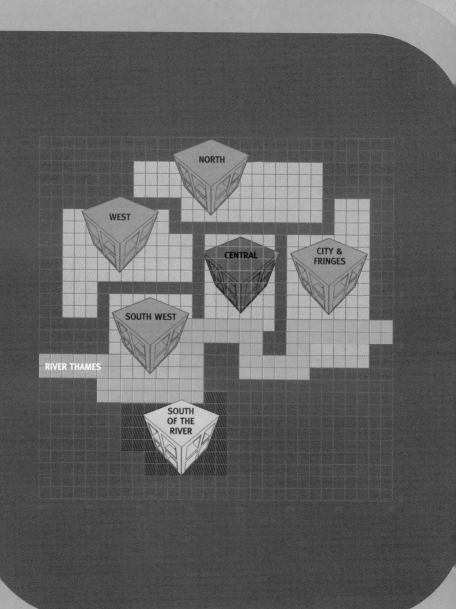

METRO

intro

SOUTH OF THE RIVER
balham
battersea
brixton
camberwell
clapham
elephant & castle
greenwich

South of the river is as far as nightlife goes, not an area that even a social Shackleton would have the stomach for. Property prices may have soared but the glitter has not rubbed off on the lamentable lack of choice and style here. As large as an estate agent's asinine grin, its case is seriously damaged by appalling traffic and a crap transport system. Tip: make friends with your black cabbie by asking him to take you back to Clapham on a Friday night.

Battersea is first port of call for those who make it over the water. The local sport here is pram-dodging, due to the amount of new mums and dads who like to think that they actually live in south Chelsea, which has resulted in a lot of bars but few of note. The most credible of these is **The Drawing Room and Sofa Bar**.

It's a fact that most of Balham's residents aspire to live in Battersea (do you see a dirty hierarchy forming here – will Orpington be next in line?). Sometimes called south Clapham (if you're that way inclined) its residents think that Balham's the next big thing, though if you'd bought in 2000 you'd have been a fool – it was the only area in London where property prices actually fell. **Exhibit** draws the Balham masseeve.

Brixton was previously known as the place to go in London if you wanted to have your hair blow-dried by a welding torch or a sawn-off shotgun; it now attracts middle-class white boys who reckon they're tuff enuff and cat-keeping 30-year-old meeja types. **Bug Bar** and **Dogstar** hold almost cult status, while **Mass** and **Fridge** are responsible for drawing some of the most interesting dressers in London for Torture Garden and Escape from Samsara.

Camberwell arguably holds the most credible and user-friendly bars in the south. Its biggest customers are the neighbouring Goldsmiths and Camberwell arts students,

who give even the most dedicated Hoxtonite a run for their money in the distressed fashion stakes.

Clapham's (or rather Cla'am darling) chattering classes are largely comprised of financial, real estate and recruitment upstarts squandering their wages in the many bars. The High Street is awash with places to drink, from cool, laid-back revamped pubs like **The Railway** to your 'know-what-you're-getting' chains, like **Bierodrome** and **The Fine Line**. Among the High Street fodder a few real gems sparkle: the rather stylish and sublime **Sequel** and so-Marrakech **So.uk**, owned by Lee Chapman and Leslie Ash of Teatro. And for the truly chi chi, both **Sand** and the triple-floored **White House** have members bar areas, it's so good the locals can forget about Soho, which is just as well considering the not-going-south cabbie syndrome.

If Ali G hadn't been born in Staines he would have come from Elephant and Castle, home to the most controversial council estate in London and the ugliest roundabout. An acceptable reason to venture into Puffa City is to check out the big-name DJs at the **Ministry of Sound**.

By far the most productive outcome of the Millennium Dome Project was the effect it had on the quantity and quality of bars in the area. Despite the hype, Greenwich never really managed to secure anything other than the cliquey but naice younger middle classes it always attracted, though **Time** is well worth the journey.

balham

BALHAM TUP

Pub, Chain
21 Chestnut Grove SW12
020 8772 0546

OPEN Mon-Sat 11am-11pm,	GETTING LUCKY	1/5
Sun 11am-10.30pm	EYE CANDY	2/5
TUBE/RAIL Balham	BIG SPENDERS	3/5
BUSES 249, 355	MIX 70%M 30%F	
	AGE 25-60	
	PRICE Cheap	

AMBIENCE Business, Conversation, Groups, Live Music
REVIEW For donkey's years this place was the infamous Balham Hotel, a haven for the area's grottiest cut-throats, uiks and spluttering coffin-dodgers. After several half-hearted attempts to revamp the site, the Tup gang got their hands on it and rapidly went about transforming the place, via the ubiquitous stripped floorboards and industrial magnolia technique. The result is a welcome addition to this, the scuzzy but improving end of Balham High Road, and predominantly attracts hordes of Balham's ever increasing yuppie population. That said, you still get the occasional smattering of 'You callin' my pint a poof' geezers who wander in to bemoan how Balham's gone all poncey.
PLACE Enormous windows give the Tup a very airy feel and the open plan layout and the long bar means it never feels overly packed. Sadly, this all adds up to a rather spartan atmosphere. At least the lack of perfection and uniformity in the furniture detracts from the 'boozer-by-numbers' feel.
PEOPLE Aside from the occasional ruddy-nosed stray who still thinks this is the old 'otel, it's strictly the post-work brigade and 'Balham's the new Clapham' type upstarts.
PROFS Bankers, estate agents, publishers, salesman, IT, advertising execs, marketers, foreign exchange dealers
CELEBS Hunter (Gladiator)
DRESS M&S suits, Jigsaw, FCUK, Nike, Zara, Levi's denim jackets. Mr Byrite trainee estate agent suits mingling with trainers and oceans of monochrome monotony
MUSIC Easy Listening, Pop
DOOR None
DRINKS Beer £2.50, Wine £2.50, Cocktail £3
FOOD Pub Food, £6.50
CARDS All
CAPACITY 420, seating 250
HIRE Venue: No · Private Room: Yes

BAR INTERLUDE

Bar
100 Balham High Road SW12
020 8772 9021

OPEN Mon-Fri midday-11pm,	GETTING LUCKY	4/5
Sat 11am-11pm,	EYE CANDY	3/5
Sun 11am-10.30pm	BIG SPENDERS	3/5
TUBE/RAIL Balham,	MIX 55%M 45%F	
Clapham South	AGE 20-35	
BUSES 155, 355	PRICE Average	

AMBIENCE Dancing, Groups, Hip/Fashionable, Party, Pulling
REVIEW A real jewel in the turd known as Balham High Road, this excellent bar attracts Balham's youthful, combat-wearing contingent by the bucketload and, along with Exhibit and Oblivion, saves locals the cab fare into Clapham. Oliver Reed once said that the only reason blokes go to the pub is to 'Get pissed, pull birds and bullshit.' If that's the case Interlude is perfect as, come the weekend, sexual frisson abounds, service is rapid and music-levels are conversation-friendly. Performance trainer-wearing girls squat on dinky beanbags nibbling sundried whatevers, as groups of Hoegaarden-sipping blokes surreptitiously cop a look at the knicker elastic on show. Meanwhile, doting couples chill out on the leather sofas sipping Rolling Rock and plotting the evening ahead. Best new bar in Balham.
PLACE Don't tell the new residents that this site once housed an Asian furniture shop selling items that'd make George and Mildred wince. When Interlude first opened, the exterior was very magnolia and Fine Line-ish, but the owners come over all Changing Rooms and painted the place in a more distinctive shade of lilac. The smart interior has lots of exposed brick, orchids, huge pot plants, backlit glass tiles, bleached wood, bizarre fireplace, flash sound system... must've cost a fortune.
PEOPLE Strangely enough, the young and the beautiful of Balham. Anyone who can't afford to live in Clapham. 20-somethings who rent nearby, locals who used to cab-it-the-hell-out of Balham for a drink, plus the odd non-sarf Londoner who's been forced there by his mates.

PROFS Estate agents, students, hairstylists, staff from other bars, fashion assistants, salespersons, set designers, admins, ITs
CELEBS Anna Friel
DRESS Bertie, Morgan, Pied à Terre, Miss Selfridge, jeans, leather biker jackets; 'Yoof' TV look: FCUK, Hilfiger, Next, Gap, Kookaï, the odd suit, Air Max, fitted cardies, Timberland, Quicksilver
MUSIC Disco, House, Funk, DJs Fri-Sat
DOOR None
DRINKS Beer £2.60, Wine £2.90, Cocktail £4.25
FOOD Snacks, Traditional British, Tapas, £6
CARDS All
CAPACITY 240, seating 50
HIRE Venue: Yes · Private Room: No

DUKE OF DEVONSHIRE

Pub
39 Balham Road SW12
020 8763 1363

OPEN Mon-Thu 11am-	GETTING LUCKY	2/5
midnight, Fri-Sat 11am-2am,	EYE CANDY	3/5
Sun midday-midnight	BIG SPENDERS	3/5
TUBE/RAIL Clapham South,	MIX 65%M 35%F	
Balham	AGE 25-40	
BUSES 355, 155	PRICE Cheap	

AMBIENCE Casual, Comfy, Dancing, Late Night Open, Outdoors
REVIEW The Duke is one of those boozers that does the simple things exceptionally well – the interior has

been beautifully refurbished, the service is swift, the music levels allow whispered conversations and there is nearly always somewhere to sit. But, as usual, it's the details that make all the difference: the brave use of candlelight throughout the main bar, for instance. Or the fact that at 11 o'clock the staff don't snarl for your glasses but gently alert you to the fact that you can continue drinking in the intimate jazz room where the booze flows and the candles and glitterballs create an ethereal atmosphere for low-level flirting in grand surrounds.

PLACE A big, old, traditional South London pub that's had a tasteful facelift to make it airy and inviting without sacrificing its heritage. The jazz bar at the rear has a 2am licence at weekends, midnight on other nights, and is tailor made for stranger-in-the-night shenanigans.

PEOPLE As befits the eclectic Balham/Clapham South catchment area, the Duke's clientele is a mix of the up and coming and the traditional: so stand-up comedians rub shoulders with local MPs, commodity brokers, journalists, builders and the old codger in the corner who has been a fixture since 1948.

PROFS Journalists, comedians, City workers, nurses, gardeners, builders
CELEBS None
DRESS Nike, Levi's, Next, M&S, Gap
MUSIC Live Jazz, Mellow Mainstream
DOOR None
DRINKS Beer £2.40, Wine £2.50
FOOD Traditional English, £4.50
CARDS No Diners
CAPACITY 300, seating 100
HIRE Venue: No · Private Room: Yes

EGA

Bar
87 Bedford Hill SW12
020 8673 6107

OPEN Mon-Sat 7pm-1am	GETTING LUCKY	**4/5**
TUBE/RAIL Balham	EYE CANDY	**3/5**
BUSES 355, 155	BIG SPENDERS	**2/5**
	MIX 65%M 35%F	
	AGE 22-35	
	PRICE Cheap	

AMBIENCE Casual, Friendly, Groups, Late Night Open, Legendary, Live Music, Party, Pulling
REVIEW One of the more colourful, chaotic and charismatic late-night drinking joints on the Balham scene. It was always dark inside, and its location at the base of Bedford Hill added to the sense of (imagined) danger. Now Roger and Chris, the two brothers who own the place, have given it a lick of paint, lined the walls with original art, sanded the floorboards and invested in a couple of light bulbs. The old, battered Tropicana sign is gone, replaced by the cryptic moniker EGA (slogan: Caffe – Bar – Fusion – excuse me?), and along with it some of the old-time, den-of-iniquity atmosphere. In its place is a bright, inviting bar run by two of the most charismatic geezers in Sarf London. There's a rum choice of cocktails (not to mention Roger's Rum Cocktail, which is psychotically more-ish) and a decent menu to boot.

PLACE Small, intimate bar where it's nigh on impossible to avoid mingling. Some of the party nights here during its Tropicana days have gone down in Balham legend, and though the name has changed and the decor may be sprucer, Roger and Chris can still party with the best of them.

PEOPLE Charles Bukowski would feel right at home in this barfly's paradise. The punters are generally Balham locals – a mix of journalists, City types, wannabe stand-up comedians, medical students et al, united by their love of booze-fuelled camaraderie.

PROFS Journalists, bankers, artists, musicians, advertising, media, students, comedians
CELEBS Arthur Smith, Boy George, Artful Dodger
DRESS Nike, Gap, M&S
MUSIC Funk, Jazz, House, Garage, Ambient, varied live musicians and groups
DOOR £3
DRINKS Beer £2.50, Wine £3, Cocktail £4.75
FOOD Global Fusion, £7
CARDS No Diners
CAPACITY 100, seating 30
HIRE Venue: Yes · Private Room: No

THE EXHIBIT

Bar, Restaurant Bar
Balham Station Road SW12
020 8772 6556

OPEN Mon-Thu 11.30am-	GETTING LUCKY	**3/5**
11pm, Fri 11.30-midnight,	EYE CANDY	**3/5**
Sat 11:00-midnight, Sun	BIG SPENDERS	**3/5**
midday-10.30pm	MIX 50%M 50%F	
TUBE/RAIL Balham	AGE 20-35	
BUSES 355, 155	PRICE Average	

AMBIENCE Conversation, Groups, Warehouse/Industrial
REVIEW These days it's all about 'location, location, location'. If this is true, spanking new Exhibit is in trouble, trouble, trouble, as it lurks behind the arse-end of Balham station and looks out over a Sainsbury's car park. Inside, this is Changing Rooms does James Bond, as Balham's barflies stand transfixed by an enormous tropical fishtank and a Blofeld-style fire. The startling lighting does little to lift the strangely fun atmosphere and, even at this early stage, the stressed-out staff appear to have lost the will to live. That said, it's still early days so teething problems are to be expected and, hopefully, corrected, as Balham needs all the trendy bars it can get.

PLACE This Lego-style industrial unit was never going to be easy to tart up. The exposed metal girders, corrugated iron roof and cement floor don't really gel with the plush fishtank, crazy lightboxes and creosoted wooden partitions.

PEOPLE Tables full of giggling girls who think Seabreezes are the best thing since sliced bread, trendy locals who dream of opening a bar and a few pre-Banana Cabaret punters.

PROFS Event organisers, carpet fitters, landscape gardeners, nursery teachers, media execs, City bods, insurance brokers, lawyers, estate agents, builders, students, accountants
CELEBS Actors from The Bill

DRESS Levi's, Jigsaw, Paul Smith, busty FCUK tops ('bit cold tonight darling?'), 'zany' Hawaiian shirts, combats and Jigsaw, Reiss and TopMan bits
MUSIC Ambient
DOOR None
DRINKS Beer £2.80, Wine £2.75, Cocktail £4.90
FOOD Modern European, £10
CARDS No Amex
CAPACITY 200, seating 90
HIRE Venue: No · Private Room: No

THE LOUNGE

Bar
76 Bedford Hill SW12
020 8673 8787

OPEN Mon-Fri 5pm-11pm,	**GETTING LUCKY**	**1/5**
Sat 11am-11pm,	**EYE CANDY**	**2/5**
Sun midday-10.30pm	**BIG SPENDERS**	**3/5**
TUBE/RAIL Balham	**MIX** 55%M 45%F	
BUSES 155, 355	**AGE** 20-60	
	PRICE Average	

AMBIENCE Casual, Groups
REVIEW Yet another spanking new bar to add to 'Blarms' burgeoning collection, this is an attractive little place plonked just by Balham Bridge, an area that, less than five years ago, was notable purely because it constantly stank of rotting pilchards, off cauliflower and dog's muck. Not that the punters in here would know much about that. Most of them are proud, new-wave Balhamites who've never had to sheepishly explain that they live 'er, near Clapham.' The Lounge is a smart and friendly bar, dotted with after-workers, unpretentious locals and the odd yuppie wine snob. It hasn't really found its footing as yet, but expect it to curry favour with the pre-Banana Cabaret crowd and upwardly mobile locals who find nearby Exhibit a tad too trendy.
PLACE Intimate corner bar with pleasant lighting, stripped floors, pot plants, pine tables and trendy uplighters. The bright exterior is painted in simple blues and creams. The staff seem accommodating enough – on our visit the Evisu-clad barman coped admirably with some pretentious ass who insisted on testing his red wine by sniffing it and then sloshing it round his gob – wise up mate, you're in Balham, not Belgravia.
PEOPLE A few attractive girls in for a post-work snifter, lovey-dovey couples who sit on the sofa and play with each other's hair, Freedom beer fans, well-dressed commuters, and locals in search of a peaceful glass of wine.
PROFS Architects, barristers, teachers, chefs, account execs, caterers, media students, receptionists, doctors, students, IT consultants
CELEBS Ainsley Harriott
DRESS Vans, Airwalk, Gap, TopShop, jeans, River Island, Jigsaw
MUSIC Jazz, Acid Jazz, Pop, Dance
DOOR None
DRINKS Beer £2.60, Wine £2.60, Champagne £4.75, Cocktail £4.50
FOOD Global Fusion, £8
CARDS No Amex
CAPACITY 130, seating 70
HIRE Venue: No · Private Room: Yes

battersea

BABEL

Bar
3-7 Northcote Road SW11
020 7801 0043

OPEN Mon-Sat midday-	**GETTING LUCKY**	**4/5**
11pm, Sun midday-10.30pm	**EYE CANDY**	**3/5**
TUBE/RAIL Clapham Junction	**BIG SPENDERS**	**3/5**
BUSES 35, 156, 170, 219	**MIX** 60%M 40%F	
	AGE 20-35	
	PRICE Average	

AMBIENCE Buzzy, Casual, Conversation, Dancing, Futuristic, Groups, Party, Pulling
REVIEW According to legend, the tower of Babel was intended to reach heaven, but Jehovah lost his rag and cursed its builders with a previously unknown confusion of languages, hence the word 'babble'. The history of this bar is decidedly less impressive, but in its previous incarnation as the Significant Half, the potential for Friday night fornication was frequently biblical in proportion. These days, minus the old grope-friendly central bar, this place attracts a party hearty mix of genitally-fixated singles, noisy couples and closet philanderers who mentally undress every new arrival with decreasing levels of discretion. The new, improved layout is conducive to shouty conversation rather than pouty flirtation, but the prospect of waking up next to a complete stranger remains a distinct possibility. Iron those pants.
PLACE Shame the only biblical allusion is the picture of a tower. Where are Sodom and Gomorrah and the plagues of locusts? Pleasant staff jerk ringpulls off Red Bull tins, and animated conversations take place amidst a selection of the ubiquitous seating pouffes, wood panelling and orange strip lighting.
PEOPLE A bloke who looks similar to Chris Evans drinks in here, but it can't be him – surely he's still in casualty having Danny Baker's tongue surgically removed from his bum cheeks. Look-a-likes aside, it's high end of the fun-o-meter for young Claphamites who have yet to succumb to the yuppy-esque trappings of Northcote Road.

PROFS Advertisers, office temps, journalists, junior investment bankers, IT salespeople, engineers, middle managers, wannabe entrepreneurs, jewellery designers
CELEBS None
DRESS Adidas, Firetrap, Third Rail, Duffer, Vans, River Island, New Balance, TopShop, Oasis, JCB, Reiss, Benetton, Jigsaw, Kookaï
MUSIC Funk, Soul, Motown
DOOR Smart casual
DRINKS Beer £2.80, Wine £2.90, Champagne £5.50, Cocktail £5
FOOD Snacks, Breakfast, Brunch, £6.50
CARDS All
CAPACITY 250, seating 40
HIRE Venue: No · Private Room: No

BAR ROOM BAR

Bar, Chain
441 Battersea Park Road SW11
020 7223 7721

OPEN Mon-Sat midday-11pm, Sun midday-10.30pm
TUBE/RAIL Battersea Park
BUSES 44, 49, 344, 345

GETTING LUCKY	**2/5**
EYE CANDY	**2/5**
BIG SPENDERS	**3/5**
MIX 55%M 45%F	
AGE 25-50	
PRICE Average	

AMBIENCE Casual, Chilled, Conversation, Elegant/Classic, Groups, Live Music
REVIEW Bar Room Bar. Bar Rum-ba. Geddit? No, I'm not sure I do either. Curious wordplay aside, this wonderfully elegant bar plays host to Battersea's well-to-do, and Chelsea's could-do-slightly-better. It's a cool, sassy place where FITS (Financially Independent 30-somethings) come to lounge around, drink Hoegaarden and pick at wood-fired pizzas. Even the DJ is unobtrusive and the eardrum-friendly volume level ensures things never get too Pete Tong. In the beautiful patio out back, some drunken twit tells everyone 'Aim not pissed. Aim fresh as a daisy'. Girlfriend Sophie remains unimpressed though and vanishes inside to fetch him an Evian. Whatever your tonic, this is a great place to pit stop en route to Chelsea.
PLACE Big and airy. Creating a relaxed synergy between old and new is not always easy (see the Liberace/Bet Lynch inspired Artesian Well), but this place has pulled it off with great aplomb. Seductive lighting, gorgeous chandeliers, twinkly wall lights, and an impressive Victorian frontage all add up to an exceptionally elegant watering hole. With its garden bar, mosaics and large metal sculpture, the patio out back would be great for a private do.
PEOPLE As this is a bit of a jaunt from the lively barcrawl area of Battersea Bridge Road, the people who come here are rarely on the pull. Consequently, the punters are usually locals chilling out and groups of couples slowly moving into that 'I must have a seat' phase of life.

PROFS Accountants, estate agents, set designers, buyers, PR agents, IT specialists, property developers, beauticians, salespeople, journalists
CELEBS None
DRESS Gap, Firetrap, Ralph Lauren, FCUK, Jigsaw, Nike, Hilfiger, Hackett

MUSIC Easy Listening, 70s, 80s, 90s, Pop, DJs Fri-Sat, Elvis impersonator first Friday of every month
DOOR None
DRINKS Beer £2.70, Wine £3.50, Cocktail £4
FOOD Pizza, Salads, £6.20
CARDS No Amex
CAPACITY 250, seating 60
HIRE Venue: No · Private Room: No

BASE

Restaurant Bar
1 Battersea Rise SW11
020 7228 6026

OPEN Mon-Sat 11am-11pm, Sun 11am-10.30pm
TUBE/RAIL Clapham Common, Clapham Junction
BUSES 49, 239, 337

GETTING LUCKY	**3/5**
EYE CANDY	**3/5**
BIG SPENDERS	**4/5**
MIX 50%M 50%F	
AGE 25-45	
PRICE Average	

AMBIENCE Conversation, Groups, Live Music, Party
REVIEW Base is an aspirational bar for the aspirational Battersea set that longs for an SW3 postcode. It tries very hard to be that little bit more sophisticated than it is, as do its customers: early 30-somethings who are clearly not short of a bob or two. This pleases the management immensely, as it means they can charge well over the odds for a gin and tonic and serve fantastic Leffe Blonde in half-pints. The clientele are happy in the belief that they must be in the right place. Still, it's a gemütlich little place: pavement tables on the street, accommodating bar stools at the front, an airy restaurant with a great menu further back, and even live music on Sundays. If only it would loosen its tie a little and relax this would be a much better venue.
PLACE Attractive enough, but contrived, with carefully-placed houseplants in silver pots complemented by exposed brick walls and large windows. Very deliberately more bar stools than tables, presumably to encourage more drinking, talking and general togetherness.
PEOPLE The obligatory Earl Jean wearing girl sporting a Caribbean tan perches on a bar stool and sniggers at the advances of an ex-army management consultant-type, probably named Alan. The clientele changes later on as the suits disappear and the SW11 crowd emerge from their garden flats, but the difference in attitude is negligible.

PROFS Solicitors, estate agents, management consultants, small business owners, TV producers, City types
CELEBS None
DRESS Blazer, Sisley, Press and Bastyan, Guess, Nicole Farhi, black DKNY, Emporio Armani, Gap, Russell & Bromley loafers, Harvey Nichols
MUSIC Jazz, Soul, Chart, Live Jazz Sun lunch, Soul Sun night
DOOR None
DRINKS Beer £3.90, Wine £2.75, Champagne £5.25, Cocktail £4.25
FOOD Modern European, Pacific Rim, South East Asian, £7.95
CARDS No Diners
CAPACITY 120, seating 60
HIRE Venue: No · Private Room: No

B@1

Bar, Cocktail Bar
85 Battersea Rise SW11
020 7978 6595

OPEN 7 days 5pm-11pm	GETTING LUCKY	4/5
TUBE/RAIL Clapham Junction	EYE CANDY	2/5
BUSES 49, 239, 337	BIG SPENDERS	3/5
	MIX 55%M 45%F	
	AGE 21-35	
	PRICE Average	

AMBIENCE Buzzy, Casual, Dancing, Groups, Party, Pulling
REVIEW Walk into B@1 and it is as if you have been teleported into a different space and time – possibly a British-run bar on a beach front in Majorca, circa 1987. The all-singing, all-dancing, Elvis-worshipping staff do the circus seal cocktail act with aplomb. B@1's holiday feel comes from the well-travelled staff, who've worked in or come from Hong Kong, Cape Town and other exotic locations. It's steamy in more ways than one; rugger or checked shirts bounce around to Robert Palmer, trying to impress a group of strapless-topped girls pretending to be those sullen lady guitarists in the 'Addicted to Love' video. Not 'cool' in any way, shape or form – but that kind of exuberance can be really infectious.
PLACE Surely this small, sweaty, vine-draped joint, bedecked with mirrors and framed photos of good times past, cannot be situated on quiet, respectable Battersea Rise?
PEOPLE A fun-loving crowd with absolutely no shame (which could be a good or a bad thing, depending on your point of view). A high public school quotient with a healthy lack of snobbery.

PROFS City workers, bankers, brokers, graduate management schemers, PAs, IT consultants, financiers, solicitors
CELEBS John Hannah, England Rugby Squad
DRESS Casual shirts and jeans, girls in Oasis handkerchief tops and knee-length skirts
MUSIC 80s, Dance, Disco, House
DOOR None
DRINKS Beer £2.70, Wine £3.20, Champagne £5, Cocktail £3.50
FOOD Paninis, £6
CARDS No Amex
CAPACITY 160, seating 60
HIRE Venue: No · Private Room: No

BOOM

Bar
165-167 St Johns Hill SW11
020 7924 3449

OPEN Mon-Thu 5pm-11pm,	GETTING LUCKY	2/5
Fri-Sat midday-midnight,	EYE CANDY	3/5
Sun 11am-11pm	BIG SPENDERS	3/5
TUBE/RAIL Clapham Junction	MIX 55%M 45%F	
BUSES 37, 39, 77, 156	AGE 25-35	
	PRICE Average	

AMBIENCE Casual, Dancing, Groups,
Late Night Open, Outdoors
REVIEW One can't help but feel intimidated asking for a packet of crisps in a bar/restaurant boasting a Modern British Pacific Rim Fusion menu. At the bar, heterosexual men wear clingy, homosexual tops, unaware of the fact straight men can only get away with such outfits if they're (A) drop dead gorgeous, and (B) under 35. Meanwhile, Wayne Hemingway lookalikes pick at food with Marlboro-light puffing girls, telling that story about the time they met Alexander McQueen. Away from the rare groove-emitting speakers, thigh-slapping locals flex their plastic, smug in the knowledge local house prices have gone up another ten grand in the past half-hour.
PLACE With its long central catwalk, this place is made for posing. Candlelit tables and sofas provide a safe haven to sip red wine and bitch about new arrivals making their way to the bar area at the back. The bar itself is very stylish, with exposed brick and stone tiled floor. Don't miss the bank-vault style toilet doors and the pebbles in the sink.
PEOPLE Yuppies who strategically place bulging wallets next to their Chardonnay and mobiles, Stella McCartney-ish girls, platonic groups and good-looking blokes who use their Vespa helmets as pulling props.

PROFS DJs, A&Rs, property developers, media layabouts, legal secretaries, account execs
CELEBS Lennox Lewis, Brian from Big Brother
DRESS Hope and Glory, crop-tops, tank tops, Hilfiger, vintage jeans, American Classics, chinos, Ted Baker, Gap, Kookaï, Prada
MUSIC Rare Groove, Funk
DOOR None
DRINKS Beer £2.50, Wine £2.50, Cocktail £5
FOOD Oceanic, Moroccan, Tapas, Burgers, £7
CARDS No Amex
CAPACITY 400, seating 150
HIRE Venue: Yes · Private Room: Yes

CIRCLE BAR

Bar
317 Battersea Park Road SW11
020 7627 1578

OPEN Mon-Fri midday-11pm,	GETTING LUCKY	1/5
Sat-Sun 11am-11pm	EYE CANDY	2/5
TUBE/RAIL Battersea Park	BIG SPENDERS	3/5
BUSES 44, 319, 344, 345	MIX 65%M 45%F	
	AGE 25-45	
	PRICE Average	

AMBIENCE Conversation, Dancing
REVIEW Formerly Galangga (wasn't that a 70s videogame?), the snappy new name certainly rolls off the tongue but has done little to pull in any more punters. In fact, like most bars on this road, Circle is rarely packed, making it the ideal place to come for a relaxing drink and chat. Although Circle pushes all the right buttons as far as decor and ambience go, it really could do with a kick up its incredibly laid-back arse, as its get up and go seems to have got up and gone. On the plus side, eavesdropping on Will from TGI Friday-style media prats does have its comedic compensations: 'I had a lambburger in focaccia last week.' 'Really... where's focaccia?' Although tempting, we resisted the urge to tell him it was near Thickotown and departed.
PLACE A large, vaguely stylish bar with candlelit tables and magazine racks. A 70s glitter ball flecks light-beams across trendy pastel walls fitted with funky uplighters.

Walk past the large central bar, and you'll find yourself in a back room with blood-red walls and an enormous butchers-style table.
PEOPLE Young-ish locals mixed with the odd post-work suit, the occasional funkster, plus creative media-ish looking blokes who lollop around drinking designer lager. The un-pubby pub grub (Piri Piri chicken, etc.) attracts a few peckish commuters and the odd Waitrose-weary couple.

PROFS Media professionals, salespeople, PRs, design consultants, journalists, DJs, IT professionals, teachers
CELEBS Sir Bob Geldof, Simon Le Bon
DRESS Think Selfridges – basically, anything and everything
MUSIC Funk, House, Dance, DJs Fri
DOOR None
DRINKS Beer £2.50, Wine £2.50, Cocktail £3.95
FOOD Modern European, £6.50
CARDS No Diners
CAPACITY 250, seating 70
HIRE Venue: No · Private Room: Yes

DRAWING ROOM AND SOFA BAR

Restaurant Bar
103 Lavender Hill SW11
020 7350 2564

OPEN Mon-Fri 5pm-midnight, Sat 10.30am-midnight, Sun 11am-10.30pm	**GETTING LUCKY**	**2/5**
	EYE CANDY	**3/5**
	BIG SPENDERS	**3/5**
TUBE/RAIL Clapham Junction	**MIX** 45%M 55%F	
BUSES 39, 77, 344, 345	**AGE** 25-40	
	PRICE Average	

AMBIENCE Conversation, Cosy, Elegant/Classic, Groups, Late Night Open, Outdoors, Romantic
REVIEW Imagine yourself transported into the pages of an Anne Rice novel – a heady, baroque, New Orleans boudoir full of crushed velvet curtains, ornate Catholic iconography and an underlying sense that taboos themselves are taboo – and you'll scratch the surface of the Sofa Bar's unique atmosphere. As you settle back into one of the sublimely relaxing sofas, you'll feel the overwhelming urge to do something bad, like puff on a big fat cigar or polish off a dusty bottle of Late Bottled Vintage port. Surrounding conversations are sotto voce with the occasional clink of glass cutting through the air like a stern librarian. The air is warm, thick and swirling with sensuality – most of the couples here are going to make mad, passionate love before the witching hour ends. Oo-er. I think I'd better get me coat...
PLACE Nicely furnished bar which in the broad light

of day possibly looks a tad shabby, with an en-suite restaurant (The Drawing Room) which offers a view on to the dismal nitrous oxide grunge of Lavender Hill.
PEOPLE Creatives from design, advertising, PR and media backgrounds jealously guard their patch – non-regulars are at first eyed suspiciously, but eventually either ignored or welcomed. Battersea estate agents are made short thrift of and politely encouraged to leave. Pronto.

PROFS Musicians, film directors, actors, designers, advertising execs, PR, media types, ITs
CELEBS None
DRESS Stüssy, Duffer, Issey Miyake, Jigsaw, Reiss, Warehouse, Gap, Joseph
MUSIC Mellow Jazz
DOOR None
DRINKS Beer £2.40, Wine £2.85, Cocktail £4.95
FOOD New World Fusion, £8
CARDS No Amex
CAPACITY 130, seating 25
HIRE Venue: Yes · Private Room: Yes

THE DUKE OF CAMBRIDGE

Gastropub
228 Battersea Bridge Road SW11
020 7223 5662

OPEN Mon-Sat 11am-11pm, Sun midday-10.30pm	**GETTING LUCKY**	**1/5**
	EYE CANDY	**3/5**
TUBE/RAIL Clapham Common	**BIG SPENDERS**	**4/5**
	MIX 70%M 30%F	
BUSES 49, 319, 345	**AGE** 25-40	
	PRICE Average	

AMBIENCE Casual, Conversation, Groups
REVIEW An upmarket pub just along from Battersea Bridge, the Duke of Cambridge has an ABC1 catchment area and it shows. Rugby shirts and Nokia Communicators are compulsory, and it helps if you boarded with Lucy's sister who went out with Barnaby's friend who was head boy at your brother's prep school. Like many pubs and bars in the area, an unwritten 'no mingling' policy seems to be in force, even during prime pulling time on a Friday night. The fact that the pub was far from full also diluted the atmosphere a little. If you're feeling left out, place your mobile on the table, sip a pint of 'Ordinary', discuss share options and revel in Brent Hoberman and the Fox's impending financial armageddon. You'll be well at home.
PLACE A large, covered front conservatory sets this apart from most South London boozers, as do the chaises longues – no plebby bar stools here, thank you very much. The colour scheme? Verdigris-and-beige, dahling.
PEOPLE A place where loud and proud public-school types blow their bonuses. A Bolshevik bomber would get good value for his gunpowder.

PROFS Property developers, contractors, actors, graphic designers, musicians, architects, bond traders, accountants, management consultants
CELEBS Jo Malone, Tracy Wilcox, Greg Rusedski, Helen Mirren, Gordon Ramsay
DRESS White Stuff, Pringle, Hush Puppies, Blazer, Land's End, Cotton Traders, Racing Green, Pink
MUSIC Jazz, Pop, Classical
DOOR None

DRINKS Beer £2.50, Wine £2.55, Champagne £5.50
FOOD Modern European, £6
CARDS All
CAPACITY 300, seating 100
HIRE Venue: No · Private Room: Yes

FICTION

Bar, Live Music Venue
47 Northcote Road SW11
020 7228 6240

OPEN Tue-Sun 9am-midnight	**GETTING LUCKY**	**2/5**
	EYE CANDY	**2/5**
TUBE/RAIL Clapham Junction	**BIG SPENDERS**	**3/5**
BUSES G1, 49, 239, 319, 337	**MIX** 60%M 40%F	
	AGE 25-40	
	PRICE Average	

AMBIENCE Airy/Bohemian, Casual, Funky, Groups, Late Night Open, Student
REVIEW If you're after that funky hippy vibe minus the noxious stench of patchouli, Fiction might just be your bag. This small, innocuous bar is perfect for a quiet drink now the experimental trio who occasionally butchered Stevie Wonder classics through a PA that sounded like a broken chainsaw have been banished. This is definitely not the place to meet the love of your life – dressed-down career women adopt that 'don't you dare talk to me' arms folded position, and handsome chaps are more interested in admiring the modern art daubed on the slightly tatty walls than the talent around them.
PLACE Sitting on a shabby/chic section of Northcote Road, Fiction's garish mosaic frontage looks down on a small front patio. The open front leads on to a whitewashed interior with a simple bar, funky backlit tiles and a static glitterball. Reminiscent of the kind of boho joint you might find in the Moroccan quarter of some trendy European city.
PEOPLE Transient punters and ponytailed mates of the barmen mingle with local toffs on their way home and girls in need of a couple of bottles of Dutch courage before presenting hubby/financial crutch with the latest Visa bill.

PROFS Musicians, PRs, media employees, interpreters, chefs, ad salespeople, property developers, TV producers, bar staff, retailers
CELEBS None
DRESS Frayed denim skirts, retro Reeboks, Gap, Reiss, Levi's, Carhartt, Hilfiger, funky shirts, Moschino, FCUK, Joseph, Acupuncture, Warehouse, Bay Trading, Camden Market gear, Oxfam
MUSIC Blues, Funk, Soul, DJ Sat
DOOR None
DRINKS Beer £2.50, Wine £2.50, Champagne £3.50, Cocktail £4.50
FOOD Tapas, £3.50
CARDS All
CAPACITY 150, seating 50
HIRE Venue: Yes · Private Room: No

THE FRONT ROOM BAR

Bar, Pub
45 Lavender Hill SW11
020 7738 1879

OPEN Mon-Sat midday-11pm, Sun midday-10.30pm	**GETTING LUCKY**	**2/5**
	EYE CANDY	**3/5**
TUBE/RAIL Clapham Common, Clapham Junction	**BIG SPENDERS**	**3/5**
	MIX 70%M 30%F	
BUSES 77, 77A, 345	**AGE** 20-55	
	PRICE Average	

AMBIENCE Backpackers, Casual, Comfy, Friendly, Groups, Lounge, Conversation
REVIEW From the moment you walk in, see the long Cheers-esque bar and hear cries of 'Hey, Norm, what you having, fat boy?' you feel comfortable. Firstly because it's, well, a front room. You half expect to bump into students drinking coffee while working on their Kant essay or writing postcards. The friendly and largely Southern hemisphere bar staff look like they should be limbering up for a match against Lawrence Dallaglio et al, yet display an epicurean knowledge of wine. Solos are comfortable here among young groups with peaked quiffs, leathered arty types and the 50-year-old rolling his own. Fine, relaxed atmosphere makes it a great starting point before Saturday's large one and perfect for that Sunday lunchtime hair-of-the-dog to get over the morning after.
PLACE Brunch off big wooden tables, relax into Chesterfields or long sofas. Whopping wood-framed screen in the corner shows off Antipodean beach volleyballers and surfer dudes. The lavender walls are replete with dancing, one-dimensional female forms in cream – Matisse's women meet Mr Tickle.
PEOPLE Antipodeans, travellers and regulars. You feel that soon, everyone will know your name. Tolerant attitude but no fools please. Media money and artistic neuroses won't impress here.

PROFS City boys, first jobbers, musicians, lawyers
CELEBS None
DRESS High Street
DOOR None
DRINKS Beer £2.40, Wine £3.50, Cocktails £3.95
MUSIC Standard airplay fare but more Missy Elliot and Stereo MCs than Hear'Say
FOOD International, Snacks, £9
CARDS All
CAPACITY 150, seating 50
HIRE Venue: No · Private Room: No

G2

Pub
339 Battersea Park Road SW11
020 7622 2112

OPEN Mon-Thu 11am-11pm, Fri, Sat 11am-1am, Sun 11am-10.30pm	**GETTING LUCKY**	**2/5**
	EYE CANDY	**3/5**
TUBE/RAIL Battersea Park	**BIG SPENDERS**	**3/5**
	MIX 50%M 50%F	
BUSES 44, 344	**AGE** 25-40	
	PRICE Average	

AMBIENCE Groups, Late Night Open
REVIEW Formerly The Legless Ladder, this place now goes under the rather abrupt name of G2, a funky contraction of King George II. Which means Queenie's E2 and Charlie'll be C3, all of which has FA to do with this swish new bar, so let's move on. On our visit, G2 was dotted with designer glamourpusses discussing Chinese horoscopes with winsome, Evisu-clad model-types, but

the majority of the punters were the usual Battersea suspects: flush yup locals, Eurotrash bankers and the hair flicking pashmina posse.
PLACE Très flash, modernised boozer decked out in, you guessed it, magnolia. It's a big, airy place with trendy uplighters, a few sofas, wooden floors, silly phrases daubed on the walls and bits of modern art. The back room leading to the beer garden is more of the same with a roaring fire. The designer barstaff are courteous and efficient, and waitresses patrol the tables providing shooters, shots and cocktails.
PEOPLE Battersea's bold and beautiful; 'mwah, mwah'-ing PR/fashion women, sleek handsome fellas, well-to-do couples and groups of reluctantly platonic yuppies. Also a few older letches who are probably friends of the owners.

PROFS PRs, bankers, IT consultants, salespeople, media planners, arts professionals, buyers, workmen, recruitment consultants
CELEBS None
DRESS Gap, Levi's, Evisu, Prada, Oxbow, Diesel, Jimmy Choo, Earl Jeans, knee high boots, denim skirts, trainers, rugger tops, thick woolies, M&S
MUSIC Pop, DJs Fri-Sat
DOOR None
DRINKS Beer £2.70, Wine £2.80, Champagne £5.75, Cocktail £4.25
FOOD Snacks, £6
CARDS All
CAPACITY 300, seating 100
HIRE Venue: Yes · Private Room: Yes

PROFS Publishing employees, graphic designers, IT consultants, students
CELEBS Tim Henman, Lee Hurst
DRESS White Stuff, rugby shirts, Gap, Next, DKNY
MUSIC Hip Hop, Disco, Ambient, Funk
DOOR None
DRINKS Beer £2.70, Wine £2.60
FOOD None
CARDS No Amex
CAPACITY 200, seating 40
HIRE Venue: No · Private Room: No

THE HOLY DRINKER

Bar
59 Northcote Road SW11
020 7801 0544

OPEN Mon-Fri 4.30pm-11pm, Sat midday-11pm, Sun 1pm-11pm	GETTING LUCKY	**4/5**
	EYE CANDY	**3/5**
	BIG SPENDERS	**2/5**
TUBE/RAIL Clapham Junction	MIX 40%M 60%F	
BUSES 37, 49, 219, 319, 349	AGE 20-35	
	PRICE Average	

AMBIENCE Buzzy, Casual, Minimalist, Student
REVIEW Named after an Italian art-house film, this joint was proudly pretentious long before the chain bars swarming the length and breadth of SW11 opened their second branch in Fulham. Cocooned from the local Nappy Valley by the thick pall of Marlboro Light smoke that would poison the infant Amelia within two toddling steps of the door, the Drinker is youthful and vibrant if not all that trendy – unless one considers White Stuff the fons et origo of urban cool. It's a tight, intimate place where 20-something trainee hepcats chatter excitedly; it's their first stop on a Friday night frolic, only five minutes' walk from their shared flat in Clapham Common.
PLACE From the street the place seems a spartan one-room affair with a starkly minimalist bar, bare plaster walls and an odd collage of ill-fitting tables and chairs. Inside, there's more space than immediately apparent and the pleasing lack of a cohesive interior style is a boon.
PEOPLE SW11 and SW4 young'uns chain-smoke and sup bottled beers and Red Bull chasers in a comfortable pastiche of what cool might be if any of them really knew.

HYDRO

Bar
137-139 St John's Hill SW11
020 7924 6167

OPEN Mon-Sat 5pm-11pm, Sun 5pm-10.30pm	GETTING LUCKY	**4/5**
	EYE CANDY	**4/5**
TUBE/RAIL Clapham Junction	BIG SPENDERS	**3/5**
BUSES 37, 39, 77	MIX 55%M 45%F	
	AGE 25-40	
	PRICE Average	

AMBIENCE Casual, Conversation, Cute Staff, Groups, Minimalist, Pulling
REVIEW Hydro's quietened down a lot since its famous talking point, a jacuzzi plonked absurdly in the middle of the floor, was removed. Idiot 30-somethings dressed as 20-somethings still come here to talk asinine media shite, but there are fewer of them than before and the steamy Saturday night crush is a thing of the past. Over at the titchy bar, sexy career girls eye up a handful of single men whilst simultaneously canoodling with their Ben Elton-ish partners, who, in turn, eye up the statuesque barmaids.
PLACE With its oval mirrors in dralon frames, sexy lighting and smart minimalist decor, this is reminiscent of Captain Scarlett's house, mid-cocktail party. NB: Don't drive here; parking's impossible.
PEOPLE Media veterans who think Armand van Helden's a WWF wrestler, mixed with flush locals and a few glammy girls who 'Cruella-de-Vil' their way round the place flashing their g-strings at a selection of solvent pushovers.

PROFS PR agents, entrepreneurs, City bods, media creatives, accountancy execs, bankers, traders, IT consultants, students
CELEBS None
DRESS Fitted black anything, combats, fashiony body-warmers/gilets, vanity specs, Next, Gap, Adidas, Paul Smith, Gucci, Levi's, Prada, chinos, Tag Heuer
MUSIC House, Dance, Funk DJ Fri
DOOR None
DRINKS Beer £2.80, Wine £3.70, Cocktail £4.95
FOOD Bar Snacks, £4
CARDS No Amex or Diners
CAPACITY 200, seating 80
HIRE Venue: Yes · Private Room: No

MASON'S ARMS

Gastropub
169 Battersea Park Road SW8
020 7622 2007

OPEN Mon-Sat midday-11pm, Sun midday-10.30pm	**GETTING LUCKY**	**2/5**
	EYE CANDY	**2/5**
TUBE/RAIL Battersea Park	**BIG SPENDERS**	**3/5**
BUSES 44, 137, 344	**MIX** 50%M 50%F	
	AGE 25-35	
	PRICE Average	

AMBIENCE Children/Families, Groups, Conversation
REVIEW Local gastropub serving the new Battersea (part Fulham/Clapham overflow, part Sarf London, part Mummy-and-Daddy-funded student). It overlooks the Gotham Cityesque Battersea Power Station, directly opposite the railway and near the mongrels' home. The Mason's Arms is a convenient place to stop for a spot of lunch before going to see a man about a new dog. The gastro element really comes into its own on Sundays when hordes of weekend boho Ikea couples leaf through The Observer over a roast with all the trimmings. It can be a touch pricey for what is ostensibly pub grub, though. £4.50 for soup? Behave.
PLACE Usual gastropub template: lots of wood, dubious artwork, tables and chairs rather than benches. Open kitchen in the corner.
PEOPLE Mix-match of punters who dream of being spikey-haired web designers; punters who dress like spikey-haired web designers; and, just occasionally, the odd bona fide spikey-haired web designer who's now looking for a new career.

PROFS ITs, teachers, students, new media profs, advertising, tradesmen, music industry employees
CELEBS Sir Bob Geldof, Patsy Palmer, Simon Le Bon, Harry Hill, Rick Astley
DRESS Jigsaw, Nike, FCUK, the odd suede loafer, Reebok trainers, Birkenstocks, New Balance
MUSIC Chill-out, Lounge, DJs Thu-Sat
DOOR None
DRINKS Beer £2.70, Wine £2.60
FOOD Modern European, £8.50
CARDS All
CAPACITY 200, seating 120
HIRE Venue: No · Private Room: No

THE MESS

Bar
225 St John's Hill SW11
020 7207 1276

OPEN Mon-Thu 6pm-11pm, Fri-Sat midday-1am, Sun midday-11pm	**GETTING LUCKY**	**4/5**
	EYE CANDY	**2/5**
	BIG SPENDERS	**2/5**
TUBE/RAIL Clapham Junction	**MIX** 40%M 60%F	
BUSES 37, 39, 77A, 156, 170, 337	**AGE** 21-30	
	PRICE Average	

AMBIENCE Casual, Groups, Pulling, Student
REVIEW What was once an old man's pub has turned over the last two years into a scruffy young clubbers' bar, glammed up with a paint job and a few mirror mosaics. South London yups mix with regular Sarf Laarnden yoofs drawn in by the thumping-club atmosphere. One of the first 'new' bars in this particular stretch of Clapham, now home to a whole string of busy bottled beer and cocktail joints. What makes The Mess different, however, is the dance floor on the right hand side of the bar. Holding up to 80 groovers, tentative steps are made towards it by nine in the evening; by half past it's heaving, and by half ten you'll have to book space to boogie.
PLACE The Mess is the inspired name for a place that houses threadbare sofas and chairs and a random selection of mismatched tables and tobacco brown walls. The enclosed beer garden is great – it's even got a sand pit and a punchbag for taking out vodka Red Bull-fuelled aggression.
PEOPLE Local loaded yups on a St John's Hill crawl, scruffies, students, long-haired yoofs, young Reebok Classic wearing ladettes and types that even Men Behaving Badly would wag their fingers at.

PROFS Media, TV, advertising and music professionals
CELEBS Hunter, Sasha, Alistair Whitehead, Paul Oakenfold, Johnny Vaughan, Ainsley Harriott
DRESS Second-hand Levi's, Burton suits (without ties or jackets), Next, Miss Selfridge logo crop tops, Paul Smith, Acupuncture
MUSIC Funk, House, Disco, DJs Fri-Sun
DOOR None
DRINKS Beer £2.50, Wine £2.50, Cocktail £3.50
FOOD Bar snacks, £3.50
CARDS No Amex or Diners
CAPACITY 220, seating 80
HIRE Venue: No · Private Room: No

BABUSHKA

Bar, Chain
40 St Matthew's Road SW2
020 7274 3618

OPEN Mon-Fri 5pm-11pm,	**GETTING LUCKY**	**2/5**
Sat midday-midnight,	**EYE CANDY**	**2/5**
Sun midday-10.30pm	**BIG SPENDERS**	**2/5**
TUBE/RAIL Brixton	**MIX** 55%M 45%F	
BUSES 45, 59, 109	**AGE** 20-35	
	PRICE Average	

AMBIENCE Arty/Bohemian, Buzzy, Casual, Funky, Late Night Open
REVIEW We can't help thinking about Kate Bush – all trussed up in gold chain mail and thigh-high boots – whenever anyone mentions this place. Schoolboy fantasies are one thing, but this fabulous vodka bar is obviously the work of an enthusiastic acolyte of Russian sanatorium-chic. Inside this sterilised leather-clad lounge den, a marvellous Marvin Hagler lookalike orders another bottle of Molt, much to the bemused consternation of the boho barmaid whose flustered manner is reminiscent of the giggling receptionist in Alan Partridge. As a couple of chicks canoodle in a corner, Brixtonian media creatives nod to the cool, jazzy soundtrack and suspiciously spy a lone girl ordering yet another potent vodka. Altogether now, 'Babushka, Babushka, Babushka Ya Ya!'
PLACE The fact that this boxy, prefab-style building is surrounded by a council estate, and has a big red star stuck on it, only adds to the genuine Communist Lithuania circa-1963 feel. Walk past the benches out front and you enter a pristine fetishist's den with unreasonably high leather banquettes, sand-blasted walls and chain-mail clad down-lighting. The subdued lighting and lavish vodka list conspire to give the place a real 'Do you ave ze microfilm?' feel, but it's so bloomin' dark I fell over walking to the lavvy. How un-Harry Palmer of me.
PEOPLE Cool dudes, trendy locals, after-workers, pre-clubbers (downing a few shooters before hitting the nearby Bug Bar, Crypt, Dogstar), groups of reluctantly platonic ravey types, a few suits.

PROFS Soho types, bartenders, media employees, publishing employees, fashion employees, DJs, music business employees, salespeople
CELEBS None
DRESS The odd third-division footballer-style suit, retro Nike, silly TPT-style fringed jeans, retro sportswear, Firetrap, Carhartt, Gap, Ben Sherman, Oasis, Warehouse, Wallis
MUSIC Funk, Jazz, House, Latin, Reggae, Ska, Soul, DJs every night
DOOR None
DRINKS Beer £2.60, Wine £3.50, Champagne £5.75, Cocktail £4.50
FOOD None
CARDS All
CAPACITY 220, seating 100
HIRE Venue: Yes · Private Room: No

BAR ON

Bar, Café
10-12 Turnstall Road SW9
020 7737 4797

OPEN 7 days 8.30am-	**GETTING LUCKY**	**1/5**
midnight	**EYE CANDY**	**2/5**
TUBE/RAIL Brixton	**BIG SPENDERS**	**3/5**
BUSES 34, 45, 59, 109	**MIX** 65%M 35%F	
	AGE 20-35	
	PRICE Average	

AMBIENCE Conversation, Late Night Open, Minimalist, Student
REVIEW We originally thought 'Baize? Baize? = Snooker + Brixton = Blurggh!' But we were wrong. There's not a cue in sight in this groovy little bar/café, and the only tables are of the sit down and have a chat variety. Plus, you certainly wouldn't hear poncey statements such as 'Roland, have you met my student Antonia?' in your average snooker dive. Oh no, this caters to more discerning Budvar/fancy cocktail drinking Brixtonians, and attracts a mix of SW2 bohos and egg-on-face yups who fell for the estate agent codswallop about Brixton being the new Clapham. The only bummer is the curt barman who's about as welcoming as a turd in a hot tub. On top of that, his sexy colleague's grasp of English appeared equal to that of a particularly lethargic budgie. A shame, as clueless staff apart, this could be wicked.
PLACE Intimate bar/café in off-road setting. The paved area outside allows for several tables and chairs where punters can watch the comings and goings on nearby Brixton High Street Inside, this is pleasant minimalism; neutral walls, stripped boards, a large chrome-framed mirror, a dinky bar, lots of little tables and a beautiful display of orchids.
PEOPLE Brixton trendies, a few after-workers, studenty looking girls with pig tails and bicycle-riding yups. It's not often you hear 'Yah, I was rowing in Cambridge...' as reggae plays in the background and a tramp picks up dog ends.

PROFS Solicitors, doctors, market workers, lecturers, students, stylists, financiers, musicians, engineers, actors, IT specialists, sales, PR and media executives, office workers, advertising executives
CELEBS Naomi Campbell, The Cookie Crew
DRESS A bit studenty: jeans, hooded Liam tops, Camden Market stuff, sandals, t-shirts, Diesel, Duffer, Hilfiger, Levi's, the odd suit. Some smart and trendy: YSL, Ralph Lauren, Gap, Adidas
MUSIC Jazz, Latin American
DOOR None
DRINKS Beer £2.60, Wine £2.20, Champagne £2.95, Cocktail £4.50
FOOD Modern European, £6.95
CARDS None
CAPACITY 200, seating 80
HIRE Venue: Yes · Private Room: Yes

BRIXTONIAN HAVANA CLUB

Bar
11 Beehive Place SW9
020 7924 9262

OPEN 7 days 4pm-midnight
TUBE/RAIL Brixton
BUSES 109, 118, 196

GETTING LUCKY	4/5
EYE CANDY	3/5
BIG SPENDERS	3/5
MIX 50%M 50%F	
AGE 25-40	
PRICE Average	

AMBIENCE Casual, Groups, Pulling
REVIEW Brixton, as my trendy A&R friends like to tell me, is the new Notting Hill. But, obviously, with quite a bit of the old Brixton atmosphere. There's nothing so divine as watching a drive-by over your low-fat pistachio latte, is there? This bar is definitely for the trendy media types currently swamping the area – first-generation Brixtonians, if you like – but takes on board the local Caribbean flavour in the form of luscious bowls of rum punch and gorgeously calypsoesque bartending. It's peaceful early evenings, but gets sweaty around 9pm on weekends. A couple to my right were debating the definition of 'observational comedy', while two 'new lads' observed the entrance of a young Jerry Hall lookalike in a scant pink paisley dress and impossibly complicated heels. She was clutching one of those little booklets of Caribbean recipes they sell outside the tube.
PLACE Airy, white emulsioned second-floor barn conversion, tucked down an insalubrious alleyway, provoking those 'you'd never guess it was down here, would you?' comments. The bar is brightly lit and stocked with a plethora of cocktail ingredients. There's some curious pink and blue glass panelling, exposed beams and a screen with some decapitated angels on.
PEOPLE The hard work ethic of their middle-class parents has been rejected, and they've decided to give the media a whirl because it looks easy, you get to meet the stars and you don't really need to know anything about finance or computers, do you? It's also one of the few professions in which an 11am start and a hangover are indispensable fashion accessories.

PROFS Media professionals, theatre staff, council workers, contemporary writers
CELEBS Sophie Dahl, Des'Ree, Lee John (Imagination)
DRESS Hawaiian shirts, 70s gear, Diesel, Wrangler, t-shirts, charity shop finds
MUSIC Funk, Jazz, Latin, Live Percussion Fri-Sat
DOOR Smart
DRINKS Beer £2.50, Wine £3, Champagne £5.95, Cocktail £4.95
FOOD Caribbean, £14
CARDS No Amex
CAPACITY 250, seating 100
HIRE Venue: Yes · Private Room: Yes

BUG BAR

Bar
The Crypt, St Matthew's Church, Brixton Hill SW2
020 7738 3184

OPEN Wed-Thu 7pm-1am,
Fri-Sat 9pm-3am,
Sun 7pm-2am
TUBE/RAIL Brixton
BUSES 133, 196, 250

GETTING LUCKY	4/5
EYE CANDY	1/5
BIG SPENDERS	2/5
MIX 60%M 40%F	
AGE 18-35	
PRICE Average	

AMBIENCE Basement, Dancing, Funky, Groups, Late Night Open, Live Music, Party, Pulling, Student, Vampire/Gothic
REVIEW Brixton wouldn't be complete without its very own dive bar, and Bug Bar locals can relax in the knowledge that this den of iniquity falls well into that category. Evolved from the crypt of St Matthew's Church punters would be forgiven for thinking this was Buffy territory and not Brixton, as you descend the sidesteps of this imposing Gothic edifice. This venue is a double-edged sword, where the early evenings have the perfect makings of a louche lounge bar, but like all ghoul-infested church-crypt basement bars, the night brings ferocious hedonistic partying on a demonic scale. Sweat drips from the walls, bodies gyrate, and as if to maintain the theme, the management have installed two poxy fans not big enough to dry a rat's arse. This is not for the faint of heart, but if you want a debauched party (or to lose weight) this is the place to come.
PLACE Gothic, stone cellar with sweat/condensation dripping off the walls after 10pm as the punters get down to some funky sounds. Red neon glow from the bar. Definitely not for the claustro/phobic.
PEOPLE Media wits, Camberwell art students, casual young creatives, many local Brixton boyz plus a lot of first jobbers and the odd council worker.

PROFS Accounts' clerks, artists, stylists, musicians, PRs, builders, market stallholders, finance secretaries, shop workers, famous DJs, students
CELEBS Basement Jaxx, Gomez, Diesel Bug, Moby, Des'ree, David Holmes, Andrew Weatherall
DRESS Thriftstore chic meets urban streetwear and Camden market gear
MUSIC Soul, Funk, Disco, Breakbeat, House, Dub, Garage, Latin House
DOOR Wed-Thu free before 8pm, £5 after, Fri-Sat free before 9pm, 9pm-11pm £4, after 11pm £6, NUS and member discount
DRINKS Beer £2.80, Wine £3, Cocktail £4.50
FOOD None
CARDS None
CAPACITY 200, seating 100
HIRE Venue: Yes · Private Room: No

CAFÉ GOYA

Café, Restaurant Bar
85 Acre Lane SW2
020 7274 3500

OPEN Mon-Sat 5pm-11pm,
Sat-Sun 11am-5pm
TUBE/RAIL Brixton,
Clapham North
BUSES 35, 45

GETTING LUCKY	1/5
EYE CANDY	2/5
BIG SPENDERS	3/5
MIX 50%M 50%F	
AGE 25-50	
PRICE Average	

AMBIENCE Arty/Bohemian, Casual, Conversation, Funky
REVIEW Imagine if Billy Bragg and Janet Street-Porter opened a restaurant, and you'll get a rough idea of what this place is like. Despite its crappy surroundings, Goya admirably attempts to inject a bit of community spirit into this, the Clapham/Brixton border; what it lacks in finesse it more than makes up for in charm. Amidst a kind of funky Parisian boho vibe a lone regular sips coffee at a little bar area, eavesdropping

on chattering locals who discuss forthcoming hill treks in Burma. Bizarrely, although the place was empty, the Antipodean waiter turned away a lone businessman, explaining that Goya couldn't accommodate single diners. But then again, wearing a pinstripe suit in here's a bit like turning up at a Friends of the Earth meeting in a stretch limo.

PLACE Blink and you'll miss it. Charming, little shabby chic café/restaurant filled with candlelit tables. Apparently the place extends over three floors when necessary, but the majority of punters remain on the ground floor – a simple room with a few gold-framed mirrors, some religious iconography, arty farty flyers and a few Parisian brasserie-style bits and bobs.

PEOPLE Locals who probably watch Time Team but secretly earn over £35K, a few boho/ecological hippies and nibbling couples who want a late drink.

PROFS Media professionals, writers, charity workers, PRs, IT professionals, salespeople, students, graphic artists

CELEBS None

DRESS From absolutely fabulous to absolutely anything

MUSIC Jazz

DOOR None

DRINKS Beer £2.50, Wine £2.50, Champagne £4.25, Cocktail £4.75

FOOD Modern British, £9.95

CARDS All

CAPACITY 100, seating 60

HIRE Venue: Yes · Private Room: No

THE DOGSTAR

Bar, Club
389 Coldharbour Lane SW9
020 7733 7515

OPEN Mon-Thu midday-2.30am, Fri-Sat midday-4am, Sun midday-2.30am	**GETTING LUCKY**	**4/5**
	EYE CANDY	**3/5**
	BIG SPENDERS	**3/5**
TUBE/RAIL Brixton	**MIX** 55%M 45%F	
BUSES 35, 45, 250	**AGE** 18-35	
	PRICE Cheap	

AMBIENCE Chin Stroking, Dancing, Groups, Hip/Fashionable, Late Night Open, Live Music, Mashed-up, Party, Pulling, Student

REVIEW The Dogstar has single-handedly shifted the perceptions of Brixton as a drinking mecca. During the day it's a ringer for many other wood-clad drinking holes with chill-out music, a decent menu and a wide range of reasonably priced booze. But when darkness falls, the state-of-the-art sound system is pumped up to earbleed levels, UV lights and trippy video loops decorate the walls and cascades of up-for-it punters spill in off Coldharbour Lane to party on into the wee hours. The winning combination of spot-on music, (everything from nu skool breaks to speed garage to good-ol'-fashioned-raise-the-roof house), the very relaxed door policy, a late licence and fair prices creates the happiest, clappiest crowd this side of a Billy Graham revival. The launchpad for talented promoters and acts, here even the bouncers smile.

PLACE Three-levelled old Brixton backstreet pub. Still gets crowded on weekends despite the recent expansion and the stricter door policy upstairs. Sometimes a stand-up comedy club operates up top, but the joint still jumps down below.

PEOPLE They're young, they're trendy (but not that trendy, no door policy, remember) and they know how to have fun. At weekends they're not so young, somewhat less trendy and there's a helluva lot more of them. Brixtonites, energised bohos and many a fun-lovin' student.

PROFS Art students, designers, media types, fashion designers

CELEBS Moby, Super Furry Animals, Ash, Alabama 3, Darcus Howe, Ainsley Harriot, Lol Hammond

DRESS Exposed and pierced navels outnumber suits by around 1,000 to 1, vintage clothing, Mambo, Maharishi, Boxfresh, Diesel, Caterpillar, Firetrap, Duffer, Stüssy, Carhartt, Evisu, Levi's, Gap, Pink Soda, Acupuncture, Life Legend, Blue Nile, FCUK, H&M

MUSIC Breakbeat, Hip Hop, House, Chill-out, Drum 'n' Bass

DOOR Thu free before 9pm, £2 after 10pm, £3 after 11pm, Fri free before 10pm, £4 after, Sat free before 9pm, £4-5-7 after 9pm-10pm-11pm

DRINKS Beer £2.50, Wine £2.50, Cocktail £2.80

FOOD Modern Eclectic, Sunday Lunch, Traditional British, £6

CARDS No Amex or Diners

CAPACITY 350, seating 100

HIRE Venue: Yes · Private Room: Yes

FRIDGE BAR

Bar
1 Town Hall Parade, Brixton Hill SW2
020 7326 5100

OPEN Mon-Thu 5pm-2am, Fri-Sat 5pm-4am, Sun 5.30am-midday, 8pm-3am	**GETTING LUCKY**	**3/5**
	EYE CANDY	**3/5**
	BIG SPENDERS	**3/5**
TUBE/RAIL Brixton	**MIX** 55%M 45%F	
BUSES 2, 37, 108, 109	**AGE** 25-35	
	PRICE Expensive	

AMBIENCE Basement, Conversation, Dancing, Late Night Open, Outdoors

REVIEW The Fridge Bar located alongside the much larger Fridge Club and sharing the same management creates a personality bigger, better and brighter than its club daddy. The increasingly popular Fridge Bar retains its own character with a more balanced mix and the decor is chrome-lined, much cleaner than its scuff-marked neighbour. It's a place to chill out, have meaningful conversations and people watch through shades. But venture into the basement and you enter a different world: a dark, humid vortex of exposed flesh and decaying inhibitions. On the right night you can dance through dawn and well into the afternoon, with occasional sorties upstairs for fruit juice and fresh air. It's so dark you can't tell whose groin is thrusting next to you – which, of course, is a large part of this bar's unique appeal.

PLACE Compact, chrome and beech decor upstairs with bright lighting and the usual rack of designer drinks. Dark, low-ceilinged dance floor in the basement with a charming, fenced-off cage for the DJ.

PEOPLE It's an older, more sophisticated crowd than the Fridge Club or the Dogstar, and more ethnically mixed. The influx of gurning club casualties on a Saturday morning often adds to the humour of proceedings.

PROFS Students, media professionals, business people, DJs, designers, entrepreneurs
CELEBS James Dreyfus (Gimme Gimme Gimme)
DRESS Zack, TopShop, FCUK, Reiss, Adidas, Hugo Boss, Ted Baker, Police rub shoulders alongside the usual sportswear suspects, Sue Ryder, suits, combats, jeans, trainers, Dr Martens
MUSIC Funk, Garage, Reggae, R&B, Soul, Hip Hop, DJs every night from 9pm, loosely around the music of black origin theme
DOOR Fri-Sun admission charge £5 after 11pm
DRINKS Beer £3.50, Wine £3.50, Champagne £6, Cocktail £3.95
FOOD None
CARDS No Amex or Diners
CAPACITY 250, seating 25
HIRE Venue: Yes · Private Room: No

JUICE BAR

Bar, Café
407 Coldharbour Lane SW2
020 7738 4141

OPEN Mon-Thu 10am-11pm, Fri-Sat 10am-2am, Sun 10am-11pm	GETTING LUCKY	**4/5**
	EYE CANDY	**3/5**
	BIG SPENDERS	**2/5**
TUBE/RAIL Brixton	MIX 60%M 40%F	
BUSES 2, 35, 159	AGE 27-37	
	PRICE Average	

AMBIENCE Conversation, Late Night Open, Pulling
REVIEW Like Café Nervosa in Frasier only much, much cooler. And with beer. What looks like a moderately scruffy café from the outside turns out to be a spectacularly scruffy café on the inside, but one stuffed with modern beatnik style and spirit. The archetypal regular is a mocha-drinking, Duke Ellington-digging, well-travelled film buff who wears Oxfam and thinks Hideous Kinky is the best book/film/thing ever. Although it's always nice to find a bookshop that sells beer, you're better off with one of the imaginative juice concoctions. There's something to alleviate all ailments from fatigue, PMT or a hangover through to 'The Flu Fighter' and 'Hot Stuff' – a blend of carrot, apple, lettuce and ginger billed as 'the natural Viagra'. Ooh missus. Although a bit too worthy for some, the Juice Bar is a cerebral oasis, somewhere to experience Brixton's many-faceted culture first hand.
PLACE Not unlike a big school storeroom cupboard, complete with cheap metallic roof-high bookshelves and whatever furniture has been left lying around. Is it chic? Is it a scruffy dive? Strangely, it's both.
PEOPLE A too-cool-to-care crowd of writers, artists, poets, graphic designers, research students and street cleaners. Largely unpretentious, although some of the conversations get a little tedious.

PROFS Young graduates, media execs, theatre staff, artists, self-employed, tourists, writers, students
CELEBS Benjamin Zephaniah, Linton Kwesi Johnson, Darcus Howe, Sol Campbell, Michael Palin, Jean Binta Breeze, Paul Gilroy, Prof Henry Lewis Gates
DRESS Young, trendy – High Street, second-hand, independent labels thrown together in a creative way. Jarvis Cocker meets Janis Joplin. They have a kid. Kid opens a clothes shop. Shop very popular amongst Juice Bar drinkers

MUSIC Jazz, Live Jazz Band Fri-Sat
DOOR None
DRINKS Beer £2.50, Wine £2.75, Cocktail £3.50
FOOD Organic, Vegetarian, £4.99
CARDS No Amex
CAPACITY 30, seating 22
HIRE Venue: Yes · Private Room: No

LIVINGROOM BAR

Bar
443 Coldharbour Lane SW9
020 7326 4040

OPEN Mon-Fri 5pm-1am, Sat-Sun midday-1am	GETTING LUCKY	**4/5**
	EYE CANDY	**3/5**
TUBE/RAIL Brixton	BIG SPENDERS	**3/5**
BUSES 2, 3, 35, 37, 45, 109, 133, 159	MIX 50%M 50%F	
	AGE 20-30	
	PRICE Average	

AMBIENCE Funky, Late Night Open, Lounge Atmosphere, Party, Pulling, Queues
REVIEW This is no ordinary bar. In fact, it's a living room, or it's supposed to be. Put it this way, if you were David Linley then maybe you could afford the furniture in this sleek Brixton bonhomie bar, but for the rest of us it's Ikea and at a push Heals. Still, how many living rooms do you know with two floors, two bars, incumbent bar staff and regular DJs? Not many I'll wager. As it is, Livingroom has garnered a serious weekend school disco party reputation, or should I say school disco house living room party reputation. Unbelievably most of those that come here even know the words to Bon Jovi's 'Living on a Prayer'. Now that's showing your age.
PLACE Large lounge sofas, big screens showing classic movies, low level lighting for that inconspicuous sofa snog. A living room for the upwardly mobile...
PEOPLE A stronghold for Brixton's growing trustafarian population, media types, footballers, anyone from Clapham who wants to pull au pairs.

PROFS New media, footballers, students, advertising creatives
CELEBS Dennis Wise, Alan Smith
DRESS Diesel, Carhartt, Duck and Cover, Boxfresh
MUSIC Relaxed/Funky during the week, Funky House and 80s on weekends, DJs 9pm-1am nightly
DOOR No scruffiness, Fri-Sat £5 after 11pm
DRINKS Beer £2.50, Wine £2.50, Cocktail £4
FOOD None
CARDS No Amex or Diners
CAPACITY 400, seating 100
HIRE Venue: Yes · Private Room: No

MASS

Club
St Matthew's Church, Brixton Hill SW2
020 7237 7616

OPEN Fri-Sat 10pm-6am	GETTING LUCKY	**3/5**
TUBE/RAIL Brixton	EYE CANDY	**2/5**
BUSES 2, 3, 35, 37, 45, 109, 133, 159	BIG SPENDERS	**2/5**
	MIX 50%M 50%F	
	AGE 18-35	
	PRICE Average	

AMBIENCE Dancing, Gothic/Vampire, Groups, Late Night Open, Party, Student,

REVIEW A Brixton landmark transformed lazily into two gloomy dance-floor pits and a smoky sweatbox of a chill-out room, hung on a dank Dali-inspired spiral staircase. Mass pulls in good crowds when popular acts appear – and many elusive crowd pullers consent to do so, especially from the hip hop fraternities – but few punters seem keen on the venue. Staff appear to be hired on the basis of their sneering ability alone and without a baying crowd the atmosphere is distinctly underwhelming. Navigating around is a tad tedious since there is nothing to see, all ramps and swinging doors. A maze of meaninglessness. This former temple of religion has gone the way of the dark side without, to the chagrin of the clubber, the illicit thrill of iconoclastic revelry.

PLACE A multi-roomed megalopolis of mediocrity. The grandish St Matthew's Church converted into a club. From the outside it's definitely of the cathedral class, but from the inside you might as well be under the railyard. No spires, no views, no attention to detail, no vibe.

PEOPLE Depending on the night it pulls different crowds from all over. Young pranksters, West London hip hop kids, City admins, Brixtonian posers, the accelerated lollypop generation and people who don't know how to have a good time yet.

PROFS Students, retail staff, media professionals, hip hop fraternities, models
CELEBS Goldie, Dillinja
DRESS A two-coloured t-shirt and your trendiest runners
MUSIC Drum 'n' Bass, Breakbeat, Hip Hop, Trance, Hard House
DOOR £10 entry
DRINKS Beer £3.50, Cocktails £3.50
FOOD None
CARDS All
CAPACITY 1200
HIRE Venue: Yes · Private Room: No

RITZY CINEMA BAR

Bar
261 Brixton Oval, Coldharbour Lane SW2
020 7733 2229

OPEN Mon-Sat 5pm-11pm,	GETTING LUCKY	1/5
Sun 2pm-10.30pm	EYE CANDY	2/5
TUBE/RAIL Brixton	BIG SPENDERS	2/5
BUSES 2, 3, 35, 45,	MIX 55%M 45%F	
109, 118	AGE 20-50	
	PRICE Cheap	

AMBIENCE Arts/Entertainment, Casual, Conversation, Groups
REVIEW Like many other SW2 watering holes, this place attracts a mix of earnest young locals and slightly pretentious bohemians who get a strange kick out of socialising in 'da ghetto'. This basic, no-frills cinema bar acts as a convenient venue to debate the various aspects of whatever film happens to be playing, so the punters vary accordingly. That said, there seem to be two types of movie fans: genuine enthusiasts who can't wait to discuss the film and smarmy cynics who have to wait till they're at least 500 yards out of earshot before whispering their opinions. Punters aside, the Ritzy

deserves full marks for opening a pleasant, non-rip-off bar, but I doubt anyone bothers coming here solely to drink – I asked for a Coke and the barmaid plonked a can on the counter – 'Oh, sorry... do you want a glass?'

PLACE This has got a bit of an art centre/museum cafeteria-type feel to it. It's all a bit spartan, with yellow walls, glass doors, a stone-tiled floor, lots of little tables and flyers all over the place. The only genuine point of interest is the old projector sitting in the corner, although you do wonder why they've got a johnny machine in the gents – snogging in the back row has obviously progressed by leaps and bounds since my day.

PEOPLE Depends on what movie's playing. Generally, it's joe-average moviegoers but, as this is an independent cinema, you often pick up a few pretentious Islington type twats who think Arnie is the cinematic antichrist and maintain that films need to be foreign, black and white, boring as f**k and about as visually appealing as watching a skip rust to offer any intellectual stimulation.

PROFS Media students, council/social workers, speech therapists, local retailers, IT consultants, sales people, beauticians
CELEBS None
DRESS Everything: sandals, second-hand jeans, Japanese art t-shirts, retro Adidas, Nike, Timberland, Jigsaw, Diesel, Carhartt, Mambo
MUSIC Easy Listening
DOOR None
DRINKS Beer £2.25, Wine £2.50
FOOD Quiche, £4
CARDS None
CAPACITY 170, seating 40
HIRE Venue: No · Private Room: No

SATAY BAR

Restaurant Bar
447-450 Coldharbour Lane SW9
020 7326 5001

OPEN Mon-Thu midday-	GETTING LUCKY	2/5
11pm, Fri-Sat midday-1am,	EYE CANDY	3/5
Sun midday-10.30pm	BIG SPENDERS	3/5
TUBE/RAIL Brixton	MIX 55%M 45%F	
BUSES 2, 3, 35, 118, 250	AGE 25-35	
	PRICE Cheap	

AMBIENCE Casual, Chilled, Conversation, Groups, Hip/Fashionable, Late Night Open
REVIEW One word comes to mind when you step into the Satay Bar in Brixton: chilled. The music is trippy, the decor African chic and the punters are too cool to give a damn about being cool. Which is pretty damn cool. This bar/restaurant is more of a Brixton locals' haunt than the Dogstar up the road and is very much a place to go eat and talk rather than rip it up. Drop in during happy hour and you can pick up a beautifully mixed cocktail jug for eight quid. Then just sit back, sip slowly and watch the gamut of Brixton life pass by the panoramic windows. Your face won't feel the heat of an Ibiza sunset, but inside you'll find yourself warming up pretty nicely. An ideal place to tee yourself up for a big club night.
PLACE Prime location at the top of Coldharbour Lane, the interior is tastefully subdued African with low lighting and trip-hop rhythms helping to build a tropical vibe.

PEOPLE An even split between black and white, not that the colour of your skin is an issue. A relaxed attitude and a sense of style are the only prerequisites here.

PROFS Housing officers, students, advertising and media employees
CELEBS Darcus Howe
DRESS Nike, Adidas, DKNY
MUSIC Jazz, Easy Listening, Drum 'n' Bass evenings only, DJs Fri-Sat
DOOR None
DRINKS Beer £2.50, Wine £2.50, Champagne £3.50
FOOD Indonesian, £7
CARDS All
CAPACITY 150, seating 100
HIRE Venue: No · Private Room: No

SW9

Bar, Café, Gay
11 Dorell Place SW9
020 7387 3116

OPEN Mon-Wed 10am-11pm,Thu 10pm-11.30pm, Fri-Sat 10am-1am, Sun 10am-11pm	**GETTING LUCKY**	**2/5**
	EYE CANDY	**4/5**
	BIG SPENDERS	**2/5**
TUBE/RAIL Brixton	**MIX** 50%M 50%F	
BUSES 109, 118, 296, 250	**AGE** 20-45	
	PRICE Cheap	

AMBIENCE Casual, Conversation, Groups, Late Night Open, Outdoors, Student
REVIEW Gay/straight café bar with a fashion code more savage than a pack of salivating hyenas encircling Bambi with a broken paw. By day a pleasant place to imbibe caffeine, meet your clique, talk about the film you're writing or boast about the boy you blew, on weekends a late drinking bar that spills over into the alleyway where anything goes. An arty white woman with a Cleopatra haircut was spotted one night cheerily horse-pissing next to a skip a homeless person will later scour for a half-eaten baked potato. Less than a minute from the high street and a million miles from the maddening markets, this place is a respite from beggars, dealers and people wearing Tommy Hilfiger.
PLACE Window-fronted corner shop café bar. Relaxed but with a little of that Brixton tension thrown in. Food ('we have it so we can have a late licence') is not too bad, actually. During the week a good place for a drink and chat, but gets boisterous on the weekend as punters gear up to get it on, and off, at the local gay clubs.
PEOPLE Casting glances around this joint is like flicking through a style mag. A half gay half arty-farty crowd. Dress is hip, retro and sometimes outrageous. A silver sequined top with transparent mac, darling! Popular spot with single lasses who want to escape high street, and tidy gay boys.

PROFS Artists, designers, fashion and music industry professionals, art students
CELEBS Ainsley Harriot
DRESS From Moschino to Oxfam, but worn well
MUSIC Dance, Indie, Jazz, Pop, R&B
DOOR None
DRINKS Beer £2.80, Wine £2.85, Champagne £4.20, Cocktail £4.60

FOOD Full English Breakfast, Snacks, £6
CARDS No Diners
CAPACITY 100, seating 50
HIRE Venue: No · Private Room: No

Z RESTAURANT & BAR

Bar, Music Venue, Restaurant Bar
30 Acre Lane SW2
020 7501 9001

OPEN Tue-Sun midday-midnight	**GETTING LUCKY**	**3/5**
	EYE CANDY	**4/5**
TUBE/RAIL Brixton	**BIG SPENDERS**	**2/5**
BUSES 2, 3, 35, 37, 159	**MIX** 45%M 55%F	
	AGE 25-35	
	PRICE Cheap	

AMBIENCE Casual, Chilled, Conversation, Groups, Live Music, Student
REVIEW Not as banging as the Bug Bar, less stylish than Neon and lacking the familiarity of the Fridge, this is where Brixtonians come when they grow tired of posing and just fancy a drink. The decor strikes a balance between trendy eaterie and daytime TV studio, a set-up which sees workmates staging informal meetings alongside canoodling couples. And where other bars would insist on blaring out cutting-edge two-step, the music policy here is gentle R&B (appropriately, we were served by a Macy Gray lookalike). Smooth and gentle is the order of the evening and although the Z Bar probably isn't your main event venue, it will warm you up nicely.
PLACE A recent make-over improved the look of this place no end. Apricot walls now house brash, enthusiastic paintings, while the large mirrored bar-back makes everything seem twice as big and bright as it really is.
PEOPLE A vaguely individual-looking crowd, most of whom seem to know one another. No one was acting as if they had anything to prove; instead, most were content to chat about nothing much whilst mooching through the cocktail menu.

PROFS Voluntary workers, retailers, mature students, musicians, artists, doctors, singers
CELEBS Sacha Baron Cohen, Felix Jaxx
DRESS Lycra, denim, cheesecloth, DKNY, Levi's, Ben Sherman, Adidas
MUSIC Funk, Jazz, R&B, Soul, Live Jazz Singer Sun night, DJs Thu-Sat
DOOR None
DRINKS Beer £2.50, Wine £2.50, Champagne £3.75, Cocktail £3.75
FOOD Brasserie, International, £7
CARDS No Amex or Diners
CAPACITY 200, seating 100
HIRE Venue: Yes · Private Room: No

camberwell

THE FUNKY MUNKY

Bar
25 Camberwell Church Street SE5
020 7252 5222

OPEN Mon-Wed midday-midnight, Thu midday-1am, Fri-Sat midday-2am, Sun midday-10.30pm
TUBE/RAIL Oval
BUSES 12, 36, 185, 345

GETTING LUCKY	**3/5**
EYE CANDY	**3/5**
BIG SPENDERS	**3/5**
MIX 55%M 45%F	
AGE 20-35	
PRICE Average	

AMBIENCE Arty/Boho, Brightly Coloured/Cheerful, Casual, Chilled, Dancing, Funky, Groups, Historic, Late Night Open, Live Music
REVIEW Brighter than a baboon's bottom, the Funky Munky's banana-coloured walls do little to blend into the unimaginative local terrain. Being one of the only places around Camberwell with a late licence, it has become a mecca for those wanting to drink deep into the night. Its monkey magic attracts a range of species at odds with the local habitat, all being suitably domesticated and groomed to face the rigours of urban survival. DJs emerge from the trees to provide Jungle Boogie for swingers unimpressed by the Birdy Song. Definitely an ape-free zone devoid of serious predators, although the extensive cocktail list and laid-back atmosphere provide the perfect plain for subtler game-hunting.
PLACE A well-aired drinking hole with fans aplenty, bright wood, the odd plant and a scary number of windows. Lots of seating and subtle lighting. Long, thin dance floor upstairs with DJs spinning cutting-edge house and hip hop. Henry VIII's stables were once located behind the building.
PEOPLE Parkas lined with fur... fake, naturally. Also the usual 20-something, accessory-toting urban warriors.
PROFS Lawyers, students, bankers, graphic designers, DJs, artists
CELEBS Gary Mason, Basement Jaxx
DRESS Some like it hot and, then again, some don't. Basically, anything. FCUK, Firetrap, Carhartt, Diesel
MUSIC Latin, Funk, House, Hip Hop, Breaks, DJs Wed-Sat
DOOR None
DRINKS Beer £2.50, Wine £3, Cocktail £4.50
FOOD Italian, £4.50
CARDS All
CAPACITY 300, seating 80
HIRE Venue: Yes · Private Room: No

RED STAR

Club
319 Camberwell Road SE5
020 7703 7779

OPEN Mon-Thu 5pm-2am, Fri-Sat 5pm-4am, Sun midday-midnight
TUBE/RAIL Kennington
BUSES 12, 35, 45, 176, 185, 345

GETTING LUCKY	**5/5**
EYE CANDY	**2/5**
BIG SPENDERS	**1/5**
MIX 60%M 40%F	
AGE 18-25	
PRICE Average	

AMBIENCE Arty/Boho, Dancing, Late Night Open, Luvved up Clubbers, Party, Student, Warehouse/Industrial, Pulling
REVIEW New Southside louche-about and younger brother of rabid rave pit The Dogstar. Also related to The Living Room Bar, which in the genes contest may have won the looks, but lost out to the Star in the taste and funk stakes. Varied music policy from retro to all forms of house and breakbeat. Catering mainly

for students and often the most hormone driven of this learned breed. Nobody's particularly fussy and everyone's virtually rubbing their crotches against the furnishings. Open until 4am, you're more likely to get in to the Red Star than you are The Dogstar (with its perhaps undeserved legendary rep). Weeknights are more relaxed: blokes are in to play pool and drink pints, rather than irritate the hell out of any poor lass that even blinks in their direction.
PLACE Bar with decks and basic 70s retro suave. Two floors but upstairs is open only at the weekend and is heavy on the cheese and tongue tussling. Downstairs has understated decor and plenty of drinking space.
PEOPLE Jenny and Mark are first years at Goldsmiths. They think Urban Outfitters is the coolest thing on the planet and have just spent the first instalment of their student loans on Japanese gadgetry.
PROFS Creatives, music industry, artists, students
CELEBS None
DRESS Typical utility wear and up-to-the-second distressed fashions, Chrissie Hynde haircuts in abundance. Fairly smart at the weekends, casual during the week
MUSIC Funky Grooves, Breakbeat, Hip Hop, House, DJs 7 nights
DOOR Fri-Sat free before 10pm, after 10pm £4-6
DRINKS Beer £2.50, Wine £2.50, Cocktail £4
FOOD Sunday Roast, £6
CARDS No Amex or Diners
CAPACITY 500, seating 100
HIRE Venue: Yes · Private Room: No

SNUG

Bar
65 Camberwell Church Street SE5
020 7277 2601

OPEN Mon-Thu 4pm-midnight, Fri-Sat 2pm-2am, Sat midday-2am, Sun midday-11pm
TUBE/RAIL Oval, Elephant & Castle
BUSES 12, 36, 185, 345

GETTING LUCKY	**4/5**
EYE CANDY	**2/5**
BIG SPENDERS	**3/5**
MIX 55%M 45%F	
AGE 25-35	
PRICE Average	

AMBIENCE Arty/Boho, Buzzy, Dancing, Friendly, Funky, Groups, Late Night Open, Party, Pulling, Student
REVIEW Thanks to an overdose of delicious but deadly banana milkshake flavoured vodka shots, our memories of this splendidly shabby-chic outpost of the Babushka chain are as wobbly as the Russian economy. We definitely remember the impolite bouncer, the exceptionally chirpy barstaff and the two gurning mentalists who spent all evening raving it up on the dance floor. What we don't fully recall is why we foolishly moved on to vindaloo vodkas just as the place started to fill up with some frightfully attractive punters. Snug's huge vodka list and late licence ensures that the majority of customers leave hammered, happy and ready for some lurve.
PLACE This is an interesting and dimly-lit conversion with some suitably Baroque features; lavish mirrors decorate the blood-red walls, and the whole place is filled with ornate chandeliers and leather sofas. Opening an upstairs chill-out room late November 2001.

PEOPLE Über trendy boho-chic art students mix with gaw-blimey locals, the linguistically challenged, Denmark Hill media strays and lots of randoms.

PROFS Art students, salespeople, graphic designers, couriers, IT consultants, PRs, property developers, teachers, writers, fashion professionals
CELEBS None
DRESS Hilfiger, New Balance, Diesel, Prada, Hope & Glory, Mambo, Adidas, Carhartt, River Island
MUSIC Breakbeat, Dance, Disco, Funk, Hip Hop, Pop, Reggae, Ska, DJs 7 nights, Live Music Sun
DOOR Smart casual, Sun £3
DRINKS Beer £2.50, Wine £3.50, Champagne £5.75, Cocktail £4.50
FOOD Bar Snacks, Traditional English, £3.50
CARDS All
CAPACITY 280, seating 100
HIRE Venue: Yes · Private Room: Yes

SUN AND DOVES

Pub
61-63 Coldharbour Lane SE5
020 7733 1525

OPEN Mon-Fri 10am-11pm,	GETTING LUCKY	3/5
Sat midday-11pm, Sun	EYE CANDY	3/5
midday-10.30pm	BIG SPENDERS	2/5
TUBE/RAIL Brixton,	MIX 55%M 45%F	
Loughborough Junction	AGE 25-35	
BUSES 35, 45, 345	PRICE Average	

AMBIENCE Casual, Conversation, Friendly
REVIEW What to read first? The local theatre and cinema flyers? Or the Operation Trident posters, politely asking customers to dob in their gun-wielding neighbours when they've finished their beer? For all of Brixton and Camberwell's many cool spots, this stretch of Coldharbour Lane is as shabby and rundown as London gets, which is why the Sun and Doves is such a welcome addition to the area. Heaving at weekends, and never less than lively, it's a comfort zone for anyone who wants a reliable night out with soothing music, good drinks and comfy sofas. Despite a few minor quibbles – like the pun-tastic 'Coolharbour Lane' artwork, which reeks of trying too hard – this is a solid, likeable, easy-going pub, in an area that desperately needed one.
PLACE Light, airy, wooden-floored space, à la All Bar One, but marginally funkier. The designers obviously thought it might be nice to attract a few, y'know, women. Hey, it might catch on...
PEOPLE Professional, cohabiting couples in their early 30s who get a kick out of their postcode, but have stopped pretending they like drum 'n' bass. Their clubbing days are almost over, but they aren't yet ready to accept full-blown domesticity.

PROFS Hospital workers, art students, artists
CELEBS Dinos Chapman, Terry Gilliam, Jenny Eclair, Bill Bailey
DRESS Cutting-edge street-label t-shirts ordered via a Japanese website, on a foundation of Gap
MUSIC Funk, Disco, Hip Hop
DOOR None
DRINKS Beer £2.50, Wine £2.60, Cocktail £4.50

FOOD Modern European, Moroccan, £9
CARDS All
CAPACITY 250, seating 150
HIRE Venue: No · Private Room: No

clapham

100 PUB

Bar
100 Clapham Park Road SW8
020 7720 8902

OPEN Mon-Fri 4.30pm-	GETTING LUCKY	3/5
11pm, Sat midday-11.00pm	EYE CANDY	4/5
TUBE/RAIL Clapham	BIG SPENDERS	3/5
Common	MIX 50%M 50%F	
BUSES 35, 37, 137, 437	AGE 21-35	
	PRICE Average	

AMBIENCE Casual, Conversation, Dancing, Groups
REVIEW The 100 draws in young, groovy Cla'amites like moths to a flame, where they loll about drinking Staropramen or vodka and cranberry juice. Hot discussion topics are their media/marketing careers, EastEnders, and how glad they are to still be renting what with the house prices as they are, y'know. They like the 100 because it fulfils their bar needs, with not a whiff of fusty old men or brass horseshoes and bedpans. Comedy nights on Thursdays are well received, and it serves draught beers and shows the Big Match Live, thus sating the desire to just 'go down the pub'.
PLACE Slightly incongruous pub/bar crossover is bizarrely, but successfully, combined with table football and two big screens – but the best feature is the Cheers-esque central bar. Not, however, the kind of place where everybody knows your name. Outside there's a big mural on a kind of sunset beach theme – not to everyone's taste, perhaps, but then neither's the bar.
PEOPLE Hip pre-mortgage Claphamites. Not for anyone over mid-30s, nor genuine locals – heaven forbid, it might burst the 'Clapham Bubble'. This, after all, is not Real London. Youngsters who moved here after university and live in a world populated exclusively by people like them.

PROFS Media types, architects, graphic designers, PRs, students, stockbrokers, estate agents
CELEBS None
DRESS Contrived casual. Expensive 'combat' trousers (like you'd wear those in a conflict situation), cheap t-shirts or vest tops and the indispensable hooded fleece, Gap, H&M, Jane Norman, Kookaï, TopMan
MUSIC Easy Listening, Chart, Dance, DJs Fri-Sat, Comedy Night Thu
DOOR None
DRINKS Beer £2.60, Wine £3, Cocktail £4
FOOD Pizza, Snacks, £7.50
CARDS No Amex
CAPACITY 300, seating 50
HIRE Venue: Yes · Private Room: Yes

BAR OBLIVION

Bar
8 Cavendish Parade SW4
020 8772 0203

OPEN Mon-Sat midday-11pm, Sun midday-10.30pm
TUBE/RAIL Clapham South
BUSES 255

GETTING LUCKY	**3/5**
EYE CANDY	**3/5**
BIG SPENDERS	**3/5**
MIX 60%M 40%F	
AGE 20-35	
PRICE Average	

AMBIENCE Groups, Hip/Fashionable, Party
REVIEW A curious mix of pre-rave youngsters, double-barrelled Clapham-ites and fresh-off-the-tube suits jostle for service amidst Oblivion's brash riot of hideous sculptures, broken mirrors and dalek-style bar stools. With music as loud as the decor, conversing can be thirsty work – but then that's the idea. Although typically overpriced cocktails are available, most punters seem hell-bent on Red-Bulling themselves into their own private Oblivion. Rave on. Despite the unnecessary knuckleheads on the door and sporadically crappy service, Oblivion skilfully manages to blur the line between pub and club, and continues to pack 'em in, in its own inimitable 'bring your own bongos' kind of way. A great summer venue, this would be THE place to come in Clapham if only they could get hold of a late licence.
PLACE A welcome relief from the ubiquitous quasi-timberyard craze, this is a very 'Blue Peter presenter drops acid and goes mental with the tinfoil' type affair. Incidentally, don't miss the centrefold-plastered bogs complete with complimentary turd.
PEOPLE 'Hey Tobias, your Hawaiian shirt is completely wacky; where d'ya say your mum bought it?' type Theakston characters, mixed with after-workers who wouldn't say no to a shag and locals en route to some railway arch hellhole that poses as a club.

PROFS Estate agents, stockbrokers, media professionals, middle managers, recruitment consultants, salespeople, IT consultants, advertising professionals, students
CELEBS None
DRESS From shabby-chic to designer-ponce, this is a decidedly trendy affair. Clark Kent-esque transformers (by day – geeky suit, by nightfall – baggy trousered berk in loud shirt and fluorescent trainers) largin' it up with the rest of the IT department, mixed with FCUK girls who feign disdain when blokes gawp at their barely concealed boobs.
MUSIC Chart, Dance, Pop, House, Funk, Garage, DJs Thu-Sun
DOOR None
DRINKS Beer £2.60, Wine £2.50, Champagne £5.25, Cocktail £4.50
FOOD Brasserie, Modern European, £7
CARDS No Amex
CAPACITY 400, seating 75
HIRE Venue: No · Private Room: Yes

CIRCLE BAR

Bar
348 Clapham Road SW9
020 7622 3683

OPEN Mon-Sat midday-11pm, Sun midday-10.30pm
TUBE/RAIL Clapham North, Stockwell
BUSES 88, 315, 345, 348

GETTING LUCKY	**2/5**
EYE CANDY	**3/5**
BIG SPENDERS	**2/5**
MIX 65%M 35%F	
AGE 25-35	
PRICE Average	

AMBIENCE Groups
REVIEW 'Hooj choons' and 'chunky classics' are all the rage at this could-be-West-End-but-not venue. It's got an ambitious food menu that must not be described as 'pub grub' at any stage, a range of board games that everyone's too cool to play with, a retro table football table and MTV projected across the expansive walls. So far so what, you say, but hang on – the Circle is not in Noho or Hoxton Square, but actually at the arse-end of Clapham Road, next to a greasy kebab shop and bang smack between the council estates of Stockwell and Clapham North. The location means the punters are an unpretentious down to earth bunch who are a little past hitting Brixton but will gladly shake that leg for up to 20 minutes if put to the test. In this manor there's little alternative, so sling on yer glad rags and make that move... or try.
PLACE Sticks out a bit in this rather dilapidated section of Clapham. The tables are made out of old church doors and there's an outside terrace for summer barbecues.
PEOPLE The drinkers here are a friendly, down to earth bunch who just hate talk of celebrities and designer and shopping (far too shallow), prefer to tackle meatier matters like hunger strikes in Turkey and Harry Potter.

PROFS Journalists and web hacks meet picture framers and landscape gardeners. Interesting.
CELEBS Jamie Oliver, Nadia Sawalha
DRESS Desert boots and chinos mix with jeans, sweatshirts and trainers. This place is not exactly a fashion-conscious style hole but people do make a bit of an effort in that South London effortless way. Wear what you like when you like.
MUSIC Funk, House, DJs Thu-Sun
DOOR None
DRINKS Beer £2.70, Wine £2.30, Cocktails £4.50
FOOD Modern British, £7
CARDS No Amex
CAPACITY 200, seating 80
HIRE Venue: Yes · Private Room: Yes

THE FALCON

Pub
2 St John's Hill SW11
020 7924 8041

OPEN Mon-Sat 11am-11pm, Sun midday-10.30pm
TUBE/RAIL Clapham Common
BUSES 35, 37, 77, 77a

GETTING LUCKY	**3/5**
EYE CANDY	**2/5**
BIG SPENDERS	**3/5**
MIX 65%M 35%F	
AGE 25-55	
PRICE Average	

AMBIENCE Casual, Groups
REVIEW This traditional boozer has, along with department store Arcing and Hobbs, been a landmark building in Clapham for over a century and is a firm favourite with non-paunchy pub fans. Like the majority of bars round here, weekends see the place overflowing with pre-club drinkers, yet this remains a male-dominated alehouse. The central bar and squashed layout make for quite a pull-friendly atmosphere but most punters foolishly keep their options open, waiting to hit the nearby Grand. That's a big mistake, 'bird in

the hand' and all that. Apparently, the Falcon possesses the longest bar in Britain – an apocryphal claim at best. I can confirm however that the waiting time to get served in here is the longest in the universe. More staff please.
PLACE Huge corner pub, very traditional and atmospheric but squint-enduringly bright, with wood partitions, stained glass and green walls. Unbelievably, a sign outside claims the phrase 'At death's door' originated here because some shopkeeper next door's surname was 'Death'. Hmmm.
PEOPLE Local squares who hate Abbess (All Bar Ones), rugby lads, pre-clubbers and gangs of dull-looking blokes who drink Guinness professionally.

PROFS Nurses, recruitment personnel, roofers, IT profs, journalists, accountants, retail staff, City temps, builders, market stallholders
CELEBS Nigel Havers, Johnny Vaughan
DRESS Rugby shirts, tarty clubwear, Frank Skinner-esque shirt/jeans combos, Nike (whole outfit plus Grade One haircut/wet shave and plenty of gold jewellery for male AND female), Diesel, older business women in 80s Jaeger style, Argyle knit sweaters and green kagouls for old men (not forgetting the paisley tie), leatherette macs for City temps
MUSIC Music comes straight from the juke box at this venue that rarely switches its numerous screens off for long enough for you to hear a selection. Subscriptions to Sky and ITV Digital mean that no kick, hop, skip or jump is missed in the world of sport
DOOR None
DRINKS Beer £2.30, Wine £2.50
FOOD Grill, Pub Food, £5
CARDS No Amex
CAPACITY 250, seating 60
HIRE Venue: No · Private Room: No

THE FINE LINE

Bar
182-184 Clapham High Street SW4
020 7622 4436

OPEN Mon-Wed midday-	GETTING LUCKY	3/5
11pm, Thu midday-midnight,	EYE CANDY	3/5
Fri-Sat 11am-1am,	BIG SPENDERS	3/5
Sun midday-10.30pm	MIX 70%M 30%F	
TUBE/RAIL Clapham	AGE 20-30	
Common	PRICE Average	
BUSES 35, 37, 137, 437		

AMBIENCE Casual, Dancing, Groups
REVIEW More opulent than the All Bar Ones of this world, this is a beautifully designed gin palace – spacious and modern but ultimately predictable. Weekends see the mandatory inclusion of headset-wearing meatheads on the door and an Ali G lookalike spinning some phat sounds. Sadly, the latter renders all conversation futile, forcing the majority of punters to nod in pretend appreciation, when in reality they'd probably prefer a few Robbie tunes.
PLACE Exposed brick, twinkly lights and, of course, plenty of wood. The large bar area gives way to a raised restaurant/snogging section where typically pretentious new 'pub' food, eg wild boar and basil burgers, is available.
PEOPLE Clapham's new wave of upwardly mobile upstarts

rub shoulders with the sporadic provincial slack-wearer en route to Southsides, a neighbouring nightclub where sovereign-ring knuckle-dusters are a prerequisite.

PROFS City boys, bankers, insurance company employees, lawyers, solicitors, catering employees, graphic designers, PAs, account executives
CELEBS Patsy Kensit
DRESS Anything goes, but it's pretty much Clapham-meets-Chamonix-meets-Jamie Theakston
MUSIC Trip Hop, Funk, Trance, DJs Fri-Sat
DOOR Smart casual
DRINKS Beer £2.60, Wine £2.70, Champagne £6, Cocktail £5
FOOD Mediterranean, Oriental, Traditional British, £8
CARDS No Diners
CAPACITY 400, seating 150
HIRE Venue: No · Private Room: No

KAZBAR

Bar, Gay, Live Music Venue
50 Clapham High Street SW4
020 7622 0070

OPEN Mon-Fri 4pm-	GETTING LUCKY	5/5
midnight,	EYE CANDY	3/5
Sat midday-midnight,	BIG SPENDERS	3/5
Sun midday-11.30pm	MIX 80%M 20%F	
TUBE/RAIL Clapham North	AGE 25-35	
BUSES 25, 35, 37, 88,	PRICE Cheap	
137, 345		

AMBIENCE Dancing, Party, Pulling
REVIEW Kazbar is not one of the run-of-the-mill Clapham drinking holes. A superb venue; the penny drops for most when, approaching the bar, you begin to notice the references to the good gay life. It makes a change from the usual peanut pin-up packs and a board of pork scratchings. The Kazbar is not an intimidating place and straight folk are made to feel more than welcome. Happy hour all day until 8pm is a worthwhile experience, if it becomes too sweaty downstairs the more sedate can move to tables on the mezzanine floor and survey the activities below from a distance. Oh, and it has a resident VJ too, so there's always something suitably flamboyant to observe.
PLACE Stylish exterior looks a little out of place amid the Clapham North grunge, while the inside is an entertaining mix of the childlike and sophisticated, but then again I always was a sucker for glitterballs.
PEOPLE Upwardly mobile young men and women with cropped hair, toned bodies and an aversion to jokes about the nearby Clapham Common.

PROFS Bankers, doctors, theatre staff, graphic designers, architects, lawyers, DJs, artists, musicians
CELEBS Dale Winton, Brian (Big Brother), not much to report here
DRESS Tight Adidas t-shirts, Levi's, Burro, Jigsaw, FCUK
MUSIC Pop, House, Garage, Chart, Dance, 70s, 80s, DJs
DOOR None
DRINKS Beer £2.50, Wine £2.40, Cocktail £5
FOOD None
CARDS All
CAPACITY 190, seating 30
HIRE Venue: No · Private Room: No

RAILWAY

Bar, Restaurant
18 Clapham High Street SW4
020 7622 4077

OPEN Mon-Fri 11am-11pm,	**GETTING LUCKY**	4/5
Sat midday-11pm,	**EYE CANDY**	3/5
Sun midday-10.30pm	**BIG SPENDERS**	2/5
TUBE/RAIL Clapham North	**MIX** 50%M 50%F	
BUSES P5, 88, 155,	**AGE** 20-35	
345, 355	**PRICE** Average	

AMBIENCE Casual, Groups, Outdoors, Pulling, Student
REVIEW Can work but don't want to, will work but can't, gizza a job, not now though maybe next year. Clapham's laid-back come here for its unchallenging atmosphere, which means you're likely to find the place packed with joyful artisans and the work-shy. Busiest on weekend nights, when the cocktails are fast and furious and heavy shot drinkers mingle with the unadventurous House White brigade. Come here if you're single: you might score with the abundance of easy come, easy go locals cruising through this anti-Blair stronghold.
PLACE Aztec decor with a worn wooden floor that's scattered with tiled, mosaic or second-hand wooden tables and chairs. A yellow bohemian shade adorns walls, as do tropical paintings. Inspired positioning under the railway bridge.
PEOPLE Hippies and low-maintenance Claphamites. Postgraduate travellers or first jobbers just back from Thailand or Mexico.

PROFS Musicians, media execs, art students, City workers, graphic designers
CELEBS None
DRESS Department-store office gear mingles with some TopShop/Man eveningwear, Burtons, New Look, H&M, Miss Selfridge
MUSIC Dance, Alternative, Chart
DOOR None
DRINKS Beer £2.60, Wine £2.75, Cocktail £4.50
FOOD Thai, £4.95
CARDS No Amex
CAPACITY 150, seating 60
HIRE Venue: No · Private Room: Yes

RAPSCALLION

Bar, Restaurant
75 Venn Street SW4
020 7787 6555

OPEN Mon-Sat 10.30am-	**GETTING LUCKY**	2/5
midnight,	**EYE CANDY**	4/5
Sun 10.30am-11pm	**BIG SPENDERS**	4/5
TUBE/RAIL Clapham	**MIX** 50%M 50%F	
Common	**AGE** 30-40	
BUSES 155	**PRICE** Average	

AMBIENCE Arty/Bohemian, Buzzy, Conversation, Groups, Hip/Fashionable
REVIEW Tucked away from the busy High Street, this diminutive bar/restaurant attracts the upper echelons of Clapham's yuppie society. Unfortunately, identifying the exact species is rather difficult as that largely depends on what film is playing at the Picture House opposite.

At weekends, groups of glamorous PR-types discuss the latest goings-on in Sex and the City over a glass or five of Chardonnay, whilst snooty couples chomp on mussels, skilfully ignoring the passing beer boys who occasionally glance through the window like Dickensian street urchins. The friendly staff wander attentively around the smart minimalist interior, straightening the orchids as some sloshed media weasel clicks his fingers to Tony Bennett and tells the entire bar that he was into old 'Tone' years ago.
PLACE Very small, jazzy side-street affair with reddish banquettes and a smart little bar holding enormous beer taps that spew unpronounceable lagers. Reminiscent of those happening bars in Greenwich Village. That's NYC not SE10.
PEOPLE Young Monty Don/Clare Francis types and pullable 30-something women who can't believe how skinny Ally McBeal is. The occasional media type and pre-cinemagoer whose idea of a good movie involves lots of subtitles.

PROFS Actors, architects, designers, PRs, writers, artists
CELEBS Nick Moran, Anna Friel, Beth Orton, Max Clifford, Kathy Burke, David Gray, Paul Oakenfold, Sir Peter Hall, Dame Judi Dench
DRESS Anything black. DKNY, Helmut Lang and Prada power-suits combined with relaxed off-duty yachtwear and chinos. Lots of media-friendly, Olive-from-'On the Buses' style glasses
MUSIC Easy Listening, Jazz, Funk
DOOR None
DRINKS Beer £2.99, Wine £3.50, Champagne £7, Cocktail £5.75
FOOD MediterrAsian, £11
CARDS All
CAPACITY 70, seating 30
HIRE Venue: Yes · Private Room: No

SAND

Bar
156 Clapham Park Road SW4
020 7622 3022

OPEN Mon-Sat 5pm-2am,	**GETTING LUCKY**	4/5
Sun 5pm-1am	**EYE CANDY**	4/5
TUBE/RAIL Clapham	**BIG SPENDERS**	4/5
Common	**MIX** 55%M 45%F	
BUSES 35, 37	**AGE** 25-35	
	PRICE Expensive	

AMBIENCE Dancing, Late Night Open, Live Music, Pulling
REVIEW If you could bottle the atmosphere in this swish cocktail bar it would undoubtedly be marketed as 'Eau de Ponceywanker' and sold by the lorryload. Trendy Clapham stereotypes are strictly adhered to in here, as svelte girls in skimpy tops openly flirt with lecherous designer mockney geezers who offer them shots of vodka then try to guess their star sign. The evening ends for the aforementioned Oliverites in the nearest kebab shop drunkenly shouting 'chilli soss', and comparing the rotating doner to an elephant's leg. South London's young and beautiful come here to be just that, and judging by the smouldering eye-tennis going on, a fair amount of wobbly bit-fumbling occurs after Sand finally spills out at 2am. Fun. The only bummer is the over-zealous, power-crazy bouncer revelling in his role as artificial queue creator.

'the sequel'

described variously as the best thing to open in Clapham for years, the finest weekend brunch in London and the place where Max Clifford hatches his most important business coups, is as appropriate for an evening get-together with friends as for an executive dinner meeting.

Call 020 7622 4222 for reservations.
www.thesequelonline.com

PLACE Regarded as a bit of a local gem amongst the Cla'am gang. Sexy lighting, linear architecture, black leather sofas, Japanese wood theme, a designer fire and a bibliotheque at the back lend to the lounge feel of this bar.

PEOPLE Vinnie Jones meets Bridget Jones for a bit of the old eye action and maybe more.

PROFS Bankers, property developers and prize-fighters mix with IT consultants, media jockeys and the odd waif and stray from the world of television

CELEBS Strictly B and C list here only – the odd EastEnder drinks with a so-and-so from Hollyoaks

DRESS Very casual with a touch of designer meets High Street basics such as Gap, Next, H&M and TopShop blending well with a touch of Prada, dahling

MUSIC Funk, Soul, Jazz

DOOR Smart casual

DRINKS Beer £2.80, Wine £3.50, Champagne £7, Cocktail £5

FOOD Modern European, £20

CARDS No Amex or Diners

CAPACITY 200, seating 80

HIRE Venue: No · Private Room: Yes

THE SEQUEL

Bar, Restaurant
Clapham Picture House, Venn Street SW4
020 7622 4222

OPEN Mon-Fri 4.30pm-midnight, Sat 11am-midnight, Sun 11am-11pm	**GETTING LUCKY**	**1/5**
	EYE CANDY	**3/5**
	BIG SPENDERS	**4/5**
TUBE/RAIL Clapham Common	**MIX** 50%M 50%F	
BUSES 155	**AGE** 25-50	
	PRICE Average	

AMBIENCE Arty/Bohemian, Business, Conversation, Groups, Hip/Fashionable

REVIEW Me old mate Sean Connery told me that it's rude to name-drop, but I can't resist; apparently Geri-Augustus Halliwell-Gloop eats leaves here and Max Clifford used to advise on the PR side. This is the offspring of Rapscallion, a similarly bijou joint across the road. Inside, trendy media folk huddle round the teensy bar discussing the cinematic implications of Lady and the Tramp as exceptionally smart couples sit smoking Indonesian cigarettes, whilst perusing the outstanding cocktail list and hilariously pretentious menu. 'Dahling, I just can't decide between the crusted shark or the charred octopus.' Full marks though for trying something a bit different.

PLACE Unlike most sequels, this one surpasses the original, in terms of decor at least. Sadly, the whole place is a smidgen up its own arse and, unless you're up on your Estonian film trivia, the hovering staff and snooty punters can be slightly intimidating.

PEOPLE Cliquey wine gulpers, dining couples and the occasional Claphamite who can't be bothered going to Notting Hill to get his/her fix of hi-falutin' artifice.

PROFS Actors, architects, fashion designers, PRs, journalists, advertising executives

CELEBS Max Clifford, Geri Halliwell, Nick Moran, Anna Friel, Jason Flemyng, Dame Judi Dench, Sir Peter Hall, David Gray, Roachford, Paul Oakenfold

DRESS DKNY, Gap, Armani, moddish trendy, boho filmmaker with lots of black

MUSIC Jazz, Funk, World Music

DOOR None

DRINKS Beer £2.99, Wine £3.50, Champagne £7, Cocktail £5.75

FOOD Modern Global, £11

CARDS All

CAPACITY 150, seating 40

HIRE Venue: Yes · Private Room: No

SO.UK

Cocktail Bar, Restaurant Bar
165 Clapham High Street SW4
020 7622 4004

OPEN Mon-Wed 5pm-midnight, Thu-Fri 5pm-2am, Sat midday-2am	**GETTING LUCKY**	**3/5**
	EYE CANDY	**3/5**
	BIG SPENDERS	**3/5**
TUBE/RAIL Clapham Common	**MIX** 55%M 45%F	
	AGE 25-40	
BUSES 35, 37, 137, 437	**PRICE** Average	

AMBIENCE Chilled, Comfy, Funky, Hip/Fashionable, Late Night Open, Lounge

REVIEW Exactly why celeb owners Leslie Ash and Lee Chapman cheesified the name by conforming to current compu-dot zeitgeist is anyone's guess, but it certainly hasn't affected business; So.uk (souk – geddit?) is rammed. Although the late licence, lounge atmosphere and captivating decor partially explain the crowds, the star attraction is undoubtedly the fantabulous booze list: Martini cocktails, obscure beers, stupefying shooters – there's even a cigar menu. If getting hammered and chilled simultaneously is your thing, this is the place. The only bummer is the cack layout; unless you're lucky enough to get a seat there isn't really anywhere to stand without looking like a loitering prick. The bar area's an option but that's busier than the Northern Line. Still, claustrophobic surroundings can have a wonderfully positive effect on the angle of your dangle. Not 'arf.

PLACE Think Turkish Delight advert mixed with a crowded harem, and then throw in a touch of North African minimalism. The staff are astoundingly friendly, even the obligatory door meathead grunts hello and goodbye.

PEOPLE Although the majority of punters are well-to-do-Claphamites, this area appears to be pulling in a glut of beautiful people these days; we spotted several designer-clad model types sipping champagne. The only place for the true Clapham elite.

PROFS Bankers, salespeople, IT consultants, civil servants, fashion bizz people, media creatives, journos, pretend models, Photoshop wizards, photographers

CELEBS Ainsley Harriott, Leslie Ash, Lee Chapman

DRESS Predominantly smart/designer with an occasionally trendy twist; Jap-art t-shirts, chunky jewellery, tinted vanity spccs, short-sleeved Firetrap/Evisu shirts, Prada, Gaultier, combats, chinos and a Nicole Farhi and Chloe following

MUSIC Moroccan, French, Tunisian, Hip Hop, Rare Groove, Progressive French (see SO.UK CD)

DOOR None

DRINKS Beer £3, Wine £3.25, Champagne £6.50, Cocktail £3

FOOD All
CAPACITY 120, seating 70
HIRE Venue: Yes · Private Room: No

THE SUN

Bar
47 Clapham Old Town SW4
020 7622 4980

OPEN Mon-Sat 11am-11pm,	**GETTING LUCKY**	**4/5**
Sun 11am-10.30pm	**EYE CANDY**	**4/5**
TUBE/RAIL Clapham	**BIG SPENDERS**	**3/5**
Common	**MIX** 55%M 45%F	
BUSES 35, 37, 137, 437	**AGE** 25-35	
	PRICE Average	

AMBIENCE Brightly Coloured/Cheerful, Casual, Conversation, Groups, Pulling
REVIEW What used to be a dazzlingly bright boozer is now a creamy, far more mediocre affair. That said, things remain offbeat enough to ensure any venturing traditionalist CAMRA beardies would have a fit. Then there's the clientele: in contrast to their surroundings they're a pretty square bunch, most of them paired-up and enjoying their last gasp of dual-income expenditure before the kids arrive. On weekends, the atmosphere becomes decidedly 'hearty' with English rugby-shirted blokes downing pints of Staropramen and slapping each other on the back while the 'ladies' drink almost as much as the boys. The large beer garden affords a rare opportunity to sit outside in this part of Clapham, and there's plenty of furtive male-female eye contact being made. This is a superb venue to get a flavour of the Clapham scene and is neatly positioned close to the tube. A veritable must go for all who visit the area.
PLACE Three bars across two floors and, at the weekend, service that's slower than the continental drift.
PEOPLE Clapham and Battersea Rise types – the road outside is awash with flash motors belonging to these aspirational smart boys and girls.

PROFS Advertising and marketing employees, film PAs, accountants, writers, receptionists, estate agents
CELEBS Tony Slattery, Paul Kaye (Dennis Pennis), Chris Evans, David Gower, Ian Botham
DRESS Next, Gap, Levi's, Monsoon, Cotton Traders, Hilfiger, Helly Hansen
MUSIC Dance, Jazz
DOOR None
DRINKS Beer £2.60, Wine £2.50
FOOD Thai, £2.95
CARDS All
CAPACITY 400, seating 106
HIRE Venue: Yes · Private Room: No

TEAROOM DES ARTISTES

Bar
697 Wandsworth Road SW8
020 7652 6526

OPEN Fri-Sat 5.30pm-1am,	**GETTING LUCKY**	**2/5**
Sun 3pm-12.30am	**EYE CANDY**	**3/5**
TUBE/RAIL Clapham	**BIG SPENDERS**	**2/5**
Common	**MIX** 50%M 50%F	
BUSES 77, 77A	**AGE** 25-35	
	PRICE Average	

AMBIENCE Casual, Groups, Historic, Late Night Open, Star Spotting
REVIEW What was once an original 16th-century two-storey barn has survived through the years, morphing into its current incarnation as a sumptuous, successful and groovy veggie and seafood restaurant/bar. It caters for those with a keen eye and the lucky few that stumble upon its best night by far, Sunday. Local regulars get to combine the bohemian menu with their favourite DJ or band as the upstairs bar area turns into a club-like loft on a popular night. Chilled out über style merchants make for a very sociable crowd, harping on about 'their' night like old-established friends. Couples and the 'DJ crowd' usually eat first and stay at the table to listen to the night's entertainment (different each week). The music policy dictates atmosphere – from drum 'n' bass to funky jazz or mellow grooves. The pink neon sign outside is the only clue to South London's finest little groove hole.
PLACE Original wooden barn interior with a long counter bar on the ground floor, open area frontage with kitsch low-rise old car seats, stairs up to restaurant, split-level bar and stage with DJ booth.
PEOPLE Groovers, vinyl junkies debating whether the minidisc format will survive.

PROFS DJs, journalists, musicians, TV and radio pluggers, interior designers, teachers, local retailers, tradesmen
CELEBS Morcheeba, Björk, Boy George, Ross Kemp, Jacqueline Ryan, Vince Power, Alan Bennett, Richard Blackwood, Robbie Williams
DRESS Maharishi, Puma, Evisu, 'salvage' denim, Levi's, Nike Air, Rookie, Paul Smith, Lacoste
MUSIC House, Light Jazz, DJ Sun
DOOR None
DRINKS Beer £2.50, Wine £2.50, Cocktail £8

FOOD Seafood, Vegetarian, £8
CARDS All
CAPACITY 200, seating 130
HIRE Venue: Yes · Private Room: Yes

THE WHITE HOUSE

Cocktail Bar, Members Club, Restaurant
65 Clapham Park Road SW4
020 7498 3388

OPEN Tue 6pm-midnight,	GETTING LUCKY	**4/5**
Wed-Sat 6pm-midnight,	EYE CANDY	**4/5**
Sun 1pm-midnight	BIG SPENDERS	**4/5**
TUBE/RAIL Clapham	MIX 55%M 45%F	
Common	AGE 25-35	
BUSES 35, 37, 155,	PRICE Average	
345, 355		

AMBIENCE Chilled, Dancing, Elegant/Classic, Exclusive/Chic, Hip/Fashionable, Late Night Open, Lounge, Opulent, Star Spotting, Pulling
REVIEW Forget dress-staining, impeachment and vandalism. The only similarity this venue has to its Washington-based namesake is a quite ludicrous level of security. Following a caution by the surly MIB's (Meatheads In Black) for wearing trainers, we fled to the dimly lit sanctuary of the bar, only to have a clipboard-wielding bimbo barge over and ask 'Are you here for a drink?' Whilst resisting the urge to say 'No, we're here to watch Alan Titchmarsh fellate a donkey', we were then instructed to order our drinks at a different section of the bar. The somewhat oppressive atmosphere was further reinforced by the inexplicable presence of three(!) headset-wearing bouncers monitoring the gent's. Maybe we were unlucky, but at the moment this groovy-looking place is far too far up its own sumptuously designed arse.
PLACE Large, flood-lit Victorian building with three floors of chilled-out fun. The dimly-lit ground floor contains a groovy central bar serving two areas, the members' lounge is on the first floor and the second floor is home to three private dining rooms. Presumably, the bouncers are stored in the basement.
PEOPLE With Sand and So.uk within spitting distance, this enclave of SW4 is rapidly becoming a Mecca for wannabe MTV VJs and fashion-victims who, until recently, had to pretend that they lived in N1. Full of Face/i-D/Arena readers, pretend media bimbettes and trendies who probably attend more launches than an astronaut's girlfriend.

PROFS PR, publishers, writers, club promoters, assistant editors, stylists, graphic designers, art students, Mac pros
CELEBS None
DRESS Standard Theakston-wear mixed with media-specs, Evisu, Diesel, Earl, Firetrap, Gucci, Maharishi and Prada
MUSIC Jazz, Chill-out, Live, Happy House DJs Wed-Sat
DOOR None
DRINKS Beer £2.70, Wine £3, Champagne £6, Cocktail £5
FOOD International, Tapas, £6
CARDS All
CAPACITY 190, seating 60
HIRE Venue: Yes · Private Room: Yes

MINISTRY OF SOUND

Club, Live Music Venue
103 Gaunt Street SE1
020 7378 6528

OPEN Fri 10.30pm-5am,	GETTING LUCKY	**5/5**
Sat 11pm-8am	EYE CANDY	**3/5**
TUBE/RAIL Elephant &	BIG SPENDERS	**3/5**
Castle	MIX 60%M 40%F	
BUSES 12, 35, 40, 53	AGE 21-35	
	PRICE Expensive	

AMBIENCE Dancing, Euphoric, Glammed-up, Groups, Hormone-fuelled Club Kidz, Late Night Open, Luvved-up Clubbers, Mashed-up, Party, Pulling, Student, Touristy
REVIEW If Ministry was a coffee shop, it would be Starbucks. It started off with good intentions, but success and popularity led to its 'Risk' style mission of world domination. Like Coca Cola, the brand has outgrown the product, and now we associate it with the mags, the CDs, the overseas parties, the t-shirts, the holidays... and the shell of the original product is left like a relic on a whistle-stop tour of London. Major nights include Smoove with residents Masterstepz and Matt White, while Saturdays go for fresh garage and deep, deep house. While the old euphoria and beautiful crowd have all but vanished (if you can remember it, you weren't really there), the big-name DJs still make appearances, and really this is the only reason any self-respecting Londoner would ever visit.
PLACE The main bar area has full-on dancers on the counter (mind your drink); it's overlooked by a walkway where people hang-out looking for talent on the podiums below. The VIP area is possibly one of the most unglamorous in London. Tunnels lead to a huge, dark dance area.
PEOPLE Sweaty out-of-towners dancing their socks off in the main room. Watch out for gropey men. Tourists, especially pint-sized Japanese, having the best night of their lives.

PROFS Bankers, secretaries, DJs, groupies, music industry employees, media types, PRs, lots and lots of tourists
CELEBS Jay Kay, Mick Jagger, Eminem, Sisqo, Jordan, Richard Blackwood, Dreem Teem, So Solid Crew, Jo Guest, Roger Sanchez, Macy Gray, Sugababes, Richard Bacon, Goldie, Pied Piper, Outsiders, Mis-teeq, Julia Roberts, Denise van Outen, Roni Size, Caprice, Ralph Lauren (turned away for wearing a tie), Pamela Anderson, Jude Law, Geri Halliwell, Mel B, Emma Bunton
DRESS Joe Bloggs, Ministry (own label), puffa jackets, Miss Sixty, Kooka¨ı, Morgan
MUSIC Garage, Hard House, Tech House, Happy House, New York House, Ambient
DOOR Fri, no jeans or trainers, £10-12.
Sat, over 21s, no light blue denim, £12-15
DRINKS Beer £3.50, Wine £3.50
FOOD None
CARDS No Diners
CAPACITY 1,250, seating 250
HIRE Venue: Yes · Private Room: Yes

greenwich

THE ADMIRAL HARDY

Pub
7 College Approach SE10
020 8858 6452

OPEN Mon-Sat 11am-11pm,	**GETTING LUCKY**	**5/5**
Sun midday-10.30pm	**EYE CANDY**	**3/5**
TUBE/RAIL Greenwich,	**BIG SPENDERS**	**3/5**
Cutty Sark	**MIX** 60%M 40%F	
BUSES 177, 180	**AGE** 20-35	
	PRICE Average	

AMBIENCE Buzzy, Pulling, Student
REVIEW About to get married, but scared stiff of the responsibility? Baby on its way, and you're never going to dance with the devil in the pale moonlight after all? Then come to The Admiral Hardy – just don't forget to bring your wavering liberal sensibilities and the first flushes of your early-life crises. This is where the characters in TV's Cold Feet should drink. Never has a single pub contained so many 30-year-olds quite so desperate to sink their escalating responsibilities under a mountain of lager, fags and similarly-challenged friends. On a completely unrelated note, it also houses a shop, which sells such essential post-pub necessities as vanilla essence, brandy butter and grapefruit marmalade. Don't ask.
PLACE For every naval portrait, there are some cute globe candles; for every sketch of Greenwich, there's a shagged-out leather settee. This is the Funk 'n' Firkin your local could be, if only it could be arsed.
PEOPLE Weeknight drinkers tend to be younger and slightly more energetic than the weekend crowd, who have seemingly solved the problems above and whose biggest concern now centres around which part of the Independent on Sunday they should read first.

PROFS ITs, PRs, graphic designers, lecturers, students, clerical staff
CELEBS Laurie Metcalf, Timothy Spall, Glenn Tilbrook, Daryl Hannah, Anna Friel
DRESS Diesel, Hope & Glory, Duffer
MUSIC Jazz, Funk, Soul
DOOR None
DRINKS Beer £2.60, Wine £2.75, Cocktail £4
FOOD Fish, Traditional English, £9
CARDS No Amex or Diners
CAPACITY 150, seating 60
HIRE Venue: No · Private Room: Yes

CAFÉ ROUGE

Bar, Café, Restaurant
30 Stockwell Street SE10
020 8293 6660

OPEN Mon-Sat 10.30am-	**GETTING LUCKY**	**1/5**
11pm, Sun 10.30am-	**EYE CANDY**	**3/5**
10.30pm	**BIG SPENDERS**	**3/5**
TUBE/RAIL Greenwich	**MIX** 40%M 60%F	
BUSES 177, 180	**AGE** 20-45	
	PRICE Average	

AMBIENCE Casual, Children/Families, Groups, Outdoors, Touristy
REVIEW One of the largest and busiest places to drink in Greenwich, Café Rouge reminds you that you're in tourist country now, boy. Although a certain sector of SE10's well-to-do residents (semi-Sloane, jeep-driving PR gals or cigar-smoking property developers) pop in for coffee, the bulk of this crowd are tourists, stopping off to admire their antique door wedges. If you're here to eat, you'll be slavered over by tip-hungry waiters. If you just want a drink, you'll be met with the kind of respect normally reserved for Millwall supporters.
PLACE One large, L-shaped expanse with an emphasis on cleanliness and order. Vintage poster prints, bottles of sparkling water and piles of freshly-laundered cotton aprons have been scattered around to remind you that you're in the 'French Quarter'.
PEOPLE Business-lunching office workers; tourists who appreciate the pristine exterior; pub-a-phobes. At the weekend, lots of families with whinging, attention-seeking brats.

PROFS Tourists, small business owners, property developers, antique dealers, PRs
CELEBS Boy George, Prince Edward, Gianluca Vialli, Keith Duffy, Lawrence Lewellyn-Bowen, Melanie Blatt
DRESS Monsoon, Gap, Next
MUSIC Chart, Motown
DOOR None
DRINKS Beer £2.75, Wine £2.40
FOOD Anglo-French, £8
CARDS No Amex or Diners
CAPACITY 150, seating 100
HIRE Venue: Yes · Private Room: No

NORTH & SOUTH POLE

Bar, Restaurant, Cocktail Bar
131 Greenwich High Road SE10
020 8853 3020

OPEN North Pole: Mon-Sat	**GETTING LUCKY**	**3/5**
midday-11pm, Sun midday-	**EYE CANDY**	**3/5**
10.30pm. South Pole: Wed-	**BIG SPENDERS**	**4/5**
Sun 6.30pm-11pm	**MIX** 50%M 50%F	
TUBE/RAIL Greenwich	**AGE** 25-35	
BUSES 177	**PRICE** Average	

AMBIENCE Basement, Chic, Romantic
REVIEW Now that Greenwich has an established nightlife it's hard to remember that prior to the DLR inner city slickers thought the place was a Channel Island. With the maritime link on the back burner, bar operators noticed there's more to the Georgian cul-de-sac than the Cutty Sark. One of the original bohemian bars, The North Pole has become a mini-empire comprising a restaurant, café-bar and late-night drinking den. Word has spread across the river and now troupes of fully-vaccinated Docklands dwellers head over for something a little less bland than their local All Bar Lettuce.
PLACE While the first-floor restaurant errs on the side of conservative chic (save for the live goldfish in the chandeliers) the lower you go, the more funkier it gets. Ground level offers furniture swathed in industrial aluminium and animal prints. In the basement lurks the 'wittily' named South Pole, themed on an airport departure lounge.

PEOPLE Attracts Docklands lawyers, couples on their way up. Staff have illusions of glittering stage careers which makes for great service.

PROFS Architects, solicitors, designers, bankers
CELEBS None
DRESS C'mon, it might be sarf-east London, but they know their stuff. From vintage to Versace
MUSIC Jazz, Funk, Garage, House, DJs Thu-Sun
DOOR Smart casual, No white trainers
DRINKS Beer £2.50, Wine £2.50, Champagne £6, Cocktail £5.50
FOOD Modern European, £12
CARDS No Diners
CAPACITY 250, seating 70
HIRE Venue: Yes · Private Room: Yes

TIME

Bar
7a College Approach SE10
020 8305 9767

OPEN Mon-Fri 5pm-	**GETTING LUCKY**	**3/5**
midnight, Sat-Sun midday-	**EYE CANDY**	**3/5**
midnight, Sun midday 11pm	**BIG SPENDERS**	**3/5**
TUBE/RAIL North Greenwich	**MIX** 50%M 50%F	
BUSES M1, M2	**AGE** 20-35	
	PRICE Average	

AMBIENCE Buzzy, Conversation, Funky, Groups, Historic, Live Music, Party
REVIEW The revamped, classic Georgian architecture of the oldest ex-music hall in Great Britain impresses upon arrival with its volume alone. Large-scale paintings, photography and installation pieces from neighbouring Goldsmiths and Camberwell students are dramatic, often dictating the mood of the place. Popular upon opening, it moved downhill, the trendy, down to earth and artistically interesting crowd replaced by nobodies verging on the ex-offenders-side from neighbouring Charlton and Woolwich.
PLACE Impressive and uniquely designed gallery-cum-bar on a historic square in a historic site. If you like the art on the walls you can even take it home with you.
PEOPLE People who are creatively successful or interested mingle with those who aspire to be. Discreet entrance means Time manages to avoid the flock of tourists that descend upon other Greenwich pubs.

PROFS Architects, bankers, electricians, estate agents, hairdressers, retail staff, curators
CELEBS Jools Holland, Gwyneth Paltrow, Johnny Depp, John Thomson, Kathy Burke
DRESS Firetrap, Boxfresh, Diesel, Vexed Generation, Earl jeans, one-offs
MUSIC Jazz, Funk, House, Soul, Rare Groove, Live Music Wed and Sun, DJs Fri-Sat
DOOR Smart casual
DRINKS Beer £2.70, Wine £3, Champagne £6, Cocktail £5
FOOD Modern British, Modern European, £7
CARDS All
CAPACITY 280, seating 120
HIRE Venue: Yes · Private Room: No

THE TRAFALGAR TAVERN

Pub, Restaurant
6 Park Row SE10
020 8858 2437

OPEN Mon-Fri 11.30am-	**GETTING LUCKY**	**2/5**
11pm, Sat 11.30am-11.30pm,	**EYE CANDY**	**2/5**
Sun midday-10.30pm	**BIG SPENDERS**	**3/5**
TUBE/RAIL North Greenwich	**MIX** 60%M 40%F	
BUSES 177, 188	**AGE** 25-40	
	PRICE Average	

AMBIENCE Casual, Groups, Historic, Live Music, Old World, Outdoors, Student, Views, Legendary
REVIEW Let's start, if you please, in the loos, where newspaper pages have been conveniently pinned to the walls in front of you. If there's any greater pleasure than going about your business while idly browsing yesterday's second-division football scores then, please, e-mail us. The Trafalgar is an institution, thanks to its riverside location, panoramic views and rich history (Charles Dickens wrote about it in 'Our Mutual Friend'). During summer weekends, it becomes almost unbearably busy, with Pimms drinkers fighting tooth and nail for seats in the sun-trap bay windows. The lucky ones can watch practising rowers, tourist boats and the eternal Docklands developments coming to life before their eyes.
PLACE Borderline palatial, with high ceilings, wood panelling and forest-green walls. The River Thames laps at its foundations, and in summer the whole of the front opens up to embrace the sun.
PEOPLE A reasonably affluent bunch that typify Greenwich's younger, disposable income-rich sector. Lots of day-tripping Londoners who make regular visits because they would love to live here.

PROFS Students, tourists, sales, retail staff, teachers, bankers
CELEBS Prince Philip, Timothy Spall, Anna Friel, Macauley Caulkin, Michael French
DRESS Casual, high-end High Street, FCUK, Warehouse, Gap
MUSIC Funk, Soul, Lounge, Live Jazz and Funk Sat
DOOR None
DRINKS Beer £2.70, Wine £2.50
FOOD Fish, Pub Food, Seafood, £10
CARDS No Diners or Amex
CAPACITY 250, seating 60
HIRE Venue: Yes · Private Room: Yes

www.crushguide.com

© Tristan O'Neill/PYMCA

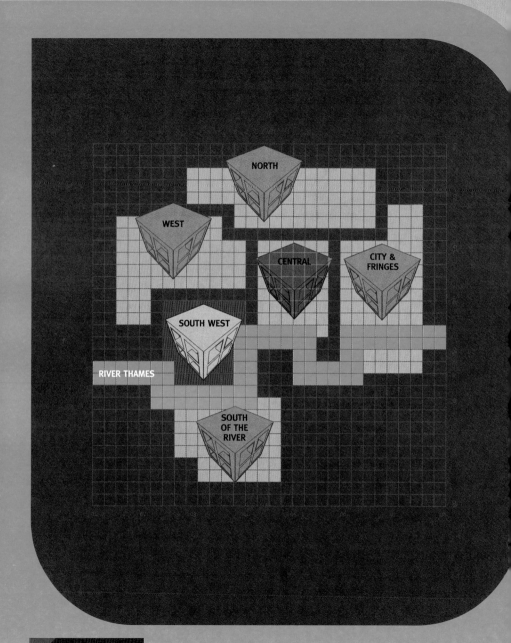

METRO

intro

SOUTH WEST
chelsea
fulham
knightsbridge
south kensington

Chelsea Boots, Chelsea Girl, Chelsea Bun – for God's sake even Clinton named his daughter after it – this part of London once had a sexy sashay few could question. We're sorry to report, however the circus that was Chelsea has left town.

What's left is the sound of powerful German motors and will-sapping commercialism. You see, the King's Road may still attract tourists like cliffs attract lemmings, but for drinkers that know, there is almost nothing of note here. Nowadays no self-respecting Sloane worth his brogues would be seen dead drinking in this commercial thoroughfare, where bars like **Big Easy** and **Henry J. Beans** accommodate a flotsam of tourists and Euro financial-somethings. However, Conran's **Bluebird** fills a much-needed style gap, drawing the well-dressed, nipped and tucked affluent set that Chelsea is now most famous for.

Walk through Knightsbridge after 7pm and you can feel a little like being in an anthrax zone, so empty are the streets. Sensible shoppers scuttle to the relative safety of department store and hotel bars; the newly opened **Wellington Club** and hard-to-miss **Isola** should breathe a little life (and youth) into the area, giving old boys **Fifth Floor** and **Foyer Bar** a run for their (new) money. Places with a bit of new rather than blue blood are the **Blue Bar** at the Berkeley Hotel and **Montes**. The latter has the irresistible combination of cocktail guru Dick Bradsell shaking it up and Jamie Oliver as consultant chef.

Move up the King's Road and Fulham Road to the so-called 'The Beach' and, much like the film of the same name, you'll find it's lost the plot. Bars come, go and change hands here with alarming rapidity; no doubt caused by the invasion of the chain bar. But then most South Westerners, whether they be Snobbish and Workshy, Sophisticated and Well-Heeled, Wage Slaves or Soaks and Wastrels, feel more than happy in conformist institutions; after all, that's where they were brought up.

The long Fulham Road and upper King's Road drags – with 'The Beach' at its centre – is set up for young, corporate hoorays to barhop through. These fresh-faced bankers, PRs and recruitment consultants spend conspicuously yet seem content to relive that student union feel in bars like **The Fine Line, Bierodrome** and the so-bad-it's-good **Purple**. Those wanting a slightly smarter drink will be hard done by unless they go to **Bardot**.

South Kensington's bars tend to be brash, flash and full of Eurotrash, though they retain more individuality than their neighbours: South Kensington is Fulham grown up. More Chelsea girls and rich kids than in Chelsea itself, a hawk and prey atmosphere pervades many bars, of which **Catch, Eclipse** and **190 Queensgate** have the most integrity.

Recent and future openings:

Babushka House, 648 King's Road
Sloane's, 87 Sloane Avenue

chelsea

151

Club, Members Club
151 King's Road SW3
020 7351 6826

OPEN Mon-Sat 11pm-3am
TUBE/RAIL Sloane Square
BUSES 11, 22

GETTING LUCKY	**4/5**
EYE CANDY	**2/5**
BIG SPENDERS	**3/5**
MIX 60%M 40%F	
AGE 20-38	
PRICE Average	

AMBIENCE Basement, Dancing, Groups, Party, Pulling, Romantic, Late Night Open
REVIEW Nicknamed '1 Dive 1' by its regulars, this bar and club is like the late-night kebab joint is for students: you know it's no good but then what's the alternative but milk that's morphed into a yoghurt and a bowl of cornflakes? Once the pubs and the few local bars have shut this is where a Fulham man goes if he thinks the West End's a bit of a schlep and far too full of ruffians wearing trainers. Fear not. If you can make it through to 2am the place swells with a younger crowd on a mission to show up the fogeys shaking their corduroyed asses.
PLACE A discreet doorway (unless the queue is swelling); the club is downstairs. Clad in red velvet, with intimate round tables and alcoves with candles, it's reminiscent of a 'classy' northern club from the 80s – the mirrored dance floor is the pièce de resistance.
PEOPLE Early on in the evening you'll be with 30-year-olds drinking wine by the bottle; they have never been anywhere else on a Friday night. Later it becomes a mixture of Essex temps, Sloaney university students on holiday from Edinburgh and Oxford Brookes and recent graduates who still think they can 'cut it' despite being trainees at PriceWaterhouseCoopers. They loosen their ties, dance around their briefcases on the tardis-like dance floor to 80s mixes while sipping tequila shots.

PROFS Professional shoppers, Sloaney uni graduates, trainees of all sorts, 30-something Fulhamites who should have grown up
CELEBS None
DRESS Early on – blazers and those dressed by Blazer. Later on – girls wearing very tight, very little dresses. Lots of sunglasses
MUSIC Dance, Chart, DJs Mon-Sat
DOOR Conservative dress; members only; non-member accompanied by member £5
DRINKS Beer £3.50, Wine £3.50, Champagne £7.50
FOOD None
CARDS All
CAPACITY 150, seating 100
HIRE Venue: No · Private Room: No

THE ADMIRAL CODRINGTON

Gastropub
17 Mossop Street SW3
020 7581 0005

OPEN Mon-Sat 11.30am-midnight, Sun midday-10.30pm
TUBE/RAIL South Kensington
BUSES 14, 19, 22

GETTING LUCKY	**1/5**
EYE CANDY	**3/5**
BIG SPENDERS	**3/5**
MIX 60%M 40%F	
AGE 25-40	
PRICE Average	

AMBIENCE Buzzy, Historic, Star Spotting, Outside
REVIEW For years, the Admiral Codrington (known as 'The Cod' to its regulars) muddled along as a classic Sloane watering hole. With its clientele loudly twanging their braces and discussing their bonuses they deterred almost anyone else from going there. Then Joel Cadbury took it over and hired a man who knows his onions – chef Stephen Terry – to sort out the menu in the new restaurant at the rear. Terry has now left, but his legacy and Cadbury's nous live on: superior pub food in a smart setting that attracts a broader crowd than before.
PLACE Classic wood pub bar with restaurant at back. Gastropub or not, the loos are stark and overpoweringly bleached. Tables are close-set, and the noise levels can be a little overwhelming. In summer the roof slides off the restaurant.
PEOPLE Typical Fl'am and Chelsea: boys in Thomas Pink shirts accessorised with BMW keyfobs and teeny mobiles. Daddy's girls with impeccable hair and latest Vogue-featured handbag – Prada, Louis Vuitton, Fendi, Loads of silver Vespas parked closeby.

PROFS Estate agents, marketing, insurance, property and advertising execs
CELEBS Tim Henman, Eddie Irvine, Sophie Rhys-Jones (Countess of Wessex), Frederick Forsyth, Ainsley Harriott, Tara Palmer-Tomkinson, Gordon Ramsay, Michael Portillo
DRESS Alarming number of people in black tie and lots of pink shirts. Suits, smart leather jackets, Karen Millen, Jane Norman, Gucci
MUSIC Jazz, Pop
DOOR None
DRINKS Beer £2.80, Wine £2.80, Champagne £6
FOOD Comfort Food, Modern European, £11
CARDS No Diners
CAPACITY 100, seating 56
HIRE Venue: Yes · Private Room: No

BIG EASY

Bar, Restaurant
332-334 King's Road SW3
020 7352 4071

OPEN Mon-Fri midday-	**GETTING LUCKY**	**2/5**
11.30pm, Sat midday-	**EYE CANDY**	**2/5**
12.30am,	**BIG SPENDERS**	**2/5**
Sun midday-11.30pm	**MIX** 60%M 40%F	
TUBE/RAIL Sloane Square	**AGE** 20-35	
BUSES 11, 22	**PRICE** Average	

AMBIENCE Casual, Children/Families, Groups, Live Music
REVIEW Okay, so Louisiana is the inspiration for the name of this joint but perhaps someone should have added some inspiration to it in the first place. For bar-goers with a nanogram of sense any venue with an American name is guaranteed to produce a fear and flight response. Nevertheless if you like mediocrity it comes with a generous happy hour and a once prime King's Road location. Early on it's colonised by the assistants of those ghastly rent-a-high-street-shops which have made the King's Road a doppelgänger for a small market town high street somewhere outside Ipswich. Later on the restaurant is largely responsible for the faces passing through the bar, in the main groups of well-off, middle-class drinkers. Summer in Chelsea can have an unusual effect on the collective King's Road libido, and combined with good cocktails and the generally boozy flavour of a busy bar, can undo the best of us. The seductive qualities of the Big Easy are, however, not apparent and, despite the name, it is neither big nor easy.
PLACE Smallish bar attached to a smallish American restaurant.
PEOPLE Thirty-somethings enjoying a bit of 80s nostalgia. Frayed-at-the-edges long-haired rockers of all ages. Lots of families and kids, too.

PROFS King's Road shop workers, caterers, shoppers, accountants, bankers, tourists
CELEBS George Best, Dennis Wise, Sir Bob Geldof, Loyd Grossman, Isla Fisher, Mel C, Brian May, Tony Adams, George Best and son
DRESS Comfortable, smart casual. Gap, DKNY, Oasis
MUSIC Classic Rock, Country and Western, Live Pop Cover Bands 7 Days
DOOR Smart casual
DRINKS Beer £2.95, Wine £2.95, Champagne £4.50, Cocktail £4.95
FOOD American, Barbeque, £12.50
CARDS No Diners
CAPACITY 190, seating 140
HIRE Venue: Yes · Private Room: No

BLUEBIRD

Bar, Café, Member's Bar, Restaurant
350 King's Road SW3
020 7559 1000

OPEN Mon-Thu 11am-11pm,	**GETTING LUCKY**	**2/5**
Fri-Sat 11am-1am,	**EYE CANDY**	**4/5**
Sun 11am-11pm	**BIG SPENDERS**	**5/5**
TUBE/RAIL Sloane Square	**MIX** 40%M 60%F	
BUSES 11, 19, 22, 211, 319	**AGE** 25-40	
	PRICE Expensive	

AMBIENCE Business, Buzzy, Cute Staff, Elegant/Classic, Groups, Hip/Fashionable, Legendary, Retro
REVIEW The Conran empire keeps expanding like Sir T's girth. All the Bluebird site needs is a colonic irrigation centre to turn this emporium into the ultimate rich gal's theme park. It houses a food shop, a household shop, a café, a bar, a private member's club, a restaurant and a flower stall. Generally critics like to sniff and grumble about Sir T, but in this case you just can't fault him. Argue with inspired and luxurious surroundings, possibly the most obliging and friendly service in London, and being surrounded by beautiful, smiling people all evening? I don't think so, unless you happen to be an Old Labour supporter. It's not a place you nip into wearing your slippers having crawled out of bed to buy the Sunday morning paper and fags, but then there's always the café downstairs...
PLACE Stunningly large open plan space which is, like Michael Jackson's children, imaginatively conceived. Unpretentious yet sophisticated atmosphere.
PEOPLE In a permanent state of jetlag. Models, playboys, moguls, titled people, movers 'n' shakers.

PROFS Managers, models, PRs, property tycoons, tourists, businessmen, Conde Nasties, kept women, doctors
CELEBS Geri Halliwell, Nicky Haslam, Robbie Williams, Ryan Phillipe and Reese Witherspoon, cast of Friends, Madonna, Kylie and Dannii Minogue, Graham Norton
DRESS Saks 5th Avenue, Burberry, Prada, Gucci, Versace, Chloe, Joseph, Whistles
MUSIC Chill-out, Chart, Ambient, Jazz, DJs Fri-Sat
DOOR None
DRINKS Beer £3.25, Wine £3.75, Champagne £6.95, Cocktail £5.50
FOOD Modern Eclectic, £5
CARDS No Diners
CAPACITY 180, seating 75
HIRE Venue: Yes · Private Room: Yes

THE BRIDGE

Bar
451 Fulham Road SW10
020 7352 8636

OPEN Mon-Wed 11am-11pm,	**GETTING LUCKY**	**2/5**
Thu-Sat 11am-midnight, Sun	**EYE CANDY**	**2/5**
midday-10.30pm	**BIG SPENDERS**	**2/5**
TUBE Fulham Broadway	**MIX** 50%M 50%F	
BUSES 14, 211	**AGE** 20-35	
	PRICE Average	

AMBIENCE Casual, Comfy, Cosy, Groups, Lounge Atmosphere
REVIEW More like a tunnel than a bridge, this doesn't feel like a chain bar, though it is. It's taken all the core components of what makes a good bar work and mixed them together. Space Invaders, tick. Fairylights, tick. Artwork, tick. Beaten-up sofas, tick. Two-for-one cocktails, tick. There's been a lot of effort but not a whole lot of love. This results in a somewhat dislocated clientele of social undesirables: the DJ and his mates have travelled up from Harlesden, a postman cries about his marriage breakdown, and it's a discreet place for Nigel the lettings director to court his secretary. Rather NGD (not geographically desirable), being situated on the arse side of Chelsea & Westminster Hospital.

PLACE Lots of black in this labyrinthine expanse of space. Big staircases and back lounge room. Upstairs there's a pseudo cocktail lounge, but neither the decor nor the clientele seem appropriate.
PEOPLE Lacklustre and random. Fashion chicks mix with sorting office totty mix with slumming bankers. Come prepared with a stretcher for recent outpatients just fallen off the wagon.

PROFS Retail staff, doctors, nurses, students, decorators, office workers, bankers, postmen, accountants, press officers
CELEBS None
DRESS Firetrap, Diesel, Jane Norman, Morgan, Levi's
MUSIC Breakbeat, House, Ambient, DJs Thu-Sat
DOOR None
DRINKS Beer £2.70, Wine £2.50, Cocktail £4
FOOD Italian, £5
CARDS No Diners
CAPACITY 190, seating 70
HIRE Venue: Yes · Private Room: Yes

THE BUILDER'S ARMS

Gastropub
13 Britten Street SW3
020 7349 9040

OPEN Mon-Sat 11am-11pm,	**GETTING LUCKY**	**3/5**
Sun midday-11pm	**EYE CANDY**	**3/5**
TUBE/RAIL South	**BIG SPENDERS**	**3/5**
Kensington, Sloane Square	**MIX** 50%M 50%F	
BUSES 11, 19, 22, 211, 319	**AGE** 20-50	
	PRICE Average	

AMBIENCE Historic
REVIEW Fair-to-middling gastropub affair that suffers in comparison with its Primrose Hill cousins, but suits this stretch of Chelsea down to the ground. The bottom line is that boozers with bookshelves, carpets and 'interesting' art are just as tiresomely theme as top-of-the-morning trad Irish efforts in Holloway. And just as phoney. Still, the locals seem to enjoy it (they also enjoy Sting albums and films with Kevin Kline in them) and it's just as good a place as any around these parts to while away a Sunday.
PLACE Imagine a gentleman's library that's been around since 1820.
PEOPLE Nice-but-dims, heirloom bohos, Antipodeans

PROFS Antique dealers, computer techs, TV producers, shopowners, gallery owners, interior designers
CELEBS Johnny Vaughan, Joseph Fiennes, Amanda de Cadenet, Bob Geldof, Ben Elton, Michael Portillo, Dani Behr, George Best
DRESS Cotton Traders, suede loafers, Ralph Lauren, Thomas Pink, Munich Beer Festival t-shirts, jeans of the non-designer variety and checked shirts. Mainly trousers and twinset tops for the women. 'Very kitsch, kitten heels, peroxide hair and lots of cleavage' says the manager
MUSIC Jazz
DOOR None
DRINKS Beer £2.60, Wine £2.60, Champagne £5
FOOD Modern British, £8
CARDS No Amex or Diners
CAPACITY 100, seating 45
HIRE Venue: No · Private Room: No

CACTUS BLUE

Restaurant Bar
86 Fulham Road SW3
020 7823 7858

OPEN Mon-Fri 3.30pm-	**GETTING LUCKY**	**4/5**
11pm, Sat midday-11pm,	**EYE CANDY**	**3/5**
Sun midday-10.30pm	**BIG SPENDERS**	**4/5**
TUBE/RAIL South	**MIX** 55%M 45%F	
Kensington	**AGE** 25-40	
BUSES 14, 345	**PRICE** Average	

AMBIENCE Casual, Groups, Live Music, Pulling
REVIEW Boys with octagonal lens eyewear and eight digit bonuses crowd a high u-shaped bar. This is a home for Euro bankers, of the sort that have colonised South Kensington and enjoy dressing up to go out in a way that few London males of similar background can be bothered to match. When mixed with locals who'd rather not drive anywhere for fear of losing their Mercedes parking spot you end up with a middle-class, middle-of-the-road crowd in an area bereft of good bars. Groups and couples recline on kilim-backed banquettes lining the walls, while singles congregate around the central bar. If only the clientele would loosen their collars a bit...
PLACE If lighting was a little less harsh CB would be one of Chelsea's better venues. On three floors it's large without being cavernous and despite its southwest-American theming has enough detail and perspective to arouse the eye. Sit at the bar and watch people ascend by lift to the 1st floor. It neatly avoids the theme park look although eponymous cacti, lots of Santa Fe-style wrought iron and Native American art adorn the sand-coloured walls.
PEOPLE Kensington and Chelsea parking permits double up as membership cards

PROFS Retail staff, bankers, brokers, embassy staff, consulate staff
CELEBS Jeremy Clarkson, Julia Roberts, Lord Gowrie, Chelsea Football Club, George Best, New York Giants, Yoko Ono, Lulu, Tara Palmer-Tomkinson
DRESS Spot Jermyn Street shirts with Levi's or chinos and black Chevignon leather jackets for the boys while flirty girls dress with Sloane Street in mind
MUSIC Jazz, Easy Listening, Live Music Tue-Thu
DOOR Smart casual
DRINKS Beer £3.15, Wine £2.95, Champagne £3.95, Cocktail £4.95
FOOD South West American, £12.95
CARDS All
CAPACITY 300, seating 220
HIRE Venue: Yes · Private Room: No

CAHOOTS

Bar, Pub
2 Elystan Street SW3
020 7584 0140

OPEN Mon-Sat 11am-11pm,	**GETTING LUCKY**	**4/5**
Sun midday-10.30pm	**EYE CANDY**	**4/5**
TUBE/RAIL Sloane Square,	**BIG SPENDERS**	**4/5**
South Kensington	**MIX** 65%M 35%F	
BUSES 11, 19, 22, 211	**AGE** 22-40	
	PRICE Average	

AMBIENCE Groups, Party, Pulling
REVIEW Say what you like about the upper classes but they certainly know how to have a good time, as Friday night at Cahoots proves. This lively, attractive bar is full of half-cut Hugh and Liz-lookalikes who clearly don't know when or how to say 'no'. The atmosphere is a cross between an office party and the Conservative party as pinstriped Henrys and well-toned Henriettas belt down the Becks and Bolly. Contrary to expectations, we enjoyed being thrust into the heart of these jolly japes – the people are far friendlier than the natives of most North London media caves, and the comparative lack of elbow room stops it all getting too cliquey. Borrow a Malvern old boys' tie and you won't have to buy a beer all night.
PLACE Brightly lit bar in the heart of prosperous Chelsea with some lovely decorative touches and two sets of men's and women's loos.
PEOPLE Imagine the champagne sponsor's tent at Henley Regatta: if it were winter they'd be discussing Val, if it were summer, swapping Algarve antics.

PROFS Property developers, interior designers, estate agents, stockbrokers, art gallery owners, lawyers, accountants, PR execs, tourists
CELEBS Pierce Brosnan, Petula Clark, Ringo Starr
DRESS From countrywide and hacking jackets to Savile Row, peppered with flashes of Hérmes or New and Lingwood. Smart girls, darling, in smart labels: Voyage, Karen Millen, Joseph
MUSIC Easy Listening, Classical, Rare Groove, 70s
DOOR None
DRINKS Beer £2.80, Wine £2.60
FOOD Belgian, Modern European, £4
CARDS All
CAPACITY 120, seating 65
HIRE Venue: Yes · Private Room: No

THE CHELSEA RAM

Gastropub
32 Burnaby Road SW10
020 7351 4008

OPEN Mon-Sat 11am-11pm,	GETTING LUCKY	2/5
Sun midday-10.30pm	EYE CANDY	2/5
TUBE/RAIL Sloane Square,	BIG SPENDERS	3/5
Fulham Broadway	MIX 65%M 45%F	
BUSES 11	AGE 25-65	
	PRICE Average	

AMBIENCE Friendly, Conversation
REVIEW 'I've made a million mate – piece of piss.' Well, what else do you expect to overhear in a residential Chelsea gastropub? Put off? Don't be. This pub was dragged from pub purgatory by Nick Elliott, a man with a fanatic's zeal for putting good plain food into pubs. Recently sold, only time will tell if the place keeps up the standards. Note: when eating you'll find no dedicated food area, so you could easily be supping your pint at the same table as a cravat-wearing old boy whose teeth are fighting a losing battle with his guinea fowl and mash. Then again, you might get lucky and be forced to squash in next to a pair of gorgeous It girl wannabes. We did, but unfortunately they seemed preoccupied with the millionaire.

PLACE Bright and airy corner pub in a quiet residential area. For the most part this is a typically modern Young's pub with saffron walls, wooden furniture, arched windows with half shutters and stripped floorboards. Interesting features include the faux bookshelf toilet doors, a few abstract nudes, clocks showing different time zones and a Frankenstein-esque light fitting.
PEOPLE Typical Chelsea, a few cashmere and pearl necklace oldies, rugger buggers who drive two-seaters (pushchairs and cars), the odd Alan Clark-style Chelsea eccentric who's given the butler the night off and lots of young girls who say 'horrid' a lot.

PROFS Estate agents, PRs, lawyers, auctioneers, OAPs, highbrow travel agents, former dotcommers moving back into estate agency
CELEBS Johnny Vaughan, Nick Ross
DRESS Bodywarmers, cravats, knitwear, Timberlands, rollneck sweaters, pie-crust collars with pearls, Tetley's t-shirts, rugger shirts with obligatory up-turned collars, chinos, combats, Fendi scarves, leather jackets and jeans
MUSIC None
DOOR None
DRINKS Beer £2.50, Wine £2.55, Champagne £5.50
FOOD Modern European, Pub Food, £10
CARDS No Amex or Diners
CAPACITY 200, seating 85
HIRE Venue: No · Private Room: No

CRAZY LARRY'S

Club
533 King's Road SW10
020 7376 5555

OPEN Thu-Sat 10pm-2.30am	GETTING LUCKY	5/5
TUBE/RAIL Fulham	EYE CANDY	2/5
Broadway	BIG SPENDERS	3/5
BUSES 11, 22	MIX 60%M 40%F	
	AGE 18-35	
	PRICE Expensive	

AMBIENCE Casual, Dancing, Groups, Late Night Open, Live Music, Party, Pulling, Student
REVIEW Crazy Larry's, Shoeless Joe's, Bad Bob's... Sickly Jim's, Deranged Pete's, Asinine Tom's... the possibilities are endless. If you're thinking of opening a bar in London, please, for God's sake, don't name it after the lead singer of a Country & Western band. This seems to guarantee only that the doormen are unnecessarily moody, the decor is naff and the clientele are people that you would not wish to share a continent with, let alone an evening. Crazy Larry's is one of those terrible places that has a 'rigid' guest list but no queue. A bit like saying it's the last one in the shop and there are five people waiting, but seeing as it's you, love, have it for a tenner.

PLACE High-end McDonalds style. Lowbrow cheesy fun at highbrow prices. Nuff said.
PEOPLE Women tend to be either suspiciously young and trying to look slightly older, or slightly older and trying to look suspiciously young. A predator's paradise.
PROFS Nurses, well-off students, estate agents, bankers
CELEBS Adam Rickett, John Leslie, S Club 7
DRESS As little as possible. For girls: tight tops. For boys: polo shirts and jeans or chinos
MUSIC 70s, 80s, 90s, Dance, Chart
DOOR Smart casual, no trainers, £7-12 admission
DRINKS Beer £3.50, Wine £3, Champagne £7, Cocktail £6
FOOD Bar snacks, £12.50
CARDS No Diners
CAPACITY 400, seating 50
HIRE Venue: Yes · Private Room: No

THE CROSS KEYS

Pub, Restaurant
1 Lawrence Street SW3
020 7349 9111

OPEN Mon-Sat 12pm-11pm, Sun 12pm-10.30pm	**GETTING LUCKY**	**3/5**
TUBE/RAIL Sloane Square	**EYE CANDY**	**3/5**
BUSES 19, 49, 319, 345	**BIG SPENDERS**	**3/5**
	MIX 50%M 50%F	
	AGE 25-40	
	PRICE Average	

AMBIENCE Groups, Conversation
REVIEW So when is a pub not a pub? When there are only two beers on tap and enough artsy interior touches to upset Carole Smillie's Changing Rooms team. This is Chelsea's answer to Beach Blanket Babylon which seems to have been around as long as the Savoy Grill. After BBB's success in Notting Hill, stylist/sculptor/ artist Rudy Weller brought his talent to the more conventional set. The crowd here seem to live by the book: public school, pensions and a semi in Fulham are distinct possibilities, all quite commendable I know, but it sure as hell ain't sexy. Mixed groups of singles and couples sit at a few large tables or get in the scrum by/for the bar, while badly parked Audi TTs get towed away outside.
PLACE Stylishly successful pub overhaul, overlooked by popular private party room. 90s medieval – stone floor, dimly lit by a huge wrought-iron chandelier; a sculpted monk dances over the fireplace. Conservatory restaurant at rear. When it's busy, it's not nearly big enough.
PEOPLE They rave about Dido, spend their honeymoons in the Maldives and can't wait to get back to the slopes. 'What will we do now Swissair's gone?'

PROFS Bankers, lawyers, shop staff, estate agents, property developers, PRs, chalet girls, secretaries, PAs
CELEBS David Cotter, Viscount Linley, Ulrika Jonsson, Bill Wyman, Michael Winter, Julia Bradbury, Mike Atherton, Eric Clapton, George Best
DRESS Fleeces, chinos, Levi's, Ralph Lauren shirts, Gap, Jigsaw, Karen Millen
MUSIC Pop, Rock, Easy Listening
DOOR None
DRINKS Beer £2.60, Wine £2.95, Champagne £5.95, Cocktail £5.50
FOOD Mediterranean, Modern British, £12

CARDS No Diners
CAPACITY 360, seating 70
HIRE Venue: Yes · Private Room: Yes

DÔME

Bar, Café
354 King's Road SW3
020 7352 2828

OPEN Mon-Sat 9am-11pm, Sun 9.30am-10.30pm	**GETTING LUCKY**	**2/5**
TUBE/RAIL South Kensington, Sloane Square, Earl's Court	**EYE CANDY**	**3/5**
	BIG SPENDERS	**4/5**
	MIX 50%M 50%F	
BUSES 29, 328	**AGE** 18-55	
	PRICE Average	

AMBIENCE Conversation, Groups
REVIEW This Dôme has long been a landmark hangout for Chelsea's affluent residents – phonies and genuine alike. Alone at the bar, Hugh Grant wannabes mull over espressos and broadsheets, as precocious Tory boys look forward to the day their balls drop, thus enabling them to consummate that on/off relationship with Arabella who's going into PR. Meanwhile, waiters destined for the catwalk clear tables for Alain Prost lookalikes who sit with the wife/mistress surrounded by designer carrier bags. The place is a window shop for those wanting a window on 21st-century Chelsea: smart, successful and monied but dull as Neff dishwasher water.
PLACE Perfectly positioned for Saturday afternoon posing, this corner bar/café is standard Dôme, with French windows, chandeliers and ceiling fans. The decor's largely irrelevant though – it's each other that everyone comes here to gawp at.
PEOPLE It's all a bit Lalaland in here and so are the punters – transient shoppers who 'lurrve London', girls whose credit card bills go straight to papa, blokes who invent glamorous pretend professions to explain their wealth and genuinely minted locals who think poor people smell.

PROFS Millionaire's offspring, Chelsea layabouts, pretend pro-skateboarders, PRs, designers, IT consultants, musicians, window shoppers, actors, hairdressers, restaurateurs, estate agents
CELEBS Chris Eubank, Spice Girls, Ross Kemp, Paul Young, Kevin Spacey, Martine McCutcheon, Minnie Driver, Jason Priestley, Damon Hill
DRESS Joseph, Miu Miu, Whistles, Karen Millen, Earl jeans, Evisu, Firetrap, Voyage, Chloe, Helmut Lang, vintage Levi's, Prada, Gap
MUSIC House, Garage, Easy Listening
DOOR None
DRINKS Beer £2.60, Wine £3, Champagne £4.55
FOOD Brasserie, Continental Breakfast, French, Full English Breakfast, £6
CARDS No Diners
CAPACITY 150, seating 120
HIRE Venue: No · Private Room: No

HENRY J. BEAN'S BAR & GRILL

Bar, Restaurant
195-197 King's Road SW3
020 7352 9255

OPEN Mon-Sat 10am-11pm, Sun midday-10.30pm
TUBE/RAIL Sloane Square, South Kensington
BUSES 11, 19, 49, 211, 375

GETTING LUCKY	**5/5**
EYE CANDY	**4/5**
BIG SPENDERS	**3/5**
MIX 45%M 55%F	
AGE 21-39	
PRICE Average	

AMBIENCE Children/Families, Conversation, Groups, Historic, Outdoors, Pulling, Student
REVIEW This is the place that post-pubescent Sloanes come to hang out during half-term. And this is the place they bring their dates to partake in pre-party hamburgers (admittedly good, but you try negotiating a taffeta sleeve with greasy fingers) before working it all off to the sound of Juliana's Discotheque. Contrast that to the steady stream of luvverly and oh-so-innocent Eastern European beauties, supplied by a local modelling agency, who have adopted the bar as a second home. Mere cannon fodder to the rotund Chelsea estate agents who have it particularly easy on weekends when an over-21 door policy bars entrance to lither – and younger – competitors. As sophisticated as a burger – and like one, does no more than fill a gap.
PLACE Huge barn of a place in typical American-eatery style. Follows the principle that the faster the music, the more people drink. Hank's Heated Garden at the back is an address to remember on London's few warm summer evenings. The site is steeped in history dating back to the 16th century. The garden, formerly the bowling green of The Six Bell, extended to the Thames and was popular with King Charles II.
PEOPLE An odd mix of Chelsea yuppies, out-of-townies and Euros, all oozing self-confidence.

PROFS Media employees, models, office workers, estate agents, retail staff, tourists, lawyers, students, secretaries, models
CELEBS George Best, Chelsea Football Club, Henry Kelly, Jo Guest, Caprice, England Cricket team
DRESS Casual weekdays (Next, Gap, chinos, jeans) to more clubby-style weekends
MUSIC 60s, 70s, 80s, 90s, Pop
DOOR Over 21s Fri-Sat, no football shirts/work clothes
DRINKS Beer £2.85, Wine £2.60, Champagne £5, Cocktail £4.25
FOOD American, £7
CARDS All
CAPACITY 200, seating 125
HIRE Venue: Yes · Private Room: No

K BAR

Bar
266a Fulham Road SW10
020 7352 6200

OPEN Tue-Sat 9pm-2am
TUBE/RAIL Earl's Court
BUSES 14, 211, 345

GETTING LUCKY	**4/5**
EYE CANDY	**4/5**
BIG SPENDERS	**3/5**
MIX 50%M 50%F	
AGE 25-40	
PRICE Expensive	

AMBIENCE Basement, Dancing, Groups, Late Night Open, Pulling

REVIEW Once the shiny new K-id on the Chelsea/Fulham block, this bar was sold in 2001. Piers Adam has since gone on to bigger and better things, but only time will tell whether the 20-something Sloane set will follow in his dust trail. Nevertheless, its location predominantly attracts the traditional Fl'am/Chelsea/Euro crowd, with a minority of trendier desirables. Fresh-faced Suits, 'Yah, Adam, he's the boy, yah'. Blokes whose names are abbreviated to end in 'ers' or 'o'. Girls named after their uncles. So be it Paddo by the long bar, Tara on the dance floor, Henry in an alcove or alone with an orchid, this is the most fun you'll have in SW10.
PLACE Minimalist, middle Asian decor, with tasteful Buddha by the bar and candlelit conversation nooks.
PEOPLE Rich kids in Ralph Lauren jeans. A few scantily clad Essex girls trying to bag some rich totty. Lots of suits.

PROFS Bankers, media movers and shakers, PRs, trustafarians, retired dotcommers
CELEBS Lady Victoria Hervey, Tamara Beckwith, John Leslie, England Rugby team members, Big Brother contestants
DRESS Chinos, blazers, cufflinks, mixed with surf dudes returning from St Andrews and perfectly formed and presented Euros – especially the Italians
MUSIC R&B, Disco, Funky House, Chill-out, DJs
DOOR Smart casual, trainers accepted in good condition. Tue-Sat, £5-15
DRINKS Beer £4, Wine £4.50, Champagne £7, Cocktail £7
FOOD None
CARDS No Diners
CAPACITY 150, seating 40
HIRE Venue: Yes · Private Room: Yes

ORIEL

Bar, Restaurant
50-51 Sloane Square SW1
020 7730 2804

OPEN Mon-Sat 8.30am-10.45pm, Sun 9am-10pm
TUBE/RAIL Sloane Square
BUSES 19, 22, 137, C1, 319, 211, 11

GETTING LUCKY	**2/5**
EYE CANDY	**2/5**
BIG SPENDERS	**3/5**
MIX 50%M 50%F	
AGE 22-45	
PRICE Average	

AMBIENCE Basement, Business, Conversation, Groups, Outdoors
REVIEW Being two doors down from Sloane Square tube is as much of a blessing as a curse for the Sloane Square institution that is Oriel. On the one hand, the bar is packed pretty continuously from 6pm with commuters on their way to or from the tube. On the other hand, just how much fun can a combination of City Sloanes and Peter Jones regulars be? Happily for those among us whose tastes stretch beyond, the clientele here is actually quite diverse, with jaunty Chelsea pensioners chatting up Sloane Street shoppers, while at the bar downstairs, self-restrained fathers of two are secretly champing at the bit for an opportunity to really let rip with those 'naice' young girls down from uni for the hols.

PLACE The upstairs bar is sedate with seating on rattan furniture for small groups: music here stops at 8pm. The bar below is comfortably set up with tattered velvet sofas, armchairs and plenty of space, but with sickly salmon-ochre walls that take that party urge straight out of you. Good people watching from pavement tables.
PEOPLE Day shoppers and the occasional Antiquarius stallholder. Evening: sensible afterwork and pre-dinner drinkers, soon to be joined by the hip and arty crowd from the Royal Court theatre.

PROFS Tourists, office workers, PRs, advertising agents, TV and film professionals, estate agents, surveyors, accountants, lawyers, professional shoppers
CELEBS Chelsea Football Club, Pierce Brosnan, Kevin Spacey, Sally Gray, Liz Hurley, Charles Dance, Right Said Fred
DRESS Situated a short Gucci loafer stroll from Hackett and its more fashionable neighbours in Sloane Street, the dress here reflects this
MUSIC Jazz, Chart
DOOR None
DRINKS Beer £2.50, Wine £3.20, Champagne £4.95
FOOD French, £10
CARDS All
CAPACITY 120, seating 100
HIRE Venue: Yes · Private Room: No

PITCHER & PIANO

Bar, Chain
316-318 King's Road SW3
020 7352 0025

OPEN Mon-Fri midday-11pm,	GETTING LUCKY	3/5
Sat 11am-11pm, Sun 11am-	EYE CANDY	3/5
10.30pm	BIG SPENDERS	3/5
TUBE/RAIL Sloane Square	MIX 55%M 45%F	
BUSES 11, 19, 22	AGE 18-40	
	PRICE Average	

AMBIENCE Conversation, Groups
REVIEW The 'ID required' sign is a clear indication of the age group this place predominantly attracts. This is where young Sloanes come when they're not in Val or Rock. Tiggy Burk-Piddlewit and her boyfriend Ed De Biactol often drop in for a 'snifter' before hitting Po Na Na's next door. Infuriatingly fresh-faced chaps buy Veuve Clicquot for obsequious babes on laps, as vowel butchering 20-somethings stand shoeless, clutching designer rollerblades – don't they know they went out in the 90s? By the entrance, groups of suburban shoppers do their best to blend in, but fake TAGs and big knicker VPLs are a dead give-away in joints like this.
PLACE Small-ish, young-ish P&P with a few chairs out the front and a couple of sofas at the back.
PEOPLE Girls who spend all night tucking their Jo Malone scented hair behind their ears, rich Chelsea snowboarders, Prince William lookalikes, passers by (no oiks), pre-cinema crowd and singles on a King's Road bar crawl in search of chalet girl totty.

PROFS Doctors and nurses, students, retailers, estate agents, media, fashion executives, designers
CELEBS David Beckham, Chelsea Football Club, Ant & Dec, Ross Kemp, Minnie Driver, Robbie Williams

DRESS City suits, DKNY, FCUK, Levi's, Ralph Lauren, surfwear, chinos/blazer, Thomas Pink, Hackett, the latest must-have accessories for the girls
MUSIC Easy Listening
DOOR None
DRINKS Beer £2.95, Wine £2.75, Cocktail £4.85
FOOD Modern British, £7
CARDS All
CAPACITY 150, seating 90
HIRE Venue: No · Private Room: No

PO NA NA SOUK BAR

Bar, Club, Theme, Chain
316 King's Road SW3
020 7352 7127

OPEN Mon-Sat 9.30pm-1am	GETTING LUCKY	4/5
TUBE/RAIL Sloane Square	EYE CANDY	3/5
BUSES 11, 22	BIG SPENDERS	3/5
	MIX 50%M 50%F	
	AGE 20-30	
	PRICE Average	

AMBIENCE Basement, Cosy, Dancing, Funky, Late Night Open, Party, Pulling
REVIEW The original Moroccan theme bar, set up by Rob Sawyer and Christian Arden nine years ago and now a stock exchange listed company with 54 venues. The style has been done to death around town and even its most famous exponent Momo is slipping well below its peak of popularity. Nevertheless with so little else in Chelsea of note this place still has a sexy, fun atmosphere. Ok, for some it can be rather 'Poo Yah Yah' but it attracts the roving eyes of a young, friendly mix of local Sloanes, alongside the more trendy/clubby set. Good sounds all week long, with room to wiggle just a little bit. Expect to queue as members and their guests get priority. Groups of girls get in with ease, whereas no more than three guys at a time are allowed.
PLACE Moroccan souk style cosy basement bar, on a buzzy stretch of the King's Road. Dimly lit, with sexy decor and secluded corners although the place is looking a bit worn now.
PEOPLE 21s-30s young, funky things. Cross-section of Chelsea/Fl'am set with money to enjoy themselves, out for fun and games.

PROFS Retail, restaurant and club staff, City boys, secretaries
CELEBS Natalie Imbruglia, Matt Goss, Mark Hughes, Chelsea Football Club, Ant & Dec
DRESS Barbours and suits meet club gear and high street chic. No trainers at weekends
MUSIC Breakbeat, Funk, Garage, Hip Hop, House, Rare Groove, Soul
DOOR Smart casual, Wed-Sat £5
DRINKS Beer £3, Wine £3, Champagne £4, Cocktail £5.50
FOOD None
CARDS All
CAPACITY 120, seating 50
HIRE Venue: Yes · Private Room: No

fulham

606 CLUB

Jazz Club, Live Music Venue
90 Lots Road SW10
020 7352 5953

OPEN Mon-Wed 7.30pm-1am, Thu 8pm-1.30am, Fri-Sat 8pm-2am, Sun 8pm-midnight	**GETTING LUCKY** 3/5
	EYE CANDY 3/5
	BIG SPENDERS 3/5
	MIX 50%M 50%F
TUBE/RAIL Earl's Court, Fulham Broadway	**AGE** 18-55
	PRICE Average
BUSES C3, 328	

AMBIENCE Basement, Chin Stroking, Late Night Open, Live Music, Underground, Warehouse/Industrial
REVIEW Behind the forbidding black grille off Lots Road, the 606 vibe has not changed since the club opened in 1958. This is not an elevator muzak venue; jazz here is taken seriously and most of the time you can rely on an exciting line-up. Musicians jam on the same floor level as drinkers and diners, who sit pouring out plonk and puffing on Marlboros in intense candlelit clusters. Unlike Ronnie Scott's or The Vortex, talking is permitted during the performances but the majority of the clientele are too involved in the sounds to consider it. Because the 606 is a private club, if you want to drink alcohol you must either be a member or have booked a meal in advance.
PLACE Functional but cosy basement crammed with wooden chairs and tables, nightlights on each. Brickwork and exposed piping in the US jazz club tradition. Yellowing mural on back wall depicts jazz greats. Members mill in the slightly raised bar section to the right of the door.
PEOPLE Jazz fans from late teens to late middle age, in twos or fours. Occasional parties of tanked-up Sloanes get a bit too raucous but most punters are so caught up in the music, they're oblivious to their companions. The odd spinstery muso sitting alone, eyes closed, hypnotised.

PROFS Musicians, doctors, actors, lawyers, media professionals, antique dealers
CELEBS John Critchenson, Jim Mullen, Claire Martin
DRESS Gone are the days of the black polo neck and Chris Evans specs. Men in sharp suits (with the odd jazzy tie) to dishevelled Tom Baker-style get-ups. Older women in chiffon animal prints and fuschia lipstick, younger groups in Gap/Urban Outfitters.

MUSIC Live Jazz every night
DOOR Live music Sun-Thu £5, Fri-Sat £6
DRINKS Beer £1.95, Wine £2.20
FOOD Fish, Modern European, £12.50
CARDS No Diners
CAPACITY 150, seating 150
HIRE Venue: Yes · Private Room: No

THE ATLAS

Gastropub
16 Seagrave Road SW6
020 7385 9129

OPEN Mon-Sat midday-11pm, Sun midday-10.30pm	**GETTING LUCKY** 2/5
	EYE CANDY 3/5
TUBE/RAIL West Brompton	**BIG SPENDERS** 3/5
BUSES 74, 190	**MIX** 60%M 40%F
	AGE 25-65
	PRICE Average

AMBIENCE Casual, Conversation, Groups, Mature/Older, Outdoors
REVIEW A centuries old two-bar pub, The Atlas has recently been transformed into a bar-bistro in one much larger room. It's almost a shame to let the secret out about this brilliant little gastro-oasis – it's one of the best foodie pubs to be found in London. Note, however, this is not preen-and-be-seen territory – if you want that head up the road towards South Ken.
PLACE The floors are well-scrubbed; the walls are wood-panelled; the chairs and tables are well-spaced. Staff are ultra-friendly and informed and they actually smile with no electrical stimulation. There's a nice little walled beer garden with awning and those outdoor heaters to take the chill out of a July evening.
PEOPLE The clientele includes recently-acquired regulars, lots of PRs from the firms nearby and workers from the Earl's Court Exhibition Centre. There are also a few charity workers from CCC around the corner, too – an easygoing mix.

PROFS PRs, charity workers, exhibition centre workers, local residents who should be thanking the landlord for increasing their house value
CELEBS Guy Ritchie, Liv Tyler
DRESS High Street suits, khakis and t-shirts
MUSIC Latin Jazz, Salsa, Bossa Nova
DOOR No children in the evening
DRINKS Beer £2.50, Wine £2.50
FOOD Mediterranean, £8
CARDS No Amex or Diners
CAPACITY 200, seating 80
HIRE Venue: Yes · Private Room: Yes

BARDO

Bar
196-198 Fulham Road SW10
020 7351 1711

OPEN Mon-Thu 5.30pm-midnight, Fri-Sat 5pm-1am	**GETTING LUCKY** 3/5
	EYE CANDY 3/5
TUBE/RAIL Fulham Broadway	**BIG SPENDERS** 4/5
	MIX 50%M 50%F
BUSES 19	**AGE** 25-55
	PRICE Expensive

AMBIENCE Conversation, Groups, Late Night Open

REVIEW With Kartouche shut down and 'The Beach' becoming increasingly chain infested this bijou bar is a Fulham find... if you can put up with a lot of wedged-up 35+ Fulhamites shoving blazered elbows in your face. Locals come to chat up coquettish girls while suits sit drinking wine and puffing cigars. While there we witnessed some overweight, media spec-wearing tool in his late 50s camp it up at the bar with a pair of sycophantic girls: 'I just can't go to Spain sweetheart... it's too damn clichéd.' And so, my friend, are you.

PLACE The brown suede banquette in here looks like something out of The Bitch; We half expected to see Oliver Tobias groping up Joannie and stinking the place out with his Hai Karate. This is a small, bustling bar with a teensy chill-out room in the back and a central table with a backgammon board. It's got a bit of a Far Eastern feel with orchids and Japanese-ish chairs. The open windows are great for spying on youngsters falling out of the Goat & Boots over the road. Look out for the 'lady's hand' door handles – oo-er, missus. Nice selection of vodkas – at a price.

PEOPLE Annoying media types who constantly speak in acronyms – 'Yah, lets throw in some FAQs on the web page and really highlight our USPs... Pippa, be a dahling and get me a VAT.' Estate agents, property types, bankers, PAs, faded Page 3 girls looking for 'posh blokes'.

PROFS Producers, PRs, financial advisers, project managers, bankers, estate agents, PAs

CELEBS Hugh Grant, Dannii Minogue, Steps, James Hewitt

DRESS Bespoke Savile Row, Rolex, Omega Seamaster, Gucci, Helmut Lang, Tommy Hilfiger, Prada, Miu Miu, designer baguettes, combats, Polo Sport, Aquascutum

MUSIC Jazz, Easy Listening

DOOR Smart casual

DRINKS Beer £3, Wine £3.25, Champagne £6.25, Cocktail £6

FOOD Japanese, Sushi, £9

CARDS No Diners

CAPACITY 120, seating 40

HIRE Venue: Yes · Private Room: Yes

BIERODROME

Bar, Restaurant, Chain
678 Fulham Road SW6
020 7751 0789

OPEN Mon-Sat midday-11pm, Sun midday-10.30pm	**GETTING LUCKY**	**3/5**	
TUBE/RAIL Parsons Green, Fulham Broadway	**EYE CANDY**	**3/5**	
	BIG SPENDERS	**3/5**	
BUSES 14	**MIX** 60%M 40%F		
	AGE 25-40		
	PRICE Average		

AMBIENCE Groups

REVIEW Bierodromes seem to be cropping up all over the place lately and this one's much the same as the rest: mega-efficient staff dressed up in comedy Xena/Hercules tabards, a humungous selection of ludicrously potent beer, and plenty of Belgian-style nibbles and snacks. But shandy drinkers beware – this is undoubtedly a pisshead's paradise, and the emphasis

is on getting completely blotto. Take it from us, these beers bite. Most excellent. It's just a shame they didn't exploit the whole Belgian thing a bit more – we reckon a few kagoul-wearing mulletheads behind the bar and a bit of naff Eurodisco would've gone down a storm. Then again, with this much beer inside you, a Jehovah's Witness singalong would keep you happy.

PLACE Double-fronted bierkeller-type affair with restaurant bit on the left side (serving mussels, sausages etc) and a bar area on the right. At the back there's an interesting out-of-focus forest mural (maybe it was the booze), and the area behind the bar is backed by coloured glass. The long banquettes' proximity to the bogs make them the ideal place to sample the dinky but deceptive beer samples. Rather noisy, but that's the idea.

PEOPLE The majority of punters are business bods who talk mundane money-matters over lethal doses of cloudy beer. Overheard (slurred): 'Tell me, do you feel comfortable earning that kinda money?' As for the ladies, it's amazing what a couple of glasses of Lucifer can do – on our visit a tipsy duo were in hysterics over the prospect of Bierodrome's forthcoming 'Sausagefest'.

PROFS Estate agents, web designers, PAs, PRs, financial whizzes, salespeople, property developers, local businessman blotting out the last VAT return

CELEBS None

DRESS Fleeces, Omega watches, post-work suits minus ties, jeans, Caterpillars, Timberland, North Face, Hackett, Ralph Lauren, FCUK, Jigsaw, Office, Prada

MUSIC Pop, Easy Listening

DOOR None

DRINKS Beer £2.60, Wine £2.50

FOOD Belgian, £11

CARDS All

CAPACITY 200, seating 74

HIRE Venue: Yes · Private Room: No

THE CRESCENT

Bar, Restaurant, Wine Bar
99 Fulham Road SW3
020 7225 2244

OPEN Sun 11am-10pm, Mon 11am-11pm,	**GETTING LUCKY**	**1/5**	
	EYE CANDY	**3/5**	
Tue-Sat 10am-11pm	**BIG SPENDERS**	**5/5**	
TUBE/RAIL South Kensington	**MIX** 55%M 45%F		
	AGE 25-55		
BUSES 22, 49, 71	**PRICE** Average		

AMBIENCE Casual, Conversation, Groups

REVIEW This chic little wine bar/restaurant is within a Jimmy Choo heel of both Bibendum and Voyage, so the punters are of the 'links with nobility, holiday in St Kitts' variety. It's quite a plain kinda bar, with a small downstairs restaurant, but it's the clientele that make the place interesting. As the smell of coffee mingles with hops and posh tobacco, a trio of babes sip Freedom lager and chat to lugubrious men friends about the Maldives. Meanwhile, the friendly barman straightens the papers on the bar and pours another drink for a single American.

PLACE Good place to meet for some pre-Bibendum boozing, this is a simple, clean-as-a-cat's-bum bar, with stripped floorboards, a chrome bar, and a blue banquette running along the wall. It's unostentatious and relatively easy to miss. The only eyesore is the door by the bar that looks like one of those depressing doors from a school science block. Do say 'Magnum of your finest vintage.' Don't say 'Oi guv'nor, pint o' wallop and some smokes.'

PEOPLE Blokes whose parents are half-famous but fully loaded and girls who've probably been to the Priory Clinic but keep it under their pashminas. Also, Sada from Big Brother-types, who think they're hippies but couldn't function without gold plastic.

PROFS Sales directors, designers, captains of industry, rich hippies, property developers, trust fund layabouts, PR agents, fashion buyers, writers, office workers, business owners, estate agents, bankers, film employees, theatre staff
CELEBS Madonna
DRESS Suits, chinos, Rolexes, cashmere sweaters, pashminas, skimpy tops, designer everything
MUSIC Classical Jazz, Pop
DOOR None
DRINKS Beer £2.95, Wine £2.75, Champagne £8.50, Cocktail £6.95
FOOD Continental Breakfast, Full English Breakfast, International, Modern Eclectic, Modern European, Snacks, £8.50
CARDS All
CAPACITY 110, seating 60
HIRE Venue: Yes · Private Room: Yes

EMBARGO

Club
533b King's Road SW10
020 7351 5038

OPEN Tue-Sat 10pm-2am	**GETTING LUCKY**	**4/5**
TUBE/RAIL Sloane Square,	**EYE CANDY**	**4/5**
Fulham Broadway	**BIG SPENDERS**	**4/5**
BUSES 11, 22	**MIX** 60%M 40%F	
	AGE 21-35	
	PRICE Average	

AMBIENCE Dancing, Late Night Open, Party, Pulling, Opulent
REVIEW If your idea of a great time is standing in the middle of a dance floor, holding a bottle of Becks and making 'Woo! Woo!' noises to Sister Sledge songs then the Embargo is the club for you. You will also live in Chelsea, Fulham or Battersea, be in your late 20s and earn a salary well in excess of your age. Oh, and your idea of 'club dress' is brogues, chinos and a fleece with the collar turned rakishly upwards. Amazingly, Embargo is not kneecapped by its clientele. It is a beautiful venue with state-of-the-art facilities, and the good-looking punters are out to have a good old-fashioned, drug-free laugh. You may look around at 1am and think you've gatecrashed the Eton sixth-form disco, but by then you'll be having too much fun to give a monkeys.
PLACE One of the prettiest clubs in London with Bedouin-style draped ceilings, a candlelit chill-out room and loos clean enough to drop sprogs on. The management have thoughtfully provided poles on the dance floor to allow drunken females to tease their even more inebriated menfolk.

PEOPLE A million miles from the 'street' – these are the people who drive around SW7 in Audi TTs with the stereo tuned into Capital Gold. Bless 'em.

PROFS Bankers, lawyers, accountants, property developers, luxury car dealers, estate agents
CELEBS Hugh Grant
DRESS Suits, blazers, Earl jeans, Snow+Rock, leather trousers
MUSIC House, Garage; 70s-90s DJs Wed-Sat
DOOR Smart casual, club night on weekends £5
DRINKS Beer £3, Wine £3.50, Cocktail £5
FOOD Snacks, £4
CARDS No Amex or Diners
CAPACITY 200, seating 100
HIRE Venue: Yes · Private Room: Yes

THE FULHAM TUP

Pub
268 Fulham Road SW10
020 7352 1859

OPEN Mon-Sat midday-	**GETTING LUCKY**	**2/5**
11pm, Sun midday-10.30pm	**EYE CANDY**	**2/5**
TUBE/RAIL Fulham	**BIG SPENDERS**	**3/5**
Broadway, Earl's Court	**MIX** 65%M 35%F	
BUSES 211	**AGE** 23-45	
	PRICE Cheap	

AMBIENCE Backpacker, Casual, Conversation, Groups, Sports
REVIEW The Tup is a real modern pub, traditional but with enough of a twist to keep it successful despite tough competition from neighbouring bars. It tends to attract the less prim of Chelsea types – more rugger bugger than hooray fop and girls without pearls – generally those who can stomach the wooden chairs, scuff marks on the floor and the scrummage for service at the bar. The staff are friendly and usually foreign, in fact, enough Antipodeans work here to give an immigration officer an aneurysm.
PLACE Bright, open plan, wood and more wood. Close to Stamford Bridge, a large and generously staffed bar to fuel celebration or drown sorrows after a match.
PEOPLE Predominantly male. Either rugby enthusiasts who have slipped from active to armchair and from stocky to sofa. Or the non-notorious type of Chelsea football fan if they are playing at home.

PROFS Bankers, nurses, PAs, PRs, football managers, lawyers, tourists, office workers
CELEBS Suggs, Jeremy Clarkson, Kylie, Bob Geldof
DRESS Pringle, sports casual and rugby shirts, fleeces, combats, high street suits, jeans, sweatshirts, TopShop
MUSIC Easy Listening, Jazz
DOOR None
DRINKS Beer £2.70, Wine £2.50
FOOD International, Pub Food, £5
CARDS All
CAPACITY 600, seating 130
HIRE Venue: No · Private Room: No

GOAT IN BOOTS

Cocktail Bar, Pub
333 Fulham Road SW10
020 7352 1384

OPEN Mon-Sat 11am-11pm,
Sun midday-10.30pm
TUBE/RAIL South
Kensington
BUSES 14, 211

GETTING LUCKY	3/5
EYE CANDY	3/5
BIG SPENDERS	3/5
MIX 55%M 45%F	
AGE 18-35	
PRICE Cheap	

AMBIENCE Casual, Groups, Party, Student
REVIEW If you dressed up all the youngsters in here
in gowns and tuxedos, this gaff would resemble one
of those hilariously debauched aristo-balls that all
the papers frown upon. Soppy young girls with blokes'
names (George, Charlie etc.) 'shite viry lidely' into
mobiles, as James Major-style boyfriends pull up on
mopeds to clumsily high-five with mates. Meanwhile,
in the boisterous cocktail section downstairs, a
blackboard suggests you 'Fcuk your Mind'. Most of
the lads stand squashed on the stairs drinking daft-
sounding cocktails and phwoaring at the tight bums
and trim tums emerging from the small basement.
PLACE Fun pub in prime corner location. Green canopies
and a few benches out front. On some nights this triple-
level boozer resembles a house party and often gets
rammed to a standstill. The cocktail bar downstairs can
be very cliquey and the basement is more like a sixth-
form common room. Forget pulling if you've grown out
of Oxy10.
PEOPLE Assorted Chelsea/Fulham types who use the
Goat as a place to get tanked up early, pre-club; plus
attractive girls who always hug bouncers when queue-
jumping, and blokes who make out they understand
baseball by playing rounders every Sunday wearing
a pitcher's glove.

PROFS Students, retailers, ITs, pine dealers, City types,
trustafarians, fashion designers, doctors, nurses
CELEBS Hugh Grant, Guy Ritchie, Tara Palmer-Tomkinson,
John Hannah, Stereophonics
DRESS For girls: skimpy Miss Selfridge stuff with
navel-rings and waist chains. For blokes: clueless
mummyboywear and surfy dudewear, through to
supercool Lenny Kravitz-style gear worn by ageing
predators on the prowl for impressionable totty.
MUSIC Pop, Chart, Rock; Thu-Sun Commercial Dance,
Ambient DJs, Sat House DJ
DOOR None
DRINKS Beer £2.40, Wine £2.50, Cocktail £4.50
FOOD Pub Food, £4
CARDS No Diners
CAPACITY 200, seating 50
HIRE Venue: No · Private Room: No

HAVANA

Bar, Theme
490 Fulham Road SW6
020 7381 5005

OPEN Mon-Thu 4pm-2am,
Fri-Sat midday-2am,
Sun midday-12.30am
TUBE/RAIL Fulham
Broadway
BUSES 14, 11, 28

GETTING LUCKY	4/5
EYE CANDY	3/5
BIG SPENDERS	3/5
MIX 45%M 55%F	
AGE 21-28	
PRICE Average	

AMBIENCE Buzzy, Casual, Dancing, Groups, Kitsch,
Late Night Open, Live Music, Party, Pulling, Cute Staff
REVIEW Havana looks as tired as the concept. It's
another place that's heavy on those sexy Latin beats:
salsa, mambo, Latin house, you name it. They even
teach salsa dancing every Tuesday, Thursday and Sunday
night and feature live bands, usually from
Cuba. Open until 2am it's a pub-restaurant-cum-club.
According to the manager, Havana is a very sexy place.
He takes pride in the fact that many women come here
just to drool over the hunky bar staff, who flirt to an
astronomical degree and go all Tom Cruise on the
cocktails. Much flirting and gyrating of hips goes on,
not just on the dance floor, but anywhere a space to
schmooze presents itself as Havana packs them in.
Advanced civilisation is evidenced by providing spirits
by the bottle. If you don't finish it all in one go, they
put your name on the bottle and hold it until next time.
PLACE Decor is Changing Rooms tack, with ironwork,
uneven tiled floors and tables plus the inevitable fake
leopard and tiger skin print sofas and chairs. Walls are
muted greens, oranges and terracotta. Latin cool meets
a Jonathon Ross show set in a kitsch clash of cultural
styles that barely manages to keep its integrity. Due for
refurbishment soon.
PEOPLE Double-cheek grazing, dizzied yahoos. Rugger-
buggers in back-slapping frenzies. The girls all read
Lady Victoria Hervey's column over a latte with vanilla
syrup. Chelsea and Fulham residents.

PROFS PAs, production co-ordinators, buyers, cleaning
supervisors, photographers, accountants, bankers,
students, City workers
CELEBS Ben Hollioake, Surrey Cricket Team, Daley
Thompson, Ricky Martin
DRESS Next, TopShop, Jigsaw, Ciro Citerrio, Gap, FCUK,
Mango, Levi's, t-shirts
MUSIC Latin, Salsa, Funk, Jazz, Soul; Dance, Latin,
Funk DJs 7 Days, Live Bands Fri-Sat
DOOR Sun-Mon Free, Tue £2 after 10pm,
Wed £4 after 10pm, Thu £5 after 10pm,
Fri-Sat £6 after 9pm, £8 after 11pm
DRINKS Beer £2.90, Wine £3, Champagne £4.50,
Cocktail £5
FOOD Cuban, Mexican, South West American,
Spanish, £8, Tapas, £3
CARDS No Diners
CAPACITY 245, seating 70
HIRE Venue: Yes · Private Room: No

THE IFIELD

Gastropub
59 Ifield Road SW10
020 7351 4900

OPEN Mon-Thu 5pm-11pm,	GETTING LUCKY	3/5
Fri-Sun midday-11pm	EYE CANDY	3/5
TUBE/RAIL Earl's Court,	BIG SPENDERS	3/5
Fulham Broadway	MIX 60%M 40%F	
BUSES N14	AGE 20-55	
	PRICE Average	

AMBIENCE Casual, Star Spotting
REVIEW Right, no beating about the bush: The Ifield is a bogus pub. You'd have thought the cobalt blue paint job plus the rosemary growing in square terracotta pots outside would be a bit of a giveaway, but I bet there's many a local oldster who's wandered in hoping for a barley wine and a singalong to 'Snooker Loopy' (as in nuts are we) on the jukebox and immediately had to be sectioned under the relevant provision of the Mental Health Act. No, The Ifield is a suave and delightful bar/restaurant entirely for the benefit of the chattering middle classes. A luxurious squidgy-sofaed bar area leads through to a wider restaurant space you wouldn't be ashamed to take your girlfriend to – surely a first for the arse-end of Earl's Court/Fulham and its peeling stucco.
PLACE Stylishly converted pub by Ed 'pretty boy' Baines – big mirrors, candelabras, a nice picture of some apples, the sort of fresh flower arrangements you don't have to dry-clean or iron, flattering lighting – with fab food.
PEOPLE Well-to-do, hip locals back from stressful media-related jobs up west. Husky-voiced Mariella Frostrup-o-grams. Some Barbour-jacketed Henries but not the hooray type.
PROFS Account execs, journalists, film and media professionals, designers
CELEBS Ed Baines, Madonna, Guy Ritchie, Rod Stewart, Lennox Lewis, Mick Jagger, Elaine Paige, Kris Akabussi, England Rugby team, Martine McCutcheon
DRESS Relaxed. Largely a hard core of regulars who've been home first to change into something sloppy
MUSIC Pop
DOOR None
DRINKS Beer £2.80, Wine £3, Champagne £5.50, Cocktail £5.50
FOOD Mediterranean, Modern British, £12
CARDS No Diners
CAPACITY 100, seating 75
HIRE Venue: No · Private Room: No

LA PERLA

Bar, Restaurant
803 Fulham Road SW6
020 7471 4895

OPEN Mon-Fri 5pm-11pm,	GETTING LUCKY	1/5
Sat midday-11pm,	EYE CANDY	3/5
Sun midday-10.30pm	BIG SPENDERS	3/5
TUBE/RAIL Parsons Green	MIX 50%M 50%F	
BUSES 14	AGE 25-55	
	PRICE Average	

AMBIENCE Chilled, Conversation, Groups
REVIEW Having recently returned from a trip to jolly old Mehico, I can confirm that this place is pretty authentic in terms of Mexican booze. Thankfully though, La Perla's attempts at realism don't extend to turning the heating up to 130 degrees, surrounding each table with packs of anorexic cats and swarms of flies and then playing a broken guitar an inch from your face. So, as far as sanitised versions of Mexico go, La Perla is a real winner. It stocks dozens of different tequilas and the helpful staff will be more than happy to advise you on which lager to shove your lime wedge into. Bueno.
PLACE Not as rowdy as your usual Mexican, this place relies on its chilled atmosphere to pull in the punters. More spacious than you may imagine, it's a bright and airy place with neon Corona ads, mounted swordfish and a large aquatic mural by the entrance.
PEOPLE Local regulars, well-to-do geezers who fancy a nibble with their firewater, groups of girls who don't want any hassle (and subsequently eyeball every single man), and quiet couples who dig bottled beer.
PROFS Stockbrokers, PRs, salespeople, retailers, estate agents, promoters
CELEBS Richard Dunwoody, Brad Pitt, John McEnroe
DRESS Casual Fulhamish stuff – from fleeces and jeans to blazers and a bit of designer glitz
MUSIC Latin American
DOOR None
DRINKS Beer £2.85, Wine £2.80, Cocktail £4.75
FOOD Mexican, £10
CARDS No Diners
CAPACITY 150, seating 60
HIRE Venue: Yes · Private Room: No

THE MARTINI GRILL

Bar, Restaurant
308-310 North End Road SW6
020 7385 5005

OPEN Closed Mondays,	GETTING LUCKY	2/5
Tue-Sat 6pm-midnight,	EYE CANDY	3/5
Sun Midday- 6pm	BIG SPENDERS	4/5
TUBE/RAIL Fulham Broadway	MIX 40%M 60%F	
BUSES 295	AGE 25-45	
	PRICE Average	

AMBIENCE Casual, Conversation, Cute Staff, Kitsch
REVIEW The Martini Grill is going for the comfort factor but doesn't provide much by the way of material comfort – the only seating is a hard, dark leather banquette running along one wall or a selection of small red leather pouffes. On the plus side, the staff are welcoming, knowledgeable and cute and it's a colourfully inviting place. The original bar left over from the Grill's previous reincarnation as a dodgy boozer has been buffed to within an inch of its life and brightened up with an acrylic light box. Velvet purple sausage cushions add a louche feel and pink frosted windows cast a rosy glow on the proceedings, helped along by the bar's range of six Martinis.
PLACE A tongue-in-cheek, kitsch creation mixing old Hollywood glamour, 50s US diner and New York city

cocktail bar, with a hint of old pub thrown in for good measure.
PEOPLE Slim, suede-coated kittens flick their Jemima Khan hair and moan about 3 hours of lectures a week before skipping off to Harvey Nicks and whacking a bundle on daddy's charge card.

PROFS Ex army blokes turned dotcommers, lawyers, thespians, investment bankers
CELEBS None
DRESS Anything from Gucci to Gap, but more label than style
DOOR None
MUSIC Chill-out
DRINKS Beer £2.75, Wine £2.75, Champagne £6, Cocktail £4.50
FOOD International, £10
CARDS No Amex
CAPACITY 70, seating 40
HIRE Venue: Yes · Private Room No

PURPLE

Club
Chelsea Village, Fulham Road SW10
020 7434 2933

OPEN Thu 9pm-1am,	GETTING LUCKY	**5/5**
Fri-Sat 9pm-2.30am	EYE CANDY	**4/5**
TUBE/RAIL Fulham	BIG SPENDERS	**4/5**
Broadway	MIX 60%M 40%F	
BUSES 14, 211	AGE 18-30	
	PRICE Expensive	

AMBIENCE Brightly Coloured/Cheerful, Dancing, Friendly, Groups, Kitsch Decor, Late Night Open, Party, Pulling
REVIEW 'Club Tropicana drinks are freee'. Stepping into Purple you are instantly transported from Chelsea Village into Magaluf Town. Typical of a Mediterranean port complex club, with its strobe lighting, garish decor, cheesy tunes and high percentage of tanned 18-30s. Did you ever hear about those balls where 14-year-olds shag each other? Well, when they grow up they all go to Purple, and it's clear that the Chelsea kids can't get enough of it, spending their hard-earned trust funds on champagne and the £15 entrance fee. For that you get not an iota of sophistication: the decor is Stringfellows meets your worst Purple nightmare. Gross. Worryingly,

when the music stops the disco dolls burst into an impromptu rendition of 'Hey Baby' by DJ Otzi...
PLACE All the class of the tasteful wall mural in the EastEnders B&B. Impossible to hear yourself speak, but that doesn't matter when you have young, nubile body language.
PEOPLE Suits (come on boys, it's a Saturday). Lots of randy rich totty and the standard clusters of dusky, sharking men around the edges.

PROFS Fundraisers, PRs, butlers, events organisers, recruitment consultants, researchers, sportsmen, bankers, estate agents, ITs
CELEBS Johnny Lee Miller, Martine McCutcheon, Fulham and Chelsea Footballers, Boy George, John Leslie, EastEnders
DRESS Girls: fresh-faced and raunchy, tiny dresses or corsets with jeans, heels obligatory. Boys: suits, suits and more suits; the dangerous ones opt for shirt and trouser combos
MUSIC Chart, House, 70s, 80s, Disco, DJs
DOOR Over 21s. No jeans or baseball caps, Thu £5, Fri-Sat £15
DRINKS Beer £3.50, Wine £4, Champagne £6, Cocktail £6.50
FOOD None
CARDS All
CAPACITY 650, seating 140
HIRE Venue: Yes · Private Room Yes

THE WHITE HORSE

Gastropub
1-3 Parsons Green SW6
020 7736 2115

OPEN Mon-Sat 11am-11pm	GETTING LUCKY	**4/5**
Sun 11am-10.30pm	EYE CANDY	**4/5**
TUBE/RAIL Parsons Green	BIG SPENDERS	**4/5**
BUSES 11, 22	MIX 50%M 50%F	
	AGE 25-35	
	PRICE Cheap	

AMBIENCE Casual, Groups, Pulling
REVIEW Voted National Pub of the Year of 2000, the White Horse or 'Sloaney Pony' combines top-quality traditional bevvies with an innovative approach to promoting drink from beer festivals to wheat beer competitions and a terrifying sounding oyster stout with bourbon and vanilla pods for St Patrick's Day, plus an awesome wine list stretching back to a Margaux 1979, and more than a dozen single malts. Energetic atmosphere generated by a hard core of trustafarians, stockbrokers and design babes, stimulated by passing trade from the local recording and photographic studios. There are 60 beer styles around and most of them have passed through here – from Harvey's Sussex to Rooster's Yankee. Just the place to put real ale back on the map.
PLACE Refurbished in 1999 to include the original coach house with flagstone floor. The bar itself is one of the longest around – some 80 feet. Leather sofas, oak benches, semi-panelled walls, art for sale on the walls and gourmet food.
PEOPLE Much of the army and rugby crowds have disappeared leaving an inspiring and eclectic community of the young and discerning.

PROFS Music employees, media employees, IT consultants, musos, models, stockbrokers, extra-curricular skiers
CELEBS Oz Clarke, Jeremy Clarkson, Rick Astley, Carol Thatcher
DRESS It's trendy but not intimidating. Just wear what you want and enjoy the experience. Suits, fleeces and snowboarding/skating labels, King's Road and High Street labels for women, designer-label shirts and rugby shirts for men.
MUSIC No background music
DOOR No scruffy clothes/shoes
DRINKS Beer £2.80, Wine £2.95
FOOD Modern British, £8
CARDS No Diners
CAPACITY 350, seating 150
HIRE Venue: Yes · Private Room: Yes

knightsbridge

BLUE BAR

Hotel Bar
The Berkeley Hotel, Wilton Place SW1
020 7201 1680

OPEN Mon-Sat 4pm-11pm	GETTING LUCKY	1/5
non-residents,	EYE CANDY	4/5
4pm-1am residents	BIG SPENDERS	5/5
TUBE/RAIL Hyde Park	MIX 60%M 40%F	
Corner, Knightsbridge	AGE 25-65	
BUSES 9, 10, 14, 22,	PRICE Very expensive	
74, 137		

AMBIENCE Exclusive/Chic, Hip/Fashionable, Legendary, Opulent Star Spotting
REVIEW The Blue Bar is not just any old blue, but a grandly titled 'Lutyens Blue', after the British architect Sir Edwin Lutyens, creator of the fiddly wooden carvings that decorate the room. Elton J. would adore it: faux ostrich leather, a mock croc print leather floor and all that lush blue. It's an elegant little tête à tête of a bar, that wouldn't have merited much mention except it was christened by the great lady herself, Madonna. With friends like these visiting his interiors David Collins really doesn't need PR. However, she's unlikely to appear again, since last time she stayed at the Berkeley she flounced out when the air-con broke down mid Ashtanga pose. That's pri-Madonna for you.
PLACE David Collins displays his knack of blending original details with a contemporary style in this bijou hotel bar. Deluxe, divine details include faux ostrich leather stools and a white onyx bar.
PEOPLE Sugar daddies and their toyboys, examining purchases after a shopping spree to Harvey Nicks/ Westwood, businessmen from the dapper to the dull, fashion queens of both sexes and Knightsbridge ladies and gents.

PROFS Designers, actors, musicians, international businessmen, people of influence
CELEBS Madonna, Mario Testino, Bruce Oldfield, Vivienne Westwood
DRESS Just don't wear blue. Chanel, Vivienne Westwood, Pink, Prada, Gucci, MaxMara, Jaeger, Harvey Nichols, Dolce & Gabbana

MUSIC Middle Eastern, Classical, Opera, Jazz
DOOR No trainers, no jeans
DRINKS Beer £4.20, Wine £5.50, Champagne £12, Cocktail £10
FOOD Tapas, £4.75
CARDS All
CAPACITY 60, seating 40
HIRE Venue: Yes · Private Room: No

FACES

Bar, Restaurant
138 Brompton Road SW3
020 7584 0552

OPEN Mon-Sun midday-	GETTING LUCKY	5/5
midnight	EYE CANDY	2/5
TUBE/RAIL Knightsbridge	BIG SPENDERS	4/5
BUSES 14, 74	MIX 50%M 50%F	
	AGE 30-50	
	PRICE Expensive	

AMBIENCE Basement, Buzzy, Mature/Older, Pulling
REVIEW Imagine a bar where everyone's up for it all of the time. Oh, you went to one last night? Well, if you WLTM other romantically challenged young-at-hearts but-getting-longish-of-tooth out for fun, friendship and maybe more, come to Faces. The line drawings of Patrick Swayze, the soft porn soundtrack caressing your ears, the zebra print chairs and the beautiful hostess – just airbrush the customers and it's a soft focus 80s wet dream. 'I love romance, I love kissing, I have a cheeky side.' So says Greg, one of the Faces on the books of this dating agency-cum-bar-cum-restaurant. All it costs is £600 a year to meet like-minded people with a GSOH.
PLACE Cheap-looking tourist traffic restaurant with a dodgy salon/beach-style bar in basement.
PEOPLE Soulmates, people who feel happiest in organised social engagements. Men who like paint-balling, women who love Ally McBeal and 'forgot' to get married.

PROFS Bankers, lawyers, doctors, singers, journalists, architects, accountants, PRs
CELEBS None, though there is an 'Elite' section on the books
DRESS Chanel, Versace, Gucci, Ralph Lauren
MUSIC House, Garage, Salsa, DJ Thu, Live Jazz Fri
DOOR Members only
DRINKS Beer £2.50, Wine £3.50, Champagne £6, Cocktail £8
FOOD Italian, Bar Snacks, £7.50
CARDS All
CAPACITY 300, seating 100
HIRE Venue: Yes · Private Room: No

FIFTH FLOOR BAR & RESTAURANT

Bar, Cocktail Bar, Restaurant
Harvey Nichols, 109-125 Knightsbridge SW1
020 7823 1839

OPEN Mon-Sat 11am-11pm,	GETTING LUCKY	4/5
Sun midday-6pm	EYE CANDY	5/5
TUBE/RAIL Knightsbridge	BIG SPENDERS	5/5
BUSES 19, 22, 137	MIX 50%M 50%F	
	AGE 28-60	
	PRICE Expensive	

AMBIENCE Business, Buzzy, Elegant/Classic, Groups, Hip/Fashionable, Jet Set, Live Music, Mature/Older, Star Spotting, Views

REVIEW On the fifth floor of designer department store Harvey Nicks, this is a vibrant, upscale pitstop, perfect for post-retail rehab; a place to rest those worn Manolos and overworked credit cards. By day it meanders along as a stylish haven for weary shoppers, by night the bar's reputation as a pickup joint precedes itself – and is well reflected in its clientele, who queue up outside with the impatience of mares kept waiting outside the stud. The bar offers 360 degrees of contemplation, in contrast to the low, closely-knit cluster of tables at the end of the room.

PLACE Horse shoe-shaped dark brown bar, portraits by Hollywood favourite Graham Knuttell line the walls. The faces are eerie, though not as pained as the businessmen out shopping with their young girlfriends. Booked for makeover in February 2002.

PEOPLE City boys on the pull, unsophisticates, Essex commuters, Middle Eastern middle to high rollers looking to spend some petro-dollars. You can well imagine that the shelves have been cleared of aftershave and foundation.

PROFS Fashion professionals, beauticians, bankers, PRs, stylists, media professionals, models, tourists, ladies who lunch

CELEBS Uma Thurman, Pamela Anderson, David and Victoria Beckham, Lulu, Ainsley Harriott, Hear'Say

DRESS McQueen, Gucci, Prada, Gaultier, Kenzo, Galliano

MUSIC Soul, Jazz

DOOR Smart casual

DRINKS Beer £3.35, Wine £3.50, Champagne £7, Cocktail £7.50

FOOD Snacks, £8.50

CARDS All

CAPACITY 200, seating 100

HIRE Venue: Yes · Private Room: No

FOYER BAR

Bar, Hotel Bar
Berkeley Hotel, Wilton Place SW1
020 7235 6000

OPEN 7 days 8am-11pm non-residents, 8am-1am residents
TUBE/RAIL Hyde Park Corner, Knightsbridge
BUSES 9, 10, 52, 34, 19, 22

GETTING LUCKY	2/5
EYE CANDY	3/5
BIG SPENDERS	5/5
MIX 70%M 30%F	
AGE 35-65	
PRICE Very expensive	

AMBIENCE Business, Conversation, Elegant/Classic, Groups, Jet Set, Romantic

REVIEW Sadly, since the opening of the Blue Bar, the Foyer seems to have picked up the sloppy seconds, the ones who feel threatened by the unconventional, yet love extreme sports. This Knightsbridge sanctum, in one of London's finest hotels, offers such librarian composure that you find yourself whispering your drinks order. Men sit alone and read or chew over the day's business with colleagues and cigars (selection available). Opposing loveseats by windows provide perfect seclusion for chattering ladies or illicit couplings. This is definitely the ideal retreat after a local shopping spree, for those girls who want to be left alone to enjoy the post-retail flush. Everyone here has their own agenda and interaction is generally 'not encouraged'. Shame, because if you're feeling forward it's a great spot to pick up some City tips, a wealthy American banker or a Euro sugar daddy.

PLACE The three large banquettes facing the window are a little beaten up these days, but due for a refurb in the New Year.

PEOPLE Japanese and American businessmen are the key protagonists in this hedonistic funfair of unabandoned pleasure chasing.

PROFS Bankers, tourists, shoppers

CELEBS Tara Palmer-Tomkinson

DRESS Prada, Gucci, Gap, Casual

MUSIC No background music

DOOR None

DRINKS Beer £4.50, Wine £6.50, Champagne £12.94, Cocktail £8

FOOD Snacks, Entrées, £12

CARDS All

CAPACITY 70, seating 40

HIRE Venue: No · Private Room: No

ISOLA BAR

Bar, Restaurant
145 Knightsbridge SW1
020 7838 1044

OPEN Mon-Sat 5pm-11pm
TUBE/RAIL Knightsbridge
BUSES 9, 10, 22, 52, 74, 137

GETTING LUCKY	4/5
EYE CANDY	4/5
BIG SPENDERS	5/5
MIX 60%M 40%F	
AGE 28-50	
PRICE Expensive	

AMBIENCE Business, Buzzy, Cute Bar Staff, Futuristic, Exclusive/Chic, Mature/Older, Pulling, Retro, Views

REVIEW Dapper man about town Oliver Peyton has at last turned his expensive upper dining room at Isola into a bar that serves 30 wines by the glass and a huge range of cocktails, including the richly stinky 'Isola Martini' with Truffle-infused vermouth. Head bartender Tony Conigliaro oversees operations with charm and, you know, that old-fashioned thing called manners. For those who appreciate the finer things in life, this is your bar; (straight) olive-skinned men in pink cords, Italiano guys in expensive bespoke suits practising that 'Fugedaboutit' air of indifference, groomed ladies, English gents in checked shirts and braces (evidently sooo autumn 2001). If you prefer to rough it then bounce through the door, get lost in the music (great sounds) and dream of the dusty, booted denim cowboy taking you in his stride.

PLACE Fantastic, futuristic Andy Martin designed bar with funky parquet wood wall, chunky chrome pillars, Pillar Box red leather booth seating, groovy, huge green UFO lights and giant cowboy portrait.

PEOPLE Knightsbridge homeowners and businessmen, wine lovers, Eurotrash. People who have three loves in common: money, fashion and drinking nice cocktails.

PROFS Bankers, tourists, chairmen, company directors, models, fashionistas, PRs, journalists

CELEBS Sophie Dahl, Ben Fogle, Tamara Beckwith, Dani Behr, Emma B, Donna Air, David Furnish, Johnny Lee Miller, Ruby Wax, Claudia Schiffer, David Coulthard, Reese Witherspoon, Harry Enfield, Jude Law, Sadie Frost

DRESS Nicole Farhi, Harvey Nichols, Harrods, Boateng, John Smedley, Shanghai Tang, Jaeger, Patrick Cox

MUSIC Jazz, Acid Jazz

DOOR Smart casual

DRINKS Beer £3, Wine £3.90, Champagne £7.50, Cocktail £6.50

FOOD Antipasti, £7

CARDS All

CAPACITY 250, seating 90

HIRE Venue: Yes · Private Room: No

MANDARIN BAR

Bar, Restaurant, Hotel Bar
Mandarin Oriental, 66 Knightsbridge SW1
020 7235 2000

OPEN Mon-Sat 11am-2am,	GETTING LUCKY	4/5
Sun 11am-10.30pm	EYE CANDY	4/5
TUBE/RAIL Knightsbridge	BIG SPENDERS	5/5
BUSES 9, 10, 14, 52	MIX 60%M 40%F	
	AGE 23-60	
	PRICE Very expensive	

AMBIENCE Business, Buzzy, Elegant/Classic, Late Night Open, Legendary, Mature/Older Clientele, Network, Opulent, Pulling,

REVIEW Past the ludicrously formal lobby area, with its walking relic guests, in this frightfully superior hotel the bar comes as a breath of contemporary air. Part mad professor's laboratory, part airport lounge, part catwalk, the interior references to China are kept, thankfully, to a minimum. It looks great – and it should do. Two years ago four hundred million pounds was spent refurbishing the bar, restaurants, spa area and hotel. Just imagine how gutted Mr Oriental must have been to discover that some guy called Ian had just popped in to London, where an old fabric showroom rather caught his eye.

PLACE Leather 'bar within the bar'. Main counter designed like a catwalk, drinks prepared behind a screen lined with multi-coloured bottles no doubt to avoid staff having Japanese rice crackers thrown at them (over the slow service?). Cocktails are exceptional, particularly the Moltinis.

PEOPLE Old, balding businessmen, suspicious-looking highly groomed single Eastern European women, rich people, seasonally and geographically confused Americans wearing shorts and deck shoes in November.

PROFS Company directors, international businessmen, lawyers, models, politicians, sportsmen, shoppers, tourists

CELEBS Christy Turlington, The Three Tenors, The Corrs, Mariah Carey

DRESS Chanel, Prada, Bespoke, Ozwald Boateng, Gucci, Issey Miyake

MUSIC Live Jazz Mon-Sat

DOOR None

DRINKS Beer £4.30, Wine £4.70, Champagne £8.50, Cocktail £8.50

FOOD Oriental, £9

CARDS All

CAPACITY 90, seating 42

HIRE Venue: No · Private Room: Yes

MONTE'S

Bar, Club, Cocktail Bar, Members Club, Restaurant
164 Sloane Street SW1
020 7245 0896

OPEN Mon 11am-11pm,	GETTING LUCKY	1/5
Tue 11am-2am,	EYE CANDY	3/5
Wed-Sat 11am-3am	BIG SPENDERS	4/5
TUBE/RAIL Knightsbridge,	MIX 70%M 30%F	
Sloane Square	AGE 25-60	
BUSES C1, 19, 22, 137	PRICE Very expensive	

AMBIENCE Business, Conversation, Elegant/Classic, Groups

REVIEW Everything about the bar screams of OTT opulence, so any puritans with a social conscience should avoid it. This is the townie, Nouveau deco equivalent of a 1920s ocean liner, all oak panelling, fibre optics, silver leafing, mirrors and velvet upholstery. Enjoying the general decadence, and fuelled by one of London's finest cellars, are a mixed bag of paunchy international businessmen hoping to impress their clients, smooth PR executives and leggy It girls. The club is gradually being taken over by the new Knightsbridge brigade, that crowd of young professionals who usually lunch at Joseph's L'Express across the road before going on to Harvey Nicks for an Aveda massage. Take someone pretty and call the caterers to ensure everything's as smooth as foie gras for the Formula 1 lunch you're holding tomorrow.

PLACE Liner-inspired membership club spanning four floors. Includes a private room kitted out with a

David Linley specially commissioned dining table, a swanky restaurant, nightclub and cigar shop. All that's missing is a casino.
PEOPLE Private bankers, bankruptcy lawyers, entrepreneurs, horse breeders and anyone else who either has a lot of money or is surrounded by people who do.

PROFS Fashion workers, media professionals, bankers, lawyers, PRs
CELEBS Pierce Brosnan, Darcey Bussell, David Ginola, Casey Keller, Paul McKenna, Colin Montgomerie, Tara Palmer-Tomkinson, Normandie Keith, Rory Bremner, Geoff Boycott, David and Victoria Beckham, Graham Norton, Chris Evans, Billie Piper, Hugh Grant
DRESS Women: little black dresses, Chanel, Escada, Joseph. Men: blazers and loafers
MUSIC Chart, R&B, House
DOOR Members only in the evening. Smart casual
DRINKS Beer £4, Wine £7, Champagne £9.50, Cocktail £9
FOOD Snacks, £10
CARDS All
CAPACITY 170, seating 45
HIRE Venue: Yes · Private Room: Yes

THE WELLINGTON CLUB

Members Club
116a Knightsbridge SW1
020 7823 8211

OPEN Mon-Sat 6pm-1am	GETTING LUCKY	4/5
TUBE/RAIL Knightsbridge	EYE CANDY	5/5
BUSES 9, 10, 52	BIG SPENDERS	4/5
	MIX 50%M 50%F	
	AGE 20-40	
	PRICE Expensive	

AMBIENCE Arty/Bohemian, Basement, Buzzy, Comfy, Cute Staff, Destination/Wishlist, Elegant/Classic, Exclusive/Chic, Funky, Hip/Fashionable, Late Night Open. Lounge Atmosphere, Minimalist, Party
REVIEW Byzantine excess, celebrity patronage, a strict – and we mean strict, not the old 'sorry guv she said her brother was inside and she looked really cold in that tiny dress' – member's policy are all factors that contribute to the creation of a legend in barland. Browns badboy Jake Panayiotou and his son Christian have opened The Wellington Club – a mansion away from mansion for those leading the high life. When he's not pouring from a personalised vodka bottle (it has the owner's name printed on the label), the learned barman reads Proust, while behind him sits The Tibetan Book of the Dead. Damien Hirst installed the artwork, Tong and Oakie set up the sound system, and the walls to the downstairs loos (which, mercifully, don't have ears or cameras) are lined with photos of friends of the management as kids – Yasmin, Sophie and Trevor – their mums must be so proud.
PLACE Minimalist space in Georgian townhouse set across two floors, each with its own distinct feel. Comfy six-seater leather bean bag downstairs for tête à têtes and bonhomie.
PEOPLE Low-profile hedonists, high-profile artistes, no wankers or flash gits please.

PROFS Arts, music and media professionals and pioneers
CELEBS Pete Tong, Paul Oakenfold, Mick Hucknall, Sophie Dahl, Ronnie Wood, Max Beesley, Mel B, Damien Hirst, Yasmin Le Bon, Trevor Sorbie, Tara Palmer-Tomkinson
DRESS Levi's, Evisu, Prada, Voyage, Gucci, Miss Sixty, Whistles, Balenciaga
MUSIC Hip Hop, Ambient, Garage, R&B, Funk, DJs Wed-Sat
DOOR Members only
DRINKS Beer £3.30, Wine £4.40, Champagne £8, Cocktail £5.50
FOOD Bar Snacks, £9
CARDS No Diners
CAPACITY 300, seating number 120
HIRE Venue: Yes · Private Room: No

THE ANGLESEA ARMS

Pub, Restaurant
15 Selwood Terrace SW7
020 7373 7960

OPEN Mon-Sat 11am-11pm,	GETTING LUCKY	3/5
Sun midday-10.30pm	EYE CANDY	3/5
TUBE/RAIL South	BIG SPENDERS	4/5
Kensington, Gloucester	MIX 70%M 30%F	
Road	AGE 20-70	
BUSES 14, 49, 345	PRICE Average	

AMBIENCE Outdoors, Conversation, Historic, Mature/Older, Old World
REVIEW A South Ken institution approved of by Charles Dickens who was a regular before he joined the Inn crowd. Great location, fab food and beer. Switch your mobile to silent when inside, for if it goes you risk profound disapproval from regulars. Someone's did, and the impertinent swine took the call indoors, whereupon 'Angry of Kensington', a silver-haired Kingsley Amis lookalike, roared, 'Decent people would go outside.' The bounder. Tourists seeking to sample a taste of genuwine English pub culture descend like whores in a Roller, as it's wood-panelled and full of wealthy claretheads with grogblossom noses. Enjoy your pint, behave yourself, and as Björk once sensibly advised, be quiet, at least, indoors.
PLACE A proper old school English boozer, so much so that possibly the most famous old English boozer, George Best, was once a regular. During summer the forecourt gets full to bursting.
PEOPLE Boozy, rich regulars arriving via Bank tube. Sample dialogue: 'I'm so emotionally drained. I will deliver on that, but tonight is not the night. I'm going to New York.'

PROFS Financiers, tourists, stockbrokers, media professionals, estate agents, doctors, antique dealers, the independently wealthy
CELEBS Jeremy Clarkson, Julian Lloyd Webber, Charles Dickens
DRESS Blue blazers and what older gents would probably call 'sneakers'. Suits and their immaculate girlfriends, American movers and shakers in Burberry scarves
MUSIC No background music

DOOR No soiled clothes
DRINKS Beer £2.80, Wine £2.85
FOOD Traditional English, Mediterranean, £6
CARDS No Amex or Diners
CAPACITY 100, seating 24
HIRE Venue: Yes · Private Room: Yes

BAR AT 190

Bar, Cocktail Bar, Hotel Bar, Restaurant
Gore Hotel, 190 Queensgate SW7
020 7581 5666

OPEN Mon-Wed 10am-1am,	GETTING LUCKY	3/5
Thu-Sat 10am-2am,	EYE CANDY	3/5
Sun 10am-midnight	BIG SPENDERS	4/5
TUBE/RAIL Gloucester Road	MIX 50%M 50%F	
BUSES 70	AGE 28-50	
	PRICE Expensive	

AMBIENCE Buzzy, Casual, Comfy, Conversation, Cute
Staff, Dancing, Groups, Late Night Open, Old World
REVIEW One of South Kensington's few bars that attract
a grown-up crowd in very grown-up surroundings.
Imagine walking into the drawing room of a Scottish
country pile full of sofas, paintings and armchairs where
you can relax with drinks served by very attractive
waitresses. Used to have a real pulling reputation and
was a haunt for sexy singletons of a certain age on
their way to the Collection. Recommended for
sophisticated courting rather than in-yer-face-pulling,
though it has been known. An old fashioned regulars'
bar which attracts a good cross-section of the affluent
set, from models to tycoons to students: impromptu
bar-top dancing makes for entertaining viewing.
PLACE Think gentleman's club: dark panelled walls
and bar, sumptuous sofas showing their age and
large oil paintings in a period Queensgate building.
PEOPLE Range from Range Rover locals and Euro
Kensington crowd to pre-Albert Hallers and models
staying in the hotel during fashion week.

PROFS Musicians, tennis players, bankers, dentists,
media execs, MPs
CELEBS Martina Navratilova, Darcey Bussell, Darryl Hall,
Robert De Niro, Al Pacino, Sting, Slash, Robbie Williams,
Elle McPherson, Dustin Hoffman
DRESS From Barbours, City suits and Dunhill blazers
to Gucci and Versace
MUSIC Dance, Lounge
DOOR 7 days, selective door policy after 10pm
DRINKS Beer £3.95, Wine £3.45, Champagne £6.95,
Cocktail £7.50
FOOD Oysters, Bar Snacks, £8

CARDS All
CAPACITY 180, seating 50
HIRE Venue: Yes · Private Room: Yes

BIBENDUM OYSTER BAR

Bar, Restaurant
Michelin House, 81 Fulham Road SW3
020 7581 5817

OPEN Mon-Sat midday-	GETTING LUCKY	2/5
11pm, Sun midday-10.30pm	EYE CANDY	4/5
TUBE/RAIL South	BIG SPENDERS	4/5
Kensington	MIX 40%M 60%F	
BUSES C1, 14, 74	AGE 25-65	
	PRICE Expensive	

AMBIENCE Conversation, Elegant/Classic,
Historic, Romantic
REVIEW Ladies who launch and lunch favour this
venue, don't be surprised to overhear greetings like
'My God, you look knockout, Stanick's a genius'. Not a
grease monkey in sight in this unique, sophisticated
Euro café bar on the former site of a Michelin garage.
This famous Conran development services the smart
local Chelsea/Continental set and neighbouring designer
retail posse at the end of the working day. 'Seating
only' means that eating soon becomes a priority and
summons a new wave of faces and agendas. Sitting
back, you can also watch the serious head upstairs to
the stiffer Bibendum Restaurant. You could well spot
someone you fancy, but the overall set-up makes it
hard to make moves.
PLACE Cool and clean as oysters on ice, immaculately
pale and interestingly tiled. Quietly romantic, French
Edwardian seafood bar in the forecourt of this landmark
Michelin building.
PEOPLE Wealthy Chelsea meets after-hours local media
and designer retail clan. At the weekends the pretty-
pack, like designer sherpas, drag engorged shopping
bags in scenes reminiscent of Pretty Woman.

PROFS Account execs, media professionals, fashion
retailers, City boys, kept women
CELEBS Sir Elton John, Lenny Henry, Dawn French,
Lucien Freud, Brian Sewell
DRESS Designer suits, girls look immaculate in Joseph
MUSIC Country, Classical, Chill-out
DOOR Smart casual
DRINKS Beer £2.95, Wine £3.50, Champagne £6.95,
Cocktail £7
FOOD Salad, Seafood, £12
CARDS No Visa
CAPACITY 45, seating 45
HIRE Venue: Yes · Private Room: No

BLAKES HOTEL BAR

Bar, Hotel Bar
Blakes Hotel, 33 Roland Gardens SW7
020 7370 6701

OPEN 7 Days midday-11pm	**GETTING LUCKY**	**2/5**
TUBE/RAIL South	**EYE CANDY**	**4/5**
Kensington	**BIG SPENDERS**	**5/5**
BUSES C1, 14, 74	**MIX** 60%M 40%F	
	AGE 25-65	
	PRICE Expensive	

AMBIENCE Basement, Business, Conversation, Cute Staff, Elegant/Classic, Exclusive/Chic, Jet Set, Romantic, Star Spotting
REVIEW Sorry, the Jade's become well... jaded and Anouska's star has descended. Hempel's world-famous hotel has, in its time, graced 101 interior design pages but the pages are getting dog-eared. The bar and its extension, 'The Chinese Room', reflect a once-celebrated design flair. Young, attractive staff in black tie attend to the local Euro/Chelsea in-crowd and hotel guests of the sort who never need carry their own Vuitton luggage. Big, bold, blue and rust signature stripes dominate the walls; copious cushions and banquettes are set off by red lacquer Chinese antiques. 'The Chinese Room' boasts enviable glossy hardbacks. Rather useful should present company bore you. Still, better to bring that date than hope to meet one.
PLACE Two small, chi-chi areas downstairs from the restaurant in this incredibly smart hotel guaranteed to drain the colour from your black card. Intimate, sexy and romantic, this is a bar to launch a thousand seductions.
PEOPLE Predominantly professional stylish 30-somethings. A lot of dates and a pre-dinner crowd.

PROFS Bankers, financiers, international business executives, tourists, lawyers, advertising executives, MDs
CELEBS Michael Flatley, Eric Clapton, Liam Gallagher, Robert De Niro, Uma Thurman, Helena Christensen, George Michael
DRESS Versace, Armani, Hugo Boss, Vivienne Westwood, Katherine Hamnett, Monsoon, Burberry. Smart suits, designer casual, a definite Gucci zone
MUSIC Ambient, Chill-out
DOOR None
DRINKS Beer £4.60, Wine £6.50, Champagne £12.50, Cocktail £12
FOOD Modern Eclectic, £20
CARDS All
CAPACITY 20, seating 10
HIRE Venue: No · Private Room: Yes

CATCH

Bar, Restaurant
158 Old Brompton Road SW5
020 7370 3300

OPEN Tue-Thu 6pm-	**GETTING LUCKY**	**4/5**
12.30am, Fri-Sat 6pm-1am	**EYE CANDY**	**4/5**
TUBE/RAIL Gloucester Road,	**BIG SPENDERS**	**4/5**
Earl's Court	**MIX** 40%M 60%F	
BUSES C1	**AGE** 22-35	
	PRICE Expensive	

AMBIENCE Basement, Conversation, Elegant/Classic, Friendly, Hip/Fashionable, Jet Set, Romantic, Star Spotting
REVIEW Catch. Of course, it's a fish restaurant. As in '... of the day.' Enter through the street entrance, past the unnecessarily burly doormen or, if eating, take the backstairs which leads to a basement bar where there are plenty more fish in the sea. Brilled-back Italiano princes, bronzed yachties, spineless bankers and petite, blonde PRs exchange numbers and fluids in this den of unbridled name-dropping. When dining you can nip down for a quick flirt and be back up before your date starts wondering what you meant by 'fixing your nose' in the ladies.
PLACE Owned by posh-bird Sophia Burrell of the much publicised Birth of Venus photo. Basement bar is all leather scatter-cubes, smooth banquettes and alcoves for those looking to joint-account their trustfunds.
PEOPLE Basement bar gets a younger party crowd who specialise in snogging the sons or daughters of Europe's rich and famous. (Oh, it's a Ferragamo! I snogged his...)

PROFS Media moguls, models, trustafarians, City boys, rich boys
CELEBS Prince Andrew, Hugh Grant, Jeremy Guscott, Chelsea Football Club, Robbie Williams
DRESS Prada, Gucci, city chic, Jigsaw, Armani, Whistles, Paul Smith, Joseph
MUSIC Funk, Euro House, R&B, DJs Tue-Sat
DOOR Thu-Sat £5 on the door after 11pm
DRINKS Beer £3.50, Wine £3.50, Champagne £6.50, Cocktail £6.50
FOOD Bar Snacks, Seafood, £5
CARDS All
CAPACITY 100, seating 50
HIRE Venue: Yes · Private Room: Yes

THE COLLECTION

Bar, Restaurant
264 Brompton Road SW3
020 7225 1212

OPEN Mon-Sat 5pm-11pm,	**GETTING LUCKY**	**4/5**
Sun 5pm-10.30pm	**EYE CANDY**	**3/5**
TUBE/RAIL South	**BIG SPENDERS**	**3/5**
Kensington	**MIX** 55%M 45%F	
BUSES C1, 14, 74	**AGE** 25-40	
	PRICE Expensive	

AMBIENCE Conversation, Elegant/Classic, Jet Set, Pulling
REVIEW The collection... mmm... a great name for a museum or art gallery. Well, there are enough oldies (Okay, 35+s) hanging around this mega-bar to fill the British Museum or at least one of its European annexes. You see, The Collection is full of Euro-bankers, suits and heavily made-up single 30-something gals who throng here having heard about the place's (justifiable) pulling reputation. Looking single at The Collection is the equivalent of arriving with a string of onions around your neck at a cannibal's cocktail party. You will be prodded, winked at and shamelessly chatted up by men who stalk the Bull and the Bear by day and the totty by night.
PLACE One of London's largest bars in a former fashion warehouse just opposite the Bibendum/Michelin building, formerly owned by Mogens Tholstrup. 60ft catwalk-style entrance to what must be one of the longest bars in London.

PEOPLE Draws broad group of clients from the City to Essex. Home of ageing 30+ 'Girl's Guide to Hunting, Shooting and Fishing' singles travelling from all over London – sadly many of the 'mothers-of-former-page-three-lookalikes' have to get trains back home so leave early.

PROFS Bankers, financiers, actors, PRs, film, TV and music professionals
CELEBS Madonna, Sting, George Michael, Johnny Vaughan, Chris Evans, Sir Elton John, Mariella Frostrup, Tara Palmer-Tomkinson, Denise van Outen, Prince Andrew
DRESS Smartish suits, too much St Tropez and a lot of cleavage tucked into tight lycra. Ralph Lauren, Hugo Boss, Versace, Joseph, Whistles, Guess
MUSIC Funky House, DJs Mon-Sat
DOOR Smart casual
DRINKS Beer £3.50, Wine £3.50, Champagne £8, Cocktail £7
FOOD Bar Snacks, £9
CARDS All
CAPACITY 350, seating 250
HIRE Venue: Yes · Private Room: No

THE ECLIPSE

Bar, Cocktail Bar
113 Walton Street SW3
020 7460 7109

OPEN Mon-Thu 5.30pm-1am, Fri 4pm-1am, Sat 2pm-1am, Sun 2pm-midnight	GETTING LUCKY	**4/5**
	EYE CANDY	**3/5**
	BIG SPENDERS	**3/5**
TUBE/RAIL South Kensington	MIX 50%M 50%F	
BUSES 11, 19, 22, 211, 319	AGE 27-47	
	PRICE Expensive	

AMBIENCE Hip/Fashionable, Late Night Open, Minimalist, Pulling
REVIEW The staff at Eclipse were loathe to discuss their venue or its impending transformation. Perhaps that's the reason they're so seldom mentioned in the press. In this heaving, narrow cocktail bar, the enthusiastic clientele might make you think that Eclipse could change your life; but, if uninitiated and/or unaccompanied, your first visit here may leave you scared and running from this side of South Ken and its invading hordes of Eurotrash. The banker boys attract the girls and vice versa, so everyone's happy, and if you're open to new experiences you, too, may be swept up in the heady, hormonal harangue. The bar's limited dimensions aid the interaction process as subtly as a can of Lynx.
PLACE Eclipse is a Jimmy Choo-shoebox of a bar with trendy, minimalist decor; it's just taken over the adjoining site which is to become a table-serviced lounge bar in a similarly earth-toned, minimalist style.
PEOPLE Americans, affluent locals, European aristocracy, It girls, Formula One drivers.

PROFS Merchant bankers, Greek and Italian marketing professionals and advertisers, lawyers
CELEBS Liz Hurley, Hugh Grant, Tara Palmer-Tomkinson, Kylie Minogue, Dannii Minogue
DRESS Suits, clothes made by your family's label, Prada, Versace, MaxMara
MUSIC Deep House, Ambient
DOOR Smart casual

DRINKS Beer £3.50, Wine £4, Champagne £8.50, Cocktail £6.50
FOOD Snacks, Sushi, £4.25
CARDS All
CAPACITY 180, seating 110
HIRE Venue: Yes · Private Room: Yes

THE ENTERPRISE

Bar, Gastropub
35 Walton Street SW3
020 7584 3148

OPEN Mon-Sat midday-11pm, Sun midday-10.30pm	GETTING LUCKY	**1/5**
	EYE CANDY	**4/5**
TUBE/RAIL South Kensington, Knightsbridge	BIG SPENDERS	**5/5**
	MIX 30%M 70%F	
BUSES 11, 19, 22, 211, 319	AGE 25-65	
	PRICE Average	

AMBIENCE Buzzy
REVIEW Although this looks like a pub, it isn't – they don't even sell pints. Well, they probably do, but asking for a pint of champagne is frightfully gauche, dahling. This is where the rich come to drink, eat and fool themselves into thinking they're in a normal boozer. Diana used to pop in here for lunch but, to be honest, she was far too closely related to that Barbara Cartland to become a regular. That said, the Enterprise still attracts a rather large amount of Di lookalikes, who sit picking at quail's eggs and fiddling with their platinum plastic. By the bar, doddery Mrs Slocombe-like relics slop G&T all over their pampered, rat-like pooches, while checking purchases from old Al Fayed's nearby hypermarket.
PLACE One room containing a small bar area, though a large, ornate mirror gives the illusion of more space. The bar itself is lined with interesting warrior-figurine lamps. Fascinating furnishings pale into insignificance compared with the punters, though.
PEOPLE Women who are named after countries that their parents used to run (Persia, India, Syria etc.), mixed with seriously flush locals, nobs looking for a post-Harrods snifter, ladies who lunch, captains of industry, and the odd guffawing polo-player.

PROFS Stockbrokers, property dealers, fashion executives, millionaires, estate agents
CELEBS Gwyneth Paltrow, John Hannah, Brendan Fraser, Nell McAndrew
DRESS Designer everything, period
MUSIC 70s, 80s, Jazz
DOOR No soiled work clothes. Smart casual
DRINKS Beer £3, Wine £3.25, Champagne £5.95, Cocktail £5.95
FOOD Hors d'ouevres, £14
CARDS No Diners
CAPACITY 90, seating 50
HIRE Venue: No · Private Room: No

ITSU BAR

Bar, Cocktail Bar, Restaurant Bar
118 Draycott Avenue SW3
020 7590 2401

OPEN Mon-Sat midday-11pm, Sun midday-10pm	**GETTING LUCKY** 1/5
	EYE CANDY 4/5
TUBE/RAIL South Kensington	**BIG SPENDERS** 4/5
	MIX 50%M 50%F
BUSES 11, 19, 22, 211, 319	**AGE** 30-45
	PRICE Average

AMBIENCE Business, Hip/Fashionable, Star Spotting
REVIEW Next to Daphnes and Bibendum with Joseph a mere credit card width away, you'd expect this bar to be stuffed with South Kensington Euros and local shop staff; you won't be disappointed. Immaculately turned-out groups of Italian hairdressers sip £7 cocktails while their customers fiddle with their shiny manes. The place itself – unless you get the prime spot on the leather sofas – is poorly lit and uncomfortable. Expensive-looking, as indeed are the few punters present, but the lack of unique character makes it seem more like a hotel lobby than a 'real' bar. Perhaps it might suit business travellers who want to relax in a flawless, orderly and impersonal ambience, but if you're looking to loosen your tie and have some fun you'd be better off booking a table downstairs.
PLACE Uniform minimalism and table service completes the 'Business First' atmosphere, with more cabin crew than punters. Very friendly staff.
PEOPLE Prosperous jet-setters who don't know London that well. Businessmen with attaché cases, sipping Kirin while tweaking a spreadsheet on their Toshiba laptop.

PROFS PRs, property agents, inscrutable business types, bankers, marketing execs, designers, footballers, models, pop stars
CELEBS Robbie Williams, Helena Christensen, Gianfranco Zola, Roberto di Matteo, Madonna, Boy George, Lawrence Dallaglio
DRESS Think gold card takes walk down the rue Faubourg-St-Honoré. Prada, Gaultier, Issey Miyake, Nicole Farhi, Patrick Cox
MUSIC Contemporary Jazz, Acid Jazz
DOOR None
DRINKS Beer £2.95, Wine £3.95, Champagne £7, Cocktail £7
FOOD Sushi, £3.50
CARDS No Diners
CAPACITY 35, seating 28
HIRE Venue: Yes · Private Room: No

LATITUDE

Bar, Members Bar
163 Draycott Avenue SW3
020 7589 8464

OPEN Mon-Sat 3pm-11pm, Sun 3pm-10.30pm	**GETTING LUCKY** 4/5
	EYE CANDY 3/5
TUBE/RAIL South Kensington	**BIG SPENDERS** 4/5
	MIX 50%M 50%F
BUSES 11, 19, 22, 211, 319	**AGE** 25-40
	PRICE Very expensive

AMBIENCE Basement, Buzzy, Pulling
REVIEW Like a World War II bunker but without the camaraderie, Latitude is cramped and dimly lit with a vague sense of desperation among its clientele. Meet the made-it but lonely thirties set at their lowest. Wage and label slaves sit tightly by their overpriced

drinks and Vuitton bags, concealing a burning desire to mingle. The girls give out the old, 'I'm really happy sharing a bottle of Grigio with my successful-but-on-the-shelf-friends' routine, but still cast furtive glances around the room. Groups of receding men stand near the door, asking every woman who leaves where she's going to next. Sadly, the law of averages would dictate that, sooner or later, someone's going to be drunk enough to spill the beans.
PLACE A brown version of Café Rouge but with nicer chairs. Long, wooden bar, benches line the perimeters, glass-fronted with nondescript fruit prints on the walls.
PEOPLE V drunk and v haggard. Smoked thirty fags, spent fifty quid and drank six cocktails. Latitude's the best bar in London, everyone's bitter like me.

PROFS Bankers, stockbrokers, financial advisers, PRs, lawyers, shop owners, fashionistas
CELEBS Vinnie Jones, Lady Victoria Hervey
DRESS Prada and Gucci worn like security blankets, Armani, Ghost, Nicole Farhi
MUSIC Funk, Lounge, House, Jazz
DOOR Smart casual
DRINKS Beer £4.50, Wine £5, Champagne £6, Cocktail £7.50
FOOD MediterrAsian, £7
CARDS No Diners
CAPACITY 150, seating 45
HIRE Venue: Yes · Private Room: No

NAM LONG-LE SHAKER

Bar, Restaurant
159 Old Brompton Road SW5
020 7373 1926

OPEN Mon-Sat 6.30pm-1am	**GETTING LUCKY** 4/5
TUBE/RAIL Gloucester Road, South Kensington	**EYE CANDY** 4/5
	BIG SPENDERS 4/5
BUSES C1	**MIX** 55%M 45%F
	AGE 25-50
	PRICE Expensive

AMBIENCE Hip/Fashionable, Jet Set, Late Night Open, Pulling, Queues
REVIEW East meets West meets Chelsea. Incorrigible Vietnamese entrepreneur, Thai Dang, and French World Cocktail Shaking Champion, Marc Boccard Schuster, have been responsible for intoxicating Londoners for over a dozen years with the most yummy yet pricey cocktails around. A terminal rush hour, get there early in the week and early in the evening if you want to enjoy a very limited, smart seated service, as weekends have club-like queues banging on the door. Naturally, the intoxicating reputation and probable consequences are a big pull, and the limited size makes for effortless interaction, whether you like it or not. Dutch courage here can quickly develop into a desperate need for Viagra. So boys, if you've always hoped to follow in your father's footsteps, avoid the 'Flaming Ferrari'. Better still, drive one ...
PLACE Not for the faint-hearted. Small narrow bar, with Vietnamese restaurant at the rear. Pretty in peach, fairy lights and foliage – short on space, big on atmosphere. Great place to spot Le Schiffer leaving Noor Jahan opposite with current arm-holder Matthew Vaughan.
PEOPLE Local Sloaney/Euro, Chelsea/Fulham

professionals who can afford aprés-ski high drink and food prices. Some irregulars at weekends.

PROFS Bankers, stockbrokers, brokers, artists, athletes, property developers, PAs
CELEBS Brad Pitt, Kevin Keegan, David Ginola, Hugh Grant, David Coulthard, Caprice Bourret, Prince Ernst of Hanover, Mick Jagger, Sir Sean Connery, Kylie
DRESS Strict warning sign on door 'No trainers, please tuck in your shirts.' Suits, designer casual, the odd fleece and rugby shirts – it goes with the postcode
MUSIC No Background Music
DOOR Smart casual, No trainers
DRINKS Beer £4, Wine £4, Champagne £8, Cocktail £8.60
FOOD Vietnamese, £8
CARDS All
CAPACITY 100, seating 60
HIRE Venue: No · Private Room: No

ZAIKA BAZAAR

Bar
2a Pond Place SW3
020 7584 6555

OPEN Mon-Sat 6pm-11pm	**GETTING LUCKY**	**2/5**
TUBE/RAIL South	**EYE CANDY**	**2/5**
Kensington	**BIG SPENDERS**	**4/5**
BUSES C1, 14, 49, 74	**MIX** 40%M 60%F	
	AGE 25-40	
	PRICE Expensive	

AMBIENCE Basement, Brightly Coloured/Cheerful, Chilled, Conversation, Opulent, Romantic
REVIEW Take one basement, sprinkle on some ethnic features (as you prefer, but stone idolatry, wicker fans and pebble water features are particularly flavoursome). Mix in sounds from the Buddha Bar or Café del Mar then leave to simmer for 20 minutes. Decorate with a largely immigrant staff so that the rich bastard clientele can reminisce about that lost summer in Phuket or gap-year in Nepal. Now you are ready to open your very own Developing Theme Bar. Ling Ling, Opium, Chinawhite, Momo... the list goes on, but the question remains – has London got room for another post-colonial big boy? Probably not, but I doubt that Momo et al are going to lose sleep over a puddle of a bar in Pond Place whose clientele has about as much life in them as the occupants of Père Lachaise.
PLACE Lots of earth colours, pebbles, urns, split-level space, very suitable for pre-dinner drinks and 'How're things going with Nigel since the op?' type chat.
PEOPLE Couples looking serious, friends looking serious, families looking serious, staff looking serious... If only Blair would really Drop The Debt.

PROFS Bankers, retailers, doctors, art collectors, estate agents
CELEBS Julien McDonald, Rupert Everett
DRESS Smart casual, verging on the conservative
MUSIC Ambient, Chill-out
DOOR None
DRINKS Beer £3, Wine £3.50, Champagne £6, Cocktail £5.50
FOOD Modern Indian, Tapas £6
CARDS All
CAPACITY 40, seating 20
HIRE Venue: Yes · Private Room: No

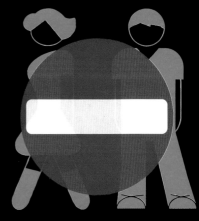

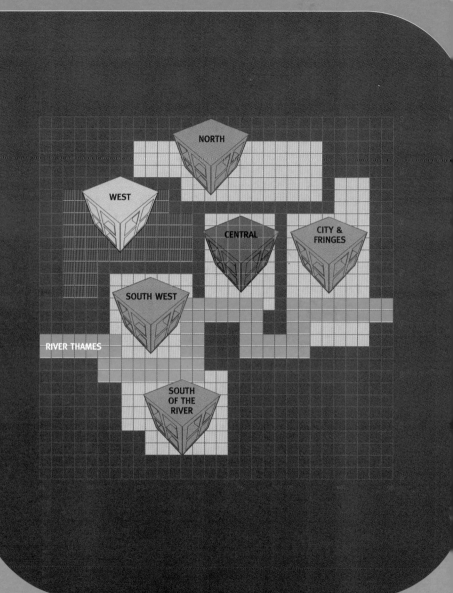

METRO

intro

WEST
hammersmith
holland park
kensington
maida vale
notting hill
portobello
shepherd's bush
westbourne park

Whatever North Londoners tell you, West London's hip pulse is still a-throbbing.

Notting Hill, from run-down Rachman ghetto and centre of racial tension to one of the most sought-after areas of London. Always an edgy, mixed bag of ethno-inspired fashion and artistes, its fashionability goes from strength to strength. Recent converts include Madonna and Guy Ritchie, Elle MacPherson and Robbie Williams; with friends like these the neighbourhood has fast outrun Hampstead in the celebrity stakes.

The Bonaparte's patrons sport more new labels than HMV and is one of the few worthwhile stops on an otherwise distinctly tourist trail. Drinking here offers a reasonably wide choice of venue but not of punters. From classic pub with great beer garden – **The Windsor Castle** – to classic bar and never-say-die **192**. **Pharmacy**'s been redeveloped (yawn) and old soldier **Beach Blanket Babylon** still exists if only as a historical curiosity to show us what one of London's first destination bars looked like. Even Will Ricker, owner of some of East London's hippest bars, has gone west and opened the celeb-friendly **e&o** bar and restaurant in the heart of Notting Hill.

The reiki-loving, rune-reading, retreat-goers of Portobello are a specialist breed. The bars here reflect this; diverse and funky, they retain more individuality than many in London.

If Portobello is the face of Notting Hill, then Westbourne Park is the underbelly, with bars like **The Cow** and **The Westbourne** still drawing the youngish, trendy urbanites. **The Cobden Club** wins the all-London prize for most unlikely location for a members club, lurking in the shadow of the Trellick Tower.

Kensington has a frightfully, frightfully, good shopping street but precious little by way of bars. You'd be wise to steer clear of **Cuba** or **Souk**, rather try the **Scarsdale Tavern**, **Bar 6** or **Wodka**. But don't expect dancing in the streets; this is, after all, an area full of overwrought bankers and their offspring.

Beautiful Holland Park is just that, and since when have scenic beauty and electrodes-in-your-shorts nightlife ever shared the same space in London? It's the kind of place your parents would like. **The Halcyon** and **Julies** are firmly established old-school watering holes.

Shepherd's Bush is now picking up the Notting Hill rejects, and with it a steady cash injection has gone into an area which, only a couple of years ago, was about as appealing as coiled black hair in your latte. **The Bush Bar and Grill** has drawn out the beautiful birds in the Bush, and the eagerly anticipated K-West Hotel will be the first five star in the area.

Really no reason to make the long journey to Hammersmith, and indeed few do. Back in the day, office workers travelled far and wide to cop off in the Hammersmith Palais of a Saturday night, nothing much has changed other than it's now called **Po Na Na** and they're wearing school uniforms.

What do music entrepreneurs and property tycoons do when their bellies get too big for the Lotus? Trade it in for a Benno and move north and westish to Maida Vale. Located in Nouveau Circus, **Le Cochonnet** remains a staple for the gold Rolex-wearing wheelers and dealers of West London, while the recently rejigged **Otto** holds more paunch than punch and **Woody**s despite its recent sale remains a fab destination for under 30s.

Recent and future openings:

Steam Bar, London Hilton, Paddington
Canvas, 177 Portobello Road
K-Lounge, K-West Hotel, Richmond Way
Grand Union, 45 Woodfield Road

hammersmith

THE GROVE

Bar, Restaurant, Restaurant Bar
83 Hammersmith Grove W6
020 8748 2966

OPEN Mon-Sat 11am-midnight, Sun 11am-11pm	**GETTING LUCKY**	**2/5**
	EYE CANDY	**3/5**
TUBE/RAIL Hammersmith, Goldhawk Road	**BIG SPENDERS**	**3/5**
	MIX 50%M 50%F	
BUSES 9, 10, 33, 209, 94, 237	**AGE** 20-39	
	PRICE Average	

AMBIENCE Brightly Coloured/Cheerful, Children/Families, Conversation, Friendly, Groups, Outdoors
REVIEW The Cinderella of Hammersmith Grove transformed from a grotty old boozer into an REM pub for the shiny happy people of W6. It has a real neighbourhood feel, an echo of the local it once was. At weekends, when the outside tables fill up, the air is thick with cries of 'ohmygodimagineseeingyou' and 'Camillayoulookamaaaazing'. Blond pony tails swing, long lost friends embrace, 'Perfect Day' plays on a loop and organic house champagne costs £16.95 a bottle in happy hour.
PLACE Summery yellow walls and sage green woodwork. Stripped floorboards, pine furniture, a comfy Chesterfield and two wing-backed armchairs in the bar area complete the Homes and Gardens feel. A Goethe quote is scribbled across the back wall, above a mural of lemons. At its best when the sun is shining.
PEOPLE Well-moisturised smart girls in skirts and pumps and pairs of boys in suits. Non-predatory singles feel comfortable, hence a few lone females with books.

PROFS TV, film and motor industry professionals
CELEBS Ralph Fiennes, Victor Ubogu
DRESS Middle-class informal, Muji, Gap, sleeveless puffas
MUSIC Jazz, Blues, Soft Rock
DOOR None
DRINKS Beer £2.85, Wine £2.75, Champagne £5.50
FOOD Modern European, £12.50
CARDS No Amex or Diners
CAPACITY 130, seating 100
HIRE Venue: Yes · Private Room: Yes

PO NA NA

Club, Theme
242 Shepherd's Bush Road W6
0800 7837 485

OPEN Tue 10pm-3am, Fri 10pm-3am, Sat 9pm-3am	**GETTING LUCKY**	**5/5**
	EYE CANDY	**2/5**
TUBE/RAIL Hammersmith	**BIG SPENDERS**	**3/5**
BUSES 72, 220, 283, 295	**MIX** 50%M 50%F	
	AGE 18-30	
	PRICE Average	

AMBIENCE Bump 'n' Grind, Dancing, Groups, Late Night Open, Live Music, Party, Pulling, Student
REVIEW If you enjoy the oily aftertaste of 70s budget porn then Po Na Na (formerly the 'Ammersmiff Palay)

is the discotheque for you. One of the original superclubs, it now offers that particular variety of watered-down, Kiss FM-bolstered clubbing 'experience' that gets the more seasoned beat freak seething into his chewed water bottle. Special nights include two-step giants The Dreem Teem's monthly, as well as regular 'Balearic excursions', offering acne'd clubbers the chance to relive summers in Oibeefa. Top of the pops, however, is Saturday's temple of tack, the peculiarly British School Disco. Can you picture young Italians discarding their Dolce in favour of pencilled-on freckles and a shrunken games kit? Thought not.
PLACE A Hercules air hanger-sized dance floor still leaves you contemplating lobbying for the introduction of a national dancing licence. It's typical Po Na Na bohème à la budget, all white trash whorehouse lanterns and leopard print, just on a very large scale.
PEOPLE House nights witness a lively bunch, out to get bladdered and groped in the nearest fire exit. Garage nights see oiled-up, greased-down teens bumping and grinding in ways that would shock their mothers and probably their sisters.

PROFS Office workers, retail staff, students, bar staff, PRs, secretaries
CELEBS Steps, Mick Jagger, EastEnders and Hollyoaks cast
DRESS Miss Selfridge/Burtons on a week when the fashion director was off sick, with a few designer logos thrown in.
MUSIC Commercial Dance, Disco, UK Garage, Handbag House, R&B, 80s, Balearic Beats
DOOR Smart, no tracksuits or hoods; Sat school uniform only; entrance £7-£12
DRINKS Beer £3, Wine £3, Cocktails £4
FOOD Snacks, £5
CARDS All
CAPACITY 2230, seating 350
HIRE Venue: Yes · Private Room: Yes

THE STONEMASON'S ARMS

Gastropub
54 Cambridge Grove W6
020 8748 1397

OPEN Mon-Sat midday-11pm, Sun midday-10.30pm	**GETTING LUCKY**	**4/5**
	EYE CANDY	**3/5**
TUBE/RAIL Hammersmith	**BIG SPENDERS**	**3/5**
BUSES 9, 10, 33, 209, 211, 266	**MIX** 50%M 50%F	
	AGE 25-39	
	PRICE Average	

AMBIENCE Casual, Cute Staff, Groups, Pulling
REVIEW Yet another former salt 'n' vinegar crisps boozer joining the gastropubbery stampede across London. The Stonemason's Arms lurks in the nether regions of the Hammersmith one-way system, but once inside, everyone swears they're in Fulham. As a rule, the place manages to get busy enough to make you feel you're somewhere popular, but not so busy that you can feel your hair grey as you wave your hopeful tenner at the bar. Full marks for the staff, incidentally, who are helpful, informed, friendly and – oh yes – alarmingly good-looking.
PLACE Exactly what you would see if you closed your eyes, clicked your heels three times and murmured 'gastropub': stripped wood floors, white-ish walls, experienced-looking wooden tables of varying sizes and chairs and benches of ecclesiastical provenance.
PEOPLE A young-ish crowd of the 'New W6-ers'. Groups and couples sit at the tables and pairs of girly singles perch at the bar drinking long, brightly-coloured drinks and chewing their straws in a way that would delight Helmut Newton.

PROFS Media girls, IT boys, musicians, traffic wardens, local retailers, cab drivers, hairdressers
CELEBS The Bluetones, The Alarm, Hugh Scully, John Torode, Jody Morris
DRESS Lots of neutral colours, Gwyneth Paltrow hairdos and young men in old jumpers
MUSIC Pop, Jazz, Latin American, House, Reggae
DOOR None
DRINKS Beer £2.70, Wine £2.70, Cocktail £4.50
FOOD Nouveau European, £8
CARDS No Diners
CAPACITY 150, seating 60
HIRE Venue: No · Private Room: No

holland park

THE ACADEMY

Restaurant Bar
57 Princedale Road W11
020 7221 0248

OPEN Mon-Sat midday-11pm, Sun midday-10.30pm TUBE/RAIL Holland Park BUSES 94	GETTING LUCKY	**4/5**
	EYE CANDY	**3/5**
	BIG SPENDERS	**4/5**
	MIX 45%M 55%F	
	AGE 25-45	
	PRICE Average	

AMBIENCE Cute Staff, Pulling, Conversation
REVIEW We've bought enough Marlboro Lights to sit out the evening until my friend's dress gets a propitious reaction from the well-to-do Lock, Stock types who frequent the Academy. The first thing we notice, though, is that lots of other women seem to have had the same idea. They're everywhere: tanned and impeccably dressed, sipping demurely at their wine and flicking ash like Lauren Bacall wannabes. But when some guys finally do show up later it appears The Academy is Holland Park's answer to 'Cheers' – everyone knows nearly everyone else, and if they don't, they're not interested.
PLACE Behind the wooden slatted blinds it's a mix of modern and antique, with cream walls, wooden floors, original oils and pen and ink drawings in gold frames.
PEOPLE Camilla and Emma both live locally in their parents' townhouses which they now have pretty much to themselves. They're young professionals with Holmes Place memberships and use Harvey Nick's bags to line their pedal bins.

PROFS Media, advertising, TV and music executives
CELEBS None
DRESS Joseph, Whistles, Harvey Nichols
MUSIC Jazz
DOOR Kevin Spacey, Dire Straits, Terrorvision
DRINKS Beer £2.40, Wine £2.65, Cocktails £3
FOOD Modern Eclectic, £9
CARDS No Amex or Diners
CAPACITY 100, seating 50
HIRE Venue: No · Private Room: No

THE CASTLE

Pub
100 Holland Park Avenue W11
020 7313 9301

OPEN Mon-Sat 11am-11pm, Sun midday-10.30pm TUBE/RAIL Holland Park BUSES 94	GETTING LUCKY	**4/5**
	EYE CANDY	**3/5**
	BIG SPENDERS	**3/5**
	MIX 55%M 45%F	
	AGE 20-45	
	PRICE Average	

AMBIENCE Buzzy, Casual, Conversation, Groups, Grunge, Party, Pulling
REVIEW Seedy pub in neo-grunge style. Live DJs spin deep funk and funky house from Thursdays till Saturdays. A spilt-beer, sticky tables kind of place, The Castle is packed with a mix of groovers and suits who all seem totally up for a messy night out. The only pub in the area which combines fusion food (British/Mediterranean) with great music and a happening vibe. Very matey, buzzy atmosphere, but not too naff or sleazy. Even though it's one of the last bastions of Notting Hill's old boozers there's not an American tourist in sight. It's one of those pubs where another quick one always seems like the best idea you ever had.
PLACE Very much a small, old-style local with 150 years of history. High and heavy scuffed bar stools; dark-wood veneer tables in the front bar.
PEOPLE Young, well-off local media groovesters mix happily with pissed suits on their way home. Everyone seems well on the road to getting cheerfully lashed.

PROFS Musicians, city workers, lawyers, publicists, hotel staff
CELEBS Richard Branson, Robbie Williams, Ian Brown, Chris Penn, John Cleese, Dani Behr, Ed Harris
DRESS Carhartt, Pink, jeans and combats
MUSIC Dance, House, Funk DJs Thu-Sat
DOOR None
DRINKS Beer £2.90, Wine £2.85
FOOD Mediterranean, Modern British, £8
CARDS No Amex or Diners
CAPACITY 350, seating 100
HIRE Venue: No · Private Room: Yes

THE HALCYON

Cocktail Bar, Hotel Bar
81 Holland Park W11
020 7727 7288

OPEN 7 days 11am 11pm	**GETTING LUCKY**	**1/5**
TUBE/RAIL Holland Park	**EYE CANDY**	**4/5**
BUSES 94	**BIG SPENDERS**	**4/5**
	MIX 50%M 50%F	
	AGE 30-60	
	PRICE Expensive	

AMBIENCE Basement, Conversation, Exclusive/Chic, Jet Set, Star Spotting
REVIEW With Richard Branson as its next-door neighbour you wouldn't expect this Holland Park bar to be anything other than quietly stylish and achingly expensive. They filmed parts of Mission Impossible here, and its clientele are made up of film and music stars who love the faux English country house look and the I'm-not-here-but-really-I-am exclusivity. The scent of money fills The Halcyon's hallowed halls, filtering down to the basement bar where hotel residents, pre-diners and locals chat quietly and nibble on probably the most expensive cashews in the world.
PLACE A baby pink period building on a stunning corner of Holland Park Avenue. Enter through the hotel lobby and go down a tiny staircase to the bar. (You'll get lost if you don't ask.)
PEOPLE The hotel is a retreat for the stars – music and showbiz – who sometimes come to the bar but are more than likely to be secreted away in the restaurant. Mariella Frostrup was chortling into her mobile on the night we were there.

PROFS Music execs, TV execs, brokers, traders, PRs, property developers, writers, artists
CELEBS Mick Jagger, Van Morrison, Elvis Costello, Al Pacino, Robert De Niro, Tom Cruise, Nicole Kidman, Mariella Frostrup, Noel Edmonds, Andrew Morton, Mick Jagger, Mick Hucknall, Kate Moss
DRESS Gieves & Hawkes for the men, MaxMara for the women, jeans and Gucci sunglasses for the stars
MUSIC Jazz, Chill-out
DOOR Open to non-residents until 11pm
DRINKS Beer £3.25, Wine £4.25, Champagne £9, Cocktail £7.50
FOOD Modern French, £13
CARDS All
CAPACITY 50, seating 30
HIRE Venue: No · Private Room: No

JULIE'S BAR

Bar, Restaurant, Wine Bar
137 Portland Road W11
020 7727 7985

OPEN Mon-Sat 9am-11.30pm, Sun 10am-10.30pm	**GETTING LUCKY**	**1/5**
	EYE CANDY	**3/5**
TUBE/RAIL Holland Park	**BIG SPENDERS**	**3/5**
BUSES 94	**MIX** 50%M 50%F	
	AGE 30-55	
	PRICE Average	

AMBIENCE Business, Conversation, Cosy, Groups, Old World, Outdoors, Romantic
REVIEW It may be just a few minutes down the road from Portobello, but you can bet your bottle of Montrachet you'll be safe from the noodle-slurping market hordes. Tucked away from it all on a leafy residential road, this well-established bar offers a secluded retreat from the feeding-time-at-the-zoo W11 frenzy. A classy old-school wine bar (and proud of it), it's the sort of place you'd take your parents/grandparents/clients, or where you'd go with your friends to reassure yourselves that you've really made it.
PLACE If the small shabby chic ground-floor bar area or the tables on the street should somehow prove too hectic, withdraw yourself to the upstairs room where Gothic wood pews and stained windows create a hushed timewarp.
PEOPLE Ageing old-money locals rub shoulders with distinctly less charming moneyed young Notting Hill/Holland Park professionals in an atmosphere of sedate opulence.

PROFS Film, TV and radio professionals
CELEBS Joseph Fiennes, Madonna, Prince Charles, Eric Clapton, Helen Mirren, Sting, Tina Turner, Kate Moss, Naomi Campbell, Richard Branson, Sarah Cracknell, Robbie Williams, Jeremy Clarkson
DRESS Voyage, Whistles, Donna Karan, Nicole Farhi, Paul Smith, Timothy Everest, Savile Row
MUSIC Easy Listening, Jazz
DOOR None
DRINKS Beer £3, Wine £3, Champagne £6, Cocktail £5.50
FOOD Modern European, £10.95
CARDS No Diners
CAPACITY 100, seating 50
HIRE Venue: Yes · Private Room: No

kensington

BAR 6

Bar
6 Holland Street W8
020 7937 3367

OPEN Tue-Sat 6pm-11pm	GETTING LUCKY	**2/5**
TUBE/RAIL Kensington High	EYE CANDY	**3/5**
Street, Notting Hill	BIG SPENDERS	**3/5**
BUSES 27, 28, 52, 70, 328	MIX 40%M 60%F	
	AGE 25-45	
	PRICE Average	

AMBIENCE Conversation, Casual
REVIEW Bar 6 is set on one of those London streets that caused collective sighs from US tourists... when we had them. Improbably quaint with dolls house terraces, you're as likely to bump into Laura Bailey and Jeremy Irons as one of the glass milk bottles standing on guard outside the multi-million-pound houses. Bar 6 fits the Lilliputian dimensions of this one way backwater perfectly. Housed next to a cutesy tea room, if you stopped to blow your nose you'd miss it. Peach, oblong and candlelit, Bar 6 is home to some of the most uncomfortable seats ever designed but has a charm and idiosyncrasy so many places lack. Which is perhaps why it is either totally empty – apart from an Eastern-Euro babe who brings the drinks or a rather scary looking bloke – or very full. Either way, don't worry yourself as to how it stays in business, just savour the fact that it's a great spot to relax and chat in this virtually bar-free quarter.
PLACE Modern, peach and rather small but nicely lit at night. Rather bare downstairs chill-out room.
PEOPLE A rag tag of local residents, professional shoppers or star players at McKinsey or Yahoo! out for a quick post-work beer.

PROFS Media employees, gym workers, publishing doyennes, nannies
CELEBS None
DRESS Suits, Jigsaw, Barker's best
MUSIC Lounge Music
DOOR None
DRINKS Beer £3.50, Wine £3.50, Champagne £6.50, Cocktail £5.50
FOOD Peanuts
CARDS No Amex or Diners
CAPACITY 35, seating 30
HIRE Venue Yes · Private Room Yes

CUBA

Bar, Live Music Venue, Restaurant, Theme
11-13 Kensington High Street W8
020 7938 4137

OPEN Mon-Sat midday-2am,	GETTING LUCKY	**3/5**
Sun 2pm-10pm	EYE CANDY	**3/5**
TUBE/RAIL High Street	BIG SPENDERS	**2/5**
Kensington	MIX 50%M 50%F	
BUSES 9, 10, 52, 70	AGE 21-40	
	PRICE Average	

AMBIENCE Casual, Dancing, Groups, Late Night Open, Live Music, Party, Student,
REVIEW Opposite Kensington Palace – where tourists come for an authentic Diana experience – Cuba attempts to recreate a Cuban one. Often very busy and always noisy, Cuba is as downmarket as most central Latin locations. It caters mainly for local retail workers, residents and tourists, but it also pulls in a real Latin American crowd who like nothing better than dragging the Brits on to the dance floor for that salsa initiation/ humiliation. It can get hot, sweaty and sexy down there as the Chilean chiquitas do their thing. The tightly packed bar (think Tube width) encourages mingling, but volume levels/language barriers require postgraduate sign-language skills.
PLACE The grotesque, papier-mâché, caricatured Cuban in the window could have been forklifted straight out of a regional theme park. Inside it's splashed with cheap and cheerful Dulux: a hint of a tint of terracotta, cactus green and banana republic yellow. You drink at ground level, dine on the raised platform and dance downstairs.
PEOPLE Shop assistants with media studies degrees, impressed by a mulch of crushed mint in their cocktails. They'd all probably be working on an album/collection/ novel/exhibition after work if they didn't spend all their time out gossiping about Will & Grace and Ally McBeal ('I mean, she's looking sick'). Students with Saturday jobs ('no grant will cover the price of these drinks').

PROFS Students, journalists, shop workers, stallholders, caterers, hotel staff
CELEBS Terry Venables, Brian May, Anita Dobson, The Honeyz, Jordan Knight, Meatloaf, Jo Guest, Liam Gallagher, Mark Owen
DRESS Unisex uniforms, Gap, FCUK, Whistles, dumb slogan t-shirts, combats, Diesel, the odd suit and Kensington-cred threads
MUSIC Fri-Sat salsa/live bands; Mon 80s, 90s, salsa; Tue-Wed Latin American sounds; Thu Brazilian
DOOR Fri-Sat £5 10.30pm-1am, Mon-Thu £3 after 9.30pm, Fri-Sat £5 from 9.30-10.30pm, post-10.30pm £8
DRINKS Beer £2.95, Wine £3.45, Champagne £4.65, Cocktail £5.25
FOOD Cuban, Spanish, Tapas, £8
CARDS All
CAPACITY 297, seating 68
HIRE Venue: Yes · Private Room: Yes

DEVONSHIRE ARMS

Pub
37 Marlowes Road W8
020 7937 0710

OPEN midday-11pm,	GETTING LUCKY	**3/5**
midday-10.30pm	EYE CANDY	**3/5**
TUBE/RAIL High Street	BIG SPENDERS	**3/5**
Kensington	MIX 65%M 35%F	
BUSES 9, 10, 27, 28,	AGE 25-50	
49, 328	PRICE Average	

AMBIENCE Conversation, Groups, Historic, Old World, Outdoors
REVIEW While many men go out in the hope of ensnaring those of multiple mammaries, here is a pub devoted to the double breasted. From pinstripes to charcoal-grey-clad architects, enter a world where the chaps turn up in turn-ups. Not a place to let your hair down or roll your shirtsleeves up, but if you want to be with gallery owners, antique dealers, architects and their ilk, you could do a lot worse. The real ale's great (Guinness, Pedigree, Burton's), the atmosphere is familiar but not cramped, the music hardly adventurous top tens, the service is friendly and there's a pretty, heated beer garden at the front. Not a theme in site, so undo the top button, hoick down the tie and relax.
PLACE Halfway between Earl's Court and High St Kensington, the Devonshire is a haven in residential W8. It's clean, well-kept and traditional in feel with wall upon wall of real oak panelling.
PEOPLE Local professionals, office workers with time for a quickie, rich locals; it's an Antipodean-Free Zone – surprising, given its proximity to Earl's Court.

PROFS Bankers, IT specialists, travel agents, medium-ranking executives, drama students, secretaries/PAs, antique dealers, editors, record industry execs
CELEBS Dennis Wise, Tom Parker Bowles, Gwyneth Paltrow, Eddie Izzard, Hugh Grant, Pamela Armstrong
DRESS For the girls, from local Ken purchases to Nicole Farhi and Betty Barclay. For the guys, Tom Pink shirts to Paul Smith. Tuck your shirts in here.
MUSIC Blues, Jazz, 60s, Dance, Pop, Rock
DOOR None
DRINKS Beer £2.60, Wine £2.70
FOOD Pub Food, £6.50

CARDS No Diners
CAPACITY 150, seating 30
HIRE Venue: No · Private Room: No

GOOLIES

Restaurant Bar, Wine Bar
21 Abingdon Road W8
020 7938 1122

OPEN Mon-Fri 12.30pm-	GETTING LUCKY	**2/5**
10.30pm, Sat 6.30pm-11pm,	EYE CANDY	**3/5**
Sun 12.30pm-10pm	BIG SPENDERS	**4/5**
TUBE/RAIL High Street	MIX 50%M 50%F	
Kensington	AGE 25-60	
BUSES 28, 31	PRICE Average	

AMBIENCE Brightly Coloured/Cheerful, Business, Casual, Conversation
REVIEW The silly name is the fault of Aussie owner, Mike Goolie, who clearly wasn't ribbed about it nearly enough at school. Legend has it that in its previous incarnation, this was Mike's favourite bar. As the owner of Trailfinders he took a few months off to travel and on his return found the bar closed down, so he bought it. He who drinks Australian etc... Anyhow, Goolies is far from being the Foster's mean's pub. It's a refined little wine bar/restaurant tucked away from the Ken High St tourists, where you can get a decent slug of Lagavulin in the winter, or a bottle of Dom Perignon in the summer.
PLACE Even though it's gone for a 'modern' look with its bright yellow and blue colour scheme, pop music and laid-back bar staff, Goolies tends to attract a rather tweedy set who can make fourth or fifth generation money feel dreadfully nouveau.
PEOPLE Of the Nicole/Papa school. Well groomed, buffed and guffawed. These are people who buy their kids brand new cars on their 17th birthdays and 'get a man in to hang the curtains.'

PROFS Bankers, financiers, advertising executives, travel agents, tour operators, those for whom the state pension pays their dog-food bills
CELEBS Sean Scott, Diana Rigg, Jennifer Powell, Noel Edmonds, Vanessa Mae, Terry Venables
DRESS Jaeger for the Russell & Bromley-booted ladies, Gieves & Hawkes for men in suits
MUSIC Easy Listening
DOOR None
DRINKS Beer £3, Wine £3, Champagne £7.50
FOOD Pacific Rim, Seafood, £12
CARDS All
CAPACITY 65, seating 40
HIRE Venue: Yes · Private Room: Yes

PO NA NA SOUK BAR

Bar, Club, Theme
20 Kensington Church Street W8
020 7795 6656

OPEN Mon-Sat 7.30pm-2am	GETTING LUCKY	**2/5**
TUBE/RAIL High Street	EYE CANDY	**2/5**
Kensington, Notting Hill	BIG SPENDERS	**2/5**
Gate	MIX 50%M 50%F	
BUSES 27, 28, 52, 70, 328	AGE 22-38	
	PRICE Average	

AMBIENCE Basement, Dancing, Late Night Open
REVIEW Converted from the tawdry Gothic dungeon that was Kensington's 'Za Zu Bar', the takeover by Po Na Na ensures that this cellar retains a ridiculous three-syllable name and Aussie staff. The makeover hasn't been entirely successful. Although they're aiming for that genuinely exotic 'Turkish delight' atmosphere, the place has ended up looking more like a low-budget Indiana Jones set. Much of the original gothy wrought-iron work remains, helped along by a few arches and alcoves and some red and blue lighting. They've also popped a traditionally exotic pool table out the back. They seem to have been successful in chasing away the sleazier clientele from its former incarnation as Za Zu.
PLACE Through the 'lost civilisation'-style doorway of Kensington Church Street, down a convincingly dingy staircase, Po Na Na Souk Bar is a cavernous joint with endless nooks and crannies. Fairly tame, BHS homeware decor in ethnic themes.

PEOPLE Junior professionals from local media companies, in awkward or conspiratorial groups.
PROFS Retail workers, music industry and publishing execs, travel/estate agents, students
CELEBS REM, Anna Friel
DRESS From media-black suits with polo necks through BHS greys to Kensington Market freshman grunge. Most of these people don't give a FCUK about fashion
MUSIC House, Garage, Funk, Hip Hop, Soul, R&B, DJs Mon-Sat
DOOR Smart casual, no trainers; £3-5 after 9.30pm
DRINKS Beer £2.50, Wine £3, Champagne £5, Cocktail £5.50
FOOD Snacks, £15
CARDS No Diners
CAPACITY 100, seating 20
HIRE Venue: Yes · Private Room: Yes

SCARSDALE TAVERN

Pub
23a Edwardes Square W8
020 7937 1811

OPEN Mon-Sat midday-	GETTING LUCKY	3/5
11pm, Sun midday-10.30pm	EYE CANDY	3/5
TUBE/RAIL Earl's Court,	BIG SPENDERS	3/5
High Street Kensington,	MIX 50%M 50%F	
Kensington (Olympia)	AGE 25-45	
BUSES 9, 10, 27, 28, 49	PRICE Cheap	

AMBIENCE Casual, Conversation, Cosy, Friendly, Historic, Intellectual/Literary, Outdoors, Romantic
REVIEW A great country-style pub stuck in the middle of residential Kensington for those that can't afford the country pad, given the exodus on Friday nights round here, is not many. In a splendidly tree-lined residential square – forgive the Estate Agent patois – it's an ideal spot to settle yourself on the patio with a cold one. In winter it's a pretty attractive prospect, too, with its open fire, bare brick walls, oil paintings, subtle lighting and small tables à deux. Actually, there is a bit of a French theme here in Edwardes Square, which Louis Changeur built for the Emperor Napoleon in anticipation of his forthcoming occupation of London. Bit cheeky, but he did a good job.

PLACE French glass-and-wrought iron porch, Napoleonic baggage wagon and pretty English hanging baskets outside. Inside, it's North Downs rural.
PEOPLE Friendly mishmash of arties and young Piaggio-scooting trendsters. Writers, publishers, locals, web weavers, coppers from the local station and record industry employees come together. No shop talk, just great beer, good gastropub food, unobtrusive music and a glowing ambience.

PROFS Journalists, property developers, lawyers, bankers, brokers, estate agents, police, blue-chip company directors, antique dealers, A&R men
CELEBS Dustin Hoffman, Catherine Zeta Jones, Dan Strauss, Madonna, Guy Ritchie, Philip Seymour-Hoffman, The Bill cast, Casualty cast
DRESS Mature businessmen in Huntsman and Gieves & Hawkes tailor-made, younger guys in Uth and trainers, older smoothies in black Armani, estate agents in blue Thomas Pink shirts, yellow ties and 9ct gold signet rings. A few females spotted wearing Racing Green
MUSIC Easy Listening, Chart, Pop
DOOR None
DRINKS Beer £2.60, Beer £2.50
FOOD Modern European, Pub Food, £9
CARDS All
CAPACITY 100, seating 60
HIRE Venue: Yes · Private Room: No

WODKA

Restaurant Bar
12 S. Alban's Grove W8
020 7937 6513

OPEN Lunch Mon-Fri	GETTING LUCKY	2/5
12.30pm-2.30pm, Mon-Sun	EYE CANDY	3/5
Dinner 7pm-11.15pm	BIG SPENDERS	3/5
TUBE/RAIL High Street	MIX 50%M 50%F	
Kensington	AGE 25-40	
BUSES 9, 31, 49, 73, 74	PRICE Average	

AMBIENCE Conversation
REVIEW The last thing you would expect to find on a smart little tucked-away Kensington street like St Alban's Grove is a Polish restaurant, which gives Wodka an air of eccentricity. Forget nasty balalaikas, this bar and restaurant is an altogether smarter interpretation of Eastern European eating and drinking. The eponymous drink, of course, is the mainstay of the bar, with dozens of different varieties flavoured with everything from honey to gold leaf, as well as a range of cocktails. Drunkenness, needless to say, is commonplace, although it is generally of the genteel, Kensington variety: this is not, after all, a place for vodka louts.
PLACE The interior is more like a moody, modern club than a Polish restaurant: calm, bare rooms with original features and the odd bit of art.
PEOPLE Lunchtime – freelance journalists (Evening Standard, Mail). Evening – US tourists, 25-40s, media (professional types, locals).

PROFS Bankers, tourists, media professionals, journalists, savvy shoppers
CELEBS Ken Livingstone, David Bowie, Ian Holme, Jerry Hall, Brian Sewell, Mick Jagger, Hugh Grant, Stephen Dorff

DRESS Clothes that are always pressed and look like they've just come from the dry cleaners from shops/ designers that end in -ium or -ius somewhere in 'the centre of town'
MUSIC Jazz
DOOR None
DRINKS Beer £2.75, Wine £2.75, Champagne £4.50
FOOD Polish, £11.50
CARDS All
CAPACITY 60, seating 60
HIRE Venue: Yes · Private Room: Yes

maida vale

LE COCHONNET

Restaurant, Restaurant Bar
1 Lauderdale Road W9
020 7289 0393

OPEN Mon-Sat midday-midnight, Sun midday-11pm	GETTING LUCKY	4/5
TUBE/RAIL Maida Vale	EYE CANDY	3/5
BUSES 6, 36	BIG SPENDERS	2/5
	MIX 50%M 50%F	
	AGE 25-45	
	PRICE Average	

AMBIENCE Conversation, Groups, Outdoors, Pulling
REVIEW Like your neighbour's conifer, this mature wine bar and pizzeria has grown rapidly over the years to accommodate the never-ending flow of good-looking singles passing through this wealthy first-time-buyers' neighbourhood. Owner Peter Colman claims The Cosh keeps the satellite areas of Queens Park, Brondesbury and West Hampstead supplied with couples who marry, breed and spend their joint incomes in the restaurants and baby shops of West London. So what does he want? Commission?
PLACE Anonymous spread in a quaint shopping parade in the middle of a high-density residential area. Extensive pavement seating area adds a Riviera touch (river area touch when wet).
PEOPLE Home to most of the younger sections of the music, fashion and media industry mixed with an older gold Rolex and Range Rover crowd.
PROFS Estate agents, PRs, TV and radio execs, stylists, models, DJs
CELEBS Kate Moss, Meg Matthews, Nicole Appleton, Jamie Theakston, Susie Bick
DRESS Result dressing: Joseph, Paul & Joe, Diesel, Voyage
MUSIC Jazz, Chart
DOOR None
DRINKS Beer £2.75, Wine £2.50, Champagne £4.50
FOOD Italian, Pizza, £8.50
CARDS All
CAPACITY 130, seating 97
HIRE Venue: No · Private Room: No

OTTO DINING LOUNGE

Bar, Restaurant
215 Sutherland Avenue W9
020 7266 3131

OPEN Mon-Sat 6pm-11pm	GETTING LUCKY	1/5
TUBE/RAIL Maida Vale	EYE CANDY	3/5
BUSES 6, 187	BIG SPENDERS	5/5
	MIX 50%M 50%F	
	AGE 20-70	
	PRICE Expensive	

AMBIENCE Business, Conversation, Lounge Atmosphere, Mature/Older
REVIEW The Otto Dining Lounge seemed like such a good idea; a designer-dwarf's throw from the Starck-designed Yoo apartments in this affluent neighbourhood largely bereft of bars. However, it's hard to imagine it ever heaves with people or atmosphere. The bar, with its Esso-Tesco Express vista, has the unsalutary air of a motorway phone booth, so unsettling that most of the drinkers behave like they're in an airport terminal, texting and talking on mobiles, staring out of the window, waiting for that gate call that never comes. The cocktails are sickeningly sweet, vodka espresso Martinis taste like Tia Maria straight up and the Margarita may well just be pure lime juice. Shame, because Otto looks nice, but then it's concrete and glass proof that looks ain't everything.
PLACE Aspen ski-lodge meets Scandinavian airport lounge bar and restaurant with flight-observation-sized windows, wood panelling, low chunky sofas and not a wonky line in sight.
PEOPLE Vuitton-tanned local residents nod hello to each other across the room, spoilt little rich girls with preppy boyfriends, 'mature' couples, Botox-ed mamas, sugar papas, Middle Eastern dandies, the odd trendy fashion dahlin'.
PROFS Oil barons, diplomats, fashionistas, retired people, chairmen
CELEBS None
DRESS Polo necks and pink pashminas abound, a sequinned top here and there, Hermes bag there. John Smedley, Ronit Zilkha, Liberty, Dunhill, Earl Jeans, Manolo Blahnik, Agnés B
MUSIC Lounge Music
DOOR Smart
DRINKS Beer £3.50, Wine £4.20, Champagne £6.50, Cocktail £7
FOOD Modern European, £9
CARDS All
CAPACITY 120, seating 60
HIRE Venue: Yes · Private Room: No

THE VALE

Restaurant Bar
99 Chippenham Road W9
020 7266 0990

OPEN Mon-Sat 7pm-11pm	GETTING LUCKY	2/5
TUBE/RAIL Maida Vale	EYE CANDY	2/5
BUSES 31, 36, 328	BIG SPENDERS	3/5
	MIX 50%M 50%F	
	AGE 35-65	
	PRICE Average	

AMBIENCE Basement, Conversation, Groups, Mature/Older
REVIEW Buried a few feet beneath a blossoming restaurant, The Vale's sunken bar is a bit of a looker –

shame about the personality. Although this bar has plenty of potential, it's clearly under heavy sedation and desperately needs a jump lead. The Vale bar's history to date is a bit like the Titanic's – glamorously decorated with an air of indestructibility, overshadowed by the fact that it sunk like a stone. Not a bad place for an undisturbed chat and a sit down, but most customers stay firmly rooted in the better-known upstairs restaurant.
PLACE Uneasy access via a sophisticated spiral staircase leading into what looks like a second-hand furniture store with an endless assortment of seating. Fifties two-tone blue and subtle lighting in a coffin-sized bar.
PEOPLE A rather small cross-section of local residents and diners unable to renegotiate the complicated stairs.

PROFS Media, film and TV professionals, doctors, catering workers, writers
CELEBS None
DRESS Suits for the starchier workers, middle-aged media-luvs in more casual jeans
MUSIC Anything and everything
DOOR None
DRINKS Beer £2.50, Wine £2.75, Champagne £4.50, Cocktail £5
FOOD Modern British, £11.50
CARDS No Amex
CAPACITY 140, seating 70
HIRE Venue: Yes · Private Room: Yes

WOODY'S

Bar, Cocktail Bar, Members Club
41-43 Woodfield Road W9
020 7266 3030

OPEN Tues-Sat 7.30pm-2am	GETTING LUCKY	5/5
TUBE/RAIL Westbourne Park	EYE CANDY	4/5
BUSES 28, 31, 328	BIG SPENDERS	4/5
	MIX 60%M 40%F	
	AGE 26-40	
	PRICE Average	

AMBIENCE Basement, Conversation, Dancing, Groups, Late Night Open, Party, Pulling
REVIEW This place is just soooo West London. Although it's marked on the map at Westbourne Park tube, regulars just roll out of bed and they're in. It's not private (except for the top floor) but the doorman gets more abrasive as 11pm approaches. The first-floor lounge cocktail bar is an attractive scrum of guys and girls celebrating their own cool fabness beneath Mario Testino Calvin Klein pant-ad style photos. Willowy models sway obliviously in the disco-bar while a scary looking door gorilla prevents lesser mortals from entering the upstairs members attic. Don't feel like you're missing out if you don't make it – it's only Tristram and his loaded school chums slumming house-party style in jeans and scruffy trainers. Overheard: 'Go on, lend me a tenner, you can have my BUPA card.'
PLACE A Trustafarian house-cum-old-school-Soho-members club set over four floors in an area you wouldn't want to hang around in late at night. A stairway porthole allows a bird's-eye view of the main bar. One unimpressed passer-by described the scene as 'a sea of twats'. Fair enough.
PEOPLE Trustafarians and offspring of bohemian 60s parents, music execs, fashionistas, artists, ex-Met bar crowd, cocktail lovers and bartenders.

PROFS Fashion, music/TV/film/advertising execs, photographers, models
CELEBS Hugh Grant, Johnny Depp, Joseph Fiennes, Jeremy Paxman, Julien Macdonald, Bella Freud
DRESS Vintage/thrift/boho chic. So Jade, so Stella, so Phoebe...
MUSIC Soul, Funk, House, DJs Tue-Sun
DOOR Members Only, Entrance £3-10
DRINKS Beer £3, Wine £3.50, Champagne £7, Cocktail £7
FOOD Bar food, £6
CARDS No Amex or Diners
CAPACITY 325, seating 150
HIRE Venue: Yes · Private Room: No

notting hill

192

Bar, Restaurant
192 Kensington Park Road W11
020 7229 0482

OPEN Mon-Fri 12.30pm-3pm	GETTING LUCKY	3/5
6.30pm-11pm, Sat 12.30pm-	EYE CANDY	4/5
3.30pm 6.30-11.30pm, Sun	BIG SPENDERS	4/5
12.30pm-3.30pm 7pm-11pm	MIX 50%M 50%F	
TUBE/RAIL Notting Hill	AGE 28-60	
Gate, Ladbroke Grove	PRICE Expensive	
BUSES 23, 28, 31, 52, 295		

AMBIENCE Business, Conversation, Destination/Wishlist, Friendly, Hip/Fashionable, Star Spotting, Outdoors
REVIEW Once fiercely independent, now the Groucho's younger sister. Fashionable for two decades, the old girl may have expanded round the middle and gained a few wrinkles but she still parties on a nightly basis. Immortalised by Bridget Jones, this is a place where pop and film stars help with the washing up, dance on the bar and nurse hangovers behind oversized Gucci shades. On a regular basis. Democratic almost to the point of communism, most everyone gets the same treatment: understated but friendly service from the offspring of early customers. Be warned – heavy drinking is encouraged.

PLACE 192's post-modern interior nods knowingly to most styles. The banquette seats and eye-level mirrors helpfully ensure maximum people watching with minimum neck craning.
PEOPLE The place where the cool let their hair down. Some find it's enduring popularity slightly baffling, but 192's charm is more slow and sure, less wham bam.

PROFS Media, ladies who lunch, pop musicians, publishers, PRs, TV profs, film producers, actors, journalists, models, restaurant staff
CELEBS Alan Yentob, Robbie Williams, Madonna, Johnny Depp, Liam Neeson, Helena Bonham-Carter, Jade Jagger, Kate Moss, Steve Martin, Anjelica Huston, Viscount Ovenden, Patsy Kensit, Mick Jagger, Harry Enfield, Alistair Scott, Kristin Scott Thomas, Ruby Wax, Mariella Frostrup, Michelle Collins
DRESS The famous dress down, the less so more up
MUSIC Jazz, Dance, Funk, World Music
DOOR None
DRINKS Beer £3, Wine £3.80, Champagne £6.60, Cocktail £4.50
FOOD Modern British, £12
CARDS All
CAPACITY 95, Seating 95
HIRE Venue: No · Private Room: No

BEACH BLANKET BABYLON

Bar, Restaurant
45 Ledbury Road W11
020 7229 2907

OPEN 7 days midday-midnight	GETTING LUCKY	4/5
TUBE/RAIL Notting Hill Gate	EYE CANDY	3/5
BUSES 7, 23, 28, 31, 52, 328,	BIG SPENDERS	3/5
	MIX 55%M 45%F	
	AGE 25-45	
	PRICE Average	

AMBIENCE Groups, Chilled, Funky, Conversation, Star Spotting, Vampire/Gothic, Pulling
REVIEW Gone are the heady days when the multi-award-winning Beach Blanket Babylon was lauded as the capital's most fashionable boozer. While getting in is revealingly easy these days – you just walk through the door – BBB retains more than a hint of its former glory. The Gothic exterior and interior are still impressively decadent but the crowds have dwindled. Customers have aged with the bar and the previously hedonistic atmosphere has been replaced by a more warming-glass-of-wine-on-a-chilly-night comfortable air. Kind of strange for a bar that looks like a cross between the Sagrada Familia and Dracula's holiday home.
PLACE It might be somewhat past its sell by date, but the smart topiaried Notty Ash townhouse (outside) and Gaudíesque bat cave decor (inside) remain as off-the-wall as ever.
PEOPLE Successful, confident and trendy-ish local crowd, creative, media and advertising people.

PROFS Fashion, media, music and advertising employees
CELEBS Nelly Furtado, Robbie Williams, Geri Halliwell, Noel Gallagher, Liam Gallagher, Sophie Dahl, Jasmine Guinness, Yasmin and Simon le Bon
DRESS Muji, Ghost, Jigsaw, DKNY, FCUK and trainers

MUSIC Dance, Soul, Funk, Jazz, Latin
DOOR Smart casual
DRINKS Beer £3, Wine £3.80, Champagne £5, Cocktail £6
FOOD Modern British, £12
CARDS All
CAPACITY 143, seating 50
HIRE Venue: Yes · Private Room: Yes

CAFÉ MED

Bar, Restaurant, Restaurant Bar
184a Kensington Park Road W11
020 7221 1150

OPEN Mon-Fri midday-11.30pm,	GETTING LUCKY	2/5
Sat midday-11.30pm,	EYE CANDY	4/5
Sun midday-10.30pm	BIG SPENDERS	4/5
TUBE/RAIL Notting Hill Gate, Ladbroke Grove	MIX 50%M 50%F	
BUSES 7, 23, 28, 31, 52, 328	AGE 20-60	
	PRICE Average	

AMBIENCE Casual, Children/Families, Comfy, Conversation, Friendly, Groups, Outdoors
REVIEW When Notting Hill began its metamorphosis from boho to boutique, along came Café Med. And what perfect timing. As the tables of nearby eateries 192 and First Floor began to groan under the pressure of extra mouths to feed, in stepped Café Med, providing yet another home-from-home for the Notting Hill hordes to be seen on the scene. Now established as the place where it's OK to have a burger (chopped steak on rosemary focaccia) and chips and still stay close to fashionable.
PLACE Three dark 'n' moody floors and a glass frontage that opens up on sunny days to allow maximum people watching and air-kissing. Built for speed but still comfortable, the tiny bar sees plenty of action upstairs. In winter warm fires heat things up and couples snuggle and nuzzle on banquettes.
PEOPLE A surprisingly glittery bunch given the democratic style of the place. Madonna managed to close the street off with 200 paparazzi and fans desperate to get a glimpse of the Material Girl's 'informal' tryst with then unpublicised partner Guy Ritchie. Families happily munch alongside young funksters.

PROFS Media and music professionals, creatives, PRs, pop stars, club promoters, gallery owners, journalists
CELEBS Madonna, George Michael, Mick Jagger, Jade Jagger, Alan Rickman, Johnny Depp, Robbie Williams, Claudia Schiffer, Björk, Angela Rippon, Richard Curtis, Natalie Imbruglia, Noel Gallagher
DRESS To look as though you're going to or coming from a hot party, premiere, opening, meeting, screening etc. without having made any discernible effort
MUSIC Jazz, Funk, World Music, Lounge
DOOR None
DRINKS Beer £2.60, Wine £2.95, Champagne £3.95, Cocktail £5.50
FOOD Modern Mediterranean, £10.50
CARDS All
CAPACITY 100, seating 70
HIRE Venue: No · Private Room: No

THE CHEPSTOW

Pub, Restaurant
39 Chepstow Place W2
020 7229 0323

OPEN Mon-Sat 11am-11pm,	**GETTING LUCKY**	**2/5**
Sun midday-10.30pm	**EYE CANDY**	**3/5**
TUBE/RAIL Notting Hill	**BIG SPENDERS**	**3/5**
Gate, Bayswater	**MIX** 40%M 60%F	
BUSES 7, 27, 28, 31	**AGE** 25-40	
	PRICE Average	

AMBIENCE Brightly Coloured/Cheerful,
Comfy, Conversation
REVIEW Tucked away in the middle of a fine Georgian
terrace, The Chepstow is not as loud or in-your-face
as some of the nearby Portobello haunts. Braying
trustafarians and de rigueur drum 'n' bass are
replaced by slightly wealthier, less hip professionals
tapping their feet to a gentle mix of jazz and blues.
As a result, this is more a place to come for a quiet
drink, a bite to eat, a lounge on a sofa and a chat than
to pose, pull or party. For some people, the atmosphere
is just too polite, oozing well-off calm and inoffensive
style in place of character and energy. If it's all too
refined and dainty for you, Ladbroke Grove and the
Notting Hill Arts Club are only a short trainer traipse away.
PLACE Well-converted pub, painted in strong bright
colours and filled with sofas, wooden tables and church
chairs. Large restaurant area.
PEOPLE On the wealthy side of trendy, with a smattering
of oldies and Americans who just loved the film. More
cutting wedge than cutting edge.

PROFS Corporate managers, marketing employees,
publishers, bankers, TV producers, financiers
CELEBS Jeremy Clarkson, Louis Theroux
DRESS Dressed-up (Paul Smith, DKNY, Ghost) versus
off-duty casual (Gap, Oasis, the occasional polo shirt).
MUSIC Jazz, Funk, Blues, Live Jazz Wed
DOOR None
DRINKS Beer £2.60, Wine £2.50, Champagne £5.95,
Cocktail £5
FOOD Modern Eclectic, £14
CARDS No Amex
CAPACITY 100, seating 30
HIRE Venue: Yes · Private Room: No

DAKOTA

Bar, Restaurant
127 Ledbury Road W11
020 7792 9191

OPEN Mon-Sat midday-	**GETTING LUCKY**	**1/5**
3.30pm, 7pm-11pm,	**EYE CANDY**	**3/5**
Sun 11am-6pm	**BIG SPENDERS**	**4/5**
TUBE/RAIL Ladbroke Grove,	**MIX** 50%M 50%F	
Westbourne Park,	**AGE** 20-50	
Notting Hill Gate	**PRICE** Expensive	
BUSES 7, 23, 52, 70		

AMBIENCE Basement, Buzzy, Children/Families,
Conversation, Groups, Hip/Fashionable, Outdoors
REVIEW The first real competitor to 192 in the
Westbourne Grove social stakes, Dakota mixes City
moneymakers with hip local thoroughbreds to great
effect. During the day, like the state, Dakota is flat
and empty – high prices and slick lines keep the broke
bohos away. Come night time, a tight seating policy
means that early tables are filled with local parents
training their young ones in the art of fine dining
while later bookings bring a touch of glamour to the
proceedings. Service is good, but harsh acoustics
induce protracted bouts of trader-style shouting.
PLACE Corner site with discreet outside seating
area protected from views of the facing chippy by
hedges and a canopy. Interior ground floor has
bare boards and dark high banquettes for comfort.
A Fort Apache wooden screen hides the kitchen and
downstairs bar.
PEOPLE A corporate-meets-fashion hang-out for shakers
and fakers. Local good lookers 'sponsored' by City
investors come to see and be seen.

PROFS Music, film, marketing and media execs,
City bankers, PRs, models, investment capitalists,
make-up artists, furniture designers
CELEBS Madonna, Bill Amberg, Dinny Hall,
Lulu Guinness, Chris Evans, Alan Rickman,
Gwyneth Paltrow, Miranda Richardson, Ben Affleck
DRESS City boys wear smart braces, locals wear
smart casual
MUSIC Background
DOOR None
DRINKS Beer £3, Wine £3, Champagne £5,
Cocktail £5.50
FOOD Contemporary American, £12
CARDS No Diners
CAPACITY 100, seating 80
HIRE Venue: Yes · Private Room: Yes

e&o

Bar, Restaurant
14 Blenheim Crescent W11
020 7229 5454

OPEN Mon 6pm-11pm,	**GETTING LUCKY**	**3/5**
Tues-Sat midday-11pm,	**EYE CANDY**	**3/5**
Sun midday-10.30pm	**BIG SPENDERS**	**4/5**
TUBE/RAIL Ladbroke Grove	**MIX** 45%M 55%F	
BUSES 7, 23, 52	**AGE** 25-60	
	PRICE Average	

AMBIENCE Conversation, Party, Groups, Buzzy
REVIEW Formerly a dodgy pub of ill repute, e&o is Will 'Cicada & Great Eastern Dining Rooms' Rickers' third neighbourhood joint. Bridget 'hic' Jones would most definitely have preferred this place to 192, as various sightings of blonde media singleton Mariella Frostrup confirm. Very much a local, but with residents like Robbie Williams, who needs long-distance restaurants or destination diners? Sunday brunch is a baby-fest, when the restaurant transforms into a 4x4 buggy jogger rally. By night, the bar collects shabby public schoolboys debating the price of a pint while tables of pretty girls run up a tab drinking Caipirinhas, content in the knowledge that Daddy's paying off the Amex.
PLACE Cosy and cool neighbourhood cocktail bar plus dining room on a Notting Hill street corner. Decor is plain and simple; dark timber slats feature heavily as do large, broad pendant lights.
PEOPLE 'Darling, did I tell you I got the book deal?', 'Yeah, great... I thought we could have a launch at the gallery, whaddya reckon?'

PROFS Trustafarians, musicians, entrepreneurs, journalists, writers, advertising creatives
CELEBS Robbie Williams, Mariella Frostrup, Charles Saatchi, Nigella Lawson, Liv Tyler, Angela Rippon, Richard Branson, AA Gill
DRESS Effortlessly hip, from trainers and jeans to little black ensembles, fancy fripperies from overpriced boutiques, Maharishi, Uth, Jigsaw etc.
MUSIC Funk, Breakbeat
DOOR None
DRINKS Beer £2.90, Wine £3.50, Champagne £6.50, Cocktail £6.50
FOOD Dim Sum, £5
CARDS All
CAPACITY 80, seating 40
HIRE Venue: No · Private Room: Yes

THE GATE

Bar, Restaurant
87 Notting Hill Gate W11
020 7727 9007

OPEN Mon-Sat 5pm-1am,	GETTING LUCKY	4/5
Sun 5pm-midnight	EYE CANDY	3/5
TUBE/RAIL Notting Hill Gate	BIG SPENDERS	2/5
BUSES 12, 70, 94	MIX 60%M 40%F	
	AGE 22-30	
	PRICE Average	

AMBIENCE Basement, Funky, Late Night Open, Party
REVIEW Probably referred to by its urbanite regulars as 'da gate', they don't even remove their puffas, they're so damn tuff. It's hit or miss, each night of the week has various different promoters and the crowd varies accordingly, although bottled beer and vodka & Red Bull drinkers seem to be a regular fixture. The bar service can be haphazard at best, what with lipstick-smudged glasses and manhandling the ice into drinks, but hey, it's dark in here and the big kids don't care. Sometimes they hold jammin' nights, just pray that the ginger bloke and his mate don't try their Zig 'n' Zag schoolyard rap, the calibre's such school yardie nonsense.

When decent DJs play the place goes wild, tables are pushed back and the joint is jumpin' jumpin'. Crazy cool, but sometimes like stepping into a Bacardi Breezer advert with the distinct whiff of Clearasil.
PLACE Funky basement diner and bar with decks, horizontally fixed vodka bottles form the back bar display and plastic screens separate the standing bar area from the dining section.
PEOPLE Nobody old enough to know better; local 20-somethings; girls in strappy tops revealing backs, belly rings and breasts, blokes in t-shirts, jeans and trainers.

PROFS Retail staff, fashion employees, music promoters
CELEBS Neneh Cherry
DRESS Outdoor wear worn inside; Lacoste puffas and assorted head wear, jeans and trainers rule, slogan t-shirts, H&M, Converse, Adidas, Zara
MUSIC Hip Hop, House, DJs 7 nights
DOOR None
DRINKS Beer £3, Wine £3, Champagne £6.50, Cocktail £6
FOOD Sushi, Bar snacks, £5
CARDS All
CAPACITY 120, seating 55
HIRE Venue: Yes · Private Room: Yes

NOTTING HILL ARTS CLUB

Bar, Club
21 Notting Hill Gate W11
020 7460 4459

OPEN Mon-Wed 6pm-1am,	GETTING LUCKY	4/5
Thu-Sat 4pm-2am, Sun	EYE CANDY	3/5
4pm-11pm	BIG SPENDERS	2/5
TUBE/RAIL Notting Hill Gate	MIX 50%M 50%F	
BUSES 12, 31, 27, 28, 328	AGE 20-35	
	PRICE Average	

AMBIENCE Arty/Bohemian, Basement, Casual, Dancing, Groups, Hip/Fashionable, Late Night Open, Live Music, Party, Pulling, Student
REVIEW Should you ever lose sleep over the definition of post-modern, get up, put on 'some weird shit' and get down to the NHAC around 10pm. Throbbing with nouveau punk attitude, this subterranean den specialises in all things experimental in arts and minds. There's a programme of weekly and monthly happenings, all listed on a generic flyer. Sunday's Lazy Dog with DJ Ben Watt is well recommended, as is Brazilian Love Affair with Patrick Forge. Insurance men and accountants? No chance.
PLACE Rough and ready, distressed art space-cum-lounge with armchairs and a circular bar. Adjoining dance room interchangeable as catwalk/performance/exhibition space. A slightly scuzzy blank canvas where you are the artwork.
PEOPLE Young hyper-hip locals and that's just the staff. Babes and babettes, Hawaiian dudes, Tinkerbell 'Hello Kitty' girlies, laid-back cool dudes, Westbourne regulars, art students and fashion junkie Japanese.

PROFS Freelancers, photographers, art students, DJs, A&R types, fashion execs, make-up artists, stylists, musicians, writers, dancers
CELEBS Sophie Dahl, Robbie Williams, Howie B, Jade Jagger, Lucien Freud, Kate Moss, Stella McCartney

DRESS Down and out there – exhibitionists unite. Think i-D and The Face. Self-creations mutate with Hysteric Glamour, retro t-shirts, Maharishi, Evisu, Westwood, Urban Outfitters, Diesel, Fuct, swamping flares, shell-toed trainers, old-style Reeboks and fleamarket chic

MUSIC Jazz, Indie, Latin, World Music, Funk, Dub, Breakbeat, Hip Hop, UK and US Garage, Deep House, Asian Fusion, Soul, Brazilian

DOOR No suits, no team colours, after 8pm £5-6

DRINKS Beer £2.40, Wine £2.80, Champagne £3.75, Cocktail £5.50

FOOD Snacks, £4.80

CARDS No Amex

CAPACITY 200, seating 30

HIRE Venue: Yes · Private Room: No

PHARMACY

Bar, Restaurant Bar
150 Notting Hill Gate W11
020 7221 2442

OPEN Mon-Thu midday- 1am, Fri-Sat midday-2am TUBE/RAIL Notting Hill Gate BUSES 27, 31, 28	GETTING LUCKY	**2/5**
	EYE CANDY	**4/5**
	BIG SPENDERS	**4/5**
	MIX 60%M 40%F	
	AGE 25-50	
	PRICE Expensive	

AMBIENCE Buzzy, Cute Staff, Friendly, Late Night Open

REVIEW A few years ago some suits got together with millionaire Damien Hirst and brainstormed ways to make money out of other's people's pain. The result was Pharmacy – possibly the first and last medically themed bar in the world. The prognosis wasn't good though, so it went under the knife. There's still Prozac in the windows but there aren't any suppositories in the loos any more. Before, you could hardly move without tripping over a DNA sculpture or aspirin stool but now it's just about possible to choose a cocktail without falling headlong into the clinical trap. The relentless and somewhat chilling pharmaceutical theme has been ditched in favour of a warmer lounge area and DJ booth. Wonder if Damien minds?

PLACE Once you've passed the obligatory plate-glass doors into the main cocktail bar, you can relax. Wall to wall medicine cabinets are no more. Instead there's pill motif wallpaper and squashy green banquettes, albeit of a molecular design.

PEOPLE The artists have headed east now, so you're left with local rich kids and their mates. And the odd suit or tourist who wondered what all the fuss was about.

PROFS Journalists, record label executives, PRs, film production

CELEBS Kate Moss, Gerard Depardieu, Terence Stamp

DRESS Armani and Gucci sling it out with distressed denim from Portobello market and suits through the week

MUSIC Funky House, DJs Thu-Sun

DOOR None

DRINKS Beer £3, Wine £3.50, Champagne £7, Cocktail £6.50

FOOD Bar snacks, £6

CARDS All

CAPACITY 300, seating 300

HIRE Venue: Yes · Private Room: Yes

THE PRINCE BONAPARTE

Gastropub, Pub
80 Chepstow Road W2
020 7313 9491

OPEN Wed-Mon midday- 11pm, Tues 5pm-11pm, Sun midday-10.30pm TUBE/RAIL Westbourne Park, Royal Oak BUSES 7, 28, 31	GETTING LUCKY	**5/5**
	EYE CANDY	**5/5**
	BIG SPENDERS	**3/5**
	MIX 55%M 45%F	
	AGE 24-45	
	PRICE Average	

AMBIENCE Casual, Conversation, Groups, Hip/Fashionable, Pulling

REVIEW West London local sharing the same seriously cool clientele as the Westbourne. Easy to pull if you're looking streamlined and sassy. If not, the lights dim gradually over the evening which can help. Early evening, a few City boys prop up the bar, but as the light fades the Nike and Adidas bounce in, mixing with indie musos and Um and Aah (A&R) men kitted out from their last NYC trip. It's a Portobello crowd, a uniquely bohemian marriage of fleamarket chic and Joseph. Famed for its Sunday Bloody Mary recovery sessions, The Prince Bonaparte also does a legendary sticky toffee pudding.

PLACE Huge plain glass windows, dark floorboards and basic reclamation yard wooden furniture. There is plenty of standing space around the large horseshoe bar; the carpeted area at the back is less hectic.

PEOPLE By day they're between jobs artists/writers/journos/ designers, as night falls they're joined by City bankers whose W2 postcodes make them cool by association.

PROFS Advertising executives, music executives, graphic designers, TV producers, presenters and researchers, music lawyers, A&R execs, publishing executives, TV executives, PRs, designers, models, city traders
CELEBS Stella McCartney, Chemical Brothers, Jamie Theakston, Damon Albarn, Ewan McGregor, Paul Weller, Texas, Kate Winslet, Kate Moss, Chrissie Hynde, Tim Roth
DRESS Combat, skate wear, Maharishi, Evisu, Nike, Adidas, Gaultier, Lulu Guiness, Whistles, Prada, Ted Baker, Paul Smith. Black never ceases to please...
MUSIC Drum 'n' Bass, House, Jazz, Dance, DJs Fri-Sat
DOOR None
DRINKS Beer £2.80, Wine £2.50, Cocktail £3.50
FOOD Modern Eclectic, £8
CARDS No Diners
CAPACITY 200, seating 90
HIRE Venue: No · Private Room: No

THE WALMER CASTLE

Pub, Restaurant
58 Ledbury Road W11
020 7229 4620

OPEN Mon-Fri midday-11pm,	**GETTING LUCKY**	**2/5**
Sat 11am-11pm,	**EYE CANDY**	**2/5**
Sun midday-10.30pm	**BIG SPENDERS**	**3/5**
TUBE/RAIL Notting Hill Gate	**MIX** 50%M 50%F	
BUSES 7, 23, 52	**AGE** 25-40	
	PRICE Average	

AMBIENCE Casual, Conversation, Groups
REVIEW Catering mainly for a mix of youngish locals and lads who find The Cow or The Westbourne too stilettos-and-legwarmers trendy. Early evenings find bitter types nursing pints at the bar, while the white wines curl up on corner tables with a Penguin Modern. By 8.30pm the pub fills up with sociable groups of locals buying rounds and catching up on the gossip. They're smartly dressed but informal – this may be one of Notting Hill's least conspicuous boozers but it's still W11 and certain standards are assumed. In the summer drinking begins earlier and there's a beach towel-on-the-sunlounger-style scrummage for pavement tables.
PLACE Standard pub layout with some terracotta Dulux and Gothic wall-torch/chandelier touches. The Easyjet-orange Thai menus decorate several conspicuous ledges. A 2ft statue of a scantily clad woman, of the sort painted on to WWII planes, stands atop the bar rail. Not sure what that's all about.
PEOPLE Middle-class professionals in their early thirties meeting up with local mates they've known since university. Boys taking a break from the Playstation.
PROFS Media, publishing, PR, recruitment consultants, lawyers, financiers, professional trustafarians
CELEBS Chemical Brothers, Kate Moss, Mariella Frostrup, Robert Carlyle
DRESS Jeans, white t-shirts and a linen Armani jacket would do in summer. Chinos, woolly knits and long woollen overcoats in winter
MUSIC Easy Listening, Dance
DOOR Over 21s
DRINKS Beer £2.50, Wine £2
FOOD Thai, £5.75

CARDS All
CAPACITY 125, seating 60
HIRE Venue: Yes · Private Room: Yes

THE WINDSOR CASTLE

Pub
114 Campden Hill Road W8
020 7243 9551

OPEN Mon-Sat midday-	**GETTING LUCKY**	**2/5**
11.30pm, Sun midday-	**EYE CANDY**	**3/5**
10.30pm	**BIG SPENDERS**	**3/5**
TUBE/RAIL Notting Hill Gate	**MIX** 60%M 40%F	
BUSES 12, 52, 31, 328	**AGE** 20-60	
	PRICE Cheap	

AMBIENCE Casual, Conversation, Cosy, Groups, Historic
REVIEW Sensationally dark, wood interiored pub (suggested rechristening: 'The Tree Man'), rich in cosy nooks and sequestered crannies, with no shortage of pictures of the eponymous royal pile. Not really like a London pub at all, it has a sort of Kentish smugglers' inn feel which doubtless explains its appeal to a largely sloaney/touristy clientele. Outside, an appealing Ye Olde English Pubbe frontage with cascading greenery plus benches for carbon monoxide lovers. Inside, a good place to hang out and look pale and interesting, which you're likely to remain if you sit here long enough.
PLACE Village-inn style pub in mid-Kensington: a series of snug, interconnected panelled rooms, a separate food bar to your left and a no-smoking area with open fire to your right. Perfect for Americans.
PEOPLE Popular haunt of the upper-crust middle-aged, especially lunchtimes. Younger, but equally sloaney crowd evenings. A constant stream of clueless tourists so totally missing the point of Notting Hill.

PROFS Barristers, film producers, actors, advertising execs, musicians
CELEBS None
DRESS Old school collar-up rugby shirts with girls in Boden, trendier Sloanes in dishevelled, studied Portobello market stuff, Burberry and Aquascutum bag-laden tourists
MUSIC None
DOOR None
DRINKS Beer £3, Wine £2.90
FOOD Modern English, £7.95
CARDS All
CAPACITY 350, seating 100
HIRE Venue: No · Private Room: No

portobello

BED

Bar
310 Portobello Road W10
020 8969 4500

OPEN Mon-Sat midday-	**GETTING LUCKY**	**4/5**
11pm, Sun midday-10.30pm	**EYE CANDY**	**3/5**
TUBE/RAIL Ladbroke Grove	**BIG SPENDERS**	**3/5**
BUSES 7, 23, 52, 70	**MIX** 50%M 50%F	
	AGE 25-35	
	PRICE Average	

AMBIENCE Arty/Bohemian, Chilled, Comfy, Conversation, Cosy, Funky, Lounge, Pulling, Romantic, Souk
REVIEW Wonder how many times the gag 'Let's go to Bed' will remain funny. In case you didn't know, the word 'bed' also means 'a layer of small animals, especially reptiles, congregated thickly in some particular spot'. Come here on a Friday or Saturday night and you'll find the reptiles out in full force. While there are plenty of decent blokes in here, there are probably two posing snakes for every one of them. Visit early in the week when the inviting piles of ethnic cushions are relatively bum-free; later in the week you risk getting crushed by nests of networking vipers.
PLACE A schizophrenic orange 70s pastiche exterior contrasts bizarrely with a Moroccan souk interior, all candlelight, carved wooden thrones, cushions and ethnic paraphernalia. Upstairs is similar but with more nooks and cushions. A DJ, hidden mysteriously behind a potted palm, plays funky dance, jazz and soul.
PEOPLE They read 'Dazed and Confused', love lava lamps, shop in Urban Outfitters and dance to the hip world music CD du jour.

PROFS TV researchers, radio production assistants, journalists
CELEBS Damon Albarn, Melanie Sykes
DRESS Young career bods in tailored leather jackets and Uth or APC dark denims. Some vintage seconds
MUSIC Jazz, Funk, House, Soul, DJs 7 days
DOOR Over 25s; Smart casual
DRINKS Beer £2.50, Wine £2.60, Champagne £5.75, Cocktail £5
FOOD None
CARDS All
CAPACITY 300, seating 120
HIRE Venue: Yes · Private Room: Yes

GROUND FLOOR BAR

Bar
186 Portobello Road W11
020 7243 8701

OPEN Mon-Sat 11am-11pm,	GETTING LUCKY	3/5
Sun midday-10.30pm	EYE CANDY	3/5
TUBE/RAIL Ladbroke Grove,	BIG SPENDERS	3/5
Notting Hill Gate	MIX 40%M 60%F	
BUSES 23, 52, 70, 295	AGE 20-35	
	PRICE Average	

AMBIENCE Chilled, Comfy, Conversation, Friendly, Funky, Groups, Lounge, Outdoors
REVIEW Many locals are still cursing the owners for turning the dark, wild Ground Floor of yore into a modern, well-lit, snug sofas Central Perk kind of place. As a result, most have not set foot in the bar ever since. Perhaps because of this embargo, Ground Floor has collected a more new-to-the-area than lived-here-for-years crowd, attracted by the spacious interior and outside tables. At weekends, however, with the market in situ, it's predictably rammed, with regulars getting serious competition from similarly be-trainered weekenders with bare midriffs and/or boyband hair. Not as hip as some in the neighbourhood, but as this is Portobello, that could be a blessing.
PLACE Large corner pub converted into a politely-terracotta-and-blue lounge bar, with a deliberately

ragged collection of high-backed thrones, Chesterfields and pub pews with the obligatory oversized gilt-framed mirrors for people gawping.
PEOPLE Young relatively trendy Grove residents loaf about with their customary nonchalance, although if they were that hip they'd probably be somewhere else. Slightly calmer and older locals go there simply because they like it.

PROFS Portobello market types, artists, hairdressers, retailers, architects, musicians, creatives
CELEBS Chris Evans, Tim Roth, Robbie Williams, Jamie Oliver, Finley Quaye, Sophie Dahl, Marcel Desailly
DRESS Vintage vs urban streetwear with a dash of High Street chic
MUSIC Ambient, Jazz, House, Breakbeat
DOOR None
DRINKS Beer £2.80, Wine £2.50, Champagne £5
FOOD Modern European, £6
CARDS No Amex
CAPACITY 120, seating 56
HIRE Venue: No · Private Room: Yes

ION BAR

Bar
161-165 Ladbroke Grove W10
020 8960 1702

OPEN Mon-Fri 5pm-midnight,	GETTING LUCKY	2/5
Sat-Sun midday-midnight	EYE CANDY	3/5
TUBE/RAIL Ladbroke Grove	BIG SPENDERS	3/5
BUSES 23, 52, 70, 295	MIX 50%M 50%F	
	AGE 28-35	
	PRICE Average	

AMBIENCE Buzzy, Conversation, Dancing, Futuristic, Groups, Late Night Open, Live Music
REVIEW The light from the glass-fronted bar by Ladbroke Grove tube has probably put dozens of muggers out of business. Every graffiti tag and lichen curl on the underside of the railway bridge is now illuminated by the dazzling light from the Ion fishtank. A beacon of wealth and sophistication amid the local launderettes, kebab shops and second-hand fridge emporia, Ion Bar keeps its Prada'd-up punters flooding in with nightly DJs playing soul, hip hop and R&B. Don't even attempt to come near the place at Carnival, when the bar is busier than the first day of the Gucci sale and punters would sell their limited edition Evisus to squeeze their way in.
PLACE Tall, bright, slim, glassy box. An uneasy fusion of glamour and sixth-form common room, complete with low budget Barbarella-style futuristic touches. You wobble on perilous bar stools or share rectangular orange cushions.
PEOPLE Media, PR, fashion, City – all youngish, richish and very stylish

PROFS A&R people, advertising execs, designers, students, computer programmers
CELEBS Natalie Imbruglia, Mel B, Anna Friel, Eddie Izzard, Goldie, Ruby Wax, Kate Moss, Heather Small, Richard Blackwood, Tim Westwood, Eternal, Damage, Paul Smith, Celestine Babayaro, Audley Harrison
DRESS Prada, Gucci, Evisu, shiny shiny trainers
MUSIC Reggae, Salsa, Rare Groove, Soul, R&B, Hip Hop, Disco. Live music Wed

DOOR Smart casual, no baseball caps
DRINKS Beer £2.80, Wine £4, Champagne £7,
Cocktail £5
FOOD Modern European, £12
CARDS Cash only in bar
CAPACITY 200
HIRE Venue: No · Private Room: Yes

THE MARKET BAR

Bar
240a Portobello Road W11
020 7229 6472

OPEN Mon-Sat midday-		
11pm, Sun midday-10.30pm	GETTING LUCKY	3/5
TUBE/RAIL Ladbroke Grove	EYE CANDY	3/5
BUSES 23, 52, 70, 295	BIG SPENDERS	3/5
	MIX 50%M 50%F	
	AGE 20 35	
	PRICE Average	

AMBIENCE Casual, Chilled, Conversation, Cosy, Friendly, Funky, Groups, Live Music, Souk
REVIEW Still a perennial favourite in this famously fickle neighbourhood, the Market Bar thrives on a mix of regulars, from Jamie Oliver-a-likes and bed-head boiled-wool students to ancient Rastas and rollie-smoking slackers. Although it starts getting busy at about five, the long bar is a relatively suit-free zone. Instead, a vibrant blend of young and young at heart Portobello-ites stream in and out, and there's usually a handful of drinkers loitering with intent outside the front door in all but the most inclement of weathers. In a neck of the woods more concerned with cool than conviviality, the lively, welcoming vibe of the Market is almost an anomaly.
PLACE Converted old corner pub, mixing scuffed pub decor with lavish carved wood knick-knacks, tall dripping candles and warm colours. Good Thai food in the glowing 'Market Thai' restaurant upstairs.
PEOPLE Everyone from try hard trust-funders to market traders and local professionals of many years' standing. Occasional dead-ringer for Lenny Kravitz. Market shoppers Fri & Sat.

PROFS Market traders, hairdressers, photographers, tourists, artists
CELEBS Shaznay Lewis
DRESS Diesel, Carhartt, market seconds, sheepskin and leather jerkins
MUSIC Jazz, Hip Hop, Trance, House, DJs Fri-Sat, Live Jazz Sun
DOOR None
DRINKS Beer £2.60, Wine £2.60, Cocktail £4.50
FOOD Thai, £6
CARDS No Amex
CAPACITY 160, seating 70
HIRE Venue: Yes · Private Room: No

THE MAU MAU BAR

Bar, Café Bar
265 Portobello Road W11
020 7229 8528

OPEN Mon-Sat 11am-11pm,		
Sun midday-10.30pm	GETTING LUCKY	2/5
TUBE/RAIL Ladbroke Grove,	EYE CANDY	4/5
Notting Hill Gate	BIG SPENDERS	3/5
BUSES 7, 23, 52, 70	MIX 50%M 50%F	
	AGE 20-55	
	PRICE Average	

AMBIENCE Chilled, Arty/Bohemian, Relaxed, Brightly Coloured, Comfy, Cute Staff
REVIEW You'd think Portobello needs another arty/bohemian café bar as much as Donatella Versace needs another sparkly dress. How wrong you'd be. It's gone through a refurbishment (it was the Beat Bar pre-July) and come out the other side with a relaxed, organic feel. Everything about this place smacks of laid-back cool – you can bring in your own food from The Grain Shop next door, they make up original cocktails to order and the chocolate brown leather sofas are a couch potato's dream. What more could you want? Maybe a little selection of weekly art stuff, from classical music and Portobello film festival shenanigans to standup comedy from new and established acts.
PLACE Large, funky Andy Warhol-esque paintings of stars from Audrey Hepburn to George Best plus white walls, banquettes, leather bean bags and a long postcard-pasted bar.
PEOPLE Middle-aged ladies who lunch sip coffee next to students discussing chaos theory and Britney. BBC presenters pop in for a quiet one and stay for the 20-30 year olds who arrive later to chill-out and funk it up until last orders.

PROFS Media types, students, locals, artists, painters, comedians
CELEBS None
DRESS Street cool, expensive shoes mixed with perfect vintage pieces from a charity place nearby
DOOR None
MUSIC Ambient Trance, Chill-out
DRINKS Beer £2.60, Wine £2.80, Cocktail £3.50
FOOD None
CARDS All
CAPACITY 100, seating 45
HIRE Venue: Yes · Private Room No

PORTOBELLO GOLD

Bar, Hotel Bar, Restaurant Bar
95 Portobello Road W11
020 7460 4900

OPEN Mon-Sat 10am-		
midnight, Sun midday-	GETTING LUCKY	1/5
10.30pm	EYE CANDY	3/5
TUBE/RAIL Notting Hill Gate	BIG SPENDERS	5/5
BUSES 7, 23, 52, 70	MIX 50%M 50%F	
	AGE 25-65	
	PRICE Average	

AMBIENCE Casual, Groups, Outdoors, Student
REVIEW Long ago, in an age of glam rock, Thatcher and loon pants (before Julia and Hugh), there was a pub known to all as The Alex. On entering, one would be greeted by Lemmy from Motorhead standing at the bar, vodka and orange in hand and a tasty young chick on each arm. In the mid-80s, in pursuit of the tourist dollar/yen/peseta, The Alex was reinvented as The Portobello Gold. A conservatory was built out back

and turned into a restaurant and one of the first Internet cafes was built on the first floor. At least Lemmy'd be pleased with the 12 bottled and five draft beers served behind the bar. As to pulling, it was better in the old days. (Motorcycle Irene, where are you now?)
PLACE The medium-sized bar is half consumed by the excellent restaurant. The decor is plain and simple, with only the Jocasta Innes colourwash in the bathrooms to remind you of where you are.
PEOPLE A definite split between weekends and the rest of the week. Monday to Friday, pretty much what you would expect in an area with the highest housing prices in history. At the weekends, Invicta rucksacks, knee socks and the Lonely Planet rule.

PROFS Stockbrokers, artists, lawyers, media execs, marketing execs, TV professionals, radio staff
CELEBS Bill Clinton, Hillary Clinton
DRESS Not including weekends, when lycra and bad taste are de rigueur, working clothes – that is, if you work in a chi chi antiques shop or a painfully trendy boutique
MUSIC World, Progressive, Fusion, Blues
DOOR No trainers
DRINKS Beer £2.30, Wine £2.90, Champagne £5, Cocktail £4.50
FOOD Modern British, MediterrAsian, £12
CARDS No Amex
CAPACITY 200, seating 80
HIRE Venue: Yes · Private Room: Yes

PORTOBELLO STAR

Pub
171 Portobello Road W11
020 7229 8016

OPEN Mon-Sat 11am-11pm, Sun midday-10.30pm	GETTING LUCKY	3/5
TUBE/RAIL Notting Hill Gate, Ladbroke Grove	EYE CANDY	3/5
	BIG SPENDERS	2/5
BUSES 7, 15, 52	MIX 65%M 35%F	
	AGE 25-75	
	PRICE Average	

AMBIENCE Arty/Bohemian, Buzzy, Casual, Cosy, Friendly
REVIEW A regular hang-out of Blur, Pulp, Suede and Elastica during the birth of Britpop, the down-at-heel Tudor beamed pub is propped up by a real selection of Parklife-style cheeky chappies with frazzled mid-length hair and basic disdain for fashion. When we dropped in, conversation ranged from a proposed trip to the Imperial War Museum, through potential sources for a second-hand bumper for Ron's Escort, to Jordan's latest tits. If you wanna live like common people in an area inhabited by possibly the least common in the world, then The Portobello Star's the boozer for you.
PLACE Narrowish standard Britpub with plaster and beam walls. Inside, a muddle of wooden and plastic furniture with some gold and silver stars stencilled on in honour of the name. It widens out towards the back, where the mirrored walls give the impression of more space.
PEOPLE Kevin and John have just closed up their market stalls for the night and are filling in their pools coupons at the bar, chatting to the youngish barman. Luke and Cassandra are freelance arty types who live in a studio off the Great Western Road and like nothing better than a bit of experimental theatre on a Friday night.

PROFS Musicians, market stallholders, media profs
CELEBS Chris Evans, Damon Albarn
DRESS Wrangler jeans, battered leather, Reebok Classics
MUSIC Jukebox
DOOR None
DRINKS Beer £2.50, Wine £2.60
FOOD Pub food, Sat only £3.50
CARDS None
CAPACITY 75, seating 30
HIRE Venue: No · Private Room: No

RUBY IN THE DUST

Bar, Café, Restaurant
299 Portobello Road W10
020 8969 4626

OPEN Mon-Fri 10am-11pm, Sat 9am-11pm, Sun 9am-10.30pm	GETTING LUCKY	3/5
	EYE CANDY	5/5
TUBE/RAIL Ladbroke Grove	BIG SPENDERS	3/5
BUSES 7, 23, 52, 70	MIX 50%M 50%F	
	AGE 20-40	
	PRICE Average	

AMBIENCE Arty/Bohemian, Buzzy, Casual, Comfy, Conversation, Groups
REVIEW Bleach-blonde, dreadlocked girls with Latin American tans carrying as much weight in silver jewellery as daddy's name does at Coutts. They spit measuring out their afternoons with long latte spoons, sinking into battered sofas and comparing Portobello purchases of organic soaps and veg. It's bright, colourful, comfortable and classily boho. Just this side of zany, it features largish fabric flowers, one pink wall and a presque-Basquiat oil painting on another with cutesy scribblings on the walls: 'I never knew I loved you till I saw you rock and roll' and 'how sweet it is to be loved by you'. A little too much saccharine, maybe. But the women come and go, talking of Michaelangelo (the Italian ambient DJ they slept with at Glastonbury).
PLACE Bright, cool canopied entrance with a couple of cast-iron tables outside. The café area is very informal

with solid wooden tables, comfy battered seating, aqua glass-tiled bar and restaurant out back.
PEOPLE Olivia's just got back from her yoga class, and she can really feel the spaces between her bones starting to breathe now... she just feels so PURE, you know? Which is clearly why it's time for a roll-up, an espresso and something chocolatey.

PROFS Musicians, actors, artists, film professionals
CELEBS Damon Albarn, Robbie Williams, John Malkovich, Rik Mayall, Emmanuel Petit, former All Saints
DRESS Stüssy, Nike, Adidas, Vivienne Westwood, combat gear, Maharashi
MUSIC Jazz, Reggae, Chill-out
DOOR None
DRINKS Beer £2.55, Wine £2.90, Cocktail £3.50
FOOD International, £7.50
CARDS All
CAPACITY 80, seating 20
HIRE Venue: Yes · Private Room: Yes

WINE FACTORY

Bar, Restaurant, Wine Bar
294 Westbourne Grove W11
020 7229 1877

OPEN Mon-Sat midday-3.30pm, 6pm-11pm, Sun midday-4pm	**GETTING LUCKY**	**2/5**
	EYE CANDY	**3/5**
	BIG SPENDERS	**3/5**
TUBE/RAIL Notting Hill Gate	**MIX** 50%M 50%F	
BUSES 23, 28, 31, 52	**AGE** 20-50	
	PRICE Average	

AMBIENCE Casual, Conversation, Groups, Minimalist
REVIEW Anyone who objects to the extortionate price of plonk in London's restaurants (and, frankly, who doesn't?) will love Wine Factory. Owned by Brinkley's, an enlightened Chelsea wine merchant, Wine Factory sells its bottles at virtually shop prices, making it an absolute bargain compared with other restaurants. Hic. The food is distinctly ordinary, although fairly priced. Come for a snack, and drink to excess is our advice: a bottle of champagne will set you back a mere £15 (so that's £60 each, then).
PLACE Sparsely-decorated – bare plaster walls and simple tables – Wine Factory spreads over two floors; the outside tables, in good weather, are the best bet. Atmosphere is not a strong point and the restaurant is often bafflingly empty.
PEOPLE Thin-on-the-ground. When they are around, a cross-section of humanity drawn together by love of cheap wine: media (especially new media) people, posh locals, a visible BBC contingent and Portobello market traders.

PROFS TV and radio professionals, antique dealers
CELEBS Robbie Williams, Mick Jagger, Annie Lennox
DRESS From casual jeans and tiny backpacks to boho chic and Prada bags
MUSIC Easy Listening, Jazz
DOOR None
DRINKS Beer £2.50, Wine £2.25
FOOD Pizza, Pasta, Mediterranean, £8
CARDS No Amex or Diners
CAPACITY 300, seating 75
HIRE Venue: No · Private Room: No

shepherd's bush

ALBERTINE

Wine Bar
1 Wood Lane W12
020 8932 3531

OPEN Mon-Fri midday-11pm, Sat 6.30pm-11pm	**GETTING LUCKY**	**1/5**
	EYE CANDY	**3/5**
TUBE/RAIL Shepherd's Bush	**BIG SPENDERS**	**3/5**
BUSES 72, 95, 220	**MIX** 50%M, 50%F	
	AGE 20-60	
	PRICE Average	

AMBIENCE Conversation, Cosy, Friendly
REVIEW One of the most common drinker's gripes is from red/white stuff aficionados looking for a simple bar serving little more than copious varieties of wine and great food to soak it up. Gripe no longer and head straight to Albertine, serving bottle after bottle to the good people of Shepherd's Bush for over 20 years. It offers literally hundreds of world wines, from £2.50 for a glass of house plonk to £4.60 for a tipple of Broken Wood Semillion. Whether you're a serious oenophile in search of that elusive claret or a juice of the grape ignoramus with arthouse pretensions, you're sure to find something to please. Just don't bother asking for a Caipirinha – serving no spirits, no cocktails and only one beer, Albertine is a wine bar and proud of it.
PLACE A green-fronted set piece from a Stella Artois commercial. Eccentrically decorated by the owner, an eclectic mix of knick knacks set amongst the wooden tables and pews provide a lived-in, homely feel.
PEOPLE Lots of regulars and a mixed bag of ages plus a semi-permanent selection of old BBC soaks.

PROFS BBC workers, media types, presenters, students
CELEBS None
DRESS FCUK, Jigsaw, M&S, Jaeger, Aquascutum
DOOR None
MUSIC Chill-out, Jazz
DRINKS Beer £3, Wine £2.50, Champagne £4.40
FOOD International, £6
CARDS No Amex
CAPACITY 70, seating 70
HIRE Venue: No · Private Room Yes

BUSH BAR & GRILL

Bar, Restaurant, Restaurant Bar
45a Goldhawk Road W12
020 8746 2111

OPEN Mon-Sat midday-11pm, Sun midday-10.30pm	**GETTING LUCKY**	**4/5**
	EYE CANDY	**4/5**
TUBE/RAIL Goldhawk Road	**BIG SPENDERS**	**4/5**
BUSES 237, 94, 49, 295	**MIX** 50%M 50%F	
	AGE 20-55	
	PRICE Average	

AMBIENCE Buzzy, Gourmet/Foodie, Hip/Fashionable, Minimalist, Pulling, Star Spotting
REVIEW Housed in an old milk-bottling factory, the Bush Bar and Grill has been about as successful as the white stuff since its opening a year ago. Backed

by the same moneymen as the Groucho but without its reverence of culture, Da Bush veers towards 70s minimalism rather than Jeffery Bernard indulgence. You'll be greeted by a small bush (ahem!) at the entrance, led down a terracotta-paved courtyard and faced with a wall of glass windows and a leather-coated Putin lookalike on the door. Packed on weeknights, Bush brings style to the Dial-a-Cab detritus of Goldhawk Road, winkling local professionals out of their overpriced, Heals-furnished flats. Stylishly designed and miles ahead in the race to gentrify W12.

PLACE White walls, steel plant pots and curvy banquettes. Airy, spacious and immaculately clean, the industrial-style space has been broken up in to three sections. Bar on the left, with dais seating and backlit panels that morph soporifically from one colour to the next.

PEOPLE A conversationally competent mix of Bush dwellers from media suits talking shares dealing to Amy and Rafael debating oil versus watercolour.

PROFS Media suits, traders, models, artists
CELEBS Ralph Fiennes, Billy Zane, Bono, Louis Theroux, Nigella Lawson, Francesca Anis, Jack Nicholson, Lara Flynn-Boyle
DRESS Framed glasses, Paul Smith jumpers, Agnès B suits and the more vintage end of Portobello
MUSIC Jazz, Chill-out, Funk
DOOR None
DRINKS Beer £2.50, Wine £3.95, Champagne £6, Cocktail £5
FOOD Modern Mediterranean, £10
CARDS No Diners
CAPACITY 50, seating 20
HIRE Venue: Yes · Private Room: Yes

westbourne park

BABUSHKA

Bar, Chain
41 Tavistock Crescent W11
020 7727 9250

OPEN Mon-Fri 5pm-11pm,	**GETTING LUCKY**	**2/5**
Sat, Sun midday-10.30pm	**EYE CANDY**	**3/5**
TUBE/RAIL Westbourne Park	**BIG SPENDERS**	**3/5**
BUSES 7, 23, 31, 70, 328	**MIX** 50%M 50%F	
	AGE 20-35	
	PRICE Average	

AMBIENCE Arty/Bohemian, Buzzy, Comfy, Conversation, Cosy, Funky, Party
REVIEW Tucked under the Westway, on what used to be a famously dodgy corner, Babushka has been plying its trade to the Notting Hill cognoscenti for a few years now. Previously incarnated as a scuzzy old boozer, hardened drinkers will be gladdened by the fact they're downing their double scotch chasers in a pub featured in Withnail & I. Ostensibly part of a small chain of vodka bars, the management has been given a relatively free rein and the result is a laid-back music-orientated bar, popular with locals decked out in ironic golf jumpers, Burberry scarves and Guy Ritchie-esque flat caps. The deep-red upstairs room has occasional screenings, while downstairs the inevitable DJs play an even more inevitable mix of funk and house.

PLACE Exterior is coated in deep blue tiles and distinctive graphics. Dark interior, kitted out with mismatched benches, chairs and snuggly sofas.
PEOPLE Funky, up-for-it clubby crowd. Thursdays bring waves of urban surfers from the skate park round the corner.

PROFS DJs, record industry professionals, musicians, video producers
CELEBS Clive James, Robbie Williams, Melanie Sykes, Howard Marks
DRESS NYC trainers, combats, urban streetwear
MUSIC House, Funk, Disco, Daily DJs
DOOR None
DRINKS Beer £2.60, Wine £2.50, Champagne £5.75, Cocktail £4.50
FOOD None
CARDS All
CAPACITY 250, seating 150
HIRE Venue: Yes · Private Room: Yes

THE COBDEN CLUB

Bar, Members Club
170-172 Kensal Road W10
020 8960 4222

OPEN Mon-Sat 6pm-1.30am	**GETTING LUCKY**	**3/5**
TUBE/RAIL Westbourne Park	**EYE CANDY**	**4/5**
BUSES 7, 23, 31, 70, 328	**BIG SPENDERS**	**4/5**
	MIX 60%M 40%F	
	AGE 25-45	
	PRICE Average	

AMBIENCE Arty/Bohemian, Comfy, Cute Staff, Dancing, Historic, Late Night Open, Live Music, Network, Opulent, Vampire/Gothic
REVIEW Ex-working men's club without a labourer on site. Half of this lot probably don't surface before 11am and wouldn't know a cement mixer if they were thrown into one. More of a slouching around chatting than a waving your hands in the air kind of place, The Cobden is the last word in laid-back boho chic. Founded in 1996 by a group of pedigree chums including Nicholas Coleridge, Jade Jagger, Kate Moss and Malcolm McLaren, this is where multi-million-pound music deals are forged, contracts are signed and Chrissie Hynde and our Stella watch the football of a Saturday afternoon. Overheard in-crowd swapses, 'I know. You take us to the Groucho and then we'll take you to Soho House, deal yeah?'
PLACE Restored Victorian Grade II grandeur, with first-floor restaurant and second-floor Grand Hall bar. Comfy warmth with rich russets and golds, red velvet drapes and huge mirrors. Chesterfields, sofas and easy chairs provide lounge seating while the raised platform at the end is great for eyeing the crowd.
PEOPLE The art/fashion/design/music/media crew who grace Home House, Momo, Soho House and The Groucho with their fabber-than-thou moniker. Also Woody's, The Cow and Westbourne regulars.

PROFS Musicians and music industry, fashion designers, models, film directors and producers, TV presenters, jewellery makers, advertising execs, musicians, pop stars, radio journalists, ex-art schoolers, PRs, stylists, actors, bankers

CELEBS Jade Jagger, Jay Kay, Hugh Grant, Kate Moss, Dan MacMillan, Will Self, Isabella Blow, Tom Dixon, Dinny Hall, Alexandra Shulman, Sadie Coles, Bella Freud, Bill Amberg, Huey Fun Lovin' Criminal, Damon Albarn, Marilyn Manson, Daryl Hannah, Ruby Wax, Chrissie Hynde, Stella McCartney
DRESS Rockstar scruffy. Evisu, Earl Jeans, Paul Smith, Ghost, Patty Shelabarger, Voyage, Koh Samui
MUSIC Funk, Soul, World Music, Nightly DJs
DOOR Members Only
DRINKS Beer £3, Wine £3, Champagne £6, Cocktail £6
FOOD Modern British, Modern European, £11.50
CARDS All
CAPACITY 300, seating 200
HIRE Venue: Yes · Private Room: Yes

THE COW

Gastropub, Restaurant
89 Westbourne Park Road W2
020 7221 5400

OPEN Mon-Sat midday-	GETTING LUCKY	2/5
11pm, Sun midday-10.30pm	EYE CANDY	3/5
TUBE/RAIL Westbourne	BIG SPENDERS	3/5
Park, Royal Oak	MIX 50%M 50%F	
BUSES 28, 31, 70, 328	AGE 22-55	
	PRICE Average	

AMBIENCE Conversation, Cosy, Star Spotting
REVIEW To realise what a triumph The Cow is, just pop in to one of the plague of cod-Oirish theme bars infesting London as we speak. Tom son-of-Terence Conran's joint concentrates on the important things (well-kept Guinness and fresh shellfish) rather than the repulsive things (Ballykissangel tat and potato-digging implements), making it one of the few successful Gaelic new-old bars in town. The combination of authenticity and relatively diminutive proportions create a simultaneously bustling and laid-back atmosphere. Attracting an older and calmer crowd than the neighbouring Westbourne, The Cow is thankfully free of the latter's 'look-at-me' element. Word of warning – the pub gets very, very busy, so make sure you get there early or you may be dancing jigs and warbling Danny Boy before your food arrives.
PLACE Small, traditional-looking pub space, done out in unobtrusive old-style burgundy and cream. Regulars gather around the bar, while eaters head for the back or upstairs to the dining-room.
PEOPLE Mix of locals with a refreshing dearth of post-work packs of suits.

PROFS TV and radio professionals, musicians, bankers, art and design students, film crews, painters, sculptors
CELEBS Madonna, Robbie Williams, Nick Cave, Hugh Grant, Mick Jagger, Jamie Theakston, Louis Theroux, Brett Anderson, Mariella Frostrup
DRESS Notting Hill trendy, combats, Gap, DKNY, Levi's, ironic slogan t-shirts
MUSIC Jazz, Chill-out
DOOR None
DRINKS Beer £2.80, Wine £2.85, Champagne £5
FOOD Seafood, £8
CARDS All
CAPACITY 250, seating 80
HIRE Venue: No · Private Room: Yes

THE ELBOW ROOM

Pool Bar, Chain
103 Westbourne Grove W2
020 7221 5211

OPEN Mon-Sat midday-	GETTING LUCKY	1/5
11pm, Sun midday-10.30pm	EYE CANDY	3/5
TUBE/RAIL Westbourne Park	BIG SPENDERS	3/5
BUSES 7, 23, 31, 328	MIX 70%M 30%F	
	AGE 18-35	
	PRICE Average	

AMBIENCE Buzzy, Casual, Comfy, Conversation, Cosy, Friendly, Funky, Groups, Hip/Fashionable
REVIEW Not for pulling but for potting balls. The first of many, this bar-cum-cool-pool hall has spawned sequels across Leeds, Bristol and London. Frequented by a wide range of young professionals who fancy a game of pool in surroundings more MTV-friendly than your average pub games room or seedy pool hall, The Elbow Room is manna from heaven for ball 'n' booze loving W2ers. A bit like a destination youth club for big kids who like bottled beer and Seabreezes, you pay £9 for an hour's play and hang out with the boys and girls who live round your neighbourhood.
PLACE Paul Daly's woody design is funky and tactile with sand-blasted wood divisions creating intimate areas in the bar. The tripod table in the front window must be highly desirable as it's chained to the floor.
PEOPLE A broad mix of West Londoners, from urban surfers to suited City boys. Word of warning girls – the tight-skirt-and-cleavage hustler look is a definite no-no. The only way to impress here is to beat your opponent fair and square.

PROFS Advertisers, photographers, journalists, TV professionals, bankers, graphic designers
CELEBS Finley Quaye, Sinead O'Connor, Tim Roth, Fun Lovin' Criminals, Vanessa Mae, Brett Anderson, Shaznay Lewis, Toploader
DRESS Urban street labels and a bit of military chic
MUSIC House, Dance, Funk, Breakbeat
DOOR None
DRINKS Beer £2.80, Wine £3
FOOD American Grill, £7
CARDS No Amex
CAPACITY 250, seating 70
HIRE Venue: Yes · Private Room: No

GOLBORNE HOUSE

Gastropub
36 Golborne Road W10
020 8960 6260

OPEN Mon-Sat midday-	GETTING LUCKY	2/5
11pm, Fri-Sat midday-	EYE CANDY	3/5
midnight,	BIG SPENDERS	3/5
Sun midday-10.30pm	MIX 50%M 50%F	
TUBE/RAIL Westbourne Park	AGE 25-50	
BUSES 23, 28, 31, 52, 328	PRICE Average	

AMBIENCE Conversation, Arty/Bohemian, Cute Staff, Hip/Fashionable
REVIEW Five minutes away from Westbourne Park tube, Golborne House is a prime target for gastropub hoppers.

Located near a cluster of recording studios, it's a little bit of pub heaven smack bang in the middle of da 'hood. Lunchtime sees middle-brow media and mainstream record industry professionals mulling over release strategies with a bottle of Chilean Chardonnay and the occasional celeb chowing down with their marketing handlers. On weekend nights, it's rammed with Ladbroke groovers and pre-Subterrania club kids, so the mood swings like Tiger Woods on steroids. Huge frosted windows soak up the scenic (or not, depending on taste) views of Trellick Tower.
PLACE Open-plan Victorian refurb. Oak-panelled floor and bare-brick walls frame an L-shaped bar.
PEOPLE Music and media professionals, along with an assortment of PRs and artists. The family-oriented Sunday lunch is much more low-key.

PROFS Media and music professionals, PRs, artists
CELEBS Kate Moss, Stella McCartney, Damon Albarn, Jarvis Cocker, Jon Carter, Beth Orton, Sarah Cox, Samuel L Jackson, Ewan McGregor, Tom Cruise
DRESS Paul Smith, Nicole Farhi, Stüssy, FCUK, Ralph Lauren, Pepe, Gotcha
MUSIC Ambient, Chill-out, House
DOOR None
DRINKS Beer £2.70, Wine £2.60, Champagne £5.50, Cocktail £5
FOOD Modern European, £10
CARDS No Amex
CAPACITY 200, seating 60
HIRE Venue: Yes Private Room: Yes

LIQUID LOUNGE

Bar, Restaurant Bar
209 Westbourne Park Road W11
020 7229 5050

OPEN Mon-Thu 5pm-midnight, Sat, Sun 10am-midnight	**GETTING LUCKY**	**3/5**
	EYE CANDY	**4/5**
	BIG SPENDERS	**3/5**
TUBE/RAIL Westbourne Park	**MIX** 60%M 40%F	
BUSES 7, 28, 31, 328	**AGE** 23-35	
	PRICE Average	

AMBIENCE Brightly Coloured/Cheerful, Chilled, Conversation, Lounge
REVIEW The Boyzone Pepsi ad was shot here, although you'd never guess, as the Liquid Lounge has far more cartoon cool blue paint than the Americanised commercial reveals. Music biz loungers loll around at the bar, flicking hair out of their eyes while discussing new sounds and promotional gimmicks through a haze of Marlboro. Some sit alone at tables scribbling frantic notes, nodding incessantly as hennaed waitresses supply food. Despite being the only 'bar' in the area and popular with the pre-club drinkers, pulling is not a priority here. They're colleagues or local residents out for conversation – not consummation.
PLACE Ladbroke Grovey lounge dunked in matte blue Dulux with 3D plastic fish murals created by children's TV artist Jay Burridge. Central bar, uncomfortable royal blue plastic canteen chairs – grab a diner-booth for comfort and confidentiality.
PEOPLE They're into their music in a big way, and despite the laid-back-horizontal impression, most probably have their CDs catalogued alphabetically.

PROFS Producers, promoters, music journos, media professionals, PRs, TV professionals, account execs
CELEBS Sacha Baron Cohen, Katy Hill, Hugh Grant, Melanie Sykes, Jamie Theakston, Claudia Winkleman, former All Saints, Lighthouse Family
DRESS Urban sportswear, corduroy, combats, Calvin Klein t-shirts, DKNY touches. Wearing tour t-shirts will get you nowhere. Hair cropped or flopped by Toni & Guy. Camden silver jewellery. Vans trainers
MUSIC Trip Hop, House, Soul, Hip Hop DJs Fri-Sat
DOOR None
DRINKS Beer £2.80, Wine £2.50, Champagne £5, Cocktail £4.50
FOOD Modern British, Modern Eclectic, £6
CARDS No Amex
CAPACITY 150, seating 60
HIRE Venue: Yes · Private Room: No

SUBTERRANIA

Club
12 Acklam Road W10
020 8960 4590

OPEN Mon-Fri 8pm-2am, Sat-Sun 10pm-3am	**GETTING LUCKY**	**3/5**
	EYE CANDY	**3/5**
TUBE/RAIL Ladbroke Grove	**BIG SPENDERS**	**3/5**
BUSES 6, 52	**MIX** 50%M 50%F	
	AGE 23-32	
	PRICE Average	

AMBIENCE Arty/Bohemian, Dancing, Groups, Late Night Open, Minimalist, Party, Student
REVIEW Walking in the shadow of the Westway, it feels more like you're about to score crack than go clubbing. Like a scene from 1984, the impasse to Subterrania is bleak and hostile. With boarded-up shops surrounding it, all it needs is searchlights and Rottweilers to complete the picture. The club itself is cramped and underground, though its four-year strong Rodigan's Reggae on a Wednesday night is still a firm favourite among followers. Subterrania is a concert and club venue that pulls West London's liggers and makers for a few hours of fun. Fashion here may be understated cool, but the atmosphere is easygoing and vaguely local, with themed weeknights. Occasional big name trendy rappers and bands add to the diverse clientele making the most of this minimalist space.
PLACE Like the sticky wall in fairgrounds, Subterrania's two-floor layout allows a balcony of talent to survey the punters below.
PEOPLE A homey club-around-the-corner feel attracts everyone from Penelope Prada and her Notting Hill mob, to meeja midweekers and Queens Park crews.

PROFS Music producers, record company staff, PRs, fashion designers, students, market stallholders
CELEBS Coolio, Fun Lovin' Criminals, Jarvis Cocker, Anna Friel, Finley Quaye, Les Ferdinand
DRESS Trustafarian appliquéd girlie-chic meets wide-leg South Central know how
MUSIC Funk, Garage, Hip Hop, House, Reggae, R&B, DJs
DOOR £5-8
DRINKS Beer £3, Wine £3, Cocktail £7
FOOD Junk, £2
CARDS All

CAPACITY 600, seating 100
HIRE Venue: Yes · Private Room: Yes

THE WESTBOURNE

Gastropub, Pub
101 Westbourne Park Villas W2
020 7221 1332

OPEN Tue-Sat 11am-11pm,	**GETTING LUCKY**	**4/5**
Sun midday-10.30pm	**EYE CANDY**	**5/5**
TUBE/RAIL Westbourne	**BIG SPENDERS**	**4/5**
Park, Royal Oak	**MIX** 50%M 50%F	
BUSES 28, 31, 70, 328	**AGE** 25-35	
	PRICE Average	

AMBIENCE Conversation, Cute Staff, Groups, Hip/Fashionable
REVIEW Remember the snotty shop assistants in Pretty Woman? Now imagine them with Liam hair do's and pierced body parts, serving behind a bar in Portobello. Our advice is to start sleeping with one of them if you want to guarantee service in under 15 minutes. Despite this, the über-trendy masses keep on rollin' in, by motorised skateboard, micro-scooter, kitten heel or TVR Tuscan. A fashionista's paradise, The Westbourne's got about as little in common with a trad boozer as a plate of bresaola and a packet of pork scratchings. This is W2 at its self-confident, posturing best, where popping out for a pint equals a two-hour wardrobe crisis of Elton John proportions. Just fell out of bed? Must have been uncomfortable sleeping in those shoes, sweetheart.
PLACE Shabby chic nicotine white walls and dankest, darkest green. Plenty of tables and chairs, but never enough. Anyone intent on illegal toilet antics, beware the layers of mountainous paint atop the cisterns.
PEOPLE Beautifully crumpled models too gorgeous for make-up, Jamie Theakston wannabes and backgammon playing bohos.

PROFS Media, music, film and TV professionals, models
CELEBS Sir Paul McCartney, Robbie Williams, Jamie Theakston, Neneh Cherry, David Baddiel, Melanie Sykes, Paul Kaye, Maxwell, Lenny Beige, Kate Moss, Anna Friel, Bono
DRESS 'I've spent hours making absolutely no effort whatsoever.'
MUSIC Acid Jazz, Cuban, Hip Hop, Jazz, World Music
DOOR None
DRINKS Beer £2.60, Wine £2.50, Champagne £5, Cocktail £3
FOOD International, Modern Eclectic, £8
CARDS No Amex
CAPACITY 200, seating 150
HIRE Venue: No · Private Room: No

© Costas Anastasakis

© Costas Anastasakis

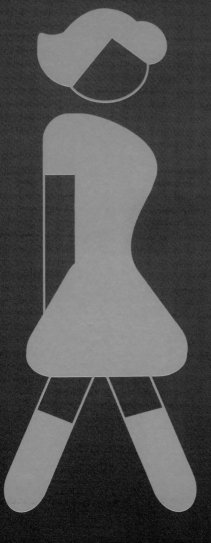

METRO

BIRMINGHAM | BRISTOL EDINBURGH | GLASGOW LEEDS | MANCHSTER

Not so long ago, the only reason a Londoner left the capital for the UK's other cities was the plague or a wrong turn on the M25. The prospect of a weekend spent style bar hopping and drinking in say, Glasgow or Birmingham, would have had 'em rolling in Shoreditch's minimalist aisles.

Such southern arrogance is running out of puff. Not least because so many are ready to quit the capital for a better standard of living. And who wouldn't be tempted given a K2-sized mortgage on a Lilliputian flat in SE1000 and half-thimbles of beer at the equivalent of £20 a pint? In fact this outflux of high spending London professionals has speeded the transformation; Leeds and Birmingham, for example, have moved from backwater boozers to full-on party cities with branches of Harvey Nicks in little more than five years.

So now you've got friends working at the Lloyds TSB or Orange HQ in Bristol you've got a great reason to visit the university city, home to a super-flash waterfront development as well as a private member's bar run by the Massive Attack crew. You don't get much cooler than that.

While Edinburgh has always been on the tourist circuit thanks to the Festival, royal connections and much more liberal Scottish licensing laws, it has had a reputation for being a bit stick-in-the-mud. The arrival of the Scottish Parliament and the ever-growing student population has boosted the city's bar scene. Out go crusty 19th century boozers in favour of a healthy dose of gay-friendly, funky style bars. Even Glasgow, the spiritual home of Begbie-style boozers and hard as nails Neds, has moved upmarket, with two new arts developments, a thriving techno scene and it's own Groucho Club outpost.

Manchester, too, has had a Beckham-style kick up its behind. The acid scene has burnt out and big money has created New York-style lounge bars, loft conversions and private member's clubs. With Man United, Man City and the Hollyoaks cast, Manchester even has a celeb scene of it's own. They're a sussed up crowd of Northern boys and girls who don't need to head to London to sip Cristal and show off their latest designer threads.

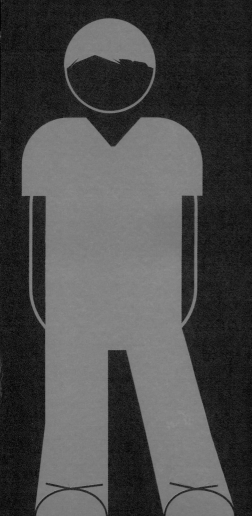

Birmingham

Home of the balti, the country's first gay superclub and the 1998 Eurovision song contest, Birmingham is finally finding a form of expression beyond its concrete image. The 'Second City' has come a long way baby – it's even got its own branch of Harvey Nicks.

The concrete jungles of Queensway and Horsefair have been completely revamped and the opening of The Mailbox is easily the most sophisticated and city-slicker sexy development to hit Brum in years. Home to chichi eateries like Fish, Café Lazeez and the ever-popular **Bar Room Bar**, it's the city's answer to millionaire's row.

The Arcadian is a buzzing mecca in the heart of Chinatown. The starting point for fashionable pre-clubbers and the city's most stylish drinkers, you could base a whole evening's bacchanalia around The Arcadian's rich choice of venues – this is where you'll find **52 Degrees North, Arca, Sobar** and **Indi**.

Broad Street, on the other hand, is Birmingham's answer to Blackpool, complete with bright lights, inebriated tourists and tack by the sack. Still churning out middle-of-the-road venues after all these years, this is where the mainstream masses head for light entertainment.

Brindley Place, just off the main strip, is the jewel in its crown, where city living flourishes for high flyers and daddy's darlings – we recommend New York-style lounge bar **Bank** and the sexy Latin-themed **Ipanema**.

birmingham

52° NORTH

Bar, Restaurant
The Arcadian Centre, Hurst Street
0121 622 5250

OPEN Mon-Wed 5pm-1am,	GETTING LUCKY	4/5
Thu-Sat 5pm-2am,	EYE CANDY	5/5
Sun 5pm-midnight	BIG SPENDERS	4/5
	MIX 50%M 50%F	
	AGE 25-40	
	PRICE Average	

AMBIENCE Hip/Fashionable, Conversation, Destination/
Wishlist, Late Night Open, Outdoors, Pulling
REVIEW Part Studio 54, part West Coast lounge, the
sophistication of this neutrally glamorous space belies
the techno-30s London Underground station interior.
Inside, it's all high-end hotel chic, with dark wood
panelling and be-seen-on raised banquettes. The bar
itself is beautiful, glassy and classy, with abstract
shapes forming a witty canopy. Two balcony areas have
blocky driftwood seats and dingy views – if you want to
gaze at the stars, you're better off inside. The Met Bar
for the Midlands, if you're not in, you're definitely out.
PLACE Vegas penthouse meets New York lounge.
Understatedly stylish, it harks back to US 70s glamour –
think Sharon Stone in Casino and you're there.
PEOPLE Suave, tanned Romeos with Rembrandt smiles;
cellulite-free glamour girls with Aniston-perfect hair.

PROFS Actors, promoters, financiers, footballers, DJs
CELEBS Eddie Izzard, Lennox Lewis, Sid Owen, Michael
Greco, Jay Kay, former All Saints, Aston Villa footballers
DRESS To impress. Even if you've only spent a hundred
dollars, you've got to look a million
MUSIC Easy Listening, Funk, Disco, DJs Tue, Fri-Sat
DOOR None
DRINKS Beer £2.80, Wine £2.20, Champagne £4.90,
Cocktail £4.50
FOOD Modern British, £17 (2 courses)
CARDS All
CAPACITY 350, seating 120
HIRE Venue: Yes · Private Room: Yes

ARCA

Bar
The Arcadian Centre, Ladywell Walk
0121 666 7777

OPEN Mon-Sat 11am-2am,	GETTING LUCKY	3/5
Sun 3pm-12.30pm	EYE CANDY	4/5
	BIG SPENDERS	3/5
	MIX 50%M 50%F	
	AGE 18-24	
	PRICE Average	

AMBIENCE Chilled, Destination/Wishlist, Funky,
Hip/Fashionable, Late Night Open, Lounge, Queues,
REVIEW Why 'Arca'? Well, seeing as it's in the heart of
the Arcadian Centre it's probably a better moniker than
'Dian'. The pre-club bar of the moment, it's Birmingham's
answer to the Queen Vic. Not because the barmaids

look like Sharon, but because it attracts a loyal band
of core regulars who can be seen in the same spot
every weekend without fail. Their eyes move like
characters in Nick Park's cartoons: male or female
they're scanning and computing labels and limbs faster
than a Gatso camera on a catwalk. You see, this is the
ultimate place for Birmingham's young spenders to preen
and be seen.
PLACE Split over two floors. The chilled and bright top
half's a lounge lizards' paradise, where all the beautiful
people hang. The more facially challenged stay
downstairs where it's decidedly darker and one face
looks very much like another.
PEOPLE Young, cocky and up for it. Conspicuous
champagne-drinking and note-waving from kids who
probably still live at home with their mums and dads.

PROFS PRs, PAs, designer shopgirls and boys, media
people, nine to fivers
CELEBS Birmingham City & Aston Villa footballers
DRESS High Street chic – TopShop, Karen Millen,
Oasis, H&M – accessorised with designer bags galore.
There's nothing like a bit of Louis Vuitton to smarten
up an outfit
MUSIC House, Garage, Dance Classics, DJs Fri-Sat
DOOR None
DRINKS Beer £2.30, Wine £2.40
FOOD Fusion, £7
CARDS All
CAPACITY 600, seating 250
HIRE Venue: Yes · Private Room: No

BACCHUS BAR

Restaurant, Bar
Burlington Arcade, New Street
0121 616 7991

OPEN Mon-Sat midday-	GETTING LUCKY	1/5
11pm, Sun midday-6.30pm	EYE CANDY	3/5
	BIG SPENDERS	3/5
	MIX 40%M 60%F	
	AGE 25-45	
	PRICE Average	

AMBIENCE Chilled, Conversation, Lounge, Opulent,
Vampire/Gothic
REVIEW Like the Crystal Maze, zone leads to zone.
There's a trompe l'oeil Oxfordian library zone filled
with fake antique spines, a cathedral window alcove
zone where footsie-playing couples canoodle beneath
chandeliers of dancing neon-orange candle bulbs as
well as an Egyptian-themed champagne bar for when
you're feeling flush. The place overflows with upscale
Harvester-style floral arrangements, 'olde worlde'
artefacts and velvet drapes. The music is almost as
schizophrenic as the flashy Vegas-style faux-historical
interior, lurching from jazz to Moby and Neil Diamond
classics. Despite its name, bacchanalian behaviour is
not accepted; try behaving like Cleopatra and the
management will be coming atcha.
PLACE A mish-mash of mock medieval French and regal
dungeon gothic combined with the latest in Ptolemy
chic. The design was executed by over 100 interior
specialists – and it shows.
PEOPLE A popular hang-out with older, sensible
business types, courting couples and ironic students.

PROFS Lawyers, football managers, TV producers, secretaries, retail staff, students
CELEBS Central News presenters, Aston Villa players, Nigel Havers
DRESS Suits, office wear, Jigsaw, M&S
MUSIC Jazz, Easy Listening, Mellow
DOOR Smart casual
DRINKS Beer £2.60, Wine £3.10, Champagne £5.25
FOOD International, £10.95
CARDS All
CAPACITY 470, seating 120
HIRE Venue: Yes · Private Room: Yes

BANK

Bar, Restaurant
4 Brindley Place
0121 643 9259

OPEN Mon-Sat 11am-11pm, Sun midday-10.30pm		
GETTING LUCKY	**1/5**	
EYE CANDY	**3/5**	
BIG SPENDERS	**4/5**	
MIX 50%F 50%M		
AGE 25-35		
PRICE Average		

AMBIENCE Business, Conversation, Destination/Wishlist, Exclusive, Network
REVIEW A New York-style lounge bar in the heart of Birmingham's swanky business metropolis, serving up cocktails and brunch to the city's Palm-toting suit brigade. With the largest range of spirits in Brum, a certain amount of decorum (and self-control) is required to hold your own in the chic surroundings, so do yourself a favour and don't try to get through them all in one night. More Manhattan than Midlands, Sarah Jessica Parker would be happy to have her Cosmopolitans shaken and stirred by the folk at Bank.
PLACE Slick, moneyed look, with a long chrome bar, red leather diner seating and funky artwork by local artists.
PEOPLE The suits file in during the day replaced by sassy, young urbanites when the lights go down. Bring your business card.

PROFS Bankers, lawyers, office execs, financial analysts, media people, arts administrators
CELEBS Cherie Blair, Vinnie Jones, Aston Villa footballers
DRESS Ralph Lauren, Gucci, Armani, Dolce & Gabbana, Prada, Reiss
MUSIC Ambient, Chill-out
DOOR Smart casual
DRINKS Beer £2.60, Wine £2.90, Champagne £6, Cocktail £5
FOOD French, £11
CARDS All
CAPACITY 300, seated 250
HIRE Venue: Yes · Private Room: Yes

BAR ROOM BAR

Bar
166-168 Salvage Wharf, The Mailbox
0121 632 1199

OPEN Mon-Wed midday-11pm, Thu-Sat midday-midnight, Sun midday-10.30pm		
GETTING LUCKY	**3/5**	
EYE CANDY	**3/5**	
BIG SPENDERS	**4/5**	
MIX 50%M 50%F		
AGE 25-35		
PRICE Average		

AMBIENCE Casual, Conversation, Late Night Open, Lounge, Outdoors, Views
REVIEW This swish bar likes to think of itself as a bit of an executive home from home; certainly the city slickers have claimed it as their local for after-work drinkies. And why not – after a hard night's boozing they've only got a few yards to stagger to their £200 grand luxury wharf-side apartments. It's definitely a 'my wallet's bigger than yours' kind of show. In fact, the whole Mailbox development reeks of Midlands' money and now Harvey Nicks has opened they can live, drink, eat and look the part too. With great views across the newly revamped canals, you can almost see the commoners partying on Broad Street, smug in the knowledge that your Diamond White days are over. Whoever said Birmingham didn't have class?
PLACE The interior is nothing special, all laid-back, understated style with lots of wood and metal, but they certainly nabbed a great location. Close your eyes and you could be in Docklands.
PEOPLE No one earning under 25k. City slickers from the swanky apartments come to splash the cash, Birmingham babes come to snatch the cash.

PROFS Bankers, financial whiz-kids, media execs, IT consultants and entrepreneurs
CELEBS None
DRESS Smartly dressed in Armani suits and Prada loafers, Dolce & Gabbana casual and Gucci shirts
MUSIC Disco, Funk, Old Skool, DJs Thu-Sat
DOOR None
DRINKS Beer £3, Wine £2.50, Champagne £3.50, Cocktail £4.50
FOOD Pizzas, £6
CARDS No Diners
CAPACITY 300, seating 80
HIRE Venue: No · Private Room: No

CODE

Club
49 Heath Mill Lane, Lower Trinity Street
0121 665 6333

OPEN Mon-Thu 7pm-2am,
Fri-Sat 9pm-4am

GETTING LUCKY	**1/5**
EYE CANDY	**2/5**
BIG SPENDERS	**2/5**
MIX 60%M 40%F	
AGE 18-23	
PRICE Average	

AMBIENCE Dancing, Destination/Wishlist, Futuristic/
High-tech, Industrial, Late Night Open, Queues
REVIEW Billed as the best purpose-built dance venue
outside of the Big Smoke, Code is the new home
of major dance superbrand Gods Kitchen. Set up in
down and dirty Digbeth, it's hardly the West End, but
they go on the principle that they'd rather be leaders
than followers. Awesome sound and lighting from the
team behind Fabric have turned this disused warehouse
in back-street Birmingham into the hottest property in
club-land. It's futuristic and high-tech on a major scale,
a haven for the freaky and up-for-it, playing to a jam-
packed house of full-on ravers every Friday and
Saturday night.
PLACE The opulent Gods Kitchen decor of golden angels
and drapes adds a touch of the finer things in life. Not
that the clubbing fraternity really care, they're too busy
doing big fish, little fish, cardboard box to notice.
PEOPLE Gods Kitchen fanatics, generally a few French
fries short of a happy meal, but causing no harm to
anyone but themselves.

PROFS Art, design and fashion students, office-based
nine to fivers letting their hair down, web designers,
promoters, advertising execs, DJs
CELEBS None
DRESS Weird and wonderful (depending on taste)
clubbing costumes prevail – furry boots, bare flesh,
PVC and glow-in-the-dark face paints
MUSIC Hard House
DOOR Entrance £5-10
DRINKS Beer £2.50, Wine £2.40
FOOD None
CARDS No Diners
CAPACITY 1,600, seating 100
HIRE Venue: Yes · Private Room: Yes

HIDDEN

Bar, Club
Kotwall House, Wrottesley Street
0121 622 5700

OPEN Tue midday-2am,
Wed midday-1am,
Thu midday-2am,
Fri midday-4am,
Sat 8pm-6am

GETTING LUCKY	**2/5**
EYE CANDY	**4/5**
BIG SPENDERS	**3/5**
MIX 60%M 40%F	
AGE 18-24	
PRICE Average	

AMBIENCE Basement, Dancing, Destination, Exclusive/
Chic, Funky, Late Night Open
REVIEW Managing to successfully house serious clubbers
alongside Birmingham's style set, Hidden is slap bang

opposite the thriving Arcadian Centre and this is as
good as it gets for late-night eye candy. A basement
VIP bar means celebs and pretenders only have to
mingle with the common people if the urge takes them.
But remember, we're mostly talking footballers here,
who regularly leave the confines of the VIP area to pick
up a friend for the night.
PLACE Impressively large, but so is my Tescos.
Nevertheless, not just another mainstream gaff,
Hidden's subtle oriental theme is a nod to its location
in the heart of Chinatown. Set over three floors with
a basement-level VIP lounge, a lively ground-floor bar
and a top-floor clubbers haven.
PEOPLE Industry players and the clubbing elite
mingle with Birmingham's cool cats and club kittens.
Serious clubbers throw shapes alongside the 'I'm only
here to be seen' poseurs. There's plenty of fine Midlands
T&A which has yet to see or need the surgeon's knife.

PROFS Industry players, promoters, local media,
fashion types, students
CELEBS Hear'Say, Aston Villa players
DRESS Studenty on weeknights – relaxed and
casual but wearing it well. Dressed to kill Fri-Sat
in Chloe, D&G, Evisu, Prada, Gucci, Karen Millen
MUSIC House, Rare Groove, Drum 'n' Bass, R&B,
Garage, Breakbeat, Funk
DOOR Entrance £2-12
DRINKS Beer £2.60, Wine £3.50
FOOD Bar snacks, £4
CARDS No Amex or Diners
CAPACITY 1,000, seating 500
HIRE Venue: Yes · Private Room: Yes

INDI

Bar, Restaurant
Arcadian Centre, Hurst Street
0121 622 4858

OPEN Mon-Sat midday-2am,
Sun midday-midnight

GETTING LUCKY	**2/5**
EYE CANDY	**3/5**
BIG SPENDERS	**3/5**
MIX 60%M 40%F	
AGE 20-26	
PRICE Average	

AMBIENCE Buzzy, Destination, Funky, Futuristic,
Hip/Fashionable, Late Night Open, Minimalist
REVIEW Minimalism and late-night drinking meets
Indian tapas menu for lasting relationship. Sounds
spicy. Actually Indi is as cool as it gets, with a space-
age canteen feel induced by whiter than white floors,
sunken seating and school-style benches. One of the
newer Arcadian venues, it's funky enough to attract the
trendies, but thankfully lacks any mainstream masses-
alienating attitude. A quirky little place to mix and
munch til late, sitting happily somewhere between
Bombay and Birmingham. It smells good too – follow
your nose and you'll be there.
PLACE Futuristic space-age glamour with a top sound
system, funky layout and cute yellow cushions for toned
tushes. The lighting's particularly kind, a sort of sober
equivalent of beer goggles. An abundance of glass
creates a fishbowl effect – avoid if you vant to be alone.
PEOPLE Sassy, young urbanites in the search of top
tunes and culinary diversity.

PROFS PR people, DJs, students, advertising execs, office folk
CELEBS None
DRESS Top-end High Street – Reiss, Karen Millen, FCUK, Jigsaw
MUSIC Funk, House
DOOR None
DRINKS Beer £2.30, Wine £2.30
FOOD Indian Tapas, £9.95
CARDS No Diners
CAPACITY 210, seated 40
HIRE Venue: No · Private Room: No

IPANEMA

Bar, Restaurant
9 Brindley Place, 60 Broad Street
0121 643 5577

OPEN Mon-Tue 10am-midnight, Wed-Sat 10am-2am, Sun midday-10.30pm	**GETTING LUCKY**	**4/5**
	EYE CANDY	**4/5**
	BIG SPENDERS	**3/5**
	MIX 50%M 50%F	
	AGE 21-30	
	PRICE Average	

AMBIENCE Chic/Elegant, Dancing, Groups, Late Night Open, Lounge, Opulent, Outdoors, Pulling
REVIEW You get the impression they're striving for something really classy and apart from the location slap bang in the middle of Birmingham's answer to Blackpool strip, they've got it. The South American-themed Ipanema arrived just in time for the Latin explosion, providing the perfect backdrop for wannabe J-Lo's and poor men's Enrique's to shake their bon-bons to a selection of salsa beats. Inspired by a 50s hotel lobby in Panama, it's all bamboo effect wallpaper, marble floor, fig trees and touchy-feely tan leather. Unfortunately the punters are not quite as tall and tan and young and lovely as the name might suggest, but what they lack in looks they make up for in enthusiasm, wiggling their way around the dance floor like condoms in a wind tunnel. The place screams sex, and many people seem to be quite literally having it on the dance floor.
PLACE Plush and very, very smooth. If this bar were a man, he'd have a rose between his teeth and a comb in his back pocket.
PEOPLE Monied, affluent types, successful brokers and financial floosies, urbanites, ageing playboys, media execs and social butterflies reliving their holiday in Havana/Rio/Cancun.

PROFS Media execs, art students, top-dog managers, financial consultants
CELEBS Local footballers
DRESS The more conservative end of the label stable – sharp suits, Armani, DKNY, Gucci, Karen Millen and Joseph

MUSIC Salsa, Latin, House, Funk
DOOR None
DRINKS Beer £2.60, Wine £4, Cocktail £4.50
FOOD Caribbean, South American, £12.95
CARDS All
CAPACITY 400, seating 200
HIRE Venue: No · Private Room: No

SOBAR

Bar, Restaurant
The Arcadian Centre, Hurst Street
0121 693 5084

OPEN Mon-Sat 11am-2am, Sun midday-midnight	**GETTING LUCKY**	**2/5**
	EYE CANDY	**4/5**
	BIG SPENDERS	**3/5**
	MIX 60%M 40%F	
	AGE 21-26	
	PRICE Cheap	

AMBIENCE Chilled, Destination/Wishlist, Funky, Hip/Fashionable, Late Night Open, Lounge, Outdoors
REVIEW Almost too chilled for its own good, if you're looking for boozed-up bacchanalia you're in the wrong place. Hence the name. If, however, you're looking for a chic venue to debut your latest Harvey Nichols purchases, then you've got it. Up there in the style stakes, it's mellow and fashionable without trying too hard. Slick, minimalist and functional, Sobar serves up tasty noodles and dim sum to a funky crowd who don't feel hard done by if their designer labels are sewn onto the inside, rather than the outside, of their expensive threads.
PLACE Bauhaus meets Ikea, with natural wood, neutral colours and floor to ceiling windows so you can check out the action on the Arcadian's main piazza. They've also got patio heaters for the terrace, so the atmosphere's sometimes hotter outside than in.
PEOPLE Hip locals pop in for a beverage with a Pacific Rim influence, staying just long enough to be seen. Funky students dance around their dim sum, and music fans and wannabe DJs wax lyrical about vinyl.

PROFS Fashion students, designers, city workers, DJs, journalists, musicians
CELEBS None
DRESS Funky street style. The more obscure the label, the better
MUSIC Funk, Breakbeat, Old Skool, DJs Wed-Sat
DOOR None
DRINKS Beer £2.40, Wine £2.30, Champagne £4.80, Cocktail £4.80
FOOD Thai, Noodles, £6.95
CARDS No Diners
CAPACITY 160, seating 80
HIRE Venue: No · Private Room: Yes

Bristol

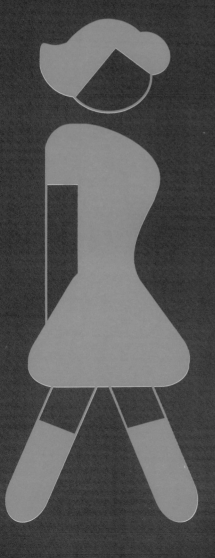

Bristol has long had a reputation as a centre of musical excellence. Thanks to Massive Attack, Reprazent and Tricky, the 90s air was thick with the cutting-edge sounds of trip-hop and breakbeat. However, it's only recently that the city's nightlife has matched the verve and style of the natives.

You see, ten years ago, Brizzle had little to recommend it. Twin gorgons of commercial nightclubs ruled the city centre and the tattooed lager lout was king. It's telling that one of these, IQ, was slain three years ago to become **Creation**, the first superclub in the South West. This was the spearhead for a rebirth of cool, and now new bars and clubs are opening up faster than you can say Portishead.

The waterfront area has been completely regenerated: warehouses are now huge sprawling bars, and boats and boathouses have mutated into restaurants or clubs. A one hundred metre stretch of the Waterfront now consists of a Babylonian commercial club, an arts cinema and seven bars. After years of neglect, the area's vitality has been restored.

The main central area away from the waterfront groans under the weight of soulless chain bars, but with the influx of young wallets that this brings come opportunities to open fiercely independent venues such as **Arc** and **The Dojo Lounge**.

There are several key satellite hubs: Clifton is the Hampstead of the city, an established and rich cultural centre, clinging to the side of the Avon Gorge. To the north is Whiteladies Road, a five hundred metre strip saturated with student-orientated pubs, bars and clubs conveniently leading up to the student halls of residence.

As for students, Bristol is well known for its university – traditionally the haunt of Oxbridge rejects. Rugby-mad Harry and groupie Henrietta are still up to their usual tricks nicking traffic cones. However, the inexorable rise of UWE, the former poly, has lent the student population a less Sloaney image.

THE ACADEMY

Club, Live Music Venue
Frogmore Street
0870 771 2000

OPEN Fri 9.30pm-6am, Sat 9.30pm-3am	**GETTING LUCKY** **4/5**
	EYE CANDY **2/5**
	BIG SPENDERS **2/5**
	MIX 50%M 50%F
	AGE 18-26
	PRICE Average

AMBIENCE Dancing, Glammed-up, Late Night Open, Live Music, Mashed-up, Pulling
REVIEW This is what you get for the £8 million Piers Adam spent re-fitting a huge cinema under an ice-rink. Formerly known as Rock, The Academy provides a sausage-factory club experience and books the biggest-name house DJs available. Friday night's Scream has become a south-west institution with Top of the Pops dancers on the stage and inflatables flying around the room. If you like DJ sets that sound like Pete Tong's Essential Selection, then this is the place for you. Academy club nights are as mainstream as Cilla and Brucie with no pretence of alluding to the underground. Which is fine if an unsophisticated high is what you're after, but discerning clubbers may prefer something more challenging.
PLACE Enormous barn of a main room with a gallery for eyeballing the talent. There's an intimate back room the size of most of the other Bristol clubs.
PEOPLE Young and on the pull from all over town. Hardened mainstream clubbers.

PROFS Students, office workers, callcentre workers, catering, sales and marketing
CELEBS Boy George, Groove Armada, Roni Size
DRESS Tiny dresses, flares, shirts
MUSIC Mainstream House, 80s, Live dance acts
DOOR Smart casual, Fri £12, Sat £5
DRINKS Beer £2.50, Wine £3, Champagne £7, Cocktail £5
FOOD None
CARDS All
CAPACITY 1700, seating 250
HIRE Venue: No · Private Room: Yes

ARC BAR

Bar, Live Music Venue
27 Broad Street
0117 922 6456

OPEN Mon-Wed 6pm-11pm, Thu-Sat 6pm-2am, Sun 6pm-10.30pm	**GETTING LUCKY** **2/5**
	EYE CANDY **2/5**
	BIG SPENDERS **2/5**
	MIX 50%M 50%F
	AGE 21-39
	PRICE Average

AMBIENCE Chilled, Dancing, Friendly, Funky, Late Night Open, Live Music
REVIEW In an area tied up by chain bars Arc is doing its best to assert its individuality. DJs pilot decks from a pod in the corner as lasers zap around above the dance floor. This sounds like it should be a bar solely for Bliss readers, but funky young things come here to check out the music while avoiding the dad-dancing posses from the office. Arc books a range of different DJs and live acts and so can be said to have a pleasingly varied atmosphere throughout the week. The flipside is that it does try too hard to be all things to all people. The result is a somewhat grating mash of styles, but the consistent quality of the music manages to keep it a step above other bars in the area.
PLACE Rough stone walls encase a narrow, candlelit grotto while a DJ overlord sits in a booth straight out of Flash Gordon. For that post-apocalyptic feel there's a bar fashioned from steel off-cuts down one side and metal tables down the other.
PEOPLE Head home from the office in the Astra, rip off the jacket and tie, get into something more comfortable and dance the night away.

PROFS Sales and marketing, insurance, recruitment
CELEBS Roni Size, Casualty cast
DRESS New looking casual, not-at-the-office-wear
MUSIC Tech House, Ambient, Rare Groove, Beats, Hip Hop
DOOR None
DRINKS Beer £2.60, Wine £2, Champagne £5.50, Cocktails £4
FOOD None
CARDS None
CAPACITY 200, seating 40
HIRE Venue: Yes · Private Room: No

BAR HUMBUG

Bar, Chain
89 Whiteladies Road
0117 904 0061

OPEN Mon-Thu 5pm-11pm, Fri-Sat 11am-11pm, Sun midday-10.30pm	**GETTING LUCKY** **3/5**
	EYE CANDY **4/5**
	BIG SPENDERS **2/5**
	MIX 50%M 50%F
	AGE 18-35
	PRICE Average

AMBIENCE Buzzy, Comfy, Groups, Hip/Fashionable
REVIEW Down you go! Park yourself on a leatherette cube with a cooling Hoegaarden. It's been a tough day on the History of Art course and Mummy has been on the phone

crying over another of Daddy's flings. So you gesticulate and exclaim to your six best friends. They sympathise, they've all been through it, but it's scant relief. Maybe food will be of comfort. You have the organic chuck steak burger with Argentinian salsa. Damn it, why shouldn't you, especially since you're never more than 27 grams from your ideal weight. But there's that fox from your tutorial discussing the relative merits of Goldfrapp and Zero 7. Now there's a thing to cheer you up.

PLACE The front bar attempts to marry minimalist and comfy. The result is a bit like an old pub fitted out by a swedish mass market furniture company. The restaurant area is stark and wavy and looks as if it's just stepped out of a Kubrick film.

PEOPLE Beautiful students in Bench and Carhartt t-shirts contemplate creative facial hair among a few of the funkier denizens of the working world.

PROFS Students, office workers, waitresses
CELEBS Portishead, Casualty cast
DRESS Mambo, Bench, Carhartt
MUSIC Ambient, Funk, DJs bi-monthly
DOOR None
DRINKS Beer £2.40, Wine £2.50, Champagne £5.50, Cocktails £5
FOOD Modern British, £10
CAPACITY 150, seating 60
HIRE Venue: Yes · Private Room: Yes

CREATION

Club
13-21 Baldwin Street
0870 444 8666

OPEN Tue-Sat 9.30pm-3am	GETTING LUCKY	3/5
	EYE CANDY	3/5
	BIG SPENDERS	2/5
	MIX 50%M 50%F	
	AGE 18-30	
	PRICE Average	

AMBIENCE Dancing, Glammed-up, Hip/Fashionable, Late Night Open, Mashed-up

REVIEW Creation wants to be the world's biggest underground club. Most of the time it succeeds. It brings the streetwise posses from around town to queue in beer boy city centre. Miraculous really, considering that the previous occupant of the building, the super cheesy IQ, was largely responsible for the area being a cool void in the first place. Creation tends to play host to breakthrough DJs like Roni Size or Fatboy Slim in the pulsing cavern of the main room. The red, slightly sleazy upstairs room usually shows off local talent. At no point should you attempt conversation, even with your best Dom Joly on the mobile impersonation, communication is virtually impossible. There's no choice but to dance, luckily the music is always cutting-edge.

PLACE Huge, forbidding main room oozes street style as lasers flash overhead. Nuclear-powered speakers turned up to 11 ensure that every alcove vibrates to the sound of the bass. The small room upstairs hardly makes for a chill-out sanctuary.

PEOPLE A wide mix of backgrounds come together to out-posture each other. Back bar crawls with enormous guys wielding tiny champagne flutes and gold cards.

PROFS Students, promoters, bar workers, DJs, secretaries, telesales
CELEBS Dannii Minogue, Sol Campbell, Norman Cook, Massive Attack, Goldie, Roni Size, Darren Campbell
DRESS Duffer, Abercrombie & Fitch, Carhartt, Diesel, Hope & Glory for the drum 'n' bass and hip-hop sessions. House nights get very glamorous with underwear as outerwear and short skirts on the girls and short-sleeved shirts and shiny shoes on the boys
MUSIC Drum'n'Bass, House, Hip Hop, UK Garage
DOOR Smart casual
DRINKS Beer £2.50, Wine £3, Cocktail £5
FOOD None
CARDS All
CAPACITY 1,400, seating 200
HIRE Venue: Yes · Private Room: Yes

THE DOJO LOUNGE

Club
12-15 Park Row
0117 925 1177

OPEN Tue-Sat 10pm-2am	GETTING LUCKY	3/5
	EYE CANDY	3/5
	BIG SPENDERS	2/5
	MIX 50%M 50%F	
	AGE 18-30	
	PRICE Average	

AMBIENCE Basement, Dancing, Funky, Hip/Fashionable, Late Night Open, Outdoors, Studenty

REVIEW Dojo is Bristol's smallest club and is always packed by midnight on a Saturday. Hip hop is da 'ting here and so the club attracts the baggiest jeans in town and the most expensive trainers. If you can go into a head-spin from a standing back somersault, chances are that you perfected the move here. The rest of the crowd consists of well-oiled locals having fun and wondering why they don't know the words to the tunes. The two groups never interact. As the place fills, the lagered-up home in on the B-boys' territory and do the one-foot-in, one-foot-out in the allotted 15cm of space. At the weekend there's a bit more room on the heated terrace, but it's still never going to be somewhere for the agoraphobic.

PLACE Tiny subterranean club with oriental motifs on the wall and metal dragons as light shades. Padded red walls and banquettes give the place that louche opium den feel. Clearly hasn't been refitted for a while but isn't run-down yet and is always so busy that all you can see is people anyway. The outside terrace is a godsend in summer.

PEOPLE Cooler than thou staff. Fly boys in bandanas doing head-spins while groupies look on. Funky, laid-back, non-posy students.

PROFS Students, bar workers, DJs
CELEBS Sophie Ellis-Bextor, Courtney Walsh
DRESS Vexed Generation, Sean John, Phat Farm, Stüssy, Quiksilver, Adidas, Puma, Vans, DCs
DOOR Entrance £5
MUSIC Hip Hop, Funk, Soul, R&B, UK Garage
DRINKS Beer £2.50, Wine £2.50
FOOD None
CARDS All
CAPACITY 200, seating 50
HIRE Venue: Yes · Private Room: No

THE ELBOW ROOM

Bar, Pool Bar, Chain
64 Park Street
0117 930 0242

OPEN Mon-Sat midday-2am,	**GETTING LUCKY**	**3/5**
Sun midday-1am	**EYE CANDY**	**3/5**
	BIG SPENDERS	**2/5**
	MIX 50%M 50%F	
	AGE 18-35	
	PRICE Average	

AMBIENCE Buzzy, Dancing, Late Night Open
REVIEW A knowing, retro cool oozes out of every wood panel and funky picture light in this new pool bar. Shoot the eyes off them balls downstairs, having left an array of spurned lovers all over town clutching empty aspirin bottles, then swagger in the gloom up to the dance floor, where seasoned disk spinners fill the small but perfectly formed air with the sounds of obscure 60s and 70s funk. The Elbow Room is co-owned by seminal house and hip-hop producer, Arthur Baker. As you would expect from control by such an arbiter of cool, it manages to stay just the right side of the thin purple line between chic and geek.
PLACE Downstairs is surely the design of Prince's Paisley Park poolroom: mirrors and mood lighting around purple velvet booths flanking the purple baize tables. The upstairs dance floor gives the place its name.
PEOPLE The cool end of the student spectrum shows off its studied nonchalance alongside young PRs and musos who would rather be out with Damon Albarn.

PROFS Students, musicians, sound engineers, media types
CELEBS Arthur Baker, Dan the Automator, Andrew Lincoln (Egg from This Life)
DRESS Mainly High Street with a few Hooch, Bench type urban surfer labels on the boys
MUSIC Funk, Soul, Hip Hop, US House and Garage
DOOR £2.50-4 after 10pm at weekends
DRINKS Beer £2.50, Wine £4, Cocktail £4.50
FOOD Bar Food, £7
CARDS All
CAPACITY 200, seating 80
HIRE Venue: Yes · Private Room: Yes.

E-SHED

Bar
Canons Road
0117 907 4287

OPEN Mon-Sat midday-1am,	**GETTING LUCKY**	**3/5**
Sun midday-12.30am	**EYE CANDY**	**2/5**
	BIG SPENDERS	**2/5**
	MIX 55%M 45%F	
	AGE 18-30	
	PRICE Average	

AMBIENCE Buzzy, Cute Staff, Dancing, Funky, Late Night Open, Party, Studenty
REVIEW Three words. Trying too hard. From the mildly risqué name to the redder than red decor, E-Shed exudes a heartfelt desire to play with the cool kids. But the design is too trendy and the dull poseurs are only here to get prestige through association. Ponytailed DJs lend an almost convincing air to E-Shed's quest for club style credibility. They're let down by the punters, clueless Johnny-come-latelies pretending to really get into the breakbeat when really they prefer tunes they can sing along to. It's not that the place is a phony, it just lacks soul.
PLACE Decked out in nail-varnish rouge, with kitsch tables and sofas. The sheer redness of the place is a bit much during the day, but at night helps to foster the illusion of a Dutch cattle market.
PEOPLE Shaun's attempting to large-it with fake labels, tan and musical knowledge. Quite a few larger ladies shaking their not-inconsiderable booty on the dance floor.

PROFS First jobbers in telesales, finance, law clerks, insurance, shop workers
CELEBS None
DRESS To impress. Short-sleeved black shirts, River Island, TopShop, Debenhams, strappy sandals
MUSIC Breakbeat, Hip Hop, House, DJs
DOOR None
DRINKS Beer £2.50, Wine £2.45, Champagne £3.45, Cocktail £3.95
FOOD Tapas, £4
CARDS No Amex or Diners
CAPACITY 150, seating 50
HIRE Venue: Yes · Private Room: No

ETHER

Bar
2 Trenchard Street
0117 922 6464

OPEN Tue-Sat 5.30pm-2am	**GETTING LUCKY**	**3/5**
	EYE CANDY	**4/5**
	BIG SPENDERS	**3/5**
	MIX 50%M 50%F	
	AGE 25-35	
	PRICE Average	

AMBIENCE Buzzy, Funky, Hip/Fashionable, Late Night Open, Party, Queues
REVIEW Reminiscent of a set from Barbarella, the retro-futuristic capsule that is Ether has seen some similarly sexy shenanigans. Its opening in 2000 heralded a new era for Bristol's bar scene. The rule of the megapub was over and a slick breed of late night boutique style drinking establishments began to ply their alluring trade. Tucked away down a side street just off the teeming city centre, Ether has proved that you can make a small, exclusive bar work outside the capital. But now the rash of slick bars such as Delfter Krug and Sukoshi may mean little Ether's days could be numbered. Still very chilled during the week, but clubby at the weekends.
PLACE Near the entertainment centres of The Academy, the Bristol Hippodrome and Colston Hall, sleek sexy and impressively contemporary. Cool tones, industrial rubber flooring and pure whites dominate both the ground floor bar and the upstairs lounge. Air conditioning, light-boxes and surprisingly comfortable retro chairs. How they keep all that white leather clean is a mystery.
PEOPLE Bristol's It people lead the way here with the usual music suspects making an appearance. Their entourage of local waitresses and bar staff join in the fun.

PROFS Musicians, waiting staff, bar staff, property developers, club owners
CELEBS Andrew Lincoln (Egg from This Life)
DRESS Diesel, Carhartt, Duffer, Abercrombie & Fitch, Linea, Karen Millen, FCUK
MUSIC Breakbeat, Funk, Hip Hop, House, DJs 7 days
DOOR £2 after 10pm Fri-Sat
DRINKS Beer £2.50, Wine £2.50, Cocktail £5
FOOD Bar Food, £4
CARDS No Amex or Diners
CAPACITY 100, seating 50
HIRE Venue: Yes · Private Room: Yes

LEVEL

Club
24 Park Row
0117 373 0473

OPEN Mon-Sat 9pm-2am,	**GETTING LUCKY**	**3/5**
Sun 8pm-1am	**EYE CANDY**	**3/5**
	BIG SPENDERS	**2/5**
	MIX 50%M 50%F	
	AGE 18-32	
	PRICE Average	

AMBIENCE Dancing, Funky, Hip/Fashionable, Late Night Open, Views
REVIEW Funkier than Pam Grier at the Paradise, Level struts its stuff in sequinned splendour. Its decor is based on a 60s/70s airport lounge, Charlie's Angels sort of thing. As a result, there's a significant cheese factor and an attendant campness in the air. Having said that, it does make for an all-together friendly atmosphere and a ripping night's boogie. The corners are bulging with funky chicks and groovy guys and there's a party atmosphere busting out all over. Although it depends on who's in session, the resident DJs are always top class and tend to fill two rooms with funky house. Sundays are of a very different hue as Roni Size and the Full Cyclers fill the place with black, frantic breakbeat for party die-hards and musos alike.
PLACE Downstairs dance floor with understated disco lights and seating in the gloom. Upstairs bright chill-out space with huge picture window looking over the city. Veneer and pastel shades throughout, studded with big neon maps.
PEOPLE Wide mix of good time arty-party people out to meet the like-minded or show off their knowledge of the latest hot tunes.

PROFS Students, office workers, musicians, PR, artists, bar workers
CELEBS Roni Size, Massive Attack
DRESS Glam, flares, 70s, funky
MUSIC Drum 'n' Bass, US House and Garage, Funk, Hip Hop
DOOR Entrance around £5
DRINKS Beer £2.60, Wine £2.50, Cocktail £5
FOOD None
CARDS None
CAPACITY 400, seating 100
HIRE Venue: Yes · Private Room: Yes

NOCTURNE

Club, Members Club
1 Unity Street
0117 929 1181

OPEN Mon-Sat 6pm-2am,	**GETTING LUCKY**	**3/5**
Sun 6pm-12.30am	**EYE CANDY**	**4/5**
	BIG SPENDERS	**4/5**
	MIX 50%M 50%F	
	AGE 21-39	
	PRICE Average	

AMBIENCE Basement, Exclusive/Chic, Destination/ Wishlist, Late Night Open
REVIEW Down a dark, dark hole there's a dark, dark club where the über cool chew the fat over what's phat. Massive Attack, the band who put Bristol on the map and are to blame for the phrase trip-hop have opened their own drinking den. The door's so strict on membership you'd be advised to bring OJ's lawyer with you. Once granted entry it's tempting to remain in the super plush subterranean passages but you'd be missing out. As you'd expect from the group who spawned Tricky, the place reeks of murky twilight. Darkness oozes from each distressed leather fitting as George Clinton gloops out of immaculate panel speakers. Cocktails come expertly mixed but don't expect a paper umbrella. Wear your troubles on your expensive sleeve.
PLACE A candle-lit vault stretching under Park Street in the centre of the city. Once your eyes adjust to the gloom, you notice the club has more raw hide than World of Leather.
PEOPLE This is as good as its gets. Having had your application for membership vetted by some of the darkest musicians of all time, you know you've made it if you spend the night here.

PROFS DJs, musicians, actors, models, writers, sound engineers, graphic designers, IT
CELEBS Massive Attack, Robert Carlyle, Air, Groove Armada
DRESS Black, understated cool. Prada, Gucci, DKNY, Evisu, Miu Miu, Commes des Garçons
MUSIC Funk, Jazz, Hip Hop
DOOR Smart casual, members only
DRINKS Beer £2.40, Wine £4, Champagne £8, Cocktail £5
FOOD Bento Box, £15
CARDS All
CAPACITY 150, seating 50
HIRE Venue: Yes · Private Room: No

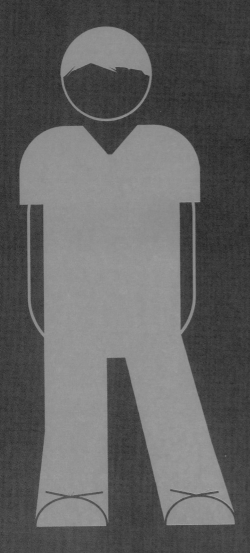

Edinburgh

Edinburgh has traditionally had a reputation for being a wee bit parochial, 'all fur coats and nae knickers' as they say on the West Coast. This certainly spilled over to the licensed trade, with a raft of pubs that looked like they hadn't seen a change or carpet clean in 50 years.

At about the time of the arrival of the Scottish Parliament Edinburgh was given the kiss of life by style-led ventures, while the student population, one of the largest in the UK, bolstered the affluence and mix of the local bar scene.

One of the first areas to tune into this new dynamic was Broughton Street. Littered with junk shops and off-beat boutiques, it set the pace with gay-friendly and funky bars. Broughton Street is now the heartbeat of the city's bar scene, introducing a state of mind that would have been pretty radical a decade ago.

Still at the top of the pile, **The Basement** gives the most vibrant snapshot of the area, drawing the young, the beautiful and the downright weird. **Pop Rokit** capitalised on this appeal, as a sleek, shiny Mecca for sleek, shiny club kids.

The city centre took a little longer to move on, and only the perennially reliable confines of the **City Café** offered any defence against the tartan-infused High Street, attracting winding-down QCs, wealthy post grads and art school idlers. Then along came **Iguana**, with a chic, buzzy appeal and, like, a whole philosophy of its own, man. This is real 90s bar material and looks set to take its place in Edinburgh bar folklore. But it's about more than just drinking, as newcomer **Beluga** underlines, with an in-house restaurant and a first for the East Coast, the VIP room. Edinburgh may still have the fur coat, but as for the knickers, only time will tell...

edinburgh

THE BASEMENT

Bar, Restaurant, Club
10a Broughton Street
0131 557 0097

OPEN Mon-Sun midday-1am		
GETTING LUCKY	4/5	
EYE CANDY	3/5	
BIG SPENDERS	2/5	
MIX 50%M 50%F		
AGE 18-35		
PRICE Cheap		

AMBIENCE Basement, Conversation, Groups, Late Night Open, Party, Pulling
REVIEW Cough, cough, wheeze, wheeze. It's not just smokers who get a nicotine hit in this low-ceilinged subterranean bar/restaurant. Whilst space, light and clean air are not in abundance, people are. Born in the dark days of 1994 when the hungry went to a restaurant, clubbers went to a club and drinkers went to a boozer, the owners set up a triple whammy where the good people of Edinburgh could go to 'get hammered, get stuffed, get down and maybe get lucky, without getting wet'. Catering fully to the professional reveller, The Basement's amply stocked bar includes possibly the most expensive tequila in the world at £70 a shot and a range of vodkas including bison grass flavour. Bison grass, in case you didn't know, is the stuff bison piss on.
PLACE Dark, cave-like basement of a traditional tenement building with two distinct eating and drinking areas split by a circular wooden bar.
PEOPLE Old skool bohemians, hungry students, jeans and t-shirts crowd, crews of drinking buddies.

PROFS Record shop owners, students, retail staff
CELEBS None
DRESS Whatever, however – just avoid Hawaiian shirts, they're reserved for the bar staff
MUSIC Funk, Hip Hop, Pop
DOOR None
DRINKS Beer £2.20, Wine £2.20, Cocktail £3
FOOD Modern Eclectic, Mexican, £5
CARDS No Amex
CAPACITY 120, seating 50
HIRE Venue: No · Private Room: Yes

BELUGA BAR & CANTEEN

Bar, Restaurant
30a Chambers Street
0131 624 4545

OPEN Mon-Sun 10pm-1am		
GETTING LUCKY	3/5	
EYE CANDY	3/5	
BIG SPENDERS	3/5	
MIX 60%M 40%F		
AGE 20-40		
PRICE Average		

AMBIENCE Basement, Buzzy, Conversation, Groups, Late Night Open
REVIEW Beluga tries hard to inject glamour into Edinburgh's drinking classes. Filling in the gap left by the city's Dental Hospital, chi-chi cocktails have replaced pink mouthwash and low-slung seating has pushed aside the dentist's chairs. If you're expecting icy Russian glam and cut-glass decadence, think again. Beluga is Changing Rooms on acid, with stained glass windows and blonde wood colliding with purple and orange 70s retro graphics. More goldfishy than sturgeon-esque, weekdays, it attracts trust fund thoroughbreds and horsey professionals.
PLACE A striking stacked slate waterfall gives a suitably subterranean feel at basement level, emphasised by a murky, muddy palette which is surprisingly effective when the lights go down. The VIP area and braided rope are somewhat unnecessary but the light, modern restaurant makes amends.
PEOPLE The key word here is 'trying'. Trying to be cool, trying to be stylish, trying so hard to look aloof that the loo-paper on your spike heel goes unmentioned until only you aren't aware of it.

PROFS Lawyers, accountants, doctors, rugby and football players, students
CELEBS Prince William, Hibernian players
DRESS Scrubbed up TopShop, Racing Green and Pink (upturned collars optional)
MUSIC Jazz, House DJs Thu-Sat
DOOR None
DRINKS Beer £2.60, Wine £2.50, Cocktail £3.50
FOOD Cross-continental Pick and Mix, £6
CARDS All
CAPACITY 650, seating 150
HIRE Venue: No · Private Room: Yes

THE CITY CAFÉ

Bar
19 Blair Street
0131 220 0125

OPEN Mon-Sun 11am-1am		
GETTING LUCKY	3/5	
EYE CANDY	4/5	
BIG SPENDERS	3/5	
MIX 50%M 50%F		
AGE 20-35		
PRICE Average		

AMBIENCE Chilled, Cute Staff, Hip/Fashionable, Late Night Open, Legendary
REVIEW With a place like the City Café, you either love it or loathe it. Like a favourite pair of trainers, it lingers

in your affections and nowhere fresher and newer really makes the grade. It's distinctively seedy appeal is confirmed by it's status as Irvine Welsh's old stomping ground, and they don't come much seedier than him. A veritable fossil on the Edinburgh scene, the City Café is 15 years old and looks not a day past 30. What it lacks in sleekness, it makes up for in class and charm by the bucketload, from the shady confines of the pool tables to the tuck shop by the door. Even the fish are cool, like some aquatic messenger has told them to like, just hang, man.

PLACE Americana without the kitsch, this is all diner-style booths, moodily lit pool tables and sulky staff. The lower floor is an altogether different animal, taking a cue from Tom Cruise's 'Cocktail', with 80s references and club-style antics come the weekend.

PEOPLE Every new wave of bar staff and every new batch of out-there freshers feel like they've discovered the place all for themselves. As a result, there's always a high level of people-watching from spindly, sexy club-hoppers and lazy lounge lizards to rich students roughing it.

PROFS Court judges, solicitors, DJs, PR, students
CELEBS Irvine Welsh
DRESS A dash of street wear, a splash of TopShop and a sprinkling of obligatory second-hand chic
MUSIC Funk, Soul, House, DJs Thu-Sun
DOOR None
DRINKS Beer £2.60, Wine £2.75, Cocktail £5
FOOD Club Sandwiches, All-Day Breakfasts, £5
CARDS All
CAPACITY 250, seating 140
HIRE Venue: No · Private Room: Yes

THE HONEYCOMB

Club
15-17 Niddry Street
0131 530 5540

OPEN Tue-Sun 11pm-3am		
GETTING LUCKY		3/5
EYE CANDY		3/5
BIG SPENDERS		2/5
MIX 50%M 50%F		
AGE 20-40		
PRICE Average		

AMBIENCE Buzzy, Dancing, Funky, Late Night Open
REVIEW In 1995, Edinburgh entrepreneur Warren Deighan cleaned up capital clubbing by opening The Honeycomb, the city's first tailor-made underground club venue. Four years later he sold the business, leaving a gaping hole in the market for dressed-up clubbers seeking underground sounds. Deighan came to the rescue once again this year, transforming legendary dive The Vaults into the new Honeycomb, a cutting-edge club space boasting a clean, fresh look, a booming sound system and a superior selection of credible club nights. Some of the city's most respected nights are based here, collectively forming a roster that includes everything from dance-floor jazz and funk, through Drum 'n' Bass to real deal house.

PLACE Cavernous club space comprised of three main vaults: the main dance floor, the white leather bar area and the low-lit brown leather back room which includes a small dance floor.

PEOPLE Given the range of nights on offer, you're just as likely to encounter a slacker student wearing a soiled and saggy sweat top as you are a kitted-out clothes horse for the new Prada collection.

PROFS Musicians, media execs
CELEBS Darius Ganesh, Trevor Nelson
DRESS Casual club wear to dressed-up designer gear
MUSIC Funk, Drum 'n' Bass, Underground House, Techno, DJs
DOOR Entrance £6-15
DRINKS Beer £2.80, Wine £2.20
FOOD None
CARDS All
CAPACITY 650, seating 150
HIRE Venue: Yes · Private Room: No

THE HUMAN BE-IN

Bar, Café Bar
2-8 West Cross Causeway
0131 662 8860

OPEN Mon-Sun 11am-1am		
GETTING LUCKY		3/5
EYE CANDY		4/5
BIG SPENDERS		3/5
MIX 45%M 55%F		
AGE 22-35		
PRICE Average		

AMBIENCE Conversation, Groups, Outdoors, Late Night Open, Legendary, Lounge Atmosphere
REVIEW Do you like your best friend any less because he's called Englebert? No. So it is with The Human Be-In. It may be one of the most irritating word-plays since Paul Anka hit the school boy top ten but this is a dreamy bar and we like it. Even if they did steal the name from a festival held in San Francisco in the late 60s where hippy legend has it there was 'a gathering of tribes, a social point and a meeting place for like-minded people'. Just as you think you might spy a young Sartre with one hand on a copy of Being and Nothingness and the other on Simone's behind, in reality, what you actually get is a place full of bunking students wasting their intellect over coffees and chic office girls whiling away lunch hours over hot chocolate.

PLACE Subdued ivory walls are brightened up with downlighting and a fancy wooden and glass bar. Tables outside in summer for posing and choking on petrol fumes.

PEOPLE Trainee It girls in pink pashminas with VW Golfs and a grand a week allowance from Daddy. Stylish professionals who work round the corner.

PROFS Academics, students, lawyers, philosophers, poets, artists, actors
CELEBS Honor Fraser, Lord Lovat, John Leslie, Finley Quaye, Kate Winslet, Mick Jagger
DRESS Racing Green, Ralph Lauren, White Stuff
MUSIC Live Jazz Sun, Live Acoustic Tue, Wed, Hip Hop DJs Thu, Funk DJs Fri, Breakbeat DJs Sat
DOOR None
DRINKS Beer £2.60, Wine £2.70, Cocktail £3.50
FOOD International, £7
CARDS All
CAPACITY 180, seating 120
HIRE Venue: No · Private Room: No

THE IGUANA

Bar
41 Lothian Street
0131 220 4288

OPEN Sun-Tue 9am-1am,	GETTING LUCKY	2/5
Wed-Sat 9am-3am	EYE CANDY	4/5
	BIG SPENDERS	3/5
	MIX 50%M 50%F	
	AGE 18-35	
	PRICE Average	

AMBIENCE Buzzy, Friendly, Late Night Open, Legendary
REVIEW Before The Iguana, Edinburgh's boozers were all blood, sweat and sawdust affairs. Then along came The Iguana, the city's first style bar, and the rest is history. Still crazy after all these years, fashionably bald-headed punters may have a full head of the stuff by the time their pint is served from the crowded curved blonde wood bar. What the bar lacks in speed of service, however, it makes up for in music. At least you'll be able to tap your toes to vinyl spun by a variety of the city's best DJs whilst waiting interminably for Iguana's popular range of 'shooters, sippers and pitchers'. Providing a permanent Friday feeling, Iguana is packed out with style-conscious workers and students who find securing a table as challenging as stretching their loans to accommodate serious vodka Red Bull habits.
PLACE Wood and colour are blended to great effect. Seating – school-style chairs or ludicrously slippy red leather stools – might be in ample supply but close proximity to Edinburgh Uni mean they are usually taken up by loafing students.
PEOPLE Followers of fashion from the university and neighbouring hospital mix with Southside trendies.

PROFS Dentists, doctors, hairdressers, sales personnel, students, lawyers
CELEBS Prince William
DRESS Denim, denim and more denim. Hats, wigs, dreads or bald heads optional
MUSIC Jazz, Funk, Hip Hop, Soul, House, DJs Wed-Sun
DOOR Smart casual
DRINKS Beer £2.50, Wine £2.65, Champagne £5, Cocktail £3.65
FOOD Fusion, £6
CARDS All
CAPACITY 240, seating 120
HIRE Venue: No · Private Room: No

PIVO CAFFÉ

Bar
2-6 Calton Road
0131 557 2925

OPEN Mon-Sat 10am-1am,	GETTING LUCKY	2/5
Sun 11am-1am	EYE CANDY	3/5
	BIG SPENDERS	2/5
	MIX 50%M 50%F	
	AGE 20-30	
	PRICE Average	

AMBIENCE Casual, Chilled, Conversation, Late Night Open
REVIEW Moody Prague shots provide a clue to the bar's identity – please don't call it theme – as well as a good talking point for wannabe travellers, 'of course, that's the totally touristy bit in Berlin... I mean Prague'. Placed in a fairly foreboding stretch of Old Town, the location is reassuringly offbeat enough to entice a jelly-limbed band of skaters and musos, who spend the evening locking on to the hip pre-club beats like a bunch of hypnotised lemmings. However, the place has more than surface appeal, and the chunky monkey benches and tables are perfectly condusive to drink quaffing, if not comfort. Don't they have cushions in Eastern Europe?
PLACE Hailed as a beer hall, or 'bier halle', this is more beer hut. While not very big, it is clever, the low ceilings enhancing a luvved-up pre-club atmosphere and forcing close contact for movement and warmth.
PEOPLE Grown-up skaters who still can't find trousers to fit properly, students with more money than sense and savvy media types guffawing loudly on phones or at friends.

PROFS Radio station employees, journalists, DJs
CELEBS None
DRESS Maharishi, Lady Soul, Stüssy
MUSIC Hip Hop, US House, DJs Thu-Sun
DOOR None
DRINKS Beer £2.60, Wine £2.30, Cocktail £4
FOOD Eastern European, £5
CARDS All
CAPACITY 220, seating 60
HIRE Venue: No · Private Room: No

THE POND

Bar
2 Bath Pond Road, Leith
0131 467 3825

OPEN Mon-Wed 4pm-1am,	GETTING LUCKY	3/5
Thu-Fri 2pm-1am,	EYE CANDY	3/5
Sat-Sun 1pm-1am	BIG SPENDERS	2/5
	MIX 60%M 40%F	
	AGE 20-40	
	PRICE Average	

AMBIENCE Conversation, Groups, Lounge, Outdoors
REVIEW When the former co-promoter of Edinburgh's much-missed easy-listening night Going Places invested his faith and cash in an old men's boozer stuck out in the arse-end of Leith, you had to question his wisdom. The gamble paid off, though, and it's now one of the best bars you'll find in Edinburgh, period. There's been no major refurbishment and it doesn't look any different to any other bar; The Pond's success is purely down to its laid-back, relaxed vibe. Night or day the atmosphere is inviting and comfortable. It's almost like hanging out round your mate's house, except sadly the beer isn't free. Sunday afternoons were made for this.
PLACE An assortment of beaten-up and decrepit furniture, including two suspended wicker chairs, pictures of Corrie stars and original Space Invader machines. Feel free to admire the tropical fish but resist the drunken urge to feed them. Although you might like unpronounceable bottled foreign beer and crisps for tea, fish don't.
PEOPLE An assortment of Edinburgh's weird and wonderful, including strange punky looking people smoking fat cigars and creatives from Leith's waterfront developments. Students give The Pond a wide berth, so being off the beaten track has its advantages.

PROFS Artists, writers, musicians, web designers, advertising copywriters
CELEBS None
DRESS Battered leather, tracksuit tops, brothel creepers, fake fur coats, grubby macs, trainers
MUSIC Easy Listening, Film Scores, Funk
DOOR None
DRINKS Beer £2.20, Wine £2.30
FOOD None
CARDS None
CAPACITY 100, seating 50
HIRE Venue: Yes · Private Room: No

POP ROKIT

Club
2a Picardy Place
0131 556 4272

OPEN Mon-Sun 11am-1am		
GETTING LUCKY	**3/5**	
EYE CANDY	**4/5**	
BIG SPENDERS	**4/5**	
MIX 40%M 60%F		
AGE 20-30		
PRICE Average		

AMBIENCE Buzzy, Cute Staff, Hip/Fashionable, Minimalist, Late Night Open
REVIEW Pop Rokit attracts bright young things like RuPaul to a make-up counter. With its trendy Broughton Street location and solemn but sexy staff, the place rocks, though the only movement is the odd spot of table-hopping and the overflow of midriff from low-slung hipsters. Previously known as The Catwalk, many of Pop Rokit's customers look like they should be on one. Bearing this in mind, tables are helpfully and strategically placed for checking out new arrivals/potential conquests/competition.
PLACE Something of a goldfish bowl, this steel and glass-walled venue shamelessly encourages narcissists. The basement is more forgiving, with sleep-inducing sofas, wrinkle-resistant lighting and late-night dance-floor action.
PEOPLE A mix of Edinburgh's prettiest people, from glossy haired, clicky-heeled promoters to boggle-eyed, baggy-trousered bedroom DJs.

PROFS Media and advertising employees, promoters, DJs
CELEBS None
DRESS Karen Millen and TopShop for girls, Uth and FCUK for boys
MUSIC R&B, Drum 'n' Bass, House
DOOR None
DRINKS Beer £2.70, Wine £2.60, Champagne £6, Cocktail £4.50

FOOD Finger Food, £4
CARDS No Amex or Diners
CAPACITY 240, seating 80
HIRE Venue: No · Private Room: Yes

RICK'S

Bar, Restaurant, Hotel
55a Frederick Street
0131 622 7800

OPEN Mon-Sun midday-1am		
GETTING LUCKY	**4/5**	
EYE CANDY	**4/5**	
BIG SPENDERS	**4/5**	
MIX 50%M 50%F		
AGE 25-40		
PRICE Average		

AMBIENCE Chic/Fashionable, Conversation, Cute Staff, Groups, Pulling
REVIEW If the Sex and the City girls were to find themselves in Edinburgh, this is where they'd drink. Set in a neo classical townhouse in the heart of Edinburgh's Georgian New Town, Rick's is a particular favourite with footballers' wives, girlfriends of club-owners and hairdressers. Don't let that put you off, though, for it's also one of the prettiest spots in town. In every way. Gorgeous staff – they probably all model on the side – can't do enough for you. Light streaming in through the glass roof illuminates the straight-off-the-catwalk crowd and the unusually friendly doormen make you feel most welcome. There's even a boutique hotel upstairs – handy if you can't make it home after one perfect Martini too many.
PLACE The bright, airy mezzanine area is great for daytime lounging while the rear of the bar gets lively and crowded. The crisp, chrome bar co-ordinates perfectly with the expensive clientele's designer threads.
PEOPLE Gawping gents who are happy to spend their inheritances on tanned, toned and teasing Amazonian lovelies who flutter their eyelashes in time to the music.

PROFS Sportsmen, media folk, loaded students
CELEBS Dwight Yorke, Graham Norton, Richard Whiteley, Gary Rhodes, John Leslie, Hibernian players
DRESS To impress. Men follow the Chris Eubank school of fashion, ladies go for va-va-voom
MUSIC R&B, Soul, Lounge
DOOR Smart casual
DRINKS Beer £2.75, Wine £2.75, Champagne £5, Cocktail £4.95
FOOD Fusion, £12
CARDS All
CAPACITY 300, seating 100
HIRE Venue: No · Private Room: No

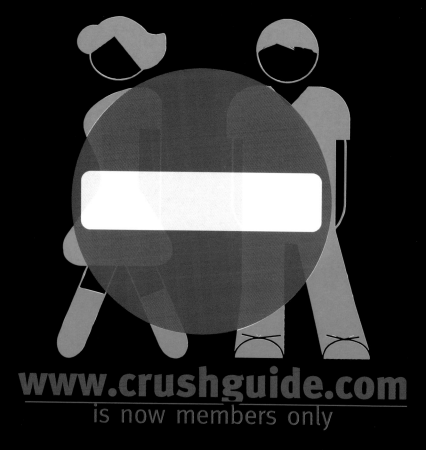

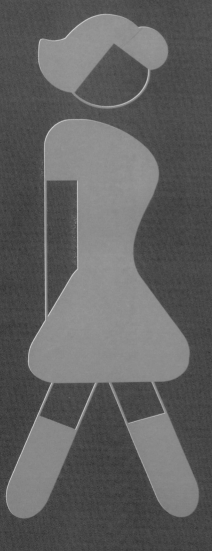

METRO

Glasgow

The mere mention of the name Glasgow evokes images of smog-choked grey skylines and foul-mouthed Rab C Nesbitt types swigging whisky in shell suits and string vests. This is the Glasgow of the past, which began to take its final gasps around the mid-80s, shortly before it was voted European City of Culture.

One by one the bleak high-rise blocks began to fall, closely followed by the infamous dive bars.

A recent drive, backed by the Scottish Parliament and City Council, which encourages the development of new architecture, is helping to revitalise once infamous areas of the city. The Gorbals, known for its 19th-century slums, is a fast-changing place with projects such as The Lighthouse Complex and CCA Gallery helping to evolve a new generation of artists. The River Clyde is the subject of a hundred million pound revival project which, it is predicted, will attract over a thousand times that figure in fresh investment along the water.

Glasgow's nightlife rocks; areas such as the Merchant City and West End are overflowing with fashionable and welcoming bars, including Bargo and Bar 91 in the Merchant Quarter and the Cul De Sac on Ashton Lane.

These areas are rivalled by the environs of Sauchiehall Street, home to bars like Variety, **Spy**, **Groucho Saint Jude's** and **Lowdown**. The area around Kelvingrove Park also has a wealth of original venues such as McPhabbs, McChuills, **54 Below** and **Air Organic**.

Glasgow was voted the second most techno city in the world after Detroit, according to *Muzik* magazine. Clubs such as **Alaska, The Arches** and **Mas** provide some of the best house nights around, with names like Jon Carter, Carl Cox and Masters at Work making the wintry journey north for regular guest appearances.

Not forgetting, of course, that Glasgow is also a big university city, with no fewer than four campuses in and around the centre. The town also has its A-list side, with **Candy Bar** and Corinthian being fashionable hang-outs for the hip.

And all without a string vest in sight.

glasgow

54 BELOW

Bar
3 Kelvingrove Street
0141 357 5454

OPEN Mon-Sun midday-midnight	GETTING LUCKY	2/5
TUBE/RAIL Partick	EYE CANDY	3/5
	BIG SPENDERS	3/5
	MIX 60%M 40%F	
	AGE 20-40	
	PRICE Average	

AMBIENCE Arty/Bohemian, Business, Buzzy, Conversation, Cute Staff, Late Night Open, Lounge Atmosphere
REVIEW Some bars burst on to the scene like Jordan, all flagrant self-promotion and in-yer-face design with two big guys up front to push back the crowds. 54 Below is from the old school. Doing it by word of mouth, this low-key venue lies in an area famous for its artistic community, next to Kelvingrove Park. The oddly urban concrete exterior places it somewhere between an office and a lockup, but step indoors and things are just peachy. It's a refreshing blend of sofas that you wish you had in your living room, drinkers who don't need to be heard by the whole bar, and staff so cute you could put them in your pocket and take them home.
PLACE Like the place, the decor is quiet, coming on to you with a nudge and a whisper, all caramel hues, earthy tones and touchy-feely wood, brick and stone.
PEOPLE The punters here may dress down, but if they're in during happy hour, it's a coincidence rather than the budget bar bill.
PROFS Art students and lecturers, lawyers, publishing, new media, music industry employees
CELEBS Arab Strap, Belle & Sebastian
DRESS Whistles, Gap, Pied à Terre, Urban Outfitters
MUSIC Ambient, Chill-out
DOOR No tracksuits, scruffy trainers or baseball caps
DRINKS Beer £2.50, Wine £2.70, Champagne £4, Cocktail £3.95
FOOD Eastern European, £5
CARDS All
CAPACITY 220, seating 100
HIRE Venue: No · Private Room: Yes

AIR ORGANIC

Bar
36 Kelvingrove Street
0141 564 5200

OPEN Mon-Sat 10am-midnight,	GETTING LUCKY	2/5
Sun midday-midnight	EYE CANDY	3/5
TUBE St George's Cross	BIG SPENDERS	3/5
	MIX 50%M 50%F	
	AGE 25-45	
	PRICE Cheap	

AMBIENCE Arty/Bohemian, Buzzy, Hip/Fashionable, Late Night Open, Minimalist
REVIEW Hang-out for rich hippies. A temple of minimalism almost to the point of sterility – all white walls, chic laminated surfaces and additive-free cuisine – the clientele treat it as a soothing sanctuary. The chat buzzing round the art-hung walls is of oxygen therapy and reiki and though the air is organic you won't find a New Age zealot near this joint – the atmosphere thankfully falls well short of the preachy, po-faced sensibility associated with other healthy-living establishments. The well-toned clientele may be ardently body conscious but the spiky-haired bartenders still sell more Chardonnay than wheatgrass juice.
PLACE Previously Bar Miro with a zany Changing Rooms style primary colour scheme, this West End bar dramatically restyled itself to emerge as the culinary equivalent of Kryptonite.
PEOPLE Some genuine grungers and lots of suits who would love to be slackers if their crippling mortgages would allow it. Weekend boarders and bladers who extol the virtues of small wheels over 18" alloys, but still drive to the park in gas-guzzling off-road vehicles.
PROFS Fashion stylists, ad and TV execs, ITs, lecturers, graphic designers, architects, snowboard retailers, couriers, management consultants
CELEBS Gillian Anderson, Robert Carlyle, Jay Kay, Jarvis Cocker, Anna Ryder-Richardson (her boyfriend owns the gaff), Neil Morrissey, Iain Glen
DRESS Stüssy, Phat Farm, Voyage, Ghost, Whistles
MUSIC House, Bongos, Funk, Rock, DJs, Live Bands
DOOR None
DRINKS Beer £2.30, Wine £1.90, Cocktail £4
FOOD Traditional Scottish, Thai, £6
CARDS All
CAPACITY 220, seating 50
HIRE Venue: Yes · Private Room: No

ALASKA

Club
142 Bath Lane
0141 248 1777

OPEN Tue, Thu-Sun 11pm-3am	GETTING LUCKY	2/5
TUBE/RAIL Buchanan Street, Charing Cross	EYE CANDY	3/5
	BIG SPENDERS	3/5
	MIX 55%M 45%F	
	AGE 18-30	
	PRICE Cheap	

AMBIENCE Casual, Chin Stroking, Dancing, Funky, Friendly, Industrial/Warehouse, Late Night Open, Party
REVIEW Alaska has quietly established itself as Glasgow's premier underground dance club, showcasing a variety of home-based DJ talent. In the year since the club was taken over by the Slam Events/Soma Records team the venue has hosted a number of international guests including Gene Farris, Carl Cox, Master H and Jon Carter. The range of happy ravers is pleasantly broad; nobody bats an eyelid, whether you're an over-dressed glamour girl or a sweat-covered urban surfer chick. Wear what you like and do what you want, just don't monopolise the dance floor.
PLACE Hidden away in a quiet lane, Alaska is one of the hardest clubs to find in Glasgow. Although the plan was for a downstairs chill-out area, in reality the temperature is so high you'd only cool off if you'd just spent a night in the sack with J-Lo.

PEOPLE Despite the overall friendliness of the crowd one twat on the upstairs dance floor can wreak absolute havoc due to the size of the place. The loos often resemble an episode of Casualty, but behind the slack jaws and thousand-yard stares there's always a very happy person 'just catching their breath'.

PROFS Students, stylists, journalists, musicians
CELEBS Sara Cox, Jon Carter, Carl Cox
DRESS From scuffed trainers to stilettos
MUSIC Deep House, Techno, Hip Hop, DJs
DOOR Entrance £10
DRINKS Beer £2.20, Wine £2.40, Cocktail £4
FOOD None
CARDS None
CAPACITY 300, seating 30
HIRE Venue: Yes · Private Room: No

THE ARCHES

Bar, Café, Club
Bar: Argyll Street
Club: Midland Street
0901 022 0300

OPEN Bar: Mon-Sat 11am-midnight, Sun midday-midnight. Club: Fri-Sat 10.30pm-3am, 1st Sun of every month 4pm-midnight	GETTING LUCKY	3/5
	EYE CANDY	4/5
	BIG SPENDERS	2/5
	MIX 65%M 35%F	
	AGE 18-40	
TUBE/RAIL St Enoch, Central Station	PRICE Cheap	

AMBIENCE Casual, Chin-Stroking, Dancing, Friendly, Funky, Industrial/Warehouse, Late Night Open, Legendary, Luvved-up, Mashed-up, Party, Queues
REVIEW The Arches has attained legendary status as Scotland's best-known dance club. Recently renovated to accommodate a café bar, the venue also serves as a concert hall, theatre and occasional television set. The club side of the operation features some of the city's finest house acts, including Silicone Soul and Funk D'Void, emerging talents, such as the Traxx DJs, and big club nights Colours and Inside Out. On any given night you can find badly dressed Neds (Celtic for Kevins) grooving alongside dance-floor veterans. The atmosphere rocks and if you ask Scottish clubbers to name their best nights you'll find that a trip to The Arches is always top of the list.
PLACE About as well furnished as a Romanian hospital, but the spartan set-up seems to only heighten the dance-obsessed atmosphere.
PEOPLE Glasgow does have a reputation as one of Britain's 'harder' cities but The Arches dispels some of the scarier stereotypes. You'll make as many new mates as records played including that large, sweaty, bug-eyed man telling you he's having the best night of his life.

PROFS Teachers, drag artists, postroom boys, couriers, artists, musicians
CELEBS Howard Marks, Irvine Welsh, Sara Cox, Evan Dando
DRESS Flares to fur bikinis
MUSIC Funk, Hip Hop, House, Techno, DJs
DOOR Entrance £10-20
DRINKS Beer £2.20, Wine £2.20

FOOD Modern British, £6
CARDS All
CAPACITY 1,700, seating 100
HIRE Venue: Yes · Private Room: Yes

CANDY BAR

Bar, Restaurant
185 Hope Street
0141 353 7420

OPEN Mon-Sat midday-midnight,	GETTING LUCKY	4/5
	EYE CANDY	4/5
Sun 4pm-midnight	BIG SPENDERS	3/5
TUBE/RAIL Buchanan Street	MIX 50%M 50%F	
	AGE 20-30	
	PRICE Average	

AMBIENCE Funky, Kitsch, Late Night Open, Party, Pulling
REVIEW Not to be confused with the designer dyke bar in Soho, this humbug-coloured cutey is run by two friends from way back when. They're men of many talents, applying their technical expertise in the kitchen through the day and mastering the decks come the weekend. The be-seen kids flock to Candy like winos to a Belgravia dustbin. The most self-consciously cool drinkers in the city have perfected a shabby casual chic look to rival Portobello's finest.
PLACE Taking inspiration from Polo mints, the huge central seating arrangement acts as a good barometer of who's in and who's out. Don't worry if you're standing, because the music is never less than jaw-crackingly cheerful and the retro-happy decor is feel-good through and through.
PEOPLE Glammed-up PR girls and super-quiffed hair boys meet for a dazzling showdown of white teeth and St. Tropez tans with untucked shirts and knowingly obscure mobile ring tones.

PROFS Media and advertising professionals, musos, PR, club organisers
CELEBS Kelly MacDonald
DRESS Duffer, Diesel, Polo Sport, Karen Millen, TopShop, Camper
MUSIC Lounge, Dance, DJs Fri-Sun
DOOR Smart casual
DRINKS Beer £2.30, Wine £2.70, Cocktail £4.50
FOOD Modern European, £4
CARDS No Amex or Diners
CAPACITY 150, seating 50
HIRE Venue: No · Private Room: No

CUBE

Bar, Club
32 Queen Street
0141 226 8990

OPEN Mon-Tue 11.30pm-3am, Wed 11pm-3am,	GETTING LUCKY	4/5
	EYE CANDY	4/5
Thu-Sat 5pm-3am,	BIG SPENDERS	3/5
Sun 11pm-3am	MIX 50%M 50%F	
TUBE/RAIL Buchanan Street, Queen Street	AGE 18-25	
	PRICE Average	

AMBIENCE Basement, Comfy, Dancing, Glammed-up, Fashionable, Late Night Open, Party, Pulling

REVIEW Take one dingy Glasgow nightspot (Planet Peach), liberally add red leather panelling, give it a new layout and moniker and what do you get? Cube, an upmarket club carving a niche for itself as one of Glasgow's hottest new party places. Despite the wannabe poncey punters, the general mood of the place is friendly, although a smile wouldn't hurt from the cut-out tough guy bouncers.
PLACE The bar area is generally packed with well-groomed youngsters, still idealistic enough to think they can pull while steaming drunk. The dance floor is home to the usual collection of predatory females and staggering would-be romeos.
PEOPLE Cube is home to a posey, pissed-up posse. In addition to the 'do you know who I am' crew there are plenty of underdressed lasses knocking back alcopops, as well as random fools gripping free surfaces and straining under the weight of their eighth Aftershock.

PROFS Market research, students, accountants, admin workers
CELEBS The occasional Celtic or Rangers football player
DRESS Saturday night best. Designer labels, Christmas and birthday presents from Mum and that classy number they've been saving for since they were sixteen
MUSIC Chart, Party Hits, Commercial Dance, R&B
DOOR Smart casual, £2-8
DRINKS Beer £2.60, Wine £2.50, Cocktail £2.50
FOOD None
CARDS All
CAPACITY 600, seating 100
HIRE Venue: Yes · Private Room: Yes

GROUCHO SAINT JUDE'S

Bar, Restaurant, Hotel Bar
190 Bath Street
0141 352 8800

OPEN Mon-Sat midday-midnight,	**GETTING LUCKY**	**1/5**
	EYE CANDY	**4/5**
Sun 12.30pm-11pm	**BIG SPENDERS**	**4/5**
TUBE/RAIL Cowcadden	**MIX** 60%M 40%F	
	AGE 25-40	
	PRICE Cheap	

AMBIENCE Basement, Business, Elegant/Classic, Late Night Open, Lounge Atmosphere
REVIEW The offspring of its Soho namesake, baby Groucho is nothing if not exclusive, though you don't need an Equity card or a Hampstead mansion to get in. Like a well-polished by-product of a Roxy Music video, every surface spells cool 70s chic. With a distinctly members bar look to it (though it's open to everyone) the bulk of customers seem to have a real sense of purpose behind their presence, whether it's getting that Latvian film project off the ground or working their way through the whole cocktail menu. This imbues everything with an air of intelligence so that even sipping a Cosmopolitan seems considered rather than frivolous.
PLACE Discreet to the point of invisible, only the little neon cocktail sign rescues that optimistic night on the tiles from going West End-wards. There's space out front for those that like to see their own breath, otherwise grab the big square sofa to the left for your own private party.

PEOPLE Successful, well-adjusted professionals content to switch off the mobile for a big night out. Smart 30-something ladies living it up like Carrie and co.

PROFS Media and advertising professionals, finance executives, lawyers
CELEBS Fran Healey, Ewan McGregor, Baz Luhrmann, Jarvis Cocker, Steve Coogan, Sian Phillips, Dougray Scott
DRESS Jigsaw, Joseph and Whistles
MUSIC Funk, Soul, DJs Thu-Sun
DOOR No Kappa tracksuit and gold sovereign ring combos
DRINKS Beer £2.40, Wine £2.30, Champagne £5.90, Cocktail £5
FOOD Modern European, £6
CARDS No Amex or Diners
CAPACITY 240, seating 80
HIRE Venue: Yes · Private Room: Yes

LOWDOWN

Bar, Restaurant, Club
154-158 Bath Street
0141 331 4060

OPEN Mon-Thu 11.30am-1am, Fri-Sun 11.30am-3am	**GETTING LUCKY**	**3/5**
	EYE CANDY	**3/5**
TUBE/RAIL Buchanan Street	**BIG SPENDERS**	**3/5**
	MIX 60%M 40%F	
	AGE 30-45	
	PRICE Average	

AMBIENCE Basement, Groups, Late Night Open, Mature/Older Clientele, Network, Party
REVIEW Sweet and low down, this basement venue sits in the abyss marked 'good bars for grown-ups'. Now Bar 38 down the road has become the latest victim of consumer absenteeism and an ever-increasing gap between venues for club kids and domino-playing Help the Aged recipients, Lowdown is the real deal. Attracting paunchy, wealthy suits and their pared-down female contemporaries, this is the type of place where 30-somethings can unashamedly let rip to M People with likeminded corporate air guitarists.
PLACE In comparison to the usual broom cupboard-sized pre-club affairs dotted around Glasgow, Lowdown is positively gargantuan. Stripped-back stone walls, piles of crumbly candles, squidgy smooching booths and a massive island bar.
PEOPLE The perfect place to wind down after clinching that all-important deal, dance with rolled-up shirt sleeves, get up close to Karen from finance and drink lager you can't pronounce the name of.

PROFS Merchant bankers, solicitors, editors, ladies who lunch
CELEBS Nick Nairn, Gordon Ramsay
DRESS Gap, Jigsaw, Gant, Guess, Ralph Lauren
MUSIC Lounge, Chart, DJs Thu-Sun
DOOR Fri-Sat £6-7 after 11pm
DRINKS Beer £2.50, Wine £2.50, Champagne £6, Cocktail £6
FOOD Asian, Mediterranean, American, £5
CARDS No Diners
CAPACITY 560, seating 200
HIRE Venue: No · Private Room: Yes

MAS

Club
29 Royal Exchange Square
0141 221 7080

OPEN Tue, Thu-Sun 11pm-3am
TUBE/RAIL Buchanan Street, Queen Street Station

GETTING LUCKY	**4/5**
EYE CANDY	**4/5**
BIG SPENDERS	**3/5**
MIX 50%M 50%F	
AGE 18-35	
PRICE Average	

AMBIENCE Arty/Bohemian, Buzzy, Casual, Dancing, Friendly, Hip/Fashionable, Late Night Open, Lounge Atmosphere, Party Pulling

REVIEW As the summer of 2001 drew to a close, Mas became the official substitute venue for local favourite Sub Club, which burned down in 1999. Now the Sub's former residents play here and have brought their fans with them. Every week is a sell-out with immensely talented mix-men blending house, electro, techno for an up-for-it crowd. Mas has a reputation for being super friendly to both new residents and non-Scots, so go on your own and leave with a busload of new best friends.

PLACE A lot of money has been spent on making Mas one of the most modern, state-of-the-art clubs in Scotland. The sound system is perfect and the layout is both eye-catching and comfortable. A large and sociable bar leads on to a dark and atmospheric dance floor.

PEOPLE Since taking on the Sub Club as lodgers, Mas has inherited some of the city's most fashionable and music-conscious clubbers. There can be a bit of a pretentious element to the crowd, although in general the people are friendly and there is never any grief.

PROFS Journalists, musicians, artists, designers, film and TV executives, students, architects, teachers, music industry
CELEBS Local DJs and music industry faces
DRESS Carhartt, Evisu, Urban Outfitters, Firetrap, Diesel, Mango, FCUK, Puma
MUSIC Deep House, Underground Disco, Techno, Electronica, Tribal House
DOOR Entrance £5-10
DRINKS Beer £2.40, Wine £2.20
FOOD None
CARDS None
CAPACITY 600, seating 100
HIRE Venue: Yes · Private Room: No

SPY BAR

Bar, Hotel Bar
152 Bath Street
0141 221 7711

OPEN Mon-Sat midday-midnight,
Sun 6pm-midnight
TUBE/RAIL Cowcadden

GETTING LUCKY	**2/5**
EYE CANDY	**4/5**
BIG SPENDERS	**2/5**
MIX 50%M 50%F	
AGE 18-40	
PRICE Average	

AMBIENCE Basement, Chilled, Comfy, Funky, Late Night Open, Party

REVIEW Used to look like Austin Power's shag pad, but with its red and grey makeover now looks more Miss Moneypenny, restrained and classy but with a delicious hint of kinkiness. Rumpled staff come from the Prince Philip school of charm and do great Stasi impressions, curling their lips and acting superior. Cheap, imaginative bar grub, gallons of vodka and Red Bull and up to the minute DJs (Spy is well known for its cutting-edge music policy) fuel a hip, pre-club crowd, although the daytime customers are a squarer mob. By ten o'clock it's always heaving with a young, loud crowd who believe they're cooler than they are – someone should tell those sparkle-cheeked girls that leg warmers are 5000 2000.

PLACE Basement bar in fashionable Bath Street, a few blocks up from its posher sister, The Arthouse Hotel. Frosted glass windows and comfy couches are perfect for snuggling up and conspiring.

PEOPLE Teenagers with wallet chains and bum-fluff goatees chat up gaggles of flesh-baring Atomic Kitten fans alongside preening liggers on the lookout for free club passes.

PROFS Students, hairdressers, lawyers, computer programmers, insurance agents, shop assistants
CELEBS Dan Ackroyd, Gillian Anderson, Celtic Football Team
DRESS Clubby but inexpensive; Morgan, Base, Miss Selfridge
MUSIC Breakbeat, Funk, Hip Hop, Disco, House, DJs Tue, Thu-Sun
DOOR No Neds
DRINKS Beer £2.20, Wine £2.60, Cocktail £4.50
FOOD Pacific Rim, Bar Snacks, £5
CARDS No Diners
CAPACITY 250, seating 120
HIRE Venue: No · Private Room: Yes

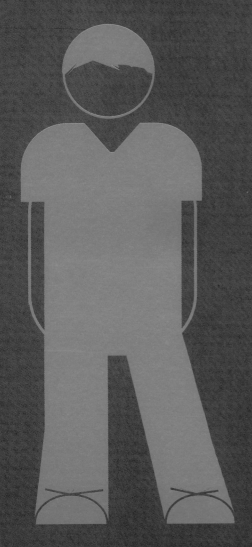

Leeds

Leeds learnt to fly before it could bar crawl, moving from land of the boozer to bar-crazy metropolis in five hectic years. It wasn't too long ago that the fishnetted legs on Call Lane belonged to an ancient hooker, rather than a dressed-up Northern glamourpuss enjoying the city's cocktail carnival.

The credit for this transformation should go to Art's Bar-Café, the first venue that didn't stock ladies glasses for soft drinks and halves of lager 'n' lime. Soon after, Wallpaper* readers favourites **Norman**'s and The Townhouse opened their stylish doors for the first time.

There aren't any no-go areas any more, but there are places where you wouldn't want to be visibly minted. New Briggate, to the north of the retail centre, is the real deal. Peppered with pound shops and people of no fixed abode, it's the spiritual home of The White Stripes and The Dandy Warhol's. **Mojo, Mint** and **North** are highlights in this insalubrious part of the city.

The Exchange Quarter is where a taxi driver might take you if you asked for a good time. The myriad of dressy bars and the lifestyle whores criss-crossing the streets make it easily the buzziest part of the city. We recommend **MPV** and **Space**. Leeds' small but perfectly formed gay quarter is here too – **Bar Fibre** and Velvet are probably the best on offer.

York Place, home to **Bambu** and **Babylon,** is much more Square Mile. The city's burgeoning legal and financial offices are located here, and though it's not as stuffy as it could be, it isn't as charismatic or edgy as elsewhere. The concrete and glass equivalent of Jamiroquai, it's where the pierced-beneath-their pinstripes professionals let their hair down.

leeds

BABYLON

Restaurant Bar
10 York Place
0113 234 3344

OPEN Mon-Wed midday-		
11pm, Thu-Sat midday-1am	GETTING LUCKY	2/5
	EYE CANDY	3/5
	BIG SPENDERS	4/5
	MIX 60%M 40%F	
	AGE 25-35	
	PRICE Average	

AMBIENCE Conversation, Friendly, Funky, Late Night Open
REVIEW Babylon is a grown-up bar for the Ritchie/Oliver Loaded generation. Tucked away in the business quarter, it opens late from Thursday to Saturday, catering for new lad dads and professionals who like to party. Wannabe wide-boys in pinstripe suits and fat-knotted Windsor ties tuck into Oliveresque 'Well Big Steak and Kidney Pie' – none of that Michelin star bollocks for them. No, they want 'good, honest grub' just like mam used to make and would honestly be more than happy to eat down the transport caff except it's too far from the office and the Vespa's in the garage. It's a little bit of heaven for try-hard geezers waiting for the day their law firm transfers to London so they can shack up with the missus in a Clerkenwell loft with Pop Art on the walls and a vintage Aston Martin in the garage.
PLACE Plasma screens, a pool table and cascading water features make Babylon unique to the city. It has loafers' sofas for Johnny Vaughan wannabes, a pool table for plastic gangstas and large fish tanks with real-life pretend fish. The restaurant is separate, underground and unfussy.
PEOPLE The spawn of Guy Ritchie and Jamie Oliver come here to be geezers, spend it large, laugh like only the successful can and buy expensive things that you, me and even they can't afford.

PROFS Bankers, solicitors, blondes, sports agents
CELEBS Lee Chapman and Leslie Ash
DRESS Armani, Hugo Boss, Karen Millen
MUSIC Funk, Soul
DOOR None
DRINKS Bottles £2.50, Wine £3, Champagne £6, Cocktail £6
FOOD Modern European/Fusion, £13
CARDS All
CAPACITY 160, seating 120
HIRE Venue: Yes · Private Room: Yes

BAMBU

Club
The Food Emporium, York Place
0113 243 6288

OPEN Thu-Sat 10pm-2am	GETTING LUCKY	3/5
	EYE CANDY	4/5
	BIG SPENDERS	4/5
	MIX 40%M 60%F	
	AGE 21-35	
	PRICE Average	

AMBIENCE Dancing, Groups, Late Night Open
REVIEW Bambu promised Leeds a unique clubbing experience. Guess what? They lied. In reality, Bambu is inimitable only because it feels exclusive. It has the same music, same vibe, same drinks, same sameness of every other club you've ever been to, but there's more money per square inch than any other club in Leeds. Perhaps that's what makes it unique. That, and the bloody great big sticks of bamboo. It's the kind of place where dancing comes third to standing in the right room and wearing the right clothes. But whoever said that was a bad thing?
PLACE Bambu is much bigger than it looks from the outside. There are three rooms, but everyone in the know heads for the smallest as that's where they stash the atmosphere. There is a secluded, bambooed 'I'm important' area for boys who drive fast cars.
PEOPLE The contact pages for Bambu: 'self-made new lad WLTM second-generation daddy's girl for no-nonsense fun time. Must be solvent.' Of course no venue is so two-dimensional and there are all sorts of other people here... like err, rich students and more rich students.

PROFS Solicitors, entrepreneurs, rich students
CELEBS Emmerdale stars, Rio Ferdinand, Gilles Peterson
DRESS Prada, Jimmy Choo, Gucci, Versace, key rings by BMW and Porsche
DOOR Smart club wear
MUSIC Funk, Soul, DJs Thu-Sat
DRINKS Beer £3, Wine £3, Champagne £5.50, Cocktail £5
FOOD Eclectic, £7.50
CARDS All
CAPACITY 1,100, seating 70
HIRE Venue: Yes · Private Room: No

BAR FIBRE

Bar, Café, Gay
168 Lower Briggate
0113 234 1304

OPEN Mon-Wed 11am-		
midnight, Thu 11am-1am,	GETTING LUCKY	4/5
Fri-Sat 11am-2am,	EYE CANDY	4/5
Sun midday-midnight	BIG SPENDERS	3/5
	MIX 60%F 40%M	
	AGE 20-30	
	PRICE Average	

AMBIENCE Conversation, Groups, Party, Pulling
REVIEW The Leeds gay scene has long been dominated by dodgy old geezers' back street pubs of dubious reputation. At last we have a chic, sleek, gay-owned and run café bar that doesn't rely on two-bit tacky drag 'artistes' or waffle-arsed strippers to pull in the punters. OK, so it's not exactly Canal Street, but it's a step in the right direction and has all the elements to make a guy go weak at the knees: top local talent, choice cut choonz of the highest order and an interior that would make Laurence Llewellyn Bowen emerald with envy. During the day Fibre is a great chill-out spot, with a mooching crowd who come for the bar snacks and a drink. At around seven, the music is turned up, the lights down and furniture is swept aside to make room for the vibrant, if somewhat cliquey, evening set.

PLACE A goldfish bowl facade, plush sofas and floor-to-ceiling heated steel coils greet you in the petite lounge area out front. The bar's a couple of steps up, gleaming with glass bricks, luscious lighting and stainless steel. The toilets verge on the Ally McBeal with minimal signage and communal washbasins.

PEOPLE A stylish funky crowd, with more women and heteros than your average gay bar, though the cocktail of designer fragrances and hairspray may leave you gasping for oxygen.

PROFS Lawyers, designers, retail staff, nurses
CELEBS Mr Gay UK, Emmerdale cast
DRESS Shiny, sparkly, sharp, smooth, sexy
MUSIC Funk, House, Dance, DJs Wed-Sun
DOOR Smart casual
DRINKS Beer £2.60, Wine £2.50
FOOD Modern European, £3.50
CARDS All
CAPACITY 170, seating 60
HIRE Venue: No · Private Room: No

MINT

Club
Harrison Street
0113 244 3168

OPEN Fri-Sat 9.30pm-6am		
GETTING LUCKY		**3/5**
EYE CANDY		**4/5**
BIG SPENDERS		**2/5**
MIX 50%M 50%F		
AGE 18-25		
PRICE Average		

AMBIENCE Party, Late Night Open, Dancing, Groups, Hip/Fashionable

REVIEW At the tender age of three, Mint has managed to snare Back to Basics, probably Leeds' most prestigious club night and a pot of gold for any venue. Like Basics, Mint trades in the style and sass of Leeds' famed house era and, like the music, it's well-toned, slick and minty fresh. Small but perfectly formed, Mint's door staff are justifiably picky. Shell-suited council estate beer monsters get short shrift with this lot, making way for a glammed-up party crowd – think Ibiza-tanned glamour queens and cooler-than-thou tank-topped boys paying homage to the biggest names in the business, from Carl Cox and Eric Morillo to Junior Sanchez and Sasha.

PLACE Disco balls of all shapes and sizes hang from the ceiling like chunks of meat in a butcher's back room. Lighting is – you guessed it – green, and the chairs, stools and tables are designed like oversized Polos. Again, Ally McBeal style unisex loos – the people of Leeds love to mix.

PEOPLE The young and the beautiful. You'll fit right in if you know how to pull a good pout, if you've appeared in a promotional video for Cream or your picture appears on a Hard Times flyer.

PROFS Students, office clerks, solicitors, retail assistants
CELEBS Emmerdale cast
DRESS Heels and Helen Big Brother-style glittery numbers for the girls, practical clubbers gear for the boys
MUSIC House

DOOR Smart casual; entrance £5-10
DRINKS Beer £2.50, Wine £2.50
FOOD None
CARDS None
CAPACITY 550, seating 60
HIRE Venue: Yes · Private Room: No

MOJO

Bar
18 Merrion Street
0113 244 6387

OPEN Mon-Thu 5pm-11pm, Fri-Sat 5pm-1am		
GETTING LUCKY		**3/5**
EYE CANDY		**3/5**
BIG SPENDERS		**3/5**
MIX 70%M 30%F		
AGE 25-35		
PRICE Average		

AMBIENCE Casual, Groups, Late Night Open, Party

REVIEW Tiny and not particularly stylish with an atmosphere you want to kiss, Mojo was featured in The Independent as one of the top 50 bars in the world. Not the north, not the UK, but the world. Now that's saying something. The walls are a rock 'n' roll hall of fame, plastered with guitar memorabilia and black and white images of music's greatest from Bobs D to M and what you see is what they play. Unsurprisingly, the bar is a hang-out for the city's musos, but also attracts drinks connoisseurs in droves, eager to crack the 60-strong cocktail list mixed by some of the best barmen known to mankind.

PLACE You won't believe how small it is but as soon as you walk through the door you'll love it. Getting people to leave has been known to be a problem.

PEOPLE Musicians and music lovers as well as out-of-towners flooding in to sample some pretty damn fine cocktails.

PROFS Retail assistants, musicians, producers, writers
CELEBS Dave Stewart, Chris Moyles, Gomez, Fun Lovin' Criminals, Sara Cox
DRESS Beatnik second-hand 60s gear. Jim Morrison for the pretty boys, although most settle for Morrissey
MUSIC Rock, Indie, Reggae
DOOR None
DRINKS Beer £2.50, Wine £2.50, Champagne £6, Cocktail £3.20
FOOD None
CARDS No Amex or Diners
CAPACITY 130, seating 30
HIRE Venue: No · Private Room: No

MPV

Bar, Club
1 Church Walk
0113 243 9486

OPEN Mon-Thu 5pm-2am, Fri 5pm-3am, Sat midday-3am, Sun midday-12.30am		
GETTING LUCKY		**4/5**
EYE CANDY		**3/5**
BIG SPENDERS		**3/5**
MIX 50%M 50%F		
AGE 25-35		
PRICE Cheap		

AMBIENCE Dancing, Groups, Hip/Fashionable, Late Night Open, Outdoors, Party, Pulling

REVIEW Talk about risky business. Build a bar on the wrong side of the tracks, mix contemporary and retro styling within industrial railway arches and hope to appeal to both the student crowd and monied Premiership footballers. Tricky. Any bar in this part of the world featuring 'posh hotdogs' (bread rolls courtesy of Harvey Nichols and wild boar and Calvados dogs shipped in from London) and a cigar menu (Trinidad Fundadores, £24.60) should expect a little choppy water. But it's been smooth sailing so far, especially during the summer when MPV's outside courtyard for up to 1,000 drinkers becomes the number one cruising spot in town.

PLACE Instead of the normal exposed brickwork and arched roofs you might expect in an industrial railway setting, the designers have created a fantasy 70s airport interior, all cream, chocolate brown, beige and glass, with smooth curves and sleek furnishings.

PEOPLE Really stylish as opposed to expensively dressed people shimmy alongside students and mad-for-it party punters.

PROFS Clothes shop entrepreneurs, hairdressers, DJs, savvy students

CELEBS Leeds United players (Rio Ferdinand, Harry Kewell), Chris Moyles, Damien Hirst

DRESS 60s originals, Paul Smith, Prada, Joseph, Westwood, Dolce & Gabbana

MUSIC House, Northern Soul, R&B, Soul DJs every night

DOOR None

DRINKS Beer £1.50, Wine £2, Champagne £5, Cocktail £3.50

FOOD Posh Hot Dogs, £3

CARDS All

CAPACITY 450, seating 70

HIRE Venue: Yes · Private Room Yes

NORMAN

Bar, Restaurant
36 Call Lane
0113 234 3988

OPEN Mon-Sat midday-2am,	**GETTING LUCKY**	**5/5**
Sun 1pm-10.30pm	**EYE CANDY**	**3/5**
BUSES X220	**BIG SPENDERS**	**3/5**
	MIX 65%M 35%F	
	AGE 24-35	
	PRICE Average	

AMBIENCE Conversation, Groups, Late Night Open, Party, Pulling

REVIEW Billed as the greatest drinking hole in Yorkshire since The Woolpack, Norman had the whole of Leeds at its feet when it opened in 1998. The city's first style bar, featuring weird inflatable wobbly walls, doors made of toast and novelty seating. Two years down the line, it's still got an atmosphere most publicans would sell their pint-pulling arm for, packed out with city slickers trying hard to look like they haven't tried at all. Offering a grown-up, Muji menu of sushi and noodles along with designer beers and designer tunes, it's a far cry from Leeds' darts-'n'-Diamond White boozers. Weekend queues mean you may have to wait to get in, but many

a love match has been forged outside Norman's doors. Not bad for a bar with no mates.

PLACE Tate Modern meets Play School. Much slicker than the city's other bars and a bit too modern-like for some. Done with an eye for humour as well as fashion.

PEOPLE Trendily scruffy and achingly cool, but nice with it.

PROFS Fashion, new media, music

CELEBS Emmerdale cast, Leeds United footballers

DRESS Engineered jeans, messy hair and Mandarina Duck jackets

MUSIC Reggae, House, Breakbeat, Hip Hop, Live Band Mon, DJs Tue-Sun

DOOR None

DRINKS Beer £2.50, Wine £2.40, Cocktail £4.40

FOOD Pacific Rim, £6

CARDS No Amex

CAPACITY 240, seating 80

HIRE Venue: No · Private Room: No

NORTH

Bar
24 New Briggate
0113 242 4540

OPEN Mon-Tue midday-midnight,	**GETTING LUCKY**	**3/5**
Wed-Thu midday-1am,	**EYE CANDY**	**3/5**
Fri-Sat midday-2am	**BIG SPENDERS**	**2/5**
	MIX 60%M 40%F	
	AGE 18-75	
	PRICE Average	

AMBIENCE Chilled, Conversation, Lounge Atmosphere, Late Night Open

REVIEW This bar would be the weird but vaguely cool kid at school – a bit different to the others, but worth hanging around with all the same. A narrow space with muted decor verging on the grubby, North is the kind of place you wouldn't expect to work but somehow does. Serving the widest selection of beers in Yorkshire probably helps. Boasting the oldest DJ mixing desk in the world (it's wooden), you are always guaranteed retro tunes and funky people. It's got the feel of an in-the-know neighbourhood joint rather than a city centre joint and with the Grand Opera House just a few doors down, it's also something of an unofficial Green Room for local actors.

PLACE Not in the least bit slick, but there's always bucketloads of atmosphere and interesting art on the walls.

PEOPLE Casual folk singing along to Beatles' tunes playing out on the old mixing deck. Attitude-free, they're just out to hang out.

PROFS Actors, bar staff, students

CELEBS Liv Tyler, Griff Rhys Jones, Su Pollard

DRESS Sturdy shoes and denim. Wacky glasses, homespun and some hemp

MUSIC Hip Hop, Funk, Jazz, Indie, Rock

DOOR None

DRINKS Beer £2.50, Wine £2.50, Cocktail £4.50

FOOD Bar snacks, £3

CARDS No Amex

CAPACITY 150, seating 50

HIRE Venue: No · Private Room: No

and not yearn for a simple boozer that closes at a sensible hour.

PROFS Barristers, students, solicitors, secretaries, fashion employees
CELEBS None
DRESS Turn up as Luke Skywalker and Princess Leia. If you've got kids, they can go as Ewoks
MUSIC World Jazz, New Disco, R&B, Deep House, Funk, Breakbeat, DJs Wed-Sun
DOOR Dress up for the door pickers
DRINKS Beer £2.50, Wine £3, Cocktail £3
FOOD Tapas, £3
CARDS All
CAPACITY 300, seating 100
HIRE Venue: Yes Private Room: No

SPACE

Club
Hirst's Yard, Duncan Street
0113 246 1030

OPEN Tue-Thu 10pm-2.30am, Fri-Sat 10pm-4am		
GETTING LUCKY	**4/5**	
EYE CANDY	**4/5**	
BIG SPENDERS	**3/5**	
MIX 50%F 50%M		
AGE 18-25		
PRICE Average		

AMBIENCE Dancing, Groups, Late Night Open, Minimalist, Party, Pulling
REVIEW A shiny piece of minimalist sci-fi design hidden off the monstrous Boar Lane. Reserved and classy, all pure white walls and soft blue lights, you could imagine a cat-stroking, leather armchair-reclining arch-villain sipping Martinis and contemplating plans for world domination over a giant console in one of the back rooms. Diverse nights – from funk and house to Drum 'n' Bass – pull in a crowd of glammed-up northern clubbers, undeterred by long queues and hefty entrance fees. Designed more to feel like a space-age labyrinth than it actually is, look out for odd steps where you didn't expect them and little corridors going in opposite directions to the ones you thought. With a little imagination and a lot of alcohol you could almost get lost in the beautifully explorable surroundings.
PLACE We know white and shiny is very trendy, but it can also mean muddy and slippery – you might regret the mini skirt and heels when you topple over on the way to the ladies loos.
PEOPLE Trendy, dressy students, hard-looking groups of men standing around looking bored (usually the promoters) and lashed-up boys and girls on the pull.

PROFS Bankers, lawyers, stockbrokers, accountants, secretaries, students
CELEBS None
DRESS Ben Sherman, Ted Baker, Paul Smith, Giant, Kookaï, Morgan
MUSIC Hard House, Drum 'n' Bass, Soul, R&B, Garage
DOOR Smart casual; entrance £4-10
DRINKS Beer £3, Wine £2.90
FOOD None
CARDS All
CAPACITY 490, seating 60
HIRE Venue: Yes · Private Room: Yes

OSLO

Bar, Members Bar
174 Lower Briggate
0113 245 7768

OPEN Mon-Wed 7pm-2am, Thu 5pm-2am, Fri-Sat 5pm-4am, Sun 8pm-12.30am		
GETTING LUCKY	**4/5**	
EYE CANDY	**4/5**	
BIG SPENDERS	**3/5**	
MIX 50%M 50%F		
AGE 20-30		
PRICE Average		

AMBIENCE Comfy, Conversation, Groups, Lounge, Late Night Open, Pulling
REVIEW Leed's first members bar (now open to all), bringing the luxury and style of Soho oop North. A funky fusion of North African chic, Scandinavian cool and 70s retro, Oslo looks spookily like the Star Wars bar sans aliens. Don't worry if things go a bit Pete Tong and the clientele start to resemble Chewbacca and chums – just call over an obliging waitress and order one of Oslo's bewildering range of coffees and fresh juices. They'll sort you out a treat. Filled with innovative little touches – an enigmatically numbered rather than named cocktail list, a ban on noise-polluting blenders and bar snacks served on hot plates so you don't have to rush – Oslo would give central London's finest a northern run for their money.
PLACE A crazed futuro-Moroccan-industrial-themed interior, with curved earthenware-effect walls, lop-sided windows and enough seating to accommodate an entire colony of lounge lizards.
PEOPLE Young and fairly cool, these are people still unsullied enough to enjoy the slightly gimmicky interior

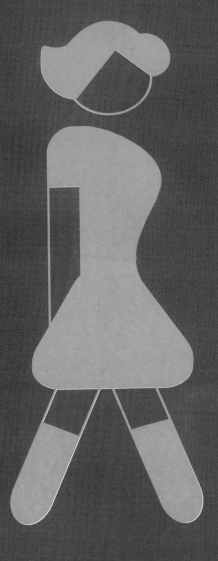

Manchester

Around ten years ago Manchester was home to the birth of the British club scene thanks to the Hacienda. Who can forget the time when Madchester dominated the charts and everyone wore jeans the size of army tents, accessorised with floral beanie hats? Now, like most buildings in the city centre, the Hacienda is being converted into trendy apartments called, of course, Acid House.

So, clubbing is dead, Madchester is long forgotten and the flares and glo-sticks have been put away. Today's Mancunians are dolled up in designer clothing, enjoying the city's burgeoning bar scene.

The compact city centre makes it easy to find a bar to suit your mood. The far end of Deansgate offers contemporary sophistication in the form of the loungey **Living Room** or the chic **Zinc Bar & Grill**. At the other end of the street is the new Deansgate Locks development – a row of smart bars, including the New York style **Loaf** (get there early on a Friday to avoid the queues) and the exclusive new **Sugar Lounge**. For the gay crowd, Canal Street remains the focus, with old favourites **Manto**, Velvet and Via Fossa enjoying a renaissance.

If you're looking for a more casual night out and fancy mingling with a few veterans of the Manchester club scene, head up to **Sankey's Soap** in the bohemian Northern Quarter (like Hoxton before the people with stupid haircuts moved in) or down to **The Ox** in Castlefield – the city's first gastropub.

Members clubs are on the up with upstarts such as the Circle Club looking to challenge the Press Club and the **Living Room** as Manchester's ultimate drinking den. Like London, Manchester's bar scene is divided into city centre dwellers and workers during the week, making way for out-of-towners at the weekends. Weekdays are quiet and casual, but at weekends it's full-on glamour as everyone tries to find either a soap star or a footballer to go home with.

manchester

LIME

Bar, Restaurant, Club
2 Booth Street
0161 233 2929

OPEN Mon-Wed 11am-11pm,
Thu 11am-midnight,
Fri-Sat 11am-1am
TRAINS Victoria

GETTING LUCKY	**3/5**
EYE CANDY	**3/5**
BIG SPENDERS	**4/5**
MIX 50%M 50%F	
AGE 21-60	
PRICE Average	

AMBIENCE Chilled, Cosy, Late Night Open, Relaxed
REVIEW Mission Impossible: locate Lime. Nobody around
Piccadilly knew where it was. Hidden away in the heart
of Manchester's legal and financial district, just behind
the city's flagship Armani store. Supposedly 'lime' is
Grenadian for 'chill', as in 'I feel like limeing today,
man', something you wouldn't expect the property
developers, lawyers and brokers in here to do. The
ground floor holds the quieter bar-cum-restaurant while
the oh-so-cleverly named basement SubLime is an
altogether cooler, clubbier place. Sister of the London
Lime, this hybrid provides metropolitan minimalism for
Manchester's chattering classes.
PLACE Classic bespoke bar. Lighting and technology are
used to great effect. SubLime is in the basement and is
just large enough to be atmospheric.
PEOPLE Lunch: suit meltdown. Weekends: the stuff
of office man's fantasies – 20 year-old nubiles
in fluffy bras rub shoulders and nothing else with
uptight lawyers trying to put off the siren call of
the golf club.
PROFS Property developers, lawyers, brokers, the
Cheshire set
CELEBS None
DRESS Jackets and ties and shirtsleeves are the
weekday uniform. Armani, DKNY, Calvin Klein rule
at weekends
MUSIC Classics, Funk, House
DOOR None
DRINKS Beer £2.50, Wine £3.95, Champagne £6.95
FOOD Pacific Rim, £5.95
CARDS All
CAPACITY 600, seating 175
HIRE Venue: Yes · Private Room: No

LIVING ROOM

Bar
80 Deansgate
0161 832 0083

OPEN Mon-Wed 10am-
midnight, Thu 10am-1am,
Fri-Sat 10am-2am,
Sun 10am-11pm
TUBE/RAIL Deansgate

GETTING LUCKY	**5/5**
EYE CANDY	**3/5**
BIG SPENDERS	**3/5**
MIX 40%M 60%F	
AGE 20-40	
PRICE Average	

AMBIENCE Buzzy, Hip/Fashionable, Late Night Open,
Lounge Atmosphere, Pulling

REVIEW Located in a part of town where mutton often
arrives dressed as bare legs of lamb and Cheshire set
wannabes sip spritzers in identi-bars, Living Room has
created its own space. A Nu Yawk style lounge with
an interior that's a cross between boutique hotel bar
and Caffé Uno, it's been a raging success with daytime
shoppers, a later loft-living crowd and local footie
players because it's not as high profile or flash as
Reform. It's got a rather dubious live music policy – the
bar's focal point is a white baby grand but you also get
a massive and accomplished cocktail list which should
help drown the Sinatra sound-a-like.
PLACE Café bar meets lounge bar in relaxed leather
sofa setting. The most coveted seats are the booths
along one wall which can be reserved for parties. The
sofa area at the back by the piano is worth getting here
early for.
PEOPLE Smart groups, Manchester's urban elite, football
players and their entourage of shopgirls, hairdressers
and journalists.
PROFS Record industry execs, journalists, musicians,
advertising, graphic designers
CELEBS Manchester United players and the occasional
after-show for the Manchester Evening News Arena
DRESS DKNY, FCUK. Blokes should aim for a boy
band/Hugo Boss model look. Girls must have smooth
hair and look as much like Davinia Murphy as possible
MUSIC Live Jazz, DJs play Funk at weekends
DOOR Smart casual
DRINKS Beer £2.50, Wine £2.30, Champagne £4.95,
Cocktail £4.50
FOOD Modern British, £8.95
CARDS All
CAPACITY 320, seating 55
HIRE Venue: No · Private Room: No

LOAF

Bar, Club, Restaurant
Deansgate Locks, Whitworth Street
0161 819 5858

OPEN Sun-Wed midday-
12.30am,
Thu-Sat midday-2am
TUBE/RAIL Deansgate

GETTING LUCKY	**3/5**
EYE CANDY	**4/5**
BIG SPENDERS	**4/5**
MIX 50%M 50%F	
AGE 22-30	
PRICE Average	

AMBIENCE Buzzy, Hip/Fashionable, Late Night Open
REVIEW Now that all the most expensive bars in Manchester have closed (Mash, Ampersand), Loaf is the new playground for the Martin with an Aston set. The equivalent of at least two weeks of Beckham's wages must have been ploughed into the stunning interior, it's just a shame that the food and service don't quite match up. During the day, it's a favourite place for liquid refreshment for Manchester's media crowd, at night there are biblical queues round the block as people throng to take advantage of the late licence and lack of entry charge.
PLACE New York loft by way of Didsbury with some fantastic Italian furniture and marble flooring. Upstairs is grandly minimal with imposing mirrors, neutral boxy furniture and plenty of obligatory chrome.
PEOPLE They look like the cast of Beverly Hills 90210, but sound like the cast of Hollyoaks.

PROFS PR, fashion, music, advertising, property
CELEBS David and Victoria Beckham, Manchester United players, Blackburn Rovers players
DRESS Armani, Gucci, Louis Vuitton, Diesel
MUSIC House and Garage, DJs Thu-Sun
DOOR No sportswear, over 21s
DRINKS Beer £2.60, Wine £3.40, Champagne £5, Cocktail £4.95
FOOD Modern British, £8
CARDS No Diners
CAPACITY 1,200, seating 300
HIRE Venue: Yes · Private Room: Yes

THE LOWRY

Bar
Pier 8, Salford Quays
0161 876 2121

OPEN Mon-Sat 11am-11pm	**GETTING LUCKY**	**1/5**
Sun 11am-10.30pm	**EYE CANDY**	**3/5**
RAIL Harbour City	**BIG SPENDERS**	**3/5**
	MIX 40%M 60%F	
	AGE 25-60	
	PRICE Average	

AMBIENCE Conversation, Views
REVIEW Money, money money. That's the story behind The Lowry, Manchester's answer to the Pompidou Centre set in the heart of Salford Quays. Unlike its French counterpart, the reaction to this well-kept Northern secret has been utterly positive. Having cost £96 million, it better be. The two theatres and four art galleries initially lured visitors out of the city centre, and now they're staying later in one of the complex's three bars. Hexagon, Quays and the Circle Bar offer a relaxed atmosphere and heart-swelling views over the waterfront. Word of mouth is largely responsible for the popularity of the bars as they aren't being pushed as dedicated drinking venues. The design is what really stands out – impressive and cool.
PLACE Michael Wilford, the architect, described his vision of a building to get lost in, and that vision has been realised. Silver clad on the outside, it famously resembles the Guggenheim in Bilbao. Inside, the riot of angles and colours is not to everyone's taste, but it's certainly worth a chin-stroke.

PEOPLE By and large, an arty and well-informed bunch who have visited The Lowry for some other reason – ballet, opera, Italian futurism – and haven't left. Quite pleased with themselves for making the effort and no regret over missing Coronation Street.

PROFS Doctors, lawyers, students, graphic designers, translators, academics
CELEBS Robert Powell, Michael Parkinson, Rula Lenska, cast of Corrie
DRESS Prada and Gucci spotted among the monochrome outfits for highbrow events and more high street on ABBA tribute nights
MUSIC Occasional live music
DOOR None
DRINKS Beer £2.50, Wine £2.85, Champagne £6, Cocktail £4.50
FOOD Snacks, £3
CARDS All
CAPACITY 600, seating 200
HIRE Venue: Yes · Private Room: Yes

MALMAISON

Bar, Hotel Bar
Joshua Hoyle Building, Auburn Street
0161 278 1000

OPEN Mon-Sun 11am-11pm	**GETTING LUCKY**	**2/5**
	EYE CANDY	**3/5**
	BIG SPENDERS	**3/5**
	MIX 50%M 50%F	
	AGE 22-45	
	PRICE Average	

AMBIENCE Business, Conversation, Elegant/Classic, Hip/Fashionable, Romance

REVIEW The Manc Malmaison (part of a chain of five) has had more than its fair share of celeb sleepers since its opening. Despite becoming something of a bolthole for rock gods and pop princesses, Malmaison's guests keep their expensive booties firmly tucked up in bed, leaving the barstools to less illustrious punters. Since its recent refurbishment the place has lightened up dramatically – it used to be so dark you thought there'd been an electricity cut and drinkers would have to remove their sunnies or risk tripping over local gangsters spending their ill-earned cash, middle-aged couples on a posh night out and glammed-up students on loan-busting missions. Still, it's one of the best spots in Manchester for lazy lovers of luxury, and one of only two bars in town with table service.

PLACE Small continental style bar and brasserie – think dark, rich and atmospheric rather than bright, light and breezy.

PEOPLE Romancing couples, rich students with visiting parents, Old Trafford other halves.

PROFS Actors, company directors, boutique owners, visiting film crews

CELEBS Janet Jackson, The Pet Shop Boys, Noel Gallagher, Cher, Kylie, Lionel Ritchie, Claire Sweeney, Simon le Bon, Robert Carlyle

DRESS Smart suits for the guys, fairly sober for the ladies. Not a place for flashing flesh

MUSIC R&B, Soul

DOOR None

DRINKS Beer £2.90, Wine £3.95, Champagne £6.95, Cocktail £6.95

FOOD French, £6.95

CARDS All

CAPACITY 80, seating 50

HIRE Venue: No · Private Room No

MANTO

Bar, Club, Gay
46 Canal Street
0161 236 2667

OPEN Mon-Thu midday-midnight, Fri midday-1.30am, Sat 2.30am-7am, midday-1.30am, Sun 3am-8am, midday-1.30am	**GETTING LUCKY**	**5/5**
	EYE CANDY	**4/5**
	BIG SPENDERS	**3/5**
	MIX 80%M 20%F	
RAIL Piccadilly	**AGE** 20-28	
	PRICE Average	

AMBIENCE Late Night Open, Legendary, Pulling, Party

REVIEW Manchester's first gay café bar, Manto kicked off Canal Street's metamorphosis into the thriving bar circuit it is now. Used to be as camp as a row of pink tents, with boys who like boys who look like girls who are boys, but things have changed on the street since the arrival of Bar Med. Manto still retains a dedicated gay crowd, though on weekend evenings you'll also find a good crop of teenage trainee fag hags. Expect tight white tops and lots of energetic dancing. Although the industrial decor might seem a bit dated now, that doesn't deter the mixed-up crowd. The after-hours sessions starting in the middle of the night until the early hours are suitably debauched.

PLACE Industrial in the bar, minimal in the restaurant. Manto has been built to withstand a decade of dancing.

PEOPLE Out and proud. Ever wondered where the ravers went when you hung up your glow-sticks. They're all here, still monged, still hugging each other and still spending every weekend dancing 'til their feet bleed.

PROFS All walks of life from designers to dustmen

CELEBS None

DRESS Sorry to say it but that techno-punk thing is still going on. Accessorize with a gurn and a bottle of poppers

MUSIC House DJs Fri-Sun

DOOR £5 for the weekend after-hours sessions

DRINKS Beer £2.40, Wine £2.75

FOOD Mediterranean, £4

CARDS No Amex

CAPACITY 400, seating 60

HIRE Venue: Yes · Private Room: Yes

THE OX

Bar, Restaurant Bar
71 Liverpool Road
0161 839 7740

OPEN Mon-Sat 11am-11pm, Sun 11am-10.30pm	**GETTING LUCKY**	**3/5**
	EYE CANDY	**3/5**
RAIL Deansgate	**BIG SPENDERS**	**3/5**
	MIX 65%M 35%F	
	AGE 25-45	
	PRICE Cheap	

AMBIENCE Buzzy, Friendly, Groups
REVIEW Ox has shed its original pub mantle and is staking a claim on restaurant bar territory. Its success and charm stems from the fact that such a crazily disparate selection of tribes have all fixed on Ox as their bar of choice. Sunday league footballers jostle gay bikers at the bar, and 40-something real-ale aficionados share a table with Alicia Silverstone lookalikes. A little tip: make sure you know your male/female symbols – there's no other indication of which lav is yours.
PLACE Casual restaurant bar with purple walls, hardwood floors and abstract art, clay jugs and mugs in rough-hewn display cabinets over the bar. Actually, it's just like Snifters, a Chorley wine bar circa 1983. Apparently. The guy at the next table told me so.
PEOPLE Where to begin? Groups of blokes with blonde-highlights out on a beery night, leather lads with really big moustaches. Nervous couples on first dates and old marrieds just taking the air.

PROFS Lawyers, creative directors, marketing execs, accountants, bus drivers, dinner ladies
CELEBS None
DRESS Anything goes here from tracksuits to morning suits
MUSIC Chart, Pop, R&B, 70s, 80s
DOOR None
DRINKS Beer £2.10, Wine £2.25
FOOD Modern British, £8
CARDS No Amex
CAPACITY 150, seating 60
HIRE Venue: Yes · Private Room: No

SANKEY'S SOAP

Club, Live Music Venue
Beehive Mill, Jersey Street
0161 661 9085

OPEN Thu-Fri 10pm-3am,	GETTING LUCKY	2/5
Sat 10pm-3am	EYE CANDY	3/5
RAIL Piccadilly	BIG SPENDERS	3/5
	MIX 50%M 50%F	
	AGE 20-30	
	PRICE Average	

AMBIENCE Dancing, Groups, Hip/Fashionable, Late Night Open, Legendary
REVIEW Sankey's Soap is scrubbing up nicely. The Mancunian clubbers' club has just had a new refurbishment and is delivering on all fronts. Having re-opened in 2000 after a three-year hiatus Sankey's is still home to the venerable Friday club night institution, Tribal Sessions, and still pulling in names like Laurent Garnier, Richie Hawtin and Sasha. Saturday night's Golden has been replaced by the Red Light boasting Eric Morillo as resident. It may have had a very impressive facelift and even stuff to sit on, but let's face it, Sankey's is a straight-down-the-line, four-to-the-floor dance club and that's the way we like it.
PLACE Small room in converted mill and warehouse decked out with red slatted walls and red cubed leather booths. The DJ is nice and near in a little box only two feet above the dance floor, proving Faithless wrong. You see God is not a DJ, so DJs don't need to be set up in some massive altar just to play a few records.

PEOPLE The two weekend nights draw different sets. Saturday nights see a glammed-up crew enjoying classic anthems, hands in the air and everything. Fridays see a few techno old-timers filling in time till the after party. Now come on, put those white gloves away.

PROFS Media workers, dance music diehards
CELEBS Steve Coogan, Corrie cast
DRESS Skatewear on Fridays and a little more dressy on Saturday
MUSIC House, Techno
DOOR No scruffy clothes £9-13
DRINKS Beer £2.80, Wine £3
FOOD Snacks, £5
CARDS None
CAPACITY 850, seating 100
HIRE Venue: Yes · Private Room: Yes

SUGAR LOUNGE

Bar
Arch 12, Deansgate Lock, Whitworth Street
0161 833 3200

OPEN Wed 5pm-1am,	GETTING LUCKY	3/5
Thu to Sat midday-2am,	EYE CANDY	4/5
Sun 6pm-1am	BIG SPENDERS	4/5
RAIL Deansgate	MIX 50%M 50%F	
	AGE 18-40	
	PRICE Average	

AMBIENCE Destination/Wishlist, Hip/Fashionable, Jet Set, Late Night Open
REVIEW Sugar Lounge is the latest addition to the rejuvenated Deansgate Lock bar scene. It opened in November, with Jenson Button and Eddie Irvine on the guest list. The owner is seriously connected. The bar teeters on the tightrope between cool and frigid. In addition to stocking in-demand L'or Cannabis vodka, they also hold bottles of cognac that will set you back £3,500 or enough to buy a Man City player. It's all a far cry from the Hacienda, but then Manchester isn't Madchester any more. Smart suited soap stars brandish bellinis and compare fake tans.
PLACE It might look like another black and tan Manchester bar, but Sugar Lounge throws in some exposed brickwork for good measure. The velvety black furniture is bespoke and the floor is stunning – shiny black pebbles inlaid into concrete.
PEOPLE In terms of people, this bar is still finding its Prada-shod feet. VIPs are kept in blissful isolation. Smell the readies as you enter.

PROFS Entrepreneurs, media folk, clothes shop staff, architects, racing drivers
CELEBS Jenson Button, Eddie Irvine, David and Victoria Beckham
DRESS Dolce & Gabbana, Gucci, Jimmy Choo, Prada
MUSIC Rare Groove, Funk, Old Skool House
DOOR Attitude policy
DRINKS Beer £2.80, Wine £3.30, Champagne £6, Cocktail £5
FOOD British, £4.95
CARDS All
CAPACITY 250, seating 75
HIRE Venue: Yes · Private Room: No

ZINC BAR & GRILL

Bar, Restaurant
The Triangle, Exchange Square
0161 827 4200

OPEN Mon-Thu 10am-midnight, Fri-Sat 10am-2am, Sun midday-10.30pm	**GETTING LUCKY**	**2/5**
	EYE CANDY	**3/5**
	BIG SPENDERS	**3/5**
RAIL Victoria	**MIX** 60%F 40%M	
	AGE 25-50	
	PRICE Moderate	

AMBIENCE Conversation, Elegant/Classic, Hip/Fashionable, Late Night Open, Network

REVIEW Following the current trend for London names to open a northern flagship (see Harvey Nichols in Leeds, Selfridges in Manchester) bar and restaurant operators are jumping on the bandwagon. Lime here has a sister in the capital so why shouldn't Terence have a restaurant bar? Now he does, with Zinc. The interior is cleaved in two, the top mezzanine level is food focused and the lower section designated for drinkers. This is where Manchester's new ruling class go to eat food that their dads would have ordered.

PLACE Zinc Bar & Grill is a cool, modern venue, located opposite the new Printworks space in the heart of rejuvenated Manchester. All chrome and pine, two-seater sofas and the odd brilliant flash of electric colour. A trademark Conran open kitchen gives you the chance to watch your steak sizzle.

PEOPLE Happy, rounded businessmen tucking into rare fillets, gay media darlings dipping their tiger prawns in chilli sauce, and ambitious, determined young women eating linguine with wild mushrooms, dreaming of hot chocolate pudding.

PROFS Accountants, media, television, butchers
CELEBS Fabien Barthez, Tracey Shaw
DRESS Armani, DKNY, Gap
MUSIC Classical, Funk, Jazz
DOOR None
DRINKS Beer £2.50, Wine £2.75, Champagne £5.25, Cocktail £4.50
FOOD Bar menu from £5.50, main menu from £8
CARDS All
CAPACITY 300, seating 200
HIRE Venue: Yes · Private Room: No

BALTIC BAR AND RESTAURANT | 74 BLACKFRIARS RD. (CORNER OF THE CUT) | LONDON | SE1 8HA

Baltic is housed in a beautifully refurbished 18th century coachbuilders, with a large and comfortable bar, serving great cocktails, forty flavours of frozen Polish Vodka and an extensive bar food menu. The hundred cover restaurant with its high vaulted ceiling serves East European and Scandinavian cuisine, while there is a private room available seating up to thirty.

Sunday is jazz day at Baltic with musicians playing from 2pm until 10pm. The bar and restaurant are open all day serving a light à la carte menu and bar food.

Opening Hours:
Bar: Monday to Sunday 12am-11pm
(Closed Saturday Lunch)
Restaurant: Lunch: Mon-Fri 12-3pm
Dinner: Mon-Sat 6-11:30pm
Sunday open from midday until 10:30pm

Tel: 020 7928 1111
Fax: 020 7928 8487
E-mail: info@balticrestaurant.co.uk
Web: www.balticrestaurant.co.uk

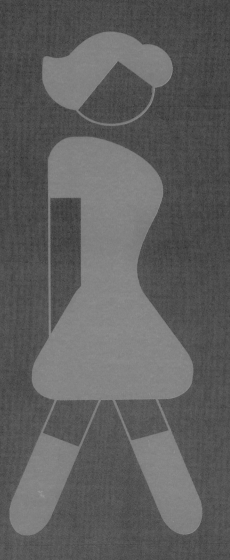

METRO

Venue finder

at a glance guide to
venues and ratings

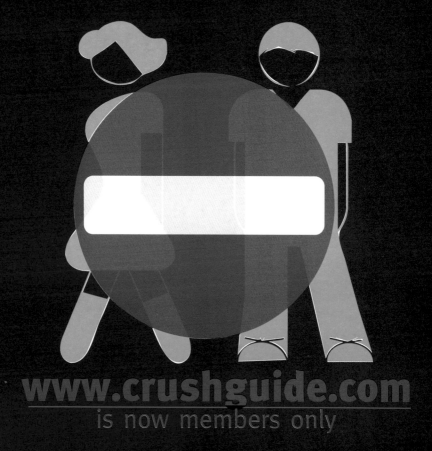

NAME	TYPE	PAGE	PROFESSIONS	LATE	GETTING LUCKY	EYE CANDY	BIG SPENDERS

LONDON

NAME	TYPE	PAGE	PROFESSIONS	LATE	GETTING LUCKY	EYE CANDY	BIG SPENDERS
10 Room	MB, CB	32	Rag trades, office types	Yes	■■■■	■■■	■■■■
10 Tokyo Joe's	B, CB	31	Dancers, hairdressers	Yes	■■■■■	■■■■	■■■■■
100 Pub	B	161	Media types, PRs	No	■■■	■■■■	■■■
151	C, MB	174	Professional shoppers, sloanes	Yes	■■■■	■■	■■■
192	B, R	207	Media, ladies who lunch	No	■■■	■■■■	■■■■
19:20	B, PLB	103	Printers, lawyers	Yes	■■	■■■	■■■
25 Canonbury Lane	B	132	Fashion profs, media execs	No	■■	■■■	■■■
291	RB	123	Media profs, design consultants	Yes	■■■	■■■■	■■
333	C, LMV	123	Artists, media types	Yes	■■■	■■■	■■
57 Jermyn Street	C, MC	81	Lawyers, bankers, musicians	Yes	■■■	■■■	■■■■
6 Degrees	B	56	PRs, actors, musicians	No	■■■	■■■	■■
606 Club	LMV	181	Musicians, doctors, lawyers	Yes	■■■	■■■	■■
93 Feet East	B, C	93	Artists	Yes	■■■	■■■■	■■■
Abigail's Party	MB	57	Advertising, artists, designers	Yes	■■■	■■■■	■■■
Academy, The	B, R	201	Media, advertising	No	■■■■	■■■	■■■■
Adelaide, The	P	139	Bank clerks, secretaries	No	■■■■	■■■	■■
Admiral Codrington, The	GP	174	Estate agents, insurance execs	No	■	■■■	■■■
Admiral Hardy, The	P	169	IT, graphic designers	No	■■■■■	■■■	■■■
AKA	B, R	21	Media, young creatives	Yes	■■	■■■■	■■■■
Akbar	B, R	57	Media, music, film	Yes	■■■	■■■■	■■■■
Albertine	WB	217	BBC workers, students	No	■	■■■	■■■
All Bar One (WC2)	B	33	Office workers, shop assistants	No	■■■■	■■	■■
All Bar One (EC2))	B	94	Bankers, support staff	No	■	■	■■■
All Bar One (N1)	B, R	133	Shop staff, doctors	No	■■	■■■	■■■
Alloro	RB	44	Bankers, lawyers, CEOs	No	■	■■■	■■■■
Alphabet Bar	B, CB	58	Musicians, media, PRs	No	■■■	■■■■	■■■
Amber	B, R	58	Media, PRs, art directors	Yes	■■■■	■■■	■■■■
American Bar, The	HB	84	Politicians, lawyers, accountants	No	■	■■	■■■■
Anglesea Arms	P, R	190	Financiers, antiques dealers	No	■■■	■■■	■■■■
Annabel's	C, MC	44	Oil tycoons, rulers of countries, royalty	Yes	■■■■	■■■	■■■■■
Arizona Bar & Grill	B, R	117	Market traders, office workers	Yes	■■■	■■	■■
Atlantic Bar & Grill	RB, CB	33	Bankers, fashion profs	Yes	■■■	■■■	■■■■
Atlas, The	GP	181	PRs, charity workers	No	■■	■■■	■■■
Attica	C, R	60	Pop stars, traders, models	Yes	■■■■■	■■■■■	■■■■■
Avenue, The	B, R	81	Bankers, art dealers, auctioneers	No	■■	■■■■	■■■■
Axis	CB, HB	84	Lawyers, bankers, stockbrokers	No	■	■■■■	■■■■
Babel	B	146	Advertisers, temps, middle managers	No	■■■	■■■	■■■
Babushka (SW2)	B	153	Fashion employees, DJs, salespeople	No	■■	■■	■■
Babushka (W11)	B	218	DJs, record industry profs	No	■■	■■■	■■■
Babushka (Caledonian Rd)	B, R	133	Marketing staff, publishers	Yes	■■	■■■	■■■
Babushka (New North Rd)	B, R	134	New media, fashion execs	No	■■■	■■■■	■■■
Balham Tup	P	144	Bankers, estate agents, publishers	No	■	■■	■■■
Balls Brothers	WB	94	Lawyers, Bankers	No	■	■■	■■■■
Baltic	RB	111	Actors, academics	No	■	■■■	■■■
Bam-bou	B, R	49	Media, film, PR	No	■■	■■■	■■■
Bank	CB, RB	85	Insurance agents, brokers, lawyers	No	■■■	■■■	■■■
Bar 38	B	22	Office girls, admin staff	No	■■■■	■■	■■■
Bar 6	B	203	Media employees, gym workers	No	■■	■■■	■■■
Bar at 190	B, HB	192	Musicians, tennis players, bankers	Yes	■■■	■■■	■■■■
Bar Chocolate	B	60	Publishers, students, PRs	No	■■■	■■■■	■■■
Bar Gansa	B, R	117	Theatre staff, students	Yes	■■	■■	■■
Bar Interlude	B	144	Estate agents, hairstylists, bar staff	No	■■■	■■■	■■■

B = Bar, C = Club, G = Gay, P = Pub, R = Restaurant, T = Theme, CB = Cocktail Bar, CF = Café, GP = Gastropub, HB = Hotel Bar, LMV = Live Music Venue, MB= Members Bar, MC = Members Club, PLB = Pool Bar, RB = Restaurant Bar, SC = Strip Club, WB = Wine Bar

NAME	TYPE	PAGE	PROFESSIONS	LATE	GETTING LUCKY	EYE CANDY	BIG SPENDERS
Bar Italia	B, R	61	Actors, singers, journalists	Yes	■■■■	■■■	■■■
Bar Madrid	B, C, R	49	Students, tourists, restaurant staff	Yes	■■■■■	■■■■	■■■
Bar Oblivion	B	161	Estate agents, middle managers	No	■■■	■■■	■■■
Bar On	B, CF	153	Office workers, stylists	Yes	■	■■	■■■
Bar Red	B, R	61	Account execs, PRs, graphic designers	No	■■■	■■■	■■■■
Bar Room Bar (SW11)	B	146	Accountants, estate agents	No	■■	■■	■■■
Bar Room Bar (NW3)	B	122	Lawyers, media profs	No	■■■■	■■■■	■■■
Bar Rumba	B, C	34	Retail workers, advertisers	Yes	■■	■■■	■■
Bar Vinyl	B, CF	117	DJs, clubbers	No	■■■■	■■■	■■
Bardo	B	181	Producers, PRs, financial advisers	Yes	■■■	■■■	■■■■
Bartok	B	121	Nurses, graphic designers	Yes	■	■■■	■■
Base	RB	147	Solicitors, estate agents, city types	No	■■■	■■■	■■■■
Be@1	B, CB	148	Brokers, bankers, PAs	No	■■■■	■■	■■■
Beach Blanket Babylon	B, R	208	Media, advertising employees	Yes	■■■■	■■■	■■■
Bear, The	GP	103	Lawyers, stockbrokers	No	■■	■■■■	■■■
Bed	B	212	TV researchers, journalists	No	■■■■	■■■	■■■
Bibendum Oyster Bar	B, R	192	Account execs, City boys	No	■■	■■■■	■■■■
Bierodrome	B, R	182	Estate agents, web designers, PAs	No	■■■	■■■	■■■
Big Easy	B, R	175	Caterers, accountants, bankers	No	■■	■■	■■
Blacks	C, MB	61	Artists, account execs, journalists	Yes	■■	■■■	■■■■■
Blakes	RB	118	Musicians, advertising execs	No	■■	■■■	■■■
Blakes Hotel Bar	B, HB	193	Bankers, financiers, lawyers	No	■■	■■■■	■■■■■
Blue Bar	HB	187	Designers, actors, musicians	No	■	■■■■	■■■■■
Bluebird	B, C, R	175	PRs, property tycoons, Conde Nasties	Yes	■■	■■■■	■■■■■
Blues Bar	B, R	62	PRs, ad execs, sales personnel	Yes	■■■	■■■	■■■
Bluu	B	124	Media execs, editors	Yes	■■■	■■■	■■■
Boardwalk	B, R	62	Artists, tourists, office workers	Yes	■■■■	■■	■■
Boom	B	148	Property developers, account execs	No	■■	■■■	■■■
Box, The	B, G	22	Marketing execs, actors	No	■■■	■■■■	■■■
Brasserie Max	HB	22	Bankers, fashion designers	No	■	■■■	■■■■
Brasserie Rocque	B	95	Stockbrokers, lawyers	No	■■	■■■	■■■■
Bricklayers Arms, The	P, R	124	Media employees, artists	Yes	■■■■	■■	■■
Bridge, The	B	175	Retail staff, doctors, nurses	No	■■	■■	■■
Brixtonian Havana Club	B	153	Media profs, theatre staff	Yes	■■■■	■■■	■■■
Bug Bar, The	B	154	Artists, students	Yes	■■■■	■	■■
Builder's Arms, The	GP	176	Antique dealers, interior designers	No	■■■	■■■	■■■
Bush Bar & Grill	B, R	217	Media suits, traders	No	■■	■■■	■■■
Cactus Blue	RB	176	Retail staff, brokers, consulate staff	No	■■■■	■■■	■■■■■
Café Boheme	B, LMV	63	Actors, students, dancers	Yes	■■■	■■■	■■■
Café de Paris	C	34	Account execs, PRs	Yes	■■■■	■■■	■■■■
Café des Amis du Vin	WB	23	Marketing staff, publishers	No	■■■	■■■	■■■
Café Goya	RB, CF	154	Media profs, charity workers	No	■	■■	■■■
Café Kick	B	104	Journalists, designers	No	■■■	■■■	■■
Café Lazeez	RB	104	City workers, lawyers	No	■■	■■■	■■■
Café Med	B, CF, R	208	Media and music profs	No	■■	■■■■	■■■■
Café Rouge	B, CF	169	Tourists, antique dealers	No	■	■■■	■■■
Cahoots	B, P	176	Interior designers, estate agents	No	■■■■	■■■■	■■■■
Camden Brewing Co.	P, B	118	Music, media employees	Yes	■■■	■■■	■■■
Candy Bar	B, L	63	PRs, directors, journalists	Yes	■■■■■	■■■	■■■
Cantaloupe	B	125	Accountants, graphic designers	Yes	■■■■■	■■■■	■■■
Cargo	B, C	125	Hoxton creatives, students	Yes	■■■■	■■■■	■■
Castle, The	P	201	City workers, publicists	No	■■■■	■■■	■■■
Catch	B, R	193	Media moguls, models, trustafarians	Yes	■■■■	■■■■	■■■■
Cecconi's	RB	31	Art dealers, auctioneers	No	■■	■■■	■■■■■

B = Bar, C = Club, G = Gay, P = Pub, R = Restaurant, T = Theme, CB = Cocktail Bar, CF = Café, GP = Gastropub, HB = Hotel Bar, LMV = Live Music Venue, MB= Members Bar, MC = Members Club, PLB = Pool Bar, RB = Restaurant Bar, SC = Strip Club, WB = Wine Bar

NAME	TYPE	PAGE	PROFESSIONS	LATE	GETTING LUCKY	EYE CANDY	BIG SPENDERS
Che	B	81	Bankers, auctioneers, hotel staff	No	■■	■■	■■■■
Cheers	B, R, T	35	Office workers, retail staff	Yes	■■■■	■	■
Chelsea Ram, The	GP	177	Estate agents, PRs, lawyers	No	■■	■■	■■■
Chepstow, The	P, R	209	Corporate managers, marketing	No	■■	■■■	■■■
Chinawhite	C, MC	35	TV execs, models, bankers	Yes	■■■	■■■■■	■■■■■
Churchill Bar & Cigar Divan	HB, MB	50	MPs, lawyers, ambassadors	No	■■	■	■■■
Cicada	B, R	104	Publishers, designers	No	■■	■■■	■■■
Circle (SW11)	B	148	Salespeople, DJs, teachers	No	■	■■	■■■
Circle (SW9)	B	162	Journalists, web hacks	No	■■	■■■	■■
Circus	B, R	63	Media, film and TV execs	Yes	■■	■■■■	■■■■
Clerkenwell House	B, PLB	105	New media, lawyers	No	■	■■■	■■■
Clinic	B	36	Students, teachers, musicians	Yes	■■■	■■■	■■
Cobden Club, The	B, MC	218	Music industry, advertising execs	Yes	■■■	■■■■	■■■■
Cocomo	CB, CF	126	Music industry employees	No	■■■	■■■	■■■
Collection, The	B, R	193	Bankers, financiers, actors	No	■■■■	■■■	■■■
Conrad Gallagher	B, R	36	Bankers, retailers, solicitors	No	■	■■■	■■■
Coq d'Argent	RB	95	City boys, bankers	No	■	■■	■■■■
Corks	B, C	14	Retailers, office staff	Yes	■■■■	■■■	■■
Corney & Barrow	B, WB	96	Lawyers, bankers	No	■■	■■	■■■■
Covent Garden Brasserie	RB	23	Theatre staff, shoppers	Yes	■	■	■■
Cow, The	GP, R	219	TV and radio profs	No	■■	■■■	■■■
Crazy Larry's	C, LMV	177	Nurses, students, estate agents	Yes	■■■■■	■■	■■■
Crescent, The	WB, R	182	Designers, property developers	No	■	■■■	■■■■■
Cross Keys, The	P, R	178	Bankers, lawyers, shop staff	No	■■■	■■■	■■■
Cuba	B, R, T	203	Students, shopworkers	Yes	■■■	■■■	■■
Dakota	B, R	209	Music, film, media execs	No	■	■■■	■■■■
Davy's	B, WB	96	Solicitors, barristers	No	■■	■■	■■■
Denim	RB, B	36	Brokers, traders, models	Yes	■■■■	■■■■■	■■■■■
Detroit	B, CB, R	24	Media, PRs	No	■■■■	■■■■	■■■
Devonshire Arms	P	204	Bankers, IT specialists	No	■■■	■■■	■■■
Digress	B, CB	64	Civil servants, support staff	Yes	■■■■	■■	■■
DK Bar	B, R	50	Media, advertising and TV execs	No	■■■■	■■■	■■■
Dog House, The	B	64	Sales assistants, solicitors, publishers	No	■■■	■■■	■■■
Dogstar, The	B, C	155	Art students, media types	Yes	■■■■	■■■	■■■
Dome	B, C	178	PRs, designers, IT consultants	No	■■	■■■	■■■■
Dorchester Bar	HB, R	45	Bankers, ambassadors, sports stars	No	■■	■■■■	■■■■■
Dover Street Wine Bar	WB, LMV	14	Lawyers, bankers	Yes	■■■■	■■■	■■■
Dragon	B	126	Artists, media profs	No	■■	■■■	■■■
Drawing Room & Sofa Bar	RB	149	Musicians, actors, designers	No	■■	■■■	■■■
Duke of Cambridge (N1)	GP	134	Journalists, comedians, builders	No	■■	■■■	■■■
Duke of Cambridge (SW11)	P	149	Media employee, PR agents	No	■■	■■	■■■■
Duke of Devonshire	P	144	Journalists, City workers	No	■■	■■■	■■■
Duke's Bar	HB	82	Bartenders, journalists	No	■	■■	■■■■
Dust	B	105	Photographers, graphic designers	Yes	■■	■■■	■■■
e&o	B, R	209	Trustafarians, advertising creatives	Yes	■■■■	■■■	■■
Eagle, The	GP	106	Publishers, journalists	No	■	■■■	■■■
Eclipse, The	B, CB	194	Bankers, lawyers, advertising execs	Yes	■■■■	■■■	■■■
Edge, The	B, G	65	Media employees, theatre workers	Yes	■■■	■■■■	■■■
Edwards	B	119	Estate agents, office workers	No	■■	■■	■■
EGA	B	145	Journalists, bankers, musicians	Yes	■■■■	■■■	■■
El Vino	B, WB	96	Lawyers, bankers	No	■	■	■■■■
Elbow Room, The (N1)	B, PLB	134	Record industry workers, PRs	Yes	■■■■	■■■	■■
Elbow Room, The (W2)	PLB	219	Advertisers, journalists	No	■	■■■	■■■
Embargo	C	183	Bankers, lawyers, accountants	Yes	■■■■	■■■■	■■■■

B = Bar, C = Club, G = Gay, P = Pub, R = Restaurant, T = Theme, CB = Cocktail Bar, CF = Café, GP = Gastropub, HB = Hotel Bar, LMV = Live Music Venue, MB= Members Bar, MC = Members Club, PLB = Pool Bar, RB = Restaurant Bar, SC = Strip Club, WB = Wine Bar

www.crushguide.com

NAME	TYPE	PAGE	PROFESSIONS	LATE	GETTING LUCKY	EYE CANDY	BIG SPENDERS
Embassy Bar	B	135	Students, media profs	Yes	■■■	■■■	■■■
Emporium	C, R	37	Footballers, boxers, shop staff	Yes	■■■■	■■	■■■■
End, The	C	24	Music industry, students	Yes	■■■	■■■	■■■
Engineer, The	GP	139	Media, computer geeks	No	■	■■■	■■■■
Enterprise, The	B, GP	194	Stockbrokers, property developers	No	■	■■■■	■■■■■
Escape	B, G	65	Shop assistants, students, media	Yes	■■■■	■■■■	■■■■
Eve Club, The	C	51	Music, TV, media	Yes	■■■■	■■■	■■■
Exhibit, The	B, R	145	Events organisers, teachers	No	■■■	■■■	■■■
Extra Time	B	97	Bankers, lawyers	Yes	■■■	■■■	■■■
Fabric	C, LMV	106	Students, DJs	Yes	■■■■	■■■■	■■■
Faces	B, R	187	Bankers, lawyers, doctors	No	■■■■■	■■	■■■■
Falcon, The	P	162	Nurses, City temps	No	■■■	■■	■■■
Fiction	B, LMV	150	Chefs, bar staff, retailers	No	■■	■■	■■
Fifth Floor	CB, R	187	Beauticians, bankers, models	No	■■■■	■■■■■	■■■■■
Fine Line, The	B	163	City boys, account execs	No	■■■	■■■	■■■
First & Last	B, CF	97	Bankers, stockbrokers	No	■■■	■■	■■■
Fluid	B, C	107	Media, students	Yes	■■■■	■■■	■■
Form	B, MB	66	Advertising execs, designers, musicians	Yes	■■	■■■■	■■■
Foundry, The	B	126	Programmers, designer	No	■■■	■■	■■
Foyer Bar	B, HB	188	Bankers, shoppers	No	■■■	■■■■	■■■■■
Freedom Brewing Co. (WC2)	P	24	Marketing execs, actors	No	■■■	■■■	■■■
Freedom Brewing Co. (W1)	B, R	66	Actors, artists, lawyers	No	■	■■■■	■■■
French House	B	66	Actors, artists, advertising	No	■■	■■	■■■
Freud	B	25	Advertising employees, art students	No	■■■	■■■	■■■
Fridge Bar	B	155	Students, media profs	Yes	■■■	■■■	■■■
Front Room Bar, The	B, P	150	City boys, musicians, lawyers	No	■■	■■■■	■■■
Fuego	B, R	98	Bankers, brokers	Yes	■■■■■	■■	■■■
Fuel	B, CB	25	Advertising, PR agents	Yes	■■■■	■■■	■■■
Fulham Tup	P	183	Bankers, nurses, lawyers	No	■■	■■	■■■
Funky Munky	B	159	Lawyers, graphic designers	Yes	■■■	■■■	■■
G2	P	150	PRs, bankers, IT consultants	No	■■	■■■	■■■
Garlic & Shots	B, R, T	67	Musicians, PRs, journalists	Yes	■■	■	■
Gate, The	B, R	210	Retail staff, fashion employees	Yes	■■■■	■■■	■■
GE Club	C, MC	98	Fashion designers, account execs	Yes	■■	■■■	■■■■
George	P, R	98	Bankers, lawyers	No	■■	■■	■■■■
Glenfiddich Bar	B, CB	67	Copywriters, recruitment consultants	Yes	■■■■■	■■■	■■■
Goat in Boots	CB, P	183	Students, retailers, doctors	No	■■■	■■■	■■■
Golborne House	GP	219	Media and music profs	Yes	■■	■■■	■■■
Gold Bar Café	B, CF	68	Media and advertising execs, retail staff	No	■■	■■■■	■■■
Goodge	B	51	Media, graphic designers, retail staff	No	■■■■	■■■	■■■
Goolies	RB, WB	204	Bankers, advertising execs	No	■■	■■■	■■■■
Gordon's	B, WB	85	Brokers, lawyers, actors	No	■■	■■■	■■■
Grand Central	CB, CF	127	Web designers, media employees	Yes	■■	■■■	■■■
Great Eastern Dining Room	B, CB	127	Writers, music industry execs	Yes	■■■	■■■	■■■
Groucho Club, The	MC	68	Producers, directors, writers	Yes	■	■■■■	■■■■■
Ground Floor Bar	B	213	Retailers, creatives	No	■■■	■■■	■■■
Grove, The	B, RB	200	TV, film and motor industry profs	No	■■	■■■	■■■■
Halcyon, The	HB, CB	202	Music execs, brokers	No	■	■■■■	■■■■
Hanover Square	WB	14	Advertising execs, media execs	No	■■	■■	■■■
Havana (W1)	B, C	15	Students, retailers	Yes	■■■■	■	■■■
Havana (SW6)	B, T	186	Bankers, students, photographers	Yes	■■■■	■■■	■■■
Heaven	C, G	86	DJs, fashion designers	Yes	■■■	■■■■	■■■
Heeltap & Bumper	B, CF	99	Bakers, media	No	■■■	■■■	■■■
Henry J Beans Bar & Grill	B, R	178	Estate agents, retail staff, students	No	■■■■■	■■■■	■■■

B = Bar, C = Club, G = Gay, P = Pub, R = Restaurant, T = Theme, CB = Cocktail Bar, CF = Café, GP = Gastropub, HB = Hotel Bar, LMV = Live Music Venue, MB= Members Bar, MC = Members Club, PLB = Pool Bar, RB = Restaurant Bar, SC = Strip Club, WB = Wine Bar

NAME	TYPE	PAGE	PROFESSIONS	LATE	GETTING LUCKY	EYE CANDY	BIG SPENDERS
Herbal	B, C	128	Photographers, designers	Yes	■■	■■■■	■■■
Holy Drinker, The	B	151	Graphic designers, IT consultants	No	■■■■	■■■	■■
Home	B, R	128	Publishers, designers	Yes	■■■	■■■■	■■■
Home House	MC, B, R	52	Media, law, finance	No	■■■	■■■■	■■■■
House on the Hill, The	B, RB	122	Stockbrokers, divas	Yes	■■■■	■■■■	■■■■
Hoxton Square Bar & Grill	B	120	Designers, writers	Yes	■■	■■■	■■
Hush	RB	15	Bankers, actors	Yes	■■■	■■■■	■■■■
Hydro	B	151	PR agents, bankers, traders	No	■■■■	■■■	■■■■■
ICA	B, CF	82	Artists, musicians, civil servants	Yes	■■	■■	■■■
Ifield, The	GP	185	Account execs, journalists	No	■■■	■■■	■■■
Ion Bar, The	B	213	A&R people, designers	Yes	■■	■■■	■■■
Isola	RB	188	Bankers, PRs, models	No	■■■■	■■■■	■■■■■
Itsu Bar	CB, B, R	194	PRs, property agents, bankers	No	■	■■■■	■■■■
Jacomo's	B, G	107	Investment bankers	No	■	■	■■
Jamie's at Pavilion	B	99	Lawyers, stockbrokers	No	■■	■■	■■■■
Jazz Café	B, LMV	119	Lawyers, creatives	Yes	■■	■■■	■■■
Jerusalem	B, RB	52	PRs, TV and record producers	No	■■■■■	■■■	■■■
Juice Bar	B, CF	156	Young graduates, media execs	Yes	■■■■	■■■	■■
Julie's Bar	WB, R	202	Film, TV and radio profs	No	■	■■■	■■■
K Bar (SW10)	B	179	Bankers, PRs, trustafarians	Yes	■■■■	■■■■	■■■
K Bar (W1)	B	68	Bankers, PRs, office girls	Yes	■■■■	■■■■	■■■
Kabaret	MC	69	Bankers, fashionistas, journos	Yes	■■■■	■■■■■	■■■■■
Katabatic	B, C	129	City types, media employees	Yes	■■■	■■■	■■■
Kazbar	B, G	164	Bankers, theatre staff	Yes	■■■■■	■■■	■■■
Kettners	B, R	69	Salespeople, travel agents, PRs	No	■■	■■■	■■■
King's Head & Dive Bar	P	37	Everything, anything and nothing	Yes	■■	■■■■	■■■
L'Equipe Anglaise	C, MC	42	Bankers, oil fat cats, estate agents	Yes	■■■■	■■■■■	■■■■
L'Odeon	B, R	16	Profs, media execs	Yes	■■■	■■■■	■■■■
La Perla	B, R	185	Brokers, retailers, promoters	No	■	■■■	■■■
La Grande Marque	B	100	Bankers, lawyers	No	■■	■■	■■■■
Lab	B, CB	70	PRs, bar staff, advertising execs	No	■■■	■■■■	■■■■
Landsdowne, The	GP	139	Writers, designers	No	■■	■■■	■■■
Latitude	B, MB	195	Bankers, stockbrokers, financiers	No	■■■■	■■■	■■■■
Le Cochonnet	RB	206	Estate agents, PRs	Yes	■■■■	■■■	■■
Le Pont de la Tour	B, R	112	Media, politicians	No	■■	■■■	■■■■■
Library, The	HB, CB	45	Lawyers, bankers, estate agents	No	■■■	■■■	■■■■■
Light Bar	HB, MB	25	Fashion, music execs	Yes	■■	■■■■■	■■■■■
Light, The	B, MB	130	Traders, analysts	Yes	■■	■■	■■■■
Limelight	C	38	Retailers, shop assistants, students	Yes	■■■■	■■■■	■■
Ling Ling	B, R	52	Actors, businessmen, doctors	Yes	■■	■■■■	■■■■
Liquid Lounge	B, R	220	Producers, promoters	Yes	■■■	■■■■	■■■
Livingroom Bar	B	156	New media, advertising creatives	Yes	■■■■	■■■	■■■
Long Bar & Purple Bar, The	HB, CB	53	Models, fashionistas, stylists	Yes	■■■	■■■■■	■■■■■
Long Island Iced Tea	RB	26	Administrative staff, insurance brokers	Yes	■■■■■	■■■	■■■
Lord Stanley, The	P	120	Media execs, IT profs	No	■■■	■■■	■■■
Lounge, The	B	146	Architects, barristers, teachers	No	■	■■■	■■■
Lounge-jing	B	121	Media employees, office workers	No	■■	■■■■	■■■
Lupo	B, R	70	Media, advertising, PR	Yes	■■■	■■■■	■■■
Mac Bar	B	120	Students, meeja types	No	■■■	■■■	■■■
Madame JoJo's	C, LMV	70	Actors, students, journalists	Yes	■■■■	■■■■	■■
Mandarin Bar	B, HB	189	Businessmen, lawyers, politicians	Yes	■■■■	■■■■	■■■■■
Manto	B, G, R	71	Students, bankers, accountants	No	■■■	■■■■	■■■
Market Bar, The	B	214	Market traders, artists	No	■■■	■■■	■■■
Martini Grill	B, R	185	Lawyers, thespians, investment bankers	No	■■	■■■	■■■■

B = Bar, C = Club, G = Gay, P = Pub, R = Restaurant, T = Theme, CB = Cocktail Bar, CF = Café, GP = Gastropub, HB = Hotel Bar, LMV = Live Music Venue, MB= Members Bar, MC = Members Club, PLB = Pool Bar, RB = Restaurant Bar, SC = Strip Club, WB = Wine Bar

NAME	TYPE	PAGE	PROFESSIONS	LATE	GETTING LUCKY	EYE CANDY	BIG SPENDERS
Mash	B, R	54	Accountants, salespeople, receptionists	Yes	■■	■■■	■■
Mason's Arms	GP	152	Teachers, students, tradesmen	No	■■■	■■	■■■
Mass	C	156	Students, retail staff	Yes	■■■	■■	■■
Match	B	54	Media employees, magazine staff	No	■■■	■■■	■■■
Match EC1	CB, B	107	Media, account execs	Yes	■■■	■■■	■■■
Matt & Matt Bar	B, CB	135	Office workers, students	Yes	■■■■	■■■	■■■
Mau Mau Bar	B, CF	214	Media types, students	No	■■	■■■■	■■■
Mean Fiddler	LMV, C	71	Musicians, bikers, students	Yes	■■■	■■■	■■
Medicine Bar	B	136	Fashion designers, DJs	Yes	■■■	■■■■	■■
Mess, The	B	152	Media, TV and advertising profs	No	■■■■	■■	■■
Met Bar, The	HB	46	Models, musicians, film execs	Yes	■■■■■	■■■■■	■■■■■■
Mezzo	B, R	72	Account execs, media and music profs	Yes	■■■■	■■■■	■■■■
Ministry of Sound	C, LMV	168	Music industry employees, groupies	Yes	■■■■■	■■■	■■■
Mint 182	CB, B	108	Designers, bankers	No	■	■■■■	■■■
Momo	B, R	16	Bankers, gold-diggers	Yes	■■	■■■■■	■■■■
Mondo	B, C	73	Promoters, singers, musicians	Yes	■■■	■■■	■■
Monte's	CB, MB, R	189	Bankers, lawyers, PRs	Yes	■	■■■	■■■■
Moorgate Oriental	B	100	Bankers, brokers	No	■■	■■■	■■■■
Mother	B, CB	130	Sound engineers, IT consultants	Yes	■■■	■■	■■
Nam Long Le Shaker	B, R	195	Bankers, stockbrokers, artists	Yes	■■■■	■■■■	■■■■
Navajo Joe	B, R	26	Brokers, PR agents	Yes	■■■	■■■	■■■
Nicole's	B, R	16	Bankers, media	No	■	■■■■	■■■■
No 10	B, C, WB	17	Music profs, publishers	No	■■■	■■	■■■
Noble Rot	MB, R	17	Bankers, models	Yes	■■■■■	■■■	■■■■■
Nordic	B	54	Media, TV, advertising	No	■■■■■	■	■■
North & South Pole	CB, R	169	Solicitors, designers	No	■■■	■■■	■■■■
Notting Hill Arts Club	B, C	210	Freelancers, stylists	Yes	■■■■	■■■	■■
Nylon	B, C, R	100	Bankers, lawyers	Yes	■■■	■■■	■■■■
O Bar	B	73	PRs, students, retailers	Yes	■■■■	■■	■■■
Odette's	B, WB	140	Music and film industry	Yes	■	■■	■■■■■
Office	B	55	Assistants, media and film wannabes	Yes	■■■■■	■■	■
On Anon	B, C	38	Bankers, accountants, traders	Yes	■■■■	■■	■■■
Opium	B, MB	73	PRs, artists, models	Yes	■■■	■■■■	■■■■■
Oriel	B, R	179	Surveyors, accountants, lawyers	No	■■	■■	■■■
Otto Dining Lounge	B, R	206	Diplomats, chairmen	No	■	■■■	■■■■■
Oxo Tower	B	113	Bankers, media	No	■	■■■	■■■
Oxygen	CB, T	39	Students, bar staff, accountants	Yes	■■■■	■■■	■■■■
Pacific Oriental	RB	101	Bankers, brokers	No	■	■■	■■■■
Pages	B	83	Civil servants, politicians, lawyers	No	■■■	■	■■
Palais du Jardin	RB	28	Media execs, advertising execs	Yes	■■	■■■■	■■■■
Palm Court at The Ritz	HB	32	Politicians, aristocrats	No	■	■■■	■■■■
Papa Gaio	C, MC	74	Models, fashionistas, media types	Yes	■■■■	■■■■	■■■■
Paparazzi Lounge	B, MC	18	Rich kids, PRs	Yes	■■■■	■■■■	■■■■■
Peasant, The	GP	108	Bankers, students	No	■■■	■■■■	■■■■
Pharmacy	B, R	211	Journalists, record label execs	Yes	■■	■■■■	■■■■
Pitcher & Piano (W1)	B	74	Bankers, PRs, secretaries	No	■■■■	■■■	■■■
Pitcher & Piano (SW3)	B	180	Doctors, retailers, students	No	■■■	■■■	■■■
Plastic People	C, LMV	130	Copywriters, computer programmers	Yes	■■■	■■	■■
Po Na Na (W6)	C, T	200	Office workers, PRs	Yes	■■■■■	■■■	■■■
Po Na Na Souk Bar (SW3)	C, T	180	Retail workers, publishing execs	Yes	■■	■■	■■
Po Na Na Souk Bar (W8)	B, T	204	Retail, restaurant and bar staff	Yes	■■■■	■■■	■■■
Poet, The	B	101	Lawyers, stockbrokers	No	■■■	■	■■■
Pool, The	PLB	131	IT profs, DJs	Yes	■■■■	■■■■	■■■
Pop	B	74	Salespeople, PRs, students	Yes	■■■■■	■■■■	■■■

B = Bar, C = Club, G = Gay, P = Pub, R = Restaurant, T = Theme, CB = Cocktail Bar, CF = Café, GP = Gastropub, HB = Hotel Bar, LMV = Live Music Venue, MB= Members Bar, MC = Members Club, PLB = Pool Bar, RB = Restaurant Bar, SC = Strip Club, WB = Wine Bar

NAME	TYPE	PAGE	PROFESSIONS	LATE	GETTING LUCKY	EYE CANDY	BIG SPENDERS
Porters Bar	B	28	PRs, bankers	No	■■■	■■■	■■■
Portobello Gold	HB, RB	214	Stockbrokers, media execs	Yes	■	■■■	■■■■■
Portobello Star	P	216	Market stall holders, media profs	No	■■■	■■■	■■
Potemkin	B, R	109	Media, IT	Yes	■■■	■■■	■■■
Prince Bonaparte, The	GP	211	Advertising execs, PRs	No	■■■■■	■■■■■	■■■
Prism	B, R	102	Bankers, traders	No	■■	■■	■■■■
Purple	C	186	PRs, sportsmen, bankers	Yes	■■■■■	■■■■	■■■■
Q Bar	B,C	18	Bankers, PRs	Yes	■■■■	■■■■	■■■■
Quaglino's	B, R	83	Accountants, management consultants	Yes	■■■	■■■	■■■■
Queens, The	GP	140	Music and media profs	No	■	■■■■	■■■
Railway	B, R	164	Media execs, City workers	No	■■■■	■■■	■■
Rapscallion	B, R	164	Architects, PRs	Yes	■■	■■■■	■■■■
Red Cube	C, B, R	39	Soap stars, admin girls, traders	Yes	■■■■	■■	■■■
Red Star	C	160	Creatives, students	Yes	■■■■■	■■	■
Rhythm Factory, The	C, LMV	93	Students, designers	Yes	■■■	■■■	■■
Ritzy Cinema Bar	B	158	Media students, salespeople	No	■	■■	■■
Roadhouse, The	B, LMV	29	Media profs	Yes	■■■	■■■	■■■■
Rock	C	86	Students, office workers, trustafarians	Yes	■■■■	■■■	■■■
Rocket	RB	18	Solicitors, office workers	No	■■■	■■■■	■■■■
Rockwell	B, HB	88	City boys, PRs, ladies who lunch	Yes	■	■■	■■■■
Ruby in the Dust (N1)	B, R	136	Lawyers, PRs	Yes	■■■■	■■■■	■■
Ruby in the Dust (W10)	B, CF	216	Musicians, film profs	No	■■■	■■■■■	■■■
Ruby Lounge	B	137	Designers, PR agents	Yes	■■■	■■■	■■
Saint	B	40	Artists, students, models	Yes	■■■■	■■■■	■■■
SAK	B, CB	76	Students, designers, musos	Yes	■■■	■■■■	■■■
Salmon & Compasses	P, C	137	Tattoo artists, advertising employees	Yes	■■■	■■■	■■
Salsa	B, C, T	40	Students, dancers, solicitors	Yes	■■■■	■■	■■■
Sand	B	164	Bankers, media jockeys	Yes	■■■■	■■■■	■■■
Satay Bar	B, R	158	Housing officers, media employees	Yes	■■	■■■	■■■
Scarsdale Tavern	P	205	Journalists, property developers	No	■■■	■■■	■■■
Scotts	B, R	46	Bankers, traders, lawyers	No	■■	■■■	■■■■
Sequel, The	B, R	166	Architects, advertising execs	Yes	■	■■■	■■■■
Shadow Lounge, The	C, G, MC	76	Designers, stylists, hairdressers	Yes	■■■■■	■■■■	■■■■
Shoreditch Elec Showrooms	B, R	131	Fashion, web, interiors	Yes	■■■■	■■■■	■■■
Singapore Sling	RB, CB	120	Media, advertising	Yes	■■■	■■■	■■■
Slug & Lettuce	B	137	Designers, estate agents	No	■■	■■■	■■
Smiths of Smithfield	B, CB, R	109	Bankers, lawyers	No	■■	■■■	■■■■
Snug	B	160	Salespeople, writers	Yes	■■■■	■■	■■■
So.uk	CB, RB	166	Bankers, media creatives	Yes	■■■	■■■	■■■
Social, The (W1)	B	55	A&R, producers, engineers	Yes	■■	■■■	■■
Social, The (N1)	B, R	138	Musos, photographers	No	■■■	■■■■	■■■
Soho House	MC	77	Film industry, actors, directors	Yes	■■■	■■■■■	■■■■■
Soho Spice	B	77	Accountants, bankers, doctors	Yes	■■■	■■	■■■
Sosho	B, CB	132	Media profs, lawyers	Yes	■■■■	■■■	■■■■
Sports Academy	P	102	Bankers, traders	No	■	■	■■
St John	RB	110	Designers, journalists	No	■	■■■	■■■
Stonemason Arms	GP	200	Media girls, IT boys	No	■■■■	■■■	■■■
Strawberry Moons	B, C	20	Office workers, students	Yes	■■■■■	■■■	■■
Stringfellows	B, SC	30	Bankers, hairdressers	Yes	■■■■■	■■	■■■■
Studio Six	B, R	113	Creatives, IT	No	■■■	■■■■	■■■
Subterrania	C	220	Music producers, record company staff	Yes	■■■	■■■	■■■
Sugar Reef	B, C, R	41	Glamour models, admin staff	Yes	■■■■	■■■	■■■■
Sun & Doves	P	161	Hospital workers, artists	No	■■■	■■■	■■
Sun, The	B	167	Advertising and media employees	No	■■■■	■■■■	■■■

B = Bar, C = Club, G = Gay, P = Pub, R = Restaurant, T = Theme, CB = Cocktail Bar, CF = Café, GP = Gastropub, HB = Hotel Bar,
LMV = Live Music Venue, MB= Members Bar, MC = Members Club, PLB = Pool Bar, RB = Restaurant Bar, SC = Strip Club, WB = Wine Bar

NAME	TYPE	PAGE	PROFESSIONS	LATE	GETTING LUCKY	EYE CANDY	BIG SPENDERS
SW9	B, G, CF	159	Artists, fashion and music industry	No	■■	■■■■	■■
Sway	B, MB, C	30	Bankers, PRs	Yes	■■■	■■	■■■
Tearoom des Artistes	B	167	DJs, journalists	Yes	■■	■■■	■■■
Teatro	MC, R	78	TV execs, journalists, fashionistas	Yes	■■	■■■■	■■■■
Tiger Tiger	B, C, R	41	Bankers, accountants, admin staff	Yes	■■■■	■■	■■
Time	B	170	Estate agents, hairdressers	No	■■■	■■■	■■
Titanic	B, R	42	DJs, secretaries, brokers	Yes	■■■■■	■■■	■■■
Toast	CB, MC	123	Lawyers, bankers, models	Yes	■■■■	■■■■	■■■■
Trader Vic's	CB, T	47	Designers, bankers, arms dealers	Yes	■■■	■■	■■■■
Trafalgar Tavern, The	P, R	170	Students, teachers	No	■■	■■	
Tramp	C, MB	84	Bankers, models, property developers	Yes	■■■■	■■■■■	■■■■■
Tsar Bar	B	56	BBC execs, film execs, city types	No	■■	■■■■	■■■■■
Turnmills	C	110	Students, promoters	Yes	■■■	■■	■■■
Two Floors	B	78	Marketing reps, sales execs, PRs	No	■■■	■■■■	■■
Vale, The	B, R	206	Media, film and TV professionals	No	■■	■■	■■■
Velvet Room, The	C	79	Students, DJs, musicians	Yes	■■■	■■■	■■■
Vertigo	B, R	102	Bankers, lawyers	No	■■	■■	■■■
Vibe Bar	B	94	Media, musicians	Yes	■■■	■■■	■■■
Vic Naylor's Bar & Grill	RB	111	Lawyers, marketing execs	Yes	■■	■■■	■■■
Village, The	B, G	79	Retail staff, students, businessmen	Yes	■■■■■	■■■■	■■■
Walmer Castle, The	P, R	212	Media, PR	No	■■	■■	■■■
Well, The	GP	111	Advertising, sales	No	■	■■	■■■
Wellington Club, The	MC	190	Actors, models, media profs	Yes	■■■■	■■■■■	■■■■
Westbourne, The	GP	221	Media, music, film and TV profs	Yes	■■■■	■■■■■	■■■■
White Horse, The	GP	186	IT consultants, stockbrokers, musos	No	■■■	■■■■	■■■■
White House, The	CB, MC	168	PRs, assistant editors	Yes	■■■■	■■■■	■■■■
Wild	MC	30	Actors, advertising	Yes	■■■	■■■■■	■■■■■
Windows Bar	HB	47	World leaders, bankers, financiers	Yes	■■	■■■	■■■■
Windsor Castle, The	P	212	Barristers, advertising execs	No	■■	■■■	■■■
Wine Factory	WB, R	217	TV and radio professionals	no	■■	■■■	■■■
WKD	B, C, CF	121	Advertising, PR	Yes	■■■■	■■■	■■■
Wodka	RB	205	Bankers, media profs	No	■■	■■■	■■■
Woody's	CB, MC	207	Fashion, photographers	Yes	■■■■■	■■■■	■■■■
Yo! Below	B, R	80	Media and music employees	Yes	■	■■■	■■
Z Restaurant and Bar	RB, LMV	159	Voluntary workers, retailers	Yes	■■■	■■■■	■■■
Zaika Bazaar	B	196	Bankers, retailers, doctors	No	■■	■■	■■■■
Zander	B, R	48	Solicitors, civil servants, MPs	No	■■	■■■	■■■
Zeta	B, HB	48	Footballers, models, beauty therapists	Yes	■■■■■	■■■■	■■■■■
Zilli Bar	B	80	Actors, advertising directors, PRs	No	■■	■■■	■■■
Zinc Bar & Grill	RB, CB	20	Film industry, PRs	No	■	■■■	■■■■

BIRMINGHAM | BRISTOL | EDINBURGH | GLASGOW | LEEDS | MANCHESTER

NAME	TYPE	PAGE	PROFESSIONS	LATE	GETTING LUCKY	EYE CANDY	BIG SPENDERS
52° North	B, R	226	Actors, promoters, financiers	Yes	■■■■	■■■■■	■■■■
54 Below	B	244	Lawyers, solicitors, lecturers	Yes	■■	■■■	■■■
Academy, The	C, LMV	232	Students, office workers, music	Yes	■■■■	■■	
Air Organic	B	244	Stylists, designers, architects	Yes	■■	■■■	■■■
Alaska	C	244	Students, journalists, musicians	Yes	■■	■■■	■■■
Arc Bar	B, LMV	232	Marketing, insurance, recruitment	Yes	■■	■■	■■
Arca	B	226	PRs, PAs, media employees	Yes	■■■	■■■■	■■■
Arches, The	B, C	245	Teachers, drag artists, musicians	Yes	■■■	■■■■	■■
Babylon	RB	250	Bankers, solicitors, sports agents	No	■■	■■■	■■■■
Bacchus Bar	R, B	226	Lawyers, football managers, students	No	■	■■■	■■■
Bar Humbug	B	232	Students, waitresses	No	■■■	■■■■	■■

B = Bar, C = Club, G = Gay, P = Pub, R = Restaurant, T = Theme, CB = Cocktail Bar, CF = Café, GP = Gastropub, HB = Hotel Bar, LMV = Live Music Venue, MB= Members Bar, MC = Members Club, PLB = Pool Bar, RB = Restaurant Bar, SC = Strip Club, WB = Wine Bar

NAME	TYPE	PAGE	PROFESSIONS	LATE	GETTING LUCKY	EYE CANDY	BIG SPENDERS
Bambu	C	250	Solicitors, entrepreneurs, students	Yes	■■■	■■■■	■■■■
Bank	B, R	227	Bankers, lawyers, office execs	No	■	■■■	■■■■
Bar Fibre	B, CF	250	Lawyers, designers, nurses	Yes	■■■	■■■■	■■■
Bar Room Bar	B	227	Bankers, finance, media execs	No	■■■	■■■	■■■■
Basement, The	B, R	238	Students, retail and bank staff	Yes	■■■■	■■■	■■
Beluga Bar & Canteen	B, R, C	238	Lawyers, accountants, doctors	Yes	■■■	■■■	■■■
Candy Bar	B, R	245	Media and advertising profs	Yes	■■■■	■■■■	■■■
City Café, The	B	238	DJs, PRs, students	Yes	■■■	■■■■	■■■
Code	C	228	Students, designers, promoters	Yes	■	■■	■■
Creation	C	233	Students, secretaries, promoters	Yes	■■■	■■■	■■■
Cube	B,C	245	Students, accountants, admin workers	Yes	■■■■	■■■■	■■■■
Dojo Lounge, The	C	233	Students, bar workers, DJs	Yes	■■■	■■■	■■
E Shed	B	234	Finance, law clerks, shop workers	Yes	■■■	■■	■■
Elbow Room, The	B, PLB	234	Students, musos, media	Yes	■■	■■■	■■
Ether	B	234	Musos, bar staff, club owners	Yes	■■■	■■■■	■■■
Groucho Saint Jude's	B, R, HB	246	Media, finance, law	No	■	■■■■	■■■■
Hidden	B, C	228	Promoters, media, fashion	Yes	■■	■■■■	■■■
Honeycomb, The	C	239	Musicians, media executives	Yes	■■■	■■■	■■
Human Be-In, The	B, CF	239	Academics, students, lawyers	Yes	■■■	■■■■	■■■■
Iguana, The	B	240	Dentists, students, lawyers	Yes	■■	■■■■	■■■
Indi	B, R	228	PRs, DJs, students	Yes	■■	■■■	■■■
Ipanema	B, R	229	Media execs, students, financiers	Yes	■■■■	■■■■	■■■
Level	C	235	Students, musicians, PRs	Yes	■■■	■■■	■■
Lime	B, R, C	256	Lawyers, brokers, property developers	No	■■■	■■■	■■■■
Living Room	B	256	Journalists, musicians, designers	Yes	■■■■■	■■■	■■■
Loaf	B, C, R	256	PRs, fashion, music	Yes	■■■	■■■■	■■■■
Lowdown	B, R, C	246	Bankers, solicitors, editors	Yes	■■■	■■■	■■■
Lowry, The	B	257	Doctors, lawyers, students	No	■	■■■	■■■
Malmaison	B, HB	257	Actors, film crew, boutique owners	No	■■	■■■	■■■■
Manto	B, C	258	Designers, dustmen	Yes	■■■■■	■■■■	■■■
Mas	C	247	Journalists, musos, designers	Yes	■■■■	■■■■	■■■
Mint	C	251	Students, office clerks, solicitors	Yes	■■■	■■■■	■■■
Mojo	B	251	Musicians, producers, writers	Yes	■■■	■■■	■■■
MPV	B, C	251	Hairdressers, students, DJs	Yes	■■■	■■■	■■■
Nocturne	C, MC	235	DJs, musicians, actors, models	Yes	■■■	■■■■	■■■■
Norman	B, R	252	Fashion, new media, music	Yes	■■■■■	■■■	■■■
North	B	252	Actors, bar staff, students	Yes	■■■	■■■	■■
Oslo	B, MB	253	Lawyers, students, solicitors	Yes	■■■■	■■■	■■■
Ox, The	B, RB	258	Lawyers, accountants, dinner ladies	No	■■■	■■■	■■■
Pivo Caffè	B	240	Radio employees, journos, DJs	Yes	■■	■■■	■■
Pond, The	B	240	Artists, writers, musicians	Yes	■■■	■■■	■■
Pop Rokit	C	241	Advertising, promoters, DJs	Yes	■■■	■■■■	■■■■
Rick's	B, R	241	Sportsmen, media, students	Yes	■■■■	■■■	■■■■
Sankey's Soap	C, LMV	259	Media, dance diehards	Yes	■■	■■■	■■■
Sobar	B, R	229	Students, designers, city workers	Yes	■■	■■■■	■■■
Space	C	253	Bankers, lawyers, stockbrokers	Yes	■■■■	■■■■	■■■
Spy Bar	B, HB	247	Students, hairdressers, lawyers	Yes	■■	■■■■	■■■
Sugar Lounge	B	259	Media, shop staff, racing drivers	Yes	■■■	■■■■	■■■■
Zinc Bar & Grill	B, R	260	Accountants, media, television	Yes	■■	■■■	■■■

B = Bar, C = Club, G = Gay, P = Pub, R = Restaurant, T = Theme, CB = Cocktail Bar, CF = Café, GP = Gastropub, HB = Hotel Bar, LMV = Live Music Venue, MB= Members Bar, MC = Members Club, PLB = Pool Bar, RB = Restaurant Bar, SC = Strip Club, WB = Wine Bar

School Disco.com

The Best Days of Your life™

40 Rock Pop Disco Anthems
School Disco.com
The Best Days of Your Life
CD Out Now!

SCHOOLDISCO.COM

LONDON
Fridays at the Hanover Grand, 6 Hanover Street, W1, £10.
Saturdays at Po Na Na Hammersmith, 230 Shepherds Bush Road, W6, £12.

DUBLIN
Saturdays at the
Ambassador Theatre,
Upper O'Connell St. Dublin 1, £12.

Dresscode School Uniform.
Visit SchoolDisco.com for info, fun and tickets.
Tickets and info **0871 717 7475** (24 hours).

Arní thinks he makes his vodka for Icelandic
fishermen.

Clearly, Arní should get out more often.

Arní's vodka is well known all over Iceland. Since the end of prohibition in '36 not only the fisherman have used his vodka to keep out the bleak Atlantic chill. Icelanders have kept their spirits high with an appreciation of the smooth strength of Pölstar Vodka that is achieved through the purity of ingredients and the integrity of the processes used to make it.

That's why Arní insists on only the finest grain spirit, triple distilled, which he marries with Icelandic spring water, ideal for the making of vodka, because of its unparalleled purity and softness.

Icelanders believe their natural resources are also their natural treasures,

non-polluting geothermal energy that literally bursts from the earth, and rivers of the purest water on earth. Pölstar is also one of Iceland's natural treasures, and as such is a jealously guarded secret - always in short supply. Now, albeit grudgingly, Arní's vodka is being released for export, and is available in better bars and restaurants in London. Hand crafted in small batches, soft and delicate, with a sweetness and refinement that belies its strength, Pölstar Vodka is the embodiment of the Spirit of Iceland, "Styrkur Vegna Hreinleika" -

Strength through Purity.

PÖLSTAR
VODKA

Spirit of Iceland
SINCE 1936

AVAILABLE IN LIMITED QUANTITIES TO FINER BARS AND RESTAURANTS IN CENTRAL LONDON
EXPORTED FROM ICELAND BY THE REFORMED SPIRITS COMPANY
DISTRIBUTED THROUGH VENUS AND CO - 020 8801 0011 - OR YOUR USUAL SUPPLIER

HTTP//WWW.POLSTARVODKA.COM